MAZDA 323/PROTEGE/MX3/MX6/626/MIATA
1990-93 REPAIR MANUAL

CHILTON'S

President, Chilton Enterprises	David S. Loewith
Senior Vice President	Ronald A. Hoxter
Publisher and Editor-In-Chief	Kerry A. Freeman, S.A.E.
Executive Editors	Dean F. Morgantini, S.A.E., W. Calvin Settle, Jr., S.A.E.
Managing Editor	Nick D'Andrea
Special Products Manager	Ken Grabowski, A.S.E., S.A.E.
Senior Editors	Jacques Gordon, Michael L. Grady, Debra McCall, Kevin M. G. Maher, Richard J. Rivele, S.A.E., Richard T. Smith, Jim Taylor, Ron Webb
Project Managers	Martin J. Gunther, Will Kessler, A.S.E., Richard Schwartz
Production Manager	Andrea Steiger
Product Systems Manager	Robert Maxey
Director of Manufacturing	Mike D'Imperio

CHILTON BOOK COMPANY

ONE OF THE **DIVERSIFIED PUBLISHING COMPANIES,**
A PART OF **CAPITAL CITIES/ABC, INC.**

Manufactured in USA
© 1993 Chilton Book Company
Chilton Way, Radnor, PA 19089
ISBN 0-8019-8411-4
Library of Congress Catalog Card No. 92-054905
4567890123 5432109876

Contents

Contents

7 DRIVE TRAIN

8 SUSPENSION AND STEERING

9 BRAKES

10 BODY

GLOSSARY

MASTER INDEX

SAFETY NOTICE

Proper service and repair procedures are vital to the safe, reliable operation of all motor vehicles, as well as the personal safety of those performing repairs. This manual outlines procedures for servicing and repairing vehicles using safe, effective methods. The procedures contain many NOTES, CAUTIONS, and WARNINGS which should be followed along with standard procedures to eliminate the possibility of personal injury or improper service which could damage the vehicle or compromise its safety.

It is important to note that the repair procedures and techniques, tools and parts for servicing motor vehicles, as well as the skill and experience of the individual performing the work vary widely. It is not possible to anticipate all of the conceivable ways or conditions under which vehicles may be serviced, or to provide cautions as to all of the possible hazards that may result. Standard and accepted safety precautions and equipment should be used when handling toxic or flammable fluids, and safety goggles or other protection should be used during cutting, grinding, chiseling, prying,or any other process that can cause material removal or projectiles.

Some procedures require the use of tools specially designed for a specific purpose. Before substituting another tool or procedure, you must be completely satisfied that neither your personal safety, nor the performance of the vehicle will be endangered.

Although information in this manual is based on industry sources and is complete as possible at the time of publication, the possibility exists that some car manufacturers made later changes which could not be included here. While striving for total accuracy, Chilton Book Company cannot assume responsibility for any errors, changes or omissions that may occur in the compilation of this data.

PART NUMBERS

Part numbers listed in this reference are not recommendation by Chilton for any product by brand name. They are references that can be used with interchange manuals and aftermarket supplier catalogs to locate each brand supplier's discrete part number.

SPECIAL TOOLS

Special tools are recommended by the vehicle manufacturer to perform their specific job. Use has been kept to a minimum, but where absolutely necessary, they are referred to in the text by the part number of the tool manufacturer. These tools can be purchased, under the appropriate part number, from your Honda dealer or regional distributor, or an equivalent tool can be purchased locally from a tool supplier or parts outlet. Before substituting any tool for the one recommended, read the SAFETY NOTICE at the top of this page.

ACKNOWLEDGMENTS

The Chilton Book Company expresses appreciation to Mazda Motor Co. for their generous assistance.

1

GENERAL INFORMATION AND MAINTENANCE

HOW TO USE THIS BOOK

Chilton's Total Car Care Manual for the Mazda 323, Protege, MX-3, Miata, MX-6, and 626 is intended to help you learn more about the inner workings of your vehicle and to save you money on its maintenence and operation.

The first two sections will be the most used, since they contain maintenance and tune-up information and procedures. A properly tuned and maintained car will get better gas mileage than an out-of-tune car. The other sections deal with more complex systems of your car. Operating systems from engine through brakes are covered to the point that the average do-it-yourselfer becomes mechanically involved. It will give you detailed instructions to help you change your own brake pads and shoes, replace spark plugs, and do many more jobs that will save you money, give you personal satisfaction, and help you avoid expensive problems.

A second purpose of this book is as a reference for owners who want to understand their car and/or their mechanics better. In this case, no tools at all are required.

Read through the entire procedure before removing any bolts. This gives you the overall view of what tools and supplies will be required. Each operation should be approached logically and all procedures thoroughly understood before attempting any work.

All sections contain adjustments, maintenance, removal and installation procedures, and repair or overhaul procedures. When repair or overhaul is not considered practical, you are told how to remove the part and then how to install the new or rebuilt replacement. In this way, you at least save the labor costs.

Two basic mechanic's rules should be mentioned here. One, whenever the left side of the car or engine is referred to, it is meant to specify the driver's side of the car. Conversely, the right side of the car means the passenger's side. Secondly, most screws and bolts are removed by turning counterclockwise, and tightened by turning clockwise unless otherwise noted.

Safety is always the most important rule. Constantly be aware of the dangers involved in working on an automobile and take the proper precautions. (See the section in this Section on Servicing Your Vehicle Safely and the SAFETY NOTICE on the acknowledgment page.)

Pay attention to the instructions provided. There are 3 common mistakes in mechanical work:

1. Incorrect order of assembly, disassembly or adjustment. When disassembling something or putting it together, doing things in the wrong order usually only costs you extra time; however, it CAN cause component damage or failure. Read the entire procedure before beginning disassembly. Do everything in the order in which the instructions say you should do it, even if you can't immediately see a reason for it. When you're taking apart something that is very intricate, you might want to draw a picture of how it looks when assembled at one point in order to make sure you get everything back in its proper position. (Exploded views will be provided whenever possible). When making adjustments, especially tune-up adjustments, do them in order; often, one adjustment affects another, and you cannot expect even satisfactory results unless each adjustment is made only when it cannot be changed by any other.

2. Overtorquing (or undertorquing): While it is more common for overtorquing to cause damage, undertorquing can cause a fastener to vibrate loose causing serious damage. Especially when dealing with aluminum parts, pay attention to torque specifications and utilize a torque wrench in assembly. If a torque figure is not available, remember that if you are using the right tool to do the job, you will probably not have to strain yourself to get a fastener tight enough. The pitch of most threads is so slight that the tension

you put on the wrench will be multiplied many, many times in actual force on what you are tightening. A good example of how critical torque is can be seen in the case of spark plug installation, especially where you are putting the plug into an aluminum cylinder head. Too little torque can fail to crush the gasket, causing leakage of combustion gases and consequent overheating of the plug and engine parts. Too much torque can damage the threads or distort the plug, which changes the sp ark gap.

There are many commercial products available for ensuring that fasteners won't come loose, even if they are not torqued just right (a very common brand is Loctite®). If you're worried about getting something together tight enough to hold, but loose enough to avoid mechanical damage during assembly, one of these products might offer substantial insurance. Read the label on the package and make sure the product is compatible with the materials, fluids, etc. involved.

3. Crossthreading. This occurs when a part such as a bolt is screwed into a nut or casting at the wrong angle and forced. Cross threading is more likely to occur if access is difficult. It helps to clean and lubricate fasteners, and to start threading with the part to be installed going straight in. Then, start the bolt, spark plug, etc. with your fingers. If you encounter resistance, unscrew the part and start over again at a different angle until it can be inserted and turned several turns without much effort. Keep in mind that many parts, especially spark plugs, use tapered threads so that gentle turning will automatically bring the part you're threading to the proper angle if you don't force it or resist a change in angle. Don't put a wrench on the part until it's been turned a couple of turns by hand. If you suddenly encounter resistance, and the part has not seated fully, don't force it. Screw it back out and make sure it's clean and threading properly.

TOOLS AND EQUIPMENT

Without the proper tools and equipment it is impossible to properly service your vehicle. It would be impossible to catalog each tool that you would need to perform each or every operation in this book. It would also be unwise for the amateur to rush out and buy an expensive set of tools on the theory that he may need one or more of them at sometime.

Proceed slowly, gathering together a good quality set of those tools that are used most frequently. Don't be misled by the low cost of bargain tools. It is far better to spend a little more for better quality. Forged wrenches, 6- or 12-point sockets and fine tooth ratchets are by far preferable than their less expensive counterparts. As any good mechanic can tell you, there are few worse experiences than trying to work on a car with bad tools. Your monetary savings will be far outweighed by frustration and mangled knuckles.

Start accumulating those tools that are used most frequently; those associated with routine maintenance and tune-up.

In addition to the normal assortment of pliers and screwdrivers, you should have the following tools for routine maintenance jobs:

1. Metric wrenches, sockets and combination open end/box end wrenches in sizes from 3mm to 19mm, and a $^{13}/_{16}$ in. spark plug socket.

If possible, buy various length socket drive extensions. One break in this department is that the metric sockets available in the U.S. will all fit the ratchet handles and extensions you may already have (1/4in., 3/8in., and 1/2in. drive).

2. Jackstands for support.
3. Oil filter wrench.
4. Oil filler spout or funnel.
5. Hydrometer for checking the battery.
6. A container for draining oil.
7. Many rags for wiping up the inevitable mess.

In addition to the above items there are several others that are not absolutely necessary, but handy to have around.

These include oil dry, a transmission funnel and the usual supply of lubricants, antifreeze and fluids, although these can be purchased as needed. This is a basic list for routine maintenance, but only your personal needs and desire can accurately determine your list of tools.

The second list of tools is for tune-ups. While the tools involved here are slightly more sophisticated, they need not be outrageously expensive. There are several inexpensive tachometers on the market that are every bit as good for the average mechanic as a more expensive professional model. Just be sure that the meter goes to at least 1500 rpm on the scale and that it can be used on 4 or 6 cylinder engines. A basic list of tune-up equipment could include:

8. Tachometer.
9. Spark plug wrench.
10. Timing light (a DC light that works from the car's battery is best, although an AC light that plugs into 110V house current will suffice at some sacrifice in brightness).
11. Wire spark plug gauge/adjusting tools.

In addition to these basic tools there are several other tools and gauges you may find useful. These include:

12. A compression gauge. The screw in type is slower to use but it eliminates the possibility of a faulty reading due to escaping pressure.

13. A manifold vacuum gauge.
14. A 12V test light.
15. An induction meter. This is used for determining whether or not there is current in a wire. These are handy for use if a wire is broken somewhere in a wiring harness.

As a final note, you will probably find a torque wrench necessary for all but the most basic work. The beam type models are perfectly adequate although the newer click types are more precise.

Special Tools

Normally, the use of special factory tools is avoided for repair procedures, since these are not readily available for the do-it-yourself mechanic. When it is possible to perform the job with more commonly available tools, it will be pointed out, but occasionally, a special tool was designed to perform a specific function and should be used. Before substituting another tool, you should be convinced that neither your safety nor the performance of the vehicle will be compromised.

Some special tools are available commercially from major tool manufacturers. Others can be purchased from a Mazda dealer or from other tool suppliers.

SERVICING YOUR VEHICLE SAFELY

It is impossible to anticipate all of the hazards involved with automotive maintenance and service but care and common sense will prevent most accidents.

The rules of safety for mechanics range from "don't smoke around gasoline" to "use the proper tool for the job." To avoid injuries one must develop safe work habits and take every possible precaution.

Do's

• Do keep a fire extinguisher and first aid kit within easy reach.

• Do wear safety glasses or goggles when cutting, drilling, grinding or prying, even if you have 20/20 vision. If you wear glasses for the sake of vision, then they should be made of hardened glass that can serve also as safety glasses, or

wear safety goggles over your regular glasses.

• Do shield your eyes whenever you work around the battery. Batteries contain sulphuric acid; in case of contact with the eyes or skin, flush the area with water or a mixture of water and baking soda and get medical attention immediately.

• Do use safety stands for any under-car service. Jacks are for raising vehicles; safety stands are for making sure the vehicle stays raised until you want it to come down. Whenever the vehicle is raised, block the wheels remaining on the ground and set the parking brake.

• Do use adequate ventilation when working with any chemicals. Like carbon monoxide, the asbestos dust resulting from brake lining wear can be poisonous in sufficient quantities.

• Do disconnect the negative battery cable when working on the electrical system. The primary ignition system can contain up to 40,000 volts.

• Do follow manufacturer's directions whenever working with potentially hazardous materials. Both brake fluid and antifreeze are poisonous if taken internally.

• Do properly maintain your tools. Loose hammerheads, mushroomed punches and chisels, frayed or poorly grounded electrical cords, excessively worn screwdrivers, spread wrenches (open end), cracked sockets, slipping ratchets, or faulty droplight sockets can cause accidents.

• Do use the proper size and type of tool for the job being done.

• Do when possible, pull on a wrench handle rather than push on it, and adjust your stance to prevent a fall.

• Do be sure that adjustable wrenches are tightly adjusted on the nut or bolt and pulled so that the face is on the side of the fixed jaw.

• Do select a wrench or socket that fits the nut or bolt. The wrench or socket should sit straight, not cocked.

• Do strike squarely with a hammer. Avoid glancing blows.

• Do set the parking brake and block the drive wheels if the work requires that the engine be running.

Don'ts

• Don't run an engine in a garage or anywhere else without proper ventilation — EVER! Carbon monoxide is poisonous; it takes a long time to leave the human body and you can build up a deadly supply of it in your system by simply breathing in a little every day. You may not realize you are slowly poisoning yourself. Always use power vents, windows, fans or open the garage door.

• Don't work around moving parts while wearing a necktie or other loose clothing. Short sleeves are much safer than long, loose sleeves. Hard-toed shoes with neoprene soles protect your toes and give a better grip on slippery surfaces. Jewelry such as watches, fancy belt buckles, beads or body adornment of any kind is not safe working around a car. Long hair should be hidden under a hat or cap.

• Don't use pockets for toolboxes. A fall or bump can drive a screwdriver deep into your body. Even a wiping cloth hanging from the back pocket can wrap around a spinning shaft or fan.

• Don't smoke when working around gasoline, cleaning solvent or other flammable material.

• Don't smoke when working around the battery. When the battery is being charged, it gives off explosive hydrogen gas.

• Don't use gasoline to wash your hands; there are excellent soaps available. Gasoline may contain lead, and lead can enter the body through a cut, accumulating in the body until you are very ill. Gasoline also removes all the natural oils from the skin so that bone dry hands will suck up oil and grease.

• Don't service the air conditioning system unless you are equipped with the necessary tools and training. The refrigerant is extremely cold and when exposed to the air, will instantly freeze any surface it comes in contact with, including your eyes. Although the refrigerant is normally non-toxic, R-12 becomes a deadly poisonous gas in the presence of an open flame. One good whiff of the vapors from burning refrigerant can be fatal.

HISTORY

The 323 was originally introduced in 1977 as the GLC model. In 1986 Mazda renamed the GLC as the 323. In 1990 Mazda introduced a new 323 hatchback. The 323 is equipped with a 1.6L, fuel injected 4 cylinder engine.

The Protege was originally introduced in 1989 as a 1990 model. The Protege is available with one of two 1.8L, fuel injected, 16 valve engines.

The MX-3 was originally introduced in 1991 as a 1992 model. The MX-3 is available in two models, the base model and the GS model. The base model features the 1.6L, 16 valve 4 cylinder engine. The GS model is equipped with the 1.8L V-6 engine.

The 626 was originally introduced in 1979 as a rear wheel drive 2 door coupe and 4 door sedan. In 1983 Mazda introduced the first front wheel drive 626 models. The 1990 model 626 was introduced in 1989. This model 626 was available with a normally aspirated or turbocharged 2.2L, fuel injected engine. In 1992, Mazda introduced an all new 1993 626 model. The 1993 626 is available with either a 2.0L or a 2.5L engine.

The MX-6 was originally introduced in 1987 as a 1988 model. This model MX-6 was equipped with a normally aspirated or turbocharged 2.2L, 4 cylinder, fuel injected engine. In 1992 Mazda introduced an all new 1993 MX-6 model. The 1993 MX-6 is available with a 2.0L or 2.5L engine.

The MX-5 Miata was originally introduced in 1989 as a 1990 model. The Miata is equipped with a 1.6L, DOHC, fuel injected, 16 valve engine.

SERIAL NUMBER IDENTIFICATION

Vehicle

▶ See Figures 1 and 2

The Vehicle Identification Number (VIN) is stamped on a metal plate that is riveted to the instrument panel adjacent to the windshield. It can be seen by looking through the lower corner of the windshield on the driver's side. The VIN number is also stamped on the firewall directly behind the engine.

The VIN is a 17 digit combination of numbers and letters. The first 3 digits represent the world manufacturer identifier which is Mazda. The 5th digit is a passenger car identifier, indicating the vehicle is imported from outside North America or built by another manufacturer in North America for Mazda. The 9th digit is a check digit for all vehicles. The 10th digit indicates the model year: L for 1990, M for 1991, N for 1992 or P for 1993. The 11th digit is the assembly plant code. The 12th through 17th digits indicate the production sequence number.

Vehicle Certification Label

▶ See Figure 3

The Vehicle Certification Label is attached to the left hand door jamb below the latch striker. The label contains the name of the manufacturer, month and year of manufacture, Gross Vehicle Weight Rating (GVWR), Gross Axle Weight Rating (GAWR), and the certification statement. The vehicle certification label also contains the VIN and the paint color code.

Engine Identification Label

▶ See Figure 4

The engine identification number label is located on the engine block.

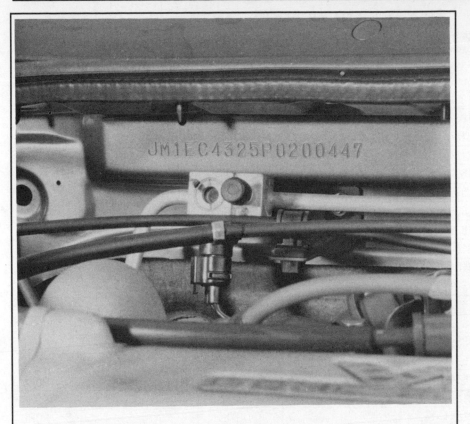

Fig. 2 Underhood vehicle serial number location

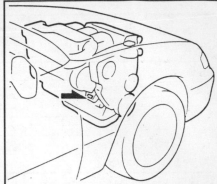

Fig. 4 Engine identification number location

Transmission

▶ See Figure 5

The transmission identification label can be found on the side of the transmission housing next to the shift mechanism.

Transaxle

▶ See Figures 5 and 6

The transaxle identification label can be found either on the top of the transaxle or on the right side.

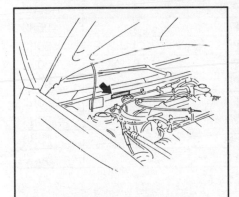

Fig. 1 Underhood vehicle serial number location

Fig. 3 Vehicle certification label location

ROUTINE MAINTENANCE

Air Cleaner

The air cleaner is a paper element contained in a housing located in the engine compartment. The air filter element should be serviced according to the Maintenance Intervals Chart at the end of this Section.

➡ Check the air filter element more often if the vehicle is operated under severe dusty conditions and replace, as necessary

REMOVAL & INSTALLATION

▶ See Figures 8, 9, 10 and 11

1.6L Engine

1. Disconnect the negative battery cable.
2. Disconnect the airflow meter electrical connector from the cover.

ENGINE IDENTIFICATION

Year	Model	Engine Displacement Liters (cc)	Engine Series (ID/VIN)	Fuel System	No. of Cylinders	Engine Type
1990	323	1.6 (1597)	B6E	MPFI	4	SOHC
	Protege	1.8 (1839)	BPE	MPFI	4	SOHC
	Protege	1.8 (1839)	BPD	MPFI	4	DOHC
	626	2.2 (2184)	F2	MPFI	4	SOHC
	MX-6	2.2 (2184)	F2	EFI	4	SOHC
	Miata	1.6 (1597)	B6ZE	EFI	4	DOHC
1991	323	1.6 (1597)	B6E	MPFI	4	SOHC
	Protege	1.8 (1839)	BPE	MPFI	4	SOHC
	Protege	1.8 (1839)	BPD	MPFI	4	DOHC
	626	2.2 (2184)	F2	MPFI	4	SOHC
	MX-6	2.2 (2184)	F2	EFI	4	SOHC
	Miata	1.6 (1597)	B6ZE	EFI	4	DOHC
1992	323	1.6 (1597)	B6E	MPFI	4	SOHC
	Protege	1.8 (1839)	BPE	MPFI	4	SOHC
	Protege	1.8 (1839)	BPD	MPFI	4	DOHC
	MX-3	1.6 (1597)	BPE	MPFI	4	SOHC
	MX-3	1.8 (1844)	K8D	MPFI	6	DOHC
	626	2.2 (2184)	F2	MPFI	4	SOHC
	MX-6	2.2 (2184)	F2	EFI	4	SOHC
	Miata	1.6 (1597)	B6ZE	EFI	4	DOHC
1993	323	1.6 (1597)	B6E	MPFI	4	SOHC
	Protege	1.8 (1839)	BPE	MPFI	4	SOHC
	Protege	1.8 (1839)	BPD	MPFI	4	DOHC
	MX-3	1.6 (1597)	BPE	MPFI	4	SOHC
	MX-3	1.8 (1844)	K8D	MPFI	6	DOHC
	626	2.0 (1991)	FS	MPFI	4	DOHC
	626	2.5 (2496)	KL	MPFI	6	DOHC
	MX-6	2.0 (1991)	FS	MPFI	4	DOHC
	MX-6	2.5 (2496)	KL	MPFI	6	DOHC
	Miata	1.6 (1597)	B6ZE	EFI	4	DOHC

MPFI—Multi-Port Fuel Injection
EFI—Electronic Fuel Injection
SOHC—Single Overhead Cam
DOHC—Dual Overhead Cam

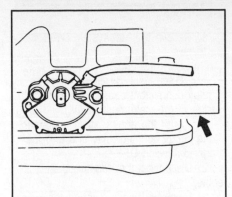

Fig. 5 Miata automatic transmission identification label location

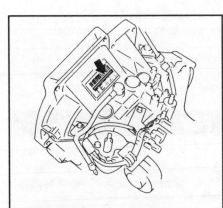

Fig. 6 323, Protege and MX-3 automatic transaxle identification label location

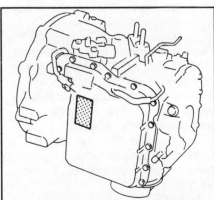

Fig. 7 1993 626 and MX-6 automatic transaxle identification label location

3. Remove the air cleaner housing cover bolts and unclip the air cleaner housing cover clips.

4. Remove the air cleaner element from the housing.

5. Inspect the air cleaner element and replace as necessary.

To install:

6. Clean any dirt or other foreign material from the air filter housing.

7. Install the air filter element and the air filter cover.

8. Install and tighten the housing cover bolts.

9. Connect the electrical connector to the air flow meter and connect the negative battery cable.

1.8L Engine

1. Disconnect the negative battery cable.

2. Remove the air cleaner housing cover bolts and remove the cover.

3. Remove the air cleaner element from the housing.

4. Inspect the air cleaner element and replace as necessary.

To install:

5. Clean any dirt or other foreign material from the air filter housing.

6. Install the air filter element and the air filter cover.

7. Install and tighten the housing cover bolts.

8. Connect the negative battery cable.

2.0L, 2.2L and 2.5L Engines

1. Disconnect the negative battery cable.

2. Disconnect the airflow meter electrical connector.

3. Remove the air duct clamp and the duct from the airflow meter assembly.

4. Remove the air filter cover mounting screws.

5. Remove the air filter cover and the filter element.

To install:

6. Clean any dirt or other foreign material from the air filter housing.

7. Install the air filter element and the air filter cover.

8. Install and tighten the cover mounting screws.

9. Connect the air duct to the airflow meter assembly and tighten the clamp.

10. Connect the electrical connector to the airflow meter and connect the negative battery cable.

Fuel Filter

The fuel filter is attached to a bracket located in the left rear of the engine compartment, next to the brake master cylinder fluid reservoir, on all except Miata. On Miata, the fuel filter is located at the rear of the vehicle, next to the fuel tank. The fuel filter should be serviced according to the Maintenance Intervals Chart at the end of this Section.

REMOVAL & INSTALLATION

▶ **See Figure 12**

Except MX-5 Miata

1. On 323, Protege and MX-3, relieve the fuel system pressure as follows:

   a. Remove the rear seat cushion and locate the fuel pump connector.

   b. Start the engine.

   c. Disconnect the fuel pump connector.

   d. After the engine stalls, reconnect the fuel pump connector and turn the ignition switch **OFF**. Install the rear seat cushion.

2. On 626 and MX-6 equipped with the 2.0L or 2.5L engines, relieve the fuel system pressure as follows:

   a. Start the engine.

   b. Remove the fuel pump relay from the relay box, located in the left side of the engine compartment.

   c. After the engine stalls, reinstall the relay and turn the ignition switch **OFF**.

3. On 626 and MX-6 equipped with the 2.2L engine, relieve the fuel system pressure as follows:

   a. Start the engine.

   b. Disconnect the circuit opening relay connector, located under the left side of the instrument panel.

   c. After the engine stalls, reconnect the circuit opening relay and turn the ignition switch **OFF**.

4. Disconnect the negative battery cable.

5. If equipped, remove the fuel line clamps.

6. Disconnect the fuel lines from the filter and plug the ends to prevent leakage.

7. Loosen the bolt and nut and remove the fuel filter from its mounting bracket. Note the direction of the flow arrow on the filter so the replacement filter can be installed in the correct position.

To install:

8. Install the fuel filter in its mounting bracket, making sure the flow arrow is pointing in the proper direction. Tighten the bracket bolt and nut.

9. Unplug the fuel lines and connect them to the fuel filter.

10. If equipped, install the fuel line clamps.

11. Connect the negative battery cable.

Fig. 8 Disconnecting the air inlet tube from the air cleaner housing

Fig. 9 Unfastening the air cleaner housing clip

MX-5 Miata

1. Relieve the fuel system pressure as follows:
   a. Start the engine.
   b. Disconnect the circuit opening relay connector, located under the left side of the instrument panel.
   c. After the engine stalls, reconnect the circuit opening relay and turn the ignition switch **OFF**.
2. Disconnect the negative battery cable.
3. Raise and safely support the vehicle.
4. Remove the fuel filter cover.
5. Disconnect the fuel lines from the fuel filter.
6. Remove the filter mounting bolts or nuts and remove the fuel filter.
7. Installation is the reverse of the removal procedure. Make sure the fuel filter is installed in the proper flow direction.

PCV Valve

The PCV valve is located in a grommet attached to the valve cover. For crankcase ventilation system testing, refer to Section 4.

REMOVAL & INSTALLATION

▶ **See Figures 13 and 14**

1. Remove the PCV valve from the valve cover grommet.
2. Disconnect the hose from the PCV valve and remove it from the vehicle.
3. Check the PCV valve for deposits and clogging. If the valve rattles when shaken, it is okay. If the valve does not rattle, clean the valve with solvent until the plunger is free, or replace it.
4. Check the PCV hose and the valve cover grommet for clogging and signs of wear or deterioration. Replace, as necessary.

To install:

5. Connect the PCV hose to the PCV valve.
6. Install the PCV valve in the valve cover grommet.

Evaporative Canister

The vapor, or carbon canister is part of the evaporative emission control system. It is located in the right rear of the engine compartment.

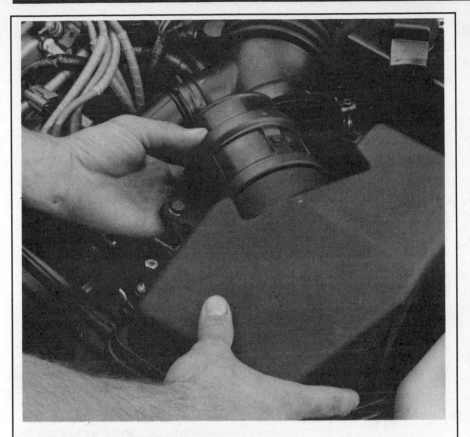

Fig. 10 Removing the air cleaner housing assembly

Fig. 11 Removing the air cleaner element

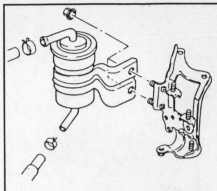

Fig. 12 Fuel filter removal and installation

SERVICING

Servicing the carbon canister is only necessary if it is clogged or contains liquid fuel, indicated by odor or by excessive weight. Remove the canister and blow into the air vent in the bottom of the canister. If air passes from the fuel vapor inlet and the canister does not contain liquid fuel, it is okay. If replacement is necessary, the canister must be replaced as a unit; it cannot be disassembled. For further evaporative emission control system testing, refer to Section 4.

Battery

The battery is located under the hood in the engine compartment in all models except the MX-5 Miata. In the MX-5 Miata, the battery is located in the right rear of the trunk. The battery in the MX-5 Miata is not a standard battery and when replacement is necessary, it must be replaced with an exact replacement battery.

GENERAL MAINTENANCE

Corrosion of battery terminals and cable clamps interferes with the flow of power out of the battery and the charge flowing into the battery from the charging system. This can result in a "no start" condition. Battery life may be shortened if the battery becomes completely discharged. In some cases, a totally discharged battery may not readily accept a charge.

To extend battery life and to reduce the need for service, keep the top of the battery, the battery terminals, and the cable clamps clean and free of corrosion. Make sure the cable clamps

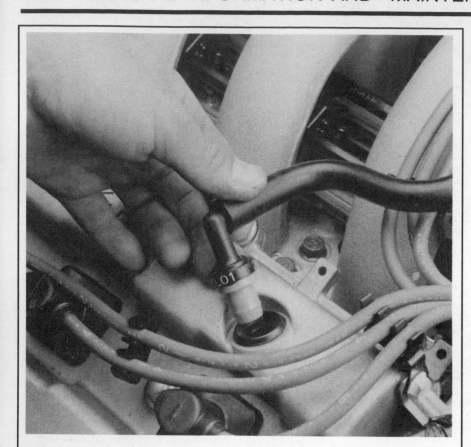

Fig. 13 Removing the PCV valve

are fastened tightly to the battery terminals. If corrosion is found, disconnect the cables and clean the clamps and terminals with a wire brush. Neutralize the corrosion with a solution of baking soda and water. After installing the cables, apply a light coating of petroleum jelly to the cable clamps and terminals to help prevent corrosion.

FLUID LEVEL (EXCEPT MAINTENANCE FREE BATTERIES)

▶ See Figure 15

Check the battery electrolyte level at least once a month, or more often in hot weather or during periods of extended car operation. The level can be checked through the case on translucent polypropylene batteries; the cell caps must be removed on other models. The electrolyte level in each cell should be kept filled to the split ring inside, or the line marked on the outside of the case.

If the level is low, add only distilled water, or colorless, odorless drinking water, through the opening until the level

is correct. Each cell is completely separate from the others, so each must be checked and filled individually.

If water is added in freezing weather, the car should be driven several miles to allow the water to mix with the electrolyte. Otherwise, the battery could freeze. If the battery needs water often, check the charging system.

CABLES

▶ See Figure 16

✳✳CAUTION

To avoid the possibility of accidently grounding the car's electrical system always remove the negative battery cable first. Failure to do so could allow a spark to occur and cause the battery gases to explode, possibly resulting in personal injury.

1. Using an adjustable or box wrench and battery pliers, loosen the negative battery cable nut. The jaws on battery pliers are specially designed for gripping the cable clamp bolts.

2. Remove the negative battery cable from the battery post, using battery pliers.

✳✳WARNING

Do not twist or pry the cable clamp off of the post using a screwdriver. This may crack the top of the battery or cause damage to the internal battery components and leakage at the terminals.

3. Repeat Steps 1 and 2 to remove the positive battery cable.
4. Clean both battery posts and the cable clamps using battery cleaning tools. There are tools available for both top post and side post batteries.
5. Remove the remaining corrosion deposits from the battery and cables by flushing with a baking soda-water solution comprising 2 teaspoons of baking soda and 1 cup of water.

✳✳WARNING

Do not allow the solution to enter the battery as this could weaken the electrolyte. Be careful not to allow the flushed deposits to come in contact with painted surfaces as paint damage may result.

6. Follow the negative battery cable to the engine block and check the connection. If it is loose or corroded, remove the cable and clean the cable end and block with sandpaper, then reconnect the cable.
7. Follow the positive cable to the starter and clean and tighten, if necessary.
8. Apply a small amount of petroleum jelly around the base of each battery post, to help reduce the possibility of corrosion. Do not coat the battery post.
9. Install the positive battery cable on the positive battery post. It may be necessary to spread the clamp slightly using a clamp spreader tool. Do not twist the clamp in an attempt to seat it on the post. When the clamp is seated, tighten the clamp nut.
10. Repeat Step 9 to install the negative battery cable.
11. After the cables are installed, coat the top of each terminal lightly with petroleum jelly.

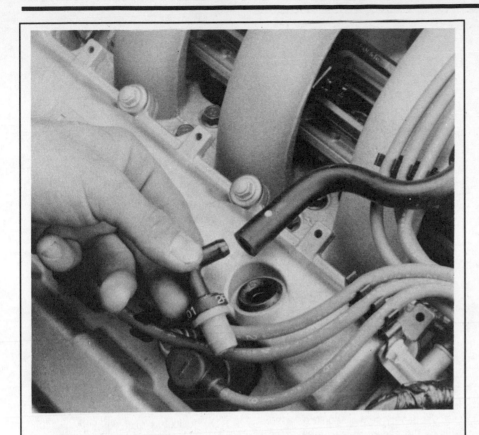

Fig. 14 Removing the PCV valve

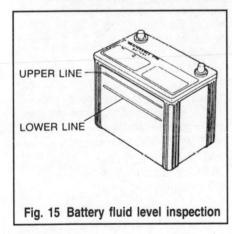

UPPER LINE

LOWER LINE

Fig. 15 Battery fluid level inspection

Fig. 16 Disconnecting the battery cables

TESTING

Specific Gravity (Except Maintenance Free Batteries)

At least once a year, check the specific gravity of the battery using a hydrometer. The hydrometer has a squeeze bulb at one end and nozzle at the other. Battery electrolyte is sucked into the hydrometer until the float is lifted from its seat. The specific gravity is then read by noting the position of the float. If the difference between cells is 50 points (0.050) or more, the battery is bad and must be replaced.

If the difference between cells is less than 50 points (0.050) and one or more cells are less than 1.225, charge the battery for 20 minutes at 35 amps and perform the capacity test. If the battery fails, it must be replaced. If it passes, add water, if necessary, and charge the battery. If the difference between cells is less than 50 points (0.050) and all cells are above 1.225, perform the capacity test. If the battery fails, replace it.

It is not possible to check the specific gravity in this manner on sealed (maintenance free) batteries. Instead, the indicator built into the top of the case must be relied on to display any signs of battery deterioration. If the indicator is dark, the battery can be assumed to be OK. If the indicator is light, the specific gravity is low and the battery should be charged or replaced.

Capacity Test

A high rate discharge battery-starter tester and a voltmeter are used for this test.

1. Turn the control knob on the tester to the **OFF** position and set the voltmeter selector switch to the 10 or 20 volt position.

2. Connect both positive test leads to the positive battery post and both negative test leads to the negative battery post. The voltmeter clips must contact the battery posts and not the high rate discharge tester clips, or actual battery terminal voltage will not be indicated.

3. Turn the load control knob on the tester until the ammeter reads approximately 3 times the ampere hour rating of the battery. For example, a 48 ampere hour battery should be tested at 150 amperes load.

4. With the ammeter reading the required load for 15 seconds, record the voltmeter reading. Do not leave the high discharge load on the battery for longer than 15 seconds.

5. If the voltmeter reading is 9.6 volts at 70°F (21°C) or more, the battery has good output capacity and will accept a charge, if necessary.

6. If the voltmeter reading is below 9.6 volts at 70°F (21°C) and the battery is fully charged, the battery is bad and must be replaced. If you are not sure about the battery's state of charge, charge the battery.

7. After the battery has been charged, repeat the capacity test. If the voltage is still less than 9.6 volts at 70°F (21°C), replace the battery. If the voltage is 9.6 or more at 70°F (21°C), the battery is good.

CHARGING

> ### ✳✳CAUTION
>
> **Keep flame or sparks away from the battery. The battery emits explosive hydrogen gas, especially when being charged. Battery electrolyte contains sulphuric acid. If electrolyte accidently comes in contact with your skin or eyes, flush with plenty of clear water. If it lands in your eyes, get medical help immediately.**

A cold battery will not readily accept a charge, so allow the battery to warm up to approximately 40°F (5°C) before charging, if necessary. This may take 4 to 8 hours at room temperature, depending on initial temperature and battery size.

A completely discharged battery may be slow to accept a charge initially and in some cases may not accept a charge at the normal charger setting. If the battery is in this condition, charging can be initiated using the dead battery switch, on battery chargers so equipped. Follow the charger manufacturers instructions on the use of the dead battery switch.

If the battery will accept a charge, it can be charged using the automatic or manual method. If the charger is equipped with an automatic setting, the charge rate is maintained within safe limits by automatic adjustment of the voltage and current in order to prevent excessive gassing and discharge of electrolyte. It will take approximately 2 to 4 hours to charge a completely discharged battery to a usable state. A full state of charge can be obtained by charging at a low current rate of 3 to 5 amps for a few more hours.

If the charger does not have an automatic setting, the battery will have to be charged manually. Initially set the charging rate for 30 to 40 amps and charge for approximately 30 minutes or as long as there is no excessive gassing or electrolyte discharge. If there is excessive gas emission, slow the charge rate to a level where the gassing stops. Excessive gas emission will result in non-replaceable loss of electrolyte.

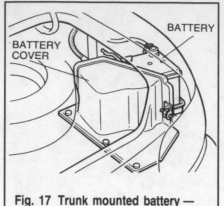

Fig. 17 Trunk mounted battery — Miata

REPLACEMENT

▶ **See Figure 17**

1. Disconnect the negative cable first and then the positive battery cable from the battery.
2. Remove the battery hold-down clamps. On the MX-5 Miata, remove the battery cover.
3. A battery carrier should be used to remove the battery. If a battery carrier is not available, grip the battery at opposite corners with your hands and carefully lift the battery from the tray.
4. Check the battery tray for corrosion or other damage. Clean the tray with a wire brush and a scraper.
5. Clean the battery and the cables.
6. Install the battery and the hold-down clamps.
7. Connect the positive and then the negative battery cables.

Belts

Accessories mounted on the front of the engine are belt-driven by the crankshaft. Some Mazda engines use one V-belt to drive the alternator and another to drive the power steering pump and air conditioning compressor. Other Mazda engines use one V-ribbed belt to drive the alternator, power steering pump and air conditioning compressor and one V-ribbed belt to drive the water pump.

INSPECTION

Inspect all belts for signs of glazing or cracking. A glazed belt will be perfectly smooth from slippage, while a good belt will have a slight texture of fabric visible. Cracks will usually start at the inner

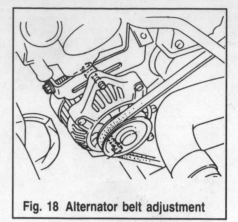

Fig. 18 Alternator belt adjustment

edge of the belt and run outward. Replace the belt at the first sign of cracking or if glazing is severe.

ADJUSTMENT

1.6L and 1.8L (except MX-3) Engines

ALTERNATOR BELT

▶ **See Figure 18**

1. Position a ruler perpendicular to the drive belt midway between the pulleys on the longest accessible belt span. Press firmly on the belt with your thumb to test the belt tension. The belt should deflect 0.31-0.35 in. (8-9mm) if it is new or 0.35-0.39 in. (9-10mm) for a used belt.
2. If the belt tension is not as specified in Step 1, loosen the alternator adjustment bolt and the through bolt. Turn the alternator adjustment screw to adjust the belt tension.
3. After adjustment, tighten the through bolt to 27-38 ft. lbs. (37-52 Nm) and the adjusting bolt to 14-19 ft. lbs. (19-25 Nm).

POWER STEERING/POWER STEERING AND AIR CONDITIONING BELT

▶ **See Figure 19**

1. Position a ruler perpendicular to the drive belt midway between the pulleys on the longest accessible belt span. Press firmly on the belt with your thumb to test the belt tension. The belt should deflect 0.31-0.35 in. (8-9mm) if it is new or 0.35-0.39 in. (9-10mm) if it is used.
2. If the belt tension is not as specified in Step 1, loosen the upper and lower air conditioning compressor through bolts.
3. Using a suitable prybar against the compressor body, move the compressor

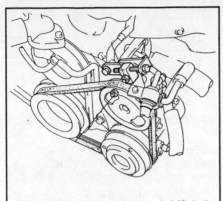

Fig. 19 Power steering and A/C belt adjustment

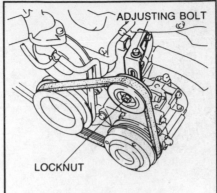

Fig. 20 Alternator and A/C belt adjustment — 1.6L engine

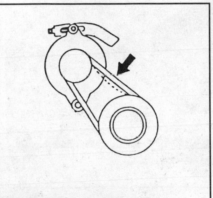

Fig. 21 A/C belt adjustment — 1990-92 626 and MX-6

until the belt tension is as specified in Step 1.

4. After adjustment, tighten the upper and lower air conditioning compressor through bolts.

AIR CONDITIONING BELT

1. Position a ruler perpendicular to the drive belt midway between the pulleys on the longest accessible belt span. Press firmly on the belt with your thumb to test the belt tension. The belt should deflect 0.31-0.35 in. (8-9mm) if it is new or 0.35-0.39 in. (9-10mm) if it is used.

2. If the belt tension is not as specified in Step 1, loosen the upper and lower air conditioning compressor through bolts.

3. Using a suitable prybar against the compressor body, move the compressor until the belt tension is as specified in Step 1.

4. After adjustment, tighten the upper and lower air conditioning compressor through bolts.

1.8L (MX-3), 2.0L and 2.5L Engines

ALTERNATOR AND POWER STEERING BELT

1. Position a ruler perpendicular to the drive belt midway between the pulleys on the longest accessible belt span. Press firmly on the belt with your thumb to test the belt tension. The belt should deflect 0.24-0.28 in. (6-7mm) if it is new or 0.28-0.31 in. (7-8mm) if it is used.

2. If the belt tension is not as specified in Step 1, loosen the idler pulley locknut. Turn the alternator adjustment bolt to adjust the belt tension.

3. After adjustment, tighten the idler pulley locknut to 23-41 ft. lbs. (31-46 Nm).

ALTERNATOR AND AIR CONDITIONING BELT

▶ See Figure 20

1. Position a ruler perpendicular to the drive belt midway between the pulleys on the longest accessible belt span. Press firmly on the belt with your thumb to test the belt tension. The belt should deflect 0.22-0.26 in. (5.5-6.5mm) if it is new or 0.26-0.30 in. (6.5-7.5mm) if it is used.

2. If the belt tension is not as specified in Step 1, loosen the idler pulley locknut. Turn the adjustment bolt to adjust the belt tension.

3. After adjustment, tighten the idler pulley locknut to 23-34 ft. lbs. (31-46 Nm).

2.2L Engine

ALTERNATOR BELT

▶ See Figure 21

1. Position a ruler perpendicular to the drive belt midway between the pulleys on the longest accessible belt span. Press firmly on the belt with your thumb to test the belt. The belt

should deflect 0.24-0.31 in. (6-8mm) if it is new or 0.27-0.35 in. (7-9mm) if it is used.

2. If the belt tension is not as specified in Step 1, loosen the alternator adjustment bolt and the through bolt. Turn the alternator adjustment screw to adjust the belt tension.

3. After adjustment, tighten the through bolt to 27-38 ft. lbs. (37-52 Nm) and the adjusting bolt to 13-18 ft. lbs. (18-25 Nm).

POWER STEERING AND AIR CONDITIONING BELT

1. Position a ruler perpendicular to the drive belt midway between the pulleys on the longest accessible belt span. Press firmly on the belt with your thumb to test the belt tension. The belt should deflect 0.27-0.35 in. (7-9mm) if it is new or 0.31-0.39 in. (8-10mm) if it is used.

2. If the belt tension is not as specified in Step 1, loosen the upper and lower air conditioning compressor through bolts.

3. Using a suitable prybar against the compressor body, move the compressor until the belt tension is as specified in Step 1.

4. After adjustment, tighten the upper and lower air conditioning compressor through bolts.

REMOVAL & INSTALLATION

1.6L and 1.8L (except MX-3) Engines

1. Loosen the alternator mounting bolt and the adjusting bolt. Rotate the alternator toward the engine and remove the drive belt.

2. Inspect the drive belts for wear or damage and replace, as necessary.

To install:

3. Position the drive belts over the pulleys.

4. Adjust the belt tension as described under Adjustment.

5. Tighten the alternator mounting bolt after belt adjustment.

1.8L (MX-3) Engine

1. Loosen the idler pulley locknut and the adjusting bolt. Remove the drive belt.

2. Inspect the drive belts for wear or damage and replace, as necessary.

To install:

3. Position the drive belts over the pulleys.

4. Adjust the belt tension as described under Adjustment.

Fig. 22 Inspecting hoses

5. Tighten the idler pulley locknut bolt after belt adjustment.

2.0L Engine

1. Loosen the alternator mounting bolt and the adjusting bolt. Remove the drive belt.
2. Inspect the drive belts for wear or damage and replace, as necessary.
To install:
3. Position the drive belts over the pulleys.
4. Adjust the belt tension as described under Adjustment.
5. Tighten the idler pulley locknut bolt after belt adjustment.

2.2L Engine

1. Loosen the air conditioning compressor upper and lower through bolts. Rotate the compressor toward the engine and remove the drive belt.
2. Loosen the alternator pivot and adjuster bolts. Rotate the alternator toward the engine and remove the drive belt.
3. Inspect the drive belts for wear or damage and replace, as necessary.
To install:
4. Position the drive belts over the pulleys.

5. Adjust the belt tension as described under Adjustment.
6. Tighten the alternator and compressor mounting bolts after belt adjustment.

2.5L Engine

1. Loosen the idler pulley locknut and the adjusting bolt. Remove the drive belt.
2. Inspect the drive belts for wear or damage and replace, as necessary.
To install:
3. Position the drive belts over the pulleys.
4. Adjust the belt tension as described under Adjustment.
5. Tighten the idler pulley locknut bolt after belt adjustment.

Hoses

✳✳CAUTION

Disconnect the negative battery cable or fan motor wiring harness connector before replacing any radiator/heater hose. The fan may come on, under certain circumstances, even though the ignition is off.

INSPECTION

▶ See Figure 22

Inspect the condition of heater and radiator hoses periodically. When you are performing other maintenance is a good time. Make sure the engine and cooling system are cold. Inspect for cracking, rotting or collapsed hoses, replace as necessary. Run your hand along the length of the hose. If a weak or swollen point is noted when squeezing the hose wall, replace the hose.

REMOVAL & INSTALLATION

1. Remove the radiator cap.

✳✳CAUTION

Never remove the radiator cap while the engine is running. Personal injury from scalding hot coolant or steam may result if the cap is removed. Wait until the engine has cooled to remove the radiator cap. If this is not possible, wrap a thick cloth around the radiator cap and turn it slowly to the first stop. Take a step back while the pressure is released from the cooling system. When you are sure that all the pressure has been released, press down on the cap, with the cloth, and turn and remove it.

2. Position a suitable container under the radiator and open the draincock to drain the radiator.

✳✳CAUTION

When draining the coolant, keep in mind that cats and dogs are attracted by the ethylene glycol antifreeze, and are quite likely to drink any that is left in an uncovered container or in puddles on the ground. This will prove fatal in sufficient quantity. Always drain the coolant into a sealable container. Coolant should be reused unless it is contaminated or several years old.

3. Loosen the hose clamps at each end of the hose requiring replacement. Pull the clamps back on the hose away from the connection.

4. Twist, pull and slide the hose off the radiator, water pump, thermostat or heater connection.

➡️**If the hose is stuck at the connection, do not try to insert a screwdriver or other sharp tool under the hose end in an effort to free it, as the connection and/or hose may become damaged. Heater connections especially are easily damaged. If the hose is not to be reused, make a slice at the end of the hose with a single edge razor blade, perpendicular to the end of the hose. Do not cut deep so as not to damage the connection. The hose can then be peeled from the connection.**

5. Clean both hose mounting connections. Inspect the condition of the hose clamps and replace them, if necessary.
   To install:
6. Coat the connection surfaces with a water resistant sealer.
7. Slide the hose clamps over the replacement hose and slide the hose ends over the connections into position.
8. Position the hose clamps. Make sure they are located beyond the raised bead of the connector, if equipped, and centered in the clamping area of the connection.
9. If the clamps are the screw type, tighten them to 22-31 inch lbs. (2.5-3.5 Nm). Do not overtighten.
10. Close the radiator draincock and fill the cooling system.
11. Start the engine and allow it to reach normal operating temperature. Check for leaks.

Air Conditioning System

SAFETY WARNINGS

1. Avoid contact with a charged refrigeration system, even when working on another part of the air conditioning system or vehicle. If a heavy tool comes into contact with a section of air conditioning line, it can easily cause the relatively soft material to rupture.
2. When it is necessary to apply force to a fitting which contains refrigerant, as when checking that all system couplings are securely tightened, use a wrench on both parts of the fitting involved, if possible. This will avoid putting torque on the refrigerant tubing. (It is advisable, when possible, to use tube or line wrenches when tightening these flare nut fittings.)
3. Do not attempt to discharge the system by merely loosening a fitting, or removing the service valve caps and cracking these valves. Wear protective gloves when connecting or disconnecting service gauge or recovery/recycling equipment hoses.
4. Discharge the system only in a well ventilated area, as high concentrations of the gas can exclude oxygen and act as an anesthetic. When leak testing or soldering this is particularly important, as toxic gas is formed when R-12 contacts any flame.
5. Never start a system without first verifying that both service valves are backseated, if equipped, and that all fittings throughout the system are snugly connected.
6. Avoid applying heat to any refrigerant line or storage vessel. Never allow a refrigerant storage container to sit out in the sun, or near any other source of heat, such as a radiator.
7. Always wear goggles when working on a system to protect the eyes. If refrigerant contacts the eye, it is advisable in all cases to see a physician as soon as possible.
8. Frostbite from liquid refrigerant should be treated by first gradually warming the area with cool water, and then gently applying petroleum jelly. A physician should be consulted.
9. Always keep refrigerant container fittings capped when not in use. Avoid sudden shock to the container which might occur from dropping it, or from banging a heavy tool against it. Never carry a container in the passenger compartment of a car.
10. Always completely discharge the system before painting the vehicle (if the paint is to be baked on), or before welding anywhere near the refrigerant lines.

SYSTEM INSPECTION

Visually inspect the air conditioning system for refrigerant leaks, damaged compressor clutch, compressor drive belt tension and condition, plugged evaporator drain tube, blocked condenser fins, disconnected or broken wires, blown fuses, corroded connections and poor insulation.

A refrigerant leak will usually appear as an oily residue at the leakage point in the system. The oily residue soon picks up dust or dirt particles from the surrounding air and appears greasy. Through time, this will build up and appear to be a heavy dirt impregnated grease. Most leaks are caused by damaged or missing O-ring seals at the component connections, damaged charging valve cores or missing service gauge port caps.

The evaporator drain tube expels the condensation that accumulates on the bottom of the evaporator housing, into the engine compartment. If the tube is obstructed, air conditioning performance can be restricted and condensation buildup can spill over onto the vehicle floor.

Any obstruction of or damage to the condenser configuration will restrict the air flow which is essential to its efficient operation. It is therefore a good rule to keep the condenser clean and in proper physical shape.

Vigorously shake the wiring harness while running the air conditioning and look for sparks (a sign of shorting) or intermittent operation (a sign of opens).

Move the refrigerant hoses and look for signs of cracks, rotted hoses or loose connections.

REFRIGERANT LEVEL CHECKS

1. Connect a manifold gauge set.
2. Run the engine at 2000 rpm.
3. Set the blower motor on high and the temperature control at cool.
4. If the compressor clutch does not engage, connect a jumper wire between the positive battery terminal and the green/black wire at the clutch connector.
5. Wait until the air conditioning system stabilizes and check the readings of the HI and LO gauges. The normal HI reading is 199-228 psi (1372-1572kpa). The normal LO reading is 19-21 psi (131-145kpa).
6. If the HI reading is 114-128 psi (786-883kpa) and the LO reading is 11.4 psi (78.6kpa), there is insufficient refrigerant in the system. The system must be leak tested and recharged with the proper amount of refrigerant.
7. If the HI reading is 284 psi (1958kpa) or more and the LO reading is 35.6 psi (245.5kpa) or more, there is excessive refrigerant in the system. Recharge the system with the proper amount of refrigerant.

GAUGE SETS

▶ **See Figure 23**

Most of the service work performed in air conditioning requires the use of a set of two gauges, one for the high pressure side of the system and the other for the low pressure side of the system.

The low side gauge records both pressure and vacuum. Vacuum readings are calibrated from 0 to 30 inches Hg and the pressure graduations read from 0 to no less than 60 psi (414kpa). The high side gauge measures pressure from 0 to at least 600 psi (4140kpa).

Both gauges are threaded into a manifold that contains two hand shut-off valves. Proper manipulation of these valves, and the use of the attached hoses allow the user to perform the following services:

1. Test high and low side pressures.
2. Remove air, moisture, and contaminated refrigerant.
3. Purge the system (of refrigerant).
4. Charge the system (with refrigerant).

The manifold valves are designed so they have no direct effect on gauge readings, but serve only to provide for, or cut off, flow of refrigerant through the manifold. During all testing and hook-up operations, the valves are kept in the closed position to avoid disturbing the refrigeration system. The valves are opened only to purge the system or to charge it.

Connect the manifold gauge set as follows:

5. Turn both manifold valves fully to the right, to close the high and low pressure hoses to the center manifold and hose.

6. Remove the caps from the high and low pressure service gauge port valves. The high pressure gauge port valve is located between the compressor and the condenser, in the high pressure vapor (discharge) line. The low pressure gauge port valve is located between the suction accumulator/drier and the compressor, in the low pressure vapor (suction) line.

7. If the manifold gauge set hoses do not have valve depressing pins in them, install fitting adapters T71P-19703-S and R or equivalent (which have pins) on the low and high pressure hoses.

8. Connect the high and low pressure hoses, or adapters, to the respective

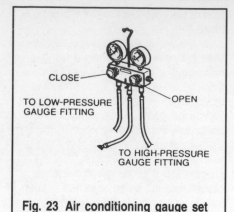

Fig. 23 Air conditioning gauge set

high and low pressure service gauge port valves.

➡ **A High side adapter set is necessary to connect the manifold gauge set to the high pressure service gauge port valve.**

DISCHARGING THE SYSTEM

➡ **R-12 refrigerant is a chlorofluorocarbon which, when released into the atmosphere, contributes to the depletion of the ozone layer in the upper atmosphere. Ozone filters out harmful radiation from the sun. Consult the laws in your area before servicing the air conditioning system. In some states it is illegal to perform repairs involving refrigerant unless the work is done by a certified technician.**

The use of refrigerant recovery systems and recycling stations makes possible the recovery and reuse of refrigerant after contaminants and moisture have been removed. When a recovery system or recyling station is used, the following general procedures should be observed, in addition to the operating instructions provided by the equipment manufacturer.

1. Connect the refrigerant recycling station hose(s) to the vehicle air conditioning service ports and the recovery station inlet fitting.

➡ **Hoses should have shut off devices or check valves within 12 in. (305mm) of the hose end to minimize the introduction of air into the recycling station and to minimize the amount of refrigerant released when the hose(s) is disconnected.**

2. Turn the power to the recycling station **ON** to start the recovery process. Allow the recycling station to pump the

refrigerant from the system until the station pressure goes into a vacuum. On some stations the pump will be shut off automatically by a low pressure switch in the electrical system. On other units it may be necessary to manually turn off the pump.

3. Once the recycling station has evacuated the vehicle air conditioning system, close the station inlet valve, if equipped. Then switch **OFF** the electrical power.

4. Allow the vehicle air conditioning system to remain closed for about 2 minutes. Observe the system vacuum level as shown on the gauge. If the pressure does not rise, disconnect the recycling station hose(s).

5. If the system pressure rises, repeat Steps 2, 3 and 4 until the vacuum level remains stable for 2 minutes.

EVACUATING

1. Properly connect a manifold gauge set.

2. Leak test all connections and components.

3. Properly discharge the refrigerant system.

4. Make sure both manifold gauge valves are turned fully to the right. Make sure the center hose connection at the manifold gauge is tight.

5. Connect the manifold gauge set center hose to a vacuum pump.

6. Open the manifold gauge set valves and start the vacuum pump.

7. Evacuate the system with the vacuum pump until the low pressure gauge reads at least 25 in. Hg or as close to 30 in. Hg as possible. Continue to operate the vacuum pump for 15 minutes. If a part of the system has been replaced, continue to operate the vacuum pump for another 20-30 minutes.

8. When evacuation of the system is complete, close the manifold gauge set valves and turn the vacuum pump **OFF**.

9. Observe the low pressure gauge for 5 minutes to ensure that system vacuum is held. If vacuum is held, charge the system. If vacuum is not held for 5 minutes, leak test the system, service the leaks and evacuate the system again.

CHARGING

1. Connect a manifold gauge set according to the proper procedure. Properly discharge and evacuate the system.

2. With the manifold gauge set valves closed to the center hose, disconnect the vacuum pump from the manifold gauge set.

3. Connect the center hose of the manifold gauge set to a refrigerant container.

4. Loosen the center hose at the manifold gauge set and open the refrigerant container valve. Allow the refrigerant to escape to purge air and moisture from the center hose. Then, tighten the center hose connection at the manifold gauge set.

5. Disconnect the wire harness snap lock connector from the clutch cycling or low pressure switch and install a jumper wire across the 2 terminals of the connector.

6. Open the manifold gauge set low side valve to allow refrigerant to enter the system. Keep the refrigerant container in an upright position.

❈❈CAUTION

Do not open the manifold gauge set high pressure (discharge) gauge valve when charging. Opening the valve can cause the refrigerant container to explode, which can result in personal injury.

7. When no more refrigerant is being drawn into the system, start the engine and set the control assembly for MAX cold and HI blower and press the air conditioning switch to draw the remaining refrigerant into the system. Continue to add refrigerant to the system until approximately 40 oz. of R-12 is in the system. Then close the manifold gauge set low pressure valve and the refrigerant supply valve.

8. Remove the jumper wire from the clutch cycling or low pressure switch snap lock connector. Connect the connector to the pressure switch.

9. Operate the system until pressures stabilize to verify normal operation and system pressures.

10. In high ambient temperatures, it may be necessary to operate a high volume fan positioned to blow air through the radiator and condenser to aid in cooling the engine and prevent excessive refrigerant system pressures.

11. When charging is completed and system operating pressures are normal, disconnect the manifold gauge set from the vehicle. Install the protective caps on the service gauge port valves.

LEAK TESTING

Electronic Leak Detector

Turn the control switch on the electronic leak detector to the **ON**position. The detector will automatically calibrate itself. Move the detector probe at approximately 1 in. per second in the suspected leak area. When escaping refrigerant gas is located, the ticking/beeping signal from the detector will increase in ticks/beeps per second. If the gas is relatively concentrated, the signal will be increasingly shrill.

Windshield Wipers

▶ **See Figure 24**

For the longest life and maximum efficiency, the windshield and wiper blades should be kept clean. Dirt, sap from trees, road tar, etc. will cause streaking, smearing and blade deterioration if not removed from the glass. It is advisable to wash the windshield carefully with a commercial glass cleaner at least once a month. Wipe the rubber blades with the wet rag afterwards. Do not attempt to move the wipers by hand; damage to the motor and drive mechanism will result.

To inspect and/or replace the wiper blades, place the wiper switch in the **LOW**speed position and the ignition switch in the **ACC**position. When the wiper blades are approximately vertical on the windshield, turn the ignition switch to the **OFF**position.

Examine the wiper blades. If they are found to be cracked, broken or torn, they should be replaced immediately. Replacement intervals will vary with usage, although ozone deterioration usually limits blade life to about one year. If the wiper pattern is smeared or streaked, or if the blade chatters across the glass, the blades should be replaced. It is easiest and most sensible to replace the blades in pairs.

There are several different types of refills, and your vehicle could have any kind, since aftermarket blades and arms may not use exactly the same type refill as the original equipment.

Most windshield wiper refills include instructions in the packaging and because of the wide variety of installation methods, these instructions should be followed.

The original equipment type of refill simply slides into a locking device at each end of the blade. By sliding the new refill through all the jaws and pushing through the slight resistance when it reaches the end of its travel, the refill will lock into position.

Regardless of the type of refill used, make sure that all of the frame jaws are engaged as the refill is pushed into place and locked. If the metal blade holder and frame are allowed to touch the glass during wiper operation, the glass will be scratched.

Tires and Wheels

Tires should be inspected often for signs of improper inflation and uneven wear, which may show a need for balancing, rotation, or wheel alignment. Check the tires frequently for cuts, stone bruises, abrasions, blisters, and for objects that may have become imbedded in the tread. More frequent inspections are recommended when rapid or extreme temperature changes occur, or where road surfaces are rough or littered with debris. Check the condition of the wheels and replace any that are bent, cracked, severely dented or have excessive runout.

The tires on your car have built-in tread wear indicators moulded into the bottom of the tread grooves. These indicators will appear as $\frac{1}{2}$in. (12.7mm) wide bands when the tread depth becomes {161}/$_{16}$ in. (1.6mm). When the indicators appear in 2 or more adjacent grooves, the tires should be replaced.

TIRE ROTATION

▶ **See Figure 25**

The tires should be rotated at the intervals recommended in the Maintenance Interval chart at the end of this Section. Rotate the tires according to the tire rotation diagram. The spare should not be included in the rotation.

TIRE DESIGN

Mazda vehicles come originally equipped with radial tires. Radial tires get their name from their construction,

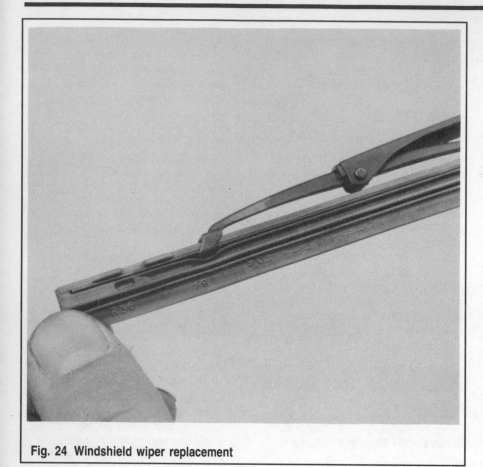

Fig. 24 Windshield wiper replacement

TIRE INFLATION

Tire inflation should be checked at least once a month, including the spare. Use an accurate tire pressure gauge. Do not trust the gauges on service station air pumps, as they are often inaccurate. The inflation specifications are listed on the tire pressure decal which is located on the right door lock pillar. Check and adjust inflation pressures only when the tires are cold, because pressures can increase as much as 6 psi (41kpa) due to heat.

A hard ride, tire bruising or damage and rapid tread wear at the center of the tire can result if inflation pressures are higher than recommended. Inflation pressures that are lower than recommended can cause tire squeal, hard steering, rim damage, high temperatures and rapid wear on the outer edges of the tires. Unequal tire pressures can compromise handling and cause uneven braking.

Radial tires have a highly flexible sidewall and this accounts for the characteristic sidewall bulge that makes the tire appear underinflated. This is normal for a radial tire, so you should not attempt to reduce this bulge by overinflating the tire.

CARE OF ALUMINUM WHEELS

Aluminum wheels are standard on some Mazda models and optional on others. These wheels are coated to preserve their appearance.

To clean the aluminum wheels, use a mild soap and water solution and rinse thoroughly with clean water. If you want to use one of the commercially available wheel cleaners, make sure the label indicates that the cleaner is safe for coated wheels. Never use steel wool or any cleaner that contains an abrasive, or use strong detergents that contain high alkaline or caustic agents, as this will damage your wheels.

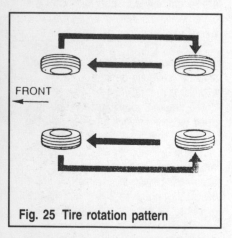

FRONT

Fig. 25 Tire rotation pattern

because the carcass plies on a radial tire run at an angle of 90° to the tire bead, as opposed to a conventional bias ply tire where the carcass plies run at an angle of 90° to each another. The radial tire's construction gives the tread a great deal of rigidity and the side wall a great deal of flexibility.

When replacing your tires, use only the size, load range and construction type (radial) originally installed on the car. This information can be found on the tire pressure decal, which is located on the right door lock pillar, and is also located on the tire sidewall. The use of any other size or type may affect ride, handling, speedometer/odometer calibration, vehicle ground clearance, and tire to body clearance.

Do not mix tires of different construction (radial, bias ply or bias belted) on the same vehicle unless it is an emergency, as vehicle handling will be seriously affected with the possibility of loss of control.

FLUIDS AND LUBRICANTS

Fluid Disposal

Used fluids such as engine oil, transmission fluid, antifreeze, and brake fluid are hazardous wastes and must be disposed of properly. Before draining any fluids, consult with the local authorities; in many areas, waste oil, etc. is being accepted as a part of recycling programs. A number of service stations and auto parts stores are also accepting waste fluids for recycling.

Be sure of the recycling center's policies before draining any fluids, as many will not accept different fluids that have been mixed together, such as oil and antifreeze.

Fig. 27 Removing oil dipstick from the engine

Fig. 29 Oil filter removal and installation

gasoline with an octane rating of 91, which usually means super unleaded.

Oil must be selected with regard to the anticipated temperatures during the period before the next oil change. Using the chart, select the oil viscosity for the lowest expected temperature and you will be assured of easy cold starting and sufficient engine protection. The oil you pour into your engine should have the designation SG marked on the container. For maximum fuel economy benefits, use an oil with the Roman Numeral II next to the words Energy Conserving in the API Service Symbol.

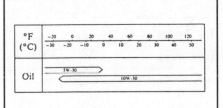

Fig. 26 Oil viscosity chart

Fuel and Engine Oil Recommendations

▶ See Figure 26

All Mazda vehicles are equipped with a catalytic converter, necessitating the use of unleaded gasoline. The use of leaded gasoline will damage the catalytic converter. Most Mazda vehicles are designed to use unleaded gasoline with an octane rating of 87, which usually means regular unleaded. The turbo models are designed to use unleaded

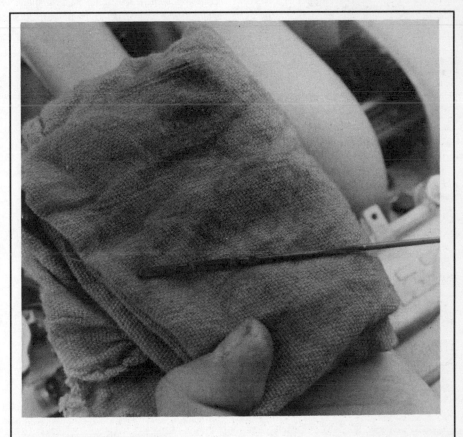

Fig. 28 Inspecting oil level

Engine

OIL LEVEL CHECK

▶ **See Figures 27 and 28**

Check the engine oil level every time you fill the gas tank. Make sure the oil level is between the F and L marks on the dipstick. The engine and oil must be warm and the vehicle parked on level ground to get an accurate reading. Also, allow a few minutes after turning off the engine for the oil to drain back into the pan before checking, or an inaccurate reading will result. Check the engine oil level as follows:

1. Open the hood and locate the engine oil dipstick.

2. If the engine is hot, you may want to wrap a rag around the dipstick handle before removing it.

3. Remove the dipstick and wipe it with a clean, lint-free rag, then reinsert it into the dipstick tube. Make sure it is inserted all the way or an inaccurate reading will result.

4. Pull out the dipstick and note the oil level. It should be between the marks, as stated above.

5. If the oil level is below the lower mark, replace the dipstick and add fresh oil to bring the level within the proper range. Do not overfill.

6. Recheck the oil level and close the hood.

OIL AND FILTER CHANGE

▶ **See Figures 29, 30 and 31**

The engine oil and oil filter should be changed at the same time, at the recommended interval on the Maintenance Intervals chart. If the vehicle is being operated under extreme conditions or in very dusty areas, the oil should be changed more frequently. Before draining the oil, make sure the engine is at operating temperature. Hot oil holds more impurities in suspension and will flow better, allowing the removal of more oil and dirt.

Change the oil and filter as follows:

1. Run the engine until it reaches the normal operating temperature. Raise and safely support the front of the car.

2. Slide a drain pan under the oil pan drain plug.

✳✳CAUTION

The EPA warns that prolonged contact with used engine oil may cause a number of skin disorders, including cancer. You should make every effort to minimize your exposure to used engine oil. Protective gloves should be worn when changing the oil. Wash your hands and any other exposed skin areas as soon as possible after exposure to used engine oil. Soap and water, or waterless hand cleaner should be used.

3. Wipe the drain plug and the surrounding area clean. Loosen the drain plug with a socket or box wrench, and then remove it by hand. If necessary, use a rag to shield your fingers from the heat. Push in on the plug as you turn it out, so that oil does not leak out until the plug is completely removed.

4. Allow the oil to drain into the pan. Be very careful; if the engine is at operating temperature, the oil is hot enough to burn you.

5. Clean and install the drain plug complete with a new drain plug washer. Tighten the drain plug to 15 ft. lbs. (20 Nm).

6. Slide the drain pan under the oil filter. Slip an oil filter wrench onto the filter and turn it counterclockwise to loosen it. Wrap a rag around the filter and unscrew it the rest of the way. Be careful of oil running down the side of the filter.

7. Clean the oil filter adapter on the engine with a clean rag.

8. Coat the rubber gasket on the replacement filter with clean engine oil. Place the filter in position on the adapter fitting and screw it on by hand. After the rubber gasket contacts the sealing surface, turn the filter ½ turn, by hand.

9. Pull the drain pan from under the vehicle and lower the vehicle to the ground.

10. Remove the oil filler cap and fill the crankcase with the proper type and quantity of engine oil.

11. On the turbocharged engine, it is necessary to pre-lube the lubricating system before starting the engine to ensure an adequate supply of oil to the turbocharger bearings. This is done as follows:

   a. Disconnect the ignition coil electrical connector from the ignition coil.

   b. Crank the engine for approximately 20 seconds. Doing this will generate a fault code in the Self-Diagnostic portion of the Electronic Control Assembly.

   c. Reconnect the electrical connector to the ignition coil.

12. Start the engine and run it at idle for approximately 30 seconds.

13. Stop the engine and disconnect the negative battery cable. Depress the brake pedal for approximately 5 seconds in order to cancel the fault code.

14. Reconnect the negative battery cable.

15. Run the engine and check for leaks. Stop the engine and check the oil level.

Manual Transmission

FLUID RECOMMENDATIONS

DEXRON®II automatic transmission fluid is required.

LEVEL CHECK

▶ **See Figures 32 and 33**

MX-5 Miata

1. Raise and safely support the vehicle.

2. Remove the check plug from the side of the transmission.

3. Verify that the oil is near the bottom of the plug hole.

4. If the oil level is low, add oil through the oil level plug hole.

5. Apply sealant to the plug and install the plug. Tighten the plug to 18-29 ft. lbs. (25-39 Nm).

6. Lower the vehicle.

DRAIN AND REFILL

MX-5 Miata

1. Raise and safely support the vehicle.

2. Slide a drain pan under the transmission. Remove the transmission drain plug with the washer and the check plug from the side of the transmission.

Fig. 30 Oil drain plug location

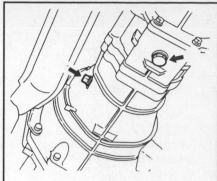

Fig. 33 Miata manual transmission fluid level check plug and drain plug

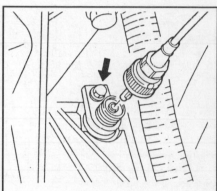

Fig. 34 Disconnecting speedometer cable from the speedometer driven gear

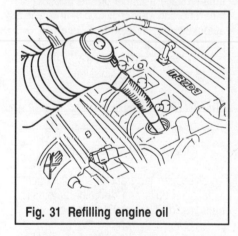

Fig. 31 Refilling engine oil

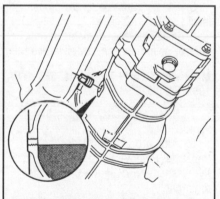

Fig. 32 Miata manual transmission fluid level check plug

Manual Transaxle

FLUID RECOMMENDATIONS

DEXRON®II automatic transmission fluid is required.

3. When the fluid has been completely drained, install the drain plug with a new washer and tighten to 29-43 ft. lbs. (39-59 Nm).

4. Fill the transmission to the proper level through the side check plug hole until the level reaches the bottom of the check plug hole.

5. Install the check plug to the side of the transmission. Tighten the check plug to 18-29 ft. lbs. (25-39 Nm).

6. Lower the vehicle.

LEVEL CHECK

⬦ See Figures 34, 35, 36 and 37

Except MX-3 with G5M-R Transaxle, 323 4WD and 1993 MX-6/626

1. Park the car on a level surface. Apply the parking brake.

2. If equipped with a digital instrument cluster, disconnect the harness from the speed sensor assembly located on the transaxle housing.

3. If equipped with an analog instrument cluster, disconnect the speedometer cable from the speedometer driven gear assembly located on the transaxle housing.

4. Remove the retaining bolt and pry out the speedometer driven gear assembly or the vehicle speed sensor from the transaxle housing.

5. Check the fluid level on the speedometer driven gear assembly or the vehicle speed sensor assembly. The level should be at the full mark, just above the gear teeth.

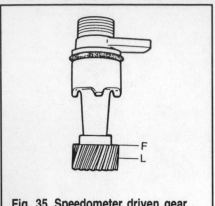

Fig. 35 Speedometer driven gear with transaxle fluid level markings

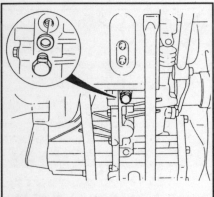

Fig. 36 Transaxle fluid drain plug location

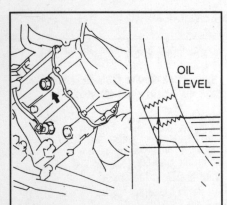

Fig. 37 Transaxle fluid level inspection — MX-3 with G5M-R transaxle, 323 4WD and 1993 MX-6/626

6. If the level is low, place a funnel in the driven gear or sensor opening in the transaxle and pour in the necessary amount of fluid. Recheck the fluid level.

7. Install the speedometer driven gear or speed sensor and connect the cable or harness.

MX-3 with G5M-R Transaxle, 323 4WD and 1993 MX-6/626

1. Park the vehicle on level ground.
2. Remove the oil level plug and washer.
3. Using a cotton swab or similar item, verify that the oil is near the bottom of the plug port.
4. If the oil level is low, add oil through the oil level plug hole.
5. Install a new washer to the oil level plug and tighten the plug to 29-43 ft. lbs. (40-58 Nm).

DRAIN AND REFILL

Except MX-3 with G5M-R Transaxle, 323 4WD and 1993 MX-6/626

1. Raise and safely support the vehicle.
2. Slide a drain pan under the transaxle. Remove the speedometer driven gear or speed sensor on the top of the transaxle case.
3. Remove the drain plug on the bottom of the transaxle case.
4. When the fluid has been completely drained, install the drain plug and tighten to 29-43 ft. lbs. (39-59 Nm).
5. Fill the transaxle to the proper level.
6. Install the speedometer driven gear or speed sensor. Lower the vehicle.

MX-3 with G5M-R Transaxle, 323 4WD, 1993 MX-6/626

1. Raise and safely support the vehicle.
2. Slide a drain pan under the transaxle. Remove the drain plug and the washer and drain the oil into the drain pan.
3. Remove the oil level plug and the washer from the side of the transaxle case.
4. When the fluid has been completely drained, install the drain plug with a new washer and tighten to 29-43 ft. lbs. (40-58 Nm).
5. Fill the transaxle through the oil level plug hole until the fluid level reaches the bottom of the oil level plug hole.
6. Install the oil level plug with a new washer and tighten to 29-43 ft. lbs. (40-58 Nm).
7. Lower the vehicle.

Automatic Transmission

FLUID RECOMMENDATIONS

DEXRON®II or M-III® automatic transmission fluid is required.

LEVEL CHECK

1. Park the car on a level surface and apply the parking brake. Run the engine to warm up the transaxle fluid.
2. Shift the transaxle through all ranges and return the lever to the **P** position.
3. Remove the dipstick and wipe it clean, then insert it firmly. Be certain that it has been pushed fully home. Remove the dipstick and check the fluid level while holding the dipstick horizontally. The level should be at or near the **F** mark. The dipstick has **F** and **L** marks, which are accurate for level indications when the fluid is hot (normal operating temperature), or at other than normal operating temperature.
4. If the fluid level is below the **L** mark, place a funnel on the dipstick tube and add Dexron®II or M-III® type automatic transmission fluid, one half pint (0.23L) at a time. Check the level often between additions, being careful not to overfill the transmission.

DRAIN AND REFILL

1. Raise and safely support the vehicle.
2. Loosen the transmission fluid pan installation bolts and drain the automatic transmission fluid into a drain pan.
3. Completely remove the transmission fluid oil pan and the gasket.
4. Clean the transmission fluid oil pan and the magnet at the bottom of the pan.
5. Install the oil pan complete with a new gasket to the transmission.
6. Tighten the transmission oil pan bolts to 52-69 in. lbs. (5.9-7.8 Nm)
7. Add approximately 4.2 quarts (4.0L) of automatic transmission fluid to the transmission.
8. After filling the transmission fluid, check the fluid level as previously described.
9. Lower the vehicle.

Automatic Transaxle

FLUID RECOMMENDATIONS

DEXRON®II or M-III® automatic transmission fluid is required.

1. Park the car on a level surface and apply the parking brake. Run the engine to warm up the transaxle fluid.

2. Shift the transaxle through all ranges and return the lever to the **P** position.

3. With the engine still idling, remove the dipstick and wipe it clean, then insert it firmly. Be certain that it has been pushed fully home. Remove the dipstick and check the fluid level while holding the dipstick horizontally. The level should be at or near the high mark. The dipstick has a high and low mark on both sides, which are accurate for level indications when the fluid is hot (normal operating temperature), or at other than normal operating temperature.

4. If the fluid level is below the low mark, place a funnel on the dipstick tube and add Dexron®II or M-III® type automatic transmission fluid, one half pint (0.23L) at a time. Check the level often between additions, being careful not to overfill the transmission.

DRAIN AND REFILL

1. Raise and safely support the vehicle.

2. Support the left-hand crossmember with a screw-type jack, or equivalent.

3. Remove the bolts and nuts from the front of the left-hand crossmember.

4. Remove the nuts and the transaxle mount through bolt from the rear of the crossmember.

5. Carefully lower the screw-type jack, allowing the crossmember to swing toward the left-hand side of the vehicle.

6. Position a drain pan under the transaxle.

7. Loosen the pan retaining bolts and drain the fluid from the transaxle.

8. When the fluid has drained to the level of the pan flange, remove the pan retaining bolts, working from the rear, to allow it to drop and drain slowly.

9. When all the fluid has been drained, remove the pan and clean it thoroughly. Discard the pan gasket.

10. Remove and discard the transmission fluid filter and the filter-to-

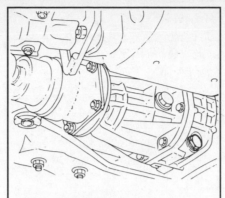

Fig. 38 1990-91 323 4WD transfer case fluid drain and fluid level inspection plugs

body gasket. The filter should not be reused or cleaned as the element material could contaminate the transaxle.

11. Install a new filter assembly using a new gasket. Tighten the retaining bolts to 69-95 inch lbs. (8-11 Nm).

12. Position a new gasket on the pan and install the pan. Tighten the pan retaining bolts to 69-95 inch lbs. (8-11 Nm).

13. Swing the left side crossmember into position and support it with the screw-type jack.

14. Install the 2 nuts and the left-hand transaxle mount through bolt to the rear of the left-hand crossmember. Tighten the nuts and through bolt to 49-69 ft. lbs. (67-93 Nm).

15. Install the 4 bolts and 1 nut to the front of the left-hand crossmember. Tighten the bolts to 27-40 ft. lbs. (36-54 Nm) and the nut to 55-69 ft. lbs. (79-93 Nm).

16. Remove the drain pan from under the vehicle. Remove the screw-type jack and then lower the vehicle to the ground.

17. Add approximately 7.2 qts. (6.8 liters) of fluid to the transaxle through the filler tube.

18. Run the engine and check for leaks. Check the fluid level according to the procedure described earlier.

Transfer Case

FLUID RECOMMENDATIONS

1990-91 323 4WD

API Service GL-5 SAE 80-90 W oil is required. Total fluid capacity is 0.53 quart (0.5 liter).

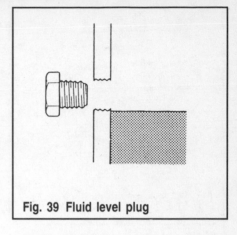

Fig. 39 Fluid level plug

LEVEL CHECK

▶ **See Figures 38 and 39**

1. Park the car on a level surface and apply the parking brake.

2. Remove the check plug from the side of the transfer carrier.

3. Check to see if oil level is at the bottom of the check plug hole.

4. If the fluid level is below the low mark, place a funnel into the plug hole and add the specified oil.

5. Install the check plug and tighten the plug to 28-43 ft. lbs. (39-58 Nm).

DRAIN AND REFILL

1. Raise and safely support the vehicle.

2. Place a drain pan below the transfer unit.

3. Remove the drain plug from the transfer unit and drain the oil.

4. When the fluid is completely drained, install the drain plug with a new washer intact. Tighten the drain plug to 28-43 ft. lbs. (39-58 Nm).

5. Remove the check plug from the side of the transfer carrier.

6. Refill the transfer unit with the specified oil.

7. Install the check plug and tighten the plug to 28-43 ft. lbs. (39-58 Nm).

Drive Axle

FLUID RECOMMENDATIONS

API Service GL-5 SAE 80-90 W oil is required. Total fluid capacity is 0.69 quart (0.65 liter).

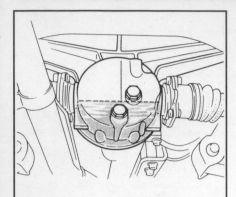

Fig. 40 Drive axle differential drain plug and fluid level check plug — Miata

LEVEL CHECK

▶ See Figure 40

1. Park the car on a level surface and apply the parking brake.
2. Remove the check plug from the differential.
3. Check to see if oil level is at the bottom of the check plug hole.
4. If the fluid level is below the low mark, place a funnel into the plug hole and add the specified oil.
5. Install the check plug with a new washer and tighten the plug to 29-40 ft. lbs. (39-54 Nm).

DRAIN AND REFILL

1. Raise and safely support the vehicle.
2. Place a drain pan below the differential.
3. Remove the drain plug from the differential unit and drain the oil.
4. When the fluid is completely drained, replace the drain plug complete with a new washer and tighten to to 29-40 ft. lbs. (39-54 Nm).
5. Remove the check plug from the differential.
6. Refill the differential unit with the specified oil.
7. Install the check plug and tighten the plug to 29-40 ft. lbs. (39-54 Nm).

Cooling System

Check the cooling system at the interval specified in the Maintenance Intervals chart at the end of this section.

Hose clamps should be tightened, and defective hoses replaced. Damp spots,

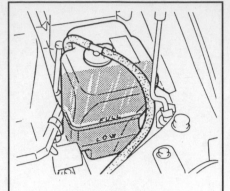

Fig. 41 Coolant overflow bottle

or accumulations of rust or dye near hoses, water pump or other areas, indicate areas of possible leakage. Check the radiator cap for a worn or cracked gasket. If the cap doesn't seal properly, fluid will be lost and the engine will overheat. A worn cap should be replaced with a new one.

Periodically clean any debris from the radiator fins. Pick the large pieces off by hand. The smaller pieces can be washed away with water pressure from a hose.

Carefully straighten any bent radiator fins with a pair of needle nose pliers. Be careful — the fins are very soft. Don't move the fins back and forth too much. Straighten them once and try not to move them again.

FLUID RECOMMENDATIONS

The recommended fluid is a 50/50 mixture of ethylene glycol antifreeze and water for year round use. Use a good quality antifreeze with water pump lubricants, rust inhibitors and other corrosion inhibitors along with acid neutralizers. Use only antifreeze that is SAFE FOR USE WITH AN ALUMINUM RADIATOR.

LEVEL CHECK

▶ See Figure 41

Coolant level should be checked at least once a month. With the engine cold, the coolant level should be even with the FULL mark on the coolant expansion tank. On some models, there is a coolant level dipstick.

DRAIN AND REFILL

1. Remove the radiator cap.

✳✳CAUTION

Never remove the radiator cap while the engine is running or personal injury from scalding hot coolant or steam may result. If possible, wait until the engine has cooled to remove the radiator cap. If this is not possible, wrap a thick cloth around the radiator cap and turn it slowly to the first stop. Step back while the pressure is released from the cooling system. When you are sure all the pressure has been released, press down on the cap, still with the cloth, and turn and remove it.

2. Position a suitable container under the radiator and open the draincock to drain the radiator.

✳✳CAUTION

When draining the coolant, keep in mind that cats and dogs are attracted by the ethylene glycol antifreeze, and are quite likely to drink any that is left in an uncovered container or in puddles on the ground. This will prove fatal in sufficient quantity. Always drain the coolant into a sealable container.

3. Clean the cooling system by flushing with clear water.
4. Close the radiator draincock.
5. Refill the system with a 50/50 mixture of antifreeze and water. Fill to the FULL mark on the reservoir and install the radiator cap only to the first stop.
6. Start the engine and run it at fast idle until the upper radiator hose feels warm, indicating the thermostat has opened and coolant is flowing throughout the system.
7. Stop the engine. Carefully remove the radiator cap and top off the radiator with the water/antifreeze mixture, if required.
8. Install the radiator cap securely and fill the coolant reservoir to the FULL mark.

FLUSHING AND CLEANING THE SYSTEM

Radiator and Engine Flush

1. Drain the cooling system. Remove the thermostat and reinstall the thermostat housing.

2. Disconnect the radiator overflow hose from the expansion tank and plug the end of the hose.

3. Disconnect the intake manifold outlet hose from the manifold nipple and plug both the nipple and the hose.

4. Disconnect the lower radiator hose from the radiator and position the hose to drain clear of the vehicle.

5. Connect a high pressure hose to the radiator lower hose outlet. Back flush the radiator and engine until water runs clear out of the lower radiator hose. Turn the water on and off several times to pulse the flow and help loosen sludge deposits.

✴✴WARNING

The flushing water flow must be limited so that pressure inside the radiator does not exceed 15 psi (103.4kpa).

6. When the system drains clear, unplug the radiator overflow hose. When water flows clear from the hose, replug it.

7. Before reconnecting the cooling system hoses, disconnect all of the hoses installed for the radiator and engine back flush procedure. The heater coolant loop must be backflushed separately to prevent loosened sediment from lodging in the heater core.

Heater Core Back Flush

1. Install and clamp a garden hose female end fitting in the heater return hose, disconnected from the bypass nipple.

2. Connect a garden hose to the hose fitting in the heater return hose and flush the heater core circuit until the drain water runs clear. Pulse the flow by turning the water on and off several times. Allow full flow for approximately 5 minutes.

3. Shut off the flushing water and remove all adapters and plugs installed for the flushing operation. Reconnect all cooling system connections and tighten the hose clamps to 22-31 inch lbs. (2.5-3.5 Nm).

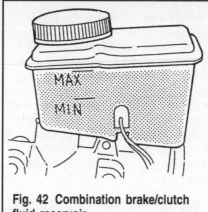

Fig. 42 Combination brake/clutch fluid reservoir

4. Install the thermostat with a new housing gasket. Tighten the retaining nuts.

5. Fill the cooling system and check for leaks.

Master Cylinder

FLUID RECOMMENDATIONS

Both the clutch and brake fluid master cylinders require brake fluid that meets or exceeds DOT 3 standards.

LEVEL CHECK

▶ See Figure 42

All except 1990-92 MX-6 and 626

All Mazda vehicles except the 1990-92 626 and MX-6 are equipped with a combination brake/clutch fluid reservoir. The fluid level should be between the MIN and MAX lines located on the side of the reservoir.

If it is necessary to add fluid, first wipe away any accumulated dirt or grease from the reservoir. Then remove the reservoir cap by twisting counterclockwise. Add fluid to the proper level. Avoid spilling fluid on any painted surface as it will harm the paint finish. Replace the reservoir cap.

1990-92 MX-6 and 626

The brake master cylinder has a translucent reservoir which enables the fluid level to be checked without removing the reservoir cap. The brake fluid level should be between the MIN and MAX lines located on the side of the reservoir.

If it is necessary to add fluid, first wipe away any accumulated dirt or grease

from the reservoir. Then remove the reservoir cap by twisting counter clockwise. Add fluid to the proper level. Avoid spilling brake fluid on any painted surface as it will harm the paint finish. Replace the reservoir cap.

Power Steering Pump

FLUID RECOMMENDATIONS

ATF Dexron®II or M-III® fluid should be used.

LEVEL CHECK

323, Protege and MX-3

The 323, Protege and MX-3 models are equipped with a power steering fluid reservoir. The reservoir is translucent with F and L fluid level markings. The fluid should be kept filled to the F mark at all times.

MX-5 Miata

1. Park the vehicle on level ground and apply the parking brake.

2. Turn the engine OFF and allow it to cool.

3. Remove the combination filler cap and dipstick.

4. Wipe the dipstick clean and reinstall.

5. Remove the combination filler cap and dipstick and inspect the fluid level.

6. The fluid level should be between the H and L marks on the dipstick. Add fluid as necessary.

1990-92 626 and MX-6

The 1990-92 626 and MX-6 models are equipped with a power steering fluid reservoir. The reservoir is translucent with FULL and LOW fluid level markings. The fluid should be kept filled to the FULL mark at all times.

1993 626 and MX-6

1. Park the vehicle on level ground and apply the parking brake.

2. Turn the engine OFF and allow it to cool.

3. Remove the combination filler cap and dipstick.

4. Wipe the dipstick clean and reinstall.

5. Remove the combination filler cap and dipstick and inspect the fluid level.

6. The fluid level should be between the Hand Lmarks on the dipstick. Add fluid as necessary.

Chassis Greasing

The ball joints and tie rod ends on Mazda vehicles are sealed at the factory and cannot be lubricated.

Body Lubrication and Maintenance

The hood latch, auxiliary catch, door, hatchback and liftgate hinges should be lubricated with multi-purpose grease and the door and window weatherstripping should be lubricated with silicone lubricant at least once a year. The body water drain holes located on the underside of each rocker panel, quarter panel and door should also be cleaned at this time.

To preserve the appearance of your car, it should be washed periodically with a mild detergent and water solution. Only wash the vehicle when the metal feels cool and the vehicle is in the shade. Rinse the entire vehicle with cold water, then wash and rinse one panel at a time, beginning with the roof and upper areas. After washing is complete, rinse the vehicle one final time and dry with a soft cloth or chamois.

Periodic waxing will remove harmful deposits from the vehicles surface and protect the finish. If the finish has dulled due to age or neglect, polishing may be necessary to restore the original gloss.

There are many specialized products available at your local auto parts store to care for the appearance of painted metal surfaces, plastic, chrome, wheels and tires as well as the interior upholstery and carpeting. Be sure to follow the manufacturers instructions before using them.

Rear Wheel Bearings

REMOVAL & INSTALLATION

1. Raise and support the vehicle safely.
2. Remove the wheel and tire assembly and the grease cap.
3. Using a cape chisel and a hammer, raise the staked portion of the hub nut.
4. Remove and discard the hub nut.
5. Remove the brake drum or disc brake rotor assembly from the spindle. Refer to Section 9.
6. Using a small prybar, pry the grease seal from the brake drum or rotor and discard it.

7. Remove the snapring. Using a shop press, press the wheel bearing from the brake drum or rotor.

To install:

8. Using a shop press, press the new wheel bearing into the brake drum or rotor until it seats and install the snapring.
9. Lubricate the new seal lip with grease and install the seal, using a suitable installation tool.
10. Position the brake drum or rotor onto the wheel spindle.
11. Install a new locknut and tighten to 73-131 ft. lbs. (98-178 Nm).
12. Check the wheel bearing endplay as follows:

   a. Rotate the drum or rotor to make sure there is no brake drag.
   b. Install a suitable dial indicator and check the wheel bearing endplay. Endplay should not exceed 0.008 in. (0.2mm).
13. Using a dull cold chisel, stake the locknut.

➡**If the nut splits or cracks after staking, it must be replaced with a new nut.**

14. Install the grease cap and the wheel and tire assembly. Tighten the lug nuts to 65-87 ft. lbs. (88-118 Nm). Lower the vehicle.

TRAILER TOWING

It is not recommended to tow a trailer with any Mazda passenger car.

PUSHING AND TOWING

In the event of a dead battery, a manual transaxle equipped car may be started by pushing. Push starting IS NOT RECOMMENDED because of possible damage to the catalytic converter. If the car must be push started, be certain that the push car bumper doesn't override the bumper of

your car. Depress the clutch pedal. Select Second or Third gear. Switch the ignition ON. When the car reaches a speed of approximately 10 mph, release the clutch to start the engine.

If towing is required, the vehicle should be flat bedded, or towed with the

front wheels off of the ground to prevent damage to the transaxle. If it is necessary to tow the vehicle from the rear, a wheel dolly should be placed under the front tires.

JACKING

The vehicle is supplied with a scissors jack for emergency road repairs. The scissors jack may be used to raise the car via the notches on either side at the front and rear of the doors. Do not attempt to position the jack in any other place. Always block the diagonally opposite wheel when using a jack.

When using stands, use the side members at the front or trailing axle front mounting crossmember at the rear for placement points.

Whenever you plan to work under the car, you must support it on jackstands or ramps. Never use cinder blocks or stacks of wood to support the car, even

if you're only going to be under it for a few minutes. Never crawl under the car when it is supported only by the tire-changing jack.

Small hydraulic, screw, or scissors jacks are satisfactory for raising the car. Drive-on trestles or ramps are also a handy and safe way to both raise and support the car. These can be bought or constructed from wood or steel. Never support the car on any suspension member or underbody panel.

CAPACITIES

Year	Model	ID	Engine Liter (cc)	Engine Crankcase With Filter	Engine Crankcase Without Filter	Transaxle/Transmission (pts.) 4-Spd	Transaxle/Transmission (pts.) 5-Spd	Transaxle/Transmission (pts.) Auto.	Drive Axle (pts.)	Fuel Tank (gal.)	Cooling System (qts.)
1990	323	B6E	1.6 (1597)	3.38	3.20	—	5.60	12.2	—	13.2	①
	Protege	BPE	1.8 (1839)	3.38	3.20	—	5.60	12.2	—	14.5	①
	Protege	BPD	1.8 (1839)	3.98	3.80	—	7.10	12.2	—	14.5	①
	626	F2	2.2 (2184)	4.23	4.10	—	②	14.4	—	15.9	7.90
	MX-6	F2	2.2 (2184)	4.23	4.10	—	②	14.4	—	15.9	7.90
	Miata	B6ZE	1.6 (1597)	3.58	3.40	—	4.20	—	1.372	11.9	6.3
1991	323	B6E	1.6 (1597)	3.38	3.20	—	5.60	12.2	—	13.2	①
	Protege	BPE	1.8 (1839)	3.38	3.20	—	5.60	12.2	—	14.5	①
	Protege	BPD	1.8 (1839)	3.98	3.80	—	7.10	12.2	—	14.5	①
	626	F2	2.2 (2184)	4.23	4.10	—	②	14.4	—	15.9	7.90
	MX-6	F2	2.2 (2184)	4.23	4.10	—	②	14.4	—	15.9	7.90
	Miata	B6ZE	1.6 (1597)	3.58	3.40	—	4.20	—	1.372	11.9	6.3
1992	323	B6E	1.6 (1597)	3.38	3.20	—	5.60	13.4	—	13.2	①
	Protege	BPE	1.8 (1839)	3.38	3.20	—	5.60	13.4	—	14.5	①
	Protege	BPD	1.8 (1839)	3.98	3.80	—	7.10	13.4	—	14.5	①
	MX-3	B6E	1.6 (1597)	3.38	3.20	—	5.60	13.4	—	13.2	6.30
	MX-3	K8D	1.8 (1844)	5.20	5.00	—	5.70	14.4	—	13.2	7.90
	626	F2	2.2 (2184)	4.23	4.10	—	②	14.4	—	15.9	7.90
	MX-6	F2	2.2 (2184)	4.23	4.10	—	②	14.4	—	15.9	7.90
	Miata	B6ZE	1.6 (1597)	3.58	3.40	—	4.20	—	1.372	11.9	6.3
1993	323	B6E	1.6 (1597)	3.38	3.20	—	5.60	13.4	—	13.2	①
	Protege	BPE	1.8 (1839)	3.38	3.20	—	5.60	13.4	—	14.5	①
	Protege	BPD	1.8 (1839)	3.98	3.80	—	7.10	13.4	—	14.5	①
	MX-3	B6E	1.6 (1597)	3.38	3.20	—	5.60	13.4	—	13.2	6.30
	MX-3	K8D	1.8 (1844)	5.20	5.00	—	5.70	14.4	—	13.2	7.90
	626	FS	2.0 (1991)	3.90	3.72	—	5.80	18.6	—	15.9	7.90
	626	KL	2.5 (2496)	5.20	5.00	—	5.80	18.6	—	15.9	7.90
	MX-6	FS	2.0 (1991)	3.90	3.72	—	5.80	18.6	—	15.9	7.90
	MX-6	KL	2.5 (2496)	5.20	5.00	—	5.80	18.6	—	15.9	7.90
	Miata	B6ZE	1.6 (1597)	3.58	3.40	—	4.20	—	1.372	11.9	6.3

① Manual trans.—5.3 qts.
  Auto trans.—6.3 qts.
② Turbo—7 pts.
  Nonturbo—7.8 pts.

Schedule 1

R: Replace or change

MAINTENANCE INTERVALS		Number of months or miles (kilometers), whichever comes first							
	Months	7.5	15	22.5	30	37.5	45	52.5	60
	Miles	7,500	15,000	22,500	30,000	37,500	45,000	52,500	60,000
MAINTENANCE ITEM	(Km)	(12,000)	(24,000)	(36,000)	(48,000)	(60,000)	(72,000)	(84,000)	(96,000)
Drive belts					I				I
Engine oil	Non-Turbo	R	R	R	R	R	R	R	R
	Turbo	Replace every 5,000 miles (8,000 km) or 5 months							
Engine oil filter	Non-Turbo	R	R	R	R	R	R	R	R
	Turbo	Replace every 5,000 miles (8,000 km) or 5 months							
Engine timing belt*1		Replace every 60,000 miles (96,000 km)							
Air cleaner element					R				R
Spark plugs					R				R
Cooling system					I				I
Engine coolant					R				R
Fuel filter									R
Fuel lines					I*2				I
Brake line hoses and connections					I				I
Drum brake					I				I
Disc brake					I				I
Steering operation and linkage					I				I
Front suspension ball joint					I				I
Drive shaft dust boots					I				I
Bolts and nuts on chassis and body					T				T
Exhaust system heat shield					I				I
All locks and hinges		L	L	L	L	L	L	L	L
Air-conditioner refrigerant		Inspect refrigerant amount annually							
Air-conditioner compressor		Inspect operation annually							

*1 Replacement of the engine timing belt is required at every 60,000 miles (96,000 km). Failure to replace this belt may result in damage to the engine.
*2 This maintenance is recommended by Mazda. However, it is not necessary for emission warranty coverage or manufacturer recall liability.

Schedule 2

I : Inspect, and if necessary correct, clean, or replace (Inspect, and if necessary replace ··· Air cleaner element only)
R : Replace or change

MAINTENANCE ITEM		Number of months or miles (kilometers), whichever comes first											
	Months	5	10	15	20	25	30	35	40	45	50	55	60
	Miles × 1000	5	10	15	20	25	30	35	40	45	50	55	60
	(km × 1000)	(8)	(16)	(24)	(32)	(40)	(48)	(56)	(64)	(72)	(80)	(88)	(96)
Drive belts							I						I
Engine oil	Non-Turbo	R	R	R	R	R	R	R	R	R	R	R	R
	Turbo	Replace every 3,000 miles (5,000 km) or 3 months											
Engine oil filter	Non-Turbo	R	R	R	R	R	R	R	R	R	R	R	R
	Turbo	Replace every 3,000 miles (5,000 km) or 3 months											
Engine timing belt *1		Replace every 60,000 miles (96,000 km)											
Air cleaner element				I*3			R			I*3			R
Spark plugs							R						R
Cooling system							I						I
Engine coolant							R						R
Fuel filter													R
Fuel lines							I*2						I
Brake line hoses and connections							I						I
Drum brake							I						I
Disc brake				I			I			I			I
Steering operations and linkage							I						I
Front suspension ball joint							I						I
Driveshaft dust boots							I						I
Bolts and nuts on chassis and body				T			T			T			T
Exhaust system heat shield							I						I
All locks and hinges		L	L	L	L	L	L	L	L	L	L	L	L
Air-conditioner refrigerant		Inspect refrigerant amount annually											
Air-conditioner compressor		Inspect operation annually											

*1 Replacement of the engine timing belt is required at every 60,000 miles (96,000 km). Failure to replace this belt may result in damage to the engine.
*2 This maintenance is recommended by Mazda. However, it is not necessary for emission warranty coverage or manufacturer recall liability.
*3 This maintenance is required in all states except California. However, we recommend that it also be performed on California vehicles.

TORQUE SPECIFICATIONS

Component	U.S.	Metric
Alternator adjusting bolt All engines	14–19 ft. lbs.	19–25 Nm
Alternator through bolt All engines	27–38 ft. lbs.	37–52 Nm
Automatic transaxle filter retaining bolts	69–95 inch lbs.	8–11 Nm
Automatic transmission pan retaining bolts	52–69 inch lbs.	5.9–7.8 Nm
Automatic transaxle pan retaining bolts	69–95 inch lbs.	8–11 Nm
Hose clamps	22–31 inch lbs.	2.5–3.5 Nm
Manual transmission drain plug	29–43 ft. lbs.	39–59 Nm
Manual transmission oil check plug	18–29 ft. lbs.	29–39 Nm
Manual transaxle drain plug	29–43 ft. lbs.	39–59 Nm
Oil pan drain plug	95 inch lbs.	11 Nm
Wheel lug nuts	65–87 ft. lbs.	88–118 Nm

2

ENGINE PERFORMANCE AND TUNE-UP

TUNE-UP PROCEDURES

To obtain the optimal performance and economy from your engine, it is essential that it be properly tuned at regular intervals. A regular tune-up will keep the engine running smoothly and will prevent the annoying minor breakdowns and poor performance associated with an untuned engine. A properly tuned engine is also important to the control of exhaust emissions.

The adjustments associated with engine tune-up should be checked every year or 12,000 miles (19,300km), whichever comes first. The engine tune-up should be checked more often if the vehicle is operated under severe conditions, such as prolonged idling, continual stop and start driving, or if starting or running problems are noticed. Refer to the Maintenance Intervals Chart in Section 1 for exact component replacement intervals. It is assumed that the routine maintenance described in Section 1 has been kept up, as this will

have definite effect on the result of a tune-up. All of the tune-up steps should be followed in order, as the result is a cumulative one.

If the specifications on the emission information label in the engine compartment do not agree with the Tune-Up Specification chart in this Section, use the label figures. The label often may include changes made during the model year.

TUNE-UP SPECIFICATIONS

Year	VIN	Engine Liters (cc)	Spark Plugs Gap (in.)	Ignition Timing (deg.) MT	AT	Com-pression Pressure (psi)	Fuel Pump (psi)	Idle Speed (rpm) MT	AT	Valve Clearance In.	Ex.
1990	B6E	1.6 (1597)	0.041	7B	7B	192	64–85	750	750	Hyd.	Hyd.
	B6ZE	1.6 (1597)	0.041	10B	—	192	64–85	850	—	Hyd.	Hyd.
	BPE	1.8 (1839)	0.041	5B	5B	173	64–85	750	750	Hyd.	Hyd.
	BPD	1.8 (1839)	0.041	10B	10B	173	64–85	750	750	Hyd.	Hyd.
	F2	2.2 (2184)	0.041	6B	6B	162	64–85	750	750	Hyd.	Hyd.
	F2	2.2 (2184)	0.041	9B	9B	139	64–85	750	750	Hyd.	Hyd.
1991	B6E	1.6 (1597)	0.041	7B	7B	192	64–85	750	750	Hyd.	Hyd.
	B6ZE	1.6 (1597)	0.041	10B	8B	192	64–85	850	850	Hyd.	Hyd.
	BPE	1.8 (1839)	0.041	5B	5B	173	64–85	750	750	Hyd.	Hyd.
	BPD	1.8 (1839)	0.041	10B	10B	173	64–85	750	750	Hyd.	Hyd.
	F2	2.2 (2184)	0.041	6B	6B	162	64–85	750	750	Hyd.	Hyd.
	F2	2.2 (2184)	0.041	9B	9B	139	64–85	750	750	Hyd.	Hyd.
1992	B6E	1.6 (1597)	0.041	7B	7B	192	64–85	750	750	Hyd.	Hyd.
	B6ZE	1.6 (1597)	0.041	10B	8B	192	64–85	850	850	Hyd.	Hyd.
	BPE	1.8 (1839)	0.041	5B	5B	173	64–85	750	750	Hyd.	Hyd.
	BPD	1.8 (1839)	0.041	10B	10B	173	64–85	750	750	Hyd.	Hyd.
	K8D	1.8 (1839)	0.041	10B	10B	193	64–85	670	670	Hyd.	Hyd.
	F2	2.2 (2184)	0.041	6B	6B	162	64–85	750	750	Hyd.	Hyd.
	F2	2.2 (2184)	0.041	9B	9B	139	64–85	750	750	Hyd.	Hyd.
1993	B6E	1.6 (1597)	0.041	7B	7B	192	64–85	750	750	Hyd.	Hyd.
	B6ZE	1.6 (1597)	0.041	10B	8B	192	64–85	850	850	Hyd.	Hyd.
	BPE	1.8 (1839)	0.041	5B	5B	173	64–85	750	750	Hyd.	Hyd.
	BPD	1.8 (1839)	0.041	10B	10B	173	64–85	750	750	Hyd.	Hyd.
	K8D	1.8 (1839)	0.041	10B	10B	193	64–85	670	670	Hyd.	Hyd.
	FS	2.0 (1991)	0.041	12B	12B	171	50–85	700	700	Hyd.	Hyd.
	KL	2.5 (2496)	0.041	10B	10B	203	64–85	650	650	Hyd.	Hyd.

NOTE: The lowest cylinder pressure should be within 75% of the highest cylinder pressure reading. For example, if the highest cylinder is 134 psi, the lowest should be 101. Engine should be at normal operating temperature with throttle valve in the wide open position.
The underhood specifications sticker often reflects tune-up specification changes in production. Sticker figures must be used if they disagree with those in this chart.
Hyd.—Hydraulic

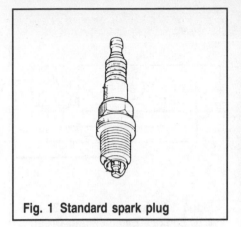

Fig. 1 Standard spark plug

Spark Plugs

▶ **See Figure 1**

A standard spark plug consists of a metal sleeve surrounding a ceramic insulator. A metal electrode extends downward through the center of the insulator and protrudes a small distance. At the end of the plug and attached to the side of the outer metal shell is the side electrode. The side electrode bends in at a 90° angle so that its tip is even with, and parallel to, the tip of the center electrode. The distance between these two electrodes (measured in thousandths of an inch or hundreths of a millimeter) is called the spark plug gap. The spark plug does not produce a spark but merely provides a gap across which the current can arc. The electrical current comes from the coil, which produces anywhere from 20,000 to 40,000 volts. This voltage then travels to the distributor where it is distributed through the spark plug wires and on to the spark plugs. The current passes along the center electrode and jumps the gap to the side electrode, and, in do doing, ignites the air/fuel mixture in the com bustion chamber.

REMOVAL & INSTALLATION

▶ **See Figures 2, 3 and 4**

Spark plugs should be removed one at a time. If all the spark plug wires and spark plugs are removed at the same time, the wires possibly could become mixed up. Number the wires with tape prior to beginning spark plug removal. Near where the wires are attached to the cap is the best location to place the numbers. Refer to the Firing Order

Fig. 2 Proper removal of spark plug wire

diagrams for the cylinder and corresponding distributor cap numbers.

1. Grasp each wire by the rubber boot. Simultaneously twist and pull the boot and wire from the spark plug. Do not ever pull directly on the plug wire, as it may become separated from the connector inside the boot.

2. Using a spark plug socket, loosen the plugs slightly by turning counterclockwise. Wipe or blow any dirt away from around the plug base.

3. Unscrew and remove the spark plugs from the engine. Check the condition of the plugs using the Spark Plug Diagnosis chart.

4. Inspect the plug gap using a feeler gauge. The correct size gauge should pass through the electrode gap with a slight drag. If the gap is not correct, carefully bend the electrode to adjust the gap.

To install:

5. Apply a drop of anti-sieze compound on the threads of the spark plug. Begin threading the spark plug into the cylinder head by hand and continue turning until it is snug. Tighten the plug to 11-17 ft. lbs. (15-23 Nm) on all vehicles except the 1993 MX-6 and 626. For 1993 626 and MX-6, tighten the plug to 11-16 ft. lbs. (15-22 Nm).

6. Connect the spark plug wire to the spark plug. If the wires were not numbered, refer to the Firing Order diagrams to make sure the wires are connected properly.

Spark Plug Wires

Inspect the spark plug wires for burns, cuts, or breaks in the insulation. Check the spark plug boots and the nipples on the distributor cap and coil. Any damaged wiring should be replaced. If no physical damage is obvious, the wires can be checked with an ohmmeter for excessive resistance and continuity. Resistance should be 16 kilo-ohms per 3.28 ft. (1m) of cable. Measure the resistance with the plug wire still attached to the distributor cap.

Replace the spark plug wires one at a time when installing a new set so there will be no mixup. The longest cable should be replaced first. Make sure that the boot is installed firmly over the spark plug. The wire routing should be exactly the same as the original. Insert the nipple into the tower on the distributor cap. Repeat the process for each wire.

Fig. 3 Removal of spark plug

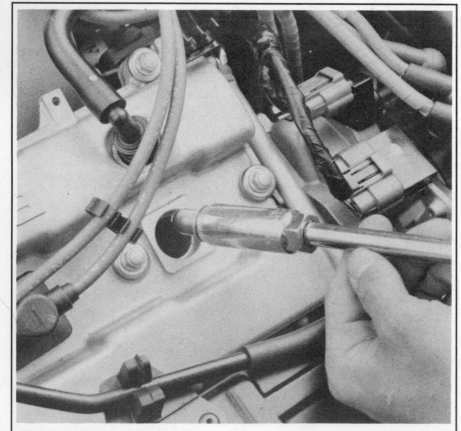

Fig. 4 Installation of spark plug

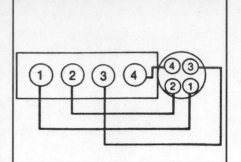

Fig. 5 1.6L (except Miata), 1.8L and 2.2L Engines Engine Firing Order: 1-3-4-2 Distributor Rotation: Counterclockwise

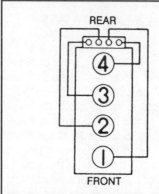

Fig. 6 1.6L Engine (Miata) Engine Firing Order: 1-3-4-2 Distributorless Ignition System

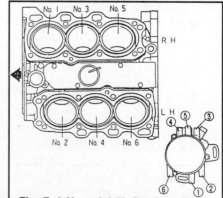

Fig. 7 1.8L and 2.5L Engines Engine Firing Order: 1-2-3-4-5-6 Distributor Rotation: Counterclockwise

Firing Orders

▶ See Figures 5, 6, 7 and 8

➡To avoid confusion, remove and tag the wires one at a time, for replacement.

ELECTRONIC IGNITION

Description and Operation

The electronic ignition on the normally aspirated engines is a fully transistorized, high energy system. It is a conventional electronic ignition system in that it operates with both centrifugal and vacuum advance mechanisms controlling ignition advance. The ignition timing is advanced by vacuum at low speeds and by the centrifugal mechanism at higher speeds. Proper engine performance and satisfactory exhaust emissions are controlled by the ECU.

The ECU controls the electronic ignition on the turbocharged engines. The system is entirely electronic. The ECU sends the spark timing signal through the ignition module to the distributor based on its triggering signal from various sensors and switches. The sensors and switches include the following:

- Vane air flow meter
- Idle switch
- Neutral gear switch
- Clutch engage switch
- EGR valve position sensor
- Knock sensor
- Throttle position sensor
- Engine coolant temperature sensor
- Engine coolant temperature switch

Other non-electronic components in the system include the starter interlock switch, battery, distributor, spark plugs, high tension leads and ignition module. The distributor provides a signal to the ECU to indicate crankshaft top dead center by means of its cylinder TDC sensors.

Both systems operate in the same manner. The power relay closes and changes the coil primary windings when the ignition switch is turned **ON**. When the engine is running, the ignition module grounds the negative side of the coil primary circuit which induces spark. This results in an inductive charge built up in the secondary circuit. Then the spark is sent to the distributor where the rotor and distributor cap work together to deliver spark to each spark plug.

Diagnosis and Testing

Before beginning any diagnosis and testing procedures, visually inspect the components of the ignition system and check for a possible discharged battery, damaged or loose electrical connections,

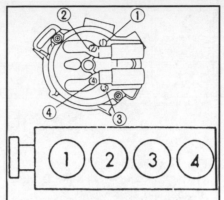

Fig. 8 2.0L Engine Engine Firing Order: 1-3-4-2 Distributor Rotation: Clockwise

blown fuses or damaged vacuum hoses. Also inspect the rotor and distributor cap for excessive wear, the spark plugs for damage and make sure that the distributor cap, rotor and spark plug wires are properly seated. Check the spark plug wires and boots for signs of poor insulation that could cause cross firing. Turn all accessories off during diagnosis and testing. Make sure the idle speed is within specification.

The following tools are required; a quality digital volt-ohmmeter, a remote starter and a spark tester for checking the ignition system. A spark tester resembles a spark plug without threads and the side electrode removed. Do not attempt to use a modified spark plug.

IGNITION COIL SPARK TEST

1. Disconnect the distributor lead wire from the distributor.
2. Hold the distributor lead wire with insulated pliers approximately 0.20-0.39 in. (5-10mm) from a ground.
3. While holding the wire in position, crank the engine.
4. A strong blue spark should be seen. If there is no spark, the ignition coil or pickup coil may be bad.
5. Replace the pickup coil or the ignition coil and test again.

DISTRIBUTOR SPARK TEST

♦ **See Figure 9**

1. Disconnect the spark plug wires from each spark plug.

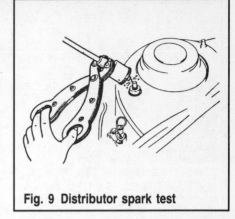

Fig. 9 Distributor spark test

2. Hold the end of the spark plug wire with insulated pliers 0.20-0.39 in. (5-10mm) from a ground. A spark tester may be connected to the plug wire end.
3. While holding the wire in position, crank the engine.
4. A strong blue spark should be seen. If there is no spark, the plug wires and the distributor should be checked.

SPARK QUALITY AND COIL WIRE TEST

1. Connect a volt-ohmmeter to the coil and make sure that 12 volts exist at the positive terminal and 6 volts exist at the negative terminal of the coil with the ignition switch **ON**. If there is no voltage, a short or open circuit exists in the wiring harness.
2. Connect the spark tester between the coil high tension wire and ground. While cranking the engine, make sure a strong spark jumps the tester gap. If there is no spark or the spark is weak, check the ignition coil or the ignition module on the turbocharged engine for carbon tracking or other damage. Measure the resistance of the coil high tension wire; replace the wire if the resistance is greater than 16 kilo-ohms per 3.28 ft.(1m). Proceed to Ignition Coil Resistance.
3. If there is a good spark at the tester in Step 2, proceed to Spark Plug Wire and Distributor Cap Resistance testing.

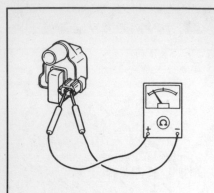

Fig. 10 Checking ignition coil primary resistance — 323, Protege and MX-3 (B6 SOHC engine)

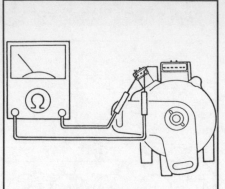

Fig. 13 Checking ignition coil primary winding — MX-3 (K8 DOHC engine) and 1993 626/MX-6

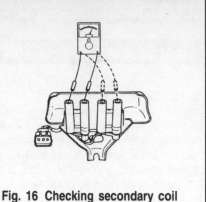

Fig. 16 Checking secondary coil winding resistance — Miata

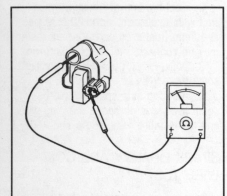

Fig. 11 Checking ignition coil secondary resistance — 323, Protege and MX-3 (B6 SOHC engine)

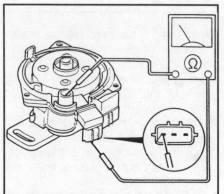

Fig. 14 Checking ignition coil secondary winding — MX-3 (K8 DOHC engine) and 1993 626/MX-6

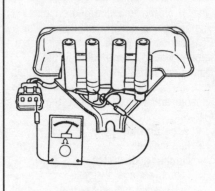

Fig. 17 Checking coil case resistance — Miata

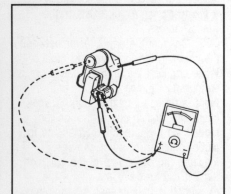

Fig. 12 Checking case insulation resistance — 323, Protege and MX-3 (B6 SOHC engine)

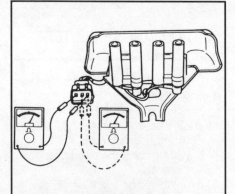

Fig. 15 Checking primary coil winding resistance — Miata

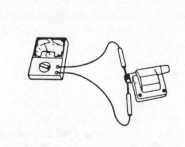

Fig. 18 Checking ignition coil primary resistance — 1990-1992 626 and MX-6

IGNITION COIL RESISTANCE TEST

▶ See Figures 10, 11, 12, 13, 14, 15, 16, 17, 18, 19 and 20

323, Protege and MX-3 (B6 SOHC)

1. Disconnect the distributor wire from the coil.

2. Disconnect the electrical connector from the coil.

3. Check the resistance of the ignition coil primary, secondary and case.

4. The resistance should be as follows:

   a. Primary coil winding — 0.81-0.99 ohms.

   b. Secondary coil winding — 10-16 kilo ohms.

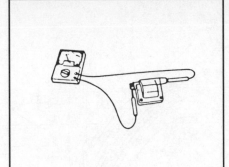

Fig. 19 Checking ignition coil secondary resistance — 1990-1992 626 and MX-6

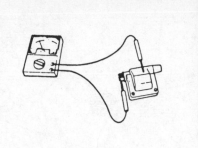

Fig. 20 Checking case insulation resistance — 1990-1992 626 and MX-6

c. Case insulation — minimum 10 mega-ohms.

5. If the ignition coil resistance is not within specifications, replace the ignition coil. If the ignition coil is within the specified limits, proceed to Spark Plug Wire and Distributor Cap Resistance.

MX-3 (K8 DOHC) and 1993 626 and MX-6

1. Disconnect the distributor wire from the coil.
2. Disconnect the 3 pin electrical connector from the coil.
3. Use an ohmmeter and check the resistance of the ignition coil primary winding.
4. The resistance should be 0.58-0.86 ohms.
5. If the resistance is not within specifications, replace the distributor assembly. If the resistance is within specifications, proceed with step 6.
6. Remove the distributor cap and use an ohmmeter to measure the secondary coil resistance.
7. The resistance should be 11.5-18.5 ohms.
8. If the resistance is not within specifications, replace the distributor assembly. If the resistance is within specifications, proceed to Spark Plug Wire and Distributor Cap Resistance.

Miata

1. Disconnect the distributor wire from the coil.
2. Disconnect the electrical connector from the coil.
3. Check the resistance of the ignition coil primary, secondary and case.
4. The resistance should be as follows:
   a. Primary coil winding — 0.78-0.94 ohms.
   b. Secondary coil winding — 11.2-15.2 kilo ohms.
   c. Case insulation — minimum 10 mega-ohms.
5. If the ignition coil resistance is not within specifications, replace the ignition coil. If the ignition coil is within the specified limits, proceed to Spark Plug Wire and Distributor Cap Resistance.

1990-1992 626 and MX-6

1. Disconnect the distributor wire from the coil.
2. Disconnect the electrical connector from the coil.
3. Check the resistance of the ignition coil primary, secondary and case.
4. The resistance should be as follows:
   a. Primary coil winding (turbo) — 0.72-0.88 ohms.
   b. Primary coil winding (non-turbo) — 0.77-0.95 ohms.
   c. Secondary coil winding — 10.3-13.9 kilo-ohms.
   d. Case insulation — minimum 10 mega-ohms.
5. If the ignition coil resistance is not within specifications, replace the ignition coil. If the ignition coil is within the specified limits, proceed to Spark Plug Wire and Distributor Cap Resistance.

SPARK PLUG WIRE AND DISTRIBUTOR CAP RESISTANCE TEST

1. Remove the distributor cap.
2. Make sure the spark plug wires are firmly seated in the cap.
3. Disconnect each spark plug wire from the spark plug and connect a volt-ohmmeter to the terminal in the distributor cap and the spark plug terminal for each wire.
4. Check the wire resistance, It should be 16 kilo-ohms per 3.28 ft. (1 m)
5. If the resistance is not within specification, replace the wire(s) or distributor cap, as required. If the resistance is as specified, check the gap and condition of the spark plugs.

DISTRIBUTOR PICKUP COIL RESISTANCE TEST — NON-TURBOCHARGED ENGINE

♦ See Figure 21

1. Remove the distributor cap, rotor and cover.
2. Connect a volt-ohmmeter and check the resistance of the pickup coil.
3. The pickup coil resistance should be 900-1200 ohms. If the resistance is not within specification, replace the pickup coil.

IGNITION TIMING

➡If the information given in the following procedures differs from that on the emission information label located in the engine compartment, follow the directions given on the label. The label often reflects production running changes made during the model year.

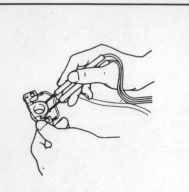

Fig. 21 Checking pick-up coil resistance — 1990-1992 626 and MX-6 non-turbo

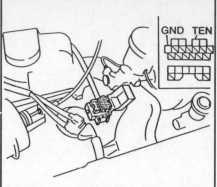

Fig. 22 Grounding connection points for ignition timing procedure — Miata

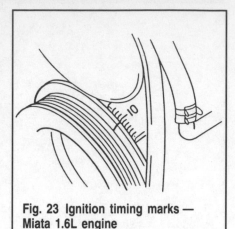

Fig. 23 Ignition timing marks — Miata 1.6L engine

Ignition

CHECKING AND ADJUSTMENT

▶ See Figures 22, 23, 24, 25, 26, 27, 28, 29 and 30

1.6L Engine

323

1. Apply the parking brake. If equipped with a manual transaxle, place the shifter in the neutral position. If equipped with an automatic transaxle, place the shift lever in **P**.
2. Locate the timing marks on the crankshaft pulley and timing belt lower cover. The engine may have to be cranked slightly to see the mark on the crankshaft pulley.
3. Start the engine and allow it to come to normal operating temperature. Make sure all accessories are **OFF**.
4. Check the idle speed and adjust, if necessary.
5. Turn the engine off. Connect a jumper wire between the TEN terminal and the GND terminal at the underhood diagnosis connector.
6. Connect an inductive timing light according to the manufacturers instructions.
7. Start the engine and allow the idle to stabilize. Aim the timing light at the timing marks.
8. The mark on the crankshaft pulley should align with the 7 degree BTDC mark on the timing cover scale, plus or minus 1 degree. If the marks are within alignment proceed with step 10. If the marks are not aligned, proceed to Step 9.
9. Loosen the distributor lock bolts just enough to turn the distributor. While aiming the timing light at the timing

marks, turn the distributor until the marks are aligned. Tighten the distributor lock bolts to 14-19 ft. lbs. (19-25 Nm) and recheck the timing.
10. The ignition timing is now set. Disconnect the jumper wire from the underhood diagnosis connector.

MIATA

1. Apply the parking brake. If equipped with a manual transmission, place the shifter in the neutral position. If equipped with an automatic transmission, place the shift lever in **P**.
2. Locate the timing marks on the crankshaft pulley and timing belt lower cover. The engine may have to be cranked slightly to see the mark on the crankshaft pulley.
3. Start the engine and allow it to come to normal operating temperature. Make sure all accessories are **OFF**.
4. Check the idle speed and adjust, if necessary.
5. Turn the engine off. Connect a jumper wire between the TEN terminal and the GND terminal at the underhood diagnosis connector.
6. Connect an inductive timing light according to the manufacturers instructions.
7. Start the engine and allow the idle to stabilize.
8. Aim the timing light at the timing marks.
9. If equipped with an automatic transmission, the mark on the crankshaft pulley should align with the 8 degree BTDC mark on the timing cover scale, plus or minus 1 degree. If equipped with a manual transmission, the mark on the crankshaft pulley should align with the 10 degree BTDC mark on the timing cover scale, plus or minus 1 degree. If the marks are within alignment proceed with step 10. If the marks are not aligned, proceed to Step 9.

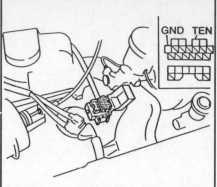

Fig. 24 Crank angle sensor location — Miata 1.6L engine

10. Loosen the crank angle sensor lock bolt just enough to turn the crank angle sensor. While aiming the timing light at the timing marks, turn the crank angle sensor until the marks are aligned. Tighten the crank angle sensor lock bolt to 14-19 ft. lbs. (19-25 Nm) and recheck the timing.
11. The ignition timing is now set. Disconnect the jumper wire from the underhood diagnosis connector. Increase the engine idle and make sure that the timing advances.

MX-3

1. Apply the parking brake. If equipped with manual transaxle, place the shifter in the neutral position. If equipped with an automatic transaxle, place the shift lever in **P**.
2. Locate the timing marks on the crankshaft pulley and timing belt lower cover. The engine may have to be cranked slightly to see the mark on the crankshaft pulley.
3. Start the engine and allow it to come to normal operating temperature. Make sure all accessories are **OFF**.

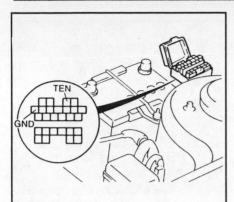

Fig. 25 Grounding connection points for ignition timing procedure — 1.6L engine

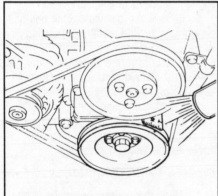

Fig. 26 Ignition timing procedure — 1.6L engine

4. Check the idle speed and adjust, if necessary.

5. Turn the engine off. Connect a jumper wire between the TEN terminal and the GND terminal at the underhood diagnosis connector as shown.

6. Connect an inductive timing light according to the manufacturers instructions.

7. Start the engine and allow the idle to stabilize. Aim the timing light at the timing marks.

8. The mark on the crankshaft pulley should align with the 10 degree BTDC mark on the timing cover scale, plus or minus 1 degree. If the marks are within alignment proceed with step 10. If the marks are not aligned, proceed to Step 9.

9. Loosen the distributor lock bolts just enough to turn the distributor. While aiming the timing light at the timing marks, turn the distributor until the marks are aligned. Tighten the distributor lock bolts to 14-19 ft. lbs. (19-25 Nm) and recheck the timing.

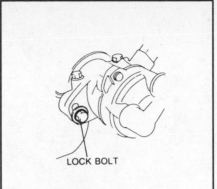

Fig. 27 Distributor lock bolt location — 1.6L engine

10. The ignition timing is now set. Disconnect the jumper wire from the underhood diagnosis connector.

1.8L Engine

PROTEGE

1. Apply the parking brake. If equipped with a manual transaxle, place the shifter in the neutral position. If equipped with an automatic transaxle, place the shift lever in **P**.

2. Locate the timing marks on the crankshaft pulley and timing belt lower cover. The engine may have to be cranked slightly to see the mark on the crankshaft pulley.

3. Start the engine and allow it to come to normal operating temperature. Make sure all accessories are **OFF**.

4. Check the idle speed and adjust, if necessary.

5. Turn the engine off. Connect a jumper wire between the TEN terminal and the GND terminal at the underhood diagnosis connector as shown.

6. Connect an inductive timing light according to the manufacturers instructions.

7. Start the engine and allow the idle to stabilize. Aim the timing light at the timing marks.

8. If equipped with the SOHC engine, the mark on the crankshaft pulley should align with the 5 degree BTDC mark on the timing cover scale, plus or minus 1 degree. If equipped with the DOHC engine, the mark on the crankshaft pulley should align with the 10 degree BTDC mark on the timing cover scale, plus or minus 1 degree. If the marks are within alignment proceed with step 10. If the marks are not aligned, proceed to Step 9.

9. Loosen the distributor lock bolts just enough to turn the distributor. While aiming the timing light at the timing

marks, turn the distributor until the marks are aligned. Tighten the distributor lock bolts to 14-19 ft. lbs. (19-25 Nm) and recheck the timing.

10. The ignition timing is now set. Disconnect the jumper wire from the underhood diagnosis connector.

MX-3

1. Apply the parking brake. If equipped with a manual transaxle, place the shifter in the neutral position. If equipped with an automatic transaxle, place the shift lever in **P**.

2. Locate the timing marks on the crankshaft pulley and timing belt lower cover. The engine may have to be cranked slightly to see the mark on the crankshaft pulley.

3. Start the engine and allow it to come to normal operating temperature. Make sure all accessories are **OFF**.

4. Check the idle speed and adjust, if necessary.

5. Turn the engine off. Connect a jumper wire between the TEN terminal and the GND terminal at the underhood diagnosis connector as shown.

6. Connect an inductive timing light according to the manufacturers instructions.

7. Start the engine and allow the idle to stabilize. Aim the timing light at the timing marks.

8. The mark on the crankshaft pulley should align with the 10 degree BTDC mark on the timing cover scale, ± 1 degree. If the marks are within alignment proceed with step 10. If the marks are not aligned, proceed to Step 9.

9. Loosen the distributor lock bolts just enough to turn the distributor. While aiming the timing light at the timing marks, turn the distributor until the marks are aligned. Tighten the distributor lock bolts to 14-19 ft. lbs. (19-25 Nm) and recheck the timing.

10. The ignition timing is now set. Disconnect the jumper wire from the underhood diagnosis connector.

2.0L Engine

1. Apply the parking brake. If equipped with a manual transaxle, place the shifter in the neutral position. If equipped with an automatic transaxle, place the shift lever in **P**.

2. Locate the timing marks on the crankshaft pulley and timing belt lower cover. The engine may have to be cranked slightly to see the mark on the crankshaft pulley.

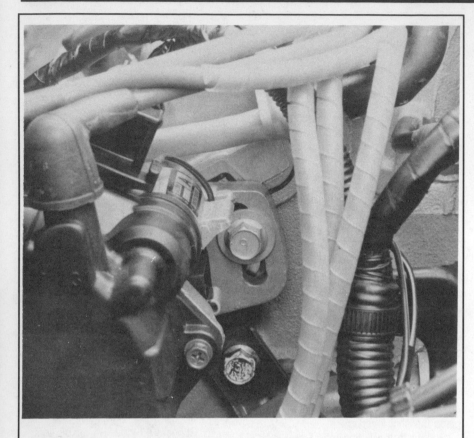

Fig. 28 Distributor lock bolt location — 1.8L engine

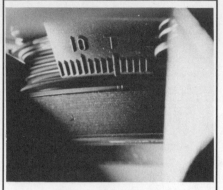

Fig. 29 Timing marks location

3. Start the engine and allow it to come to normal operating temperature. Make sure all accessories are **OFF**.

4. Check the idle speed and adjust, if necessary.

5. Turn the engine off. Connect a jumper wire between the TEN terminal and the GND terminal at the underhood diagnosis connector.

6. Connect an inductive timing light according to the manufacturers instructions.

7. Start the engine and allow the idle to stabilize. Aim the timing light at the timing marks.

8. The mark on the crankshaft pulley should align with the 12 degree BTDC mark on the timing cover scale, ± 1 degree. If the marks are within alignment proceed with step 10. If the marks are not aligned, proceed to Step 9.

9. Loosen the distributor lock bolts just enough to turn the distributor. While aiming the timing light at the timing marks, turn the distributor until the marks are aligned. Tighten the distributor lock bolts to 14-19 ft. lbs. (19-25 Nm) and recheck the timing.

10. The ignition timing is now set. Disconnect the jumper wire from the underhood diagnosis connector.

2.2L Engine

626/MX-6 NON-TURBOCHARGED ENGINE

1. Apply the parking brake. If equipped with manual transaxle, place the shift lever in neutral. If equipped with automatic transaxle, place the shift lever in **P**.

2. Locate the timing marks on the crankshaft pulley and timing belt cover. You may have to crank the engine slightly to see the mark on the crankshaft pulley. If the marks are hard to see, clean them off with some degreasing cleaner and a wire brush.

3. Start the engine and allow it to come to normal operating temperature. Make sure all accessories are **OFF**.

4. Check the idle speed and adjust, if necessary.

5. Shut off the engine. Disconnect and plug the vacuum hoses at the distributor vacuum diaphragm.

6. Connect an inductive timing light according to the manufacturers instructions.

7. Start the engine and allow the idle to stabilize.

8. Aim the timing light at the timing marks. The mark on the crankshaft pulley should align with the 6 degree

BTDC mark on the timing cover scale, ± 1 degree. If the marks are aligned, proceed to Step 10. If the marks are not aligned, proceed to Step 9.

9. Loosen the distributor lock bolt just enough to turn the distributor housing. While aiming the timing light at the timing marks, turn the distributor until the marks are aligned. Tighten the distributor lock bolt to 14-19 ft. lbs. (19-25 Nm) and recheck the timing.

10. Initial timing is now set. Remove the plugs and reconnect the vacuum hoses to the vacuum diaphragm.

626/MX-6 TURBOCHARGED ENGINE

1. Apply the parking brake. If equipped with manual transaxle, place the shift lever in neutral. If equipped with automatic transaxle, place the shift lever in **P**.

2. Locate the timing marks on the crankshaft pulley and timing belt cover. You may have to crank the engine slightly to see the mark on the crankshaft pulley. If the marks are hard to see, clean them off with some degreasing cleaner and a wire brush.

3. Start the engine and allow it to come to normal operating temperature. Make sure all accessories are **OFF**.

4. Check the idle speed and adjust, if necessary.

5. Shut off the engine. Connect a jumper wire between the test connector, located near the left strut tower, and ground.

6. Connect an inductive timing light according to the manufacturers instructions.

7. Start the engine and allow the idle to stabilize.

8. Aim the timing light at the timing marks. The mark on the crankshaft pulley should align with the 9 degree BTDC mark on the timing cover scale, ± 1 degree. If the marks are aligned,

proceed to Step 10. If the marks are not aligned, proceed to Step 9.

9. Loosen the distributor lock bolt just enough to turn the distributor housing. While aiming the timing light at the timing marks, turn the distributor until the marks are aligned. Tighten the distributor lock bolt to 14-19 ft. lbs. (19-25 Nm) and recheck the timing.

10. Shut off the engine. Remove the timing light and the jumper wire.

2.5L Engine

1. Apply the parking brake. If vehicle is equipped with manual transaxle, place the shifter in the neutral position. If the vehicle is equipped with an automatic transaxle, place the shift lever in **P**.

2. Locate the tlming marks on the crankshaft pulley and timing belt lower cover. The engine may have to be cranked slightly to see the mark on the crankshaft pulley.

3. Start the engine and allow it to come to normal operating temperature. Make sure all accessories are **OFF**.

4. Check the idle speed and adjust, if necessary.

5. Turn the engine off. Connect a jumper wire between the TEN terminal and the GND terminal at the underhood diagnosis connector.

6. Connect an inductive timing light according to the manufacturers instructions.

7. Start the engine and allow the idle to stabilize. Aim the timing light at the timing marks.

8. The mark on the crankshaft pulley should align with the 10 degree BTDC

Fig. 30 Underhood diagnostic connector location

mark on the timing cover scale, ± 1 degree. If the marks are within alignment proceed with step 10. If the marks are not aligned, proceed to Step 9.

9. Loosen the distributor lock bolts just enough to turn the distributor. While aiming the timing light at the timing

marks, turn the distributor until the marks are aligned. Tighten the distributor lock bolts to 14-19 ft. lbs. (19-25 Nm) and recheck the timing.

10. The ignition timing is now set. Disconnect the jumper wire from the underhood diagnosis connector.

VALVE LASH

The valve lash on all engines is kept in adjustment hydraulically. All Single Overhead Camshaft (SOHC) engines are equipped with hydraulic lash adjusters mounted in the rocker arms, located directly over the valve stem. All Double Overhead Camshaft (DOHC) engines are equipped with conventional type hydraulic lifters, which are located over the valve stem and driven directly by the camshaft.

No adjustment is possible with the lash adjusters or lifters, but they can be checked for function and clearance.

Lash

CHECKING

SOHC Engines

1. Warm up the engine to normal operating temperature, then shut the engine off.

2. Check the condition of the engine oil. If necessary, change the oil and filter.

3. Connect an oil pressure gauge. Start the engine and check the oil pressure. Refer to the General Engine Specifications Chart in Section 3 for the oil pressure specifications.

4. Stop the engine and remove the rocker arm cover. Refer to Section 3.

5. Push down on the hydraulic lash adjuster side of the rocker arm to make sure the hydraulic lash adjuster cannot be compressed. Use a shop rag as the rocker arm will be hot.

6. If the hydraulic lash adjuster can be compressed, it must be replaced.

DOHC Engines

On DOHC engines, the hydraulic lifters can be inspected only with the camshaft completely removed. Removal and inspection is covered in Section 3.

IDLE SPEED AND MIXTURE ADJUSTMENTS

On all Mazda engines, the air/fuel mixture is controlled by the Electronic Control Unit (ECU), therefore no idle mixture adjustment is possible or necessary.

Idle and Mixture

IDLE SPEED ADJUSTMENT

▶ See Figure 31

➡Idle speed is controlled automatically by the ECU through the Idle Speed Control (ISC) solenoid valve. Idle speed adjustment is usually not necessary.

1.6L and 1.8L Engines (Except Miata and MX-3)

1. Check the ignition timing and adjust to specification, if necessary.
2. Turn off all lights and other unnecessary electrical loads. Idle speed adjustment must be done while the radiator cooling fan is not operating.
3. Set the parking brake and place the transaxle selector lever in neutral on manual transaxle vehicles or **P**on automatic transaxle vehicles. Warm up the engine.
4. Connect a jumper wire between the TEN terminal and the GND terminal at the underhood test connector.
5. Attach a suitable tachometer according to the manufacturer's instructions.
6. Check the idle speed. It should be 750 rpm ± 50 rpm.
7. If the idle speed is not correct, adjust the idle speed by turning the air adjusting screw.
8. After adjusting the idle speed, disconnect the jumper wire from the test connector and remove the tachometer from the engine.

1.6L Engine (Miata and MX-3)

1. Check the ignition timing and adjust to specification, if necessary.
2. Turn off all lights and other unnecessary electrical loads. Idle speed adjustment must be done while the radiator cooling fan is not operating.
3. Set the parking brake and place the transaxle/transmission selector lever in neutral on manual transaxle/transmission vehicles or **P**on automatic transaxle/transmission vehicles. Warm up the engine.
4. Connect a jumper wire between the TEN terminal and the GND terminal at the underhood test connector.
5. Attach a suitable tachometer according to the manufacturer's instructions.
6. Check the idle speed. It should be 850 rpm ± 50 rpm for the Miata and it should be 750 rpm ± 50 rpm for the MX-3.
7. If the idle speed is not correct, remove the blind cap from the air adjusting screw and adjust the idle speed by turning the air adjusting screw.
8. After adjusting the idle speed, disconnect the jumper wire from the test connector and remove the tachometer from the engine.

1.8L Engine (MX-3)

1. Check the ignition timing and adjust to specification, if necessary.
2. Turn off all lights and other unnecessary electrical loads. Idle speed adjustment must be done while the radiator cooling fan is not operating.
3. Set the parking brake and place the transaxle selector lever in neutral on manual transaxle vehicles or **P**on automatic transaxle vehicles. Warm up the engine.
4. Connect a jumper wire between the TEN terminal and the GND terminal at the underhood test connector.
5. Attach a suitable tachometer according to the manufacturer's instructions.
6. Check the idle speed. It should be 670 rpm ± 30 rpm.
7. If the idle speed is not correct, adjust the idle speed by turning the air adjusting screw.
8. After adjusting the idle speed, disconnect the jumper wire from the test connector and remove the tachometer from the engine.

2.0L Engine

1. Check the ignition timing and adjust to specification, if necessary.
2. Turn off all lights and other unnecessary electrical loads. The radiator cooling fan must nut be operating while the idle speed is adjusted.
3. Set the parking brake and place the transaxle selector lever in neutral on

manual transaxle vehicles or **P**on automatic transaxle vehicles. Warm up the engine.
4. Connect a jumper wire between the TEN terminal and the GND terminal at the underhood test connector.
5. Attach a suitable tachometer according to the manufacturer's instructions.
6. Check the idle speed. It should be 700 rpm ± 50 rpm.
7. If the idle speed is not correct, adjust the idle speed by turning the air adjusting screw.
8. After adjusting the idle speed, disconnect the jumper wire from the test connector and remove the tachometer from the engine.

2.2L Engine

1. Check the ignition timing and adjust to specification, if necessary.
2. Turn off all lights and other unnecessary electrical loads. Idle speed adjustment must be done while the radiator cooling fan is not operating.
3. Set the parking brake and place the transaxle selector lever in neutral on manual transaxle vehicles or **P**on automatic transaxle vehicles. Warm up the engine.
4. Connect a jumper wire between the TEN terminal and the GND terminal at the underhood test connector.
5. Attach a suitable tachometer according to the manufacturer's instructions.
6. Check the idle speed. It should be 750 rpm ± 25 rpm.
7. If the idle speed is not correct, adjust the idle speed by turning the air adjusting screw.
8. After adjusting the idle speed, disconnect the jumper wire from the test connector and remove the tachometer from the engine.

2.5L Engine

1. Check the ignition timing and adjust to specification, if necessary.
2. Turn off all lights and other unnecessary electrical loads. Idle speed adjustment must be done while the radiator cooling fan is not operating.
3. Set the parking brake and place the transaxle selector lever in neutral on manual transaxle vehicles or **P**on automatic transaxle vehicles. Warm up the engine.

4. Connect a jumper wire between the TEN terminal and the GND terminal at the underhood test connector.

5. Attach a suitable tachometer according to the manufacturer's instructions.

6. Check the idle speed. It should be 650 rpm ± 50 rpm.

7. If the idle speed is not correct, adjust the idle speed by turning the air adjusting screw.

8. After adjusting the idle speed, disconnect the jumper wire from the test connector and remove the tachometer from the engine.

✳✳WARNING

Do not tamper with any other adjustment screws. Doing so may result in damage to the throttle body.

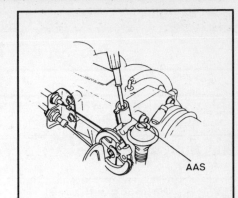

Fig. 31 Adjusting air adjustment screw — 1.6L engine (except Miata)

TORQUE SPECIFICATIONS

Component	U.S.	Metric
Distributor lock bolt All engines	14–19 ft. lbs.	19–25 Nm
Crank angle sensor lock bolt Miata	14–19 ft. lbs.	19–25 Nm
Spark plugs All engines	11–17 ft. lbs.	15–23 Nm

Diagnosis of Spark Plugs

Problem	Possible Cause	Correction
Brown to grayish-tan deposits and slight electrode wear.	• Normal wear.	• Clean, regap, reinstall.
Dry, fluffy black carbon deposits.	• Poor ignition output.	• Check distributor to coil connections.
Wet, oily deposits with very little electrode wear.	• "Break-in" of new or recently overhauled engine. • Excessive valve stem guide clearances. • Worn intake valve seals.	• Degrease, clean and reinstall the plugs. • Refer to Section 3. • Replace the seals.
Red, brown, yellow and white colored coatings on the insulator. Engine misses intermittently under severe operating conditions.	• By-products of combustion.	• Clean, regap, and reinstall. If heavily coated, replace.
Colored coatings heavily deposited on the portion of the plug projecting into the chamber and on the side facing the intake valve.	• Leaking seals if condition is found in only one or two cylinders.	• Check the seals. Replace if necessary. Clean, regap, and reinstall the plugs.
Shiny yellow glaze coating on the insulator.	• Melted by-products of combustion.	• Avoid sudden acceleration with wide-open throttle after long periods of low speed driving. Replace the plugs.
Burned or blistered insulator tips and badly eroded electrodes.	• Overheating.	• Check the cooling system. • Check for sticking heat riser valves. Refer to Section 1. • Lean air-fuel mixture. • Check the heat range of the plugs. May be too hot. • Check ignition timing. May be over-advanced. • Check the torque value of the plugs to ensure good plug-engine seat contact.
Broken or cracked insulator tips.	• Heat shock from sudden rise in tip temperature under severe operating conditions. Improper gapping of plugs.	• Replace the plugs. Gap correctly.

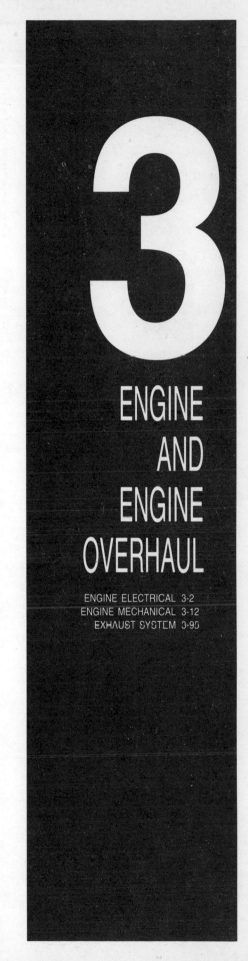

3

ENGINE AND ENGINE OVERHAUL

ENGINE ELECTRICAL

Ignition Coil

REMOVAL & INSTALLATION

323 and Protege

1. Disconnect the negative battery cable.
2. Disconnect the distributor lead wire from the coil.
3. Disconnect the electrical connector from the coil.
4. Remove the coil attaching bolts and remove the coil.
5. Installation is the reverse of the removal procedure.

Miata

▶ **See Figure 1**

1. Disconnect the negative battery cable.
2. Disconnect the coil electrical connector. Mark the location and number of the spark plug wires and disconnect the spark plug wires from the assembly.
3. Remove the 3 installation bolts and remove the coil assembly.
4. Installation is the reverse of the removal procedure. Tighten the coil assembly bolts to 14-19 ft. lbs. (19-25 Nm).

MX-3

1. Disconnect the negative battery cable.
2. Disconnect the coil electrical connector. Mark the location and number of the spark plug wires and disconnect the spark plug wires from the assembly.
3. Remove the 3 installation bolts and remove the coil assembly.
4. Installation is the reverse of the removal procedure. Tighten the coil assembly bolts to 14-19 ft. lbs. (19-25 Nm).

1990-92 626 and MX6

NORMALLY ASPIRATED ENGINE

1. Disconnect the negative battery cable.
2. Disconnect the high tension lead from the coil by first twisting, then pulling it from the coil terminal.
3. Disconnect the distributor wiring harness from the coil. Tag the wires so they can be reinstalled in their original positions.

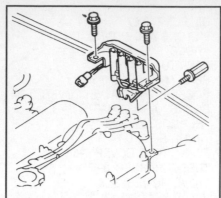

Fig. 1 Ignition coil removal — Miata

4. Remove the 2 mounting nuts and remove the coil and bracket assembly.
5. Loosen the clamp screw at the coil bracket and remove the coil.
6. Installation is the reverse of the removal procedure.

TURBOCHARGED ENGINE

1. Disconnect the negative battery cable.
2. Disconnect the high tension lead from the coil by first twisting, then pulling it from the coil terminal.
3. Disconnect the igniter wiring harness and remove the 2 nuts.
4. Lift the coil and igniter assembly and disconnect the coil and noise suppressor wiring harness. Tag the wires so they can be reinstalled in their original positions.
5. Slide the protective cover back and disconnect the coil wiring harness. Tag the wires so they can be reinstalled in their original positions.
6. Remove the noise suppressor. Remove the 2 screws and the ignitor module.
7. Remove the ignitor module mounting bracket and the coil.
8. Installation is the reverse of the removal procedure.

1993 MX-6 and 626

The ignition coil is integrated within the distributor assembly on the 1993 MX-6 and 626. Refer to the distributor section for information pertaining to the coil.

Ignition Module

REMOVAL & INSTALLATION

Refer to the Ignition Coil removal and installation procedure to remove and install the Ignition Module.

Distributor

REMOVAL

▶ **See Figures 1 and 2**

323, Protege and MX-3

1. Disconnect the negative battery cable.
2. Remove the distributor cap and position it aside, leaving the ignition wires connected.
3. On SOHC engines, remove the air intake hose from it's position next to the distributor.
4. Disconnect the distributor electrical connector(s) from the side of the distributor.
5. Using a wrench on the crankshaft pulley, rotate the crankshaft to position the No. 1 piston on Top Dead Center (TDC) of the compression stroke; the crankshaft pulley mark should align with the timing indicator.
6. Using chalk or paint, mark the position of the distributor housing on the cylinder head. Also mark the position of the distributor rotor in relation to the distributor housing.
7. Remove the distributor hold-down bolt(s) and remove the distributor.
8. Inspect the O-ring on the distributor housing and replace it, if it is damaged or worn.

INSTALLATION

Engine Not Rotated

1. Using engine oil, lubricate the O-ring.
2. Install the distributor, aligning the marks that were made in Step 6 of the removal procedure. Be sure to engage the drive gear with the slot in the camshaft.
3. Tighten the distributor hold-down bolt(s).

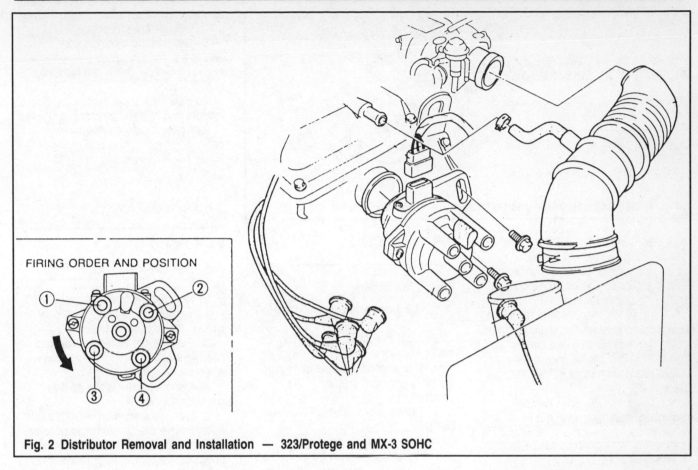

Fig. 2 Distributor Removal and Installation — 323/Protege and MX-3 SOHC

FIRING ORDER AND POSITION

FIRING ORDER AND POSITION

Fig. 3 Distributor Removal and Installation — 323/Protege and MX-3 DOHC

4. Connect the electrical connector(s) and, if equipped, air intake hose. Install the distributor cap.

5. Connect the negative battery cable. Start the engine and check or adjust the ignition timing. Refer to Section 2.

Engine Rotated

1. Using engine oil, lubricate the O-ring.

2. Disconnect the spark plug wire from the No. 1 cylinder spark plug. Remove the spark plug from the No. 1 cylinder and press a thumb over the spark plug hole.

3. Using a wrench on the crankshaft pulley, rotate the crankshaft until pressure is felt at the spark plug hole, indicating the piston is approaching TDC on the compression stroke. Continue rotating the crankshaft until the crankshaft pulley mark aligns with the timing cover indicator.

4. Place the distributor rotor in position so that it aligns with the No. 1 spark plug wire tower on the distributor cap.

5. Install the distributor. Be sure to engage the drive gear with the camshaft slot. Align the mark that was made on the distributor housing with the mark that

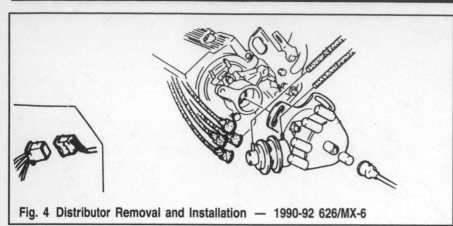

Fig. 4 Distributor Removal and Installation — 1990-92 626/MX-6

was made on the cylinder head. Tighten the distributor hold-down bolt(s).

6. Connect the electrical connector(s) and, if equipped, the air intake hose. Install the distributor cap.

7. Install the spark plug in the No. 1 cylinder and connect the spark plug wire.

8. Connect the negative battery cable. Start the engine and check or adjust the ignition timing. Refer to Section 2.

1990-92 626 and MX-6

▶ **See Figure 4**

1. Disconnect the negative battery cable.

2. Remove the distributor cap and position it aside, leaving the ignition wires connected.

3. If neccessary, disconnect the vacuum hoses from the distributor diaphragm and the wiring harness at the coil. Tag the hoses and wires prior to removal so they can be reinstalled in their original locations.

4. If neccessary, disconnect the distributor wiring harness connector located near the distributor.

5. Using a wrench on the crankshaft pulley, rotate the crankshaft to position the No. 1 piston on Top Dead Center (TDC) of the compression stroke; the crankshaft pulley mark should align with the timing plate indicator.

6. Using chalk or paint, mark the position of the distributor housing on the cylinder head. Also mark the position of the distributor rotor in relation to the distributor housing.

7. Remove the distributor hold-down bolt(s) and remove the distributor.

8. Inspect the O-ring on the distributor housing and replace it, if it is damaged or worn.

INSTALLATION

Engine Not Rotated

1. Using engine oil, lubricate the O-ring.

2. Install the distributor, aligning the marks that were made in Step 6 of the removal procedure. Be sure to engage the drive gear with the slot in the camshaft.

3. Tighten the distributor hold-down bolt(s).

4. Connect the electrical connectors and, if equipped, vacuum hoses to their original locations. Install the distributor cap.

5. Connect the negative battery cable. Start the engine and check or adjust the ignition timing. Refer to Section 2.

Engine Rotated

1. Using engine oil, lubricate the O-ring.

2. Disconnect the spark plug wire from the No. 1 cylinder spark plug. Remove the spark plug from the No. 1 cylinder and press a thumb over the spark plug hole.

3. Using a wrench on the crankshaft pulley, rotate the crankshaft until pressure is felt at the spark plug hole, indicating the piston is approaching TDC on the compression stroke. Continue rotating the crankshaft until the crankshaft pulley mark aligns with the timing cover indicator.

4. Place the distributor rotor in position so that it aligns with the No. 1 spark plug wire tower on the distributor cap.

5. Install the distributor. Be sure to engage the drive gear with the camshaft slot. Align the mark that was made on the distributor housing with the mark that

was made on the cylinder head. Tighten the distributor hold-down bolt(s).

6. Connect the electrical connectors and, if equipped, vacuum hoses to their original locations. Install the distributor cap.

7. Install the spark plug in the No. 1 cylinder and connect the spark plug wire.

8. Connect the negative battery cable. Start the engine and check or adjust the ignition timing. Refer to Section 2.

1993 626 and MX-6

▶ **See Figures 5 and 6**

1. Disconnect the negative battery cable.

2. Remove the fresh air intake duct and if neccessary, remove the air cleaner housing assembly.

3. Remove the distributor cap and position it aside, leaving the ignition wires connected.

4. Disconnect the wiring at the connectors.

5. Using a wrench on the crankshaft pulley, rotate the crankshaft to position the No. 1 piston on Top Dead Center (TDC) of the compression stroke; the crankshaft pulley mark should align with the timing plate indicator.

6. Using chalk or paint, mark the position of the distributor housing on the cylinder head. Also mark the position of the distributor rotor in relation to the distributor housing.

7. Remove the distributor hold-down bolt(s) and remove the distributor.

8. Inspect the O-ring on the distributor housing and replace it, if it is damaged or worn.

INSTALLATION

Engine Not Rotated

1. Using engine oil, lubricate the O-ring.

2. Install the distributor, aligning the marks that were made in Step 6 of the removal procedure. Be sure to engage the drive gear with the slot in the camshaft.

3. Tighten the distributor hold-down bolts to 14-18 ft. lbs. (19-25 Nm).

4. Connect the electrical connectors and install the distributor cap.

5. Connect the negative battery cable. Start the engine and check or adjust the ignition timing. Refer to Section 2.

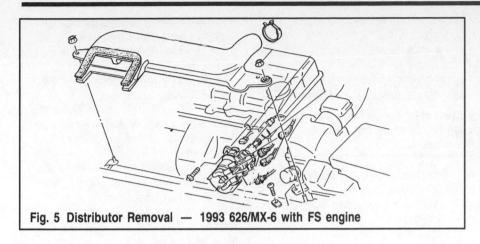

Fig. 5 Distributor Removal — 1993 626/MX-6 with FS engine

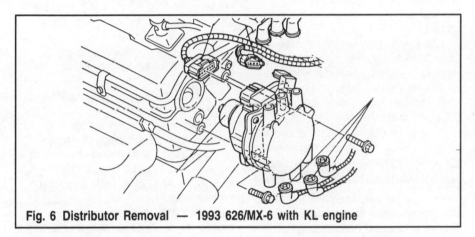

Fig. 6 Distributor Removal — 1993 626/MX-6 with KL engine

Engine Rotated

1. Using engine oil, lubricate the O-ring.

2. Disconnect the spark plug wire from the No. 1 cylinder spark plug. Remove the spark plug from the No. 1 cylinder and press a thumb over the spark plug hole.

3. Using a wrench on the crankshaft pulley, rotate the crankshaft until pressure is felt at the spark plug hole, indicating the piston is approaching TDC on the compression stroke. Continue rotating the crankshaft until the crankshaft pulley mark aligns with the timing cover indicator.

4. Place the distributor rotor in position so that it aligns with the No. 1 spark plug wire tower on the distributor cap.

5. Install the distributor. Be sure to engage the drive gear with the camshaft slot. Align the mark that was made on the distributor housing with the mark that was made on the cylinder head. Tighten the distributor hold-down bolts to 14-18 ft. lbs. (19-25 Nm).

6. Connect the electrical connectors and install the distributor cap.

7. Install the spark plug in the No. 1 cylinder and connect the spark plug wire.

8. Connect the negative battery cable. Start the engine and check or adjust the ignition timing. Refer to Section 2.

Alternator

ALTERNATOR PRECAUTIONS

Several precautions must be observed with alternator equipped vehicles to avoid damage to the unit.

• If the battery is removed for any reason, make sure it is reconnected with the correct polarity. Reversing the battery connections may result in damage to the one-way rectifiers.

• When utilizing a booster battery as a starting aid, always connect the positive to positive terminals and the negative terminal from the booster battery to a good engine ground on the vehicle being started.

• Never use a fast charger as a booster to start vehicles.

• Disconnect the battery cables when charging the battery with a fast charger.

• Never attempt to polarize the alternator.

• Do not use test lights of more than 12 volts when checking diode continuity.

• Do not short across or ground any of the alternator terminals.

• The polarity of the battery, alternator and regulator must be matched and considered before making any electrical connections within the system.

• Never separate the alternator on an open circuit. Make sure all connections within the circuit are clean and tight.

• Disconnect the battery ground terminal when performing any service on electrical components.

• Disconnect the battery if arc welding is to be done on the vehicle.

REMOVAL & INSTALLATION

All Except MX-3 1.8L Engine and 1993 MX-6/626

1. Disconnect the negative battery cable.

2. On 323/Protege, disconnect the vacuum hose and remove the solenoid bracket, if equipped.

3. On Miata, disconnect the electrical connectors for the power steering pressure switch, water thermoswitch and ISC valve, then remove the air pipe.

4. Remove the alternator drive belt.

5. Label and disconnect the electrical connectors from the alternator.

6. Remove the alternator pivot and adjusting bar bolts and remove the alternator.

7. Installation is the reverse of the removal procedure. Adjust the belt tension.

MX-3 1.8L Engine

1. Disconnect the negative battery cable.

2. Remove the fresh air duct and the radiator upper bracket.

3. Disconnect the electrical connectors and remove the cooling fan/shroud assemblies.

4. Label and disconnect the electrical connectors from the alternator.

5. Raise and safely support the vehicle. Remove the engine under cover.

6. Remove the belt tensioner and remove the alternator drive belt.

7. Remove the alternator mounting bolts and remove the alternator.

8. Installation is the reverse of the removal procedure. Adjust the belt tension.

1993 MX-6/626

2.0L ENGINE

1. Disconnect the negative battery cable.

2. Label and disconnect the electrical connectors from the alternator.

3. Raise and safely support the vehicle.

4. Remove the transverse member.

5. Remove the front exhaust pipe.

6. Loosen the belt tension and remove the accessory drive belt.

7. Remove the pivot and adjusting bar bolts and remove the alternator.

8. Installation is the reverse of the removal procedure. Install the exhaust pipe, using new gaskets, and tighten the nuts to 38 ft. lbs. (52 Nm). Tighten the transverse member bolts to 96 ft. lbs. (131 Nm). Adjust the belt tension.

2.5L ENGINE

1. Disconnect the negative battery cable.

2. Remove the fresh air duct.

3. Label and disconnect the electrical connectors from the alternator.

4. Raise and safely support the vehicle. Remove the engine under cover.

5. Remove the belt tensioner and remove the alternator drive belt.

6. Remove the A/C compressor mounting bolts and secure the compressor aside with mechanics wire, without disconnecting the refrigerant lines.

7. Remove the alternator mounting bolts and remove the alternator.

8. Installation is the reverse of the removal procedure. Tighten the alternator upper bracket bolt to 18 ft. lbs. (25 Nm) and the pivot bolt to 38 ft. lbs. (51 Nm). Tighten the A/C compressor bolts to 26 ft. lbs. (35 Nm). Adjust the belt tension.

BRUSH REPLACEMENT

1. Remove the alternator from the vehicle. Refer to the procedure in this Section.

2. Using a soldering iron, heat the alternator rear housing around the rear bearing area to expand the housing and allow the bearing to be removed.

3. Mark the relation of the alternator housing case halves for assembly reference, then remove the alternator housing case bolts. Use a small prybar to separate the stator from the alternator front housing.

❋❋WARNING

Be careful not to force the prybar in too far, as the stator may be scratched.

4. Set the alternator front housing and rotor aside.

5. Remove the nut and insulator from the B terminal at the back of the alternator rear housing.

6. Remove the rectifier retaining screw(s) and the brush holder retaining screw(s).

7. Using a small prybar, separate the stator from the alternator rear housing. Remove the stator assembly, with the brush holder and rectifier attached.

8. Remove the 2 plastic shields from the brush holder/regulator assembly.

9. Use a soldering iron to remove the solder from the rectifier and stator lead.

❋❋WARNING

Work quickly and apply the soldering iron for no more than about 5 seconds, to avoid heating and possibly damaging the rectifier.

10. Use a soldering iron to separate the brush holder from the rectifier.

11. Inspect the brushes and replace them if they are worn at or near the wear line.

12. If it is necessary to replace the brushes, remove the solder from the brush pigtails and remove the brushes.

13. When soldering the new brushes, solder the pigtail so the wear limit line of the brush projects 0.08-0.12 in. (2-3mm) out from the end of the brush holder.

14. Check the brush springs as follows:

   a. Use a spring pressure gauge to push the brush into the brush holder until the tip of the brush projects 0.08 in. (2mm).

   b. Read the force on the gauge. Replace the spring if the force is less than 7.1 oz. (200g). The force of a new brush should be 10.9-15.9 oz. (310-450g).

15. Reassemble the rectifier bridge, brush holder/regulator assembly and stator by soldering the leads in the reverse order of disassembly.

16. Use only a rosin core solder. Hold the stator leads with a pair of needlenose pliers when soldering as the pliers will act as a heat sink and protect the diodes. Do not solder for more than 5 seconds.

17. Install the 2 plastic shields to the brush holder/regulator assembly in the reverse order of disassembly.

18. Install the stator assembly with the rectifier and brush holder attached, to the alternator rear housing. Position the stator in the housing so that one of the shallow ridges in the lamination aligns with the case bolt holes.

19. Install the rectifier retaining screw(s) and brush holder retaining screw(s).

20. Install the B terminal insulator and nut.

21. Depress the brush springs and brushes. Insert a stiff piece of wire (a paperclip works well) through the rear of the alternator housing to retain the brushes in their holder while assembling the alternator.

22. Heat the alternator rear housing around the bearing area with a soldering gun. Heat the housing to no more than 122-144°F (50-60°C).

23. Install the alternator halves together, making sure the halves are indexed properly. Install the case bolts and tighten alternately and evenly to draw the halves together.

Battery

REMOVAL & INSTALLATION

1. Using a battery clamp puller and battery pliers, disconnect the negative and then the positive battery cables from the battery.

2. Remove the battery hold-down clamps.

GENERAL ENGINE SPECIFICATIONS

Year	Engine ID/VIN	Engine Displacement Liters (cc)	Fuel System Type	Net Horsepower @ rpm	Net Torque @ rpm (ft. lbs.)	Bore × Stroke (in.)	Compression Ratio	Oil Pressure @ rpm
1990	323	1.6 (1597)	MPFI	82 @ 5000	92 @ 2500	3.07 × 3.29	9.3:1	43–57 @ 3000
	Protege	1.8 (1839)	MPFI	103 @ 5500	111 @ 4000	3.27 × 3.35	8.9:1	43–57 @ 3000
	Protege	1.8 (1839)	MPFI	125 @ 6500	114 @ 4500	3.27 × 3.35	9.0:1	43–57 @ 3000
	626	2.2 (2184)	EFI	③	④	3.39 × 3.70	①	43–57 @ 3000
	MX-6	2.2 (2184)	EFI	③	④	3.39 × 3.70	①	43–57 @ 3000
	Miata	1.6 (1597)	EFI	116 @ 6500	100 @ 5500	3.07 × 3.29	②	43–57 @ 3000
1991	323	1.6 (1597)	MPFI	82 @ 5000	92 @ 2500	3.07 × 3.29	9.3:1	43–57 @ 3000
	Protege	1.8 (1839)	MPFI	103 @ 5500	111 @ 4000	3.27 × 3.35	8.9:1	43–57 @ 3000
	Protege	1.8 (1839)	MPFI	125 @ 6500	114 @ 4500	3.27 × 3.35	9.0:1	43–57 @ 3000
	626	2.2 (2184)	EFI	③	④	3.39 × 3.70	①	43–57 @ 3000
	MX-6	2.2 (2184)	EFI	③	④	3.39 × 3.70	①	43–57 @ 3000
	Miata	1.6 (1597)	EFI	⑤	⑥	3.07 × 3.29	②	43–57 @ 3000
1992	323	1.6 (1597)	MPFI	82 @ 5000	92 @ 2500	3.07 × 3.29	9.3:1	43–57 @ 3000
	Protege	1.8 (1839)	MPFI	103 @ 5500	111 @ 4000	3.27 × 3.35	8.9:1	43–57 @ 3000
	Protege	1.8 (1839)	MPFI	125 @ 6500	114 @ 4500	3.27 × 3.35	9.0:1	43–57 @ 3000
	MX-3	1.6 (1597)	MPFI	88 @ 5000	98 @ 4000	3.07 × 3.29	9.0:1	43–57 @ 3000
	MX-3	1.8 (1844)	MPFI	130 @ 6500	115 @ 4500	2.95 × 2.74	9.2:1	48–71 @ 3000
	626	2.2 (2184)	EFI	③	④	3.39 × 3.70	①	43–57 @ 3000
	MX-6	2.2 (2184)	EFI	③	④	3.39 × 3.70	①	43–57 @ 3000
	Miata	1.6 (1597)	EFI	⑤	⑥	3.07 × 3.29	②	43–57 @ 3000
1993	323	1.6 (1597)	MPFI	82 @ 5000	92 @ 2500	3.07 × 3.29	9.3:1	43–57 @ 3000
	Protege	1.8 (1839)	MPFI	103 @ 5500	111 @ 4000	3.27 × 3.35	8.9:1	43–57 @ 3000
	Protege	1.8 (1839)	MPFI	125 @ 6500	114 @ 4500	3.27 × 3.35	9.0:1	43–57 @ 3000
	MX-3	1.6 (1597)	MPFI	88 @ 5000	98 @ 4000	3.27 × 3.35	9.0:1	43–57 @ 3000
	MX-3	1.8 (1844)	MPFI	130 @ 6500	115 @ 4500	2.95 × 2.74	9.2:1	48–71 @ 3000
	626	2.0 (1991)	MPFI	118 @ 5500	127 @ 4500	3.27 × 3.62	9.0:1	57–71 @ 3000
	626	2.5 (2496)	MPFI	164 @ 5600	160 @ 4800	3.33 × 2.92	9.2:1	49–71 @ 3000
	MX-6	2.0 (1991)	MPFI	118 @ 5500	127 @ 4500	3.27 × 3.62	9.0:1	57–71 @ 3000
	MX-6	2.5 (2496)	MPFI	164 @ 5600	160 @ 4800	3.33 × 2.92	9.2:1	49–71 @ 3000
	Miata	1.6 (1597)	EFI	⑤	⑥	3.07 × 3.29	②	43–57 @ 3000

NOTE: Horsepower and torque are SAE net figures. They are measured at the rear of the transmission with all accessories installed and operating. Since the figures vary when a given engine is installed in different models, some are representative rather than exact.

MPFI—Multi-Point Fuel Injection
EFI—Electronic Fuel Injection
① Turbo—7.8:1
　　Non-turbo—8.6:1
② Manual Trans.—9.4:1
　　Auto. trans.—9.0:1
③ Turbo—145 @ 4300
　　Non-turbo—110 @ 4700
④ Turbo—190 @ 3500
　　Non-turbo—130 @ 3000
⑤ Manual trans.—116 @ 6500
　　Automatic trans.—105 @ 600
⑥ Manual trans.—100 @ 5500
　　Automatic trans.—100 @ 4000

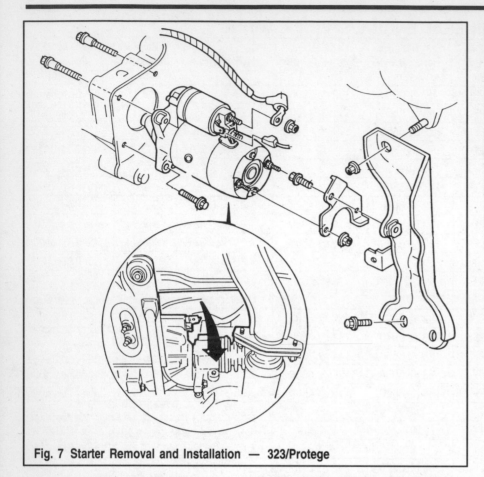

Fig. 7 Starter Removal and Installation — 323/Protege

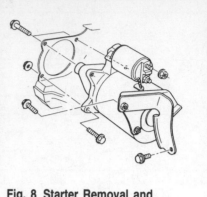

Fig. 8 Starter Removal and Installation — Miata

3. Remove the battery using a battery carrier. If a battery carrier is not available, grip the battery at opposite corners with your hands and carefully lift the battery from the tray. Be careful not to spill battery acid on yourself or the vehicle.

To install:

4. Test the battery to see if it needs to be replaced or charged. Refer to Section 1.

5. Clean the battery cable ends and battery terminals.

6. Check the battery tray for corrosion or other damage. Clean the tray with a wire brush and a scraper.

7. Install the battery and retain with the hold-down clamps.

8. Connect the positive and then the negative battery cables to the battery.

Starter

REMOVAL & INSTALLATION

All except MX-3 with 1.8L Engine and 1993 MX-6/626

▶ See Figures 7, 8 and 9

1. Disconnect the negative battery cable. On 323/Protege and MX-3 1.6L engine, disconnect the positive battery cable and remove the battery and battery tray.

2. Raise and safely support the vehicle. Remove the engine under cover.

3. On 323/Protege, MX-3 with 1.6L engine and MX-6/626 2.2L engine, remove the intake manifold bracket.

4. On 323 with 4WD, remove the differential lock assembly as follows:

a. Remove the retaining bolt.

b. Turn the differential lock shift rod 90 degrees clockwise with a flat-bladed tool.

c. Remove the differential lock assembly.

5. Remove the starter bracket, if equipped.

6. Label and disconnect the wiring from the starter.

7. Remove the starter mounting bolts and remove the starter.

To install:

8. Install the starter and install the mounting bolts.

9. Tighten the starter mounting bolts to 34 ft. lbs. (46 Nm).

10. Connect the wiring to the starter and install the bracket, if equipped.

11. On 323 with 4WD install the differential lock assembly.

12. On 323/Protege, MX-3 with 1.6L engine and MX-6/626 2.2L engine, install the intake manifold bracket.

13. Install the engine under cover and lower the vehicle.

14. Install the battery, if removed. Connect the negative battery cable.

MX-3 with 1.8L Engine

▶ See Figures 10 and 11

1. Disconnect the negative battery cable.

2. Remove the nuts and the upper strut bar from between the strut towers.

3. Remove the intake air hose from between the air cleaner and throttle body.

4. Label and disconnect the wiring from the starter.

5. Remove the mounting bolts and remove the starter.

To install:

6. Install the starter and install the mounting bolts. Tighten the bolts to 38 ft. lbs. (52 Nm).

7. Connect the wiring to the starter.

8. Install the intake air hose between the air cleaner and throttle body.

9. Install the upper strut bar to between the strut towers.

10. Connect the negative battery cable.

1993 MX-6/626

2.0L ENGINE

▶ See Figure 12

1. Disconnect the negative battery cable.

2. Remove the fresh air duct and resonance chamber.

3. Label and disconnect the electrical connectors and remove the air cleaner assembly.

4. Remove the intake manifold bracket.

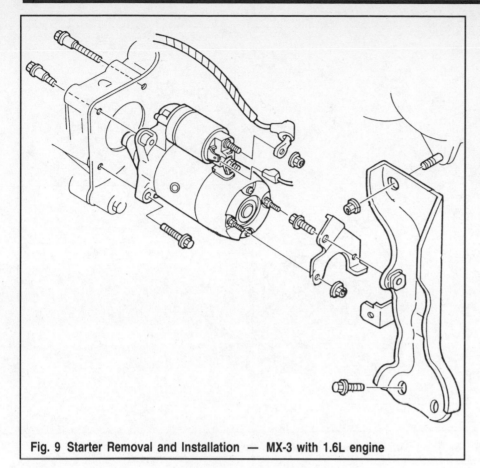

Fig. 9 Starter Removal and Installation — MX-3 with 1.6L engine

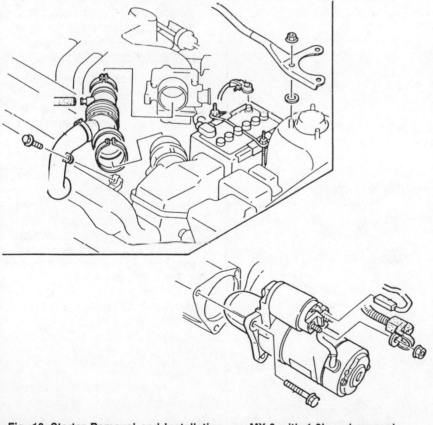

Fig. 10 Starter Removal and Installation — MX-3 with 1.8L and manual transaxle

5. Label and disconnect the wiring at the starter.

6. Remove the starter mounting bolts and remove the starter.

7. Installation is the reverse of the removal procedure. Tighten the starter mounting bolts to 33 ft. lbs. (46 Nm) and the intake manifold bracket bolts to 38 ft. lbs. (51 Nm).

2.5L ENGINE

▶ See Figures 13 and 14

1. Disconnect the negative battery cable.

2. Remove the fresh air duct. Disconnect the electrical connector and remove the air cleaner assembly.

3. If equipped with automatic transaxle, proceed as follows:

   a. Relieve the fuel system pressure. Drain the cooling system.

   b. Disconnect the accelerator cable from the throttle body. Label and disconnect the electrical connectors, vacuum hoses and coolant hoses from the throttle body.

   c. Remove the throttle body.

   d. Disconnect and plug the fuel supply and return lines.

   e. Disconnect the transaxle selector cable from the transaxle and remove the cable bracket.

   f. Remove the starter bracket.

4. Label and disconnect the wiring at the starter.

5. Remove the starter mounting bolts and remove the starter.

6. Installation is the reverse of the removal procedure. Tighten the starter mounting bolts to 38 ft. lbs. (51 Nm).

SOLENOID REPLACEMENT

1. Remove the starter according to the procedure in this Section.

2. Clamp the starter motor in a soft-jawed vise.

3. Remove the nut and disconnect the lead from the solenoid M-terminal.

4. Remove the solenoid retaining screws and remove the solenoid. If there are shims between the solenoid and the starter, save them as they are used to adjust the pinion depth clearance.

5. Install the replacement solenoid and tighten the retaining screws. Be sure to replace any shims that were removed during disassembly.

6. Proceed as follows:

   a. Leave the lead disconnected from the solenoid M-terminal.

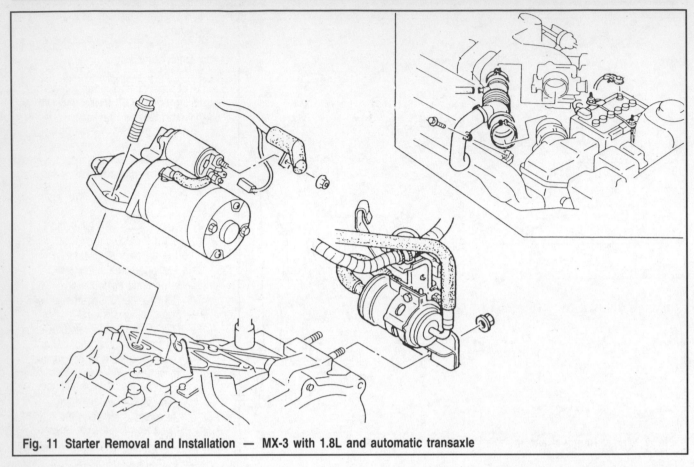

Fig. 11 Starter Removal and Installation — MX-3 with 1.8L and automatic transaxle

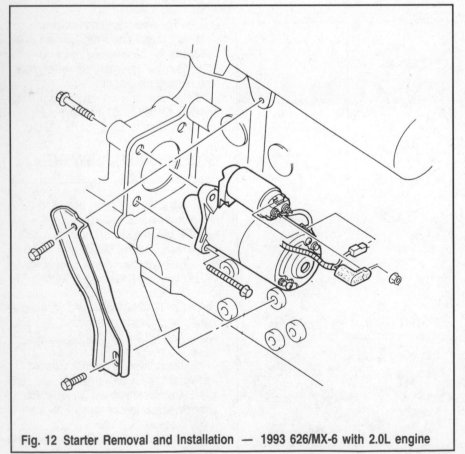

Fig. 12 Starter Removal and Installation — 1993 626/MX-6 with 2.0L engine

b. Connect the positive lead from a 12 volt battery to the S terminal of the solenoid and the negative lead to the starter motor body. When the battery is connected, the solenoid should engage and kick out the pinion.

➡**Do not engage the solenoid for more than 20 seconds at a time. If this test must be repeated, wait at least 3 minutes between attempts to allow the solenoid to cool.**

c. With the pinion extended, measure the clearance between the pinion and collar. The clearance should be 0.02-0.08 in. (0.5-2.0mm).

d. If the gap measurement falls outside the specified range, add or remove shims between the solenoid and drive end housing until the pinion gap is within specification.

e. Install the lead to the solenoid M-terminal and tighten the nut to 87-104 inch lbs. (10-12 Nm).

7. Install the starter according to the procedure in this Section.

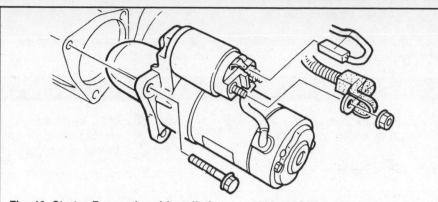

Fig. 13 Starter Removal and Installation — 1993 626/MX-6 with 2.5L engine and manual transaxle

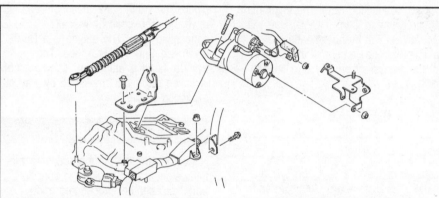

Fig. 14 Starter Removal and Installation — 1993 626/MX-6 with 2.5L engine with automatic transaxle

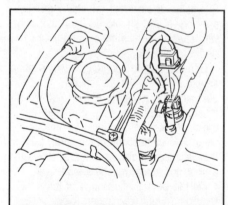

Fig. 15 Engine Coolant Temperature Sensor

Sending Units and Sensors

REMOVAL & INSTALLATION

Engine Coolant Temperature Sensor
♦ **See Figure 15**

1. Disconnect the negative battery cable.
2. Drain the cooling system.
3. Disconnect the sensor electrical connector.
4. Remove the sensor from the cylinder head.
5. Installation is the reverse of the removal procedure. Fill the cooling system.

Cooling Fan Switches

1. Disconnect the negative battery cable.
2. Drain the cooling system.
3. Disconnect the switch electrical connector.
4. Remove the switch from the coolant tube.

5. Installation is the reverse of the removal procedure. Fill the cooling system.

Oil Pressure Sender

1. Disconnect the negative battery cable.
2. Raise and safely support the vehicle.
3. Disconnect the electrical connector from the oil pressure sender, which is located on the left rear side of the engine block.
4. Remove the oil pressure sender.
5. Installation is the reverse of the removal procedure.

Oil Level Sensor

1. Disconnect the negative battery cable.
2. Raise and safely support the vehicle.
3. Drain the engine oil.
4. Remove the oil level sensor from the oil pan. Inspect the oil level sensor gasket and replace, if damaged.
5. Installation is the reverse of the removal procedure. On 3.0L engine, tighten the sensor to 25 ft. lbs. (34 Nm).

Air Charge Temperature Sensor

The air temperature sensor is an integral component of the vane air flow meter. If the temperature sensor is defective, the vane air flow meter must be replaced.

Knock Sensor

1. Disconnect the negative battery cable.
2. Disconnect the knock sensor electrical connector.
3. Raise and safely support the vehicle.
4. Remove the sensor from the engine block.
5. Installation is the reverse of the removal procedure. Tighten the sensor to 14-25 ft. lbs. (20-34 Nm).

Boost Pressure Sensor

➡**The boost pressure sensor is used for instrument gauge operation only.**

1. Disconnect the negative battery cable.
2. Remove the boost pressure line and the electrical connector from the boost sensor.
3. Remove the mounting nut from the sensor housing and remove the sensor.

Power Steering Pressure Switch

1. Disconnect the negative battery cable.

2. Raise and safely support the vehicle.

3. Disconnect the electrical connector from the switch.

4. Remove the pressure switch fitting from the hydraulic line.

5. Installation is the reverse of the removal procedure.

ENGINE MECHANICAL

Description

1.6L (B6 SOHC) ENGINE

The 1.6L engine has 4 cylinders situated in-line in a cast iron cylinder block. The pistons are aluminum and drive the crankshaft by way of connecting rods. The engine is a Single Overhead Cam (SOHC) type. The cylinder head is aluminum. The camshaft is driven off of the crankshaft by way of a cogged belt.

1.6L (B6 DOHC) ENGINE

The 1.6L engine has 4 cylinders situated in-line in a cast iron cylinder block. The pistons are aluminum and drive the crankshaft by way of connecting rods. The engine is a Dual Overhead Cam (DOHC) type. The cylinder head is aluminum. The camshafts are driven off of the crankshaft by way of a cogged belt.

1.8L (BP SOHC) ENGINE

The 1.8L engine has 4 cylinders situated in-line in a cast iron cylinder block. The pistons are aluminum and drive the crankshaft by way of connecting rods. The engine is a Single Overhead Cam (SOHC) type. There are 4 valves per cylinder, 2 intake and 2 exhaust. The cylinder head is aluminum. The camshaft is driven off of the crankshaft by way of a cogged belt.

1.8L (BP DOHC) ENGINE

The 1.8L engine has 4 cylinders situated in-line in a cast iron cylinder block. The pistons are aluminum and drive the crankshaft by way of connecting rods. The engine is a Dual Overhead Cam (DOHC) type and has 4 valve per cylinder, 2 intake and 2 exhaust. The cylinder head is aluminum.

The camshafts are driven off of the crankshaft by way of a cogged belt.

1.8L (K8) ENGINE

The 1.8L engine has 6 cylinders situated in a 60° V-configuration in a cast iron cylinder block. The pistons are aluminum and drive the crankshaft by way of connecting rods. The engine is a Dual Overhead Cam (DOHC) type with 24 valves. The cylinder heads are aluminum. The camshafts are driven off of the crankshaft by way of a cogged belt.

2.0L (FS) ENGINE

The 2.0L engine has 4 cylinders situated in-line in a cast iron cylinder block. The pistons are aluminum and drive the crankshaft by way of connecting rods. The engine is a Dual Overhead Cam (DOHC) type. The cylinder head is aluminum. The camshafts are driven off of the crankshaft by way of a cogged belt.

2.2L (F2) ENGINE

The 2.2L engine has 4 cylinders situated in-line in a cast iron cylinder block. The pistons are aluminum and drive the crankshaft by way of connecting rods. The engine is a Single Overhead Cam (SOHC) type with 12 valves. The cylinder head is aluminum. The camshaft is driven off of the crankshaft by way of a cogged belt. The engine is available in a turbocharged and a non-turbocharged configuration.

2.5L (KL) ENGINE

The 2.5L engine has 6 cylinders situated in a 60° V-configuration in a cast iron cylinder block. The pistons are aluminum and drive the crankshaft by way of connecting rods. The engine is a Dual Overhead Cam (DOHC) type with

24 valves. The cylinder heads are aluminum. The camshafts are driven off of the crankshaft by way of a cogged belt.

2.0L (FS DOHC) ENGINE

The 2.0L engine has 4 cylinders situated in-line in a cast iron cylinder block. The pistons are aluminum and drive the crankshaft by way of connecting rods. The engine is a Dual Overhead Cam (DOHC) type. The cylinder head is aluminum. The camshaft is driven off of the crankshaft by way of a cogged belt.

Engine Overhaul Tips

Most engine overhaul procedures are fairly standard. In addition to specific parts replacement procedures and complete specifications for your individual engine, this section also is a guide to accepted rebuilding procedures. Examples of standard rebuilding practice are shown and should be used along with specific details concerning your particular engine.

Competent and accurate machine shop services will ensure maximum performance, reliability and engine life. In most instances it is more profitable for the do-it-yourself mechanic to remove, clean and inspect the component, buy the necessary parts and deliver these to a shop for actual machine work.

On the other hand, much of the rebuilding work (crankshaft, block, bearings, piston, rods, and other components) is still within the scope of the do-it-yourself mechanic.

TOOLS

The tools required for an engine overhaul or parts replacement will depend on the depth of your involvement. With a few exceptions, they will be the tools found in a mechanic's tool kit (see Section 1). More in-depth work will require any or all of the following:

- dial indicator (reading in thousandths) mounted on a universal base.
- micrometers and telescope gauges.
- jaw and screw-type pullers.
- scraper.
- valve spring compressor.
- ring groove cleaner.
- piston ring expander and compressor.
- ridge reamer.
- cylinder hone or glaze breaker.
- Plastigage®.
- engine stand.

The use of most of these tools is illustrated in this section. Many can be rented for a one-time use from a local parts jobber or tool supply house specializing in automotive work.

Occasionally, the use of special tools is called for. See the information on Special Tools and the Safety Notice in the front of this book before substituting another tool.

INSPECTION TECHNIQUES

Procedures and specifications are given in this section for inspecting, cleaning and assessing the wear limits of most major components. Other procedures such as Magnaflux® and Zyglo® can be used to locate material flaws and stress cracks. Magnaflux® is a magnetic process applicable only to ferrous materials. The Zyglo® process coats the material with a flourescent dye penetrant and can be used on any material. Check for suspected surface cracks can be more readily made using spot check dye. The dye is sprayed onto the suspected area, wiped off and area sprayed with a developer. Cracks will show up brightly.

OVERHAUL TIPS

Aluminum has become extremely popular for use in engines, due to its low weight. Observe the following precautions when handling aluminum parts:

Never hot tank aluminum parts (the caustic hot-tank solution will eat the aluminum).

Remove all aluminum parts (identification tag, etc) from engine parts prior to hot-tanking.

Always coat threads lightly with engine oil or anti-seize compounds before installation, to prevent seizure.

Never over-torque bolts or spark plugs, especially in aluminum threads. Stripped threads in any component can be repaired using any of several commercial repair kits (Heli-Coil®, Microdot®, Keenserts®, etc.)

When assembling the engine, any parts that will be in frictional contact must be prelubed to provide lubrication at initial startup. Any product specifically formulated for this purpose can be used, but engine oil is not recommended as a pre-lube.

When semi-permanent (locked, but removable) installation of bolts or nuts is desired, threads should be cleaned and coated with Loctite® or other similar, commercial non-hardening sealant.

REPAIRING DAMAGED THREADS

Several methods of repairing damaged threads are available. Heli-Coil®, Keenserts® and Microdot® are among the most widely used. All involve basically the same principle — drilling out stripped threads, tapping the hole and installing prewound insert — making welding, plugging and oversize fasteners unnecessary.

Two types of thread repair inserts are usually supplied: a standard type for most Inch Coarse, Inch Fine, Metric Coarse and Metric Fine thread sizes and a spark plug type to fit most spark plug port sizes. Consult the individual manufacturer's catalog to determine exact applications. Typical thread repair kits will contain a selection of prewound threaded inserts, a tap (corresponding to the outside diameter threads of the insert) and an installation tool. Spark plug inserts usually differ because they require a tap equipped with pilot threads and combined reamer/tap section. Most manufacturers also supply blister-packed thread repair inserts separately in addition to a master kit containing a variety of taps and inserts plus installation tools.

Before effecting a repair to a threaded hole, remove any snapped, broken or damaged bolts or studs. Penetrating oil can be used to free frozen threads; the offending item can be removed with locking pliers or with a screw or stud extractor. After the hole is clear, the thread can be repaired.

CHECKING ENGINE COMPRESSION

A noticeable lack of engine power, excessive oil consumption and/or poor fuel mileage measured over an extended period are all indicators of internal engine wear. Worn piston rings, scored or worn cylinder bores, blown head gaskets, sticking or burnt valves and worn valve seats are all possible culprits here. A check of each cylinder's compression will help you locate the problems.

As mentioned earlier, a screw-in type compression gauge is more accurate than the type you simply hold against the spark plug hole, although it takes slightly longer to use. It's worth it to obtain a more accurate reading. Check engine compression as follows:

1. Warm up the engine to normal operating temperature.
2. Remove all spark plugs.
3. Disconnect the high-tension lead from the ignition coil.
4. Disconnect the cold start valve and all injector connections.
5. Screw the compression gauge into the No. 1 spark plug hole until the fitting is snug.

➡**Be careful not to crossthread the plug hole. On aluminum cylinder heads use extra care, as the threads in these heads are easily ruined.**

6. Ask an assistant to depress the accelerator pedal fully. Then, while you read the compression gauge, ask the assistant to crank the engine two or three times in short bursts using the ignition switch.
7. Read the compression gauge at the end of each series of cranks, and record the highest of these readings. Repeat this procedure for each of the engine's cylinders. Compare the highest reading to the reading in each cylinder.
8. A cylinder's compression pressure is usually acceptable if it is not less than 80% of the highest reading. For example, if the highest reading is 150 psi, the lowest should be no lower than 120 psi. No cylinder should have a reading below 100 psi.
9. If a cylinder is unusually low, pour a tablespoon of clean engine oil into the cylinder through the spark plug hole and repeat the compression test. If the compression comes up after adding the oil, it appears that the cylinder's piston rings or bore are damaged or worn. If the pressure remains low, the valves

may not be seating properly (a valve job is needed), or the head gasket may be blown near that cylinder. If compression in any two adjacent cylinders is low, and if the addition of oil doesn't help the compression, there is leakage past the head gasket. Oil and coolant water in the combustion chamber can result from this problem. There may be evidence of water droplets on the engine dipstick when a head gasket has blown.

VALVE SPECIFICATIONS

Year	VIN	Engine No. Cyl. Liters	Seat Angle (deg.)	Face Angle (deg.)	Spring Free Length (in.)	Stem-to-Guide Clearance (in.)		Stem Diameter (in.)	
						Intake	Exhaust	Intake	Exhaust
1990	B6E	4/1.6	45	45	1.720	0.0010–0.0024	0.0011–0.0026	0.2744–0.2750	0.2742–0.2748
	B6ZE	4/1.6	45	45	③	0.0010–0.0024	0.0012–0.0026	0.2350–0.2356	0.2348–0.2354
	BPE	4/1.8	45	45	④	0.0010–0.0024	0.0011–0.0026	0.2350–0.2356	0.2348–0.2354
	BPD	4/1.8	45	45	1.821	0.0010–0.0024	0.0012–0.0026	0.2350–0.2356	0.2348–0.2354
	F2	4/2.2	45	45	①	0.0010–0.0024	0.0012–0.0026	0.2744–0.2750	0.2742–0.2748
1991	B6E	4/1.6	45	45	1.720	0.0010–0.0024	0.0011–0.0026	0.2744–0.2750	0.2742–0.2748
	B6ZE	4/1.6	45	45	③	0.0010–0.0024	0.0012–0.0026	0.2350–0.2356	0.2348–0.2354
	BPE	4/1.8	45	45	④	0.0010–0.0024	0.0011–0.0026	0.2350–0.2356	0.2348–0.2354
	BPD	4/1.8	45	45	1.821	0.0010–0.0024	0.0012–0.0026	0.2350–0.2356	0.2348–0.2354
	F2	4/2.2	45	45	①	0.0010–0.0024	0.0012–0.0026	0.2744–0.2750	0.2742–0.2748
1992	B6E	4/1.6	45	45	1.720	0.0010–0.0024	0.0011–0.0026	0.2744–0.2750	0.2742–0.2748
	B6ZE	4/1.6	45	45	③	0.0010–0.0024	0.0012–0.0026	0.2350–0.2356	0.2348–0.2354
	BPE	4/1.8	45	45	④	0.0010–0.0024	0.0011–0.0026	0.2350–0.2356	0.2348–0.2354
	BPD	4/1.8	45	45	1.821	0.0010–0.0024	0.0012–0.0026	0.2350–0.2356	0.2348–0.2354
	K8D	4/1.8	45	45	1.847	0.0010–0.0024	0.0012–0.0026	0.2350–0.2356	0.2348–0.2354
	F2	4/2.2	45	45	①	0.0010–0.0024	0.0012–0.0026	0.2744–0.2750	0.2742–0.2748

VALVE SPECIFICATIONS

Year	VIN	Engine No. Cyl. Liters	Seat Angle (deg.)	Face Angle (deg.)	Spring Free Length (in.)	Stem-to-Guide Clearance (in.)		Stem Diameter (in.)	
						Intake	Exhaust	Intake	Exhaust
1993	B6E	4/1.6	45	45	1.720	0.0010–0.0024	0.0011–0.0026	0.2744–0.2750	0.2742–0.2748
	B6ZE	4/1.6	45	45	③	0.0010–0.0024	0.0012–0.0026	0.2350–0.2356	0.2348–0.2354
	BPE	4/1.8	45	45	④	0.0010–0.0024	0.0011–0.0026	0.2350–0.2356	0.2348–0.2354
	BPD	4/1.8	45	45	1.821	0.0010–0.0024	0.0012–0.0026	0.2350–0.2356	0.2348–0.2354
	K8D	4/1.8	45	45	1.847	0.0010–0.0024	0.0012–0.0026	0.2350–0.2356	0.2348–0.2354
	FS	4/2.0	45	45	1.732	0.0010–0.0024	0.0012–0.0026	0.2351–0.2356	0.2349–0.2354
	KL	6/2.5	45	45	1.847	0.0010–0.0024	0.0012–0.0025	0.2351–0.2356	0.2349–0.2354

① Intake: 1.902–1.949
   Exhaust: 1.937–1.984
② Intake:
   Outer: 1.988–2.000
   Inner: 1.819–1.835
  Exhaust:
   Outer: 2.264–2.295
   Inner: 2.063–2.091
③ Intake: 1.850–1.890
   Exhaust: 1.862–1.902

④ Intake: 1.815
   Exhaust: 1.717
⑤ Intake: 1.816
   Exhaust: 1.687

CAMSHAFT SPECIFICATIONS

All measurements given in inches.

Year	Engine ID/VIN	Engine Displacement Liters (cc)	Journal Diameter (in.)					Elevation		Bearing Clearance	Camshaft End Play
			1	2	3	4	5	In.	Ex.		
1990	B6	1.6 (1597)	1.7102–1.7112	1.7091–1.7100	1.7102–1.7112	—	—	1.4272–1.4351	1.4272–1.4351	①	0.0020–0.0080
	B6ZE	1.6 (1597)	1.0213–1.0222	1.0213–1.0222	1.0213–1.0222	1.0213–1.0222	1.0213–1.0222	1.6019–1.6098	1.6019–1.6098	0.0014–0.0060	0.0028–0.0080
	BPE	1.8 (1839)	1.7102–1.7110	1.7096–1.7106	1.7091–1.7100	1.7096–1.7106	1.7102–1.7110	1.4092–1.4170	1.4202–1.4281	②	0.0024–0.0080
	BPD	1.8 (1839)	1.0213–1.0222	1.0213–1.0222	1.0213–1.0222	1.0213–1.0222	1.0213–1.0222	1.7281–1.7360	1.7480–1.7560	0.0014–0.0060	0.0028–0.0080
	F2	2.2 (2184)	1.2575–1.2585	1.2563–1.2573	1.2563–1.2573	1.2563–1.2573	1.2575–1.2585	1.6197–1.6295	1.6396–1.6495	③	0.0030–0.0080

CAMSHAFT SPECIFICATIONS

All measurements given in inches.

Year	Engine ID/VIN	Engine Displacement Liters (cc)	Journal Diameter (in.)					Elevation		Bearing Clearance	Camshaft End Play
			1	2	3	4	5	In.	Ex.		
1991	B6	1.6 (1597)	1.7102–1.7112	1.7091–1.7100	1.7102–1.7112	—	—	1.4272–1.4351	1.4272–1.4351	①	0.0020–0.0080
	B6ZE	1.6 (1597)	1.0213–1.0222	1.0213–1.0222	1.0213–1.0222	1.0213–1.0222	1.0213–1.0222	⑤	⑥	0.0014–0.0060	0.0028–0.0080
	BPE	1.8 (1839)	1.7102–1.7110	1.7096–1.7106	1.7091–1.7100	1.7096–1.7106	1.7102–1.7110	1.4092–1.4170	1.4202–1.4281	②	0.0024–0.0080
	BPD	1.8 (1839)	1.0213–1.0222	1.0213–1.0222	1.0213–1.0222	1.0213–1.0222	1.0213–1.0222	1.7281–1.7360	1.7480–1.7560	0.0014–0.0060	0.0028–0.0080
	F2	2.2 (2184)	1.2575–1.2585	1.2563–1.2573	1.2563–1.2573	1.2563–1.2573	1.2575–1.2585	1.6197–1.6295	1.6396–1.6495	③	0.0030–0.0080
1992	B6	1.6 (1597)	1.7102–1.7112	1.7091–1.7100	1.7102–1.7112	—	—	1.4272–1.4351	1.4272–1.4351	①	0.0020–0.0080
	B6ZE	1.6 (1597)	1.0213–1.0222	1.0213–1.0222	1.0213–1.0222	1.0213–1.0222	1.0213–1.0222	⑤	⑥	0.0014–0.0060	0.0028–0.0080
	BPE	1.8 (1839)	1.7102–1.7110	1.7096–1.7106	1.7091–1.7100	1.7096–1.7106	1.7102–1.7110	1.4092–1.4170	1.4202–1.4281	②	0.0024–0.0080
	BPD	1.8 (1839)	1.0213–1.0222	1.0213–1.0222	1.0213–1.0222	1.0213–1.0222	1.0213–1.0222	1.7281–1.7360	1.7480–1.7560	0.0014–0.0060	0.0028–0.0080
	B6E	1.6 (1598)	1.7102–1.7112	1.7091–1.7100	1.7102–1.7112	—	—	1.4272–1.4351	1.4272–1.4351	①	0.0020–0.0080
	F2	2.2 (2184)	1.2575–1.2585	1.2563–1.2573	1.2563–1.2573	1.2563–1.2573	1.2575–1.2585	1.6197–1.6295	1.6396–1.6495	③	0.0030–0.0080
	K8D	1.8 (1845)	④	1.0201–1.0209	1.0201–1.0209	1.0201–1.0209	1.0213–1.0222	1.6718–1.6797	1.7054–1.7132	⑦	0.0020–0.0055
1993	B6	1.6 (1597)	1.7102–1.7112	1.7091–1.7100	1.7102–1.7112	—	—	1.4272–1.4351	1.4272–1.4351	①	0.0020–0.0080
	B6ZE	1.6 (1597)	1.0213–1.0222	1.0213–1.0222	1.0213–1.0222	1.0213–1.0222	1.0213–1.0222	⑤	⑥	0.0014–0.0060	0.0028–0.0080
	BPE	1.8 (1839)	1.7102–1.7110	1.7096–1.7106	1.7091–1.7100	1.7096–1.7106	1.7102–1.7110	1.4092–1.4170	1.4202–1.4281	②	0.0024–0.0080
	BPD	1.8 (1839)	1.0213–1.0222	1.0213–1.0222	1.0213–1.0222	1.0213–1.0222	1.0213–1.0222	1.7281–1.7360	1.7480–1.7560	0.0014–0.0060	0.0028–0.0080
	B6E	1.6 (1598)	1.7102–1.7112	1.7091–1.7100	1.7102–1.7112	—	—	1.4272–1.4351	1.4272–1.4351	①	0.0020–0.0080
	FS	2.0 (1991)	1.0213–1.0222	1.0213–1.0222	1.0213–1.0222	1.0213–1.0222	1.0213–1.0222	1.6859–1.6918	1.7003–1.7062	0.0014–0.0060	0.0032–0.0080
	KL	2.5 (2496)	④	1.0201–1.0209	1.0201–1.0209	1.0201–1.0209	1.0213–1.0222	1.7067–1.7145	1.7067–1.7145	⑧	0.0020–0.0056
	K8D	1.8 (1845)	④	1.0201–1.0209	1.0201–1.0209	1.0201–1.0209	1.0213–1.0222	1.6718–1.6797	1.7054–1.7132	⑦	0.0020–0.0055

① Bearings Number 1 and 3: 0.0014–0.0060
   Bearing Number 2: 0.0020–0.0060
② Bearings Number 1 and 5: 0.0016–0.0060
   Bearing Number 2 and 4: 0.0014–0.060
   Bearing Number 3: 0.0020–0.0060
③ Bearings Number 1 and 5: 0.0014–0.0059
   Bearings Number 2, 3 and 4: 0.0026–0.0059
④ Right exhaust and left intake: 1.0213–1.0220
   Right intake and left exhaust: 1.1801–1.1811

⑤ Manual trans.: 1.6019–1.6098
   Auto. trans.: 1.5662–1.5741
⑥ Manual trans.: 1.6019–1.6098
   Auto. trans.: 1.6018–1.6097
⑦ Numbers 1 and 5: 0.0016–0.0052
   Numbers 2, 3 and 4: 0.0028–0.0063
⑧ Numbers 1 and 5: 0.0016–0.0047
   Numbers 2, 3 and 4: 0.0028–0.0059

CRANKSHAFT AND CONNECTING ROD SPECIFICATIONS

All measurements are given in inches.

Year	Engine ID/VIN	Engine Displacement Liters (cc)	Crankshaft				Connecting Rod		
			Main Brg. Journal Dia.	Main Brg. Oil Clearance	Shaft End-play	Thrust on No.	Journal Diameter	Oil Clearance	Side Clearance
1990	B6	1.6 (1597)	1.9647–1.9668	0.0007–0.0040	0.0031–0.0120	4	1.7680–1.7699	0.0011–0.0040	0.0043–0.0120
	B6ZE	1.6 (1597)	1.9647–1.9668	0.0007–0.0040	0.0031–0.0120	4	1.7680–1.7699	0.0011–0.0040	0.0043–0.0120
	BPE	1.8 (1839)	1.9647–1.9668	0.0007–0.0040	0.0031–0.0120	4	1.7680–1.7699	0.0011–0.0040	0.0043–0.0120
	BPD	1.8 (1839)	1.9647–1.9668	0.0007–0.0040	0.0031–0.0118	4	1.7680–1.7699	0.0011–0.0040	0.0043–0.0120
	F2	2.2 (2184)	2.3597–2.3604	①	0.0031–0.0118	3	2.0055–2.0061	0.0011–0.0039	0.0040–0.0120
1991	B6	1.6 (1597)	1.9647–1.9668	0.0007–0.0040	0.0031–0.0120	4	1.7680–1.7699	0.0011–0.0040	0.0043–0.0120
	B6ZE	1.6 (1597)	1.9647–1.9668	0.0007–0.0040	0.0031–0.0120	4	1.7680–1.7699	0.0011–0.0040	0.0043–0.0120
	BPE	1.8 (1839)	1.9647–1.9668	0.0007–0.0040	0.0031–0.0120	4	1.7680–1.7699	0.0011–0.0040	0.0043–0.0120
	BPD	1.8 (1839)	1.9647–1.9668	0.0007–0.0040	0.0031–0.0118	4	1.7680–1.7699	0.0011–0.0040	0.0043–0.0120
	F2	2.2 (2184)	2.3597–2.3604	①	0.0031–0.0118	3	2.0055–2.0061	0.0011–0.0039	0.0040–0.0120
1992	B6	1.6 (1597)	1.9647–1.9668	0.0007–0.0040	0.0031–0.0120	4	1.7680–1.7699	0.0011–0.0040	0.0043–0.0120
	B6ZE	1.6 (1597)	1.9647–1.9668	0.0007–0.0040	0.0031–0.0120	4	1.7680–1.7699	0.0011–0.0040	0.0043–0.0120
	BPE	1.8 (1839)	1.9647–1.9668	0.0007–0.0040	0.0031–0.0120	4	1.7680–1.7699	0.0011–0.0040	0.0043–0.0120
	BPD	1.8 (1839)	1.9647–1.9668	0.0007–0.0040	0.0031–0.0118	4	1.7680–1.7699	0.0011–0.0040	0.0043–0.0120
	B6E	1.6 (1598)	1.9647–1.9668	0.0007–0.0040	0.0031–0.0120	4	1.7680–1.7699	0.0011–0.0040	0.0043–0.0120
	F2	2.2 (2184)	2.3597–2.3604	①	0.0031–0.0118	3	2.0055–2.0061	0.0011–0.0039	0.0040–0.0120
	K8D	1.8 (1845)	2.4382–2.4392	0.0015–0.0025	0.0031–0.0130	4	1.8872–1.8880	0.0009–0.0031	0.0070–0.0160
1993	B6	1.6 (1597)	1.9647–1.9668	0.0007–0.0040	0.0031–0.0120	4	1.7680–1.7699	0.0011–0.0040	0.0043–0.0120
	B6ZE	1.6 (1597)	1.9647–1.9668	0.0007–0.0040	0.0031–0.0120	4	1.7680–1.7699	0.0011–0.0040	0.0043–0.0120
	BPE	1.8 (1839)	1.9647–1.9668	0.0007–0.0040	0.0031–0.0120	4	1.7680–1.7699	0.0011–0.0040	0.0043–0.0120
	BPD	1.8 (1839)	1.9647–1.9668	0.0007–0.0040	0.0031–0.0118	4	1.7680–1.7699	0.0011–0.0040	0.0043–0.0120
	B6E	1.6 (1598)	1.9647–1.9668	0.0007–0.0040	0.0031–0.0120	4	1.7680–1.7699	0.0011–0.0040	0.0043–0.0120

CRANKSHAFT AND CONNECTING ROD SPECIFICATIONS

All measurements are given in inches.

Year	Engine ID/VIN	Engine Displacement Liters (cc)	Crankshaft				Connecting Rod		
			Main Brg. Journal Dia.	Main Brg. Oil Clearance	Shaft End-play	Thrust on No.	Journal Diameter	Oil Clearance	Side Clearance
	FS	2.0 (1991)	2.2020–2.2029	②	0.0031–0.0118	4	1.8872–1.8880	0.0009–0.0026	0.0043–0.0120
	KL	2.5 (2496)	2.4382–2.4392	0.0015–0.0025	0.0032–0.0125	4	2.0841–2.0848	0.0009–0.0032	0.0070–0.0160
	K8D	1.8 (1845)	2.4382–2.4392	0.0015–0.0025	0.0031–0.0130	4	1.8872–1.8880	0.0009–0.0031	0.0070–0.0160

① Numbers 1, 2, 4 and 5: 0.0010–0.0031
   Number 3: 0.0012–0.0031
② Numbers 1, 2, 4 and 5: 0.0009–0.0026
   Number 3: 0.0012–0.0026

PISTON AND RING SPECIFICATIONS

All measurements are given in inches.

Year	VIN	Engine No. Cyl. Liters	Piston Clearance	Ring Gap			Ring Side Clearance		
				Top Compression	Bottom Compression	Oil Control	Top Compression	Bottom Compression	Oil Control
1990	B6E	4/1.6	0.0015–0.0020	0.0060–0.0120	0.0060–0.0120	0.0080–0.0280	0.0012–0.0026	0.0012–0.0026	NA
	B6ZE	4/1.6	0.0015–0.0020	0.0060–0.0120	0.0060–0.0120	0.0080–0.0280	0.0012–0.0028	0.0012–0.0028	NA
	BPE	4/1.8	0.0015–0.0020	0.0060–0.0120	0.0060–0.0120	0.0080–0.0280	0.0012–0.0026	0.0012–0.0026	NA
	BPD	4/1.8	0.0015–0.0020	0.0060–0.0120	0.0060–0.0120	0.0080–0.0280	0.0012–0.0026	0.0012–0.0026	NA
	F2	4/2.2	0.0014–0.0030	0.0080–0.0138	0.0060–0.0120	0.0080–0.0276	0.0012–0.0028	0.0012–0.0028	NA
1991	B6E	4/1.6	0.0015–0.0020	0.0060–0.0120	0.0060–0.0120	0.0080–0.0280	0.0012–0.0026	0.0012–0.0026	NA
	B6ZE	4/1.6	0.0015–0.0020	0.0060–0.0120	0.0060–0.0120	0.0080–0.0280	0.0012–0.0028	0.0012–0.0028	NA
	BPE	4/1.8	0.0015–0.0020	0.0060–0.0120	0.0060–0.0120	0.0080–0.0280	0.0012–0.0026	0.0012–0.0026	NA
	BPD	4/1.8	0.0015–0.0020	0.0060–0.0120	0.0060–0.0120	0.0080–0.0280	0.0012–0.0026	0.0012–0.0026	NA
	F2	4/2.2	0.0014–0.0030	0.0080–0.0138	0.0060–0.0120	0.0080–0.0276	0.0012–0.0028	0.0012–0.0028	NA
1992	B6E	4/1.6	0.0015–0.0020	0.0060–0.0120	0.0060–0.0120	0.0080–0.0280	0.0012–0.0026	0.0012–0.0026	NA
	B6ZE	4/1.6	0.0015–0.0020	0.0060–0.0120	0.0060–0.0120	0.0080–0.0280	0.0012–0.0028	0.0012–0.0028	NA
	BPE	4/1.8	0.0015–0.0020	0.0060–0.0120	0.0060–0.0120	0.0080–0.0280	0.0012–0.0026	0.0012–0.0026	NA
	BPD	4/1.8	0.0015–0.0020	0.0060–0.0120	0.0060–0.0120	0.0080–0.0280	0.0012–0.0026	0.0012–0.0026	NA
	K8D	4/1.8	0.0011–0.0022	0.0060–0.0110	0.0100–0.0150	0.0080–0.0280	0.0012–0.0026	0.0012–0.0026	NA
	F2	4/2.2	0.0014–0.0030	0.0080–0.0138	0.0060–0.0120	0.0080–0.0276	0.0012–0.0028	0.0012–0.0028	NA

PISTON AND RING SPECIFICATIONS

All measurements are given in inches.

Year	VIN	Engine No. Cyl. Liters	Piston Clearance	Ring Gap			Ring Side Clearance		
				Top Compression	Bottom Compression	Oil Control	Top Compression	Bottom Compression	Oil Control
1993	B6E	4/1.6	0.0015–0.0020	0.0060–0.0120	0.0060–0.0120	0.0080–0.0280	0.0012–0.0026	0.0012–0.0026	NA
	B6ZE	4/1.6	0.0015–0.0020	0.0060–0.0120	0.0060–0.0120	0.0080–0.0280	0.0012–0.0028	0.0012–0.0028	NA
	BPE	4/1.8	0.0015–0.0020	0.0060–0.0120	0.0060–0.0120	0.0080–0.0280	0.0012–0.0026	0.0012–0.0026	NA
	BPD	4/1.8	0.0015–0.0020	0.0060–0.0120	0.0060–0.0120	0.0080–0.0280	0.0012–0.0026	0.0012–0.0026	NA
	K8D	4/1.8	0.0011–0.0022	0.0060–0.0110	0.0100–0.0150	0.0080–0.0280	0.0012–0.0026	0.0012–0.0026	NA
	FS	4/2.0	0.0016–0.0020	0.0060–0.0110	0.0060–0.0110	0.0080–0.0270	0.0014–0.0025	0.0012–0.0025	NA
	KL	6/2.5	0.0012–0.0022	0.0060–0.0118	0.0100–0.0150	0.0080–0.0270	0.0008–0.0026	0.0012–0.0026	NA

NA—Not available

TORQUE SPECIFICATIONS

All readings in ft. lbs.

Year	Engine ID/VIN	Engine Displacement Liters (cc)	Cylinder Head Bolts	Main Bearing Bolts	Rod Bearing Bolts	Crankshaft Sprocket Bolts	Flywheel Bolts	Manifold		Spark Plugs	Lug Nut
								Intake	Exhaust		
1990	B6E	1.6 (1597)	56–60	40–43	35–38	80–87	71–76	14–19	12–17	11–17	65–87
	B6ZE	1.6 (1597)	56–60	40–43	37–40	80–87	71–76	14–19	28–34	11–17	65–87
	BPE	1.8 (1839)	56–60	40–43	36–38	80–87	71–76	14–19	12–17	11–17	65–87
	F2	1.8 (1839)	56–60	40–43	37–40	80–87	71–76	14–19	28–34	11–17	65–87
1991	B6E	1.6 (1597)	56–60	40–43	35–38	80–87	71–76	14–19	12–17	11–17	65–87
	B6ZE	1.6 (1597)	56–60	40–43	37–40	80–87	71–76	14–19	28–34	11–17	65–87
	BPE	1.8 (1839)	56–60	40–43	36–38	80–87	71–76	14–19	12–17	11–17	65–87
	BPD	1.8 (1839)	56–60	40–43	35–37	80–87	71–76	14–19	28–34	11–17	65–87
	F2	2.2 (2184)	59–64	61–65	48–51	116–123	71–76	14–22	25–36	11–17	65–87
1992	B6E	1.6 (1597)	56–60	40–43	①	116–123	71–76	14–19	12–17	11–17	65–87
	B6ZE	1.6 (1597)	56–60	40–43	37–40	116–123	71–76	14–19	28–34	11–17	65–87
	BPE	1.8 (1839)	56–60	40–43	36–38	116–123	71–76	14–19	12–17	11–17	65–87
	BPD	1.8 (1839)	56–60	40–43	35–37	116–123	71–76	14–19	28–34	11–17	65–87
	K8D	1.8 (1844)	④	②	③	116–123	45–50	14–19	14–19	11–17	65–87
	F2	2.2 (2184)	59–64	61–65	48–51	116–123	71–76	14–22	25–36	11–17	65–87

TORQUE SPECIFICATIONS

All readings in ft. lbs.

Year	Engine ID/VIN	Engine Displacement Liters (cc)	Cylinder Head Bolts	Main Bearing Bolts	Rod Bearing Bolts	Crankshaft Sprocket Bolts	Flywheel Bolts	Manifold		Spark Plugs	Lug Nut
								Intake	Exhaust		
1993	B6E	1.6 (1597)	56–60	40–43	①	116–123	71–76	14–19	12–17	11–17	65–87
	B6ZE	1.6 (1597)	56–60	40–43	37–40	116–123	71–76	14–19	28–34	11–17	65–87
	BPE	1.8 (1839)	56–60	40–43	36–38	116–123	71–76	14–19	12–17	11–17	65–87
	BPD	1.8 (1839)	56–60	40–43	35–37	116–123	71–76	14–19	28–34	11–17	65–87
	K8D	1.8 (1844)	④	②	③	116–123	45–50	14–19	14–19	11–17	65–87
	FS	2.0 (1991)	⑤	⑥	⑦	116–123	71–76	14–18	⑧	11–16	65–87
	KL	2.5 (2496)	④	②	⑦	116–123	45–49	14–18	14–18	11–16	65–87

① 323—35–38
  MX3—35–37
② Tighten in sequence in 3 steps:
  Step 1: Inner bolts—17–18
       Outer bolts:—13–15
  Step 2: Inner bolts
       Nos. 1, 2 & 3—Turn each bolt 70°
       No. 4—Turn each bolt 80°
       Outer bolts:
       Turn each bolt 60°
  Step 3: Repeat Step 2.
③ Tighten in 3 steps:
  Step 1: 16–19
  Step 2: Turn each bolt 90°
  Step 3: Turn each bolt 90°
④ Tighten in 3 steps:
  Step 1: 17–19
  Step 2: Turn each bolt 90°, in sequence
  Step 3: Turn each bolt 90°, in sequence
⑤ Tighten in 3 steps:
  Step 1: 12.7–16.2
  Step 2: Turn each bolt 90°, in sequence
  Step 3: Turn each bolt 90°, in sequence
⑥ Tighten in 2 steps:
  Step 1: 12.7–16.2
  Step 2: Turn each bolt 90°, in sequence
⑦ Tighten in 2 steps:
  Step 1: 16.3–19.8
  Step 2: Turn each bolt 90°
⑧ Nut—15–20
  Bolt—12–16

Engine

REMOVAL & INSTALLATION

✳✳CAUTION

When draining the coolant, keep in mind that cats and dogs are attracted by the ethylene glycol antifreeze, and are quite likely to drink any that is left in an uncovered container or in puddles on the ground. This will prove fatal in sufficient quantity. Always drain the coolant into a sealable container. Coolant should be reused unless it is contaminated or several years old.

323 and Protege

▶ See Figures 16, 17, 18, 19 and 20

1. Properly relieve the fuel system pressure. Raise and safely support the vehicle, as necessary.

2. Disconnect the battery cables and remove the battery and the battery tray. Raise and safely support the vehicle.

3. Remove the splash shield(s) from under the vehicle and drain the engine and transaxle oil and the coolant.

4. Remove the air cleaner assembly and resonance chamber, including the air flow meter and all of the ducting. Remove the oil dip stick.

5. Remove the radiator hoses. If equipped with automatic transaxle, disconnect the oil cooler lines from the radiator. Disconnect the cooling fan and, if equipped, radiator switch electrical connectors and remove the radiator/cooling fan assembly. On 4WD vehicles, remove the crossmember from the underside of the vehicle.

6. Disconnect the throttle and the speedometer cable.

7. Label and disconnect the vacuum hoses and wiring.

8. Disconnect the fuel supply and return hoses and the heater hoses.

9. Disconnect the exhaust pipe from the manifold. On 4WD vehicles, remove the exhaust manifold. If equipped, remove the water inlet pipe and gasket.

10. Without disconnecting the hydraulic hoses, remove the power steering pump and hang it from the body with wire.

11. Without disconnecting the refrigerant lines, remove the air conditioning compressor and hang it from the body with wire.

12. If equipped with manual transaxle, disconnect the clutch cable and shift control rod. If equipped with hydraulic clutch, remove the slave cylinder from the transaxle without disconnecting the hydraulic line.

13. If equipped with automatic transaxle, disconnect the shift control cable.

14. Remove the nuts and disconnect the tie rod ends from the steering knuckles. Disconnect the stabilizer bar from the lower control arms.

15. Attach an engine lifting chain to the engine lifting eyes. Attach the chain to a suitable engine hoist and raise the hoist until there is tension on the chain.

16. Remove the engine mount nuts and the engine mount member bolts and nuts and remove the engine mount member. On 4WD vehicles, remove the front transaxle mount.

➡Be careful so the engine does not fall when removing the engine mount member.

17. Remove the pinch bolts from the steering knuckle and pry the control arm down to slip lower ball joint out of the knuckle.

18. If equipped, remove the bolts from the right side intermediate shaft support and, using a suitable prybar, pry the intermediate shaft from the transaxle. Insert a suitable prybar between the inner CV-joint and transaxle case and carefully pry the inner CV-joints out of the transaxle. Suspend the halfshafts with wire.

19. If equipped with 4WD, mark the position of the driveshaft on the transaxle and rear axle flanges. Remove the driveshaft, keeping all spacers, washers and bushings in order so they can be reinstalled in their original positions.

20. Remove the dynamic damper from the right side engine mount, if equipped. Remove the engine/transaxle mount nuts/bolts and right engine and, if equipped, left transaxle mounts. Carefully lift the engine/transaxle assembly from the vehicle.

21. Properly support the engine/transaxle assembly. Remove the intake manifold bracket, starter, torque converter nuts, stiffener, if equipped and No. 2 engine mount. Disconnect the throttle cable.

22. If equipped with 4WD, remove the center differential lock motor as follows:

a. Remove the set bolt and lock sensor switch.

b. Remove the plug from the end of the motor and use a small flat bladed tool to turn the shift rod ½turn clockwise.

c. Remove the retaining bolts and the center differential lock motor.

23. Remove the transaxle mounting bolts and separate the transaxle from the engine.

To install:

24. Attach the transaxle to the engine and install the transaxle-to-engine bolts. If equipped with automatic transaxle, install the torque converter nuts and tighten to 25-36 ft. lbs. (34-49 Nm).

25. Connect the throttle cable. Install the No. 2 engine mount, stiffener, if equipped, starter and intake manifold bracket. If equipped with 4WD, install the center differential lock motor as follows:

a. Install a new O-ring onto the motor. Make sure the flat edge of the shift rodis facing up.

b. Turn the shift rod ½turn counterclockwise using a small flat bladed tool.

c. Install the lock motor and tighten the bolts to 14-22 ft. lbs. (20-29 Nm). Install the set bolt and lock sensor switch and tighten to 14-22 ft. lbs. (20-29 Nm).

26. On 2WD vehicles, proceed as follows:

a. Install the engine mount member and tighten the bolts/nuts to 47-66 ft. lbs. (64-89 Nm).

b. Carefully lower the engine/transaxle assembly into the engine compartment and align the engine mount bolts with the engine mount member mounting holes. Install the mount-to-mount member nuts and tighten to 27-38 ft. lbs. (37-52 Nm).

c. Install the right side engine mount. Tighten the mount-to-engine nut(s) to 44-63 ft. lbs. (60-85 Nm) on 1989 vehicles or 54-76 ft. lbs. (74-103 Nm) on 1990-93 vehicles. Tighten the mount through bolt to 37-45 ft. lbs. (50-61 Nm) on 1989 vehicles or 49-69 ft. lbs. (67-93 Nm) on 1990-93 vehicles.

d. On 1990-93 vehicles, install the dynamic damper, to the right side mount and tighten to 41-59 ft. lbs. (55-80 Nm).

e. If equipped, install the left side transaxle mount. On 1989 vehicles, tighten the mount-to-engine nuts to 14-19 ft. lbs. (19-25 Nm) and the mount-to-body bolts to 12-17 ft. lbs. (16-23 Nm). On 1990-93 vehicles, loosely install the mount-to-transaxle nuts and align the mount bracket holes with the body holes. Install the mount-to-body bolts and tighten, in sequence, to 32-45 ft. lbs. (43-61 Nm). Tighten the mount-to-transaxle nuts to 49-69 ft. lbs. (67-93 Nm).

27. On 4WD vehicles, proceed as follows:

a. Carefully lower the engine/transaxle assembly into the vehicle.

b. Install the left and right side mounts and loosely tighten the bolts and nuts.

c. If equipped with manual transaxle, install the clutch hydraulic slave cylinder and pipe bracket assembly.

d. Install the front transaxle mount and tighten the mount-to-transaxle bolts to 27-38 ft. lbs. (37-52 Nm).

e. Align the engine mount member with the front and rear transaxle mount bolts and install the engine member-to-body bolts/nuts. Tighten the engine member-to-body bolts/nuts to 47-66 ft. lbs. (64-89 Nm) and the engine mount-to-member nuts to 47-66 ft. lbs. (64-89 Nm) on 1989 vehicles or 27-38 ft. lbs. (37-52 Nm) on 1991 vehicles.

f. On 1989 vehicles, tighten the mount-to-engine nuts to 14-19 ft. lbs. (19-25 Nm) and the mount-to-body bolts to 12-17 ft. lbs. (16-23 Nm). On 1991 vehicles. tighten the left transaxle mount-to-body bolts, in sequence, to 32-43 ft. lbs. (43-61 Nm). Tighten the mount to transaxle nuts to 49-69 ft. lbs. (67-93 Nm).

g. On 1989 vehicles, tighten the right engine mount-to-engine nuts to 44-63 ft. lbs. (60-85 Nm) and the mount through bolt to 37-45 ft. lbs. (50-61 Nm).

h. On 1991 vehicles, tighten the mount-to-engine nuts to 54-76 ft. lbs. (74-103 Nm) and the mount through bolt to 49-69 ft. lbs. (67-93 Nm). Install the dynamic damper and tighten the bolts/nuts to 41-59 ft. lbs. (55-80 Nm).

i. Install the driveshaft, aligning the marks that were made during removal. Tighten the shaft-to-flange bolts/nuts to 20-22 ft. lbs. (27-30 Nm) and the support bearing mounting nuts to 27-38 ft. lbs. (37-51 Nm).

28. Install new circlips on the inner CV-joint stub shafts and, if equipped, intermediate shaft. Grease the shaft splines and install the halfshaft/intermediate shaft into the transaxle.

29. If equipped, install the right intermediate shaft support bolts and

tighten, in sequence, to 31-46 ft. lbs. (42-62 Nm).

30. Install the lower ball joint and torque the clamping bolt to 43 ft. lbs. (59 Nm). Install the tie rod ends and torque the nut to 42 ft. lbs. (57 Nm), then tighten as required to install a new cotter pin.

31. Attach the stabilizer bar and tighten the nuts so there is ¾in. (19mm) of thread showing above the nut.

32. If equipped with manual transaxle, connect the extension bar and shift control rod. Connect the clutch cable or install the hydraulic slave cylinder, as necessary.

33. If equipped with automatic transaxle, connect the shift control cable.

34. Install a new gasket and connect the exhaust pipe to the manifold. Use new self-locking nuts and torque to 34 ft. lbs. (46 Nm).

35. Connect the wiring and all heater, fuel and vacuum hoses.

36. Install the air conditioner compressor and power steering pump, if equipped. On 4WD vehicles, install the crossmember and tighten the bolts to 69-79 ft. lbs. (93-107 Nm).

37. Install the radiator/cooling fan assembly and connect the radiator hoses and the necessary electrical connectors.

38. Connect the accelerator and speedometer cables.

39. Install the battery tray assembly and battery. Install the air cleaner and air flow meter assembly and all the ducting. Connect the air flow sensor connector.

40. Install the splash shield(s).

41. Fill the engine and the transaxle with the proper types and quantities of oil. Fill the cooling system.

42. Connect the negative battery cable, start the engine and check for leaks. Check the ignition timing and the idle speed. Check all fluid levels.

Miata

▶ **See Figures 21, 22, 23, 24 and 25**

1. Mark the position of the hood on its hinges and remove the hood.

2. Properly relieve the fuel system pressure.

3. Raise the trunk lid and disconnect the negative battery cable. Remove the fresh air duct and the air cleaner/air flow meter assembly.

4. Disconnect the accelerator cable from the throttle body.

5. Raise and safely support the vehicle and remove the under cover.

Drain the engine and transmission oil and the coolant.

6. Disconnect the radiator hoses and the cooling fan electrical connector. Remove the radiator/cooling fans assembly.

7. Remove the accessory drive belts. Without disconnecting the hydraulic hoses, remove the power steering pump and secure it aside.

8. Without disconnecting the refrigerant, remove the air conditioner compressor and secure it aside.

9. Label and disconnect the wiring and all vacuum, fuel and coolant hoses.

10. Disconnect the exhaust pipe from the exhaust manifold.

11. Without disconnecting the hydraulic line, remove the clutch slave cylinder.

12. Remove the center console and the shifter assembly.

13. Disconnect the transmission electrical connectors and the speedometer cable.

14. Mark the position of the driveshaft on the differential flange and remove the bolts. Slide the driveshaft yoke from the transmission and remove the drive shaft.

15. The frame member between the transmission and differential must be removed. With the transmission properly supported, remove the bolts at both ends and remove the frame.

➡**Do not remove the upper frame-to-differential spacers from the frame. If they are removed, the entire frame must be replaced as a unit.**

16. Install lifting equipment onto the engine and make sure all hoses, wires and cables are disconnected.

17. Remove the engine mount nuts and lift the engine and transmission as an assembly from the vehicle.

18. Remove the starter.

19. If equipped with automatic transmission, remove the torque converter-to-flywheel bolts.

20. Remove the bolts to separate the transmission from the engine.

To install:

21. Assemble the engine to the transmission and torque the bolts to 66 ft. lbs. (89 Nm). If equipped with automatic transmission, install the torque converter-to-flywheel bolts and torque to 40 ft. lbs. (54 Nm).

22. Install the starter and torque the bolts to 38 ft. lbs. (52 Nm).

23. Carefully install the engine and transmission assembly into the vehicle. Start but do not tighten the mount nuts.

24. Install the transmission-to-differential frame and torque the bolts to

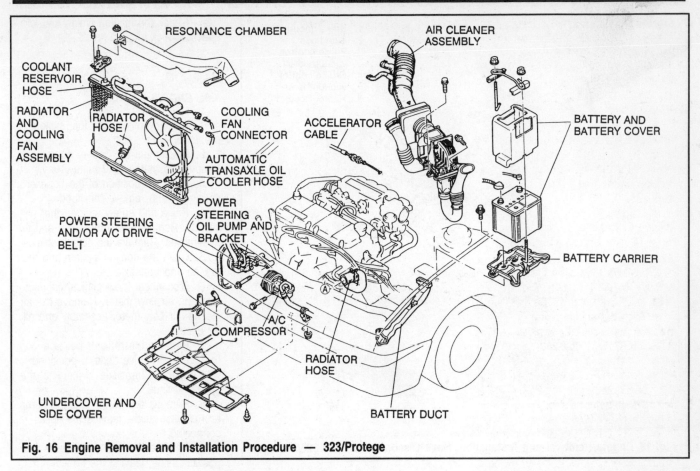

Fig. 16 Engine Removal and Installation Procedure — 323/Protege

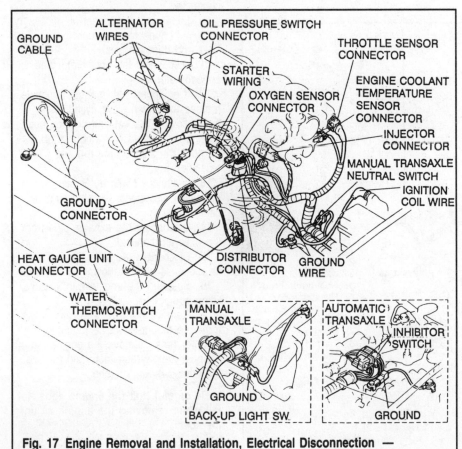

Fig. 17 Engine Removal and Installation, Electrical Disconnection — 323/Protege

91 ft. lbs. (124 Nm). Torque the engine mount nuts to 58 ft. lbs. (78 Nm).

25. Connect the transmission wiring and speedometer cable and install the driveshaft. Torque the driveshaft bolts to 22 ft. lbs. (30 Nm).

26. Use a new gasket and attach the exhaust pipe to the manifold. Torque the nuts to 34 ft. lbs. (46 Nm).

27. Install the clutch slave cylinder and torque bolts to 19 ft. lbs. (25 Nm).

28. Connect and adjust the shift linkage as required.

29. Install the air conditioner compressor and power steering pump. Install and adjust the drive belts.

30. Install the radiator and fans and connect all cooling system hoses.

31. Connect all wiring and hoses.

32. Connect and adjust the accelerator cable as required.

33. Install the air cleaner and air flow meter assembly.

34. Check to make sure all wiring and hoses are properly connected. Fill and bleed the cooling system. Fill the engine and transmission with the proper type and quantity of oil.

35. Connect the negative battery cable, start the engine and bring to normal operating temperature. Check for leaks.

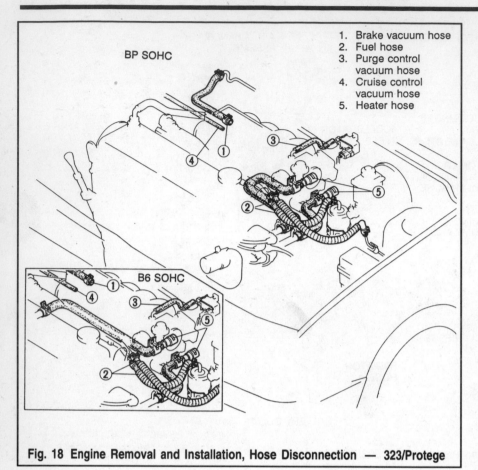

Fig. 18 Engine Removal and Installation, Hose Disconnection — 323/Protege

BP SOHC

1. Brake vacuum hose
2. Fuel hose
3. Purge control vacuum hose
4. Cruise control vacuum hose
5. Heater hose

B6 SOHC

ATX

GASKET, REPLACE

COTTER PIN, REPLACE

1. Speedometer cable
2. Clutch release cylinder
3. Shift control rod
4. Extension bar
5. Shift control cable
6. Front exhaust pipe
7. Stabilizer
8. Tie rod end
9. Engine mount member
10. Driveshaft

Fig. 19 Engine Removal and Installation Procedure — 323/Protege and MX-3 with 1.6L engine

36. Check the ignition timing and idle speed. Check all fluid levels.

MX-3

1.6L ENGINE

1. Properly relieve the fuel system pressure.

2. Disconnect the battery cables and remove the battery and battery tray.

3. Mark the position of the hood on its hinges and remove the hood.

4. Raise and safely support the vehicle. Remove the front wheel and tire assemblies. Remove the splash shields.

5. Drain the cooling system and the engine and transaxle oil.

6. Disconnect the electrical connector from the air flow meter. Remove the air cleaner/air flow meter assembly and all air ducts.

7. Remove the radiator hoses and the accessory drive belts. If equipped with automatic transaxle, disconnect the oil cooler lines.

8. Remove the power steering pump and position aside, leaving the hoses connected.

9. Remove the A/C compressor and position aside, leaving the hoses connected.

10. Label and disconnect all necessary electrical connectors, vacuum hoses, fuel lines and heater hoses.

11. Disconnect the accelerator and speedometer cables.

12. If equipped with manual transaxle, remove the clutch slave cylinder and hydraulic line bracket and position aside, leaving the hydraulic line connected. Remove the shift control rod and extension bar.

13. If equipped with automatic transaxle, disconnect the shift control cable.

14. Disconnect the exhaust pipe from the exhaust manifold.

15. Disconnect the stabilizer bar and tie rod ends from the lower control arms.

16. Suspend the engine with suitable lifting equipment.

17. Remove the front and rear transaxle mount-to-engine mount member nuts. Remove the engine mount member-to-body bolts/nuts and remove the engine mount member.

➡**Be careful that the engine does not fall when removing the engine mount member.**

18. Remove the ball joint pinch bolts/nuts from the steering knuckles. Use a suitable prybar to pull the lower

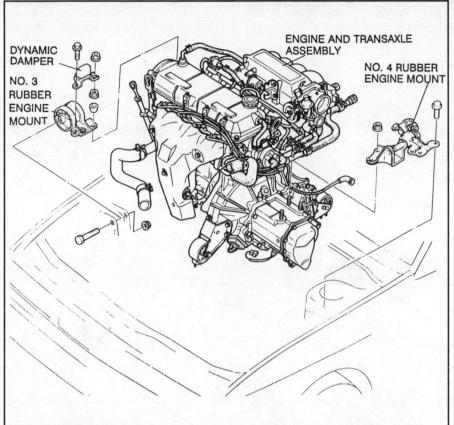

Fig. 20 Engine Removal and Installation Procedure — 323/Protege and MX-3 with 1.6L engine

control arm down and separate the ball joints from the steering knuckles. Use care so as not to damage the ball joint dust boots.

19. Insert a suitable prybar between the inner CV-joints and the transaxle case. Pry the halfshaft from the case, being careful not to damage the oil seal.

20. Remove the dynamic damper from the right side engine mount and remove the mount. Remove the left side transaxle mount and bracket.

21. Carefully lift the engine/transaxle assembly from the vehicle.

22. Safely support the engine/transaxle assembly and remove the starter and front transaxle mount.

23. If equipped with automatic transaxle, disconnect the throttle valve cable and remove the torque converter-to-flywheel nuts.

24. Remove the transaxle mounting bolts and separate the transaxle from the engine.

To install:

25. Assemble the transaxle to the engine and tighten the mounting bolts. Install the starter and front transaxle mount and tighten the bolts to 38 ft. lbs. (52 Nm).

26. If equipped with automatic transaxle, connect the throttle valve cable and install the torque converter-to-flywheel nuts. Tighten the nuts to 36 ft. lbs. (49 Nm).

27. Install the engine mount member and tighten the bolts/nuts to 66 ft. lbs. (89 Nm).

28. Carefully lower the engine/transaxle assembly into the vehicle, aligning the front and rear transaxle mount bolts with the holes in the engine mount member. Install the nuts to the front and rear transaxle mounts and tighten to 38 ft. lbs. (52 Nm).

29. Install the right side engine mount and tighten the mount-to-engine nuts to 76 ft. lbs. (103 Nm). Install the mount through bolt and tighten the nut to 69 ft. lbs. (93 Nm). Install the dynamic damper and tighten the bolt/nut to 59 ft. lbs. (80 Nm).

30. Install the left transaxle mount/bracket assembly and loosely tighten the mount-to-transaxle nuts. Install the mount-to-body bolts and tighten, in sequence, to 45 ft. lbs. (61 Nm). Tighten the mount-to-engine nuts to 69 ft. lbs. (93 Nm).

31. Apply new circlips, with the gaps positioned upward, to the inner CV-joint stubs shafts and grease the splines. Install the halfshafts in the transaxle, being careful not to damage the oil seals. After installation, pull out on the hubs to make sure the circlips are seated in the differential side gears.

32. Insert the ball joints into the steering knuckles and install the pinch bolts. Tighten the pinch bolt nuts to 43 ft. lbs. (59 Nm).

33. Insert the tie rod ends into the knuckles and install the nuts. Tighten the nuts to at least 31 ft. lbs. (42 Nm), then continue tightening until the nut castellation is lined up with the ball stud hole. Install a new cotter pin.

34. Connect the stabilizer bar to the lower control arm.

35. If equipped with manual transaxle, connect the extension bar to the transaxle and tighten the nut to 34 ft. lbs. (46 Nm). Connect the shift control rod and tighten the nut to 17 ft. lbs. (23 Nm). Install the clutch slave cylinder and pipe bracket.

36. If equipped with automatic transaxle, connect the shift cable to the transaxle.

37. Connect the speedometer and accelerator cables.

38. Using a new gasket, connect the exhaust pipe to the exhaust manifold. Tighten the flange nuts to 34 ft. lbs. (46 Nm) and the bracket bolts to 38 ft. lbs. (52 Nm).

39. Connect the electrical connectors, vacuum hoses, heater hoses and fule lines.

40. Install the A/C compressor and tighten the mounting bolts to 26 ft. lbs. (35 Nm). Install the power steering pump and bracket and tighten the bolts to 38 ft. lbs. (52 Nm). Install the accessory drive belts and adjust the belt tension.

41. Install the radiator hoses. If equipped with automatic transaxle, connect the oil cooler lines.

42. Install the battery tray and battery. Install the air flow meter/air cleaner assembly and related ducts. Connect the air flow sensor electrical connector.

43. Install the splash shields and the front wheel and tire assemblies. Lower the vehicle.

44. Install the hood, aligning the marks that were made during removal.

45. Connect the battery cables. Fill the engine and transaxle with the proper type and quantity of oil. Fill and bleed the cooling system.

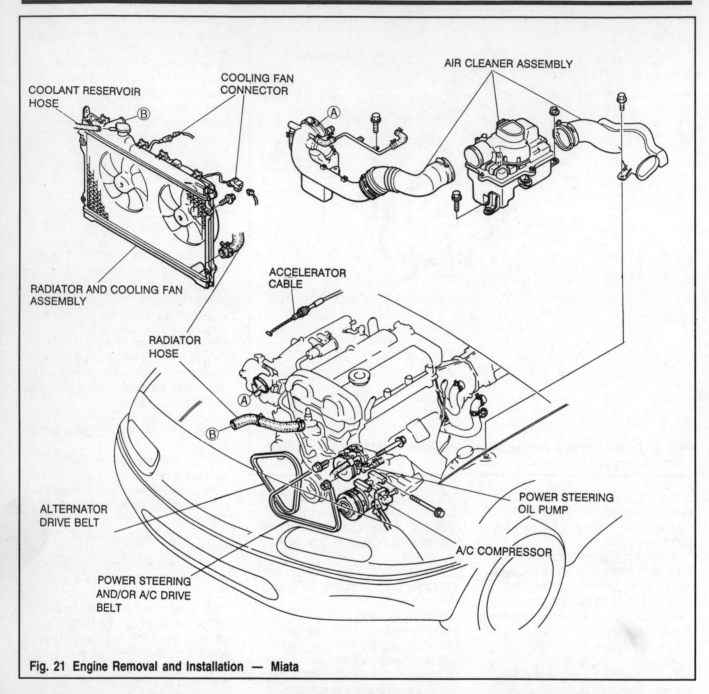

COOLANT RESERVOIR HOSE

COOLING FAN CONNECTOR

AIR CLEANER ASSEMBLY

RADIATOR AND COOLING FAN ASSEMBLY

RADIATOR HOSE

ACCELERATOR CABLE

ALTERNATOR DRIVE BELT

POWER STEERING OIL PUMP

A/C COMPRESSOR

POWER STEERING AND/OR A/C DRIVE BELT

Fig. 21 Engine Removal and Installation — Miata

46. Start the engine and bring to normal operating temperature. Check for leaks.

47. Check the ignition timing and idle speed. Check all fluid levels and road test the vehicle.

1.8L ENGINE

▶ **See Figures 26, 27 and 28**

1. Properly relieve the fuel system pressure.

2. Disconnect the battery cables and remove the battery, battery tray and duct.

3. Mark the position of the hood on its hinges and remove the hood.

4. Raise and safely support the vehicle. Remove the front wheel and tire assemblies. Remove the splash shields.

5. Drain the cooling system and the engine and transaxle oil.

6. Remove the air cleaner assembly and all air ducts. Disconnect the accelerator cable and remove the coolant reservoir.

7. Remove the radiator hoses. Disconnect the cooling fan electrical connector and, if equipped with automatic transaxle, the oil cooler hoses. Remove the radiator/shroud/cooling fan assembly.

8. Remove the accessory drive belts.

9. Disconnect the power steering hose from the engine and disconnect the

power steering pressure switch connector. Remove the power steering fluid reservoir and position aside. Remove the power steering pump pulley and mounting bolts and support the pump aside.

10. Remove the A/C compressor and position aside, leaving the hoses connected.

11. Label and disconnect all necessary electrical connectors, vacuum and heater hoses, and fuel lines.

12. If equipped with manual transaxle, remove the clutch slave cylinder and line bracket and position the slave cylinder aside, leaving the hydraulic line connected. Disconnect the shift control rod and extension bar.

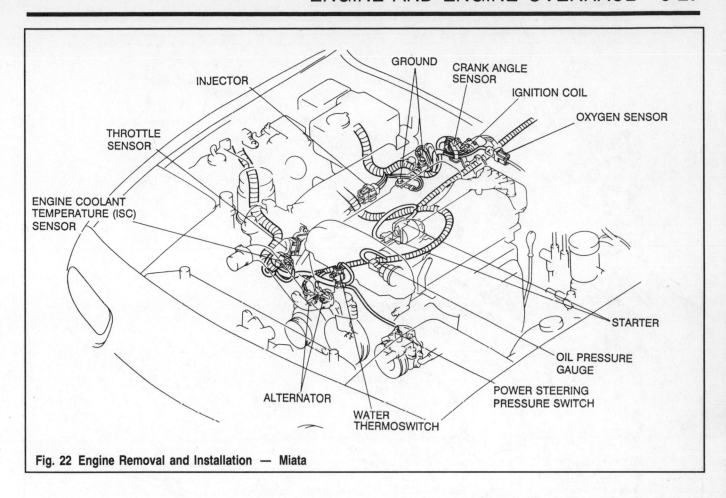

Fig. 22 Engine Removal and Installation — Miata

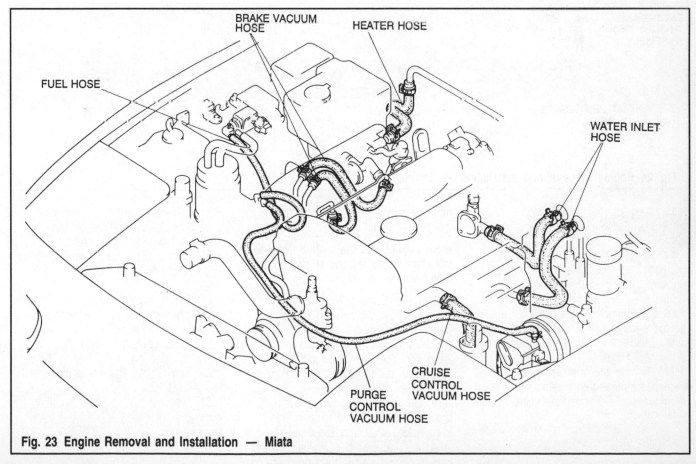

Fig. 23 Engine Removal and Installation — Miata

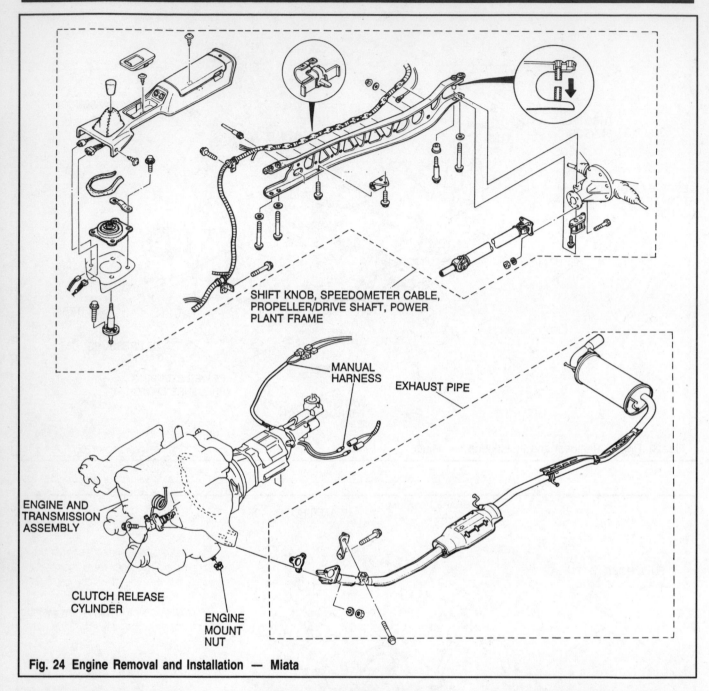

Fig. 24 Engine Removal and Installation — Miata

SHIFT KNOB, SPEEDOMETER CABLE, PROPELLER/DRIVE SHAFT, POWER PLANT FRAME

MANUAL HARNESS

EXHAUST PIPE

ENGINE AND TRANSMISSION ASSEMBLY

CLUTCH RELEASE CYLINDER

ENGINE MOUNT NUT

13. If equipped with automatic transaxle, disconnect the shift control cable.

14. Remove the transverse frame member from under the front of the vehicle. Disconnect the exhaust pipe from the exhaust manifolds.

15. Disconnect the stabilizer bar and tie rod ends from the lower control arms.

16. Suspend the engine with suitable lifting equipment.

17. Remove the front and rear transaxle mount-to-engine mount member nuts. Remove the engine mount member-to-body bolts/nuts and remove the engine mount member.

➡**Be careful that the engine does not fall when removing the engine mount member.**

18. Remove the ball joint pinch bolts/nuts from the steering knuckles. Use a suitable prybar to pull the lower control arm down and separate the ball joints from the steering knuckles. Use care so as not to damage the ball joint dust boots.

19. Remove the right intermediate shaft support bolts and remove the intermediate shaft from the transaxle. Insert a suitable prybar between the left inner CV-joint and the transaxle case.

Pry the halfshaft from the case, being careful not to damage the oil seal.

20. Remove the right engine mount and left transaxle mount. Carefully lift the engine/transaxle assembly from the vehicle.

21. Safely support the engine/transaxle assembly and remove the starter and front transaxle mount.

22. If equipped with automatic transaxle, disconnect the throttle valve cable and remove the torque converter-to-flywheel nuts.

23. Remove the transaxle mounting bolts and separate the transaxle from the engine.

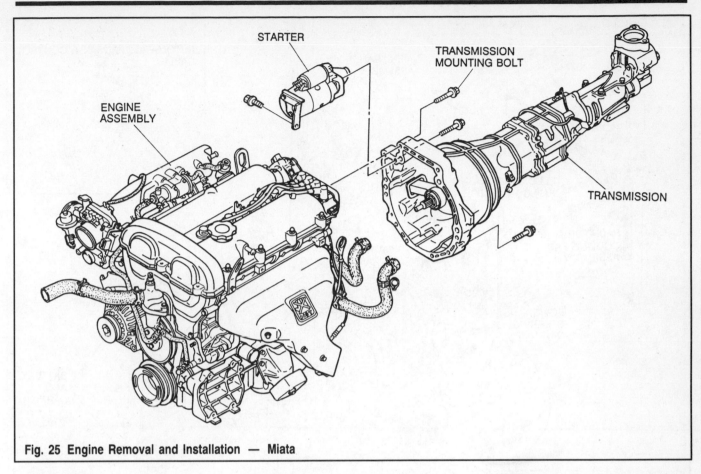

Fig. 25 Engine Removal and Installation — Miata

To install:

24. Assemble the transaxle to the engine and tighten the mounting bolts to 73 ft. lbs. (99 Nm). Install the starter and front transaxle mount and tighten the bolts to 38 ft. lbs. (52 Nm).

25. If equipped with automatic transaxle, connect the throttle valve cable and install the torque converter-to-flywheel nuts. Tighten the nuts to 36 ft. lbs. (49 Nm).

26. Install the engine mount member and tighten the bolts/nuts to 66 ft. lbs. (89 Nm).

27. Carefully lower the engine/transaxle assembly into the vehicle, aligning the front and rear transaxle mount bolts with the holes in the engine mount member. Install the nuts to the front and rear transaxle mounts and tighten to 38 ft. lbs. (52 Nm).

28. Install the right side engine mount. Tighten the mount-to-engine nuts to 76 ft. lbs. (103 Nm) and the mount through bolt to 69 ft. lbs. (93 Nm).

29. Install the left transaxle mount/bracket assembly and loosely tighten the mount-to-transaxle nuts. Install the mount-to-body bolts and tighten, in sequence, in 2-3 steps, to 45

ft. lbs. (61 Nm). Tighten the mount-to-transaxle nuts to 69 ft. lbs. (93 Nm).

30. Apply new circlips, with the gaps positioned upward, to the left inner CV-joint stub shaft and right intermediate shaft and grease the splines. Install the halfshaft and intermediate shaft in the transaxle, being careful not to damage the oil seals. Install the intermediate shaft support bolts and tighten, in sequence, to 46 ft. lbs. (62 Nm). After installation, pull out on the left hub to make sure the circlip on the left inner CV-joint stube shaft is seated in the differential side gear.

31. Insert the ball joints into the steering knuckles and install the pinch bolts. Tighten the pinch bolt nuts to 43 ft. lbs. (59 Nm).

32. Insert the tie rod ends into the knuckles and install the nuts. Tighten the nuts to at least 31 ft. lbs. (42 Nm), then continue tightening until the nut castellation is lined up with the ball stud hole. Install a new cotter pin.

33. Connect the stabilizer bar to the lower control arm.

34. If equipped with manual transaxle, connect the extension bar to the transaxle and tighten the nut to 34 ft. lbs. (46 Nm). Connect the shift control rod and tighten the nut to 17 ft. lbs. (23

Nm). Install the clutch slave cylinder and pipe bracket.

35. If equipped with automatic transaxle, connect the shift cable to the transaxle.

36. Using new gaskets, connect the exhaust pipe to the exhaust manifolds and tighten the nuts to 41 ft. lbs. (55 Nm).

37. Install the transverse member and tighten the mounting bolts to 93 ft. lbs. (127 Nm).

38. Connect the electrical connectors, vacuum hoses, heater hoses and fule lines.

39. Install the A/C compressor and tighten the mounting bolts to 38 ft. lbs. (46 Nm).

40. Install the power steering pump. Tighten all mounting bolts to 34 ft. lbs. (46 Nm) except the bolt adjacent to the belt tensioning bolt. Tighten that bolt to 19 ft. lbs. (25 Nm). Connect the power steering hose bracket to the engine and connect the power steering pressure switch.

41. Install the power steering pump pulley and loosely tighten the nut. Insert a breaker bar and 12mm socket through 1 of the pulley holes and onto a pump bolt to keep the pulley from turning.

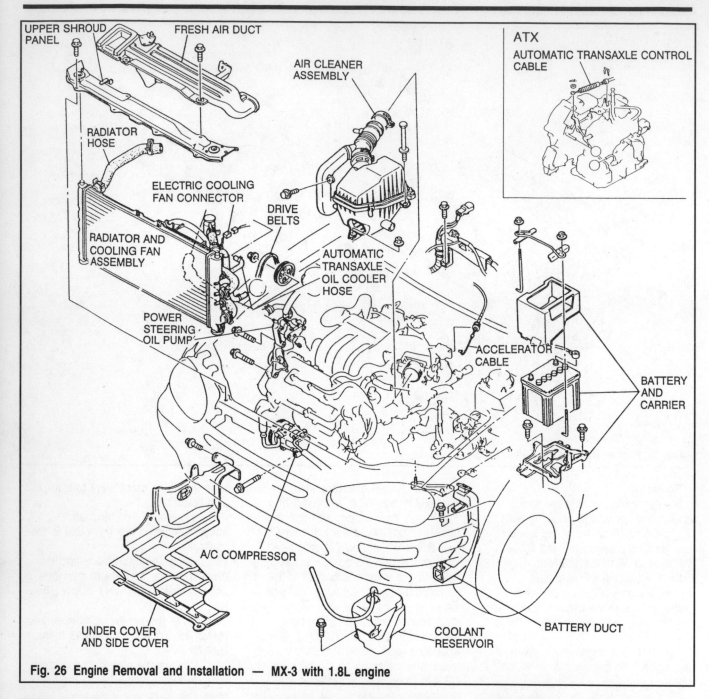

Fig. 26 Engine Removal and Installation — MX-3 with 1.8L engine

Tighten the pulley nut to 69 ft. lbs. (93 Nm).

42. Install the power steering fluid reservoir and engine ground. Install the accessory drive belts and adjust the tension.

43. Install the battery duct and coolant reservoir.

44. Install the radiator/cooling fan assembly. Connect the hoses and the cooling fan electrical connector. If equipped with automatic transaxle, connect the oil cooler lines.

45. Connect the accelerator cable. Install the battery tray and battery.

46. Install the air cleaner assembly and ducts. Connect the air flow sensor connector.

47. Install the splash shields and the front wheel and tire assemblies. Lower the vehicle.

48. Install the hood, aligning the marks that were made during removal.

49. Connect the battery cables. Fill the engine and transaxle with the proper type and quantity of oil. Fill and bleed the cooling system.

50. Start the engine and bring to normal operating temperature. Check for leaks.

51. Check the ignition timing and idle speed. Check all fluid levels and road test the vehicle.

626 and MX-6

2.0L ENGINE

▶ **See Figures 29, 30 and 31**

1. Properly relieve the fuel system pressure.

2. Disconnect the battery cables and remove the battery, battery tray and duct.

3. Mark the position of the hood on its hinges and remove the hood.

4. Raise and safely support the vehicle. Remove the front wheel and tire assemblies. Remove the splash shields.

5. Drain the cooling system and the engine and transaxle oil.

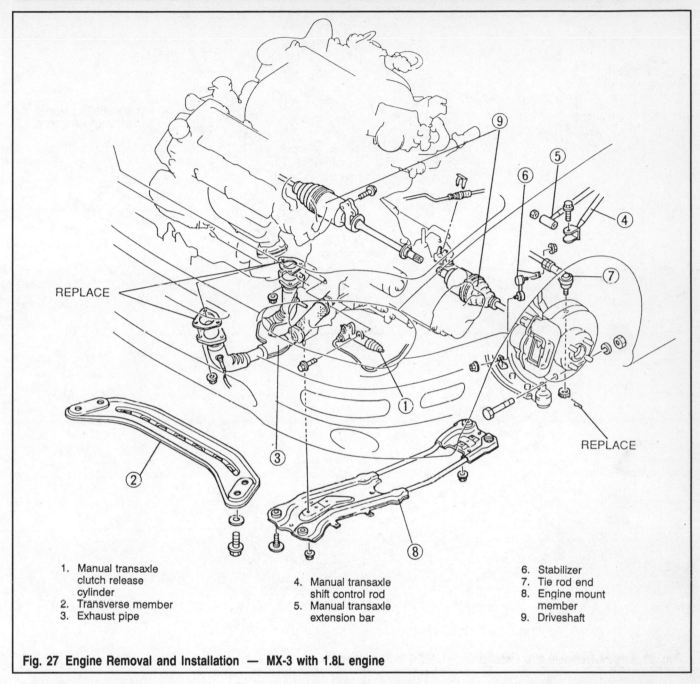

REPLACE

REPLACE

1. Manual transaxle
   clutch release
   cylinder
2. Transverse member
3. Exhaust pipe
4. Manual transaxle
   shift control rod
5. Manual transaxle
   extension bar
6. Stabilizer
7. Tie rod end
8. Engine mount
   member
9. Driveshaft

Fig. 27 Engine Removal and Installation — MX-3 with 1.8L engine

6. Disconnect the electrical connectors and remove the air cleaner/air flow meter assembly and all air ducts. Disconnect the accelerator cable.

7. Remove the radiator hoses. Disconnect the cooling fan electrical connector and, if equipped with automatic transaxle, the oil cooler hoses. Remove the radiator/shroud/cooling fan assembly.

8. Remove the accessory drive belts.

9. Remove the power steering pump and position aside, leaving the hoses connected.

10. Remove the A/C compressor and position aside, leaving the hoses connected.

11. Label and disconnect all necessary electrical connectors, vacuum hoses, fuel lines and heater hoses. Remove the fuel filter.

12. If equipped with manual transaxle, remove the clutch slave cylinder and line bracket and position the slave cylinder aside, leaving the hydraulic line connected. Disconnect the shift control rod and extension bar.

13. If equipped with automatic transaxle, disconnect the shift control cable.

14. Remove the transverse frame member from under the front of the vehicle.

15. Suspend the engine with suitable lifting equipment.

16. Remove the mount-to-engine mount member nuts. Remove the engine mount member-to-body bolts/nuts and remove the engine mount member.

➡**Be careful that the engine does not fall when removing the engine mount member.**

17. Remove the front exhaust pipe.

18. Disconnect the stabilizer bar and tie rod ends from the lower control arms.

19. Remove the ball joint pinch bolts/nuts from the steering knuckles. Use a suitable prybar to pull the lower control arm down and separate the ball joints from the steering knuckles. Use care so as not to damage the ball joint dust boots.

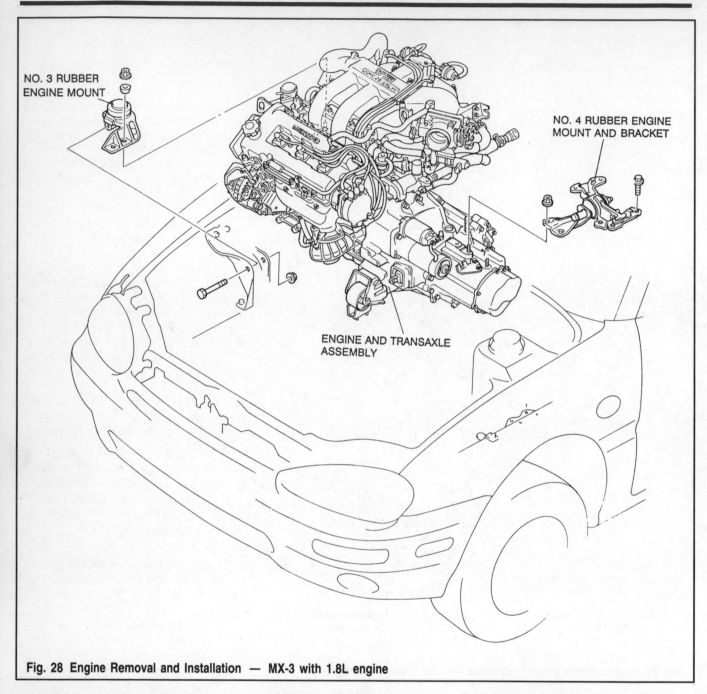

NO. 3 RUBBER
ENGINE MOUNT

NO. 4 RUBBER ENGINE
MOUNT AND BRACKET

ENGINE AND TRANSAXLE
ASSEMBLY

Fig. 28 Engine Removal and Installation — MX-3 with 1.8L engine

20. Remove the right intermediate shaft support bolts and remove the intermediate shaft from the transaxle. Insert a suitable prybar between the left inner CV-joint and the transaxle case. Pry the halfshaft from the case, being careful not to damage the oil seal.

21. Remove the fuse box.

22. Remove the rear transaxle mount stay bracket and bolts. Remove the right engine mount and the left transaxle mount.

23. Carefully remove the engine/transaxle assembly from the vehicle.

24. Safely support the engine/transaxle assembly and remove the intake manifold bracket, starter, and front transaxle mount. If equipped with automatic transaxle, remove the torque converter-to-flywheel nuts.

25. Remove the transaxle-to-engine bolts and separate the transaxle from the engine.

To install:

26. Assemble the transaxle to the engine and tighten the mounting bolts.

27. Install the front transaxle mount bracket and tighten the bolts to 44 ft. lbs. (60 Nm). Loosely tighten the mount through bolt.

28. Install the starter and intake manifold bracket and tighten the bolts to 38 ft. lbs. (51 Nm). If equipped with automatic transaxle, install the torque

converter-to-flywheel nuts and tighten to 45 ft. lbs. (60 Nm).

29. Carefully lower the engine/transaxle assembly into the engine compartment.

30. Align the front engine mount bolts with the engine mount member mounting holes. Loosely tighten the mount-to-mount member nuts and tighten the mount member-to-body bolts/nuts to 68 ft. lbs. (93 Nm).

31. Install the rear transaxle mount-to-transaxle bolts and tighten to 68 ft. lbs. (93 Nm). Install the right engine mount and tighten the mount-to-engine nuts to 76 ft. lbs. (102 Nm) and the mount through bolt to 86 ft. lbs. (116 Nm).

32. Install the left transaxle mount bracket to the body. Loosely tighten the vertical bolts. Tighten the horizontal bolts to 59 ft. lbs. (80 Nm), then tighten the vertical bolts to the same specification.

33. Install the left transaxle mount. Tighten the mount-to-transaxle bolts/nuts to 68 ft. lbs. (93 Nm) and the mount through bolt to 86 ft. lbs. (116 Nm).

34. Remove the engine lifting equipment. Tighten the front transaxle mount-to-engine mount member nuts to 77 ft. lbs. (104 Nm) and the front engine mount through bolt to 86 ft. lbs. (116 Nm).

35. Install the center transaxle mount. Tighten the mount-to-transaxle bolts to 68 ft. lbs. (93 Nm) and the mount-to-mount member nuts to 44 ft. lbs. (60 Nm). Install the rear transaxle mount stay bracket and ground wire.

36. Apply new circlips, with the gaps positioned upward, to the left inner CV-joint stub shaft and right intermediate shaft and grease the splines. Install the halfshaft and intermediate shaft in the transaxle, being careful not to damage the oil seals. Install the intermediate shaft support bolts and tighten, in sequence, to 45 ft. lbs. (61 Nm). After installation, pull out on the left hub to make sure the circlip on the left inner CV-joint stub shaft is seated in the differential side gear.

37. Insert the ball joints into the steering knuckles and install the pinch bolts. Tighten the pinch bolt nuts to 41 ft. lbs. (56 Nm).

38. Insert the tie rod ends into the knuckles and install the nuts. Tighten the nuts to at least 32 ft. lbs. (44 Nm), then continue tightening until the nut castellation is lined up with the ball stud hole. Install a new cotter pin.

39. Connect the stabilizer bar to the lower control arm and tighten to 39 ft. lbs. (53 Nm).

40. If equipped with manual transaxle, connect the extension bar to the transaxle and tighten the nut to 38 ft. lbs. (51 Nm). Connect the shift control rod and tighten the nut to 16 ft. lbs. (22 Nm). Install the clutch slave cylinder and pipe bracket.

41. If equipped with automatic transaxle, connect the shift cable to the transaxle.

42. Using new gaskets, install the exhaust pipe and tighten the nuts and bracket bolts to 38 ft. lbs. (51 Nm).

43. Install the transverse member and tighten the bolts to 97 ft. lbs. (131 Nm).

44. Connect the electrical connectors, vacuum and heater hoses and fuel lines.

45. Install the A/C compressor and tighten the mounting bolts to 26 ft. lbs. (35 Nm).

46. Install the power steering pump adjuster and tighten the mounting bolts to 16 ft. lbs. (22 Nm). Install the pump and tighten the mounting bolts to 33 ft. lbs. (46 Nm). Connect the pump pressure switch electrical connector and install the power steering line brackets to the valve cover.

47. Install the accessory drive belts and adjust the tension.

48. Install the radiator/cooling fan assembly. Connect the radiator hoses and the cooling fan electrical connector.

49. Connect the accelerator cable.

50. Install the battery tray and battery. Install the air cleaner/air flow sensor assembly and the air ducts. Connect the air flow sensor and intake air thermosensor electrical connectors.

51. Install the splash shields and the front wheel and tire assemblies. Lower the vehicle.

52. Install the hood, aligning the marks that were made during removal.

53. Connect the battery cables. Fill the engine and transaxle with the proper type and quantity of oil. Fill and bleed the cooling system.

54. Start the engine and bring to normal operating temperature. Check for leaks.

55. Check the ignition timing and idle speed. Check all fluid levels and road test the vehicle.

2.2L ENGINE

▶ See Figures 32 and 33

1. Properly relieve the fuel system pressure. Mark the position of the hood on the hinges and remove the hood.

2. Disconnect and remove the battery and the battery box. Raise and safely support the vehicle. Remove the wheel and tire assemblies.

3. Remove the splash shields at the front of the inner fenders and drain the engine and transaxle and the cooling system.

4. Remove the air cleaner assembly, including the air flow meter and all of the ducting. If equipped, remove the turbocharger pipe and hose and cover the turbocharger opening with a clean rag.

5. Remove the radiator hoses and disconnect the cooling fan electrical connector. If equipped with automatic transaxle, disconnect the oil cooler lines from the radiator. Remove the radiator/cooling fan assembly.

6. Disconnect the throttle and cruise control cables, if equipped, and the speedometer cable.

7. Label and disconnect the vacuum hoses and wiring.

8. Disconnect the fuel supply and return hoses and the heater hoses. Plug the fuel hoses to prevent leakage.

9. Disconnect the exhaust pipe from the manifold.

10. Without disconnecting the hydraulic hoses, remove the power steering pump and position it aside.

11. Without disconnecting the refrigerant lines, remove the air conditioning compressor and position it aside.

12. If equipped with manual transaxle, remove the clutch slave cylinder without disconnecting the hydraulic line. Disconnect the shift linkage.

13. If equipped with automatic transaxle, disconnect the shift cable.

14. Disconnect the stabilizer bar and the tie rod ends from the lower control arm.

15. Remove the pinch bolts from the steering knuckle and pry the control arm down to slip lower ball joint out of the knuckle.

➡ **When the halfshafts are removed from the transaxle, the differential side gears must be held in place with service tool 49 G027 003 (manual) or 40 G030 455 (automatic), or equivalent.**

16. Carefully pry the inner CV-joints from the transaxle, being careful not to damage the oil seals. Support the halfshafts so they do not hang by the outer CV-joints. Install the service tools.

17. Attach a chain to the lifting eyes on the engine and lift the engine slightly to take up the slack. Check to make sure all wiring, controls and hoses are disconnected.

18. Remove the engine/transaxle mount nuts/bolts and carefully lift the engine/transaxle assembly from the vehicle.

19. With the transaxle properly supported, remove the starter. If equipped with automatic transaxle, remove the flywheel-to-torque converter nuts.

20. Remove the transaxle mounting bolts and brackets and separate the transaxle from the engine.

To install:

21. Carefully fit the engine and transaxle together and torque the bolts to 86 ft. lbs. (117 Nm).

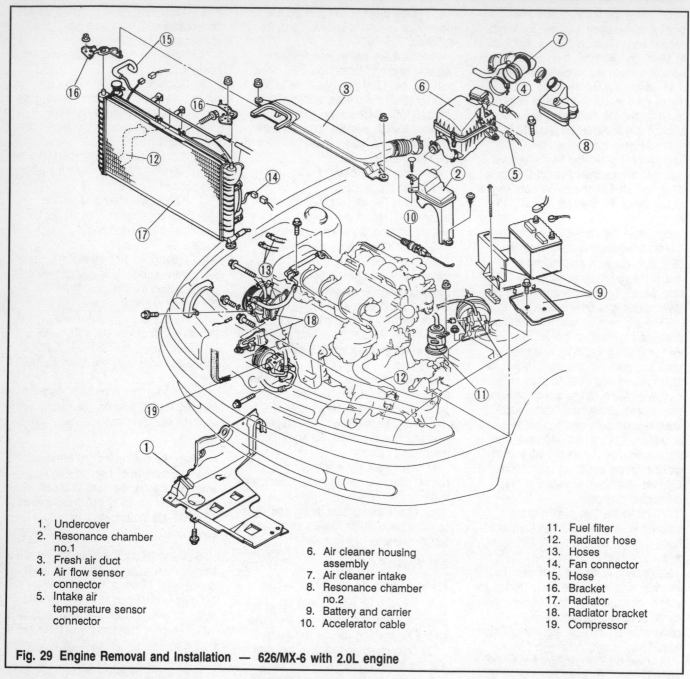

1. Undercover
2. Resonance chamber no.1
3. Fresh air duct
4. Air flow sensor connector
5. Intake air temperature sensor connector
6. Air cleaner housing assembly
7. Air cleaner intake
8. Resonance chamber no.2
9. Battery and carrier
10. Accelerator cable
11. Fuel filter
12. Radiator hose
13. Hoses
14. Fan connector
15. Hose
16. Bracket
17. Radiator
18. Radiator bracket
19. Compressor

Fig. 29 Engine Removal and Installation — 626/MX-6 with 2.0L engine

22. If equipped with automatic transaxle, install the flywheel-to-torque converter bolts and torque to 45 ft. lbs. (61 Nm).

23. On manual transaxle, when installing the clutch cover, seal the inner corners with silicone sealant.

24. Attach the stiffener brackets and torque the bolts to 38 ft. lbs. (52 Nm).

25. Attach the front transaxle mount to the engine and torque the bolts to 38 ft. lbs. (52 Nm) on non-turbocharged vehicles or to 68 ft. lbs. (92 Nm) on turbocharged vehicles.

26. Install the starter and torque the bolts to 38 ft. lbs. (52 Nm).

27. Carefully install the engine/transaxle with just the front and rear mounts attached. When the unit is in place, install the left and right mounts. Start all nuts and bolts first, then torque the following:

Left mount-to-transaxle nuts — 66 ft. lbs. (89 Nm).

Left mount-to-body bolts — 40 ft. lbs. (54 Nm).

Right mount-to-engine nuts — 76 ft. lbs. (103 Nm).

Right mount through bolt — 69 ft. lbs. (93 Nm).

Front mount-to-body nut — 69 ft. lbs. (93 Nm).

Rear mount through bolt — 86 ft. lbs. (117 Nm).

28. Use new gaskets and attach the exhaust pipe. Torque the pipe-to-

manifold or turbocharger nuts to 36 ft. lbs. (49 Nm).

29. Connect the manual shift linkage and install the clutch slave cylinder. Torque the shift rod bolt to 17 ft. lbs. (22 Nm) and the extension bar nut to 34 ft. lbs. (46 Nm).

30. Install new circlips on the inner CV-joint stub shafts with the gap facing upward. Grease the splines and push the halfshafts into the transaxle, being careful not to damage the oil seals. After installation, pull the hubs outward to make sure the circlips are seated in the differential side gears.

31. Install the lower ball joint and torque the pinch bolt to 40 ft. lbs. (54 Nm). Install the tie rod ends and torque

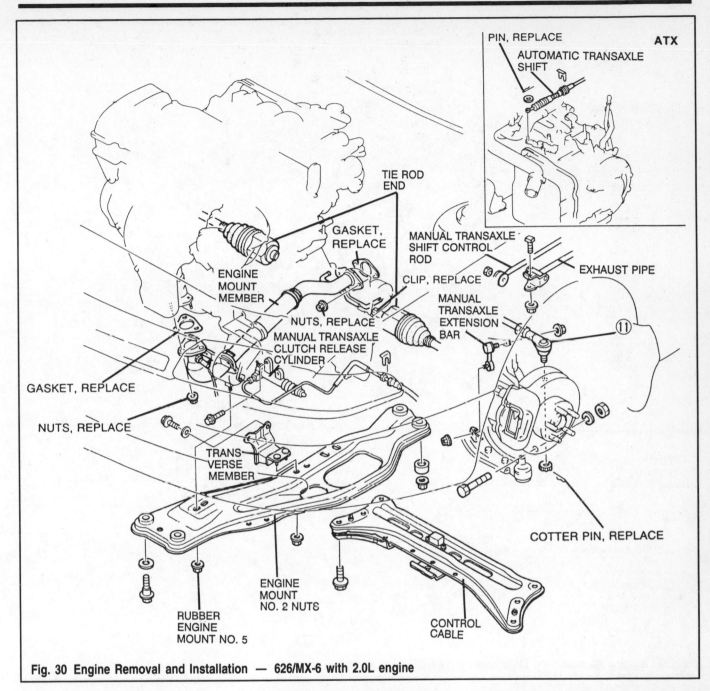

Fig. 30 Engine Removal and Installation — 626/MX-6 with 2.0L engine

the nut to 42 ft. lbs. (57 Nm), then tighten as required to install a new cotter pin.

32. Attach the stabilizer bar and tighten the nuts so there is 0.80 in. (20mm) of thread showing at the top of the long mounting bolt.

33. If equipped with automatic transaxle, connect and adjust the shift cable as required.

34. Connect the wiring and all water, fuel and vacuum hoses. Connect the accelerator cable.

35. Install the air conditioner compressor and power steering pump. Install the accessory drive belts and adjust the tension.

36. Install the radiator/cooling fan assembly and connect the hoses and cooling fan electrical connector.

37. Install the battery tray and the battery.

38. Install the air cleaner and air flow meter assembly and all the ducting. If equipped, install the turbocharger pipe and hoses.

39. Install the splash shields and the front wheel and tire assemblies. Lower the vehicle.

40. Install the hood, aligning the marks that were made during removal.

41. Connect the battery cables. Fill the engine and transaxle with the proper type and quantity of oil. Fill and bleed the cooling system.

42. Start the engine and bring to normal operating temperature. Check for leaks.

43. Check the ignition timing and idle speed. Check all fluid levels and road test the vehicle.

2.5L ENGINE

▶ See Figures 34, 35 and 36

1. Properly relieve the fuel system pressure.

2. Disconnect the battery cables and remove the battery, battery tray and duct.

3. Mark the position of the hood on its hinges and remove the hood.

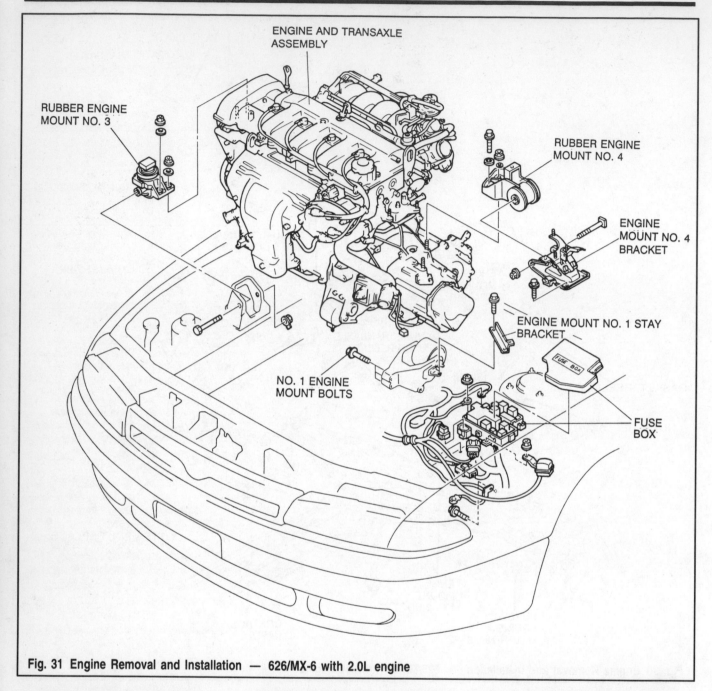

Fig. 31 Engine Removal and Installation — 626/MX-6 with 2.0L engine

4. Raise and safely support the vehicle. Remove the front wheel and tire assemblies. Remove the splash shields.

5. Drain the cooling system and the engine and transaxle oil.

6. Remove the air cleaner assembly and all air ducts. Disconnect the accelerator cable.

7. Remove the radiator hoses. Disconnect the cooling fan electrical connector and, if equipped with automatic transaxle, the oil cooler hoses. Remove the radiator/cooling fan assembly.

8. Remove the accessory drive belts.

9. Remove the power steering fluid reservoir and position aside, leaving the hoses attached. Remove the power

steering pump pulley and mounting bolts and support the pump aside, leaving the hoses attached.

10. Remove the A/C compressor and position aside, leaving the hoses connected.

11. Remove the fuel filter. Label and disconnect all necessary electrical connectors, vacuum and heater hoses, and fuel lines.

12. If equipped with manual transaxle, remove the clutch slave cylinder and line bracket and position the slave cylinder aside, leaving the hydraulic line connected. Disconnect the shift control rod and extension bar.

13. If equipped with automatic transaxle, disconnect the shift control cable.

14. Remove the transverse frame member from under the front of the vehicle. Remove the front exhaust pipe.

15. Disconnect the stabilizer bar and tie rod ends from the lower control arms.

16. Remove the ball joint pinch bolts/nuts from the steering knuckles. Use a suitable prybar to pull the lower control arm down and separate the ball joints from the steering knuckles. Use care so as not to damage the ball joint dust boots.

17. Remove the right intermediate shaft support bolts and remove the intermediate shaft from the transaxle.

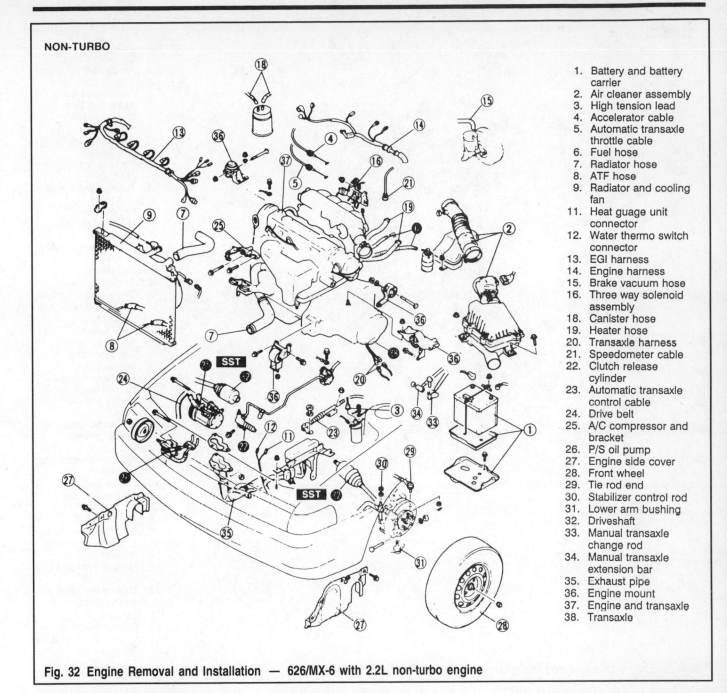

NON-TURBO

1. Battery and battery carrier
2. Air cleaner assembly
3. High tension lead
4. Accelerator cable
5. Automatic transaxle throttle cable
6. Fuel hose
7. Radiator hose
8. ATF hose
9. Radiator and cooling fan
11. Heat guage unit connector
12. Water thermo switch connector
13. EGI harness
14. Engine harness
15. Brake vacuum hose
16. Three way solenoid assembly
18. Canister hose
19. Heater hose
20. Transaxle harness
21. Speedometer cable
22. Clutch release cylinder
23. Automatic transaxle control cable
24. Drive belt
25. A/C compressor and bracket
26. P/S oil pump
27. Engine side cover
28. Front wheel
29. Tie rod end
30. Stabilizer control rod
31. Lower arm bushing
32. Driveshaft
33. Manual transaxle change rod
34. Manual transaxle extension bar
35. Exhaust pipe
36. Engine mount
37. Engine and transaxle
38. Transaxle

Fig. 32 Engine Removal and Installation — 626/MX-6 with 2.2L non-turbo engine

Insert a suitable prybar between the left inner CV-joint and the transaxle case. Pry the halfshaft from the case, being careful not to damage the oil seal.

18. Suspend the engine with suitable lifting equipment. Remove the right engine mount and left transaxle mount.

19. Remove the mount-to-engine mount member nuts. Remove the engine mount member-to-body bolts/nuts and remove the engine mount member.

20. Carefully lift the engine/transaxle assembly from the vehicle.

21. Safely support the engine/transaxle assembly and remove the starter and front transaxle mount.

22. If equipped with automatic transaxle, remove the torque converter-to-flywheel nuts.

23. Remove the transaxle mounting bolts and separate the transaxle from the engine.

To install:

24. Assemble the transaxle to the engine and tighten the mounting bolts to 73 ft. lbs. (99 Nm). Install the starter and front transaxle mount bracket and tighten the bolts to 38 ft. lbs. (52 Nm). Install the front engine mount and loosely tighten the through bolt.

25. If equipped with automatic transaxle, install the torque converter-to-flywheel nuts. Tighten the nuts to 44 ft. lbs. (60 Nm).

26. Carefully lower the engine/transaxle assembly into the engine compartment.

27. Align the front engine mount bolts with the engine mount member mounting holes. Loosely tighten the mount-to-mount member nuts and tighten the mount member-to-body bolts/nuts to 68 ft. lbs. (93 Nm).

28. Install the rear transaxle mount-to-transaxle bolts and tighten to 68 ft. lbs. (93 Nm). Install the right engine mount and tighten the mount-to-engine nuts to 76 ft. lbs. (102 Nm) and the mount through bolt to 86 ft. lbs. (116 Nm).

29. Install the left transaxle mount bracket to the body. Loosely tighten the vertical bolts. Tighten the horizontal bolts

TURBO

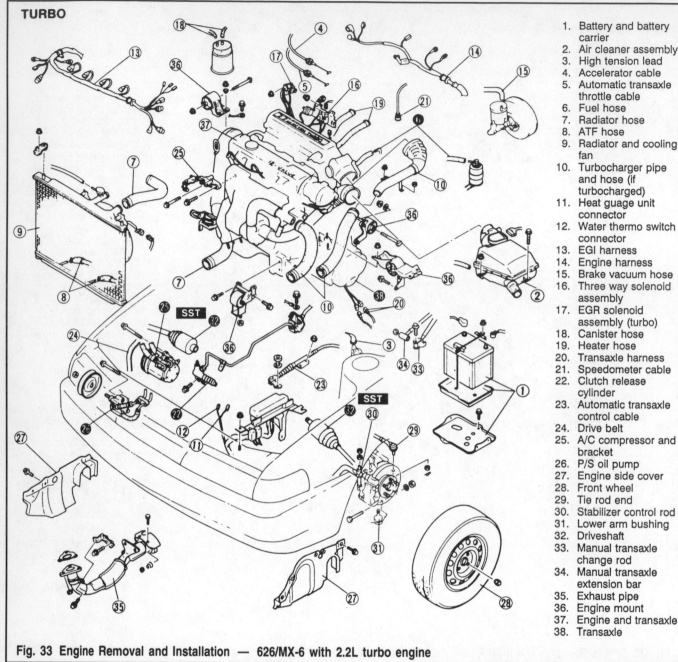

1. Battery and battery carrier
2. Air cleaner assembly
3. High tension lead
4. Accelerator cable
5. Automatic transaxle throttle cable
6. Fuel hose
7. Radiator hose
8. ATF hose
9. Radiator and cooling fan
10. Turbocharger pipe and hose (if turbocharged)
11. Heat guage unit connector
12. Water thermo switch connector
13. EGI harness
14. Engine harness
15. Brake vacuum hose
16. Three way solenoid assembly
17. EGR solenoid assembly (turbo)
18. Canister hose
19. Heater hose
20. Transaxle harness
21. Speedometer cable
22. Clutch release cylinder
23. Automatic transaxle control cable
24. Drive belt
25. A/C compressor and bracket
26. P/S oil pump
27. Engine side cover
28. Front wheel
29. Tie rod end
30. Stabilizer control rod
31. Lower arm bushing
32. Driveshaft
33. Manual transaxle change rod
34. Manual transaxle extension bar
35. Exhaust pipe
36. Engine mount
37. Engine and transaxle
38. Transaxle

Fig. 33 Engine Removal and Installation — 626/MX-6 with 2.2L turbo engine

to 59 ft. lbs. (80 Nm), then tighten the vertical bolts to the same specification.

30. Install the left transaxle mount. Tighten the mount-to-transaxle bolts/nuts to 68 ft. lbs. (93 Nm) and the mount through bolt to 86 ft. lbs. (116 Nm).

31. Remove the engine lifting equipment. Tighten the front engine mount through bolt to 86 ft. lbs. (116 Nm) and the front transaxle mount-to-engine mount member nuts to 77 ft. lbs. (104 Nm).

32. Install the center transaxle mount. Tighten the mount-to-transaxle bolts to 68 ft. lbs. (93 Nm) and the mount-to-mount member nuts to 44 ft. lbs. (60 Nm).

33. Apply new circlips, with the gaps positioned upward, to the left inner CV-joint stub shaft and right intermediate shaft and grease the splines. Install the halfshaft and intermediate shaft in the transaxle, being careful not to damage the oil seals. Install the intermediate shaft support bolts and tighten, in sequence, to 45 ft. lbs. (61 Nm). After installation, pull out on the left hub to make sure the circlip on the left inner CV-joint stub shaft is seated in the differential side gear.

34. Insert the ball joints into the steering knuckles and install the pinch bolts. Tighten the pinch bolt nuts to 43 ft. lbs. (56 Nm).

35. Insert the tie rod ends into the knuckles and install the nuts. Tighten the nuts to at least 32 ft. lbs. (44 Nm), then continue tightening until the nut castellation is lined up with the ball stud hole. Install a new cotter pin.

36. Connect the stabilizer bar to the lower control arm and tighten to 39 ft. lbs. (53 Nm).

37. If equipped with manual transaxle, connect the extension bar to the transaxle and tighten the nut to 33 ft. lbs. (46 Nm). Connect the shift control rod and tighten the nut to 16 ft. lbs. (22 Nm). Install the clutch slave cylinder and pipe bracket.

38. If equipped with automatic transaxle, connect the shift cable to the transaxle.

39. Using new gaskets, install the front exhaust pipe. Tighten the pipe-to-exhaust system nuts to 65 ft. lbs. (89 Nm) and the pipe-to-manifold nuts to 40 ft. lbs. (54 Nm).

40. Install the transverse member and tighten the bolts to 93 ft. lbs. (126 Nm).

41. Install the fuel filter. Connect the electrical connectors, vacuum and heater hoses and fuel lines.

42. Install the A/C compressor and tighten the mounting bolts to 26 ft. lbs. (35 Nm).

43. Install the power steering pump. Tighten all mounting bolts to 34 ft. lbs. (46 Nm) except the bolt adjacent to the belt tensioning bolt. Tighten that bolt to 19 ft. lbs. (25 Nm). Connect the power steering pressure switch.

44. Install the power steering pump pulley and loosely tighten the nut. Insert a breaker bar and 12mm socket through 1 of the pulley holes and onto a pump bolt to keep the pulley from turning. Tighten the pulley nut to 69 ft. lbs. (93 Nm).

45. Install the power steering fluid reservoir and engine ground. Install the accessory drive belts and adjust the tension.

46. Install the radiator/cooling fan assembly. Connect the hoses and the cooling fan electrical connector. If equipped with automatic transaxle, connect the oil cooler lines.

47. Connect the accelerator cable. Install the battery tray and battery.

48. Install the air cleaner assembly and ducts. Connect the air flow sensor connector.

49. Install the splash shields and the front wheel and tire assemblies. Lower the vehicle.

50. Install the hood, aligning the marks that were made during removal.

51. Connect the battery cables. Fill the engine and transaxle with the proper type and quantity of oil. Fill and bleed the cooling system.

52. Start the engine and bring to normal operating temperature. Check for leaks.

53. Check the ignition timing and idle speed. Check all fluid levels and road test the vehicle.

Rocker Arm (Valve) Cover

REMOVAL & INSTALLATION

323, Protege, Miata, MX-3 (B6 SOHC) and 1990-92 626/MX-6

▶ See Figure 37

1. Disconnect the vent hose from the rocker arm cover.
2. Remove the PCV valve from the rocker arm cover.
3. Remove the spark plug wires from the wire clips.
4. Remove the rocker arm cover retaining bolts and remove the rocker arm cover and gasket.

To install:

5. Clean all old gasket material from the rocker arm cover and the cylinder head.
6. Install a new gasket onto the rocker arm cover.
7. Apply silicone sealer around the groove of the cover.
8. Install the rocker arm cover on the cylinder head with the retaining bolts. Tighten the bolts to 43-78 inch lbs. (5-9 Nm).
9. Install the spark plug wires to the retaining clips and install the PCV valve. Connect the vent hose to the rocker arm cover.
10. Start the engine and bring to normal operating temperature. Check for leaks.

MX-3 (1.8L K8 DOHC Engine)

1. Disconnect the negative battery cable.
2. Remove the intake manifold stay bracket from the engine.
3. Disconnect the vent hoses from the intake manifold and from the cover assembly.
4. Remove the spark plug wires from the spark plugs, make a note of plug wire original location.
5. Remove the intake manifold assembly from the engine. Remove the bolts and disconnect the ventilation pipe from the front cover.
6. Remove the cover bolts and remove the cover assembly.

To install:

7. Clean all old gasket material from the rocker arm cover and the cylinder head.
8. Install a new gasket onto the cover.

9. Apply silicone sealer to the cylinder head perimeter.
10. Install the cover assembly and the bolts and tighten in the sequence shown over three steps to 43-78 inch lbs. (4.9-8.8 Nm).
11. Install the ventilation pipe to the front cover assembly and tighten the bolts to 69-95 inch lbs. (7.8-11 Nm).
12. Install a new gasket to the intake manifold assembly and install it to the engine.
13. Loosely tighten the bolts and nuts.
14. Install the intake manifold stay and tighten the bolts to 14-19 ft. lbs. (19-25 Nm).
15. Tighten the intake manifold nuts and bolts over three stages to 14-19 ft. lbs. (19-25 Nm).
16. Connect the vent hoses and connect the negative battery cable.
17. Start the engine and inspect for leaks.

1993 626/MX-6

FS 2.0L ENGINE

▶ See Figures 38 and 39

1. Disconnect the vent hose from the cover.
2. Disconnect the PCV hose from the cover.
3. Remove the spark plugs from the plugs.
4. Loosen the cover bolts evenly over three steps.
5. Remove the cover and the bolts from the engine.

To install:

6. Clean all old gasket material from the cover and the cylinder head.
7. Install a new gasket onto the cover.
8. Apply silicone sealer to the shaded area of the cylinder head as shown in the figure.
9. Install the cover on the cylinder head with the retaining bolts. Tighten the bolts in the order shown in fig39 to 52-69 inch lbs. (6-8 Nm).
10. Install the spark plug wires to the spark plugs. Connect the vent hose and the PCV hose to the cover.
11. Start the engine and bring to normal operating temperature. Check for leaks.

1993 626/MX-6

KL 2.5L ENGINE

▶ See Figures 40 and 41

1. Disconnect the negative battery cable.

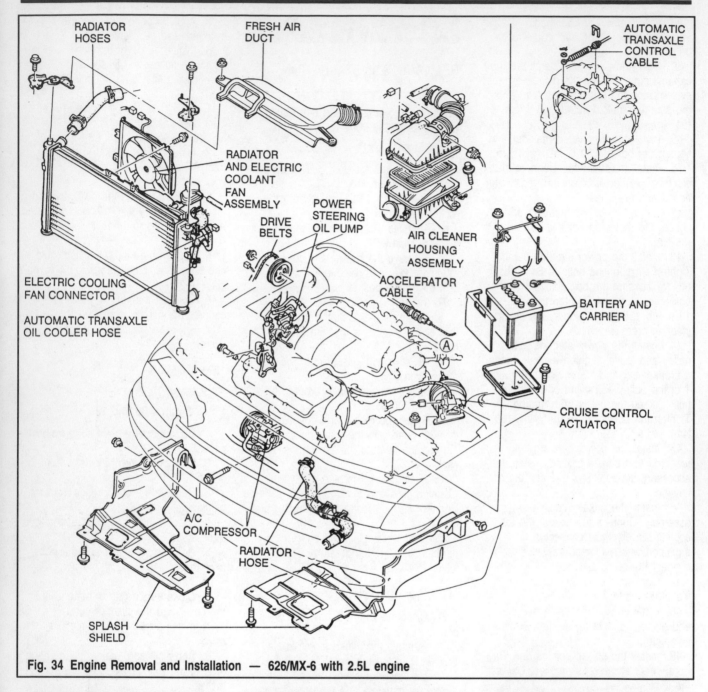

Fig. 34 Engine Removal and Installation — 626/MX-6 with 2.5L engine

2. Remove the intake manifold stay bracket from the engine.

3. Disconnect the vent hoses from the intake manifold and from the cover assembly.

4. Remove the spark plug wires from the spark plugs, make a note of plug wire original location.

5. Remove the bolts and disconnect the ventilation pipe from the front cover.

6. Remove the cover bolts and remove the cover assembly.

To install:

7. Clean all old gasket material from the rocker arm cover and the cylinder head.

8. Install a new gasket onto the cover.

9. Apply silicone sealer to the cylinder head perimeter.

10. Install the cover assembly and the bolts and tighten in the sequence shown over three steps to 43-78 inch lbs. (4.9-8.8 Nm).

11. Install the ventilation pipe to the front cover assembly and tighten the bolts to 69-95 inch lbs. (7.8-11 Nm).

12. Install a new gasket to the intake manifold assembly and install it to the engine.

13. Loosely tighten the bolts and nuts.

14. Install the intake manifold stay and tighten the bolts to 14-19 ft. lbs. (19-25 Nm).

15. Tighten the intake manifold nuts and bolts over three stages to 14-19 ft. lbs. (19-25 Nm).

16. Connect the vent hoses and connect the negative battery cable.

17. Start the engine and inspect for leaks.

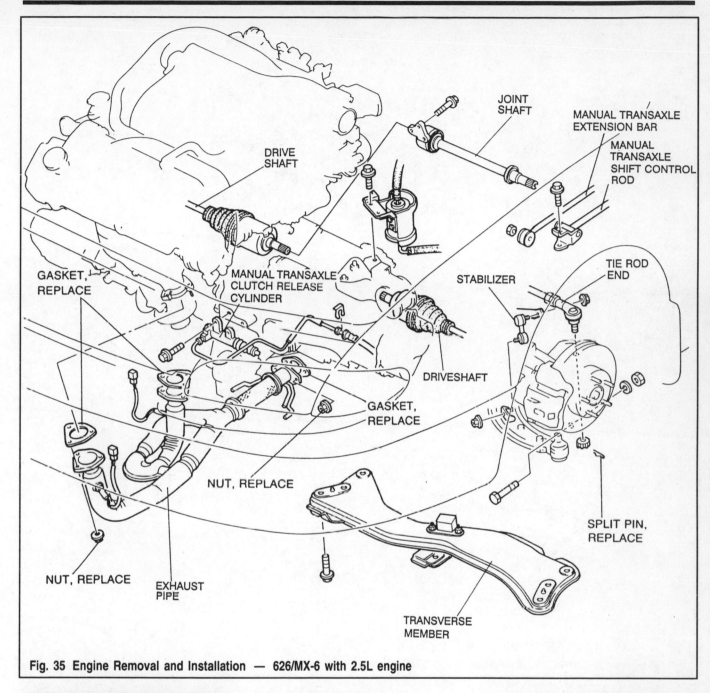

Fig. 35 Engine Removal and Installation — 626/MX-6 with 2.5L engine

Rocker Arms/Shafts

REMOVAL & INSTALLATION

1.6L (B6 SOHC) AND 1.8L (BP SOHC) Engines

▶ See Figure 42

1. Remove the rocker arm (valve) cover.

2. Remove the rocker arm and shaft assembly mounting bolts. Start at the ends and work toward the center of the shafts, when removing the bolts.

3. If necessary, separate the rocker arms and springs from the shafts; be sure to keep the parts in order for reinstallation purposes.

4. Clean and inspect the shafts and rocker arms for wear. Measure the difference between the rocker arm shaft outside diameter and the rocker arm inside diameter; this is the oil clearance. If the oil clearance exceeds 0.004 in. (0.10mm), replace the shaft and/or the rocker arm(s).

To install:

5. If they were disassembled, coat the rocker arm shafts and rocker arms with engine oil and assemble them with the springs. When assembling and installing on the cylinder head, note the notches at the ends of the shafts; they

are different on the intake and exhaust side and cannot be interchanged.

6. Install the rocker arm/shaft assemblies onto the cylinder head and torque the rocker arm shaft-to-cylinder head bolts, in sequence, to 16-21 ft. lbs. (22-28 Nm), in several steps.

7. Install the rocker arm (valve) cover.

2.2L Engine

▶ See Figure 43

1. Remove the rocker arm (valve) cover.

2. Remove the rocker arm and shaft assembly mounting bolts. Start at the

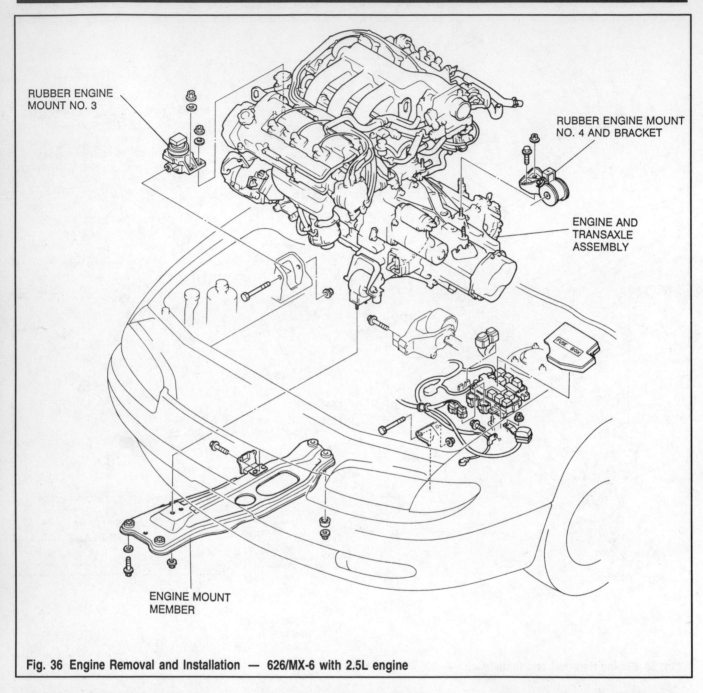

RUBBER ENGINE
MOUNT NO. 3

RUBBER ENGINE MOUNT
NO. 4 AND BRACKET

ENGINE AND
TRANSAXLE
ASSEMBLY

ENGINE MOUNT
MEMBER

Fig. 36 Engine Removal and Installation — 626/MX-6 with 2.5L engine

ends and work toward the center of the shafts, when removing the bolts.

3. If necessary, separate the rocker arms and springs from the shafts; be sure to keep the parts in order for reinstallation purposes.

4. Clean and inspect the shafts and rocker arms for wear. Measure the difference between the rocker arm shaft outside diameter and the rocker arm

inside diameter; this is the oil clearance. If the oil clearance exceeds 0.004 in. (0.10mm), replace the shaft and/or the rocker arm(s).

To install:

5. If they were disassembled, coat the rocker arm shafts and rocker arms with engine oil and assemble them with the springs. When assembling and installing on the cylinder head, note the

notches at the ends of the shafts; they are different on the intake and exhaust side and cannot be interchanged.

6. Install the rocker arm/shaft assemblies onto the cylinder head and torque the rocker arm shaft-to-cylinder head bolts, in sequence, to 13-20 ft. lbs. (18-26 Nm), in 2 steps.

7. Install the rocker arm (valve) cover.

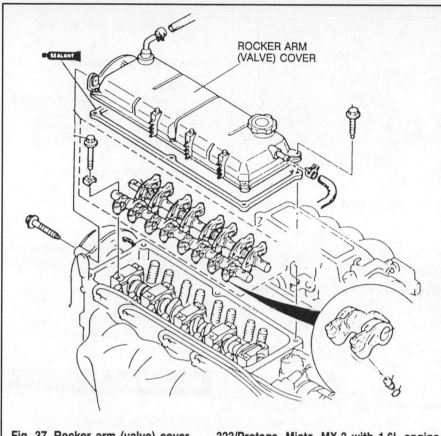

Fig. 37 Rocker arm (valve) cover — 323/Protege, Miata, MX-3 with 1.6L engine and 1990-92 626/MX-6

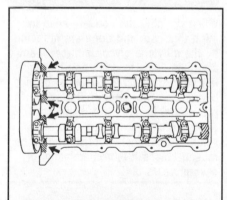

Fig. 38 Apply sealant to shaded areas — 626/MX-6 with 2.0L engine

Thermostat

REMOVAL & INSTALLATION

❊❊CAUTION

When draining the coolant, keep in mind that cats and dogs are attracted by the ethylene glycol antifreeze, and are quite likely to drink any that is left in an uncovered container or in

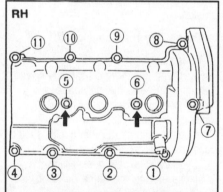

Fig. 40 Tighten the bolts in order shown — 626/MX-6 with 2.5L engine-right side

puddles on the ground. This will prove fatal in sufficient quantity. Always drain the coolant into a sealable container. Coolant should be reused unless it is contaminated or several years old.

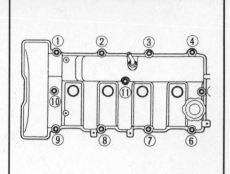

Fig. 39 Tighten the bolts in order shown — 626/MX-6 with 2.0L engine

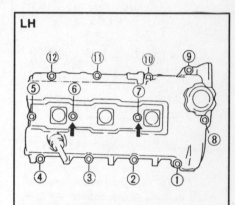

Fig. 41 Tighten the bolts in order shown — 626/MX-6 with 2.5L engine-left side

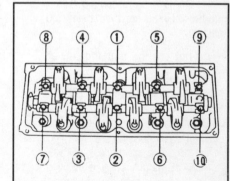

Fig. 42 Tighten the rocker arm and shaft bolts in order shown — 1.6L (B6 SOHC) and 1.8L (BP SOHC)

ALL EXCEPT MX-3 (K8 DOHC) AND 1993 626/MX-6

▸ See Figure 44

1. Disconnect the negative battery cable. Drain the radiator to below the level of the thermostat.

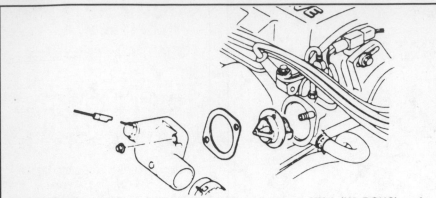

Fig. 44 Thermostat Removal and Installation all except MX-3 (K8 DOHC) and 1993 626/MX-6

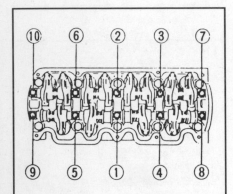

Fig. 43 Tighten the rocker arm and shaft bolts in order shown — 2.2L

2. Disconnect the coolant temperature switch at the thermostat housing.

3. Remove the upper radiator hose.

4. Remove the mounting nuts, thermostat housing, thermostat and gasket.

➡**Do not pry the housing off.**

To install:

5. Clean the thermostat housing and the cylinder head mating surfaces.

6. Insert the thermostat into the rear cylinder head housing with the jiggle pin at the top. The spring side of the thermostat should face the housing.

7. Position a new gasket onto the studs with the seal print side facing the rear cylinder housing.

8. Install the thermostat housing and 2 nuts. Tighten the nuts to 14-22 ft. lbs. (19-30 Nm).

9. Connect the coolant temperature switch and install the upper radiator hose.

10. Fill the cooling system. Connect the negative battery cable, start the engine and check for leaks. Check the

coolant level and add coolant, as necessary.

MX-3 (K8 DOHC) AND 1993 626/MX-6 (KL)

▸ **See Figure 45**

1. Disconnect the negative battery cable. Drain the radiator to below the level of the thermostat.

2. Remove the water inlet pipe mounting bolt and remove the pipe.

3. Remove the engine harness bracket bolt and position the harness aside.

4. Remove the housing bolt, thermostat housing, thermostat and gasket.

➡**Do not pry the housing off.**

To install:

5. Clean the thermostat housing and the cylinder head mating surfaces.

6. Insert the thermostat into the housing with the jiggle pin at the top. The spring side of the thermostat should face the housing.

7. Position a new gasket with the projection facing the same direction as the thermostat jiggle pin.

8. Install the thermostat housing cover and loosely install the lower bolt. Install the engine harness bracket and loosely install the bolt. Tighten both bolts to 14-19 ft. lbs. (19-25 Nm).

9. Fill the cooling system. Connect the negative battery cable, start the engine and check for leaks. Check the coolant level and add coolant, as necessary.

1993 626/MX-6 2.0L (FS)

▸ **See Figure 46**

1. Disconnect the negative battery cable. Drain the radiator to below the level of the thermostat.

2. Remove the lower radiator hose.

3. Remove the housing bolts, thermostat housing, thermostat and gasket.

➡**Do not pry the housing off.**

To install:

4. Clean the thermostat housing and the cylinder head mating surfaces.

5. Make sure that the thermostat jiggle pin is aligned with the gasket projection.

6. Install the thermostat to the housing. Align the gasket projection with the opening in the housing. The spring side of the thermostat should face into the housing.

7. Install the thermostat housing cover and tighten both bolts to 14-19 ft. lbs. (19-25 Nm).

8. Fill the cooling system. Connect the negative battery cable, start the engine and check for leaks. Check the coolant level and add coolant, as necessary.

Intake Manifold

REMOVAL & INSTALLATION

✳✳CAUTION

When draining the coolant, keep in mind that cats and dogs are attracted by the ethylene glycol antifreeze, and are quite likely to drink any that is left in an uncovered container or in puddles on the ground. This will prove fatal in sufficient quantity. Always drain the coolant into a sealable container. Coolant should be reused unless it is contaminated or several years old.

1.6L, 1.8L, 2.0L and 2.2L Engines

▸ **See Figures 47, 48 and 49**

1. Properly relieve the fuel system pressure. Disconnect the negative battery cable and drain the cooling system.

2. Disconnect the air intake hose from the throttle body. Remove the hose and air cleaner assembly if necessary.

3. Disconnect the accelerator cable. Disconnect and plug the fuel lines.

4. Label and disconnect all necessary vacuum hoses and electrical connectors. Disconnect the coolant hoses.

5. Disconnect the EGR tube, if equipped.

6. On Miata, remove the air valve and remove the fuel rail attaching bolts.

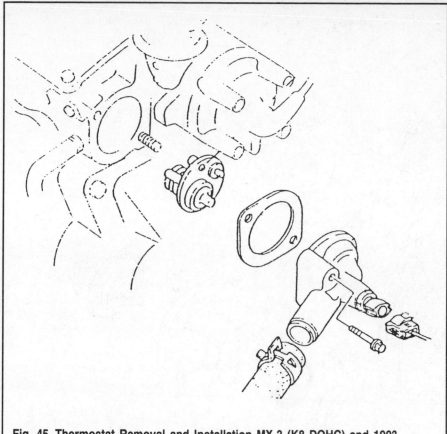

Fig. 45 Thermostat Removal and Installation MX-3 (K8 DOHC) and 1993 626/MX-6 with KL engine

Remove the fuel rail and injectors as an assembly.

7. Remove the intake manifold support bracket. If necessary, remove the bolt retaining the dipstick tube bracket to the intake manifold.

8. Remove the intake manifold-to-cylinder bolts/nuts and remove the intake manifold assembly.

9. If necessary, remove the throttle body and separate the intake manifold upper and lower halves.

To install:

10. Clean all gasket mating surfaces.

11. If separated, connect the upper and lower intake manifolds using a new gasket. Tighten the nuts/bolts to 19 ft. lbs. (25 Nm). If removed, install the throttle body using a new gasket. Tighten the retaining nuts/bolts to 19 ft. lbs. (25 Nm).

12. Install the intake manifold assembly to the cylinder head using a new gasket. Tighten the nuts/bolts to 19 ft. lbs. (25 Nm) on all except 2.2L engine. On 2.2L engine, tighten to 22 ft. lbs. (30 Nm).

➡**On all except Miata 1.6L engine and MX-6/626 2.2L engine, torque the intake manifol-to-cylinder head bolts in the proper sequence. On Miata 1.6L**

engine and MX-6/626 2.2L engine, tighten the bolts in the center of the manifold first and works outward toward the ends.

13. If equipped, install the bolt retaining the dipstick tube to the Intake manifold. Install the intake manifold bracket. Tighten the attaching nuts/bolts to 38 ft. lbs. (52 Nm) on all except 323, Protege and MX-3. On 323, Protege and MX-3, tighten the attaching nuts/bolts to 19 ft. lbs. (25 Nm).

14. On Miata, install the fuel rail and injector assembly on the intake manifold using new insulators. Tighten the fuel rail mounting bolts to 19 ft. lbs. (25 Nm). Install the air valve and tighten the bolts to 57 inch lbs. (5.5 Nm).

15. Connect the EGR tube, if equipped. Connect the coolant and vacuum hoses, electrical connectors and fuel lines.

16. Connect the accelerator cable. Install the air cleaner assembly, if removed, and connect the air intake tube to the throttle body.

17. Connect the negative battery cable. Fill and bleed the cooling system.

18. Start the engine and bring to normal operating temperature. Check for leaks. Check the idle speed.

MX-3 1.8L and MX-6/626 2.5L Engines
▶ **See Figures 50 and 51**

1. Properly relieve the fuel system pressure.

2. Disconnect the negative battery cable and drain the cooling system.

3. On MX-3, remove the upper strut bar.

4. Remove the air cleaner assembly and ducts.

5. Disconnect the accelerator cable. Label and disconnect the necessary electrical connectors and vacuum hoses.

6. Disconnect and plug the fuel lines. Disconnect the coolant hose from the air bypass valve.

7. Remove the intake manifold support bracket. Remove the intake manifold-to-cylinder head bolts and remove the intake manifold.

8. If necessary, remove the throttle body and air intake pipe from the manifold.

9. Check the intake manifold for cracks or other damage. Check the surface of the cylinder heads and intake manifold for warpage using a straightedge. Replace the intake manifold, as necessary.

To install:

10. Clean all gasket mating surfaces.

11. If removed, install the throttle body using new gaskets. Tighten the nuts/bolts to 19 ft. lbs. (25 Nm).

12. If removed, apply clean engine oil to new O-rings and install the air intake pipe to the intake manifold. Tighten the bolts to 95 inch lbs. (10.8 Nm). On 1.8L engine, the bolts must be tightened in the proper sequence.

13. Position new gaskets and install the intake manifold to the cylinder head. Install the mounting bolts and tighten, in 2-3 steps, to 19 ft. lbs. (25 Nm), working from the center toward the ends of the manifold.

14. Install the intake manifold bracket and tighten the bolts to 19 ft. lbs. (25 Nm).

15. Connect the coolant hose to the air bypass valve. Connect the fuel lines.

16. Connect the vacuum hoses and electrical connectors. Connect the accelerator cable.

17. Install the air cleaner assembly and ducts. On MX-3, install the upper strut bar.

18. Connect the negative battery cable. Fill and bleed the cooling system.

19. Start the engine and bring to normal operating temperature. Check for leaks. Check the idle speed.

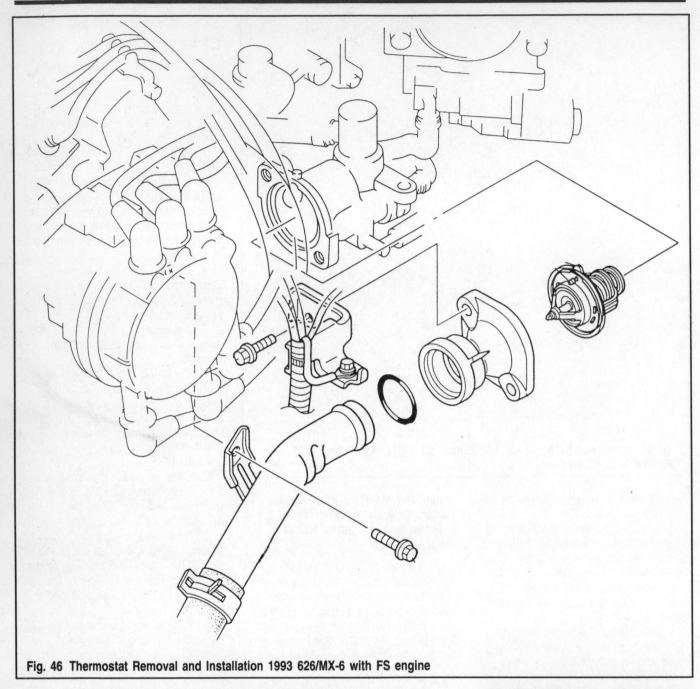

Fig. 46 Thermostat Removal and Installation 1993 626/MX-6 with FS engine

Fig. 47 BP SOHC and B6 SOHC engine intake manifold assembly

Exhaust Manifold

REMOVAL & INSTALLATION

1. Disconnect the negative battery cable.

2. Remove the retaining bolts and remove the exhaust manifold insulator.

3. Disconnect the oxygen sensor electrical connector. Remove the oxygen sensor, if necessary, if it is installed in the manifold.

4. Disconnect the EGR pipe, if equipped.

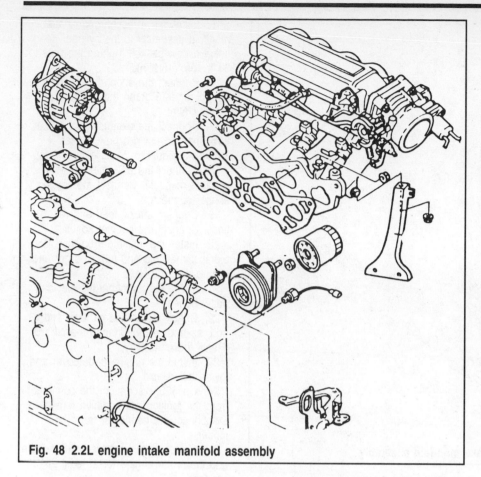

Fig. 48 2.2L engine intake manifold assembly

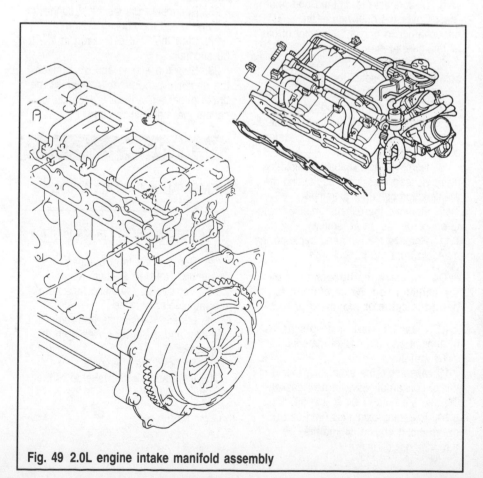

Fig. 49 2.0L engine intake manifold assembly

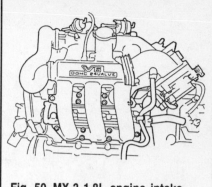

Fig. 50 MX-3 1.8L engine intake manifold assembly

5. Raise and safely support the vehicle. Remove the nuts from the exhaust pipe flange and disconnect the exhaust pipe from the manifold or turbocharger, if equipped.

6. Lower the vehicle.

7. If equipped with turbocharger, proceed as follows:

   a. Drain the cooling system.

   b. Disconnect the air hose and coolant hoses from the turbocharger.

   c. Disconnect the oil feed and return lines.

8. Remove the mounting nuts/bolts and remove the exhaust manifold. On turbocharged vehicles, the manifold and turbocharger are removed as an assembly.

9. Installation is the reverse of the removal procedure. Make sure all gasket mating surfaces are clean prior to assembly.

10. Use new gaskets and tighten the exhaust manifold-to-cylinder head nuts/bolts to 17 ft. lbs. (23 Nm) on 1.6L and 1.8L SOHC engines, 34 ft. lbs. (46 Nm) on 1.6L and 1.8L DOHC 4-cylinder engines and 2.2L engine, or 19 ft. lbs. (25 Nm) on 1.8L and 2.5L 6 cylinder engines. On 2.0L engine, tighten the nuts to 20 ft. lbs. (26 Nm) and the bolts to 16 ft. lbs. (22 Nm).

11. Use a new gasket and tighten the exhaust pipe flange-to-exhaust manifold nuts to 34 ft. lbs. (46 Nm).

Turbocharger

REMOVAL & INSTALLATION

▶ See Figure 52

Before starting the following procedure, clean the area around the turbocharger assembly with a non-caustic solution. After the turbocharger is removed, cover

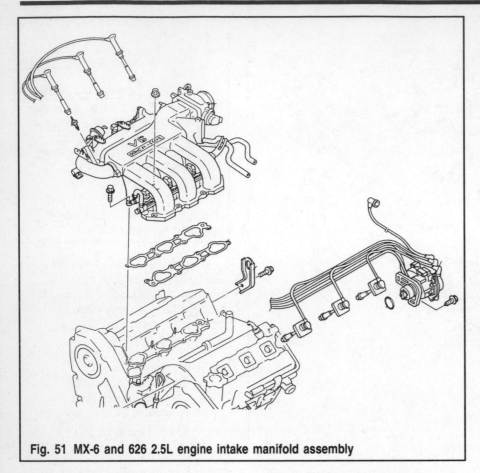

Fig. 51 MX-6 and 626 2.5L engine intake manifold assembly

the openings to prevent the entry of foreign material while it is off the engine.

During removal, be careful not to bend, nick, or in any way damage the compressor wheel blades. Damage may result in rotating assembly imbalance, and bearing and oil seal failure. Any time a turbocharger assembly has been removed, gently spin the turbine wheel before reassembly to ensure the rotating assembly does not bind.

Any time an engine bearing (main bearing, connecting rod bearing, camshaft bearing) has been damaged in a turbocharged engine, the oil and filter should be changed and the turbocharger flushed with clean engine oil to reduce the possibility of contamination.

1. Disconnect the negative battery cable.

2. Raise and safely support the vehicle. Remove the engine undercover and drain the cooling system.

3. Remove the inlet and outlet hoses from the turbocharger. Cover the turbocharger openings with clean rags to prevent the entry of dirt or foreign material.

4. Remove the retaining bolts and remove the insulator covers from the exhaust manifold and turbocharger.

5. Disconnect the coolant hoses.

6. Disconnect the oil feed and return lines. Cover the openings in the turbocharger to prevent the entry of dirt or foreign material.

7. Disconnect the oxygen sensor connector. Disconnect the EGR pipe from the exhaust manifold.

8. Remove the nuts and disconnect the exhaust pipe from the turbocharger. Remove the bolt from the turbocharger support bracket.

9. Remove the exhaust manifold-to-cylinder head nuts while supporting the manifold/turbocharger assembly.

10. Remove the exhaust manifold and turbocharger as an assembly.

11. Remove the nuts and separate the manifold from the turbocharger.

➡**Do not carry the turbocharger by the actuator rod. Be careful not to bend the actuator mounting or rod.**

12. Clean all gasket mating surfaces of sealant and old gasket material.

To install:

13. Assemble the exhaust manifold to the turbocharger, using a new gasket. Tighten the nuts to 34 ft. lbs. (46 Nm).

14. Pour approximately 0.85 oz. (25 ml) of clean engine oil into the turbocharger oil inlet.

15. Install the turbocharger/exhaust manifold assembly to the cylinder head, using a new gasket. Tighten the nuts to 34 ft. lbs. (46 Nm).

16. Connect the support bracket to the turbocharger. Tighten the bolt to 30 ft. lbs. (41 Nm).

17. Connect the exhaust pipe to the turbocharger, using a new gasket. Tighten the nuts to 34 ft. lbs. (46 Nm).

18. Connect the EGR pipe to the exhaust manifold. Connect the oxygen sensor connector.

19. Connect the oil feed and return lines. Connect the coolant hoses.

20. Install the insulators on the exhaust manifold and turbocharger and secure with the bolts.

21. Install the turbocharger inlet and outlet hoses.

22. Check the engine oil level and add, as necessary. Change the oil and filter if the oil is dirty.

23. Install the engine undercover and lower the vehicle.

24. On 323, disconnect the connector from the ignition coil negative terminal. Disconnect the connector from the igniter.

25. Connect the negative battery cable and crank the engine for at least 20 seconds.

26. Reconnect the electrical connector. Fill and bleed the cooling system.

27. Start the engine and run at idle for 30 seconds.

28. Stop the engine and disconnect the negative battery cable. Depress the brake pedal for at least 5 seconds to cancel the malfunction code.

Intercooler

REMOVAL & INSTALLATION

1. Remove the front fascia from the vehicle.

2. Remove the front bumper assembly. Refer to Section 10.

3. Remove all mounting nuts from the intercooler housing.

4. Loosen the clamps and remove the inlet and outlet air hoses from the intercooler.

5. Remove the intercooler.

6. Installation is the reverse of the removal procedure.

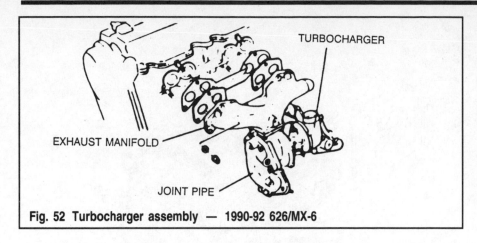

Fig. 52 Turbocharger assembly — 1990-92 626/MX-6

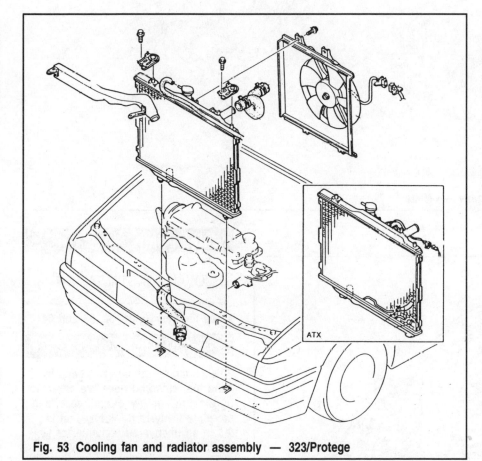

Fig. 53 Cooling fan and radiator assembly — 323/Protege

Radiator

REMOVAL & INSTALLATION

▶ See Figures 53, 54, 55, 56, 57, 58 and 59

1. Disconnect the negative battery cable.
2. Remove the engine under cover, if equipped and drain the cooling system.
3. Remove the necessary air ducts.
4. Disconnect the electric cooling fan connector and, if equipped, temperature sensor connector.
5. Disconnect the coolant reservoir and upper and lower radiator hoses. If equipped with automatic transaxle or transmission, disconnect the oil cooler lines and plug the hoses.
6. On all except MX-3 and Miata, remove the upper radiator mounting brackets. On MX-3, remove the upper shroud panel.

7. Lift the radiator/cooling fan(s) assembly from the vehicle. On Miata, support the radiator and remove the mounting bolts. Remove the radiator/cooling fans assembly.
8. If necessary, remove the cooling fan(s)/shroud assembly from the radiator.
To install:
9. If removed, install the fan and shroud assembly. Tighten the mounting bolts to 61-87 inch lbs. (7-10 Nm).
10. Install the radiator, making sure the lower tank engages the insulators.
11. Install the upper radiator insulators and tighten the retaining bolts to 69-95 inch lbs. (8-11 Nm).
12. Unplug and connect the cooler lines, if required.
13. Reattach the wiring harness to the routing clips and install the upper and lower radiator hoses to the radiator.
14. Connect the overflow tube to the radiator and connect the cooling fan wiring connectors.
15. Close the radiator drain valve and fill the system with coolant. Install the pressure cap to the first stop only.
16. Connect the negative battery cable. Start the engine and run it at fast idle until the upper radiator hose feels warm, indicating the thermostat has opened and coolant is flowing throughout the system.
17. Stop the engine. Carefully remove the radiator cap and top off the radiator with coolant, if required.
18. Install the radiator cap securely and fill the coolant reservoir to the FULL mark.
19. Run the engine and check for leaks.

Electric Cooling Fan

REMOVAL & INSTALLATION

1. Disconnect the negative battery cable and drain the cooling system.
2. Remove the radiator.
3. Remove the shroud mounting bolts and remove the shroud from the radiator.
4. Remove the mounting nut and remove the fan from the fan motor.
5. Remove the mounting bolts and remove the fan motor from the shroud.
6. Installation is the reverse of the removal procedure.

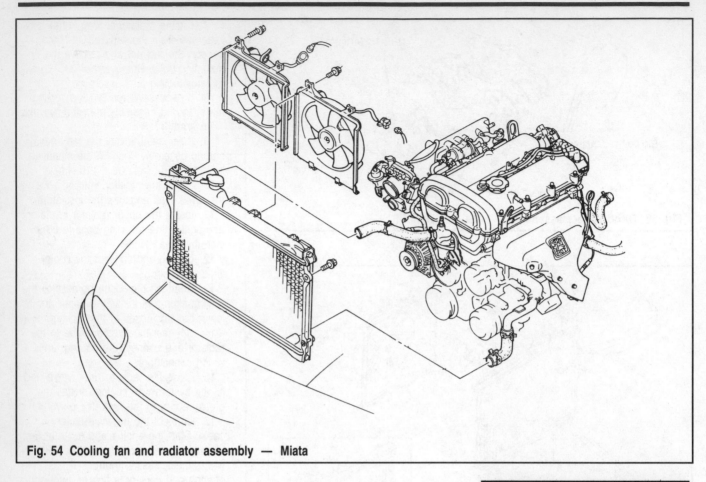

Fig. 54 Cooling fan and radiator assembly — Miata

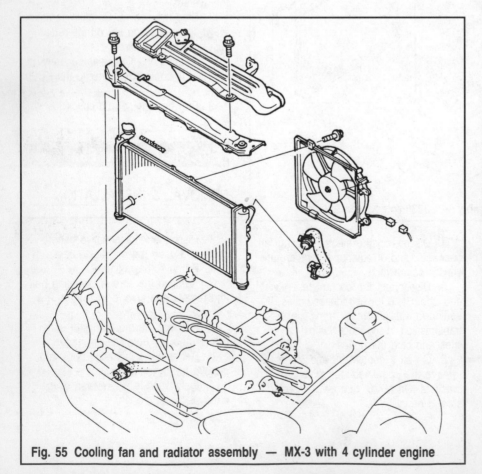

Fig. 55 Cooling fan and radiator assembly — MX-3 with 4 cylinder engine

Water Pump

REMOVAL & INSTALLATION

▶ See Figures 60, 61, 62, 63 and 64

✷✷CAUTION

When draining the coolant, keep in mind that cats and dogs are attracted by the ethylene glycol antifreeze, and are quite likely to drink any that is left in an uncovered container or in puddles on the ground. This will prove fatal in sufficient quantity. Always drain the coolant into a sealable container. Coolant should be reused unless it is contaminated or several years old.

1. Disconnect the negative battery cable. Drain the cooling system.
2. Remove the timing belt covers and remove the timing belt.
3. On Miata, remove the power steering pump and position aside, without disconnecting the hoses.
4. On 1.6L and 1.8L 4-cylinder engines, disconnect the coolant bypass pipe and remove the coolant inlet pipe from the water pump.

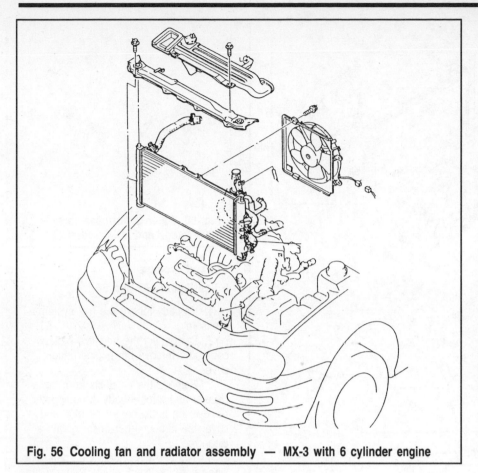

Fig. 56 Cooling fan and radiator assembly — MX-3 with 6 cylinder engine

Fig. 57 Cooling fan and radiator assembly — 1990-92 626/MX-6

5. On 2.0L engine, remove the power steering pump belt adjuster.

6. On 1.8L and 2.5L 6-cylinder engines, remove the right side engine mount bracket.

7. Remove any timing belt idler pulley(s) still attached to the water pump.

8. Remove the water pump mounting bolts and remove the water pump.

To install:

9. Clean all gasket mating surfaces.

10. If equipped, install new rubber seal(s) on the water pump.

11. Using a new gasket, install the water pump on the engine. Tighten the mounting bolts to 19 ft. lbs. (25 Nm).

12. Install any timing belt idler pulleys that were removed and tighten the bolt(s) to 38 ft. lbs. (52 Nm).

13. On 1.8L and 2.5L engines, install the engine mount bracket and tighten the bolts to 44 ft. lbs. (60 Nm).

14. On 2.0L engine, install the power steering pump adjuster and tighten the bolts to 16 ft. lbs. (22 Nm).

15. On 1.6L and 1.8L engines, install the coolant inlet pipe, using a new gasket. Tighten the bolts to 19 ft. lbs. (25 Nm). Connect the coolant bypass pipe using a new O-ring.

16. On Miata, install the power steering pump and tighten the bolts to 40 ft. lbs. (54 Nm).

17. Install the timing belt and the timing belt covers.

18. Fill the cooling system. Connect the negative battery cable, start the engine and bring to normal operating temperature. Check for leaks.

Cylinder Head

REMOVAL & INSTALLATION

✳✳CAUTION

When draining the coolant, keep in mind that cats and dogs are attracted by the ethylene glycol antifreeze, and are quite likely to drink any that is left in an uncovered container or in puddles on the ground. This will prove fatal in sufficient quantity. Always drain the coolant into a sealable container. Coolant should be reused unless it is contaminated or several years old.

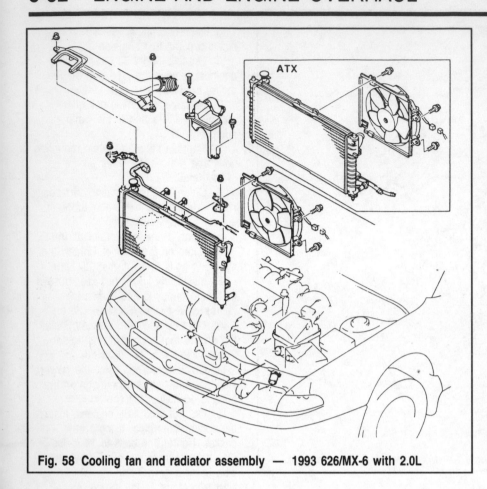

Fig. 58 Cooling fan and radiator assembly — 1993 626/MX-6 with 2.0L

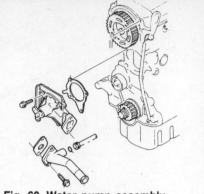

Fig. 60 Water pump assembly — 323/Protege and MX-3 with 1.6L

323 and Protege
◗ See Figures 65 and 66

1. Properly relieve the fuel system pressure.

2. Disconnect the negative battery cable and remove the engine under cover.

3. Remove the air ducts from the air cleaner and throttle body. If equipped, remove the turbocharger air pipe and cover the turbocharger opening with a clean rag.

4. Tag and disconnect the spark plug wires from the spark plugs. Remove the spark plugs and the distributor cap and wires assembly. Remove the distributor.

5. Drain the cooling system and disconnect the radiator and heater hoses. On turbocharged engines, remove the radiator/cooling fan assembly.

6. Disconnect the exhaust pipe and remove the exhaust manifold. On turbocharged engines, disconnect the turbocharger oil line and remove the manifold and the turbocharger as an assembly.

7. On DOHC engines, remove the coolant bypass pipe.

8. Disconnect the accelerator cable.

9. Label and disconnect all necessary electrical connections and vacuum hoses. Disconnect the fuel lines.

10. Remove the intake manifold bracket and the intake manifold.

11. Remove the cylinder head cover bolts and the cylinder head cover.

12. Remove the timing belt cover(s). Rotate the crankshaft, in the normal direction of rotation, until the No. 1 cylinder piston is at TDC on the compression stroke. Make sure the timing marks on the crankshaft and camshaft sprocket(s) are properly aligned and mark the direction of rotation of the belt.

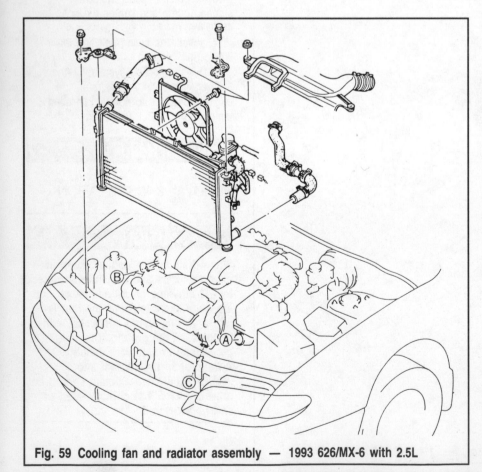

Fig. 59 Cooling fan and radiator assembly — 1993 626/MX-6 with 2.5L

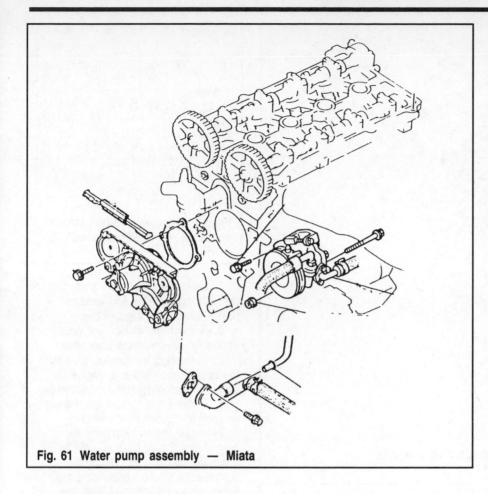

Fig. 61 Water pump assembly — Miata

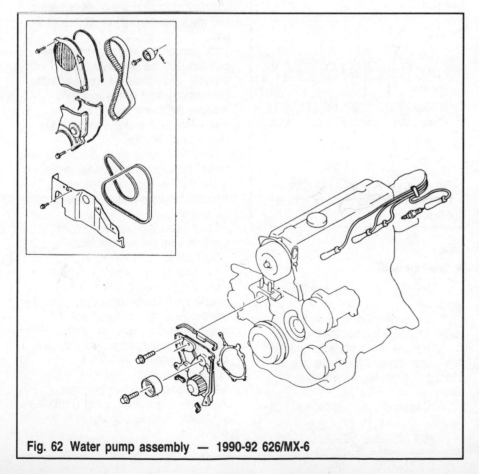

Fig. 62 Water pump assembly — 1990-92 626/MX-6

13. Loosen the timing belt tensioner and remove the belt. Do not rotate the crankshaft until the timing belt is reinstalled.

14. When everything is disconnected, loosen the cylinder head bolts in the reverse of the tightening sequence. Remove the bolts and lift the head off the engine.

To install:

15. Thoroughly, clean the cylinder head and the block contact surfaces. Examine the head gasket and check the cylinder head for cracks. Check the cylinder head for warpage using a feeler gauge and straightedge. The maximum allowable distortion is 0.006 in. (0.15mm) on 1.6L engine or 0.004 in. (0.10mm) on 1.8L engine.

16. Clean the cylinder head bolts and the threads in the block. Make sure the bolts turn freely in the block.

17. Install a new head gasket on the engine block. Make sure the camshaft sprocket timing marks are still aligned, as set during the removal procedure. Install the cylinder head.

18. Lubricate the bolt threads and seat surfaces with clean engine oil and install them. Torque the bolts in 2-3 steps to 56-60 ft. lbs. (75-81 Nm) in the proper sequence.

19. Make sure the crankshaft and camshaft sprocket timing marks are aligned, install the timing belt and set the tension. Carefully rotate the crankshaft 2 turns to make sure the timing marks still line up.

20. Apply a thin bead of sealant to the cylinder head cover and install the new gasket. Install the cover and torque the cover bolts to 78 inch lbs. (9 Nm).

21. Install the timing belt cover(s) and tighten the bolts to 95 inch lbs. (11 Nm).

22. Use new gaskets and install the manifolds. Torque the intake manifold bolts/nuts to 19 ft. lbs. (25 Nm) and install the intake manifold bracket. Torque the SOHC engine exhaust manifold bolts to 17 ft. lbs. (23 Nm). On DOHC engines, torque the exhaust manifold nuts to 34 ft. lbs. (46 Nm).

23. On turbocharged engines, connect the turbocharger oil line and install the turbocharger bracket.

24. Use a new gasket to connect the exhaust pipe and torque the nuts to 34 ft. lbs. (46 Nm).

25. If removed, install the radiator and connect all cooling system hoses. On DOHC engines, install the coolant bypass pipe.

26. Install the distributor, spark plugs, distributor cap and wires.

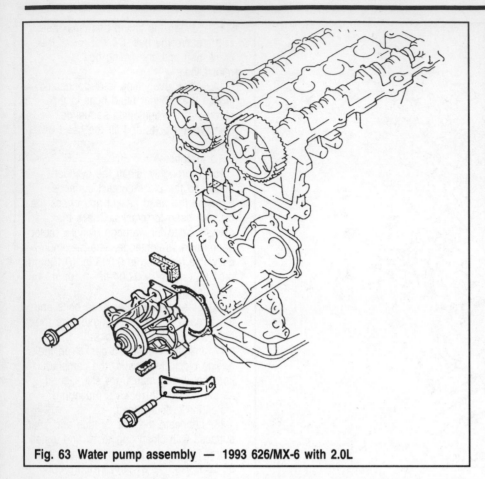

Fig. 63 Water pump assembly — 1993 626/MX-6 with 2.0L

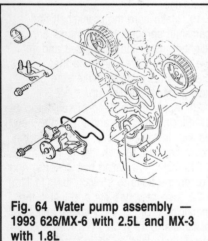

Fig. 64 Water pump assembly — 1993 626/MX-6 with 2.5L and MX-3 with 1.8L

27. Connect all vacuum and fuel system hoses and connect all wiring.

28. Connect the accelerator cable and install the air ducts and engine undercover.

29. Connect the negative battery cable. Fill and bleed the cooling system. Change the engine oil.

30. Start the engine and bring to normal operating temperature. Check for leaks. Check the ignition timing and idle speed.

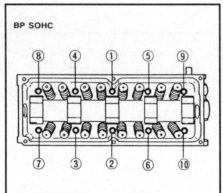

Fig. 65 Cylinder head bolt torque sequence — 323/Protege with BP SOHC

Miata

▶ See Figure 67

1. Properly relieve the fuel system pressure.

2. Disconnect the negative battery cable and drain the cooling system.

3. Remove the air cleaner and air flow meter assembly and the inlet air ducting. Disconnect the accelerator cable.

4. Disconnect the radiator and heater hoses.

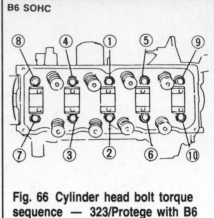

Fig. 66 Cylinder head bolt torque sequence — 323/Protege with B6 SOHC

5. Label and disconnect all necessary electrical connections and vacuum hoses. Disconnect the fuel lines.

6. Remove the ignition coil pack assembly with the spark plug wires.

7. Disconnect the exhaust pipe from the exhaust manifold and remove the exhaust manifold from the cylinder head.

8. Remove the cylinder head cover and the timing belt front covers.

9. Rotate the crankshaft, in the normal direction of rotation, until the No. 1 cylinder piston is at TDC on the compression stroke. Make sure the timing marks on the crankshaft and camshaft sprockets are properly aligned and mark the direction of rotation of the belt.

10. Loosen the timing belt tensioner lock bolt. Pry the tensioner outward with a prybar and tighten the lock bolt with the tensioner spring fully extended. Remove the timing belt.

11. Remove the intake manifold-to-engine block bracket.

12. When everything is disconnected, loosen the cylinder head bolts in the reverse of the tightening sequence. Remove the bolts and lift the head off the engine.

13. If necessary, remove the intake manifold from the cylinder head.

To install:

14. Thoroughly, clean the cylinder head and the block contact surfaces. Examine the head gasket and check the cylinder head for cracks. Check the cylinder head for warpage using a feeler gauge and straightedge. The maximum allowable distortion is 0.006 in. (0.15mm).

15. If removed, install the intake manifold using a new gasket. Tighten the intake manifold bolts to 19 ft. lbs. (25 Nm).

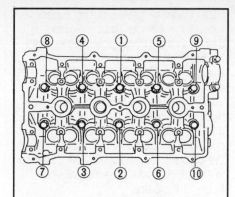

Fig. 67 Cylinder head bolt torque sequence — Miata

16. Clean the cylinder head bolts and the threads in the block. Make sure the bolts turn freely in the block.

17. Install a new head gasket on the engine block. Make sure the camshaft sprocket timing marks are still aligned, as set during the removal procedure. Install the cylinder head.

18. Lubricate the bolt threads and seat surfaces with clean engine oil and install them. Torque the bolts in 2-3 steps to 56-60 ft. lbs. (75-81 Nm) in the proper sequence.

19. Make sure the crankshaft and camshaft sprocket timing marks are aligned, install the timing belt and set the tension. Carefully rotate the crankshaft 2 turns to make sure the timing marks still line up. Install the timing belt covers.

20. Apply a thin bead of sealant to the cylinder head cover and install the new gasket. Install the cover and torque the cover bolts to 78 inch lbs. (9 Nm).

21. Using a new gasket, install the exhaust manifold and torque the nuts to 34 ft. lbs. (46 Nm). Install a new flange gasket and torque the nuts to 34 ft. lbs. (45 Nm).

22. Install the intake manifold-to-engine block bracket.

23. Install all cooling system hoses.

24. Install the ignition coil pack and spark plugs.

25. Connect all wiring and vacuum hoses. Connect the fuel lines.

26. Connect the accelerator cable. Install the air cleaner/air flow meter assembly and the air ducts.

27. Connect the negative battery cable. Fill and bleed the cooling system. Change the engine oil.

28. Start the engine and bring to normal operating temperature. Check for leaks. Check the ignition timing and idle speed.

MX-3

1.6L ENGINE

▶ See Figure 68

1. Properly relieve the fuel system pressure.

2. Disconnect the negative battery cable. Remove the engine undercover and drain the cooling system.

3. Remove the air ducts from the air cleaner and throttle body. Disconnect the accelerator and, if equipped, throttle valve cables.

4. Label and disconnect the necessary wiring, vacuum hoses and coolant hoses. Disconnect the fuel lines.

5. Remove the nut from the water bypass pipe bracket and remove the bracket from the stud.

6. Remove the accessory drive belts and the water pump pulley.

7. Remove the cylinder head and timing belt covers. Remove the crankshaft pulley.

8. Rotate the crankshaft, in the normal direction of rotation, until the No. 1 cylinder piston is at TDC on the compression stroke. Make sure the timing marks on the crankshaft and camshaft sprockets are properly aligned and mark the direction of rotation of the belt.

9. Loosen the timing belt tensioner lock bolt. Pry the tensioner outward with a prybar and tighten the lock bolt with the tensioner spring fully extended. Remove the timing belt.

10. Disconnect the xhaust pipe from the exhaust manifold. Remove the intake manifold-to-cylinder head bracket.

11. Loosen the cylinder head bolts in the reverse order of the tightening sequence. Remove the cylinder head.

12. If necessary, remove the intake and exhaust manifolds from the cylinder head.

13. Clean all gasket mating surfaces. Inspect the cylinder head for cracks or other damage. Check the cylinder head for warpage using a feeler gauge and straightedge. The maximum allowable distortion is 0.006 in. (0.15mm).

14. Clean the cylinder head bolts and the threads in the block. Make sure the bolts turn freely in the block.

To install:

15. If removed, install the intake and exhaust manifolds using new gaskets. Tighten the intake manifold bolts/nuts to 19 ft. lbs. (25 Nm) and the exhaust manifold bolts/nuts to 34 ft. lbs. (46 Nm).

16. Install a new head gasket on the engine block. Make sure the camshaft

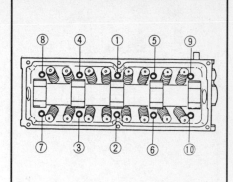

Fig. 68 Cylinder head bolt torque sequence — MX-3 with 1.6L

sprocket timing marks are still aligned, as set during the removal procedure. Install the cylinder head.

17. Lubricate the cylinder head bolt threads and seat surfaces with clean engine oil and install them. Torque the bolts in 2-3 steps to 56-60 ft. lbs. (75-81 Nm) in the proper sequence.

18. Make sure the crankshaft and camshaft sprocket timing marks are aligned, install the timing belt and set the tension. Carefully rotate the crankshaft 2 turns to make sure the timing marks still line up. Install the timing belt covers.

19. Apply a thin bead of sealant to the cylinder head cover and install the new gasket. Install the cover and torque the cover bolts to 78 inch lbs. (9 Nm).

20. Install the crankshaft pulley and tighten the bolt to 123 ft. lbs. (167 Nm). Install the water pump pulley and accessory drive belts.

21. Install the water bypass pipe bracket over the stud and install the nut. Tighten to 17 ft. lbs. (23 Nm).

22. Connect the electrical connectors, vacuum and coolant hoses, and the fuel lines.

23. Connect the accelerator and, if equipped, throttle valve cables.

24. Install the air ducts and the engine undercover.

25. Connect the negative battery cable. Fill and bleed the cooling system. Change the engine oil.

26. Start the engine and bring to normal operating temperature. Check for leaks. Check the ignition timing and idle speed.

1.8L ENGINE

▶ See Figures 69, 70, 71 and 72

1. Properly relieve the fuel system pressure.

2. Disconnect the negative battery cable and drain the cooling system.

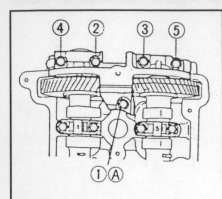

Fig. 69 Front camshaft cap bolt loosening sequence — MX-3 with 1.8L engine and 626/MX-6 with 2.5L engine

3. Remove the timing belt, then reinstall the right side engine mount to support the engine.

4. Remove the air cleaner assembly and air ducts. Remove the battery tray and battery.

5. Disconnect the accelerator and, if equipped, throttle valve cables.

6. Label and disconnect the spark plug wires, then remove the wires with the distributor cap. Disconnect the distributor electrical connector, remove the retaining bolts and remove the distributor.

7. Label and disconnect the necessary electrical connectors, vacuum hoses and coolant hoses. Disconnect and plug the fuel lines.

8. Remove the intake manifold stay. Remove the intake manifold bolts in 2-3 steps and remove the intake manifold.

9. If removing the left (front) cylinder head, disconnect the ventilation pipe from the cylinder head cover. Remove the cylinder head cover retaining bolts and remove the cylinder head cover.

10. Use a suitable wrench to hold the camshaft and remove the camshaft sprocket bolt. The wrench fits on a hexagon that is cast into the camshaft. Remove the camshaft sprocket.

11. Install engine support tool 49 G017 5A0 and support the engine. Remove the right side engine mount.

12. Remove the seal plate and water outlet from the front of the engine. Remove the engine lifting eyes.

13. Disconnect the exhaust pipe from the exhaust manifolds.

14. Turn the camshaft, using a wrench on the cast hexagon, until the camshaft

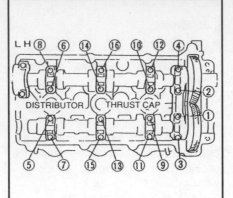

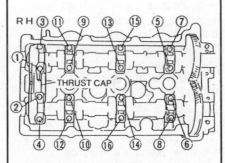

Fig. 70 Camshaft cap bolt loosening sequence — MX-3 with 1.8L engine and 626/MX-6 with 2.5L engine

knock pin aligns with the cylinder head marks.

➡**Do not remove the camshaft caps when the camshaft lobe is pressing the hydraulic lash adjuster, as this may damage the thrust journal support of the cylinder head.**

15. Loosen the front camshaft cap bolts over 5-6 steps in the proper sequence. Bolt **A** is only on the right cylinder head.

16. Loosen the remaining camshaft cap bolts in 5-6 steps in the proper sequence. Mark the position of the camshaft caps so they can be reinstalled in their original positions. Remove the thrust cap last.

17. If removing the left (front) cylinder head, remove the alternator bracket.

18. Temporarily install the right side engine mount and remove the engine support tool.

19. Loosen the cylinder head bolts in 2-3 steps in the reverse order of the tightening sequence. Remove the cylinder head bolts and the cylinder head.

20. If necessary, remove the exhaust manifold.

21. Clean all gasket mating surfaces. Inspect the cylinder head for cracks or other damage. Check the cylinder head for warpage using a feeler gauge and straightedge. The maximum allowable distortion is 0.004 in. (0.10mm).

22. Measure the length of the cylinder head bolts; replace the bolt if it exceeds 5.31 in. (135mm) from just under the bolt head to the tip of the threads. Clean the cylinder head bolts and the threads in the block. Make sure the bolts turn freely in the block.

To install:

23. If removed, install the exhaust manifold using a new gasket and tighten the bolts/nuts to 19 ft. lbs. (25 Nm).

24. Measure the height of the oil control plug from the cylinder block deck; it should be 0.315-0.354 in. (8-9mm). If not within specification, remove the oil control plug and tap in a new one, to the specified height. Apply clean engine oil to a new O-ring and install on the plug.

25. Install a new cylinder head gasket. On the left bank, the **L** mark on the gasket should be facing up. On the right bank, the **R** mark should be facing up. Be careful not to damage the oil control plug O-ring.

26. Position the cylinder head on the block. Lubricate the cylinder head bolt threads and seat faces with clean engine oil and install them with the washers. Tighten the bolts as follows:

  a. Tighten the bolts in 2-3 steps to 19 ft. lbs. (26 Nm).

  b. Put a paint mark on each bolt head.

  c. Using the paint marks for reference, turn each bolt 90 degrees, in sequence.

  d. Using the paint marks for reference, turn each bolt an additional 90 degrees, in sequence.

27. Install the engine support tool and remove the right side engine mount.

28. Lubricate the camshaft lobes, journals and gears with clean engine oil. Align the camshaft gear timing marks and install the camshafts in the cylinder head.

➡**The thrust plate positions for the right and left cylinder head camshafts are different.**

29. Make sure the camshaft cap and cylinder head surfaces are clean. Apply a small amount of sealant to the mating surface of the front camshaft cap on both cylinder heads and the rear exhaust camshaft cap on the left cylinder head.

Do not get any sealant on the camshaft rotating surfaces.

30. Install the front camshaft caps and thrust plate caps and tighten the bolts until the cap seats fully to the cylinder head. Install the remaining camshaft caps in their original locations and loosely tighten the bolts.

31. Tighten the camshaft cap bolts in 5-6 steps to 126 inch lbs. (14 Nm), in the proper sequence.

32. Apply clean engine oil to a new oil seal and the cylinder head. Install the seal, using a suitable installer. Apply sealant to a new blind cap and install, using a plastic hammer.

33. Install the engine lifting eyes and the alternator bracket. Install the seal plate and water outlet. Using new gaskets, connect the exhaust pipe to the exhaust manifolds and tighten the nuts to 41 ft. lbs. (55 Nm).

34. Temporarily install the right side engine mount and remove the engine support tool.

35. Install the camshaft sprockets. On the right cylinder head, install the sprocket so the R mark can be seen and the timing mark aligns with the camshaft knock pin. On the left cylinder head, install the sprocket so the L mark can be seen and the timing mark aligns with the camshaft knock pin.

36. Apply clean engine oil to the camshaft sprocket bolt threads and install. Hold the camshaft with a wrench on the cast hexagon and tighten the sprocket bolt to 103 ft. lbs. (140 Nm).

37. Coat a new gasket with sealant and install onto the cylinder head cover. Install the cover and tighten the bolts, in sequence, in 2-3 steps, to 78 inch lbs. (8.8 Nm). Install the ventilation pipe to the left cover.

38. Apply clean engine oil to a new O-ring and install on the distributor. Install the distributor with the blade fitting into the camshaft groove and loosely tighten the retaining bolt.

39. Install the intake manifold using a new gasket. Loosely install the bolts and nuts. Install the intake manifold stay and tighten the bolts to 19 ft. lbs. (25 Nm), then tighten the intake manifold bolts/nuts, in 2-3 steps, to 19 ft. lbs. (25 Nm).

40. Connect the wiring, vacuum and heater hoses, and the fuel lines.

41. Connect the accelerator and, if equipped, throttle valve cables.

42. Install the battery tray and the battery. Install the air cleaner assembly and the ducts.

43. Install the timing belt.

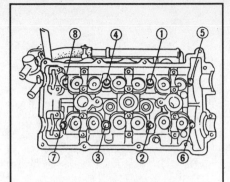

Fig. 71 Cylinder head bolt torque sequence — MX-3 1.8L engine and 626/MX-6 2.5L engine

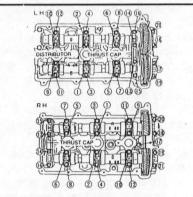

Fig. 72 Camshaft cap bolt torque sequence MX-3 1.8L engine and 626/MX-6 2.5L engine

44. Connect the negative battery cable. Fill and bleed the cooling system. Change the engine oil.

45. Start the engine and bring to normal operating temperature. Check for leaks. Check the ignition timing and idle speed.

626 and MX-6

2.0L ENGINE

▶ See Figure 73

1. Properly relieve the fuel system pressure. Disconnect the negative battery cable.

2. Mark the position of the hood on the hinges and remove the hood.

3. Remove the engine undercover and drain the cooling system.

4. Disconnect the air flow sensor and intake air temperature connectors. Remove the air cleaner assembly and air ducts.

5. Disconnect the accelerator cable. Label and disconnect the necessary wiring, vacuum and coolant hoses, and fuel lines.

6. Remove the accessory drive belts and the water pump pulley. Remove the power steering pump pulley shield.

7. Remove the power steering pump and position aside, leaving the hoses connected.

8. Hold the crankshaft pulley using a suitable tool and remove the bolt. Remove the crankshaft pulley.

9. Disconnect the spark plug wires and remove the spark plugs.

10. Loosen the cylinder head bolt cover bolts, in 2-3 steps, in the reverse order of the tightening sequence. Remove the cylinder head cover.

11. Remove the engine oil dipstick and dipstick tube.

12. Remove the timing belt covers.

13. Support the engine using engine support tool 49 G017 5A0. Remove the right side engine mount.

14. Turn the crankshaft, in the normal direction of rotation, until the crankshaft and camshaft sprocket timing marks are aligned. Mark the direction of rotation on the belt.

15. Turn the belt tensioner clockwise and disconnect the tensioner spring from the hook pin. Remove the timing belt.

16. Remove the distributor cap and spark plug wires assembly. Disconnect the electrical connector, remove the retaining bolt and remove the distributor.

17. Hold the camshaft using a wrench on the hexagon cast into the camshaft. Remove the camshaft sprocket bolts and the sprockets.

18. Loosen the camshaft cap bolts, in 2-3 steps, in the reverse order of the tightening sequence. Mark the position of the caps so they can be reinstalled in their original positions. Remove the caps and remove the camshafts.

19. Remove the intake manifold-to-engine block bracket. Disconnect the exhaust pipe from the exhaust manifold.

20. Loosen the cylinder head bolts in the reverse order of the tightening sequence. Remove the cylinder head bolts and remove the cylinder head.

21. Remove the intake and exhaust manifolds, if necessary.

22. Clean all gasket mating surfaces. Inspect the cylinder head for cracks or other damage. Check the cylinder head for warpage using a feeler gauge and straightedge. The maximum allowable distortion is 0.004 in. (0.10mm).

23. Measure the length of the cylinder head bolts; replace the bolt if it exceeds 4.154 in. (105.5mm) from just under the bolt head to the tip of the threads. Clean the cylinder head bolts and the threads

in the block. Make sure the bolts turn freely in the block.

To install:

24. If removed, install the intake and exhaust manifolds using new gaskets. Tighten the intake manifold bolts/nuts to 18 ft. lbs. (25 Nm). Tighten the exhaust manifold nuts to 20 ft. lbs. (28 Nm) and the bolts to 16 ft. lbs. (22 Nm).

25. Position a new head gasket on the cylinder block and install the cylinder head. Lubricate the bolt threads and head seat with clean engine oil and install the bolts. Tighten the bolts as follows:

  a. Tighten the bolts, in sequence, to 16 ft. lbs. (22 Nm).

  b. Make paint marks on the bolt heads.

  c. Using the paint mark as a reference, tighten each bolt, in sequence, 90 degrees.

  d. Using the paint mark as a reference, tighten each bolt, in sequence, an additional 90 degrees.

26. Install the intake manifold bracket and tighten the bolts to 38 ft. lbs. (51 Nm). Connect the exhaust pipe to the exhaust manifold and tighten the nuts to 38 ft. lbs. (51 Nm).

27. Apply clean engine oil to the camshaft lobes and journals and install the camshafts in the cylinder head.

28. Apply silicone sealant to the cylinder head on the front camshaft caps mating surface. Do not get sealant on the camshaft journals.

29. Install the camshaft caps in their original positions. Install the cap bolts and tighten in 2-3 steps, in sequence, to 125 inch lbs. (14.2 Nm).

30. Apply clean engine oil to the lips of the new camshaft seals and install the seals with a suitable seal installer. The seals must be installed so they are flush with the edge of the camshaft caps.

31. Install the camshaft sprockets, positioning the dowels at 12 o'clock. Lubricate the sprocket bolt threads with clean engine oil and install in the camshafts. Tighten to 44 ft. lbs. (60 Nm) while holding the cast hexagon on the camshaft with a wrench.

32. Apply clean engine oil to a new O-ring and install on the distributor. Apply clean engine oil to the distributor drive gear and install the distributor in the cylinder head. Loosely tighten the mounting bolts.

33. Make sure the camshaft and crankshaft sprocket timing marks are aligned and install the timing belt. There

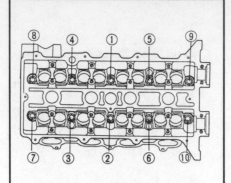

Fig. 73 Cylinder head bolt torque sequence — 626/MX-6 with 2.0L engine

should be no looseness at the idler side or between the camshaft sprockets.

34. Turn the crankshaft clockwise 2 turns and make sure the timing marks are aligned. Turn the tensioner clockwise and connect the tensioner spring to the hook pin. make sure that tension is applied to the timing belt.

35. Turn the crankshaft clockwise 2 turns and make sure the timing marks are aligned.

36. Install the right side engine mount. Tighten the mount-to-engine nuts to 86 ft. lbs. (116 Nm) and the mount through bolt to 76 ft. lbs. (102 Nm). Connect the ground harness and tighten the nut to 65 ft. lbs. (89 Nm).

37. Remove the engine support tool.

38. Install the timing belt covers, tightening the mounting bolts to 95 inch lbs. (10.7 Nm). Install the dipstick tube and dipstick.

39. Apply silicone sealer to the cylinder head cover and install a new gasket. Apply sealant to the cylinder head in the area adjacent to the front camshaft caps. Install the cylinder head cover and tighten the bolts in 2-3 steps, in sequence, to 69 inch lbs. (7.8 Nm).

40. Install the spark plugs and connect the spark plug wires.

41. Install the crankshaft pulley. Hold the pulley with a suitable tool and tighten the pulley bolt to 122 ft. lbs. (166 Nm).

42. Install the water pump pulley. Install the power steering pump and the pulley shield.

43. Install the accessory drive belts and adjust the belt tension.

44. Connect the electrical connectors, vacuum and coolant hoses, and fuel lines. Connect the accelerator cable.

45. Install the air cleaner assembly with the ducts. Connect the electrical

connectors for the air flow sensor and intake air temperature sensor.

46. Install the engine undercover. Install the hood, aligning the marks that were made during removal.

47. Connect the negative battery cable. Fill and bleed the cooling system. Change the engine oil.

48. Start the engine and bring to normal operating temperature. Check for leaks. Check the ignition timing and idle speed.

2.2L ENGINE

▶ See Figure 74

1. Properly relieve the fuel system pressure.

2. Disconnect the negative battery cable and drain the cooling system.

3. Disconnect the spark plug wires and remove the spark plugs and the distributor.

4. Disconnect the accelerator cable and if equipped, throttle valve cable.

5. Disconnect the air intake hose from the throttle body. Disconnect and plug the fuel lines.

6. Remove the upper radiator hose, water bypass hose, heater hose, oil cooler hose and brake vacuum hose. If equipped with turbocharger, disconnect the oil cooler hose.

7. Remove the 3-way solenoid and EGR solenoid valve assemblies.

8. Label and disconnect the wiring and vacuum hoses.

9. Remove the vacuum chamber and exhaust manifold shield.

10. Remove the EGR pipe, turbocharger oil pipe, if equipped, and exhaust pipe.

11. Remove the exhaust manifold. On turbocharged engines, remove the manifold and turbocharger as an assembly.

12. Remove the intake manifold bracket and the intake manifold.

13. Remove the air conditioning compressor and bracket and position the compressor aside, without disconnecting the refrigerant lines.

14. Remove the upper timing belt cover.

15. To remove the timing belt, perform the following:

  a. Rotate the crankshaft so the **1** on the camshaft sprocket is aligned with the timing mark on the front housing.

  b. When timing marks are aligned, loosen the timing belt tensioner lock bolt. Pull the tensioner outward as far as possible and temporarily tighten the lock bolt.

c. Lift the timing belt from the camshaft pulley and position it aside.

16. Remove the cylinder head cover and gasket.

17. Loosen the cylinder head bolts in the reverse of the tightening sequence, and remove the cylinder head and head gasket.

18. Thoroughly clean all gasket mating surfaces. Check the cylinder head for cracks or other damage. Check the cylinder head for warpage using a feeler gauge and straightedge. The maximum allowable distortion is 0.006 in. (0.15mm). 19.

Inspect the cylinder head bolts for damaged threads and make sure they turn freely in the threads in the block.

To install:

19. Position a new cylinder head gasket on the engine block and install the cylinder head.

20. Lubricate the bolt threads and seat surfaces with clean engine oil and install them. Torque the bolts in 2-3 steps to 59-64 ft. lbs. (80-86 Nm), in the proper sequence.

21. Apply sealant to the 4 corners of the cylinder head and install the cover with a new gasket. Torque the cover bolts to 69 inch lbs. (8 Nm).

22. Make sure the camshaft sprocket and front housing timing marks are aligned and install the timing belt. Set the tension and carefully rotate the crankshaft 2 turns to make sure the timing marks still line up. Install the timing belt cover.

23. Use a new gasket and install the intake manifold. Torque the nuts/bolts to 22 ft. lbs. (30 Nm). Install the intake manifold bracket.

24. Use new gaskets and install the exhaust manifold. Torque the nuts to 36 ft. lbs. (49 Nm). On turbocharged engines, connect the turbocharger oil line.

25. Connect the exhaust pipe with a new gasket and torque the nuts to 34 ft. lbs. (46 Nm).

26. Install the EGR pipe, exhaust manifold shield and vacuum chamber. Install the EGR solenoid and 3-way solenoid.

27. Connect all the coolant, vacuum and fuel system hoses. Connect the air intake hose to the throttle body.

28. Install the distributor and spark plugs and connect all wiring

29. Connect the accelerator cable.

30. Connect the negative battery cable. Fill and bleed the cooling system. Change the engine oil.

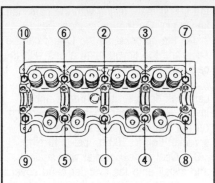

Fig. 74 Cylinder head bolt torque sequence — 626/MX-6 with 2.2L engine

31. Start the engine and bring to normal operating temperature. Check for leaks. Check the ignition timing and idle speed.

2.5L ENGINE

1. Properly relieve the fuel system pressure.

2. Disconnect the negative battery cable and drain the cooling system.

3. Remove the timing belt, then reinstall the right side engine mount to support the engine.

4. Remove the air cleaner assembly and air ducts.

5. Disconnect the accelerator cable.

6. Label and disconnect the spark plug wires, then remove the wires with the distributor cap. Disconnect the distributor electrical connector, remove the retaining bolts and remove the distributor.

7. Label and disconnect the necessary electrical connectors, vacuum hoses and coolant hoses. Disconnect and plug the fuel lines.

8. Remove the intake manifold stay, air cleaner housing bracket, fuel line and hose. Remove the intake manifold bolts/nuts in 2-3 steps and remove the intake manifold.

9. If removing the left (front) cylinder head, disconnect the ventilation pipe from the cylinder head cover. Remove the cylinder head cover retaining bolts and remove the cylinder head cover.

10. Use a suitable wrench to hold the camshaft and remove the camshaft sprocket bolt. The wrench fits on a hexagon that is cast into the camshaft. Remove the camshaft sprocket.

11. Install engine support tool 49 G017 5A0 and support the engine. Remove the right side engine mount.

12. Remove the seal plate and water outlet from the front of the engine. Remove the engine lifting eyes.

13. Disconnect the exhaust pipe from the exhaust manifolds.

14. Turn the camshaft, using a wrench on the cast hexagon, until the camshaft knock pin aligns with the cylinder head marks.

➡**Do not remove the camshaft caps when the camshaft lobe is pressing the hydraulic lash adjuster, as this may damage the thrust journal support of the cylinder head.**

15. Loosen the front camshaft cap bolts in 5-6 steps in the proper sequence. Bolt **A** is only on the right cylinder head.

16. Loosen the remaining camshaft cap bolts in 5-6 steps in the proper sequence. Mark the position of the camshaft caps so they can be reinstalled in their original positions. Remove the thrust cap last.

17. If removing the left (front) cylinder head, remove the alternator bracket.

18. Temporarily install the right side engine mount and remove the engine support tool.

19. Loosen the cylinder head bolts in 2-3 steps in the reverse order of the tightening sequence. Remove the cylinder head bolts and the cylinder head.

20. If necessary, remove the exhaust manifold.

21. Clean all gasket mating surfaces. Inspect the cylinder head for cracks or other damage. Check the cylinder head for warpage using a feeler gauge and straightedge. The maximum allowable distortion is 0.004 in. (0.10mm).

22. Measure the length of the cylinder head bolts; replace the bolt if it exceeds 5.31 in. (135mm) from just under the bolt head to the tip of the threads. Clean the cylinder head bolts and the threads in the block. Make sure the bolts turn freely in the block.

To install:

23. If removed, install the exhaust manifold using a new gasket and tighten the bolts/nuts to 19 ft. lbs. (25 Nm).

24. Measure the height of the oil control plug from the cylinder block deck; it should be 0.512-0.551 in. (13-14mm). If not within specification, remove the oil control plug and tap in a new one, to the specified height. Apply clean engine oil to a new O-ring and install on the plug.

25. Install a new cylinder head gasket. On the left bank, the **L** mark on the

gasket should be facing up. On the right bank, the **R**mark should be facing up. Be careful not to damage the oil control plug O-ring.

26. Position the cylinder head on the block. Lubricate the cylinder head bolt threads and seat faces with clean engine oil and install them with the washers. Tighten the bolts as follows:

   a. Tighten the bolts in 2-3 steps to 19 ft. lbs. (26 Nm).

   b. Put a paint mark on each bolt head.

   c. Using the paint marks for reference, turn each bolt 90 degrees, in sequence.

   d. Using the paint marks for reference, turn each bolt an additional 90 degrees, in sequence.

27. Install the engine support tool and remove the right side engine mount.

28. Lubricate the camshaft lobes, journals and gears with clean engine oil. Align the camshaft gear timing marks and install the camshafts in the cylinder head.

➡ **The thrust plate positions for the right and left cylinder head camshafts are different.**

29. Make sure the camshaft cap and cylinder head surfaces are clean. Apply a small amount of sealant to the mating surface of the front camshaft cap on both cylinder heads and the rear exhaust camshaft cap on the left cylinder head. Do not get any sealant on the camshaft rotating surfaces.

30. Install the front camshaft caps and thrust plate caps and tighten the bolts until the cap seats fully to the cylinder head. Install the remaining camshaft caps in their original locations and loosely tighten the bolts.

31. Tighten the camshaft cap bolts in 5-6 steps to 126 inch lbs. (14 Nm), in the proper sequence.

32. Apply clean engine oil to a new oil seal and the cylinder head. Install the seal, using a suitable installer. Apply sealant to a new blind cap and install, using a plastic hammer.

33. Install the engine lifting eyes and the alternator bracket. Install the seal plate and water outlet. Using new gaskets, connect the exhaust pipe to the exhaust manifolds and tighten the nuts to 41 ft. lbs. (55 Nm).

34. Temporarily install the right side engine mount and remove the engine support tool.

35. Install the camshaft sprockets. On the right cylinder head, install the sprocket so the **R**mark can be seen and

the timing mark aligns with the camshaft knock pin. On the left cylinder head, install the sprocket so the **L**mark can be seen and the timing mark aligns with the camshaft knock pin.

36. Apply clean engine oil to the camshaft sprocket bolt threads and install. Hold the camshaft with a wrench on the cast hexagon and tighten the sprocket bolt to 103 ft. lbs. (140 Nm).

37. Coat a new gasket with sealant and install onto the cylinder head cover. Install the cover and tighten the bolts, in sequence, in 2-3 steps, to 78 inch lbs. (8.8 Nm). Install the ventilation pipe to the left cover.

38. Apply clean engine oil to a new O-ring and install on the distributor. Install the distributor with the blade fitting into the camshaft groove and loosely tighten the retaining bolt.

39. Install the intake manifold using a new gasket. Loosely install the bolts and nuts. Install the intake manifold stay, bracket, fuel line and hoses, then tighten the intake manifold bolts/nuts, in 2-3 steps, to 19 ft. lbs. (25 Nm).

40. Connect the wiring, vacuum and heater hoses, and the fuel lines.

41. Connect the accelerator cable.

42. Install the air cleaner assembly and the ducts.

43. Install the timing belt.

44. Connect the negative battery cable. Fill and bleed the cooling system. Change the engine oil.

45. Start the engine and bring to normal operating temperature. Check for leaks. Check the ignition timing and idle speed.

CLEANING AND INSPECTION

1. With the valves installed to protect the valve seats, remove deposits from the combustion chambers and valve heads with a scraper and drill-mounted wire brush. Be careful not to damage the cylinder head gasket surface. If the head is to be disassembled, proceed to Step 3. If the head is not to be disassembled, proceed to Step 2.

2. Remove all dirt, oil and old gasket material from the cylinder head with solvent. Clean the bolt holes and the oil passage. Be careful not to get solvent on the valve seals as the solvent may damage them. Dry the cylinder head with compressed air, if available. Check the head for cracks or other damage, and check the gasket surface for burrs, nicks and flatness. If you are in doubt

about the head's serviceability, consult a reputable automotive machine shop.

3. Remove the valves, springs and retainers, then clean the valve guide bores with a valve guide cleaning tool. Remove all dirt, oil and old gasket material from the cylinder head with solvent. Clean the bolt holes and the oil passage.

4. Remove all deposits from the valves with a wire brush or buffing wheel.

5. Check the head for cracks in the valve seat area and ports, and check the gasket surface for burrs, nicks and flatness. If you are in doubt about the head's serviceability, consult a reputable automotive machine shop.

➡ **If the cylinder head was removed due to an overheating condition and a crack is suspected, do not assume that the head is not cracked because a crack is not visually found. A crack can be so small that it cannot be seen by eye, but can pass coolant when the engine is at operating temperature. Consult an automotive machine shop that has pressure testing equipment to make sure the head is not cracked.**

RESURFACING

Whenever the cylinder head is removed, check the flatness of the cylinder head gasket surface as follows:

1. Make sure all dirt and old gasket material has been cleaned from the cylinder head. Any foreign material left on the head gasket surface can cause a false measurement.

2. Place a straightedge across the gasket surface in the positions shown in the figure. Using feeler gauges, determine the clearance at the center of the straightedge.

3. If warpage exceeds 0.006 in. (0.15mm), the cylinder head must be resurfaced. If resurfacing is necessary, do not plane or grind off more than 0.010 in. (0.254mm) from the original gasket surface.

Valves

REMOVAL & INSTALLATION

▶ **See Figure 75**

1. Remove the cylinder head(s).

2. Remove the rocker arms/shafts assemblies and the camshaft(s).

3. Block the head on its side, or install a pair of head-holding brackets made especially for valve removal.

4. Use a socket slightly larger than the valve stem and keepers, place the socket over the valve stem and gently hit the socket with a plastic hammer to break loose any varnish buildup.

5. Remove the valve keepers, retainer, and valve spring using a valve spring compressor (the locking C-clamp type is the easiest to use).

6. Place the parts from each valve in a separate container, numbered and identified for the valve and cylinder.

7. Remove and discard the valve stem oil seal, a new seal will be used at assembly time.

8. Remove the valves from the cylinder head and place, in order, through holes punched in a stiff piece of cardboard.

9. Use an electric drill and rotary wire brush to clean the intake and exhaust valve ports, combustion chamber and valve seats. In some cases, the carbon build-up will have to be chipped away. Use a blunt pointed drift for carbon chipping, being careful around valve seat areas.

10. Use a valve guide cleaning brush and safe solvent to clean the valve guides.

11. Clean the valves with a revolving wire brush. Heavy carbon deposits may be removed with blunt drift.

➡**When using a wire brush to remove carbon from the cylinder head or valves, make sure the deposits are actually removed and not just burnished.**

12. Wash and clean all valve springs, keepers, retainers etc., in safe solvent. Remember to keep parts from each valve separate.

13. Check the cylinder head for cracks. Cracks usually start around the exhaust valve seat because it is the hottest part of the combustion chamber. If a crack is suspected but cannot be detected visually, have the area checked by pressure testing, with a dye penetrant or other method by an automotive machine shop.

14. Inspect the valves, guides, springs and seats and machine or replace parts, as necessary.

To install:

15. Install new valve seals with a valve seal installer tool. Coat each valve

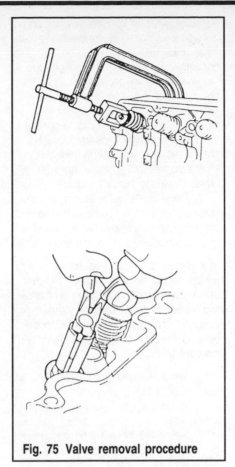

Fig. 75 Valve removal procedure

with clean engine oil and install in its original location.

16. Install any required shims, the valve spring and the retainer over the valve stem. Compress the spring with the valve spring compressor and install the keepers.

17. After all the valves and springs have been assembled, take a mallet and lightly strike each valve stem tip squarely to seat the keepers.

18. Install the camshaft and the rocker arm/shaft assemblies.

INSPECTION

▶ **See Figures 76 and 77**

1. Remove the valves from the cylinder head. Clean the valves, valve guides, valve seats and related components, as explained earlier.

2. Visually check the valves for obvious wear or damage. A burnt valve will have discoloration, severe galling or pitting and even cracks on one area of the valve face. Minor pits, grooves, etc. can be removed by refacing. Check the valve stems bends and for obvious wear that is indicated by a step between the part of the stem that travels in the valve

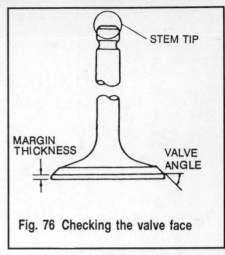

Fig. 76 Checking the valve face

guide and the part of the stem near the keeper grooves.

3. Check the valve stem-to-guide clearance. If a dial indicator is not on hand, a visual inspection can give you a fairly good idea if the guide, valve stem or both are worn. Insert the valve into the guide until the valve head is slightly away from the valve seat. Wiggle the valve sideways. A small amount of wobble is normal, excessive wobble means a worn guide and/or valve stem. If a dial indicator is on hand, mount the indicator so that gauge stem is 90° to the valve stem as close to the top of the valve guide as possible. Move the valve from the seat, and measure the valve guide-to-stem clearance by rocking the stem back and forth to actuate the dial indicator. Measure the valve stem using a micrometer and compare to specifications to determine whether stem or guide is causing excessive clearance.

4. The valve guide, if worn, must be repaired before the valve seats can be resurfaced. A new valve guide should be installed or, in some cases, knurled. Consult the automotive machine shop.

5. If the valve guide is okay, measure the valve seat concentricity using a runout gauge. Follow the manufacturers instructions. If runout is excessive, reface or replace the valve and machine or replace the valve seat.

6. Valves and seats must always be machined together. Never use a refaced valve on a valve seat that has not been machined; never use a valve that has not been refaced on a machined valve seat.

REFACING

1. Determine if the valve is usable as explained in the Inspection procedure.

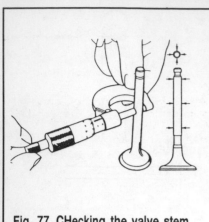

Fig. 77 CHecking the valve stem

2. Refer to specifications for the correct valve face machining angle. Make sure the valve refacer grinding wheels are properly dressed.

3. Reface the valve face only enough to remove the pits and grooves or correct any runout. If the edge of the valve head is less than 0.031 in. (0.8mm) thick after grinding, replace the valve, as the valve will run too hot in the engine.

4. Remove all grooves or score marks from the end of the valve stem, and chamfer it, as necessary. Do not remove more than 0.010 in. (0.254mm) from the end of the valve stem.

5. When the engine is reassembled, it will be necessary to check the clearance between the rocker arm pad and the valve stem tip. Refer to Section 2.

Valve Stem Seals

REPLACEMENT

Cylinder Heads Installed

1. Remove the rocker arm cover, rocker arm/shaft assemblies and camshaft. Refer to procedures in this Section.

2. Mount the valve spring compressor bar tool and angle brackets from valve spring compressor tool kit on the cylinder head.

3. Turn the crankshaft until the piston of the cylinder to be worked on is at Top Dead Center (TDC).

4. Disconnect the spark plug wire and remove the spark plug on the cylinder to be worked on.

5. Thread an adapter into the spark plug hole and connect the hose from an air compressor to the adapter. The hose

on many screw-in compression testers will accept a quick-disconnect fitting that an air compressor hose can be connected to. After all connections are made, turn the air on; this will keep the valve against the valve seat while the retainer is removed.

6. Using a socket slightly larger than the valve stem and keepers, place the socket over the valve stem and gently hit the socket with a plastic hammer to break loose any varnish buildup.

7. Depress the valve spring with the valve spring compressor until the valve keepers can be removed. Then remove the spring seat, spring and valve seal.

➡**If the air pressure has forced the piston to the bottom of the cylinder, any removal of air pressure will allow the valves to fall into the cylinder. A rubber band, tape or string wrapped around the end of the valve stem will prevent this.**

8. Install the new valve seal using a seal replacer tool.

9. Install the valve spring and upper spring seat.

10. Mount the valve spring compressor bar and spacers onto the front and rear camshaft bearing caps.

11. Compress the valve spring with the compressor until the keepers can be installed.

12. Release the air pressure. Install the spark plug and connect the spark plug wire.

13. Repeat the procedure for each cylinder.

14. Install the camshaft, rocker arm/shaft assemblies and rocker arm cover. Refer to the procedures in this Section.

Cylinder Heads Removed

1. Remove the rocker arms/shafts assemblies and the camshaft.

2. Block the head on its side, or install a pair of head-holding brackets made especially for valve removal.

3. Using a socket slightly larger than the valve stem and keepers, place the socket over the valve stem and gently hit the socket with a plastic hammer to break loose any varnish buildup.

4. Remove the valve keepers, retainer, and valve spring using a valve spring compressor (the locking C-clamp type is the easiest to use).

5. Place the parts from each valve in a separate container, numbered and identified for the valve and cylinder.

6. Remove and discard the valve stem oil seal.

7. Install new valve seals with a valve seal installer tool. Dip each valve in clean engine oil and install in its original location.

8. Install any required shims, the valve spring and the retainer over the valve stem. Compress the spring with the valve spring compressor and install the keepers.

9. After all the valves and springs have been assembled, take a mallet and lightly strike each valve stem tip squarely to seat the keepers.

10. Install the camshaft and the rocker arm/shaft assemblies.

Valve Springs

REMOVAL & INSTALLATION

1. Remove the cylinder head.

2. Remove the rocker arms/shafts assemblies and the camshaft.

3. Block the head on its side, or install a pair of head-holding brackets made especially for valve service.

4. Use a socket slightly larger than the valve stem and keepers, place the socket over the valve stem and gently hit the socket with a plastic hammer to break loose any varnish buildup.

5. Remove the valve keepers, retainer, and valve spring using a valve spring compressor (the locking C-clamp type is the easiest to use). If necessary, remove the lower spring seat or any shims that may have been under the valve spring.

6. Place the parts from each valve in a separate container, numbered and identified for the valve and cylinder.

7. Inspect the valve springs for damage or wear and replace as necessary. Check the free length and/or spring pressure.

To install:

8. Install the valve spring retainer on the valve without the spring and retain it with the keepers. Pull the valve firmly against the seat.

9. Using a suitable measuring tool (calipers, or a telescope gauge with a micrometer work well), measure the distance between the cylinder head and the retainer and compare this distance with the installed height specification. Shims are available to make up the difference and are usually necessary after a valve job.

10. Install the lower spring seat or any shims that are required under the valve spring.

11. Compress the spring using the spring compressor and install the keepers. Release the spring compressor.

12. After all the valves and springs have been assembled, take a mallet and lightly strike each valve stem tip squarely to seat the keepers.

13. Install the camshaft and the rocker arm/shaft assemblies.

14. Install the cylinder head.

INSPECTION

1. Check the springs for cracks or other damage.

2. Check each spring for squareness using a steel square and a flat surface. Stand the spring and square on end on the flat surface. Slide the spring up to the square, revolve the spring slowly and observe the space between the top coil of the spring and the square. If the space exceeds 0.067 in. (1.7mm), replace the spring.

3. Measure the free length of the spring. Compare the length to that listed in the specification chart.

Valve Seats

REMOVAL & INSTALLATION

Valve seat replacement should be left to an automotive machine shop, due to the high degree of precision and special equipment required. The following procedures can be construed as what is generally acceptable for aluminum cylinder heads; the actual method employed should be left to the qualified machinist.

Mazda engines use replaceable seat inserts. These inserts can be removed by cutting them out to within a few thousandths of their outside diameter and then collapsing the remainder, or by heating the head to a high temperature and then driving the seat out.

To install a new seat, the cylinder head is usually heated to a high temperature, then the seat, which is at room temperature or slightly chilled, is pressed into the head. The head is then allowed to cool and as it does, it contracts and grips the seat.

After a new seat is installed, it must be refaced.

REFACING

1. Inspect the valve guides to make sure they are usable. as described under valve inspection.

2. Make sure the grinding wheels on the refacer are properly dressed to ensure a good finish.

3. Grind the valve seats to a 45° angle, only removing enough metal to clean up the pits and grooves and correct valve seat runout.

4. After the seat has been refaced, measure the seat width using a suitable measuring tool and compare to specification.

5. If the seat is too wide, grinding wheels of 60° and 30° can be used to remove stock from the bottom and the top of the seat, respectively, and narrow the seat.

6. Once the correct seat width has been obtained, find out where the seat contacts the valve. The finished seat should contact the approximate center of the valve face.

7. Coat the seat with Prussian Blue and set the valve in place. Rotate the valve with light pressure, then remove it and check the seat contact.

8. If the blue is transferred to the center of the valve face, contact is satisfactory. If the blue is transferred to the top edge of the valve face, lower the valve seat. If the blue is transferred to the bottom edge of the valve face, raise the valve seat.

Valve Guides

If the valve guides are determined to be worn during the valve inspection procedure, there are two possible repair alternatives, knurling or replacement. Either procedure can be done by a competent automotive machine shop.

If guide wear is minimal, the correct inside diameter can be restored by knurling. Knurling involves using a special tool to raise a spiral ridge on the inside of the guide while it is installed in the head. This effectively reduces the inside diameter of the guide. A reamer is then usually passed through the guide to make the inside diameter smooth and uniform.

Knurling is only an alternative if there is minimum guide wear. Excessive wear can only be corrected by replacing the guide.

➡The valve seats must be refaced after guide knurling or replacement.

REMOVAL & INSTALLATION

1. Gradually heat the disassembled cylinder head in water to approximately 190°F (90°C).

✳✳CAUTION

Be careful when removing and handling the head as the water and the head will be extremely hot! Wear thick, heavy, rubber gloves during this procedure.

2. Remove the cylinder head from the water and place it on a bench. Block the head on its side, or install a pair of head-holding brackets made especially for cylinder head service.

3. Drive out the valve guide toward the camshaft side of the cylinder head using valve guide remover tool T87C-6510-A or equivalent.

4. Drive in the new guide using the same tool. Drive the guide in until 0.752-0.772 in. (19.1-19.6mm) of the guide protrudes from the top of the head.

➡Work quickly. if the head is allowed to cool, guide removal and installation will be difficult.

Oil Pan

REMOVAL & INSTALLATION

323, Protege, MX-3, MX-6 and 626
▶ See Figures 78, 79, 80 and 81

1. Disconnect the negative battery cable. Raise and safely support the vehicle.

2. Remove the engine under cover, if equipped. Position a suitable container under the oil pan. Remove the drain plug and drain the oil.

3. Remove the exhaust pipe from the exhaust manifold and from the catalytic converter. If necessary, remove the exhaust pipe bracket from the engine block.

4. On MX-3 1.8L and MX-6/626 2.5L engines, remove the transverse member from under the oil pan.

5. On 1990-93 323/Protege 1.6L engine, remove the integrated stiffener from the engine block and transaxle.

6. On MX-6/626 2.2L engine, remove the gusset plates and the clutch housing cover.

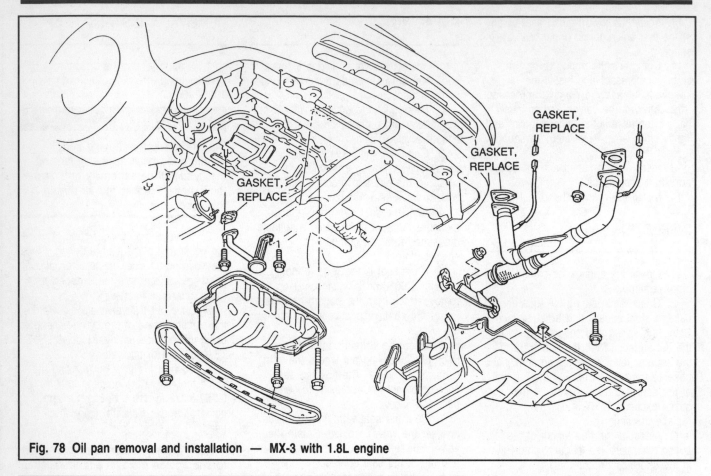

Fig. 78 Oil pan removal and installation — MX-3 with 1.8L engine

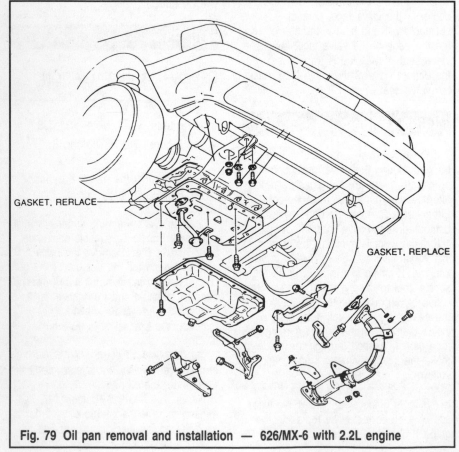

Fig. 79 Oil pan removal and installation — 626/MX-6 with 2.2L engine

7. Remove the bolts and remove the oil pan. It may be necessary to pry the pan away from the engine; be careful not to damage the gasket contact surfaces.

8. If necessary remove the oil strainer.

9. On 323/Protege, MX-3 1.6L engine and MX-6/626 2.2L engines, remove the main bearing support/stiffener plate that is installed between the oil pan and engine block.

To install:

10. Clean all oil, dirt, old gasket material and sealer from the oil pan, support/stiffener plate, oil pan bolts and all gasket mating surfaces. If removed, clean the oil strainer.

11. If equipped with the main bearing support/stiffener plate, run a bead of silicone sealer around the perimeter of the plate, going inside the bolt holes. Install the plate and tighten the bolts to 15 ft. lbs. (21 Nm) on 323/Protege/MX-3 or 104 inch lbs. (12 Nm) on MX-6/626.

➡Make sure all old sealer is removed from the bolts prior to installation. Instaling a bolt coated with old sealer could result in cracking of the bolts holes.

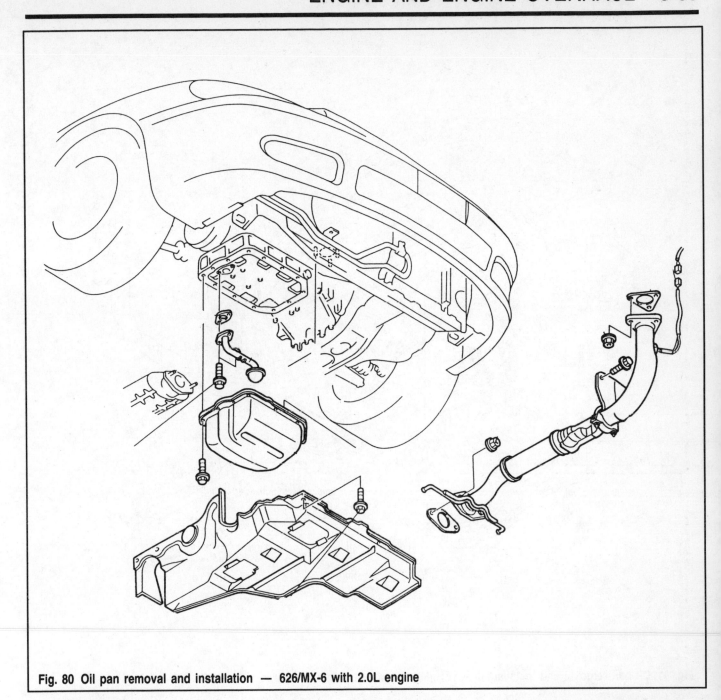

Fig. 80 Oil pan removal and installation — 626/MX-6 with 2.0L engine

12. If removed, install the oil strainer using a new gasket. Tighten the bolts to 95 inch lbs. (11 Nm).

13. If used, apply silicone sealer to new rubber end gaskets and press them into place on the engine.

14. Apply a bead of silicone to the perimeter of the oil pan, going around the inside of the bolt holes and install the pan to the engine. Install the oil pan bolts finger tight.

15. On 323/Protege 1.6L and MX-6/626 2.2L engines, tighten the oil pan bolts to 95 inch lbs. (11 Nm). On MX-6/626 2.0L engine, tighten the oil pan bolts to 18 ft. lbs. (25 Nm). On 323/Protege 1.8L and MX-3 1.6L engines, tighten bolts **A** to 95 inch lbs.

(11 Nm) and bolts **B** to 38 ft. lbs. (52 Nm). On MX-3 1.8L and MX-6/626 2.5L engines, tighten bolts **A** to 95 inch lbs. (11 Nm) and bolts **B** to 18 ft. lbs. (25 Nm).

➡**Make sure all old sealer is removed from the bolts prior to installation. Installing a bolt coated with old sealer could result in cracking of the bolts holes.**

16. On MX-6/626 2.2L engine, install the clutch housing cover and tighten the bolts to 95 inch lbs. (11 Nm). Install the gusset plates and tighten the bolts to 38 ft. lbs. (52 Nm).

17. On 323/Protege 1.6L engine, install the integrated stiffener to the

engine block and transaxle. Tighten the bolts to 38 ft. lbs. (52 Nm).

18. On MX-3 1.8L and MX-6/626 2.5L engines, install the transverse member. Tighten the bolts to 93 ft. lbs. (126 Nm).

19. Install the front exhaust pipe bracket, if equipped. Install the front exhaust pipe, using new gaskets. Tighten the exhaust manifold flange nuts to 34 ft. lbs. (46 Nm).

20. Install the oil pan drain plug using a new gasket. Tighten the drain plug to 30 ft. lbs. (41 Nm) on all except 2.2L engine, where the torque is 15 ft. lbs. (20 Nm).

21. Install the engine under cover and lower the vehicle.

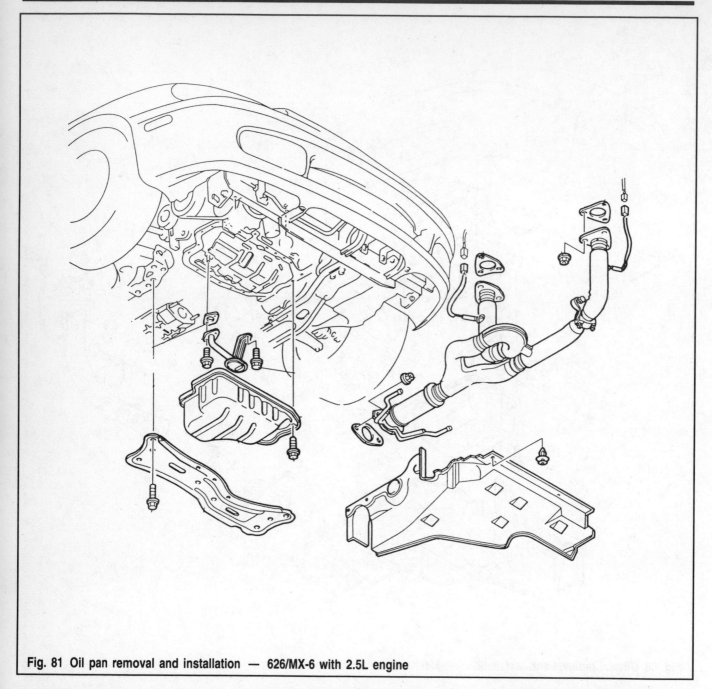

Fig. 81 Oil pan removal and installation — 626/MX-6 with 2.5L engine

22. Fill the engine with the proper type and quantity of oil.

23. Connect the negative battery cable. Start the engine and bring to normal operating temperature. Check for leaks.

Miata

▶ **See Figure 82**

1. Disconnect the negative battery cable and raise and safely support the vehicle.

2. Remove the engine under cover and drain the oil. Remove the dip stick and tube.

3. Remove both lower engine mount nuts and disconnect the steering shaft joint at the steering rack.

4. Attach lifting equipment and lift the engine slightly.

5. Support the crossmember with a jack and remove the nuts and bolts on each side. Lower the crossmember until the clearance between the oil pan and steering gear is 4 in. (100mm) or more.

6. Remove the oil pan bolts and lower the pan enough to remove the oil strainer bolts. If prying the pan is necessary, pry at the pan-to-transmission face. Be careful not to damage the block sealing surfaces.

7. Remove the oil pan and carefully pry the baffle off the block.

To install:

8. Make sure all the old sealer is cleaned off the pan, baffle, block and bolts. Make sure all surfaces are clean and dry.

9. Apply a bead of silicone sealer to the baffle, making sure the bead is inside the bolt holes. Install the baffle with a few of the pan bolts and allow the sealer to set up long enough to hold the baffle in place when the bolts are removed.

10. Apply silicone sealer to each end of the block and press the rubber end gaskets into place. Make sure the notches on the gaskets face the front and rear of the engine block.

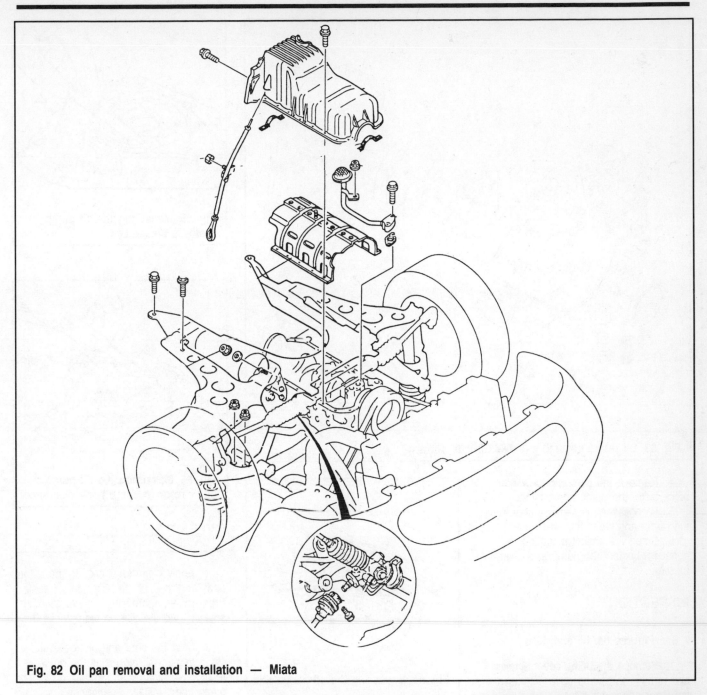

Fig. 82 Oil pan removal and installation — Miata

11. Install the oil pick-up tube with a new gasket and torque the bolts and nut to 95 inch lbs. (11 Nm).

12. Apply a bead of silicone sealer to the oil pan, making sure the bead is inside the bolt holes. Fit the pan into place and torque the pan-to-engine bolts to 95 inch lbs. (11 Nm). Start at the center and work out. Torque the pan-to-transmission bolts to 66 ft. lbs. (89 Nm).

13. Raise the crossmember and set the engine into place. Torque the crossmember nuts to 87 ft. lbs. (118 Nm) and the bolts to 61 ft. lbs. (83 Nm).

14. Torque the engine mount nuts to 58 ft. lbs. (78 Nm).

15. Connect the steering shaft to the rack and install the dip stick. Install the engine under cover and lower the vehicle.

16. Connect the negative battery cable. Fill the engine with the proper type and quantity of oil.

17. Start the engine and bring to normal operating temperature. Check for leaks.

Oil Pump

REMOVAL

▶ See Figure 83

1. Disconnect the negative battery cable. Raise and safely support the vehicle.

2. Remove the timing belt. Remove the retaining bolt and remove the crankshaft sprocket. Drain the engine oil and remove the oil pan.

3. Remove the oil pump pickup tube-to-oil pump bolts, the tube and gasket.

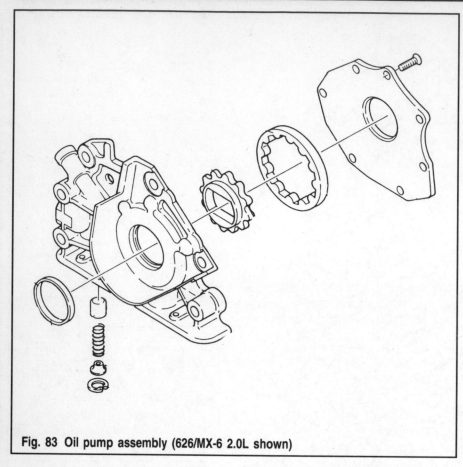

Fig. 83 Oil pump assembly (626/MX-6 2.0L shown)

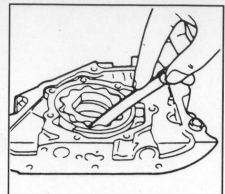

Fig. 85 Measuring the oil pump tooth-tip clearance

Fig. 86 Measuring the oil pump outer rotor to pump body clearance

4. Remove the oil pump-to-cylinder block bolts, the pump and gasket.

5. If necessary, pry the oil seal from the pump and clean the seal bore.

6. Clean the gasket mounting surfaces. Inspect the pump and gears for wear.

INSPECTION

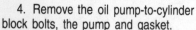 **See Figures 84, 85 and 86**

1. Remove the pump cover screws and remove the pump cover. Remove the inner and outer rotor.

2. Using snapring pliers, remove the internal snapring and remove the pressure relief valve assembly.

3. Using a small prybar, remove the oil seal from he pump body. Discard the seal.

4. Clean all parts in solvent and allow to dry. Check for obvious signs of wear: scoring, galling or distortion of the pump body or cover, worn or damaged pressure relief valve plunger, or a weak or broken spring plunger.

5. Measure the side clearance using a straightedge and feeler gauge, as shown in fig84. The clearance must not exceed 0.004 in. (0.10mm).

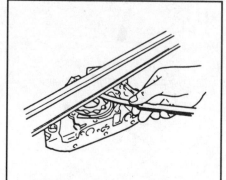

Fig. 84 Measuring the oil pump side clearance

6. Measure the tooth tip clearance using a feeler gauge as shown in fig85. The clearance must not exceed 0.007 in. (0.18mm).

7. Measure the outer rotor-to-pump body clearance using a feeler gauge, as shown in fig86. The clearance must not exceed 0.008 in. (0.20mm).

8. Replace parts or the entire assembly, as necessary.

OVERHAUL

1. Apply clean engine oil to the pump body and the outside of a new oil seal. Press in the seal using a driver slightly smaller than the outside diameter of the seal.

2. Coat the bore and plunger with clean engine oil and install the pressure relief valve plunger and spring in the pump body. Install the snapring.

3. Coat the inner and outer rotors with clean engine oil and install in the pump body with the dimples facing the pump cover, as shown in fig136.

4. Install the pump cover on the pump body. Apply thread locking compound to the cover mounting screws and tighten to 52-78 inch lbs. (6-9 Nm).

5. Make sure the rotor turns smoothly after assembly.

INSTALLATION

1. Apply a continuous bead of silicone sealer to the oil pump gasket surface.

➡**Do not allow the sealer to squeeze into the pump's outlet hole in the pump or cylinder block.**

2. Install a new O-ring into the pump body.

3. Install the oil pump to the cylinder block; be careful not to cut the oil seal lip. Tighten the 8mm oil pump-to-cylinder block bolts to 14-19 ft. lbs. (19-25 Nm) and the 10mm oil pump-to-cylinder block bolts to 27-38 ft. lbs. (37-52 Nm).

4. Install the oil pump pickup tube using a new gasket.

5. Install the oil pan and the crankshaft sprocket. Tighten the crankshaft sprocket bolt to 108-116 ft. lbs. (147-157 Nm).

6. Connect the negative battery cable and refill the crankcase. Start the engine and check for leaks.

Crankshaft Damper

REMOVAL & INSTALLATION

1. Remove the accessory drive belts. Refer to Section 1.

2. Raise and safely support the vehicle.

3. Remove the right front wheel and tire assembly.

4. Remove the right inner fender panel.

5. Remove the bolts, damper and baffle plate.

6. Inspect the damper for damage and replace, as necessary.

To install:

7. Install the crankshaft sprocket baffle with the curved lip facing outward.

8. Install the crankshaft damper with the deep recess facing out and install the bolts. Tighten the bolts to 109-152 inch lbs. (12-17 Nm).

9. Install the right inner fender panel and the wheel and tire assembly. Lower the vehicle.

10. Install the accessory drive belts. Refer to Section 1.

Fig. 87 Timing belt assembly — BP and B6 SOHC engines

Timing Belt Cover

REMOVAL & INSTALLATION

B6 and BP SOHC Engines

▶ **See Figure 87**

1. Disconnect the negative battery cable.

2. Remove the engine under splash shield.

3. Remove the accessory drive belts. Refer to Section 1.

4. Remove the crankshaft pulley.

5. Remove the inner and outer timing belt guide plates.

6. Remove the 2 bolts and remove the upper timing belt cover assembly.

7. Remove the 1 bolt and remove the lower timing belt cover assembly and gasket.

To install:

8. Install the lower cover gasket and the lower cover. Tighten the bolt to 69-95 inch lbs. (8-11 Nm).

9. Install the upper cover gasket and the upper cover. Tighten the bolts to 69-95 inch lbs. (8-11 Nm).

10. Install the timing belt inner and outer guide plates. Make sure that the inner guide plate is installed in the proper direction.

11. Install the crankshaft pulley. Tighten the bolts to 109-152 inch lbs. (12-17 Nm).

12. Install the accessory drive belts. Refer to Section 1.

13. Install the under engine splash shield.

14. Connect the negative battery cable.

BP DOHC Engines

▶ **See Figure 88**

1. Disconnect the negative battery cable.

2. Remove the engine under splash shield.

3. Remove the power steering, air conditioning and alternator drive belts. Refer to Section 1.

4. Remove the retaining bolts and remove the water pump pulley.

5. Remove the crankshaft pulley bolts and remove the crankshaft pulley.

6. Remove the inner and outer timing belt guide plates.

7. Remove the bolt and remove the upper timing belt cover assembly.

8. Remove the bolts from the middle and lower timing belt cover assembly and remove the covers and the gaskets.

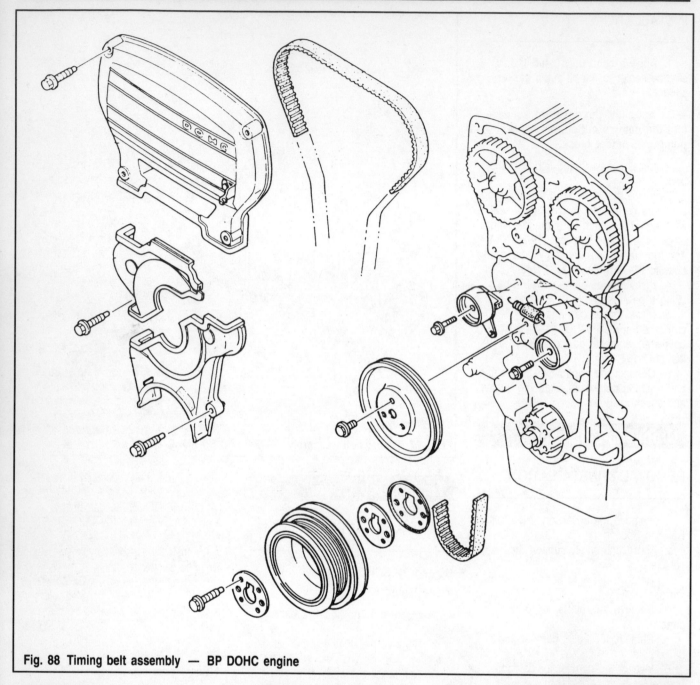

Fig. 88 Timing belt assembly — BP DOHC engine

To install:

9. Install the upper, the center and the lower timing belt covers. Tighten the bolts to 69-95 inch lbs. (8-11 Nm).

10. Install the timing belt inner and outer guide plates. Make sure that the inner guide plate is installed in the proper direction.

11. Install the crankshaft pulley. Tighten the bolts to 109-152 inch lbs. (12-17 Nm).

12. Install the water pump pulley and tighten the bolts to 69-95 inch lbs. (8-11 Nm).

13. Install the P/S, A/C and alternator drive belts. Refer to Section 1.

14. Install the under engine splash shield.

15. Connect the negative battery cable.

B6 DOHC Engines
▶ See Figure 89

1. Disconnect the negative battery cable.

2. Remove the engine under splash shield.

3. Drain the cooling system.

4. Remove the air intake pipe.

5. Disconnect the upper radiator hose and the 2 lower coolant hoses from the thermostat housing.

6. Remove the power steering, air conditioning and alternator drive belts. Refer to Section 1.

7. Remove the retaining bolts and remove the water pump pulley.

8. Remove the crankshaft pulley bolts and remove the crankshaft pulley.

9. Remove the inner and outer timing belt guide plates.

10. Disconnect the coil electrical connectors and remove coil assembly. Remove the spark plug wires. Be certain to record positioning of plug wires for assembly purposes.

11. Remove the spark plugs.

12. Remove the cylinder head cover bolts and remove the cover.

13. Remove the bolts from the timing belt covers and remove the top, the center and the lower timing belt covers.

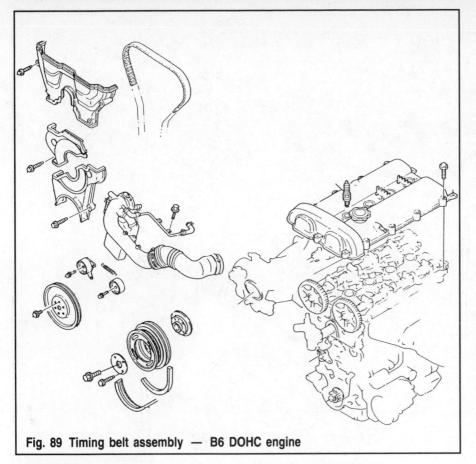

Fig. 89 Timing belt assembly — B6 DOHC engine

To install:

14. Install the timing belt covers with gaskets and tighten the bolts to 69-95 inch lbs. (8-11 Nm).

15. Apply silicone sealant to the corners of the cylinder head cover and install the cover. Tighten the bolts to 43-78 inch lbs. (5-9 Nm).

16. Install the spark plugs and tighten them to 11-17 ft. lbs. (15-23 Nm).

17. Install the coil assembly and connect the electrical connectors and the spark plug wires.

18. Install the inner and outer timing belt guide plates.

19. Install the crankshaft pulley and tighten the bolts to 109-152 inch lbs.(12-17 Nm).

20. Install the water pump pulley and tighten the bolts to 69-95 inch lbs. (8-11 Nm).

21. Install the power steering, air conditioning and alternator drive belts. Refer to Section 1.

22. Install the coolant and radiator hoses and refill the coolant to the proper level.

23. Install the air intake pipe and connect the negative battery cable.

K8 and KL Engines
▶ See Figures 90 and 91

1. Disconnect the negative battery cable.

2. Remove the engine under splash shield.

3. Remove the accessory drive belts. Refer to Section 1.

4. Remove the retaining bolts and remove the water pump pulley.

5. Remove the idler pulley bracket bolt and remove the idler pulley bracket.

6. Remove the power steering pump bolts and the pump as shown in section 8.

7. Remove the crankshaft pulley bolts and remove the pulley using a steering wheel puller.

8. Disconnect the crank angle sensor electrical connector and remove the clip from the oil dipstick tube. Remove the oil dipstick and plug the hole.

9. Remove the bolt from the knock sensor harness bracket.

10. Remove the 2 bolts that secure the engine harness to the timing cover.

11. Remove the remaining timing belt cover bolts and remove the covers and the gaskets.

To install:

12. Install the timing covers with the gaskets in place. Install the timing cover

bolts and tighten to 69-95 inch lbs. (8-11 Nm).

13. Install the 2 bolts that secure the engine harness to the timing cover and tighten the bolts to 69-95 inch lbs. (8-11 Nm).

14. Install the knock sensor harness bracket to the timing cover and tighten the bolt to 69-95 inch lbs. (8-11 Nm).

15. Install the oil dipstick tube complete with a new O-ring. Install the crank angle sensor harness clip to the dipstick tube and connect the electrical connector.

16. Install the crankshaft pulley and loosely tighten the bolt. Hold the pulley in place with special tool 49 E011 1A1 or equivalent and tighten the bolt to 116-123 ft. lbs. (157-167 Nm).

17. Install the power steering fluid pump assembly and tighten the upper bolts to 23-34 ft. lbs. (31-46 Nm) and the lower bolt to 14-19 ft. lbs. (19-25 Nm).

18. Install the power steering pump pulley nut and tighten to 46-69 ft. lbs. (63-93 Nm). Connect the power steering fluid line bracket to the engine and tighten the bolts to 69-95 inch lbs. (7.8-11 Nm).

19. Connect the power steering pressure switch electrical connector and install the power steering oil reservoir and the engine ground.

20. Install the water pump pulley and the power steering idler pulley. Install the belts and tighten the pulley bolts to 69-95 inch lbs. (8-11 Nm).

21. Install the A/C belt and adjust as necessary. Refer to section One.

22. Install the under engine splash shield and connect the negative battery cable.

F2 Engine
▶ See Figure 92

1. Disconnect the negative battery cable.

2. Remove the bolts and remove the engine side cover.

3. Remove the accessory drive belts, refer to section 1.

4. Remove the crankshaft pulley bolts and remove the crankshaft pulley.

5. Remove the timing cover bolts and remove the upper and lower covers.

To install:

6. Install the upper and lower timing belt covers with the gaskets. Tighten the bolts to 61-87 inch lbs. (7-10 Nm).

7. Install the crankshaft pulley and tighten the bolts to 109-153 inch lbs. (12-17 Nm).

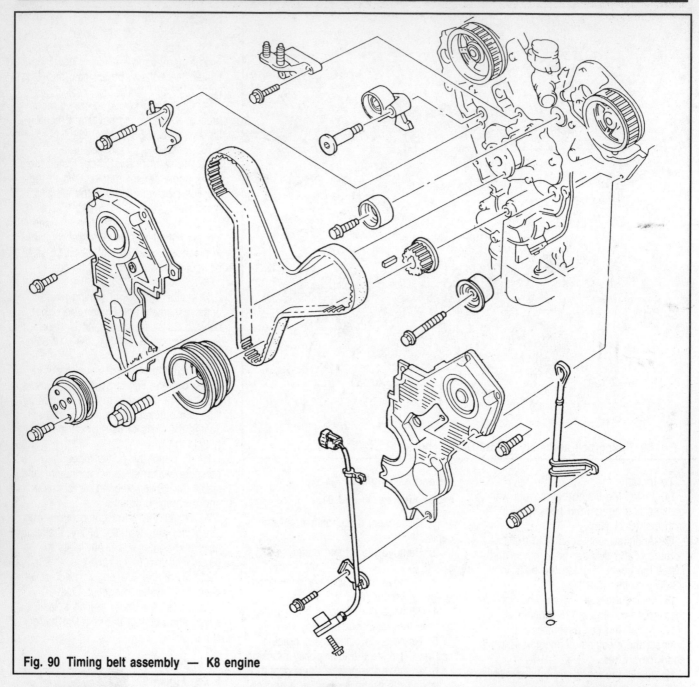

Fig. 90 Timing belt assembly — K8 engine

8. Install the accessory drive belts, refer to section 1.

9. Install the engine side cover and connect the negative battery cable.

FS Engine

▶ **See Figure 93**

1. Disconnect the negative battery cable.

2. Raise and safely support the vehicle. Remove the right front wheel.

3. Remove the engine under splash shield.

4. Remove the accessory drive belts. Refer to Section 1.

5. Remove the power steering pump pulley shield.

6. Remove the power steering pump, leaving the hoses attached and position the pump out of the way.

7. Remove the retaining bolts and remove the water pump pulley.

8. Remove the crankshaft pulley bolt and remove the pulley using a steering wheel puller.

9. Remove the spark plug wires, noting the original location of the wires for installation purposes. Disconnect the power steering hose from the cylinder head cover.

10. Remove the spark plugs and remove the cylinder head cover bolts. Remove the cylinder head cover with the gasket in place.

11. Remove the oil level dipstick bolt and remove the oil dipstick and plug the hole.

12. Remove the timing belt cover bolts and remove the upper and lower covers and the gaskets.

To install:

13. Install the timing covers with the gaskets in place. Install the timing cover bolts and tighten to 69-95 inch lbs. (8-11 Nm).

14. Install the bolt that secures the oil level dipstick and tighten the bolt to 69-95 inch lbs. (8-11 Nm).

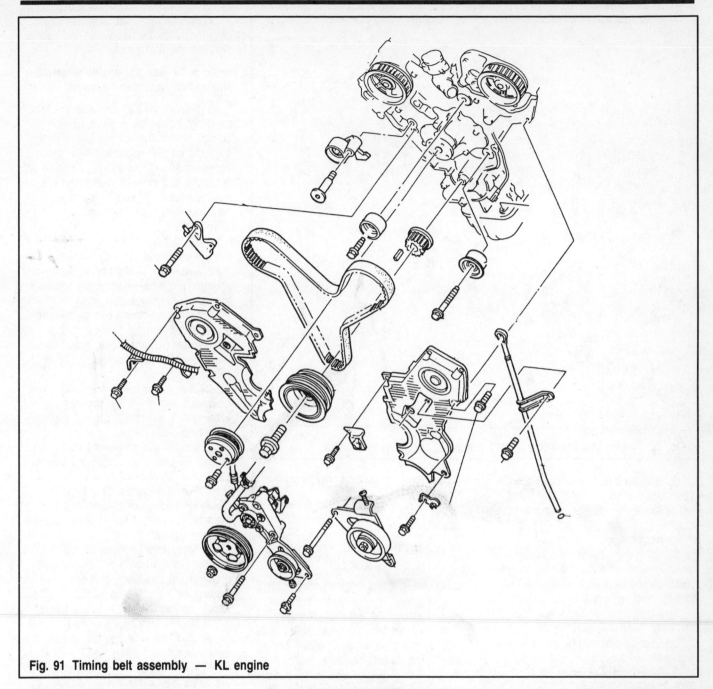

Fig. 91 Timing belt assembly — KL engine

15. Apply silicone sealant to the corners of the cylinder head cover and install the cylinder head cover to the engine and tighten the cylinder head bolts to 69-95 inch lbs. (8-11 Nm).

16. Install the spark plugs to the engine and connect the spark plug wires.

17. Install the crankshaft pulley, with the guide plate in place behind the pulley. Hold the pulley in place with special tool 49 E011 1A1 or equivalent and tighten the bolt to 116-123 ft. lbs. (157-167 Nm).

18. Install the water pump pulley and tighten the bolts to 69-95 inch lbs. (8-11 Nm).

19. Install the power steering pump. Tighten the upper bolt to 32-44 ft. lbs. (44-66 Nm) and the lower bolt to 24-33 ft. lbs. (32-46 Nm).

20. Install the power steering pump pulley shield and tighten the bolt to 60-87 inch lbs. (7-10 Nm).

21. Install the accessory belts and adjust as necessary. Refer to section One.

22. Install the under engine splash shield and install the right front wheel.

23. Lower the vehicle and connect the negative battery cable.

OIL SEAL REPLACEMENT

1. Disconnect the negative battery cable. Remove the timing belt covers and timing belt.

2. If equipped with a manual transaxle, place the shift lever in **4TH** gear and firmly apply the parking brake.

3. If equipped with an automatic transaxle, remove the lower flywheel cover and install a suitable flywheel locking tool onto the flywheel ring.

4. Remove the crankshaft sprocket-to-crankshaft bolt, the sprocket and the key.

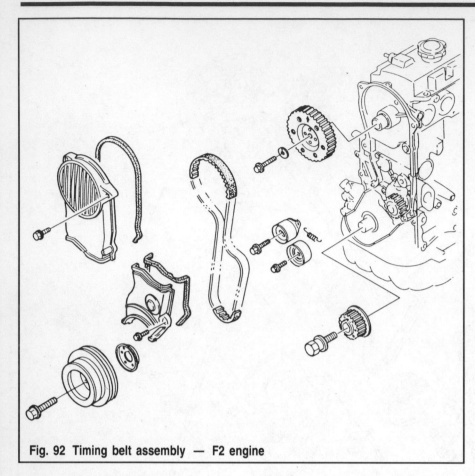

Fig. 92 Timing belt assembly — F2 engine

5. Using a small prybar, pry the oil seal from the engine block; be careful not to score the crankshaft or the seal seat.

To install:

6. Using an oil seal installation tool or equivalent, lubricate the seal lip with clean engine oil and drive the new seal into the engine until it seats.

7. Install the crankshaft key and sprocket. Torque the crankshaft sprocket-to-crankshaft bolt to 108-116 ft. lbs. (147-157 Nm).

8. If necessary, remove the flywheel locking tool.

9. Install the timing belt and connect the negative battery cable.

Timing Belt

The timing belt should be replaced every 60,000 miles. Failure to replace the belt may result in damage to the engine.

REMOVAL & INSTALLATION

323 and Protege

SOHC ENGINE

1. Disconnect the negative battery cable. Remove the engine under cover.

2. Remove the accessory drive belts.

3. Remove the water pump pulley.

4. Remove the crankshaft pulley bolts and remove the crankshaft pulley and baffle plate. Using a suitable tool to hold the crankshaft pulley, remove the pulley lock bolt. Remove the crankshaft pulley boss.

5. Remove the upper and lower timing belt covers.

6. Tag and disconnect the spark plug wires. Remove the spark plugs.

➡**Spark plugs are removed to make it easier to rotate the engine.**

7. Temporarily reinstall the crankshaft pulley boss and lock bolt.

8. Turn the crankshaft, using the bolt, until the camshaft sprocket and crankshaft sprocket timing marks are aligned. Mark the direction of rotation on the timing belt.

9. Remove the belt tensioner lock bolt, the tensioner wheel and the spring. Remove the timing belt.

➡**Do not rotate the engine after the timing belt has been removed.**

10. Inspect the belt for wear, peeling, cracking, hardening or signs of oil contamination. Inspect the tensioner for free and smooth rotation. Check the tensioner spring free length; it should not exceed 2.520 in. (64mm). Inspect the sprocket teeth for wear or damage. Replace parts, as necessary.

To install:

11. Make sure the timing marks on the sprockets are properly aligned.

12. Install the timing belt tensioner and spring. Temporarily tighten the bolt with the spring fully extended.

13. Install the timing belt so there is no looseness on the tension side. If reusing the old timing belt, make sure it is reinstalled in the same direction of rotation.

14. Turn the crankshaft 2 turns clockwise and check the timing mark alignment. If the marks are not aligned, repeat Steps 11-14.

15. Loosen the tensioner lock bolt to set the tension, then torque the bolt to 19 ft. lbs. (25 Nm).

16. Turn the crankshaft 2 turns clockwise and check the alignment of the timing marks. If they are not aligned, repeat Steps 11-16.

17. Apply approximately 22 lbs. pressure to the timing belt on the side opposite the tensioner, at a point midway between the sprockets. The belt should deflect 0.43-0.51 in. (11-13mm). If the tension is not as specified, repeat Steps 14-17 or, if necessary, replace the tensioner spring.

18. Install the spark plugs and connect the spark plug wires.

19. Install the upper and lower timing belt covers. Tighten the bolts to 95 inch lbs. (11 Nm).

20. Install the crankshaft pulley boss and tighten the lock bolt to 123 ft. lbs. (167 Nm), while holding the pulley boss with a suitable tool.

21. Install the crankshaft pulley and baffle plate.

22. Install the water pump pulley and accessory drive belts. Adjust the belt tension.

23. Install the under cover. Connect the negative battery cable.

24. Start the engine and check for proper operation. Check the ignition timing.

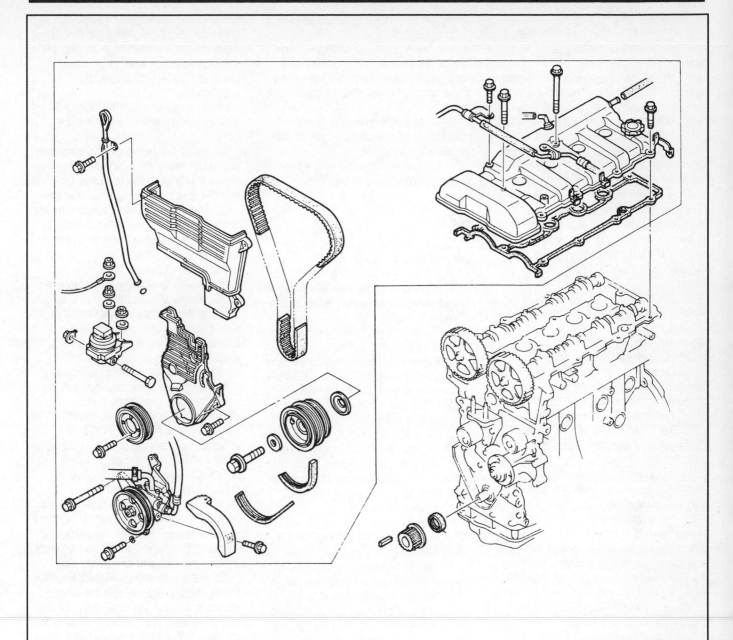

Fig. 93 Timing belt assembly — FS engine

DOHC ENGINE

1. Disconnect the negative battery cable. Remove the engine under cover.

2. Remove the accessory drive belts.

3. Remove the crankshaft pulley bolts and remove the crankshaft pulley.

4. On 1990-91 vehicles, remove the outer timing belt guide plate. On 1990-91 vehicles, remove the inner timing belt guide plate.

5. Tag and disconnect the spark plug wires. Remove the spark plugs.

➡**Spark plugs are removed to make it easier to rotate the engine.**

6. Remove the engine oil dipstick.

7. Remove the upper, middle and lower timing belt covers.

8. Turn the crankshaft until the timing marks on the crankshaft and camshaft sprockets are aligned. On 1992-93 vehicles, the pin on the pulley boss must face upward.

9. On 1992-93 vehicles, hold the crankshaft pulley boss with a suitable tool and remove the pulley lock bolt, being careful not to rotate the crankshaft. Remove the crankshaft pulley boss.

10. Mark the direction of rotation on the timing belt. Loosen the tensioner lock bolt and pry the tensioner outward. Tighten the lock bolt with the tensioner spring fully extended. Remove the timing belt.

➡**Protect the tensioner with a rag before prying on it. Do not rotate the crankshaft after the timing belt has been removed.**

11. Remove the tensioner and spring. If necessary, remove the idler pulley.

12. Inspect the belt for wear, peeling, cracking, hardening or signs of oil contamination. Inspect the tensioner for free and smooth rotation. Check the tensioner spring free length; it should not exceed 2.315 in. (58.8mm). Inspect the sprocket teeth for wear or damage. Replace parts, as necessary.

To install:

13. If removed, install the idler pulley and tighten the bolt to 38 ft. lbs. (52 Nm).

14. Install the tensioner and tensioner spring. Pry the tensioner outward and temporarily tighten the tensioner lock bolt with the tensioner spring fully extended.

15. Make sure the crankshaft sprocket timing mark is aligned with the mark on the oil pump housing and the camshaft sprocket timing marks are aligned with the marks on the seal plate.

16. Install the timing belt so there is no looseness at the idler pulley side or between the camshaft sprockets. If reusing the old belt, make sure it is installed in the same direction of rotation.

17. On 1992-93 vehicles, temporarily install the pulley boss and lock bolt.

18. Turn the crankshaft 2 turns clockwise and align the crankshaft sprocket timing mark. On 1992-93 vehicles, face the pin on the pulley boss upright. Make sure the camshaft sprocket timing marks are aligned. If they are not, repeat Steps 15-19.

19. Turn the crankshaft 1-2 turns clockwise and align the crankshaft sprocket timing mark with the tension set mark for proper belt tension adjustment. On 1992-93 vehicles, remove the lock bolt and pulley boss.

20. Make sure the crankshaft sprocket timing mark is aligned with the tension set mark. Loosen the tensioner lock bolt and allow the spring to apply tension to the belt. Tighten the tensioner lock bolt to 38 ft. lbs. (52 Nm).

21. On 1992-93 vehicles, install the pulley boss and lock bolt.

22. Turn the crankshaft 2 full turns clockwise and make sure the timing marks are correctly aligned.

23. Apply approximately 22 lbs. pressure to the timing belt at a point midway between the camshaft sprockets. The belt should deflect 0.35-0.45 in. (9.0-11.5mm). If the deflection is not correct, repeat Steps 21-24.

24. On 1992-93 vehicles, hold the pulley boss with a suitable tool and tighten the lock bolt to 123 ft. lbs. (167 Nm).

25. Install the timing belt covers and tighten the bolts to 95 inch lbs. (11 Nm). Install the engine oil dipstick.

26. Install the spark plugs and connect the spark plug wires.

27. Install the timing belt inner guide plate, if equipped. Make sure the dished side of the plate faces away from the timing belt. Install the outer guide plate, if equipped.

28. Install the crankshaft pulley and tighten the bolts to 13 ft. lbs. (17 Nm).

29. Install the water pump pulley and the accessory drive belts. Adjust the belt tension.

30. Install the engine side or undercover, as necessary. Connect the negative battery cable.

31. Start the engine and check for proper operation. Check the ignition timing.

Miata

1. Disconnect the negative battery cable. Drain the cooling system.

2. Remove the air intake pipe.

3. Remove the upper radiatro hose and disconnect the coolant hoses at the thermostat housing.

4. Remove the accessory drive belts and the water pump pulley.

5. Remove the crankshaft pulley bolts and the crankshaft pulley. On 1992-93 vehicles, hold the pulley boss with a suitable tool and remove the pulley lock bolt. Remove the pulley boss.

6. On 1990-91 vehicles, remove the outer and inner timing belt guide plates.

7. Tag and disconnect the spark plug wires from the spark plugs. Remove the ignition coil and plug wires assembly. Remove the spark plugs.

8. Remove the cylinder head cover. Remove the upper, middle and lower timing belt covers.

9. On 1992-93 vehicles, temporarily reinstall the pulley boss and lock bolt.

10. Turn the crankshaft until the crankshaft and camshaft sprocket timing marks are aligned. On 1992-93 vehicles, the pin on the pulley boss must face upward.

11. On 1992-93 vehicles, remove the pulley boss and lock bolt, being careful not to disturb the crankshaft.

12. Mark the direction of rotation on the timing belt. Loosen the tensioner lock bolt and pry the tensioner outward. Tighten the lock bolt with the tensioner spring fully extended. Remove the timing belt.

➡**Protect the tensioner with a rag before prying on it. Do not rotate the crankshaft after the timing belt has been removed.**

13. Remove the tensioner and spring. If necessary, remove the idler pulley.

14. Inspect the belt for wear, peeling, cracking, hardening or signs of oil contamination. Inspect the tensioner for free and smooth rotation. Check the tensioner spring free length; it should not exceed 2.315 in. (58.8mm). Inspect the sprocket teeth for wear or damage. Replace parts, as necessary.

To install:

15. If removed, install the idler pulley and tighten the bolt to 38 ft. lbs. (52 Nm).

16. Install the tensioner and tensioner spring. Pry the tensioner outward and temporarily tighten the tensioner lock bolt with the tensioner spring fully extended.

17. Make sure the crankshaft sprocket timing mark is aligned with the mark on the oil pump housing and the camshaft sprocket timing marks are aligned with the marks on the seal plate.

18. Install the timing belt so there is no looseness at the idler pulley side or between the camshaft sprockets. If reusing the old belt, make sure it is installed in the same direction of rotation.

19. On 1992-93 vehicles, temporarily install the pulley boss and lock bolt.

20. Turn the crankshaft 2 turns clockwise and align the crankshaft sprocket timing mark. On 1992-93 vehicles, face the pin on the pulley boss upright. Make sure the camshaft sprocket timing marks are aligned. If they are not, repeat Steps 16-20.

21. Turn the crankshaft clockwise and align the crankshaft sprocket timing mark with the tension set mark for proper belt tension adjustment. On 1992-93 vehicles, remove the lock bolt and pulley boss.

22. Make sure the crankshaft sprocket timing mark is aligned with the tension set mark. Loosen the tensioner lock bolt and allow the spring to apply tension to the belt. Tighten the tensioner lock bolt to 38 ft. lbs. (52 Nm).

23. On 1992-93 vehicles, install the pulley boss and lock bolt.

24. Turn the crankshaft 2 turns clockwise and make sure the timing marks are correctly align

25. Apply approximately 22 lbs. pressure to the timing belt at a point midway between the camshaft sprockets. The belt should deflect 0.35-0.45 in. (9.0-11.5mm). If the deflection is not correct, repeat Steps 22-23.

26. Install the timing belt covers and tighten the bolts to 95 inch lbs. (11 Nm).

27. Apply silicone sealer to the cylinder head in the area adjacent to the front and rear camshaft caps. Install the cylinder head cover and tighten the bolts to 78 inch lbs. (8.8 Nm).

28. Install the spark plugs. Install the ignition coil and tighten the bolts to 19

ft. lbs. (25 Nm). Connect the spark plug wires.

29. On 1990-91 vehicles, install the inner timing belt guide plate with the dished side facing away from the engine. Install the outer guide plate.

30. On 1992-93 vehicles, hold the pulley boss with a suitable tool and tighten the lock bolt to 123 ft. lbs. (167 Nm).

31. Install the crankshaft pulley. Tighten the bolts to 13 ft. lbs. (17 Nm).

32. Install the water pump pulley and the accessory drive belts. Adjust the belt tension.

33. Connect the coolant hoses to the thermostat housing and install the upper radiator hose.

34. Install the air intake pipe and connect the negative battery cable. Fill and bleed the cooling system.

35. Start the engine and bring to normal operating temperature. Check for leaks and proper operation. Check the ignition timing.

MX-3

1.6L ENGINE

1. Disconnect the negative battery cable. Remove the engine under cover.

2. Remove the accessory drive belts and the water pump pulley.

3. Remove the crankshaft pulley bolts and the plate. Using a suitable tool to hold the crankshaft pulley, remove the pulley lock bolt. Remove the crankshaft pulley and pulley boss.

4. Remove the upper and lower timing belt covers.

5. Tag and disconnect the spark plug wires. Remove the spark plugs.

➡**Spark plugs are removed to make it easier to rotate the engine.**

6. Temporarily reinstall the pulley boss and lock bolt.

7. Turn the crankshaft, using the bolt, until the camshaft sprocket and crankshaft sprocket timing marks are aligned. The pin on the pulley boss faces up.

8. Mark the direction of rotation on the timing belt.

9. Remove the belt tensioner lock bolt, the tensioner wheel and the spring. Remove the timing belt.

➡**Do not rotate the engine after the timing belt has been removed.**

10. Inspect the belt for wear, peeling, cracking, hardening or signs of oil contamination. Inspect the tensioner for free and smooth rotation. Check the

tensioner spring free length; it should not exceed 2.520 in. (64mm). Inspect the sprocket teeth for wear or damage. Replace parts, as necessary.

To install:

11. Make sure the timing marks on the sprockets are properly aligned.

12. Install the timing belt tensioner and spring. Temporarily tighten the bolt with the spring fully extended.

13. Install the timing belt so there is no looseness on the tension side. If reusing the old timing belt, make sure it is reinstalled in the same direction of rotation.

14. Turn the crankshaft 2 turns clockwise and check the timing mark alignment. If the marks are not aligned, repeat Steps 11-14.

15. Loosen the tensioner lock bolt to set the tension, then torque the bolt to 19 ft. lbs. (25 Nm).

16. Turn the crankshaft 2 turns clockwise and check the alignment of the timing marks. If they are not aligned, repeat Steps 11-16.

17. Apply approximately 22 lbs. pressure to the timing belt on the side opposite the tensioner, at a point midway between the sprockets. The belt should deflect 0.43-0.51 in. (11-13mm). If the tension is not as specified, repeat Steps 14-17 or, if necessary, replace the tensioner spring.

18. Remove the pulley boss and lock bolt.

19. Install the spark plugs and connect the spark plug wires.

20. Install the upper and lower timing belt covers. Tighten the bolts to 95 inch lbs. (11 Nm).

21. Install the crankshaft pulley boss and crankshaft pulley. Tighten the lock bolt to 123 ft. lbs. (167 Nm), while holding the pulley boss with a suitable tool.

22. Install the crankshaft pulley plate and tighten the bolts to 13 ft. lbs. (17 Nm).

23. Install the water pump pulley and accessory drive belts. Adjust the belt tension.

24. Install the under cover. Connect the negative battery cable.

25. Start the engine and check for proper operation. Check the ignition timing.

1.8L ENGINE

1. Disconnect the negative battery cable. Remove the engine under cover and side cover.

2. Remove the accessory drive belts.

3. Remove the water pump pulley and the accessory drive belt idler pulley bracket.

4. Disconnect the power steering pump pressure switch connector and disconnect the power steering hose from the engine.

5. Remove the power steering pump reservoir bolts and secure the reservoir aside.

6. Keep the power steering pump pulley from turning, by installing a socket on the end of a breaker bar through one of the pulley holes and engaging a pump mounting bolt. Remove the pulley nut and the pulley.

7. Remove the power steering pump mounting bolts and remove the power steering pump. Secure the pump aside, leaving the hoses connected.

8. Hold the crankshaft pulley with a suitable tool and remove the pulley bolt. Remove the crankshaft pulley, being careful not to damage the crank angle sensor rotor on the rear of the pulley.

9. Disconnect the crank angle sensor connector and remove the clip from the engine oil dipstick tube. Remove the dipstick and tube. Plug the hole after removal to prevent the entry of dirt or foreign material.

10. Remove the knock sensor harness bracket and wiring harness from the timing belt cover.

11. Support the engine with engine support tool 49 G017 5A0 or equivalent.

12. Remove the right side engine mount.

13. Remove the right and left timing belt covers.

14. Install the crankshaft pulley bolt and turn the crankshaft until the No. 1 piston is at TDC on the compression stroke. Mark the direction of rotation on the timing belt.

15. Loosen the automatic tensioner bolts and remove the lower bolt. Hold the tensioner so the bolt threads are not damaged during removal.

16. Hold the upper idler pulley to reduce the belt resistance and remove the pulley bolts and pulley. Remove the timing belt. Remove the automatic tensioner and the remaining idler pulley.

➡**Do not rotate the engine after the timing belt has been removed.**

17. Inspect the belt for wear, peeling, cracking, hardening or signs of oil contamination. Inspect the tensioner pulley for free and smooth rotation. Check the automatic tensioner for oil leakage. Check the tensioner rod projection (free length); it should be

0.55-0.63 in. (14-16mm). Inspect the sprocket teeth for wear or damage. Replace parts, as necessary.

To install:

18. Position the automatic tensioner in a suitable press. Place a flat washer under the tensioner body to prevent damage to the body plug.

19. Slowly press in the tensioner rod, but do not exceed 2200 lbs. force. Insert a pin into the tensioner body to hold the rod in place.

20. Install the tensioner and loosely tighten the upper bolts so the tensioner can move.

➡**This is done to reduce the timing belt resistance when the upper idler pulley is installed.**

21. If removed, install the lower idler pulley and tighten the bolt to 38 ft. lbs. (52 Nm).

22. Make sure the crankshaft and camshaft sprocket timing marks are aligned.

23. Install the timing belt over the crankshaft sprocket, lower idler pulley, left camshaft sprocket, tensioner pulley and right camshaft sprocket, in that order. Make sure the belt has no looseness at the tension side. If reusing the old timing belt, make sure it is installed in the same direction of rotation.

24. Install the upper idler pulley while applying pressure on the timing belt. Be careful not to damage the pulley bolt threads when installing. Tighten the upper idler pulley bolt to 34 ft. lbs. (46 Nm).

25. Push the bottom of the automatic tensioner away from the belt and tighten the mounting bolts to 19 ft. lbs. (25 Nm). Remove the pin from the tensioner, applying tension to the belt.

26. Turn the crankshaft twice in the normal direction of rotation and make sure the timing marks are aligned. If the timing marks are not aligned, repeat Steps 18-26.

27. Apply approximately 22 lbs. pressure to the timing belt at a point midway between the automatic tensioner and the crankshaft sprocket. The belt should deflect 0.24-0.31 in. (6-8mm). If the deflection is not as specified, replace the automatic tensioner.

28. Install new gaskets and the right and left timing belt covers. Tighten the bolts to 95 inch lbs. (11 Nm).

29. Install the crank angle sensor and harness brackets and tighten the bolts to 95 inch lbs. (11 Nm).

30. Install the right side engine mount. Tighten the mount-to-engine nuts to 76 ft. lbs. (103 Nm) and the mount through bolt to 69 ft. lbs. (93 Nm).

31. Remove the engine support tool.

32. Apply clean engine oil to a new O-ring and install on the dipstick tube. Remove the plug and install the dipstick tube and dipstick. Tighten the tube bracket bolt to 95 inch lbs. (11 Nm).

33. Install the crank angle sensor harness and clip to the dipstick tube. Connect the electrical connector.

34. Remove the crankshaft pulley bolt and install the crankshaft pulley. Reinstall the bolt and hold the pulley with a suitable tool. Tighten the bolt to 123 ft. lbs. (167 Nm).

35. Install the power steering pump. Tighten the mounting bolts to 34 ft. lbs. (46 Nm) except the bolt to the right of the idler pulley. Tighten that bolt to 19 ft. lbs. (25 Nm).

36. Install the power steering pump pulley and loosely tighten the nut. Hold the pulley with the socket and breaker bar and tighten the nut to 69 ft. lbs. (93 Nm).

37. Connect the power steering hose to the engine and connect the pressure switch connector.

38. Install the power steering fluid reservoir and engine ground. Tighten to 87 inch lbs. (9.8 Nm).

39. Install the water pump pulley and loosely tighten the bolts. Install the accessory drive belts and adjust the belt tension.

40. Tighten the water pump pulley bolts to 95 inch lbs. (11 Nm).

41. Install the engine under cover and side cover. Connect the negative battery cable.

42. Start the engine and check for proper operation. Check the ignition timing.

626 and MX-6

2.0L ENGINE

1. Disconnect the negative battery cable.

2. Raise and safely support the vehicle. Remove the right front wheel and tire assembly.

3. Remove the engine undercover.

4. Remove the accessory drive belts and the water pump pulley. Remove the power steering pump pulley shield.

5. Remove the power steering pump and position aside, leaving the hoses connected.

6. Hold the crankshaft pulley using a suitable tool and remove the bolt.

Remove the crankshaft pulley and the guide plate.

7. Disconnect the spark plug wires and remove the spark plugs.

8. Loosen the cylinder head bolt cover bolts, in 2-3 steps, in the reverse order of the tightening sequence. Remove the cylinder head cover.

9. Remove the engine oil dipstick and dipstick tube.

10. Remove the upper and lower timing belt covers.

11. Support the engine using engine support tool 49 G017 5A0. Remove the right side engine mount.

12. Turn the crankshaft, in the normal direction of rotation, until the crankshaft and camshaft sprocket timing marks are aligned. Mark the direction of rotation on the belt.

13. Turn the belt tensioner clockwise and disconnect the tensioner spring from the hook pin. Remove the timing belt.

➡**Do not rotate the engine after the timing belt has been removed.**

14. Inspect the belt for wear, peeling, cracking, hardening or signs of oil contamination. Inspect the tensioner pulley for free and smooth rotation and for oil leaks. Check the spring bracket and grommet for looseness or damage. Measure the tensioner spring free length; it should not exceed 1.441 in. (36.6mm). Check the sprockets for worn teeth or other damage.

To install:

15. Make sure the crankshaft and camshaft timing marks are aligned.

➡**It may be easier to check the camshaft sprocket alignment by looking behind the sprockets. The camshafts are properly aligned when the grooves on the rear of the sprockets are even with the cylinder head surface.**

16. Install the timing belt so there is no looseness at the idler side or between the camshaft sprockets. If reusing the old timing belt, make sure it is installed in the same direction of rotation.

17. Turn the crankshaft clockwise 2 turns and make sure the timing marks are correctly aligned. If the marks are not aligned, repeat Steps 15-17.

18. Turn the tensioner clockwise and connect the tensioner spring to the hook pin. Make sure that tension is applied to the timing belt.

19. Turn the crankshaft clockwise 2 turns and make sure the timing marks

are correctly aligned. If the marks are not aligned, repeat Steps 15-19.

20. Install the right side engine mount. Tighten the mount-to-engine nuts to 76 ft. lbs. (102 Nm) and the mount through bolt to 86 ft. lbs. (116 Nm). Install the ground harness and tighten the nut to 65 ft. lbs. (89 Nm).

21. Remove the engine support tool.

22. Install the timing belt covers and tighten the bolts to 95 inch lbs. (10.7 Nm). Install the dipstick tube and dipstick.

23. Apply silicone sealant to the contact surfaces of the cylinder head cover. Allso apply sealant to the cylinder head surface in the area adjacent to the front camshaft caps.

24. Install the cylinder head cover and tighten the bolts in 2-3 steps to 69 inch lbs. (7.8 Nm), in the proper sequence.

25. Install the spark plugs and connect the spark plug wires.

26. Install the guide plate and the crankshaft pulley. Hold the pulley with a suitable tool and tighten the lock bolt to 122 ft. lbs. (166 Nm).

27. Install the power steering pump and tighten the bolts to 33 ft. lbs. (46 Nm).

28. Install the power steering pulley shield and the water pump pulley.

29. Install the accessory drive belts and adjust the belt tension.

30. Install the engine under cover and the right front wheel and tire assemblly. Lower the vehicle.

31. Connect the negative battery cable. Start the engine and check for proper operation. Check the ignition timing.

2.2L ENGINE

1. Disconnect the negative battery cable. Tag and disconnect the spark plug wires and remove the spark plugs.

2. Remove the engine side cover from the fenderwell.

3. Remove the accessory drive belts.

4. Remove the retaining bolts and remove the crankshaft pulley.

5. Remove the upper and lower timng belt covers. Remove the baffle plate from in front of the crankshaft sprocket.

6. Turn the crankshaft clockwise until the **1** mark on the camshaft is aligned with the mark on top of the front housing. Unbolt and remove the tensioner and the tensioner spring.

7. Remove the timing belt. If the timing belt is to be reused, mark the direction of rotation.

➡**Do not rotate the engine after the timing belt has been removed.**

8. Inspect the belt for wear, peeling, cracking, hardening or signs of oil contamination. Inspect the tensioner pulley for free and smooth rotation. Measure the tensioner spring free length; it should not exceed 2.480 in. (63mm). Check the sprockets for worn teeth or other damage.

To install:

9. Make sure the crankshaft and camshaft timing marks are aligned.

10. Installl the timing belt tensioner and spring. Move the tensioner until the spring is fully extended and temporarily tighten the tensioner bolt to hold it in place.

11. Install the tlming belt. Make sure there is no slack at the side of the water pump and idler pulleys. If reusing the old belt, it should be installed in the original direction of rotation.

12. Turn the crankshaft 2 turns clockwise and make sure the timing marks are aligned. If the marks are not aligned, repeat Steps 9-12.

13. Loosen the tensioner lock bolt to apply tension to the belt. Tighten the tensioner bolt to 38 ft. lbs. (52 Nm).

14. Turn the crankshaft 2 turns clockwise and make sure the timing marks are aligned. If the marks are not aligned, repeat Steps 9-14.

15. Apply approximately 22 lbs. pressure to the tlming belt at a point midway between thc idler pulley and camshaft sprocket. A new belt should deflect 0.31-0.35 in. (8-9mm). A used belt should deflect 0.35-0.39 in. (9-10mm). If the deflection is not as specified, repeat Steps 12-15 or, if necessary, replace the tensioner spring.

16. Install the baffle plate wqith the dished side facing away from the engine.

17. Installl the timing belt covers and tighten the bolts to 87 inch lbs. (10 Nm).

18. Install the crankshaft pulley and tighten the bolts to 13 ft. lbs. (17 Nm).

19. Install the accessory drive belts and adjust the belt tension.

20. Install the engine side cover in the fenderwell.

21. Install the spark plugs and connect the spark plug wires.

22. Connect the negative battery cable. Start the engine and check for proper operation. Check the ignition timing.

2.5L ENGINE

1. Disconnect the negative battery cable. Remove the engine under cover and side cover.

2. Remove the accessory drive belts.

3. Remove the water pump pulley and the accessory drive belt idler pulley bracket.

4. Remove the power steering pump reservoir bolts and secure the reservoir aside.

5. Keep the power steering pump pulley from turning, by installing a socket on the end of a breaker bar through one of the pulley holes and engaging a pump mounting bolt. Remove the pulley nut and the pulley.

6. Remove the power steering pump mounting bolts and remove the power steering pump. Secure the pump aside, leaving the hoses connected.

7. Hold the crankshaft pulley with a suitable tool and remove the pulley bolt. Remove the crankshaft pulley, being careful not to damage the crank position sensor rotor on the rear of the pulley.

8. Disconnect the crank position sensor connector and remove the clip from the engine oil dipstick tube. Remove the dlpstick and tube. Plug the hole after removal to prevent the entry of dirt or foreign material.

9. Remove the crank position sensor harness bracket and wiring harness bracket from the timing belt cover.

10. Support the engine with engine support tool 49 G017 5A0 or equivalent.

11. Remove the right side engine mount.

12. Remove the right and left timing belt covers.

13. Install the crankshaft pulley bolt and turn the crankshaft until the No. 1 piston is at TDC on the compression stroke. Mark the direction of rotation on the timing belt.

14. Loosen the automatic tensioner bolts and remove the lower bolt. Hold the tensioner so the bolt threads are not damaged during removal.

15. Hold the upper idler pulley to reduce the belt resistance and remove the pulley bolts and pulley. Remove the timing belt. Remove the automatic tensioner and the remaining idler pulley.

➡**Do not rotate the engine after the timing belt has been removed.**

16. Inspect the belt for wear, peeling, cracking, hardening or signs of oil contamination. Inspect the tensioner pulley for free and smooth rotation. Check the automatic tensioner for oil

leakage. Check the tensioner rod projection (free length); it should be 0.55-0.63 in. (14-16mm). Inspect the sprocket teeth for wear or damage. Replace parts, as necessary.

To install:

17. Position the automatic tensioner in a suitable press. Place a flat washer under the tensioner body to prevent damage to the body plug.

18. Slowly press in the tensioner rod, but do not exceed 2200 lbs. force. Insert a pin into the tensioner body to hold the rod in place.

19. Install the tensioner and loosely tighten the upper bolt so the tensioner can move.

➡**This is done to reduce the timing belt resistance when the upper idler pulley is installed.**

20. If removed, install the lower idler pulley and tighten the bolt to 38 ft. lbs. (52 Nm).

21. Make sure the crankshaft and camshaft sprocket timing marks are aligned.

22. Install the timing belt over the crankshaft sprocket, lower idler pulley, left camshaft sprocket, tensioner pulley and right camshaft sprocket, in that order. Make sure the belt has no looseness at the tension side. If reusing the old timing belt, make sure it is installed in the same direction of rotation.

23. Install the upper idler pulley while applying pressure on the timing belt. Be careful not to damage the pulley bolt threads when installing. Tighten the upper idler pulley bolt to 34 ft. lbs. (46 Nm).

24. Push the bottom of the automatic tensioner away from the belt and tighten the mounting bolts to 19 ft. lbs. (25 Nm). Remove the pin from the tensioner, applying tension to the belt.

25. Turn the crankshaft twice in the normal direction of rotation and make sure the timing marks are aligned. If the timing marks are not aligned, repeat Steps 17-25.

26. Apply approximately 22 lbs. pressure to the timing belt at a point midway between the automatic tensioner and the crankshaft sprocket. The belt should deflect 0.24-0.31 in. (6-8mm). If the deflection is not as specified, replace the automatic tensioner.

27. Install the right and left timing belt covers. Tighten the bolts to 95 inch lbs. (11 Nm).

28. Install the crank position sensor and harness brackets and tighten the bolts to 95 inch lbs. (11 Nm).

29. Install the right side engine mount. Tighten the mount-to-engine nuts to 76 ft. lbs. (103 Nm) and the mount through bolt to 86 ft. lbs. (116 Nm).

30. Remove the engine support tool.

31. Apply clean engine oil to a new O-ring and install on the dipstick tube. Remove the plug and install the dipstick tube and dipstick. Tighten the tube bracket bolt to 95 inch lbs. (11 Nm).

32. Install the crank angle sensor harness and clip to the dipstick tube. Connect the electrical connector.

33. Remove the crankshaft pulley bolt and install the crankshaft pulley. Reinstall the bolt and hold the pulley with a suitable tool. Tighten the bolt to 122 ft. lbs. (166 Nm).

34. Install the power steering pump. Tighten the mounting bolts to 34 ft. lbs. (46 Nm) except the bolt to the right of the idler pulley. Tighten that bolt to 19 ft. lbs. (25 Nm).

35. Install the power steering pump pulley and loosely tighten the nut. Hold the pulley with the socket and breaker bar and tighten the nut to 69 ft. lbs. (93 Nm).

36. Install the power steering fluid reservoir and engine ground. Tighten to 87 inch lbs. (9.8 Nm).

37. Install the water pump pulley and loosely tighten the bolts. Install the accessory drive belts and adjust the belt tension.

38. Tighten the water pump pulley bolts to 95 inch lbs. (11 Nm).

39. Install the engine under cover and side cover. Connect the negative battery cable.

40. Start the engine and check for proper operation. Check the ignition timing.

Camshaft Sprocket

REMOVAL & INSTALLATION

323, Protege, Miata and MX-3 with B6 SOHC Engine

1. Disconnect the negative battery cable. Remove the timing belt.

2. Insert a small prybar through one of the camshaft sprocket holes to keep it from turning.

3. Remove the sprocket bolt and the sprocket from the camshaft.

To install:

4. Align the dowel on the camshaft with the dowel pin facing straight up. The dowel pin on the camshaft should also be facing upward. On DOHC engines, align the stamped E and I on the engine with the E and the I on the pulleys.

5. Install the camshaft sprocket bolt. Hold the sprocket with the prybar and tighten the bolt(s) to 36-45 ft. lbs. (49-61 Nm).

6. Install the timing belt and connect the negative battery cable.

MX-3 with K8 DOHC Engine

1. Disconnect the negative battery cable. Remove the timing belt.

2. Remove the cylinder head cover.

3. Hold the camshaft with a wrench at the cast point of the camshaft to keep it from turning.

4. Remove the sprocket bolt and the sprockets from the camshafts.

To install:

5. Align the timing marks with the camshaft knock pins and install the sprockets.

6. Install the camshaft sprocket bolt. Hold the camshaft in place with the proper wrench and tighten the bolt to 90-103 ft. lbs. (120-140 Nm).

7. Install the cylinder head cover.

8. Install the timing belt and connect the negative battery cable.

1990-92 626 and MX-6

1. Disconnect the negative battery cable. Remove the timing belt.

2. Insert a small prybar through one of the camshaft sprocket holes to keep it from turning.

3. Remove the sprocket bolt and the sprocket from the camshaft.

To install:

4. Align the dowel on the camshaft with the number 1 mark on the camshaft sprocket and install the sprocket.

5. Install the camshaft sprocket bolt. Hold the sprocket with the prybar and tighten the bolt to 35-48 ft. lbs. (47-65 Nm).

6. Install the timing belt and connect the negative battery cable.

1993 626/MX-6 with FS Engine

1. Disconnect the negative battery cable. Remove the timing belt.

2. Remove the cylinder head cover.

3. Hold the camshaft with a wrench at the cast point of the camshaft to keep it from turning.

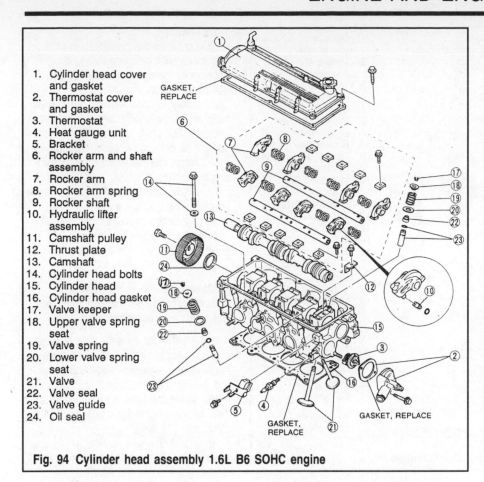

1. Cylinder head cover and gasket
2. Thermostat cover and gasket
3. Thermostat
4. Heat gauge unit
5. Bracket
6. Rocker arm and shaft assembly
7. Rocker arm
8. Rocker arm spring
9. Rocker shaft
10. Hydraulic lifter assembly
11. Camshaft pulley
12. Thrust plate
13. Camshaft
14. Cylinder head bolts
15. Cylinder head
16. Cylindor head gasket
17. Valve keeper
18. Upper valve spring seat
19. Valve spring
20. Lower valve spring seat
21. Valve
22. Valve seal
23. Valve guide
24. Oil seal

Fig. 94 Cylinder head assembly 1.6L B6 SOHC engine

4. Remove the sprocket bolt and the sprockets from the camshafts.

To install:

5. Install the camshaft sprockets so that the dowel pins are facing up. Align the E on the exhaust pulley with the I on the intake pulley.

6. Install the camshaft sprocket bolts. Hold the camshafts in place with the proper wrench and tighten the bolt to 37-44 ft. lbs. (50-60 Nm).

7. Install the cylinder head cover.

8. Install the timing belt and connect the negative battery cable.

1993 626/MX-6 with KL Engine

1. Disconnect the negative battery cable. Remove the timing belt.

2. Remove the cylinder head cover.

3. Hold the camshaft with a wrench at the cast point of the camshaft to keep it from turning.

4. Remove the sprocket bolt and the sprockets from the camshafts.

To install:

5. Align the sprocket groove with the camshaft knock pins and install the sprockets.

6. Install the camshaft sprocket bolt. Hold the camshaft in place with the proper wrench and tighten the bolt to 90-103 ft. lbs. (120-140 Nm).

7. Install the cylinder head cover.

8. Install the timing belt and connect the negative battery cable.

Camshaft

REMOVAL & INSTALLATION

1.6L and 1.8L SOHC Engines

➧ **See Figures 94 and 95**

➡**The camshaft is removed through the front of the cylinder head.**

1. Remove the cylinder head from the vehicle and position in a suitable holding fixture.

➡**Do not lay the cylinder head flat on the head gasket surface as the valves may be damaged.**

2. On 1.6L and 1.8L engines, hold the camshaft with a wrench on the hexagon cast into the front of the camshaft.

3. Remove the sprocket bolt and the sprocket.

4. Loosen the rocker arm shaft bolts in 2-3 steps, in the reverse of the torque sequence. Remove the rocker arm and shaft assemblies.

5. Pry out the camshaft seal using a small prybar, being careful not to damage the camshaft or seall bore.

6. Remove the thrust plate at the rear of the cylinder head.

7. Carefully slide the camshaft from the cylinder head, being careful not to damage the cylinder head bearing surfaces.

To install:

8. Lubricate the camshaft lobes and journals and the cylinder head bearing surfaces with clean engine oil.

9. Carefully slide the camshaft into the cylinder head, being careful not to damage the bearing surfaces.

10. Install the camshaft thrust plate. On the 1.6L 8-valve engine, tighten the thrust retaining bolt to 95 in. lbs. (11 Nm). On the 1.6L and 1.8L 16-valve engines, the thrust plate is held in place by the rocker arm and shaft assembly.

11. Lubricate the lip of a new camshaft seal with clean engine oil and install in the cylinder head, using a seal installer.

12. Lubricate the rocker arms and valve stem tips with clean engine oil. Install the rocker arm and shaft assemblies and tighten the bolts, in 2-3 steps, in the proper sequence. The final torque should be 21 ft. lbs. (28 Nm) on the 1.6L and 1.8L engines.

13. Install the camshaft sprocket and retaining bolt. Hold the camshaft with the wrench on the hexagon and tighten the bolt to 45 ft. lbs. (61 Nm).

14. Install the cylinder head and the remaining components in the reverse order of removal.

1.6L, 1.8L and 2.0L DOHC Engines

➧ **See Figures 96, 97 and 98**

1. Disconnect the negative battery cable. Drain the cooling system on Miata.

2. Label and disconnect the spark plug wires and remove the spark plugs.

3. Disconnect the hoses from the cylinder head cover, if equipped.

4. Remove the cylinder head cover bolts and remove the cylinder head cover. On 2.0L engine, loosen the bolts in 2-3 steps in the reverse of the torque sequence.

5. Remove the timing belt. Remove the distributor, or on Miata, remove the crank angle sensor.

6. Hold the camshaft with a wrench on the hexagon cast into the camshaft. Remove the sprocket bolts and remove the sprockets.

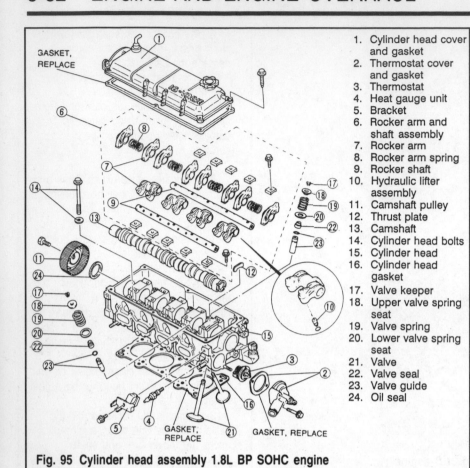

1. Cylinder head cover and gasket
2. Thermostat cover and gasket
3. Thermostat
4. Heat gauge unit
5. Bracket
6. Rocker arm and shaft assembly
7. Rocker arm
8. Rocker arm spring
9. Rocker shaft
10. Hydraulic lifter assembly
11. Camshaft pulley
12. Thrust plate
13. Camshaft
14. Cylinder head bolts
15. Cylinder head
16. Cylinder head gasket
17. Valve keeper
18. Upper valve spring seat
19. Valve spring
20. Lower valve spring seat
21. Valve
22. Valve seal
23. Valve guide
24. Oil seal

Fig. 95 Cylinder head assembly 1.8L BP SOHC engine

7. Label the caps so they can be reinstalled in their original positions. Loosen the camshaft cap bolts in 2-3 steps in the reverse of the torque sequence, then remove the camshaft caps.

8. Remove the camshafts. Remove the camshaft oil seals from the camshafts.

To install:

9. Lubricate the camshaft journals and lobes with clean engine oil. Install the camshafts in the cylinder head.

10. Apply silicone sealant to the cylinder head on the front camshaft cap mating surfaces. Do not allow any sealant on the camshaft journals.

11. Install the camshaft caps in their original positions. Loosely install the cap bolts.

12. Tighten the camshaft cap bolts in 2-3 steps to 125 inch lbs. (14 Nm) in the proper sequence.

13. Apply clean engine oil to the lip of a new camshaft seal. Push the seal slightly in by hand. Tap the seal into position, using a seall installer, until it is flush with the edge of the camshaft cap.

14. Turn the camshafts until the dowel pins face sraight up. Install the camshaft sprockets and the sprocket bolts.

15. Hold the camshaft with the wrench on the cast hexagon and tighten the sprocket bolts to 44 ft. lbs. (60 Nm).

16. Install the remaining components in the reverse order of removal.

2.2L Engine
▶ **See Figure 99**

1. Disconnect the negative battery cable.

2. Disconnect the spark plug wires and hoses from the cylinder head cover and remove the cylinder head cover.

3. Remove the timing belt and the distributor.

4. Insert a suitable tool through one of the camshaft sprocket holes to keep the camshaft from turning. Remove the sprocket bolt and remove the sprocket.

5. Remove the front and rear housings from the cylinder head.

6. Loosen the rocker arm shaft bolts, in 2-3 steps, in the reverse of the torque sequence. Remove the rocker arm and shaft assemblies with the bolts.

7. Remove the camshaft caps. Label their position prior to removal so they can be reinstalled in their original locations.

8. Remove the camshaft.

To install:

9. Lubricate the camshaft journals and lobes with clean engine oil and position in the cylinder head with the dowel pin facing straight up.

10. Apply silicone sealant the cylinder head in the area adjacent to the front and rear camshaft journals. Do not allow sealant to get on the camshaft journals.

11. Install the camshaft caps in their original locations.

12. Apply clean engine oil to the valve stem tips and rocker arms.

13. Install the rocker arm and shaft assemblies. Tighten the bolts in 2-3 steps to 20 ft. lbs. (26 Nm) in the proper sequence.

➡**Make sure the rocker arms or spacers do not get caught between the shaft and camshaft cap.**

14. Pry the old oil seal from the front housing. Apply engine oil to the front housing and a new oil seal and press the seal into the housing.

15. Install the front housing using a new gasket. Tighten the bolt and nut to 19 ft. lbs. (25 Nm).

16. Install the rear housing using a new gasket. Tighten the bolts/nuts to 19 ft. lbs. (25 Nm).

17. Apply silicone sealant at the front and rear corners of the cylinder head and install the cylinder head cover. Tighten the bolts to 69 inch lbs. (8 Nm). Connect the hoses and spark pluig wires.

18. Install the camshaft sprocket on the camshaft with the sprocket bolt. Hold the camshaft sprocket using a suitable tool inserted through a sprocket hole and tighten the bolt to 48 ft. lbs. (65 Nm).

19. Install the timing belt and the remaining components in the reverse order of removal.

MX-3 1.8L and MX-6/626 2.5L Engines
▶ **See Figure 100**

1. Properly relieve the fuel system pressure. Disconnect the negative battery cable and drain the cooling system.

2. Remove the timing belt.

3. Disconnect the accelerator cable. On 1.8L engine, disconnect the throttle cable.

4. Label and disconnect the spark plug wires.

5. Label and disconnect the necessary wiring and hoses.

6. Remove the intake manifold and the cylinder head covers.

7. Remove the distributor.

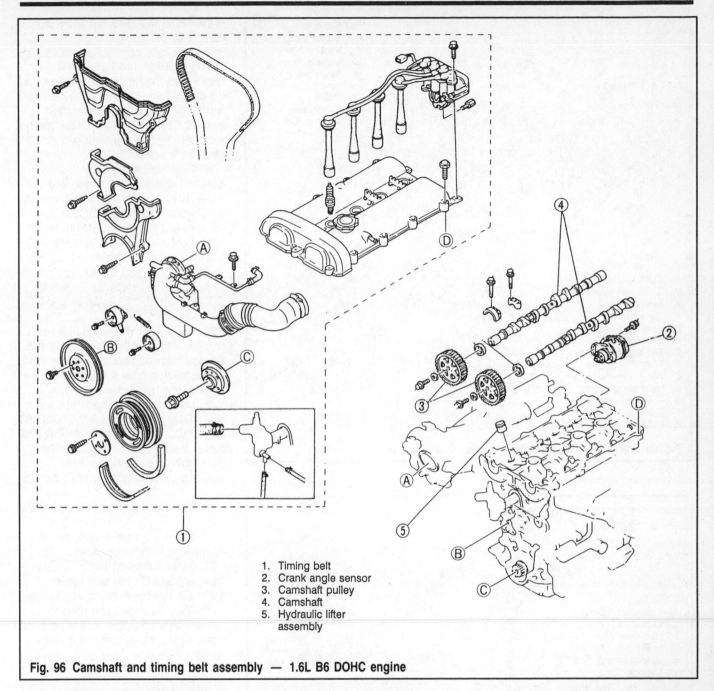

1. Timing belt
2. Crank angle sensor
3. Camshaft pulley
4. Camshaft
5. Hydraulic lifter
   assembly

Fig. 96 Camshaft and timing belt assembly — 1.6L B6 DOHC engine

8. Hold the camshaft with a wrench on the hexagon cast into the camshaft. Remove the sprocket bolt and remove the sprocket.

9. Turn the camshaft, using a wrench on the cast hexagon, until the camshaft knock pin is aligned with the cylinder head marks.

➡**Do not remove the camshaft caps when the camshaft lobe is pressing on a lifter, as the thrust journal support may become damaged.**

10. Loosen the front camshaft cap bolts in 5-6 steps, in the proper sequence. Bolt **A** is only on the right cylinder head. Remove the front camshaft cap.

11. Mark the position of the camshaft caps so they can be reinstalled in their original locations. Loosen the remaining camshaft cap bolts in 5-6 steps, in the proper sequence, then remove the caps.

12. Remove the camshafts.

To install:

13. Lubricate the camshaft journals, lobes and gears with clean engine oil. Align the intake and exhaust camshaft timing marks and install the camshafts.

➡**The thrust plate positions for the right and left cylinder head camshafts are different.**

14. Make sure the camshaft cap and cylinder head surfaces are clean. Apply a small amount of sealant to the mating

surface of the front camshaft cap on both cylinder heads and the rear exhaust camshaft cap on the left cylinder head. Do not get any sealant on the camshaft rotating surfaces.

15. Install the front camshaft caps and thrust plate caps and tighten the bolts until the cap seats fully to the cylinder head. Install the remaining camshaft caps in their original locations and loosely tighten the bolts.

16. Tighten the camshaft cap bolts in 5-6 steps to 126 inch lbs. (14 Nm), in the proper sequence.

17. Apply clean engine oil to a new oil seal and the cylinder head. Install the seal, using a suitable installer. Apply

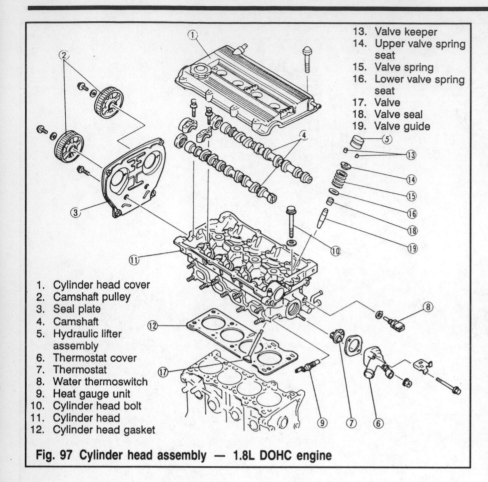

13. Valve keeper
14. Upper valve spring seat
15. Valve spring
16. Lower valve spring seat
17. Valve
18. Valve seal
19. Valve guide

1. Cylinder head cover
2. Camshaft pulley
3. Seal plate
4. Camshaft
5. Hydraulic lifter assembly
6. Thermostat cover
7. Thermostat
8. Water thermoswitch
9. Heat gauge unit
10. Cylinder head bolt
11. Cylinder head
12. Cylinder head gasket

Fig. 97 Cylinder head assembly — 1.8L DOHC engine

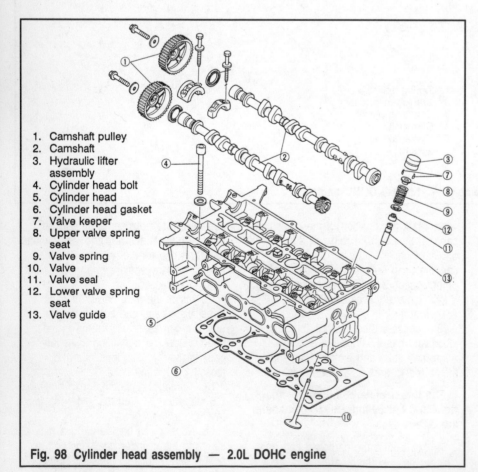

1. Camshaft pulley
2. Camshaft
3. Hydraulic lifter assembly
4. Cylinder head bolt
5. Cylinder head
6. Cylinder head gasket
7. Valve keeper
8. Upper valve spring seat
9. Valve spring
10. Valve
11. Valve seal
12. Lower valve spring seat
13. Valve guide

Fig. 98 Cylinder head assembly — 2.0L DOHC engine

sealant to a new blind cap and install, using a plastic hammer.

18. Install the camshaft sprockets. On the right cylinder head, install the sprocket so the **R** mark can be seen and the timing mark aligns with the camshaft knock pin. On the left cylinder head, install the sprocket so the **L** mark can be seen and the timing mark aligns with the camshaft knock pin.

19. Apply clean engine oil to the camshaft sprocket bolt threads and install. Hold the camshaft with a wrench on the cast hexagon and tighten the sprocket bolt to 103 ft. lbs. (140 Nm).

20. Coat a new gasket with sealant and install onto the cylinder head cover. Install the cover and tighten the bolts, in sequence, in 2-3 steps, to 78 inch lbs. (8.8 Nm). Install the ventilation pipe to the left cover.

21. Apply clean engine oil to a new O-ring and install on the distributor. Install the distributor with the blade fitting into the camshaft groove and loosely tighten the retaining bolt.

22. Install the intake manifold using a new gasket. Loosely install the bolts and nuts. Install the intake manifold stay and tighten the bolts to 19 ft. lbs. (25 Nm), then tighten the intake manifold bolts/nuts, in 2-3 steps, to 19 ft. lbs. (25 Nm).

23. Connect the wiring, hoses, and the fuel lines.

24. Connect the accelerator and, if equipped, throttle valve cables.

25. Install the timing belt.

26. Connect the negative battery cable. Fill and bleed the cooling system.

27. Start the engine and bring to normal operating temperature. Check for leaks. Check the ignition timing and idle speed.

INSPECTION

1. Clean the camshaft in solvent and allow to dry.

2. Inspect the camshaft for obvious signs of wear: scores, nicks or pits on the journals or lobes. Light scuffs or nicks can be removed with an oil stone.

3. Using a micrometer, measure the diameter of the journals and compare to specifications. Replace the camshaft if any journals are not within specification.

4. Measure the camshaft lobes across their maximum lobe height dimensions, using a micrometer. Compare your measurements with the lobe height specifications. Replace the

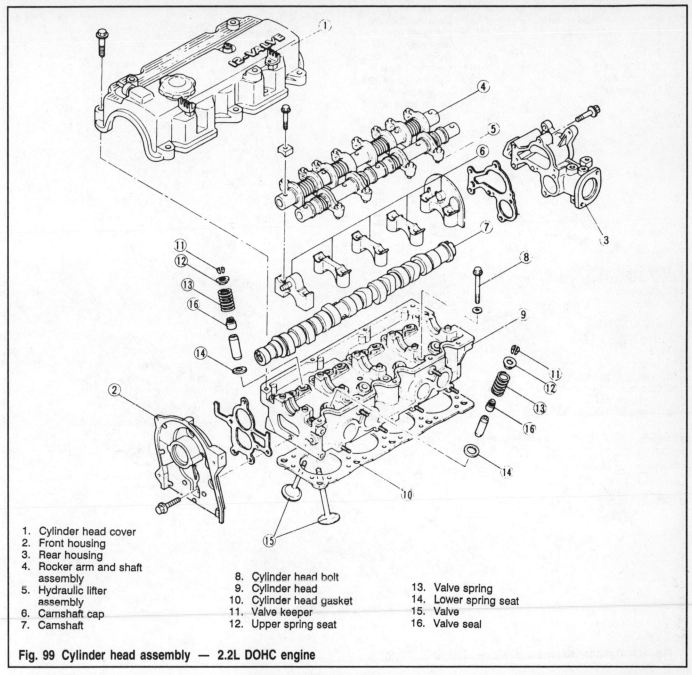

1. Cylinder head cover
2. Front housing
3. Rear housing
4. Rocker arm and shaft assembly
5. Hydraulic lifter assembly
6. Camshaft cap
7. Camshaft
8. Cylinder head bolt
9. Cylinder head
10. Cylinder head gasket
11. Valve keeper
12. Upper spring seat
13. Valve spring
14. Lower spring seat
15. Valve
16. Valve seal

Fig. 99 Cylinder head assembly — 2.2L DOHC engine

camshaft if any lobe heights are not within specification.

5. Mount the camshaft in V-blocks with the front and rear journals riding on the blocks. Check if the camshaft is bent using a dial indicator on the center bearing journal. The limit at the center journal is 0.0012 in. (0.03mm). Replace the camshaft if runout is excessive.

6. Check the camshaft endplay with the camshaft laying in the cylinder on the lower bearing journals. Mount a dial indicator to the front of the cylinder head with the indicator foot resting on the end of the camshaft. Move the camshaft back and forth and observe the indicator. Compare the reading with the specification. If endplay is excessive,

replace the camshaft or the cylinder head.

Pistons and Connecting Rods

REMOVAL

▶ See Figures 101, 102 and 103

➡**Although the pistons and connecting rods can be removed from the engine (after the cylinder head and oil pan are removed) while the engine is still in the car; it is far**

easier to work on the engine when removed from the car, and advisable for assembly cleanliness.

1. Remove the engine from the vehicle and mount it on a suitable workstand.
2. Remove the cylinder head(s) and the oil pan.
3. The position of each piston, connecting rod and connecting rod cap should be noted before any are removed, so they can be reinstalled in the same location.
4. Check the tops of the pistons and the sides of the connecting rods for identifying marks. In some engines, the top of the piston will be numbered to

1. Cylinder head cover
2. Camshaft pulley
3. Seal plate
4. Water outlet
5. Camshaft cap
6. Blind cap
7. Camshaft
8. Camshaft oil seal
9. Hydraulic lifter assembly
10. Cylinder head bolt
11. Cylinder head
12. Cylinder head gasket
13. Valve keeper
14. Upper valve spring seat
15. Valve spring
16. Lower valve spring seat
17. Valve
18. Valve seal

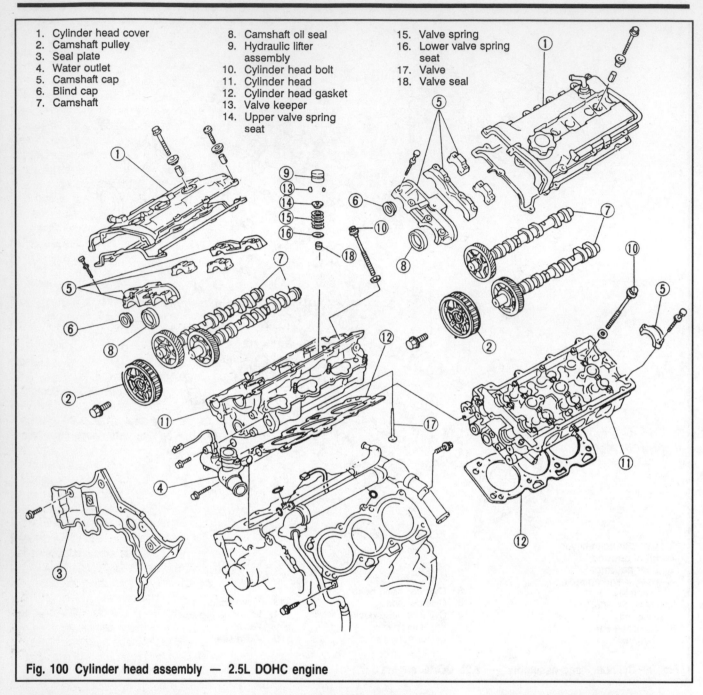

Fig. 100 Cylinder head assembly — 2.5L DOHC engine

correspond with the cylinder number. The connecting rod and connecting rod cap should have numbers stamped on them where they meet that also correspond with their cylinder number. Refer to the firing order diagrams in Section 2 to see how the cylinders are numbered. If you cannot see any identifying numbers, use a number punch set and stamp in the numbers yourself.

5. Rotate the crankshaft until the piston to be removed is at the bottom of the cylinder. Check for a ridge at the top of the cylinder bore before removing the piston and connecting rod assembly, referring to the Ridge Removal and Honing procedure.

6. Loosen the connecting rod nuts until the nuts are flush with the ends of the rod bolts. Using a hammer and a brass drift or piece of wood, lightly tap on the nuts/bolts until the connecting rod cap is loosened from the connecting rod. Remove the nuts, rod cap and lower bearing insert.

7. Slip a piece of snug fitting rubber hose over each rod bolt, to prevent the bolt threads from damaging the crankshaft during removal.

8. Using a hammer handle or piece of wood or plastic, tap the rod and piston upward in the bore until the piston rings clear the cylinder block. Remove the piston and connecting rod assembly from the top of the cylinder bore.

CLEANING AND INSPECTION

1. Remove the piston rings using a piston ring expander. Refer to the Piston Ring Replacement procedure.

2. Clean the ring grooves with a ring groove cleaner, being careful not to cut into the piston metal. Heavy carbon deposits can be cleaned from the top of the piston with a wire brush, however, do not use a wire wheel on the ring grooves or lands. Clean the oil drain holes in the ring grooves. Clean all remaining dirt, carbon and varnish from the piston with a suitable solvent and a brush; do not use a caustic solution.

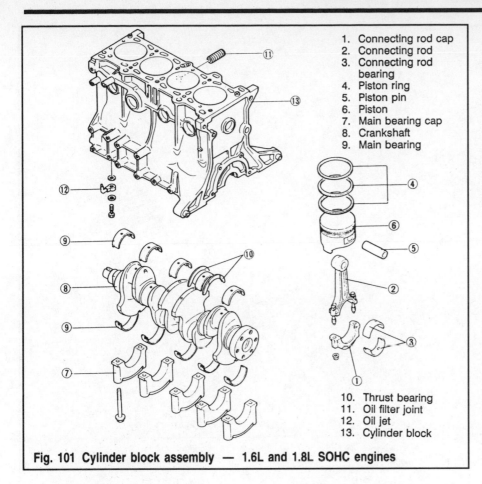

1. Connecting rod cap
2. Connecting rod
3. Connecting rod bearing
4. Piston ring
5. Piston pin
6. Piston
7. Main bearing cap
8. Crankshaft
9. Main bearing
10. Thrust bearing
11. Oil filter joint
12. Oil jet
13. Cylinder block

Fig. 101 Cylinder block assembly — 1.6L and 1.8L SOHC engines

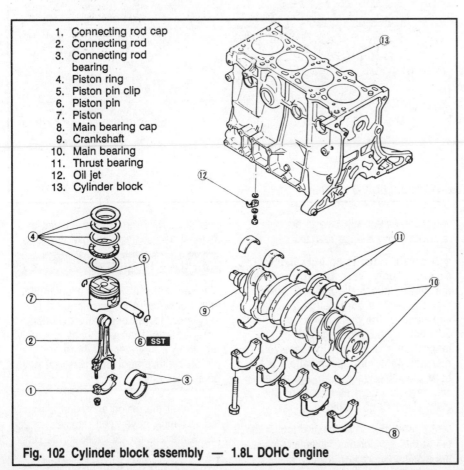

1. Connecting rod cap
2. Connecting rod
3. Connecting rod bearing
4. Piston ring
5. Piston pin clip
6. Piston pin
7. Piston
8. Main bearing cap
9. Crankshaft
10. Main bearing
11. Thrust bearing
12. Oil jet
13. Cylinder block

Fig. 102 Cylinder block assembly — 1.8L DOHC engine

3. After cleaning, inspect the piston for scuffing, scoring, cracks, pitting or excessive ring groove wear. Replace any piston that is obviously worn.

4. If the piston appears okay, measure the piston diameter using a micrometer. Measure the piston diameter in the thrust direction. On 2.2L engine, measure 0.0709 in. (18mm) below the oil ring groove. On 3.0L engine, measure in line with the centerline of the piston pin.

5. Measure the cylinder bore diameter using a bore gauge, or with a telescope gauge and micrometer. The measurement should be made in the piston thrust direction (perpendicular to the piston pin), about 2½in. (63.5mm) below the cylinder block deck.

6. Subtract the piston diameter measurement made in Step 4 from the cylinder bore measurement made in Step 5. This is the piston-to-bore clearance. If the clearance is within specification, light finish honing is all that is necessary. If the clearance is excessive, the cylinder must be bored and the piston replaced. Consult an automotive machine shop. If the pistons are replaced, the piston rings must also be replaced.

7. If the piston-to-bore clearance is okay, check the ring groove clearance. Insert the ring that will be used in the ring groove and check the clearance with a feeler gauge. Compare your measurement with specification. Replace the piston if the ring groove clearance is not within specification.

8. Check the connecting rod for damage or obvious wear. Check for signs of fractures and check the bearing bore for out-of-round and taper.

9. A shiny surface on the pin boss side of the piston usually indicates that the connecting rod is bent or the wrist pin hole is not in proper relation to the piston skirt and ring grooves.

10. Abnormal connecting rod bearing wear can be caused by either a bent connecting rod, an improperly machined journal, or a tapered connecting rod bore.

11. Twisted connecting rods will not create an easily identifiable wear pattern, but badly twisted rods will disturb the action of the entire piston, rings, and connecting rod assembly and may be the cause of excessive oil consumption.

12. If a connecting rod problem is suspected, consult an automotive machine shop to have the rod checked.

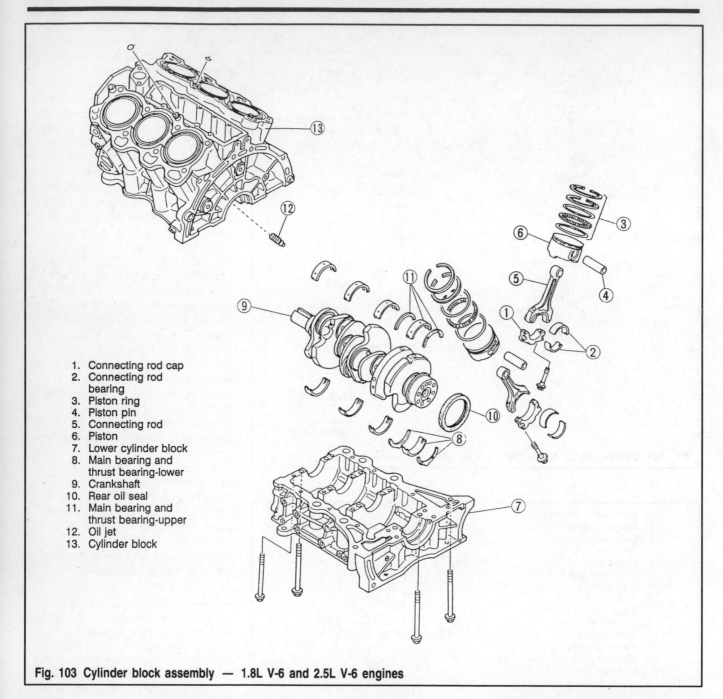

1. Connecting rod cap
2. Connecting rod bearing
3. Piston ring
4. Piston pin
5. Connecting rod
6. Piston
7. Lower cylinder block
8. Main bearing and thrust bearing-lower
9. Crankshaft
10. Rear oil seal
11. Main bearing and thrust bearing-upper
12. Oil jet
13. Cylinder block

Fig. 103 Cylinder block assembly — 1.8L V-6 and 2.5L V-6 engines

RIDGE REMOVAL AND HONING

1. Before the piston is removed from the cylinder, check for a ridge at the top of the cylinder bore. This ridge occurs because the piston ring does not travel all the way to the top of the bore, thereby leaving an unused portion of cylinder bore.

2. Clean away any carbon buildup at the top of the cylinder with sand paper, in order to see the extent of the ridge more clearly. If the ridge is slight, it will be safe to remove the pistons without damaging the rings or piston ring lands. If the ridge is severe, and easily catches

your fingernail, it will have to be removed using a ridge reamer.

➡**A severe ridge is an indication of excessive bore wear. Before removing the piston, check the cylinder bore diameter with a bore gauge, as explained in the piston and connecting rod cleaning and inspection procedure. Compare your measurement with specification. If the bore is excessively worn, the cylinder will have to bored oversize and the piston and rings replaced.**

3. Install the ridge removal tool in the top of the cylinder bore. Carefully follow the manufacturers instructions for

operation. Only remove the amount of material necessary to remove the ridge.

✳✳WARNING

Be very careful if you are unfamiliar with operating a ridge reamer. It is very easy to remove more cylinder bore material than you want, possibly requiring a cylinder overbore and piston replacement that may not have been necessary.

4. After the piston and connecting rod assembly have been removed, check the clearances as explained in the piston and connecting rod cleaning and inspection procedure, to determine

whether boring and honing or just light honing are required. If boring is necessary, consult an automotive machine shop. If light honing is all that is necessary, proceed to Step 5.

5. Honing is best done with the crankshaft removed, to prevent damage to the crankshaft and to make post-honing cleaning easier, as the honing process will scatter metal particles. However, if you do not want to remove the crankshaft, position the connecting rod journal for the cylinder being honed as far away from the bottom of the cylinder bore as possible, and wrap a shop cloth around the journal.

6. Honing can be done either with a flexible glaze breaker type hone or with a rigid hone that has honing stones and guide shoes. The flexible hone removes the least amount of metal, and is especially recommended if your piston-to-cylinder bore clearance is on the loose side. The flexible hone is useful to provide a finish on which the new piston rings will seat. A rigid hone will remove more material than the flexible hone and requires more operator skill.

7. Regardless of which type of hone you use, carefully follow the manufacturers instructions for operation.

8. The hone should be moved up and down the bore at sufficient speed to obtain a uniform finish. A rigid hone will provide a definite cross-hatch finish; operate the rigid hone at a speed to obtain a 45-65° included angle in the cross-hatch. The finish marks should be clean but not sharp, free from embedded particles and torn or folded metal.

9. Periodically during the honing procedure, thoroughly clean the cylinder bore and check the piston-to-bore clearance with the piston for that cylinder.

10. After honing is completed, thoroughly wash the cylinder bores and the rest of the engine with hot water and detergent. Scrub the bores well with a stiff bristle brush and rinse thoroughly with hot water. Thorough cleaning is essential, for if any abrasive material is left in the cylinder bore, it will rapidly wear the new rings and the cylinder bore. If any abrasive material is left in the rest of the engine, it will be picked up by the oil and carried throughout the engine, damaging bearings and other parts.

11. After the bores are cleaned, wipe them down with a clean cloth coated with light engine oil, to keep them from rusting.

PISTON PIN REPLACEMENT

All Mazda engines utilize pressed-in wrist pins, which can only be removed with a press and special fixtures. Attempting to remove the wrist pins with other than these special fixtures can result in damage to the piston and/or connecting rod. If a wrist pin problem is suspected (too tight, too loose, etc.) consult an automotive machine shop.

PISTON RING REPLACEMENT

1. Remove the piston rings from the piston using a piston ring expander.

2. Clean the piston ring grooves, check the piston-to-cylinder bore clearance and check the ring groove clearance as explained in the piston and connecting rod cleaning and inspection procedure.

3. After the cylinder bores have been finish honed and cleaned, check the piston ring end gap. Compress the piston rings to be used in the cylinder, one at a time, into that cylinder. Using an inverted piston, push the ring down into the cylinder bore area where normal ring wear is not encountered.

4. Measure the ring end gap with a feeler gauge and compare to specification. A gap that is too tight is more harmful than one that is too loose (If ring end gap is excessively loose, the cylinder bore is probably worn beyond specification).

5. If the ring end gap is too tight, carefully remove the ring and file the ends squarely with a fine file to obtain the proper clearance.

6. Install the rings on the piston, lowest ring first. The lowest (oil) ring is installed by hand; the top 2 (compression) rings must be installed using a piston ring expander. There is a high risk of breaking or distorting the compression rings if they are installed by hand.

7. Install the oil ring spacer in the bottom ring groove. Make sure the ends butt together and do not overlap. The ends must be on a solid portion of the piston, not over a drain hole.

8. Start the end of an oil ring rail ring into the oil ring groove above the spacer. The end gap must be approximately 1 in. (25.4mm) away from the spacer ends. Finish installing the rail ring by spiraling it the remainder of the way on. Repeat the rail installation with the other rail ring. Its gap must be

approximately 1 in. (25.4mm) on the other side of the spacer ends.

9. Install the lower compression ring in the piston ring expander with the proper side up. The piston ring packaging should contain instructions as to the directions the ring sides should face. Spread the ring with the expander and install it on the piston.

10. Repeat Step 9 to install the top compression ring. Space the compression ring gaps approximately 2 in. (50.8mm) on opposite sides of the oil ring gaps.

➡**If the instructions on the ring packaging differ from this information regarding ring gap positioning, follow the ring manufacturers instructions.**

ROD BEARING REPLACEMENT

1. Inspect the rod bearings for scoring, chipping or other wear.

2. Inspect the crankshaft rod bearing journal for wear. Measure the journal diameter in several locations around the journal and compare to specification. If the crankshaft journal is scored or has deep ridges, or its diameter is below specification, the crankshaft must be removed from the engine and reground. Consult an automotive machine shop.

3. If the crankshaft journal appears usable, clean it and the rod bearing shells until they are completely free of oil. Blow any oil from the oil hole in the crankshaft.

➡**The journal surfaces and bearing shells must be completely free of oil to get an accurate reading with Plastigage®.**

4. Place a strip of Plastigage® lengthwise along the bottom center of the lower bearing shell, then install the cap with the shell and torque the connecting rod nuts to specification. Do not turn the crankshaft with the Plastigage® installed in the bearing.

5. Remove the bearing cap with the shell. The flattened Plastigage® will either be sticking to the bearing shell or the crankshaft journal.

6. Using the printed scale on the Plastigage® package, measure the flattened Plastigage® at its widest point. The number on the scale that most closely corresponds to the width of the Plastigage® indicates the bearing clearance in thousandths of an inch or hundreths of a millimeter.

7. Compare your findings with the bearing clearance specification. If the bearing clearance is excessive, the bearing must be replaced or the crankshaft must be ground and the bearing replaced.

➡ If the crankshaft is still at standard size (has not been ground undersize), bearing shell sets of 0.001, (0.0254mm) 0.002 (0.050mm) and 0.003 in. (0.0762mm) over standard size are available to correct excessive bearing clearance.

8. After clearance measuring is completed, be sure to remove the Plastigage® from the crankshaft and/or bearing shell.

9. For final bearing shell installation, make sure the connecting rod and rod cap bearing saddles are clean and free of nicks or burrs. Install the bearing shells in the connecting rod, making sure the bearing shell tangs are seated in the notches.

➡ Be careful when handling any plain bearings. Your hands and the working area should be clean. Dirt is easily embedded in the bearing surface and the bearings are easily scratched or damaged.

INSTALLATION

1. Make sure the cylinder bore and crankshaft journal are clean.
2. Position the crankshaft journal at its furthest position away from the bottom of the cylinder bore.
3. Coat the cylinder bore with light engine oil.
4. Make sure the rod bearing shells are correctly installed. Install the rubber hoses over the connecting rod bolts to protect the crankshaft during installation.
5. Make sure the piston rings are properly installed and the ring end gaps are correctly positioned. Install a piston ring compressor over the piston and rings and compress the piston rings into their grooves. Follow the ring compressor manufacturers instructions.
6. Place the piston and connecting rod assembly into the cylinder bore. Make sure the assembly is the correct one for that bore and that the piston and connecting rod are facing in the proper direction. Most pistons have an arrow or notch on the top of the piston, or the letter F appears somewhere on the piston to indicate "front", meaning this side should face the front of the engine.

7. Make sure the ring compressor is seated squarely on the block deck surface. If the compressor is not seated squarely, a ring could pop out from beneath the compressor and hang up on the deck surface, as the piston is tapped into the bore, possibly breaking the ring.
8. Make sure that the connecting rod is not hung up on the crankshaft counterweights and is in position to come straight on to the crankshaft.
9. Tap the piston slowly into the bore, making sure the compressor remains squarely against the block deck. When the piston is completely in the bore, remove the ring compressor.
10. Coat the crankshaft journal and the bearing shells with engine assembly lube or clean engine oil. Pull the connecting rod onto the crankshaft journal. After the rod is seated, remove the rubber hoses from the rod bolts.
11. Install the rod bearing cap. Lightly oil the connecting rod bolt threads and install the rod nuts. Torque to specification.
12. After each piston and connecting rod assembly is installed, turn the crankshaft over several times and check for binding. If there is a problem and the crankshaft will not turn, or turns with great difficulty, it will be easier to find the problem (rod cap on backwards, broken ring, etc.) than if all the assemblies are installed.
13. Check the clearance between the sides of the connecting rods and the crankshaft using a feeler gauge. Spread the rods slightly with a screwdriver to insert the gauge. If the clearance is below the minimum specification, the connecting rod will have to be removed and machined to provide adequate clearance. If the clearance is excessive, substitute an unworn rod and recheck. If the clearance is still excessive, the crankshaft must be welded and reground, or replaced.
14. Install the oil pan and cylinder head(s).
15. Install the engine in the vehicle.

Freeze Plugs

REMOVAL & INSTALLATION

1. Raise and safely support the vehicle, as required.
2. Drain the cooling system. If the freeze plug is located in the cylinder block, it will be necessary to remove the

drain plug from the side of the block to make sure all coolant is drained.
3. Drill a ½in. (13mm) hole in the center of the plug. Remove the plug with a slide hammer or pry it out with a prybar.

➡ Be careful to stop drilling as soon as the bit breaks through the plug to prevent damaging the engine.

4. Clean all dirt and corrosion from the freeze plug bore. Check the freeze plug bore for damage that would interfere with sealing. If the bore is damaged, the bore will have to be machined for an oversize plug.
   To install:
5. Coat the plug bore and the freeze plug sealing surface with water proof sealer.
6. Install cup-type freeze plugs with the flanged edge outward. The plug must be driven in with a tool that does not contact the flange of the plug. If an improper tool is used, the plug sealing edge will be damaged and leakage will result.
7. Expansion-type freeze plugs are installed with the flanged edge inward. The plug must be driven in with a tool that does not contact the crowned portion of the plug. If an improper tool is used, the plug and/or plug bore will be damaged.
8. Replace any drain plugs that were removed and lower the vehicle.
9. Fill the cooling system, start the engine and check for leaks.

Rear Main Seal

REMOVAL & INSTALLATION

323/Protege, Miata and MX-3 with B6 engine

◢ See Figure 104

1. Disconnect the negative battery cable.
2. Raise and safely support the vehicle.
3. Remove the transaxle/transmission assembly. Refer to Section 7.
4. If equipped with a manual transaxle/transmission, remove the clutch and flywheel assembly. Refer to Section 7.
5. If equipped with an automatic transaxle/transmission, remove the flexplate-to-crankshaft bolts, the flexplate and shim plates.

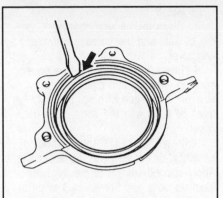

Fig. 104 Rear main seal removal — 323/Protege, Miata, and MX-3 with B6 engine

6. Cut the oil seal lip with a knife. Install a rag to the pump body and using a screwdriver, carefully pry the oil seal from the oil seal housing. Clean the gasket mounting surfaces.

To install:

7. Clean the oil seal housing. Coat the oil seal and the housing with clean engine oil.

8. Press the oil seal into the housing and tap it evenly into place with a hammer and a 4 inch diameter piece of pipe. The seal must be flush with the edge of the rear cover.

9. Install the clutch and flywheel assembly or the flexplate, as applicable. Tighten the flywheel or flexplate bolts to 71-76 ft. lbs. (96-103 Nm).

10. Install the transaxle/transmission, lower the vehicle and connect the negative battery cable.

MX-3 with K8 DOHC

1. Disconnect the negative battery cable.

2. Raise and safely support the vehicle.

3. Remove the transaxle assembly. Refer to Section 7.

4. If equipped with a manual transaxle, remove the clutch and flywheel assembly. Refer to Section 7.

5. If equipped with an automatic transaxle, remove the flexplate-to-

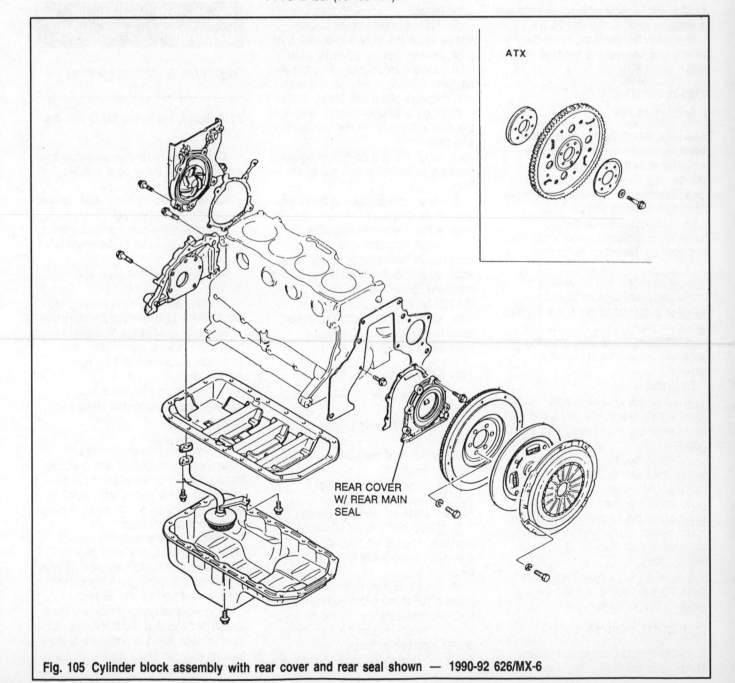

ATX

REAR COVER W/ REAR MAIN SEAL

Fig. 105 Cylinder block assembly with rear cover and rear seal shown — 1990-92 626/MX-6

crankshaft bolts, the flexplate and shim plates.

6. Cut the oil seal lip with a knife. Install a rag to the pump body and using a screwdriver, carefully pry the oil seal from the oil seal housing. Clean the gasket mounting surfaces.

To install:

7. Clean the oil seal housing. Coat the oil seal and the housing with clean engine oil.

8. Press the oil seal into the housing and tap it evenly into place with a hammer and a 3 inch diameter piece of pipe. The seal must be flush with the edge of the rear cover.

9. Install the clutch and flywheel assembly or the flexplate, as applicable. Tighten the flywheel or flexplate bolts in 3 steps to 45-50 ft. lbs. (61-68 Nm).

10. Install the transaxle, lower the vehicle and connect the negative battery cable.

1990-92 626/MX-6

▶ See Figure 105

1. Disconnect the negative battery cable.

2. Raise and safely support the vehicle.

3. Remove the transaxle/transmission assembly. Refer to Section 7.

4. If equipped with a manual transaxle/transmission, remove the clutch and flywheel assembly. Refer to Section 7.

5. If equipped with an automatic transaxle/transmission, remove the flexplate-to-crankshaft bolts, the flexplate and shim plates.

6. Remove the oil seal mounting bolts and remove the seal and the gasket.

To install:

7. Clean the oil seal gasket housing. Press a new gasket into place and coat the oil seal and the housing with clean engine oil.

8. Install the rear main seal and tighten the seal mounting bolts to 69-104 inch lbs. (8-12 Nm).

9. Install the clutch and flywheel assembly or the flexplate, as applicable. Apply sealant to the flywheel or flexplate bolts and tighten them to 71-76 ft. lbs. (96-103 Nm).

10. Install the transaxle/transmission, lower the vehicle and connect the negative battery cable.

1993 626/MX-6 with FS engine

1. Disconnect the negative battery cable.

2. Raise and safely support the vehicle.

3. Remove the transaxle/transmission assembly. Refer to Section 7.

4. If equipped with a manual transaxle/transmission, remove the clutch and flywheel assembly. Refer to Section 7.

5. If equipped with an automatic transaxle/transmission, remove the flexplate-to-crankshaft bolts, the flexplate and shim plates.

6. Remove the engine end plate and remove both portions of the oil pan and the oil strainer.

7. Remove the rear cover/seal housing bolts and remove the cover and seal.

To install:

8. Apply a small amount of clean engine oil on the lip of a new seal and push the seal into the cover by hand.

9. Use the proper tool and press the seal into the rear cover until it is flush with the edge of the rear cover.

10. Apply a bead of silicone sealant to the around the edge of the rear cover assembly.

11. Install the rear cover and tighten the bolts to 69.5-95.4 inch lbs. (8-11 Nm).

12. Install both portions of the oil pan and the oil strainer.

13. Install the engine end plate.

14. Install the clutch and flywheel assembly or the flexplate, as applicable. Apply sealant to the flywheel or flexplate bolts and tighten them to 71-76 ft. lbs. (96-103 Nm).

15. Install the transaxle/transmission, lower the vehicle and connect the negative battery cable.

1993 626/MX-6 with KL engine

1. Disconnect the negative battery cable.

2. Raise and safely support the vehicle.

3. Remove the transaxle assembly. Refer to Section 7.

4. If equipped with a manual transaxle, remove the clutch and flywheel assembly. Refer to Section 7.

5. If equipped with an automatic transaxle, remove the flexplate-to-crankshaft bolts, the flexplate and shim plates.

6. Cut the oil seal lip with a knife. Install a rag to the pump body and using a screwdriver, carefully pry the oil seal from the oil seal housing. Clean the gasket mounting surfaces.

To install:

7. Clean the oil seal housing. Coat the oil seal and the housing with clean engine oil.

8. Press the oil seal into the housing and tap it evenly into place with a hammer and piece of pipe. The seal must be flush with the edge of the rear cover.

9. Install the clutch and flywheel assembly or the flexplate, as applicable. Apply silicone sealant to the flywheel or flexplate bolts and tighten in 3 steps to 45-50 ft. lbs. (61-68 Nm).

10. Install the transaxle, lower the vehicle and connect the negative battery cable.

Crankshaft and Main Bearings

REMOVAL & INSTALLATION

323/Protege, Miata and MX-3 with B6 SOHC

1. Remove the engine assembly from the vehicle and install on a suitable workstand.

2. Remove the cylinder head, oil pan, oil pump and the flywheel.

3. Remove the piston and connecting rod assemblies. Refer to the procedure in this Section.

4. Remove the rear main seal housing.

5. Make sure the main bearing caps are numbered so they can be reinstalled in their original positions. Remove the bolts, then remove the bearing caps.

6. Lift the crankshaft from the cylinder block.

7. Inspect the crankshaft and bearings and repair and/or replace as necessary.

To install:

8. After cleaning, inspecting and measuring the crankshaft and checking the main bearing clearance, install the crankshaft. Apply engine assembly lube or clean engine oil to the upper bearing shells prior to installation.

9. Apply engine assembly lube or clean engine oil to the lower bearing shells, then install the main bearing caps in their original positions. Tighten the bolts to 40-43 ft. lbs. (54-59 Nm).

10. After each cap is tightened, check to see and feel that the crankshaft can be rotated by hand. If not, remove the bearing cap and check for the source of the interference.

11. Install the rear main seal housing and the flywheel.

12. Install the piston and connecting rod assemblies.

13. Install the oil pump and the oil pan.

14. Install the cylinder head.

15. Install the engine assembly in the vehicle.

MX-3 with K8 DOHC and MX6/626 with KL engine

1. Remove the engine assembly from the vehicle and install on a suitable workstand.

2. Remove the cylinder heads, oil pan, oil pump and the flywheel.

3. Remove the piston and connecting rod assemblies. Refer to the procedure in this Section.

4. Remove the rear main seal housing.

5. Make sure the main bearing caps are numbered so they can be reinstalled in their original positions.

6. Loosen the lower cylinder block bolts and the crankshaft cap bolts in 3 steps in the order shown in the figure. Separate the lower half of the cylinder block from the upper half by inserting M8 x 1.25 x 4.72 inch bolts into the lower cylinder block holes. Gently tap on the lower portion of the cylinder block with a plastic hammer.

7. Remove the crankshaft from the upper half of the cylinder block.

8. Inspect the crankshaft and bearings and repair and/or replace as necessary.

To install:

9. After cleaning, inspecting and measuring the crankshaft and checking the main bearing clearance, install the crankshaft. Apply engine assembly lube or clean engine oil to the upper bearing shells prior to installation.

10. Install the lower cylinder block to the upper portion. Apply clean engine oil to the bolt threads and the faces of the crankshaft cap bolts.

11. Tighten the 8 inner bolts marked as A and B to 17-18 ft. lbs. (23-25 Nm).

12. Tighten the 8 outer bolts marked as C to 13-15 ft. lbs. (18-21 Nm.

13. Tighten the 2 inner bolts marked as A (located at the transaxle end of the block) an additional 80 degrees.

14. Tighten the remaining 6 inner bolts, marked as B an additional 70 degrees.

15. Tighten the 8 outer bolts, marked as C an additional 60 degrees.

16. Tighten the lower block to upper block bolts to 14-16 ft. lbs. (19-22 Nm).

17. Install the rear main seal housing and the flywheel.

18. Install the piston and connecting rod assemblies.

19. Install the oil pump and the oil pan.

20. Install the cylinder heads.

21. Install the engine assembly in the vehicle.

1990-92 626/MX-6

1. Remove the engine assembly from the vehicle and install on a suitable workstand.

2. Remove the cylinder head, oil pan, oil pump and the flywheel.

3. Remove the piston and connecting rod assemblies. Refer to the procedure in this Section.

4. Remove the rear main seal housing.

5. Make sure the main bearing caps are numbered so they can be reinstalled in their original positions. Remove the bolts, then remove the bearing caps.

6. Lift the crankshaft from the cylinder block.

7. Inspect the crankshaft and bearings and repair and/or replace as necessary.

To install:

8. After cleaning, inspecting and measuring the crankshaft and checking the main bearing clearance, install the crankshaft. Apply engine assembly lube or clean engine oil to the upper bearing shells prior to installation.

9. Apply engine assembly lube or clean engine oil to the lower bearing shells, then install the main bearing caps in their original positions. Tighten the bolts to 48-51 ft. lbs. (65-69 Nm).

10. After each cap is tightened, check to see and feel that the crankshaft can be rotated by hand. If not, remove the bearing cap and check for the source of the interference.

11. Install the rear main seal housing and the flywheel.

12. Install the piston and connecting rod assemblies.

13. Install the oil pump and the oil pan.

14. Install the cylinder head.

15. Install the engine assembly in the vehicle.

1993 626/MX-6 with FS engine

1. Remove the engine assembly from the vehicle and install on a suitable workstand.

2. Remove the cylinder head, oil pan, oil pump and the flywheel.

3. Remove the piston and connecting rod assemblies. Refer to the procedure in this Section.

4. Remove the rear main seal housing.

5. Make sure the main bearing caps are numbered so they can be reinstalled in their original positions. Remove the bolts, then remove the bearing caps.

6. Lift the crankshaft from the cylinder block.

7. Inspect the crankshaft and bearings and repair and/or replace as necessary.

To install:

8. After cleaning, inspecting and measuring the crankshaft and checking the main bearing clearance, install the crankshaft. Apply engine assembly lube or clean engine oil to the upper bearing shells prior to installation.

9. Apply engine assembly lube or clean engine oil to the lower bearing shells, then install the main bearing caps in their original positions. Tighten the bolts to 13-16 ft. lbs. (17-22 Nm) plus an additional 90 degree turn.

10. After each cap is tightened, check to see and feel that the crankshaft can be rotated by hand. If not, remove the bearing cap and check for the source of the interference.

11. Install the rear main seal housing and the flywheel.

12. Install the piston and connecting rod assemblies.

13. Install the oil pump and the oil pan.

14. Install the cylinder head.

15. Install the engine assembly in the vehicle.

CLEANING AND INSPECTION

1. Clean the crankshaft with solvent and a brush. Clean the oil passages with a suitable brush, then blow them out with compressed air.

2. Inspect the crankshaft for obvious damage or wear. Check the main and connecting rod journals for cracks, scratches, grooves or scores. Inspect the crankshaft oil seal surface for nicks, sharp edges or burrs that could damage the oil seal or cause premature seal wear.

3. If the crankshaft passes a visual inspection, measure the main and connecting rod journals for wear, out-of-roundness or taper, using a micrometer. Measure in at least 4 places around each journal and compare your findings with the journal diameter specifications.

4. If equipped with a manual transaxle, check the fit of the clutch pilot bearing in the bore of the crankshaft. The bearing is pressed into the crankshaft and should not be loose. Inspect the inner surface of the bearing for wear or a bell-mouth condition. Check the inside diameter of the bearing for wear or damage. Check the bearing for roughness, evidence of overheating, or loss of lubricant and replace, as necessary.

5. Check journal runout using a dial indicator. Support the crankshaft in V-blocks and check the runout. Compare to specifications.

6. If the crankshaft fails any inspection for wear or damage, it must be reground or replaced.

BEARING REPLACEMENT

1. Inspect the bearings for scoring, chipping or other wear.

2. Inspect the crankshaft journals as detailed in the Cleaning and Inspection procedure.

3. If the crankshaft journals appear usable, clean them and the bearing shells until they are completely free of oil. Blow any oil from the oil hole in the crankshaft.

➡**The journal surfaces and bearing shells must be completely free of oil to get an accurate reading with Plastigage®.**

4. Place a strip of Plastigage® lengthwise along the bottom center of the lower bearing shell, then install the cap with the shell and torque the connecting rod nuts or main cap bolts to specification. Do not turn the crankshaft with the Plastigage® installed in the bearing.

5. Remove the bearing cap with the shell. The flattened Plastigage® will either be sticking to the bearing shell or the crankshaft journal.

6. Using the printed scale on the Plastigage® package, measure the flattened Plastigage® at its widest point. The number on the scale that most closely corresponds to the width of the Plastigage® indicates the bearing clearance in thousandths of an inch or hundreths of a millimeter.

7. Compare your findings with the bearing clearance specification. If the bearing clearance is excessive, the bearing must be replaced or the crankshaft must be ground and the bearing replaced.

➡**If the crankshaft is still at standard size (has not been ground undersize), bearing shell sets of 0.001 in. , (0.0254mm) 0.002 in. (0.050mm) and 0.003 in. (0.0762mm) over standard size are available to correct excessive bearing clearance.**

8. After clearance measuring is completed, be sure to remove the Plastigage® from the crankshaft and/or bearing shell.

9. For final bearing shell installation, make sure the connecting rod and rod cap and/or cylinder block and main cap bearing saddles are clean and free of nicks or burrs. Install the bearing shells in the bearing saddles, making sure the bearing shell tangs are seated in the notches.

➡**Be careful when handling any plain bearings. Your hands and the working area should be clean. Dirt is easily embedded in the bearing surface and the bearings are easily scratched or damaged.**

10. After all of the main bearing cap bolts have been tightened, mount a dial indicator on the end of the cylinder block with the indicator foot resting on the end of the crankshaft. Move the crankshaft back and forth with a prybar, being careful not to damage the crankshaft, bearings or cylinder block, and observe the dial indicator. Check the reading against the crankshaft endplay specification. If the endplay is excessive, it can be corrected using a thicker thrust bearing or by removing the crankshaft and welding and regrinding the thrust journal.

Flywheel/Flexplate

REMOVAL & INSTALLATION

▶ **See Figures 106, 107 and 108**

1. Disconnect the negative battery cable.

2. Raise and safely support the vehicle.

3. Remove the transaxle assembly. Refer to Section 7.

4. If equipped with a manual transaxle, remove the clutch assembly. Refer to Section 7.

5. If equipped with manual transaxle, remove the flywheel-to-crankshaft bolts and the flywheel. If equipped with automatic transaxle, remove the flexplate-to-crankshaft bolts and the flexplate. Remove the flexplate shims, if equipped.

6. Installation is the reverse of the removal procedure. Tighten the flywheel/flexplate bolts as follows: To 71-76 ft. lbs. (96-103 Nm) on the 323/Protege, Miata, 1990-92 626/MX-6, the MX-3 with the B6 engine and the 1993 626/MX-6 with the FS engine, To 45-50 ft. lbs. (61-68 Nm) on the MX-3 with the K8 engine and the 1993 626/MX-6 with the KL engine.

EXHAUST SYSTEM

Safety Precautions

Exhaust system work can be the most dangerous type of work you can do on your car. Always observe the following precautions:

• Support the car extra securely. Not only will you often be working directly under it, but you'll frequently be using a lot of force, say, heavy hammer blows, to dislodge rusted parts. This can cause a car that's improperly supported to shift and possibly fall.

• Wear goggles. Exhaust system parts are always rusty. Metal chips can be dislodged, even when you're only turning rusted bolts. Attempting to pry pipes apart with a chisel makes the chips fly even more frequently.

• If you're using a cutting torch, keep it a great distance from either the fuel tank or lines. Stop what you're doing and feel the temperature of the fuel bearing pipes on the tank frequently. Even slight heat can expand and/or vaporize fuel, resulting in accumulated vapor, or even a liquid leak, near your torch.

• Watch where your hammer blows fall and make sure you hit squarely. You could easily tap a brake or fuel line when you hit an exhaust system part with a glancing blow. Inspect all lines and hoses in the area where you've been working.

✳✳CAUTION

Be very careful when working on or near the catalytic converter! External temperatures can reach 1,500°F (816°C) and more, causing severe burns. Removal or installation should be performed only on a cold exhaust system.

Special Tools

A number of special exhaust system tools can be rented from auto supply houses or local stores that rent special equipment. A common one is a tail pipe expander, designed to enable you to join pipes of identical diameter.

It may also be quite helpful to use solvents designed to loosen rusted bolts or flanges. Soaking rusted parts the night before you do the job can speed the work of freeing rusted parts considerably. Remember that these solvents are often flammable. Apply only to parts after they are cool!

INSPECTION

Once or twice a year, check the muffler(s) and pipes for signs of corrosion and damage. Check the hangers for wear, cracks or hardening. Check the heat shields for corrosion or damage. Replace components as necessary.

All vehicles are equipped with a catalytic converter, which is attached to the front exhaust pipe. The exhaust system is bolted together. Replacement parts are usually the same as the original system, with the exception of some mufflers. Splash shield removal will be required, in some cases, for removal and installation clearance.

Use only the proper size sockets or wrenches when unbolting system components. Do not tighten completely until all components are attached,

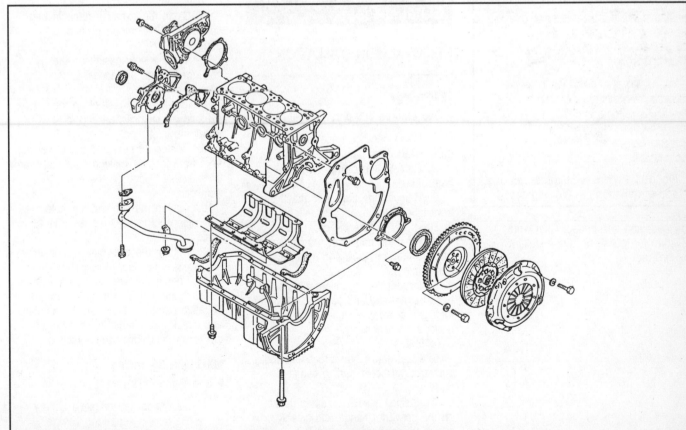

Fig. 106 Cylinder block assembly external parts — B6 and BP engines

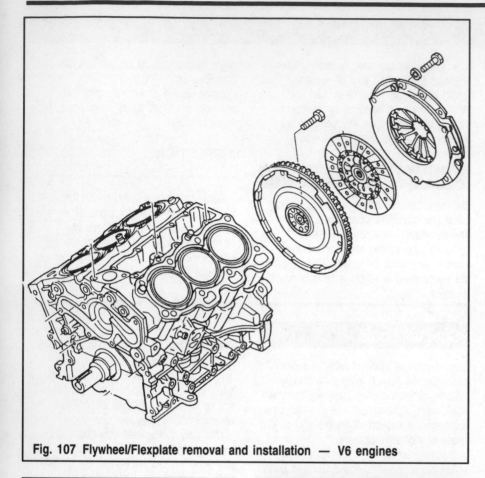

Fig. 107 Flywheel/Flexplate removal and installation — V6 engines

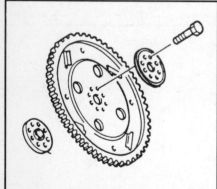

Fig. 108 Flywheel/Flexplate removal and installation — V6 engines

aligned, and suspended. Check the system for leaks after the installation is completed.

Converter Inlet Pipe (Front Exhaust Pipe)

REMOVAL & INSTALLATION

323/Protege
▶ See Figures 109 and 110

1. Disconnect the negative battery cable. Raise and safely the vehicle.
2. Remove the clamp securing the heat shield.
3. Remove the nuts that attach the front pipe to the exhaust manifold and to the front of the catalytic converter.
4. Push the converter rearward and remove the front pipe and mounting gaskets.
5. Inspect the mounting studs on the exhaust manifold and catalytic converter for signs of wear or deterioration and replace, as necessary.
   To install:
6. Clean the exhaust manifold and converter gasket mounting flange surfaces.
7. Position a new mounting gasket on the converter flange and loosely attach the inlet pipe.

8. Position a new mounting gasket on the exhaust manifold flange and loosely install the inlet pipe.
9. Tighten all nuts and bolts, working from front to rear, making sure that there is no stress placed on the exhaust manifold.
10. Tighten the exhaust manifold to inlet pipe nuts to 22-34 ft. lbs. (31-46 Nm).
11. Tighten the inlet pipe to converter nuts to 51-69 ft. lbs. (69-94 Nm).
12. Install the heat shield clamp. Connect the negative battery cable, start the engine and check for exhaust leaks. Shut off the engine and lower the vehicle.

Miata
▶ See Figure 111

1. Disconnect the negative battery cable. Raise and safely the vehicle.
2. Remove the nuts that attach the front pipe to the exhaust manifold and to the front of the catalytic converter.
3. Remove the side support bolt.
4. Push the converter rearward and remove the front pipe and gaskets.
5. Inspect the mounting studs on the exhaust manifold and catalytic converter for signs of wear or deterioration and replace, as necessary.
   To install:
6. Clean the exhaust manifold and converter gasket mounting flange surfaces.
7. Install a new gasket on the converter flange and loosely attach the inlet pipe.
8. Install a new gasket on the exhaust manifold flange and loosely install the inlet pipe.
9. Tighten all nuts and bolts, working from front to rear, making sure that there is no stress placed on the exhaust manifold.
10. Tighten the exhaust manifold to inlet pipe nuts to 22-34 ft. lbs. (31-46 Nm).
11. Tighten the inlet pipe to converter nuts to 30-41 ft. lbs. (40-55 Nm).
12. Tighten the side support bolt to 15-20 ft. lbs. (21-27 Nm). Connect the negative battery cable, start the engine and check for exhaust leaks. Shut off the engine and lower the vehicle.

MX-3 with B6 engine
▶ See Figure 112

1. Disconnect the negative battery cable. Raise and safely the vehicle.

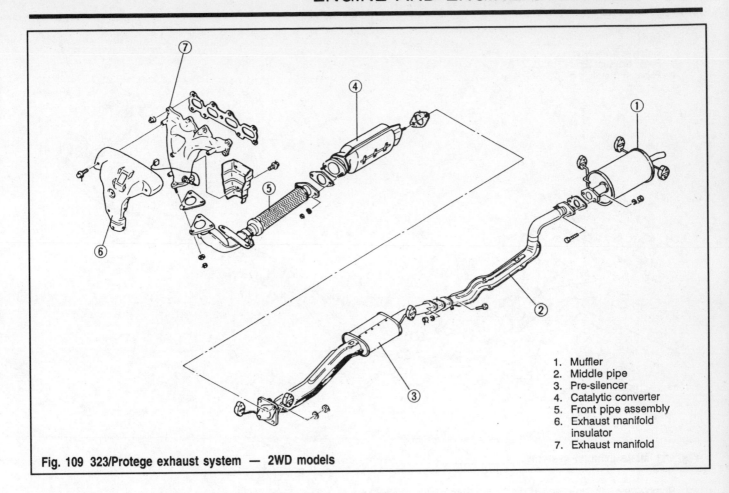

1. Muffler
2. Middle pipe
3. Pre-silencer
4. Catalytic converter
5. Front pipe assembly
6. Exhaust manifold insulator
7. Exhaust manifold

Fig. 109 323/Protege exhaust system — 2WD models

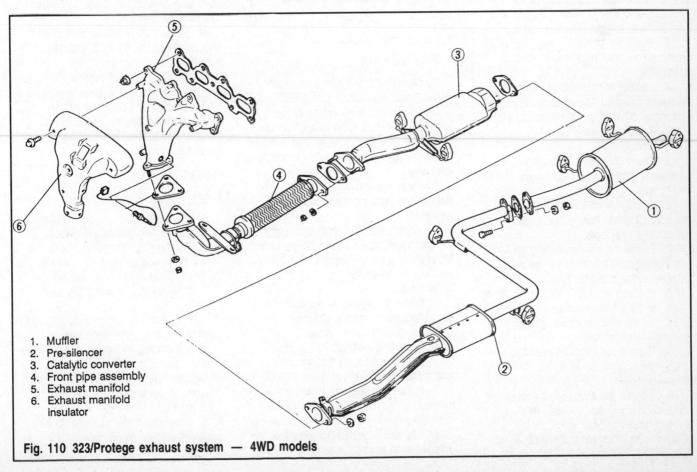

1. Muffler
2. Pre-silencer
3. Catalytic converter
4. Front pipe assembly
5. Exhaust manifold
6. Exhaust manifold insulator

Fig. 110 323/Protege exhaust system — 4WD models

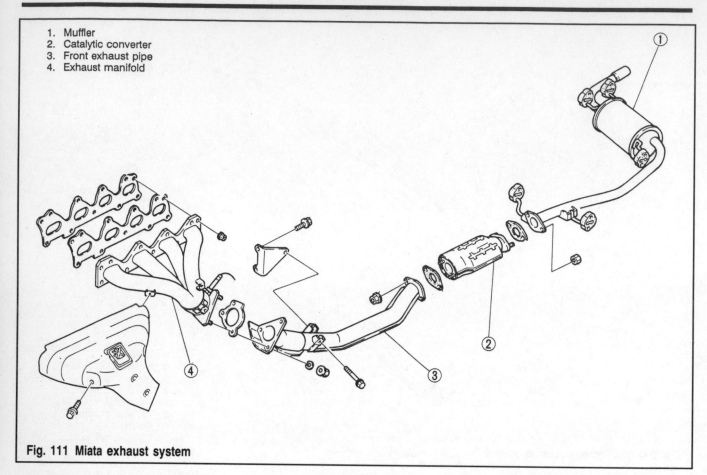

1. Muffler
2. Catalytic converter
3. Front exhaust pipe
4. Exhaust manifold

Fig. 111 Miata exhaust system

2. Remove the nuts that attach the front pipe to the exhaust manifold and to the front of the catalytic converter.

3. Push the converter rearward and remove the front pipe and mounting gaskets.

4. Inspect the mounting studs on the exhaust manifold and catalytic converter for signs of wear or deterioration and replace, as necessary.

To install:

5. Clean the exhaust manifold and converter gasket mounting flange surfaces.

6. Position a new mounting gasket on the converter flange and loosely attach the inlet pipe.

7. Position a new mounting gasket on the exhaust manifold flange and loosely install the inlet pipe.

8. Replace all nuts. Tighten all of the nuts, working from front to rear, making sure that there is no stress placed on the exhaust manifold.

9. Tighten the exhaust manifold to inlet pipe nuts to 22-34 ft. lbs. (31-46 Nm).

10. Tighten the inlet pipe to converter nuts to 51-69 ft. lbs. (69-94 Nm).

11. Install the heat shield clamp. Connect the negative battery cable, start the engine and check for exhaust leaks.

Shut off the engine and lower the vehicle.

MX-3 with K8 engine

▶ **See Figure 113**

1. Disconnect the negative battery cable. Raise and safely the vehicle.

2. Disconnect the oxygen sensor electrical connectors. Remove the nuts that attach the front pipe to both exhaust manifolds and to the front of the catalytic converter.

3. Push the converter rearward and remove the front pipe and mounting gaskets.

4. Inspect the mounting studs on the exhaust manifold and catalytic converter for signs of wear or deterioration and replace, as necessary.

To install:

5. Clean the exhaust manifold and converter gasket mounting flange surfaces.

6. Position a new mounting gasket on the converter flange and loosely attach the inlet pipe.

7. Install new gaskets to the exhaust manifold flange and loosely install the inlet pipe.

8. Replace all nuts. Tighten all of the nuts, working from front to rear, making

sure that there is no stress placed on the exhaust manifold.

9. Tighten the exhaust manifolds to inlet pipe nuts to 30-41 ft. lbs. (40-55 Nm).

10. Tighten the inlet pipe to converter nuts to 47-66 ft. lbs. (64-89 Nm).

11. Connect the negative battery cable, start the engine and check for exhaust leaks. Shut off the engine and lower the vehicle.

1990-92 626/MX-6

▶ **See Figures 114 and 115**

1. Disconnect the negative battery cable. Raise and safely the vehicle.

2. Remove the nuts that attach the front pipe to the exhaust manifold and to the front of the catalytic converter.

3. If necessary, remove the heat shield.

4. Push the converter rearward and remove the front pipe and gaskets.

5. Inspect the mounting studs on the exhaust manifold and catalytic converter for signs of wear or deterioration and replace, as necessary.

To install:

6. Clean the exhaust manifold and converter gasket mounting flange surfaces.

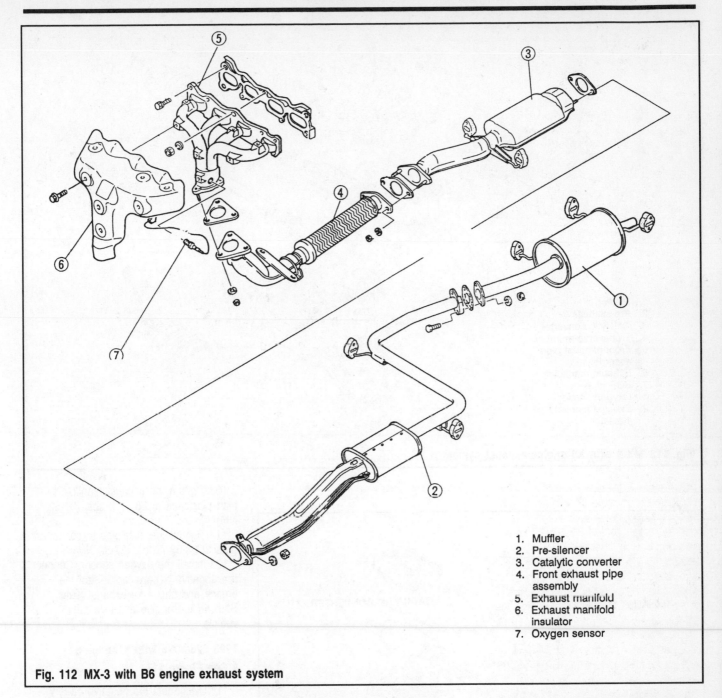

1. Muffler
2. Pre-silencer
3. Catalytic converter
4. Front exhaust pipe assembly
5. Exhaust manifold
6. Exhaust manifold insulator
7. Oxygen sensor

Fig. 112 MX-3 with B6 engine exhaust system

7. Install a new gasket on the converter flange and loosely attach the inlet pipe.

8. Install a new gasket on the exhaust manifold flange and loosely install the inlet pipe.

9. Tighten all nuts and bolts, working from front to rear, making sure that there is no stress placed on the exhaust manifold.

10. Tighten the exhaust manifold to inlet pipe nuts to 25-36 ft. lbs. (34-49 Nm).

11. Tighten the inlet pipe to converter nuts to 51-69 ft. lbs. (69-94 Nm).

12. Connect the negative battery cable, start the engine and check for exhaust leaks. Shut off the engine and lower the vehicle.

1993 626/MX-6 with FS engine
▶ **See Figure 116**

1. Disconnect the negative battery cable. Raise and safely the vehicle.

2. Remove the nuts that attach the front pipe to the exhaust manifold and to the front of the catalytic converter.

3. Disconnect and remove the oxygen sensor.

4. Push the converter rearward and remove the front pipe and gaskets.

5. Inspect the mounting studs on the exhaust manifold and catalytic converter for signs of wear or deterioration and replace, as necessary.

To install:

6. Clean the exhaust manifold and converter gasket mounting flange surfaces.

7. Install a new gasket on the converter flange and loosely attach the inlet pipe.

8. Install a new gasket on the exhaust manifold flange and loosely install the inlet pipe.

9. Tighten all nuts and bolts, working from front to rear, making sure that there is no stress placed on the exhaust manifold.

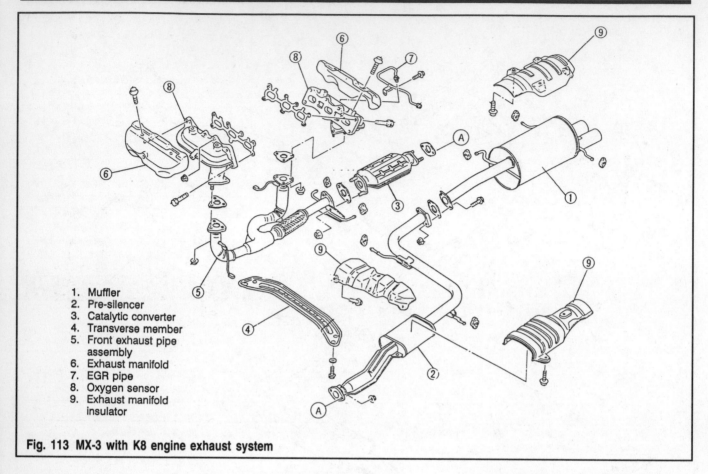

1. Muffler
2. Pre-silencer
3. Catalytic converter
4. Transverse member
5. Front exhaust pipe
   assembly
6. Exhaust manifold
7. EGR pipe
8. Oxygen sensor
9. Exhaust manifold
   insulator

Fig. 113 MX-3 with K8 engine exhaust system

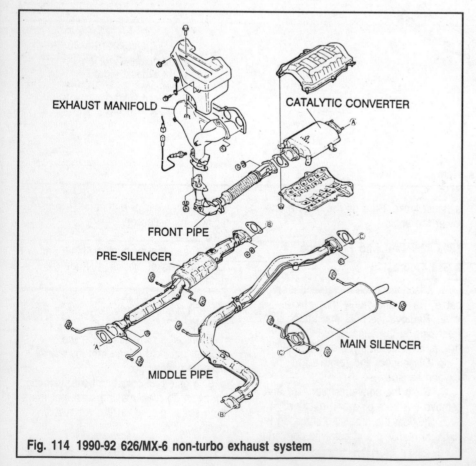

EXHAUST MANIFOLD

CATALYTIC CONVERTER

FRONT PIPE

PRE-SILENCER

MAIN SILENCER

MIDDLE PIPE

Fig. 114 1990-92 626/MX-6 non-turbo exhaust system

10. Tighten the exhaust manifold to inlet pipe nuts to 28-38 ft. lbs. (37-52 Nm).

11. Tighten the inlet pipe to converter nuts to 28-38 ft. lbs. (37-52 Nm).

12. Install the oxygen sensor. Connect the negative battery cable, start the engine and check for exhaust leaks. Shut off the engine and lower the vehicle.

1993 626/MX-6 with KL engine
▶ See Figure 117

1. Disconnect the negative battery cable. Raise and safely the vehicle.

2. Remove the nuts that attach the front pipe to the exhaust manifold and to the front of the catalytic converter.

3. Remove the 2 oxygen sensors and push the converter rearward to remove the front pipe and mounting gaskets.

4. Inspect the mounting studs on the exhaust manifold and catalytic converter for signs of wear or deterioration and replace, as necessary.

To install:

5. Clean the exhaust manifold and converter gasket mounting flange surfaces.

6. Position a new mounting gasket on the converter flange and loosely attach the inlet pipe.

ENGINE REBUILDING SPECIFICATIONS

Component	U.S.	Metric
Cylinder head warpage		
B6 Engine		
Cylinder block side (limit)	0.006 in.	0.15mm
Manifold side (limit)	0.006 in.	0.15mm
BP Engine		
Cylinder block side (limit)	0.004 in.	0.10mm
Manifold side (limit)	0.006 in.	0.15mm
F2 Engine		
Cylinder block side (limit)	0.006 in.	0.15mm
Manifold side (limit)	0.006 in.	0.15mm
FS Engine		
Cylinder block side (limit)	0.004 in.	0.10mm
Manifold side (limit)	0.004 in.	0.10mm
KL Engine		
Cylinder block side (limit)	0.004 in.	0.10mm
Manifold side (limit)	0.004 in.	0.10mm
K8 Engine		
Cylinder block side (limit)	0.004 in.	0.10mm
Manifold side (limit)	0.004 in.	0.10mm
Valve guides		
B6 Engine		
Intake		
Inside diameter	0.2744–0.2750 in.	6.970–6.985mm
Exhaust		
Inside diameter	0.2742–0.2748 in.	6.965–6.980mm
BP Engine		
Intake		
Inside diameter	0.2350–0.2356 in.	5.970–5.985mm
Exhaust		
Inside diameter	0.2348–0.2354 in.	5.965–5.980mm
F2 Engine		
Intake		
Inside diameter	0.2760–0.2768 in.	7.01–7.03mm
Exhaust		
Inside diameter	0.2760–0.2768 in.	7.01–7.03mm
FS Engine		
Intake		
Inside diameter	0.2367–0.2374 in.	6.01–6.03mm
Exhaust		
Inside diameter	0.2367–0.2374 in.	6.01–6.03mm
KL Engine		
Intake		
Inside diameter	0.2367–0.2374 in.	6.01–6.03mm
Exhaust		
Inside diameter	0.2367–0.2374 in.	6.01–6.03mm
K8 Engine		
Intake		
Inside diameter	0.2367–0.2374 in.	6.01–6.03mm
Exhaust		
Inside diameter	0.2367–0.2374 in.	6.01–6.03mm
Valves		
B6 Engine		
Minimum length:		
Intake	4.066 in.	103.27mm
Exhaust	4.022 in.	102.17mm
Stem diameter:		
Intake	0.2744–0.2750 in.	6.970–6.985mm
Exhaust	0.2742–0.2748 in.	6.965–6.980mm
Stem to guide clearance:		
Intake	0.0010–0.0024 in.	0.025–0.060mm
Exhaust	0.0012–0.0026 in.	0.030–0.065mm

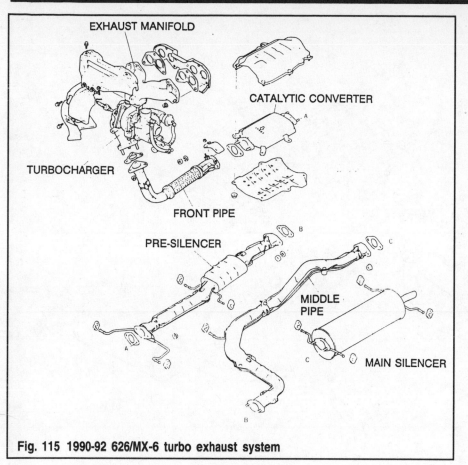

Fig. 115 1990-92 626/MX-6 turbo exhaust system

7. Position a new mounting gasket on the exhaust manifold flange and loosely install the inlet pipe.

8. Replace all nuts. Tighten all of the nuts, working from front to rear, making sure that there is no stress placed on the exhaust manifold.

9. Tighten the exhaust manifold to inlet pipe nuts to 28-38 ft. lbs. (38-51 Nm).

10. Tighten the inlet pipe to converter nuts to 48-65 ft. lbs. (64-89 Nm).

11. Install and connect the oxygen sensors. Connect the negative battery cable, start the engine and check for exhaust leaks. Shut off the engine and lower the vehicle.

Catalytic Converter

REMOVAL & INSTALLATION

1. Disconnect the negative battery cable. Raise and safely support the vehicle.

2. Place a support under the resonator pipe assembly.

3. Remove the mounting nuts from the front and rear of the converter.

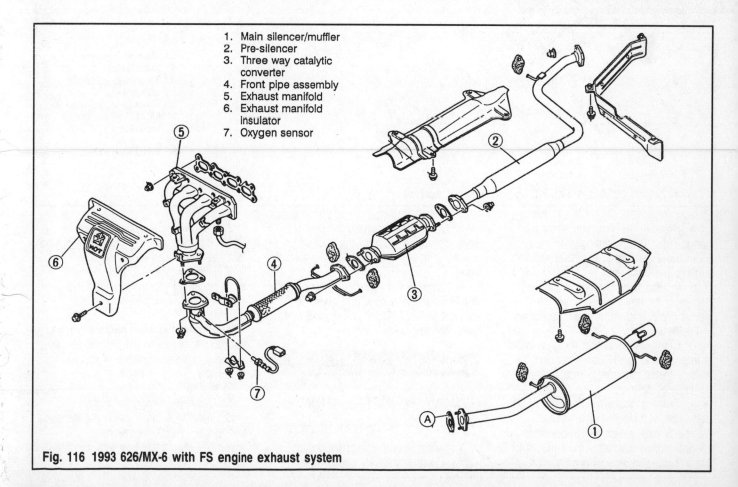

1. Main silencer/muffler
2. Pre-silencer
3. Three way catalytic converter
4. Front pipe assembly
5. Exhaust manifold
6. Exhaust manifold insulator
7. Oxygen sensor

Fig. 116 1993 626/MX-6 with FS engine exhaust system

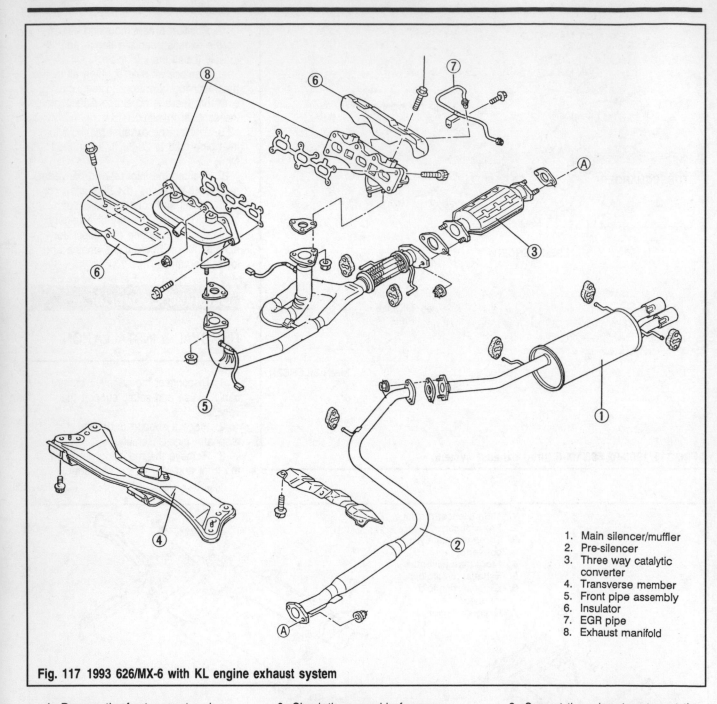

Fig. 117 1993 626/MX-6 with KL engine exhaust system

1. Main silencer/muffler
2. Pre-silencer
3. Three way catalytic converter
4. Transverse member
5. Front pipe assembly
6. Insulator
7. EGR pipe
8. Exhaust manifold

7. Check the body clearance and tighten the bolts as specified in the torque chart. Remove the support at the converter.

8. Connect the negative battery cable. Start the engine and check for exhaust leaks. Shut off the engine and lower the vehicle.

Exhaust (Middle) Pipe

REMOVAL & INSTALLATION

1. Disconnect the negative battery cable. Raise and safely support the vehicle.

2. Remove the front and rear pipe mounting nuts.

3. Remove the rubber insulator from the body mount at the middle pipe. Remove the 2 front rubber insulators from the body mounts at the muffler, if necessary.

4. Remove the pipe and discard the gaskets.

5. Inspect the mounting flanges, hangers and mounts for wear or deterioration and replace, as necessary.

To install:

6. Clean the flange surfaces.

7. Install new gaskets on the flanges and loosely install the middle pipe.

8. Install the rubber insulator to the body mount at the middle pipe and the 2 insulators to the body mounts at the muffler, if removed.

9. Check the body clearance and tighten all components, beginning at the front and working toward the rear. Tighten the nuts as specified in the torque chart.

10. Connect the negative battery cable. Start the engine and check for exhaust leaks. Shut off the engine and lower the vehicle.

Muffler

REMOVAL & INSTALLATION

1. Disconnect the negative battery cable. Raise and safely support the vehicle.

2. Remove the exhaust pipe-to-muffler mounting nuts.

3. Remove the muffler from the rubber insulators and remove the muffler assembly.

4. Inspect the mounting flange and hangers for wear or deterioration and replace, as necessary.

To install:

5. Clean the flange surfaces.

6. Install a new gasket on the flange and loosely install the muffler assembly. Mount the brackets into the rubber insulators.

7. Check the body clearance and tighten the mounting nuts.

8. Connect the negative battery cable. Start the engine and check for exhaust leaks. Shut off the engine and lower the vehicle.

4. Remove the front resonator pipe hanger from the mounting grommets. Push the assembly toward the rear and remove the converter.

5. Inspect the mounting studs on the converter for any signs of wear or deterioration and replace, as necessary.

To install:

6. Clean the mounting flanges. Install a front gasket to the converter and loosely install the front of the converter to the inlet pipe.

7. Install a gasket on the rear of the converter and loosely attach the resonator pipe assembly. Secure the resonator pipe assembly front mounting bracket into the mounting grommets.

8. Check the assembly for proper body clearance. Tighten the front mounting nuts as specified in the torque chart.

9. Connect the negative battery cable. Start the engine and check for exhaust leaks. Shut off the engine and lower the vehicle.

Resonator

REMOVAL & INSTALLATION

1. Disconnect the negative battery cable. Raise and safely support the vehicle.

2. Support the exhaust system at the catalytic converter. Remove the front and rear resonator pipe mounting nuts.

3. Remove the resonator from the body mounting grommets. Push the assembly rearward and remove the resonator.

4. Discard the used gaskets. Inspect the mounting flanges, studs and hangers for wear or deterioration and replace, as necessary.

To install:

5. Clean the flange surfaces.

6. Install new gaskets on the flanges and loosely install the resonator assembly. Mount the brackets into the body grommets.

ENGINE REBUILDING SPECIFICATIONS

Component	U.S.	Metric
Valves		
Valve head minimum margin thickness:		
Intake	0.020 in.	0.5mm
Exhaust	0.039 in.	1.0mm
BP Engine		
Minimum length:		
Intake	3.987 in.	101.27mm
Exhaust	4.034 in.	102.47mm
Stem diameter:		
Intake	0.2350–0.2356 in.	5.970–5.985mm
Exhaust	0.2348–0.2354 in.	5.965–5.980mm
Stem to guide clearance:		
Intake	0.0010–0.0024 in.	0.025–0.060mm
Exhaust	0.0012–0.0026 in.	0.030–0.065mm
Valve head minimum margin thickness:		
Intake	0.026 in.	0.65mm
Exhaust	0.028 in.	0.71mm
F2 Engine		
Minimum length:		
Intake	4.5594 in.	115.81mm
Exhaust	4.5752 in.	116.21mm
Stem diameter:		
Intake	0.2744–0.2750 in.	6.970–6.985mm
Exhaust	0.2742–0.2748 in.	6.965–6.980mm
Stem to guide clearance:		
Intake	0.0010–0.0024 in.	0.025–0.060mm
Exhaust	0.0012–0.0026 in.	0.030–0.065mm
Valve head margin thickness:		
Intake	0.020 in.	0.5mm
Exhaust	0.039 in.	1.0mm
FS Engine		
Minimum length:		
Intake	3.5150 in.	89.28mm
Exhaust	3.5189 in.	89.38mm
Stem diameter:		
Intake	0.2351–0.2356 in.	5.970–5.985mm
Exhaust	0.2349–0.2354 in.	5.965–5.980mm
Stem to guide clearance:		
Intake	0.0010–0.0024 in.	0.025–0.060mm
Exhaust	0.0012–0.0026 in.	0.030–0.065mm
Valve head margin thickness:		
Intake	0.0433 in.	1.10mm
Exhaust	0.0472 in.	1.20mm
KL Engine		
Minimum length:		
Intake	3.678 in.	93.41mm
Exhaust	3.720 in.	94.49mm
Stem diameter:		
Intake	0.2351–0.2356 in.	5.970–5.985mm
Exhaust	0.2349–0.2354 in.	5.965–5.980mm
Stem to guide clearance:		
Intake	0.0010–0.0024 in.	0.025–0.060mm
Exhaust	0.0012–0.0026 in.	0.030–0.065mm
Valve head margin thickness:		
Intake	0.0355 in.	0.9mm
Exhaust	0.0394 in.	1.0mm
K8 Engine		
Minimum length:		
Intake	3.678 in.	93.41mm
Exhaust	3.720 in.	94.49mm

ENGINE REBUILDING SPECIFICATIONS

Component	U.S.	Metric
Valves		
Stem diameter:		
Intake	0.2351–0.2356 in.	5.970–5.985mm
Exhaust	0.2349–0.2354 in.	5.965–5.980mm
Stem to guide clearance:		
Intake	0.0010–0.0024 in.	0.025–0.060mm
Exhaust	0.0012–0.0026 in.	0.030–0.065mm
Valve head margin thickness:		
Intake	0.0355 in.	0.9mm
Exhaust	0.0394 in.	1.0mm
Valve spring		
B6 Engine		
Free length:	1.720 in.	43.7mm
Squareness:	0.060 in.	1.52mm
BP Engine		
Free length:		
Intake	1.815 in.	46.1mm
Exhaust	1.717 in.	43.6mm
Squareness:		
Intake	0.063 in.	1.61mm
Exhaust	0.060 in.	1.52mm
F2 Engine		
Free length:		
Intake	1.949 in.	49.5mm
Exhaust	1.984 in.	50.4mm
Squareness:	0.060 in.	1.52mm
FS Engine		
Free length:	1.732 in.	44.0mm
Squareness:	0.061 in.	1.54mm
KL Engine		
Free length:	1.847 in.	46.92mm
Squareness:	0.0642 in.	1.63mm
K8 Engine		
Free length:	1.847 in.	46.92mm
Squareness:	0.0642 in.	1.63mm
Camshaft		
B6 Engine		
Runout:	0.0012 in.	0.03mm
Journal diameter:		
Front and rear	1.7102–1.7110 in.	43.440–43.465mm
Center	1.7091–1.7100 in.	43.410–43.435mm
Maximum oil clearance:	0.006 in.	0.15mm
Cam lobe height:		
Intake	1.4272–1.4351 in.	36.251–36.451mm
Exhaust	1.4272–1.4351 in.	36.251–36.451mm
BP Engine		
Runout:	0.0012 in.	0.03mm
Journal diameter:		
Numbers 1 and 5	1.7102–1.7110 in.	43.440–43.460mm
Numbers 2 and 4	1.7096–1.7106 in.	43.425–43.450mm
Number 3	1.7091–1.7100 in.	43.410–43.435mm
Maximum oil clearance:	0.006 in.	0.15mm
Cam lobe height:		
Intake	1.4092–1.4170 in.	35.793–35.993mm
Exhaust	1.4202–1.4281 in.	36.073–36.273mm
F2 Engine		
Runout:	0.0012 in.	0.03mm
Journal diameter:		
Front and rear	1.2575–1.2585 in.	31.940–31.965mm
Center	1.2563–1.2573 in.	31.910–31.935mm

ENGINE REBUILDING SPECIFICATIONS

Component	U.S.	Metric
Camshaft		
Maximum oil clearance:	0.006 in.	0.15mm
Cam lobe height:		
Intake	1.6256–1.6295 in.	41.290–41.390mm
Exhaust	1.6455–1.6495 in.	41.797–41.897mm
FS Engine		
Runout:	0.0012 in.	0.03mm
Journal diameter:	1.0213–1.0222 in.	25.940–25.965mm
Maximum oil clearance:	0.006 in.	0.15mm
Cam lobe height:		
Intake	1.6859–1.6918 in.	42.823–42.973mm
Exhaust	1.7003–1.7062 in.	43.188–43.338mm
KL Engine		
Runout:	0.0007 in.	0.02mm
Journal diameter:		
Number 1 (RH ex/LH in) and number 5	1.0213–1.0222 in.	25.940–25.965mm
Number 1 (RH intake and LH exhaust)	1.1802–1.1809 in.	29.975–29.995mm
Numbers 2 through 4	1.0201–1.0208 in.	25.910–25.930mm
Maximum oil clearance:	0.0050 in.	0.120mm
Cam lobe height:		
Intake	1.7067–1.7145 in.	43.349–43.549mm
Exhaust	1.7067–1.7145 in.	43.349–43.549mm
K8 Engine		
Runout:	0.0008 in.	0.02mm
Journal diameter:		
Number 1 (RH ex/LH in) and number 5	1.0213–1.0222 in.	25.940–25.965mm
Number 1 (RH intake and LH exhaust)	1.1802–1.1809 in.	29.975–29.995mm
Numbers 2 through 4	1.0201–1.0208 in.	25.910–25.930mm
Maximum oil clearance:	0.0050 in.	0.120mm
Cam lobe height:		
Intake	1.6718–1.6797 in.	42.465–42.665mm
Exhaust	1.7054–1.7132 in.	43.316–43.516mm
B6 Engine		
Piston and piston ring		
Piston diameter:	3.0690–3.0698 in.	77.954–77.974mm
Piston oil clearance:	0.0039–0.0052 in.	0.15–0.20mm
Piston ring clearance:		
No. 1	0.0012–0.0026 in.	0.030–0.065mm
No. 2	0.0012–0.0026 in.	0.030–0.065mm
Piston ring end gap:		
No. 1	0.006–0.012 in.	0.15–0.30mm
No. 2	0.006–0.012 in.	0.15–0.30mm
Oil	0.008–0.028 in.	0.20–0.70mm
BP Engine		
Piston and piston ring		
Piston diameter:	3.2659–3.2667 in.	82.954–82.974mm
Piston oil clearance:	0.0039–0.0052 in.	0.15–0.20mm
Piston ring clearance:		
No. 1	0.0012–0.0026 in.	0.030–0.065mm
No. 2	0.0012–0.0026 in.	0.030–0.065mm
Piston ring end gap:		
No. 1	0.006–0.012 in.	0.15–0.30mm
No. 2	0.006–0.012 in.	0.15–0.30mm
Oil	0.008–0.028 in.	0.20–0.70mm
F2 Engine		
Piston and piston ring		
Piston diameter:	3.3836–3.3844 in.	85.944–85.964mm
Piston to cylinder clearance:	0.0014–0.0030 in.	0.036–0.075mm

ENGINE REBUILDING SPECIFICATIONS

Component	U.S.	Metric
F2 Engine		
Piston ring clearance:		
No. 1	0.0012–0.0028 in.	0.030–0.070mm
No. 2	0.0012–0.0028 in.	0.030–0.070mm
Piston ring end gap:		
No. 1	0.008–0.014 in.	0.20–0.35mm
No. 2	0.006–0.012 in.	0.15–0.30mm
Oil	0.008–0.028 in.	0.20–0.70mm
FS Engine		
Piston and piston ring		
Piston diameter:	3.2659–3.2666 in.	82.954–82.974mm
Piston to cylinder clearance:	0.0016–0.0020 in.	0.039–0.052mm
Piston ring clearance:		
No. 1	0.0014–0.0025 in.	0.035–0.065mm
No. 2	0.0012–0.0025 in.	0.030–0.065mm
Piston ring end gap:		
No. 1	0.006–0.011 in.	0.15–0.30mm
No. 2	0.006–0.011 in.	0.15–0.30mm
Oil	0.008–0.028 in.	0.20–0.70mm
KL Engine		
Piston and piston ring		
Piston diameter:	3.3250–3.3261 in.	84.453–84.485mm
Piston to cylinder clearance:	0.0012–0.0022 in.	0.028–0.056mm
Piston ring clearance:		
No. 1	0.0008–0.0025 in.	0.020–0.065mm
No. 2	0.0012–0.0025 in.	0.030–0.065mm
Piston ring end gap:		
No. 1	0.006–0.011 in.	0.15–0.30mm
No. 2	0.010–0.015 in.	0.25–0.40mm
Oil	0.008–0.028 in.	0.20–0.70mm
K8 Engine		
Piston and piston ring		
Piston diameter:	2.9509–2.9522 in.	74.953–74.985mm
Piston to cylinder clearance:	0.0012–0.0022 in.	0.028–0.056mm
Piston ring clearance:		
No. 1	0.0008–0.0025 in.	0.020–0.065mm
No. 2	0.0008–0.0025 in.	0.020–0.065mm
Piston ring end gap:		
No. 1	0.006–0.011 in.	0.15–0.30mm
No. 2	0.010–0.015 in.	0.25–0.40mm
Oil	0.008–0.028 in.	0.20–0.70mm
Connecting rod		
B6 Engine		
Inner bushing diameter:	0.7864–0.7866 in.	19.974–19.980mm
BP Engine		
Inner bushing diameter:	0.7864–0.7866 in.	19.974–19.980mm
F2 Engine		
Inner bushing diameter:	0.8640–0.8646 in.	21.943–21.961mm
FS Engine		
Inner bushing diameter:	0.7458–0.7465 in.	18.943–18.961mm
KL Engine		
Inner bushing diameter:	0.7852–0.7858 in.	19.943–19.961mm
K8 Engine		
Inner bushing diameter:	0.7458–0.7465 in.	18.943–18.961mm
Crankshaft		
B6 Engine		
Main journal diameter:	1.9661–1.9668 in.	49.938–49.956mm
Crank pin journal diameter:	1.7693–1.7699 in.	44.940–44.956mm
Runout:	0.0016 in.	0.04mm
BP Engine		
Main journal diameter:	1.9661–1.9668 in.	49.938–49.956mm
Crank pin journal diameter:	1.7693–1.7699 in.	44.940–44.956mm
Runout:	0.0016 in.	0.04mm

ENGINE REBUILDING SPECIFICATIONS

Component	U.S.	Metric
F2 Engine		
Main journal diameter:	2.3597–2.3604 in.	59.937–59.955mm
Crank pin journal diameter:	2.0055–2.0061 in.	50.940–50.955mm
Runout:	0.0012 in.	0.03mm
FS Engine		
Main journal diameter:	2.2022–2.2029 in.	55.937–55.955mm
Crank pin journal diameter:	1.8874–1.8880 in.	47.940–47.955mm
Runout:	0.0012 in.	0.03mm
KL Engine		
Main journal diameter:	2.4385–2.4391 in.	61.938–61.955mm
Crank pin journal diameter:	2.0843–2.0848 in.	52.940–52.955mm
Runout:	0.0005 in.	0.015mm
K8 Engine		
Main journal diameter:	2.4385–2.4391 in.	61.938–61.955mm
Crank pin journal diameter:	1.8874–1.8880 in.	47.940–47.955mm
Runout:	0.0006 in.	0.015mm

TORQUE SPECIFICATIONS

Component	U.S.	Metric
Camshaft cap bolts		
1.6L, 1.8L, 2.0L, 2.5L DOHC engines	125 inch lbs.	14 Nm
Camshaft sprocket bolt		
1.6L engine		
SOHC engine	45 ft. lbs.	61 Nm
DOHC engine	44 ft. lbs.	60 Nm
1.8L engine		
SOHC engine	45 ft. lbs.	61 Nm
DOHC engine		
Protege	44 ft. lbs.	60 Nm
MX-3	103 ft. lbs.	140 Nm
2.0L engine	44 ft. lbs.	60 Nm
2.2L engine	48 ft. lbs.	65 Nm
2.5L engine	103 ft. lbs.	140 Nm
Connecting rod bolts		
1.6L engine		
SOHC engine		
323	35–38 ft. lbs.	48–51 Nm
MX-3	35–37 ft. lbs.	48–50 Nm
DOHC engine		
323	48–51 ft. lbs.	66–69 Nm
Miata	37–40 ft. lbs.	51–54 Nm
1.8L engine		
SOHC engine	36–38 ft. lbs.	49–51 Nm
DOHC engine		
Protege	35–37 ft. lbs.	48–50 Nm
MX-3		
Step 1:	19 ft. lbs.	26 Nm
Step 2:	+ 90 degrees turn	+ 90 degrees turn
Step 3:	+ 90 degrees turn	+ 90 degrees turn
2.0L engine		
Step 1:	19 ft. lbs.	26 Nm
Step 2:	+ 90 degrees turn	+ 90 degrees turn
2.2L engine	48–51 ft. lbs.	66–69 Nm
2.5L engine		
Step 1:	19 ft. lbs.	26 Nm
Step 2:	+ 90 degrees turn	+ 90 degrees turn

TORQUE SPECIFICATIONS

Component	U.S.	Metric
Crankshaft sprocket bolt		
1.6L engines		
1990–91	80–87 ft. lbs.	109–118 Nm
1992–93	116–123 ft. lbs.	158–167 Nm
1.8L engines		
1990–91	80–87 ft. lbs.	109–118 Nm
1992–93	116–123 ft. lbs.	158–167 Nm
2.0L engine	116–123 ft. lbs.	158–167 Nm
2.2L engine	116–123 ft. lbs.	158–167 Nm
2.5L engine	116–123 ft. lbs.	158–167 Nm
Cylinder head bolts		
1.6L engines	56–60 ft. lbs.	75–81 Nm
1.8L engines		
Except K8D engine	56–60 ft. lbs.	75–81 Nm
K8D engine		
Step 1:	19 ft. lbs.	26 Nm
Step 2:	+ 90 degrees turn	+ 90 degrees turn
Step 3:	+ 90 degrees turn	+ 90 degrees turn
2.0L engine		
Step 1:	16 ft. lbs.	22 Nm
Step 2:	+ 90 degrees turn	+ 90 degrees turn
Step 3:	+ 90 degrees turn	+ 90 degrees turn
2.2L engine	59–64 ft. lbs.	80–86 Nm
2.5L engine		
Step 1:	19 ft. lbs.	26 Nm
Step 2:	+ 90 degrees turn	+ 90 degrees turn
Step 3:	+ 90 degrees turn	+ 90 degrees turn
Cylinder head cover bolts		
1.6L engines	78 inch lbs.	9 Nm
1.8L engines	78 inch lbs.	9 Nm
2.0L engine	69 inch lbs.	8 Nm
2.2L engine	69 inch lbs.	8 Nm
2.5L engine	78 inch lbs.	9 Nm
Exhaust manifold nuts/bolts		
1.6L engine		
SOHC engine	12–17 ft. lbs.	17–23 Nm
DOHC engine		
323	29–42 ft. lbs.	40–57 Nm
Miata	28–34 ft. lbs.	38–46 Nm
1.8L engine		
SOHC engine	12–17 ft. lbs.	17–23 Nm
DOHC engines		
Protege	28–34 ft. lbs.	38–46 Nm
MX-3	14–19 ft. lbs.	19–25 Nm
2.0L engine		
Nuts	15–20 ft. lbs.	21–27 Nm
Bolts	12–16 ft. lbs.	17–21 Nm
2.2L engine	25–36 ft. lbs.	34–49 Nm
2.5L engine	14–18 ft. lbs.	19–24 Nm
Exhaust pipe flange nuts	34 ft. lbs.	46 Nm
Flywheel bolts		
1.6L engine	71–76 ft. lbs.	97–103 Nm
1.8L engine		
Except K8D engine	71–76 ft. lbs.	97–103 Nm
K8D engine	45–50 ft. lbs.	62–68 Nm
2.0L engine	71–76 ft. lbs.	97–103 Nm
2.2L engine	71–76 ft. lbs.	97–103 Nm
2.5L engine	45–49 ft. lbs.	62–66 Nm

TORQUE SPECIFICATIONS

Component	U.S.	Metric
Intake manifold bolts		
1.6L engine	14–19 ft. lbs.	19–25 Nm
1.8L engines	14–19 ft. lbs.	19–25 Nm
2.0L engine	14–18 ft. lbs.	19–24 Nm
2.2L engine	14–22 ft. lbs.	19–30 Nm
2.5L engine	14–18 ft. lbs.	19–24 Nm
Main bearing cap bolts		
1.6L engines	40–43 ft. lbs.	55–58 Nm
1.8L engines		
Except K8D engine	40–43 ft. lbs.	55–58 Nm
K8D engine		
Step 1:		
Inner bolts	18 ft. lbs.	24 Nm
Outer bolts	15 ft. lbs.	20 Nm
Step 2:		
Inner bolts		
Nos. 1, 2 & 3	+ 70 degrees turn	+ 70 degrees turn
No. 4	+ 80 degrees turn	+ 80 degrees turn
Outer bolts	+ 60 degrees turn	+ 60 degrees turn
Step 3:		
Inner bolts		
Nos. 1, 2 & 3	+ 70 degrees turn	+ 70 degrees turn
No. 4	+ 80 degrees turn	+ 80 degrees turn
Outer bolts	+ 60 degrees turn	+ 60 degrees turn
2.0L engine		
Step 1:	16 ft. lbs.	22 Nm
Step 2:	+ 90 degrees turn	+ 90 degrees turn
2.2L engine	61–65 ft. lbs.	83–88 Nm
2.5L engine		
Step 1:		
Inner bolts	18 ft. lbs.	24 Nm
Outer bolts	15 ft. lbs.	20 Nm
Step 2:		
Inner bolts		
Nos. 1, 2 & 3	+ 70 degrees turn	+ 70 degrees turn
No. 4	+ 80 degrees turn	+ 80 degrees turn
Outer bolts	+ 60 degrees turn	+ 60 degrees turn
Step 3:		
Inner bolts		
Nos. 1, 2 & 3	+ 70 degrees turn	+ 70 degrees turn
No. 4	+ 80 degrees turn	+ 80 degrees turn
Outer bolts	+ 60 degrees turn	+ 60 degrees turn
Oil pan bolts		
1.6L engine		
323	95 inch lbs.	11 Nm
MX-3		
Bolts A*	95 inch lbs.	11 Nm
Bolts B*	38 ft. lbs.	52 Nm
Miata		
Pan-to-engine	95 inch lbs.	11 Nm
Pan-to-transmission	66 ft. lbs.	89 Nm
1.8L engine		
Protege		
Bolts A*	95 inch lbs.	11 Nm
Bolts B*	38 ft. lbs.	52 Nm
MX-3		
Bolts A*	95 inch lbs.	11 Nm
Bolts B*	18 ft. lbs.	25 Nm
2.0L engine	18 ft. lbs.	25 Nm
2.2L engine	95 inch lbs.	11 Nm
2.5L engine		
Bolts A*	95 inch lbs.	11 Nm
Bolts B*	18 ft. lbs.	25 Nm

TORQUE SPECIFICATIONS

Component	U.S.	Metric
Oil pump bolts		
1.6L, 1.8L, 2.0L, 2.5L and 3.0L engines	19 ft. lbs.	25 Nm
2.2L engine		
8mm bolts	19 ft. lbs.	25 Nm
10mm bolts	38 ft. lbs.	52 Nm
Rocker arm shaft bolts		
1.6L and 1.8L SOHC engines	21 ft. lbs.	28 Nm
2.2L engine	20 ft. lbs.	26 Nm
Spark plugs		
All engines	11–16 ft. lbs.	15–21 Nm
Timing belt cover bolts		
Except 2.2L engine	95 inch lbs.	11 Nm
2.2L engine	87 inch lbs.	10 Nm
Water pump nuts/bolts	19 ft. lbs.	25 Nm

* Refer to the illustration in text

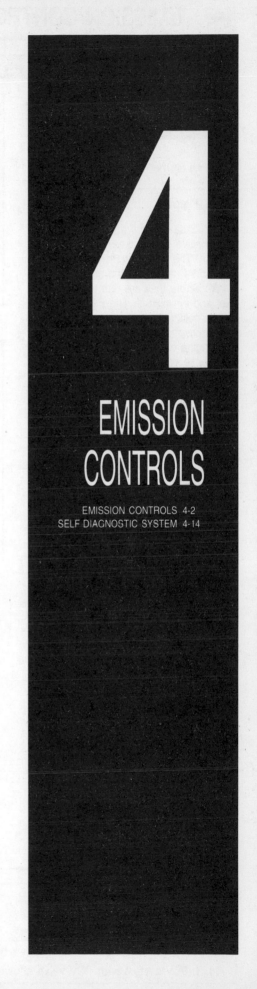

4

EMISSION CONTROLS

EMISSION CONTROLS

Crankcase Ventilation System

OPERATION

▶ See Figure 1

All Mazda engines are equipped with the Positive Crankcase Ventilation (PCV) system. The PCV system vents crankcase gases into the engine air intake where they are burned with the fuel and air mixture. The PCV system keeps pollutants from being released into the atmosphere, and also helps to keep the engine oil clean, by ridding the crankcase of moisture and corrosive fumes. The PCV system consists of the rocker arm cover mounted PCV valve, the nipple in the air intake and the connecting hoses.

The PCV valve regulates the amount of ventilating air and blow-by gas to the intake manifold. It also prevents backfire from traveling into the crankcase, avoiding the explosion of crankcase gases.

SERVICE

▶ See Figures 2 and 3

1. Visually inspect the PCV valve hose and the fresh air supply hose and their attaching nipples or grommets for splits, cuts, damage, clogging, or restrictions. Repair or replace, as necessary.

2. If the hoses pass inspection, remove the PCV valve from the rocker arm cover. Shake the PCV valve and listen or feel for the rattle of the valve plunger within the valve body. If the

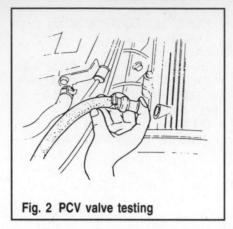

Fig. 2 PCV valve testing

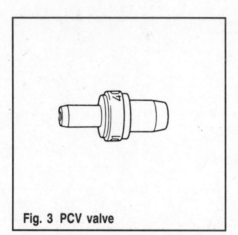

Fig. 3 PCV valve

valve plunger does not rattle, the PCV valve should be cleaned or replaced. If the valve plunger rattles, PCV valve is okay; reinstall it.

3. Start the engine and bring it to normal operating temperature. Remove the fresh air supply hose from the throttle body air hose nipple, and plug or cap the nipple immediately to keep the engine from stalling. Check for vacuum at the end of the supply hose using a stiff piece of paper. If the paper is

retained by vacuum at the end of the hose, the PCV system is okay.

4. If the paper is not held by vacuum, check the fresh air and PCV hoses for leaks or loose connections. Also check for a loose fitting oil fill cap or loose dipstick. Correct as required until vacuum can be felt at the end of the supply hose.

➡ If air pressure and oil or sludge is present at the end of the fresh air supply hose, the engine has excessive blow-by and cylinder bore or piston ring wear.

REMOVAL & INSTALLATION

1. Remove the PCV valve from the mounting grommet in the valve cover.

2. Disconnect the valve from the PCV hose and remove the valve from the vehicle.

3. Installation is the reverse of the removal procedure.

Evaporative Emission Control System

OPERATION

▶ See Figure 4

The evaporative emission control system prevents the escape of fuel vapors to the atmosphere under hot soak and engine off conditions by storing the vapors in a carbon canister. Then, with the engine warm and running, the system controls the purging of stored vapors from the canister to the engine, where they are efficiently burned. Evaporative emission control components consist of the fuel vapor valve, check valve, purge control solenoid valve(s), charcoal canister and input devices.

Charcoal Canister
▶ See Figure 5

The fuel vapors from the fuel tank are stored in the charcoal canister until the vehicle is operated, at which time, the vapors will purge from the canister into the engine for consumption. The charcoal canister contains activated carbon, which absorbs the fuel vapor. The canister is located in the engine compartment.

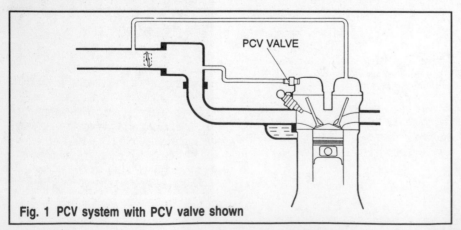

PCV VALVE

Fig. 1 PCV system with PCV valve shown

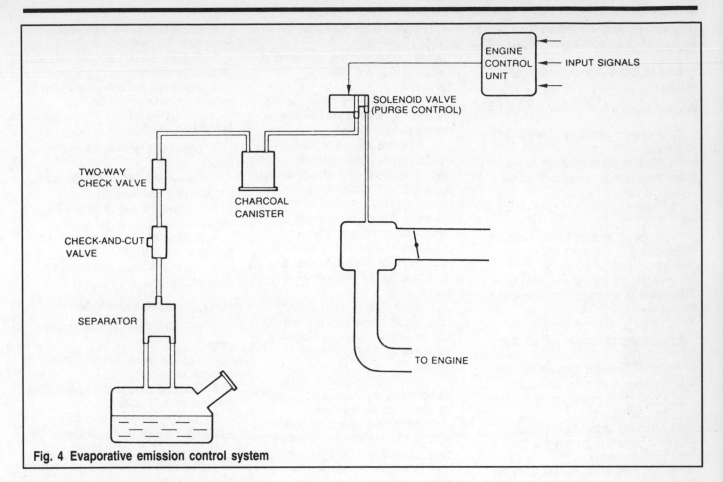

Fig. 4 Evaporative emission control system

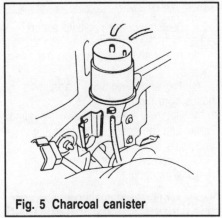

Fig. 5 Charcoal canister

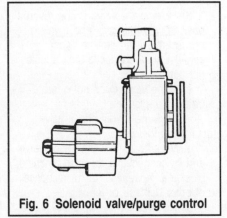

Fig. 6 Solenoid valve/purge control

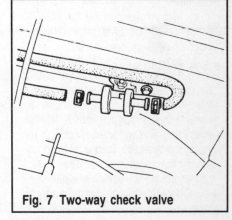

Fig. 7 Two-way check valve

Purge Control Solenoid Valves

▶ See Figure 6

The purge control solenoid valves control the flow of fuel vapor from the carbon canister to the engine. The solenoid valves are electronically controlled. Purging occurs when the engine is at operating temperature and off idle.

Check Valve

▶ See Figure 7

The check valve releases excessive pressure or vacuum in the fuel tank to atmosphere. The valve is connected in-line with the evaporative hose and rollover/vent valve. On all engines except the Miata (4 A/T), the valve is a 2-way check valve. On the Miata (4 A/T) the valve is a 3-way check valve.

Fuel Vapor Valve

The fuel vapor valve prevents fuel vapors from flowing from the fuel tank at all times through the fuel tank hose. The valve is located in the fuel tank.

SERVICE

System Inspection

1. Visually inspect the vapor and vacuum lines and connections for looseness, pinching, leakage, or other damage. If fuel line, vacuum line, or orifice blockage is suspected as the obvious cause of a malfunction, correct the cause before proceeding further.

2. Check the wiring and connectors to the solenoid, vane air flow meter, speed sensor and ECM for looseness, corrosion, damage or other problems.

This must be done with the engine fully warmed so as to activate the purging controls.

3. If all checks are okay, proceed to Testing.

Testing

1. Check the canister purge solenoid as follows:

a. Disconnect the vacuum hoses and the electrical connector from the solenoid valve.

b. Attach a clean test hose to port A.

c. Blow air through the solenoid from port A and confirm that no air exits from port B.

d. Apply 12 volts to one terminal of the solenoid connector and ground the other terminal.

e. Blow air through the solenoid from port A and confirm that air exits from port B.

f. If the solenoid does not function as specified, it must be replaced.

2. Check the carbon canister for liquid fuel as follows:

a. Run the engine long enough to warm it up and purge any fuel from the carbon canister.

b. Stop the engine and remove the canister.

c. Inspect the canister for the presence of liquid fuel, indicated by odor or by excessive weight.

d. Blow into the air vent in the bottom of the canister and verify that air exits readily from the fuel vapor inlet.

e. If the carbon canister is free of liquid fuel and air passes through it easily, proceed to Step 3. If there is fuel in the canister or air does not pass through it, replace the canister.

3. Check for purge line blockage as follows:

a. Remove the purge lines (including any orifice) leading from the carbon canister to the engine intake.

b. Check each line for blockage by blowing through it. If air flows slowly, the line may contain an orifice that may be partially plugged.

c. If the line allows air to flow freely, proceed to Step 5. If air flows very slow through the line, proceed to Step 4. If air does not flow, remove the orifice, clean it thoroughly and install it in a new line, or replace the line and orifice as an assembly; proceed to Step 5.

4. Check for purge line orifice blockage as follows:

a. Remove any orifice suspected of being restricted and clean it thoroughly.

b. Reinstall it in the purge line and recheck it for resistance to air flow by blowing through the line.

c. If the line and orifice flow air more freely than when checked in Step 3, remove the orifice, replace the purge line, and reinstall the orifice, or replace the line and orifice as an assembly. The original line may contain accumulated particles.

d. If the line and orifice do not flow air more freely, proceed to Step 5.

5. Check the fuel vapor valve as follows:

a. Visually inspect the fuel vapor valve and its connections with the fuel tank for pinched hoses, blockage, looseness, or other mechanical damage.

b. If the fuel vapor valve and its connections are not damaged, remove the valve from the fuel tank.

c. Holding the valve in an upright position, with the tank end pointing down, blow air into the valve exhaust hose connection. Air should flow freely.

d. Holding the valve in the reverse position, with the tank end pointing upward, blow air into the vapor exhaust hose connection, air should not flow.

e. If the valve does not operate properly, replace it.

6. Check the 2-way check valve function as follows:

a. Visually inspect the check valve and its connections for hose pinching, blockage, looseness, or for evidence of other damage or leakage.

b. Remove the 2-way check valve.

c. Blow air through the valve from A to B and then from B to A. Verify that air passes easily in either direction.

d. If there is no evidence of leakage, and air passes easily in either direction, the check valve is okay; system testing is completed. If the valve leaks or air will not pass easily, replace the 2-way check valve.

REMOVAL & INSTALLATION

Charcoal Canister

1. Disconnect the negative battery cable.

2. Tag and disconnect the vapor hoses from the canister.

3. Remove the canister fasteners and remove the canister.

4. Installation is the reverse of the removal procedure.

Fuel Vapor Valve

1. Disconnect the negative battery cable.

2. Relieve the fuel system pressure and drain the fuel tank.

3. Remove the fuel tank from the vehicle.

4. Remove the fuel vapor valve from the top of the fuel tank.

5. Installation is the reverse of the removal procedure.

Purge Control Solenoid Valve

1. Disconnect the negative battery cable.

2. Tag and disconnect the hoses from the valve.

3. Disconnect the electrical connector from the valve, if equipped.

4. Remove the valve from its mounting and remove it from the vehicle.

5. Installation is the reverse of the removal procedure.

Check Valve

1. Disconnect the negative battery cable.

2. Raise and safely support the vehicle.

3. Tag and disconnect the vapor hoses from the check valve.

4. Remove the check valve mounting screw and the check valve from the underside of the vehicle.

5. Installation is the reverse of the removal procedure.

Exhaust Gas Recirculation System

OPERATION

◆ **See Figure 8**

The Exhaust Gas Recirculation (EGR) System introduces exhaust gas into the intake manifold which reduces the NOx content in the exhaust gas. The system utilizes a control valve, a modulator valve, the engine control unit, a solenoid valve, throttle sensor and a water thermosensor.

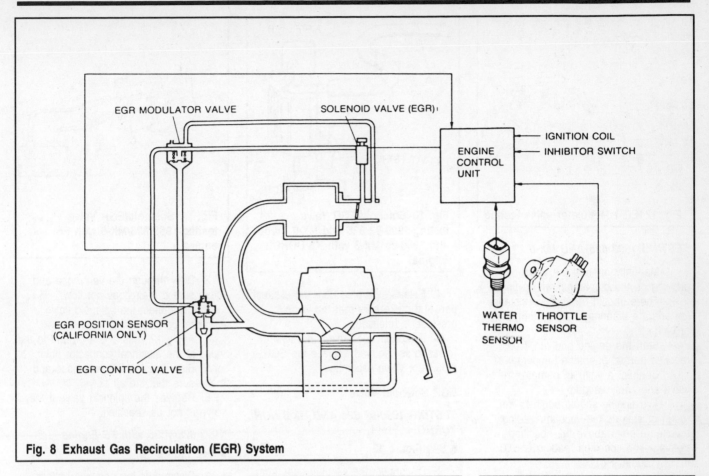

Fig. 8 Exhaust Gas Recirculation (EGR) System

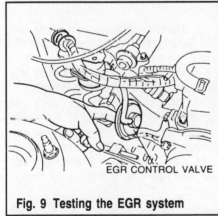

Fig. 9 Testing the EGR system

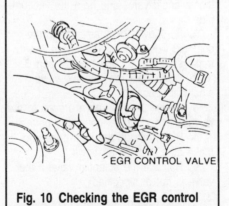

Fig. 10 Checking the EGR control valve

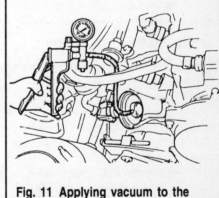

Fig. 11 Applying vacuum to the EGR control valve

SERVICE

EGR System

▶ See Figure 9

SYSTEM TESTING

1. Start the engine.
2. Accelerate the engine and verify that the EGR control valve diaphragm does not move upon acceleration with the engine cold.
3. Continue to run the engine until it reaches the normal operating temperature.

4. Accelerate the engine and verify that the EGR control valve diaphragm does move upward upon acceleration with the engine warm.

EGR Control Valve

TESTING 1990-92 626 AND MX-6

▶ See Figures 10 and 11

1. Manually operate the valve by pushing on the diaphragm with a finger.
2. There should be spring resistance felt and the diaphragm should not stick or bind.

3. Start the engine and run it until it reaches normal operating temperature.
4. Connect a vacuum pump to the valve and apply vacuum.
5. The engine should begin to run rough or stall as the vacuum reading reaches a point above the specified reading. The specified reading is 1.6-2.4 in.Hg (40-60 mm Hg).
6. If there is no change in the engine, replace the EGR control valve.

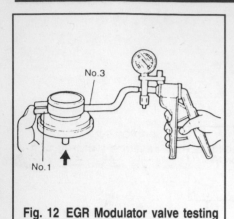

Fig. 12 EGR Modulator valve testing

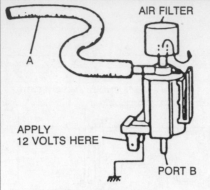

Fig. 13 Solenoid/EGR Valve testing-1990-92 626 and MX-6 Turbo and 1990-93 MX-3 with K8 DOHC Engine

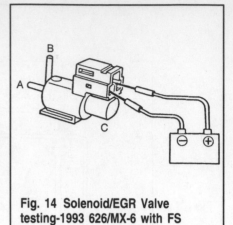

Fig. 14 Solenoid/EGR Valve testing-1993 626/MX-6 with FS engine

TESTING 1993 626 AND MX-6

1. Manually operate the valve by pushing on the diaphragm with a finger.
2. There should be spring resistance felt and the diaphragm should not stick or bind.
3. Start the engine and run it until it reaches normal operating temperature.
4. Connect a vacuum pump to the valve and apply vacuum.
5. The engine should begin to run rough or stall as the vacuum reading reaches a point above the specified reading. The specified reading is 5.91 in.Hg (150mm Hg).
6. If there is no change in the engine, replace the EGR control valve.

REMOVAL AND INSTALLATION

1. Disconnect the negative battery cable.
2. If necessary, remove the air cleaner assembly.
3. Disconnect the EGR control valve vacuum lines.
4. Remove the EGR control valve mounting bolts and remove the EGR control valve.
5. Installation is the reverse of the removal procedure.

EGR Modulator Valve

TESTING

▶ See Figure 12

1. Remove the EGR modulator valve assembly.
2. Plug the number 1 port and connect a vacuum guage to the number 3 port as shown.
3. Blow air into the exhaust port and operate the vacuum pump. Make sure that vacuum is held.

4. Release the plug from the exhaust port and make sure that the vacuum pressure is released.
5. If vacuum pressure is not held or released as required, replace the EGR modulator valve assembly.

EGR Solenoid Valve

TESTING 1990-92 626 AND MX-6 NON-TURBO

▶ See Figure 13

1. Disconnect the vacuum hose from the solenoid valve and from the vacuum pipe.
2. As shown, blow air through the solenoid valve from vacuum port A and make sure that air flows out of port B.
3. Disconnect the solenoid valve electrical connector.
4. Apply 12 volts and a ground to the valve at the electrical connector point.
5. Blow through the vent hose and make sure that the air flows.
6. Replace the solenoid valve if the valve is not as specified.

TESTING 1990-92 626 AND MX-6 TURBO AND 1990-93 MX-3 WITH K8 DOHC ENGINE — Vent Side

1. Disconnect the vacuum hoses.
2. Blow through the vent hose and make sure the air flows.
3. Disconnect the solenoid valve electrical connector.
4. Apply 12 volts and a ground to the valve at the electrical connector point.
5. Blow through the vent hose and make sure that the air does not flow.
6. Replace the solenoid valve if the valve is not as specified.

Vacuum Side

1. Disconnect the vacuum hoses.

2. Blow through the vent hose and make sure the air does not flow.
3. Disconnect the solenoid valve electrical connector.
4. Apply 12 volts and a ground to the valve at the electrical connector point.
5. Blow through the vent hose and make sure that the air flows.
6. Replace the solenoid valve if the valve is not as specified.

1993 626/MX-6 with FS Engine

▶ See Figure 14

1. Disconnect the negative battery cable.
2. Disconnect the vacuum hoses and the electrical connector from the solenoid valve.
3. Blow air into port A and verify that air does not flow from ports B or C.
4. Blow air into port B and verify that air does flow from port C.
5. Connect 12V and a ground to the terminals of the solenoid valve.
6. Blow air into port A and verify that air does flow from port B but not from port C.
7. Blow air into port B and verify that air does not flow from port C.
8. If the solenoid valve does not respond properly, replace it.

Check Engine Light

RESETTING

The Electronic Control Unit (ECU) contains a self-diagnosis system. When troubles within the engine emission and fuel control system are detected, the CHECK ENGINE light will illuminate.
The CHECK ENGINE light will illuminate briefly when the ignition is first turned ON. The light should then go off

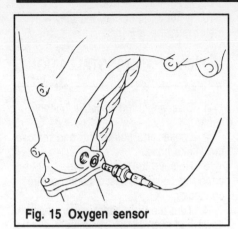

Fig. 15 Oxygen sensor

after the engine is started. If the light does stay on, the ECU has detected a fault or malfunction within the system.

If the CHECK ENGINE light is on, the system may be reset by following the steps below.

1. Disconnect the negative battery cable.

2. Wait for at least 20 seconds before connecting the negative battery cable. Connect the cable and start the engine.

3. Observe that the CHECK ENGINE light is not illuminated.

4. If the light is illuminated again, the vehicle should be inspected by a properly trained experienced technician using specialized diagnostic equipment. The steps that are involved in this procedure are normally beyond the capabilities of the DIYer.

Oxygen Sensor

OPERATION

▶ See Figure 15

The oxygen sensor reacts with the oxygen in the exhaust gases and sends a voltage signal to the ECU based on this reaction. A low voltage signal indicates too much oxygen or a lean condition while a high voltage signal indicates not enough oxygen or a rich condition. The ECU uses this information along with other sensor inputs to calculate air/fuel ratio.

The oxygen sensor is threaded into the exhaust manifold on non-turbocharged engines and into the turbocharger on turbocharged engines.

TESTING

323, Protege, Miata, MX-3 with B6 SOHC engine, 1990-92 626/MX6 and 1993 626/MX6 with FS engine

1. Start the engine and bring to normal operating temperature.

2. Disconnect the oxygen sensor connector.

3. Measure the voltage between the oxygen sensor wire and ground. With the engine speed is increased, the voltage should be 0.5-1.0 volts. When decreasing engine speed, the voltage should drop to 0-0.4 volts.

➡Voltage that remains above 0.55 volts indicates a continuously rich condition while below 0.55 volts indicates a continuously lean condition. Rich or lean conditions could be an indication of another problem.

4. If the voltage readings are not as specified, replace the oxygen sensor.

MX-3 with K8 DOHC engine and 1993 626/MX6 with KL engine

1. Start the engine and bring to normal operating temperature.

2. Disconnect the oxygen sensor connector.

3. Run the engine speed at 4500 RPM until the voltmeter indicates 0.7 volts.

4. Increase the engine speed and watch the voltage. During increased idle the voltage should read above 0.5 volts.

5. As the engine speed decreases, the voltage should drop to below 0.4 volts.

6. If the voltage readings are not as specified, replace the oxygen sensor.

REMOVAL AND INSTALLATION

All except turbocharged engines

1. Disconnect the oxygen sensor electrical connector.

2. Remove the oxygen sensor from the exhaust manifold.

3. Installation is the reverse of the removal procedure. Tighten the oxygen sensor to 22-36 ft. lbs. (29-49 Nm).

Turbocharged engines

1. Disconnect the negative battery cable.

2. Disconnect the sensor electrical connector.

3. Remove the wiring harness from the spark plug wire retaining bracket and the retaining bracket on the turbocharger heat shield.

4. Remove the sensor from the turbocharger.

5. Installation is the reverse of the removal procedure.

AIRFLOW METER

TESTING

323, Protege and MX-3 SOHC
▶ See Figures 16 and 17

1. Disconnect the negative battery cable.

2. Remove the airflow meter assembly.

3. Inspect the meter body for cracks and for smooth operation of the measuring plate.

4. Using a suitable ohmmeter, check the resistance between the terminals of the airflow meter plate.

5. When measuring the resistance between terminals E1 and FC (fuel pump switch), the reading should be infinity with the plate fully closed and 0 ohms when fully opened.

6. When measuring the resistance between terminals E2 and VS, the reading should be 200-600 ohms with the measuring plate fully closed and 20-1000 ohms when fully opened.

7. When measuring the resistance between terminals E2 and VC, the reading should be 200-400 ohms with the metering plate in any position.

8. When measuring the resistance between terminals E2 and THA (intake air thermosensor), the reading should be 13.6-18.4 kilohms at -4°F; 2.21-2.69 kilohms at 68°F and 493-667 ohms at 140°F with the metering plate in any position.

9. If not as specified, the airflow meter must be replaced.

MX-3 DOHC Engine
▶ See Figure 18

1. Disconnect the negative battery cable.

2. Remove the airflow meter assembly.

3. Inspect the meter body for cracks and for smooth operation of the measuring plate. Make sure the measuring core opens smoothly.

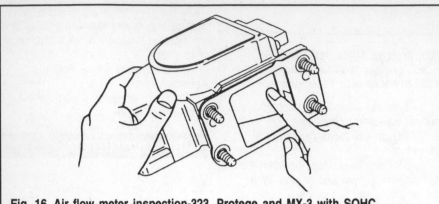

Fig. 16 Air flow meter inspection-323, Protege and MX-3 with SOHC

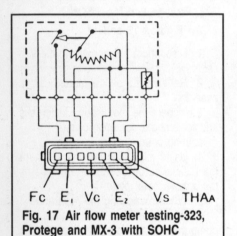

Fc E₁ Vc E₂ Vs THAₐ

Fig. 17 Air flow meter testing-323, Protege and MX-3 with SOHC

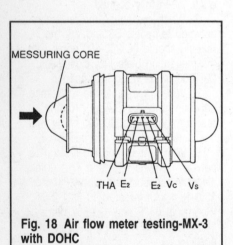

MESSURING CORE

THA E₂ E₂ Vc Vs

Fig. 18 Air flow meter testing-MX-3 with DOHC

4. Using a suitable ohmmeter, check the resistance between the terminals of the airflow meter plate fully closed and 0 ohms when fully opened.

5. When measuring the resistance between terminals E2 and VS, the reading should be 200-600 ohms with the measuring plate fully closed and 20-1000 ohms when fully opened.

6. When measuring the resistance between terminals E2 and VC, the reading should be 200-400 ohms with the metering plate in any position.

7. When measuring the resistance between terminals E2 and THA (intake air thermosensor), the reading should be 13.6-18.4 kilohms at -4°F; 2.21-2.69 kilohms at 68°F and 493-667 ohms at 140°F with the metering plate in any position.

8. If not as specified, the airflow meter must be replaced.

Miata, 626 and MX-6
▶ **See Figure 19**

1. Disconnect the negative battery cable.

2. Remove the airflow meter assembly.

3. Inspect the meter body for cracks and for smooth operation of the measuring plate.

4. Using an ohmmeter, check the resistance between the terminals of the airflow meter plate.

5. When measuring the resistance between terminals E1 and FC (fuel pump switch), the reading should be infinity with the plate fully closed and 0 ohms when fully opened.

6. When measuring the resistance between terminals E2 and VS, the reading should be 20-400 ohms with the measuring plate fully closed and 20-1000 ohms when fully opened.

7. When measuring the resistance between terminals E2 and VC, the reading should be 100-400 ohms with the metering plate in any position.

8. When measuring the resistance between terminals E2 and VB, the reading should be 200-400 ohms with the metering plate in any position.

9. When measuring the resistance between terminals E2 and THA (intake air thermosensor), the reading should be 13.6-18.4 kilohms at -4°F; 2.21-2.69 kilohms at 68°F and 493-667 ohms at 140°F with the metering plate in any position.

10. If not as specified, the airflow meter must be replaced.

REMOVAL AND INSTALLATION

1. Disconnect the negative battery cable.

2. Loosen the hose band and remove the intake hose.

3. Remove the airflow meter attaching bolts and disconnect the wire connector.

4. Turn the air cleaner cover upside down and remove the attaching nuts and remove the airflow meter.

5. Installation is the reverse order of the removal procedure.

Water Thermosensor(Coolant Temperature Sensor)

▶ **See Figures 20 and 21**

TESTING

1. Drain the engine coolant and remove the thermosensor from the rear of the engine or intake manifold.

2. Place the sensor in water with a thermometer and heat the water gradually.

3. Measure the resistance of the sensor and compare to the following values:

-4°F (-20°C) — 14.6-17.8 kilohms
68°F (20°C) — 2.2-2.7 kilohms
104°F (40°C) — 1.0-1.3 kilohms
140°F (60°C) — 0.50-0.65 kilohms
176°F (80°C) — 0.29-0.35 kilohms

4. Install a new sealing washer and thermosensor.

5. Torque the sensor to 18-22 ft. lbs. (25-29 Nm).

Throttle Position Sensor

TESTING

323

Manual Transaxle

▶ **See Figure 22**

1. Disconnect the connector from the throttle position sensor.

2. Connect an ohmmeter between terminals IDL and E.

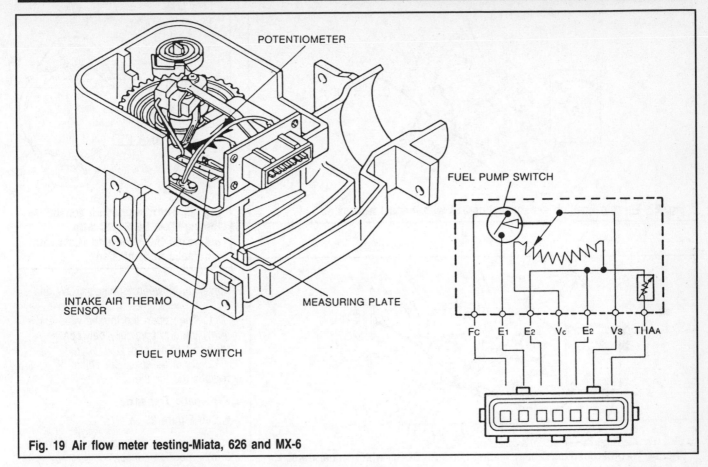

Fig. 19 Air flow meter testing-Miata, 626 and MX-6

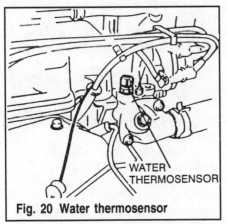

Fig. 20 Water thermosensor

3. Insert a 0.004 in. (0.1mm) feeler gauge between the throttle stop screw and stop lever.

4. Verify there is continuity between terminals IDL and E.

5. Then replace the feeler gauge with a 0.039 in. (1.0mm) feeler gauge, verify there is no continuity between terminals **IDL** and **E.**

6. Then open the throttle wide and verify there is no continuity again between terminals IDL and E.

7. Next, connect the ohmmeter between terminals POW and E.

8. Insert a 0.004 in. (0.1mm) feeler gauge between the throttle stop screw and stop lever.

9. Verify there is no continuity between terminals POW and E.

10. Then replace the feeler gauge with 0.039 in. (1.0mm), verify there is no continuity between terminals POW andE.

11. Then open the throttle wide and verify there is continuity between terminals POW and E.

12. If not as specified, adjust or replace the throttle sensor.

323

Automatic Transaxle

♦ See Figure 23

1. Disconnect the connector from the throttle position sensor.

2. Connect an ohmmeter between terminals DL and E.

3. Insert a 0.004 in. (0.1mm) feeler gauge between the throttle stop screw and stop lever.

4. Verify there is continuity between terminals DL and E.

5. Insert a 0.024 in. (0.6mm) feeler gauge between the throttle stop screw and stop lever.

6. Verify there is continuity no between terminals DL and E.

7. Connect an ohmmeter to the throttle sensor terminals Vt and E.

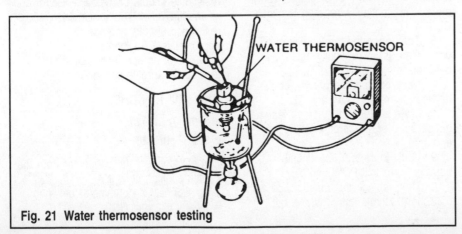

Fig. 21 Water thermosensor testing

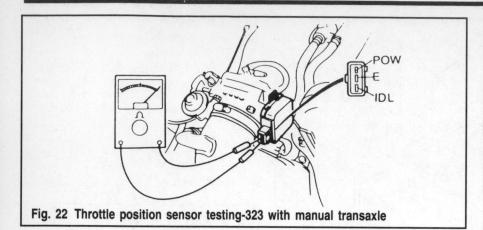

Fig. 22 Throttle position sensor testing-323 with manual transaxle

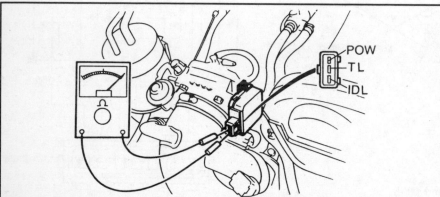

Fig. 24 Throttle position sensor testing-MX-3 B6 SOHC with manual transaxle and Miata with manual transmission

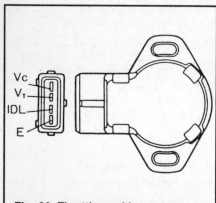

Fig. 23 Throttle position sensor testing-323 with automatic transaxle

8. Verify that resistance increases as throttle valve opening increase.

9. With throttle valve fully closed the resistance should be below 1 kilohm and as throttle valve is fully opened resistance should increase to approximately 5 kilohms.

10. If not as specified, adjust or replace the throttle sensor.

MX-3 with B6 SOHC and Miata

Manual Transaxle

▶ See Figure 24

1. Disconnect the connector from the throttle position sensor.

2. Connect an ohmmeter between terminals DL and TL.

3. Insert a 0.004 in. (0.1mm) feeler gauge between the throttle stop screw and stop lever.

4. Verify there is continuity between terminals DL and TL.

5. Then replace the feeler gauge with a 0.027 in. (0.7mm) feeler gauge, verify there is no continuity between terminals DL and TL.

6. Then open the throttle wide and verify there is no continuity again between terminals DL and TL.

7. Next, connect the ohmmeter between terminals POW and TL.

8. Insert a 0.004 in. (0.1mm) feeler gauge between the throttle stop screw and stop lever.

9. Verify there is no continuity between terminals POW and TL.

10. Then replace the feeler gauge with 0.027 in (0.7mm), verify there is no

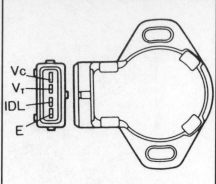

Fig. 25 Throttle position sensor testing-MX-3 B6 SOHC with automatic transaxle and Miata with automatic transmission

continuity between terminals POW and TL.

11. Then open the throttle wide and verify there is continuity between terminals POW and TL.

12. If not as specified, adjust or replace the throttle

Automatic Transaxle

▶ See Figure 25

1. Disconnect the connector from the throttle position sensor.

2. Connect an ohmmeter between the terminals IDL and E.

3. Insert a 0.004 in. (0.1mm) feeler gauge between the throttle stop screw and stop lever.

4. Verify there is continuity between terminals IDL and E.

5. Insert a 0.024 in. (0.6mm) feeler gauge between the throttle stop screw and stop lever.

6. Verify there is no continuity between terminals IDL and E.

7. Connect an ohmmeter to the throttle sensor terminals Vt and E.

8. Verify that resistance increases as throttle valve opening increase.

9. With throttle valve fully closed the resistance should be below 1 kilohm and as throttle valve is fully opened resistance should increase to approximately 5 kilohms.

10. If not as specified, adjust or replace the throttle sensor.

MX-3 with K8 DOHC

Manual Transaxle

▶ See Figure 26

1. Disconnect the connector from the throttle position sensor.

2. Connect an ohmmeter between terminals IDL and GND.

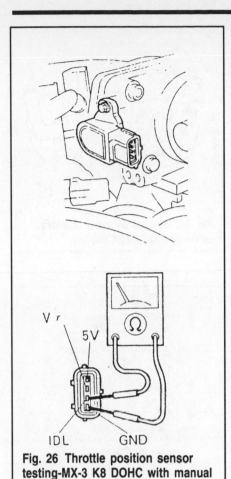

Fig. 26 Throttle position sensor testing-MX-3 K8 DOHC with manual transaxle

3. Rotate the throttle linkage by hand. With the throttle valve fully closed, the ohmmeter should read 0.1-1.1 volts.

4. With the throttle valve fully open, the ohmmeter should read 3.1-4.4 volts.

5. If not as specified, adjust or replace the throttle position sensor.

1990-92 626 and MX-6

1. Remove the air hose from the throttle body.

2. Disconnect the 3-pin throttle sensor connector.

3. Connect the 49-G018-901 testing harness or equivalent, between the throttle sensor and the wiring harness.

4. Turn the ignition switch **ON**.

5. Verify the throttle valve is fully closed.

6. Measure the voltage at the black and the red wires of the testing harness using a precision voltmeter with a scale of 0.01 volts, the voltage at the black wire should be approximately 0 volts and the voltage at the red wire should be 4.5-5.5 volts.

7. If the voltage reading is not as specified, check the battery voltage and wiring harness, if these are okay, replace the engine control unit.

8. Record the red wire voltage.

9. Measure the voltage of the blue wire, verify that the blue wire voltage is within specification according to the red wire voltage. For example; if the red wire voltage reading is 4.50-4.59 volts, then the blue wire voltage reading would have to be within 0.37-0.54 volts.

10. Hold the throttle valve fully open.

11. Measure the blue wire voltage, verify that the blue wire voltage is within specification according to that of the red wire voltage. For example; if the red wire voltage reading is 4.50-4.59 volts, then the blue wire voltage reading would have to be within 3.58-4.23 volts.

12. Check that blue wire voltage increases smoothly when opening the throttle valve from closed to fully open.

13. If the throttle sensor does not perform as specified, adjust or replace the sensor.

14. Turn the ignition **OFF**.

15. Disconnect the testing harness and reconnect the throttle sensor connector.

16. Disconnect the negative battery terminal and depress the brake pedal for at least 5 seconds to eliminate the control unit malfunction memory.

ADJUSTMENT

323 and Protege

MANUAL TRANSAXLE

1. Disconnect the connector from the throttle sensor.

2. Connect an ohmmeter to the sensor terminals **IDL** and **E**.

3. Insert a 0.016 in. (0.4mm) feeler gauge between the throttle stop screw and stop lever.

4. Loosen the mounting screws and rotate the sensor clockwise about 30 degrees and rotate it counterclockwise until continuity exists.

5. Insert a 0.027 in. (0.7mm) and verify that continuity does not exist.

6. Tighten the mounting screws.

7. Open the throttle fully a few times and recheck.

AUTOMATIC TRANSAXLE

1. Disconnect the connector from the throttle sensor.

2. Connect an ohmmeter between terminals {243}cf35 {242}E {243}cf33 {242} and {243}cf35 {242}IDL {243}cf33 {242} of the sensor.

3. Loosen the 2 attaching sensor attaching screws.

4. Insert a 0.01 in. (0.25mm) feeler gauge between the throttle stop screw and stop lever.

5. Rotate the sensor clockwise approximately 30 degrees, then rotate it counterclockwise until there is continuity.

6. Replace the feeler gauge with a 0.016 in. (0.4mm) gauge and verify there is no continuity.

7. Tighten the throttle position sensor screws.

8. Recheck the adjustment of the throttle sensor.

MX-3 and Miata

MANUAL TRANSAXLE

1. Disconnect the connector from the throttle position sensor and connect an ohmmeter to the throttle position sensor terminals IDL and TL.

2. Insert a 0.016 in. (0.4mm) feeler gauge between the throttle stop screw and throttle lever.

3. Loosen the 2 attaching screws. Rotate the throttle position sensor clockwise approximately 30 degrees, then rotate it counterclockwise until there is continuity.

4. Replace the feeler gauge with a 0.027 in. (0.7mm) feeler gauge. Verify there is no continuity.

5. If there is continuity, repeat the procedure or replace the sensor.

6. Tighten the attaching screws. Be sure not to move the throttle position sensor from the set position when tightening the screws.

7. Open the throttle valve fully a few times, then recheck the adjustment of the throttle position sensor.

AUTOMATIC TRANSAXLE

1. Disconnect the connector from the throttle position sensor and connect an ohmmeter to the throttle position sensor terminals IDL and E.

2. Insert a 0.01 in. (0.25mm) feeler gauge between the throttle stop screw and throttle lever.

3. Loosen the 2 attaching screws. Rotate the throttle position sensor clockwise approximately 30 degrees, then rotate it counterclockwise until there is continuity.

4. Replace the feeler gauge with a 0.016 in. (0.4mm) feeler gauge. Verify there is no continuity.

5. If there is continuity, repeat the procedure or replace the sensor.

6. Tighten the attaching screws. Be sure not to move the throttle position sensor from the set position when tightening the screws.

7. Open the throttle valve fully a few times, then check the adjustment of the throttle position sensor by verifying that resistance between terminals Vt and E.

8. If not as specified, replace the throttle position sensor.

1990-92 626 and MX-6

1. Remove the air hose from the throttle body.

2. Disconnect the 3-pin throttle sensor connector.

3. Connect the 49-G018-901 testing harness or equivalent, between the throttle sensor and the wiring harness.

4. Turn the ignition switch **ON**.

5. Verify the throttle valve is fully closed.

6. Measure the voltage at the red wire of the testing harness using a precision voltmeter with a scale of 0.01 volts and record it.

7. Measure the voltage of the blue wire.

8. Loosen the throttle position sensor attaching screws.

9. Turn the throttle sensor to adjust the blue wire voltage reading to within the range specified for the recorded red wire voltage reading. For example; if the recorded red wire voltage is 4.50-4.59 volts, then the blue wire voltage reading would have to be within 0.37-0.54 volts specification. Refer to the test and adjustment illustrations.

10. Tighten the throttle sensor attaching screws and recheck that the voltage is still within specification.

11. Hold the throttle valve fully open.

12. Measure the blue wire voltage, verify that the blue wire voltage is within specification according to that of the red wire voltage. For example; if the red wire voltage reading is 4.50-4.59 volts, then the blue wire voltage reading would have to be within 3.58-4.23 volts.

13. Check that blue wire voltage increases smoothly when opening the throttle valve from closed to the fully opened position. If the throttle sensor does not perform as specified, replace the sensor.

14. Turn the ignition **OFF**.

15. Disconnect the testing harness and reconnect the throttle sensor connector.

16. Disconnect the negative battery terminal and depress the brake pedal for at least 5 seconds to eliminate the control unit malfunction memory.

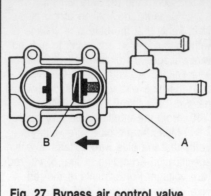

Fig. 27 Bypass air control valve testing-323 and Protege

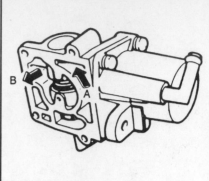

Fig. 29 Bypass air control valve testing-1990-92 626/MX-6

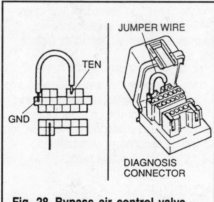

Fig. 28 Bypass air control valve testing-MX-3

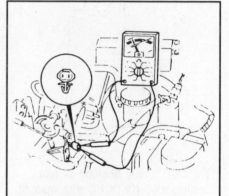

Fig. 30 Bypass air control valve testing-1990-92 626/MX-6

Bypass Air Control (BAC) valve

TESTING

323 and Protege
▶ **See Figure 27**

1. Remove the air valve from the vehicle.

2. Cool the valve to below 32°F (0°C).

3. Apply heat to the A area of the valve using a suitable tool.

4. Verify the plunger B moves away from the hose inlets.

5. If not as specified, replace the air valve.

MX-3
▶ **See Figure 28**

1. Connect the diagnostic connector terminals **TEN** and **GRN** with a jumper wire.

2. Connect a tachometer and start the engine.

3. The idle speed should decrease gradually as the engine warms.

1990-92 626 and MX-6
▶ **See Figures 29 and 30**

1. Disconnect the ISC valve connector when the engine is cold and idling.

2. Note the engine rpm and reconnect the connector.

3. Warm the engine to normal operating temperature and disconnect the connector again.

4. Verify the engine rpm is lower with the ISC disconnected when the engine is warm.

5. If not as specified, remove the BAC valve from the throttle body.

6. Blow air through the valve port A and B and verify air comes out of port B when the valve is cold.

7. If not as specified, replace the valve.

Miata
▶ **See Figure 31**

1. Using a jumper wire, connect diagnosis test terminals TEN and GND.

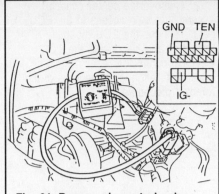

Fig. 31 Bypass air control valve testing-Miata

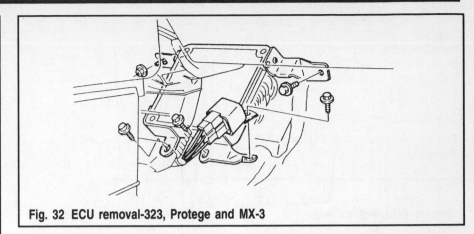

Fig. 32 ECU removal-323, Protege and MX-3

2. Verify the engine temperature is below 68°F (20°C) and start the engine.

3. Verify that engine rpm decreases gradually as engine temperature increases.

4. Remove the jumper wire.

5. Remove the air valve.

6. Cool the valve to 32°F (0°C).

7. Using a suitable tool, warm the valve slowly and note plunger movement.

8. Verify that plunger moves away from hose inlet.

9. If not as specified, replace the valve.

Idle Speed Control (ISC) valve

TESTING

323 and Protege

1. Disconnect the ISC valve wire connector.

2. Check the resistance of the valve using an ohmmeter.

3. The resistance should be approximately 11-13 ohms at 68°F (20°C).

4. If not as specified, replace the ISC valve.

MX-3

1. Warm the engine to normal temperature and turn all electric load **OFF**.

2. Connect a tachometer to the diagnostic connector **IG** terminal.

3. Check the idle speed to specifications.

4. Check the idle speed with engine loads energized with the transaxle in neutral for manual transaxle or **P** for automatic transaxle.

5. If equipped with a SOHC engine:

a. Power Steering **ON** — 700-800 rpm for manual transaxle.

b. Power Steering **ON** — 800-900 rpm for automatic transaxle.

c. A/C **ON** — 800-900 rpm for manual transaxle.

d. A/C **ON** — 750-850 rpm for automatic transaxle.

6. If equipped with a DOHC engine:

a. Power Steering **ON** — 640-700 rpm.

b. A/C **ON** — 720-780 rpm.

7. To check the BAC valve, connect the diagnostic connector terminals **TEN** and **GRD** with a jumper wire.

8. Connect a tachometer and start the engine.

9. The idle speed should decrease gradually as the engine warms.

10. To check the ISC valve, disconnect the valve and measure the resistance of the ISC valve with an ohmmeter. The resistance should be 10.7-12.3 ohms at 68°F (20°C). If not, replace the valve.

1990-92 626 and MX-6

1. Disconnect the ISC valve wire connector.

2. Check the resistance of the valve using an ohmmeter.

3. The resistance should be approximately 6.3-9.9 ohms at normal operating temperature.

4. If not as specified, replace the ISC valve.

Miata

1. Disconnect the ISC valve wire connector.

2. Check the resistance of the valve using an ohmmeter.

3. The resistance should be approximately 11-13 ohms.

4. If not as specified, replace the ISC valve.

Engine Control Unit (ECU)

REMOVAL AND INSTALLATION

323, Protege and MX-3
▶ See Figure 32

1. Disconnect the negative battery cable.

2. Remove the passenger and driver side cover walls from the center console unit.

3. Remove the ECU mounting bolts/nuts and disconnect the ECU electrical connectors.

4. Installation is the reverse of the removal procedure.

Miata
▶ See Figure 33

1. Disconnect the negative battery cable.

2. Lift the passenger side floor mat.

3. Remove the ECU protective cover.

4. Remove the ECU mounting bolts/nuts and disconnect the electrical connectors.

5. Installation is the reverse of the removal procedure.

1990-92 MX-6/626

1. Disconnect the negative battery cable.

2. Remove the passenger and driver side cover walls from the center console unit.

3. Remove the ECU mounting bolts/nuts and disconnect the ECU electrical connectors.

4. Installation is the reverse of the removal procedure.

1993 MX-6/626

1. Disconnect the negative battery cable.

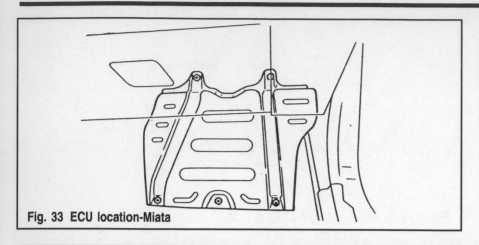

Fig. 33 ECU location-Miata

2. Remove the center console assembly to gain access to the ECU.

3. Remove the ECU mounting bolts/nuts and disconnect the ECU electrical connectors.

4. Installation is the reverse of the removal procedure.

SELF-DIAGNOSTIC SYSTEM

General Information

All Mazdas have self-diagnostic capabilities. The ECU monitors all input and output functions within the electronic engine control system. If a malfunction is detected, the information will be stored in the ECU memory in the form of a 2 or 3 digit code. These codes can be accessed only through the use of Mazda self diagnosis checker 49 H018 9A1 and system selector 49 B019 9A0 or equivalent.

When using the Mazda tools, codes will be output and displayed as numbers, such as the number 23. If codes are being read on an analog voltmeter, the needle sweeps indicate the code digits.

Clearing Codes

Codes stored within the ECM memory must be erased when repairs are completed. Also, erasing codes during diagnosis can separate hard faults from intermittents. To erase stored codes, disconnect the negative battery cable, then depress the brake pedal for at least 10 seconds. Reconnect the battery cable and recheck the system for any remaining or newly set codes.

ENGINE CODES

Code	Explanation
2	No NE signal—distributor
3	No G signal—distributor
8	Air flow meter
9	Water thermo sensor
10	Intake air thermo sensor
12	Throttle sensor
14	Atmospheric pressure sensor
15	Oxygen sensor
17	Feedback system
25	Solenoid valve for pressure regulator control
26	Solenoid valve for purge control valve
34	Open or short circuit—ISC valve
41	Solenoid valve—VICS

Fig. 34 1989-93 323/Protege and 1992-93 MX3 (1.6L) engine diagnostic codes

ENGINE CODES

Code	Explanation
2	No NE signal—distributor
3	No G signal—distributor
8	Air flow meter
9	Water thermo sensor
10	Intake air thermo sensor
12	Throttle sensor
14	Atmospheric pressure sensor
15	Oxygen sensor
17	Feedback system
25	Solenoid valve for pressure regulator control
26	Solenoid valve for purge control valve
34	Open or short circuit—ISC valve
41	Solenoid valve—VICS

Fig. 35 1989-93 323/Protege and 1992-93 MX3 (1.8L) engine diagnostic codes

ENGINE CODES

Code	Explanation
01	Ignition pulse
02	Ne signal—distributor
03	G signal—distributor
08	Airflow meter
09	Water thermosensor
10	Intake air thermosensor
14	Atmospheric pressure sensor
15	Oxygen sensor
17	Feedback system
26	Solenoid valve—purge control
34	ISC valve

Fig. 36 1990-93 Miata engine diagnostic codes

ENGINE CODES

Code	Explanation
01	Ignition pulse
08	Air flow meter
09	Water thermo sensor
10	Intake air thermo sensor
12	Throttle sensor
14	Atmospheric pressure sensor
15	Oxygen sensor
16	EGR position sensor
17	Feedback system
25	Solenoid valve—pressure regulator
26	Solenoid valve—purge control
28	Solenoid valve—EGR vacuum
34	Solenoid valve—idle speed control

Fig. 37 1989-92 626/MX6 with 2.2L engine diagnostic codes

No.	Indicator flashing pattern	Diagnosted circuit	Condition	Fail-safe	Memorized
02		Ne signal (Crankshaft position sensor)	No Ne signal while detecting 12 G signals	—	Yes
03	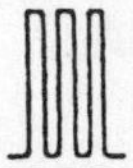	G signal (Crankshaft position sensor)	No G signal for 1.5 sec.	Cancels sequencial injection	Yes
06	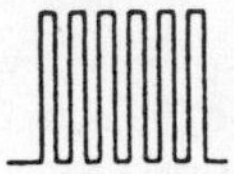	Vehicle speed sensor	No input signal from vehicle speed sensor while driving at turbine speed above 600 rpm in D.S or L range	Refer to Section K	Yes
08	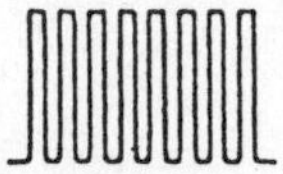	Air flow sensor		Measures intake air amount by throttle valve opening angle	Yes
09	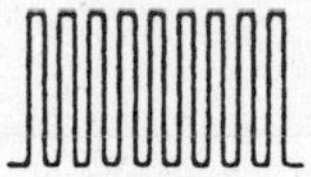	Engine coolant temperature sensor (CIS)		Maintains constant 34°C {93°F} command	Yes
11	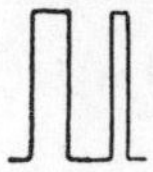	Intake air temperature sensor	Open or short circuit	Maintains constant 20°C {68°F} command	Yes
12		Throttle position sensor		Maintains constant command of throttle valve fully open	Yes
14		Barometric absolute pressure sensor		Maintains constant command of sea-level pressure	Yes
15		Heated oxygen sensor	Sensor output continues less than 0.55V 75 sec. after engine exceeds 1,500 rpm	Cancels engine closed loop operation	Yes
16		EGR function sensor (California)	Open or short circuit EGR valve stuck	—	Yes
17		Closed loop system	Sensor output continues unchanged 40 sec. after engine exceeds 1,500 rpm	Cancels engine closed loop operation	Yes
25		Solenoid valve (pressure regulator control)		—	No
26		Solenoid valve (purge control)	Open or short circuit	—	No
28		Solenoid valve (EGR control)		—	No

Fig. 38 1993 626/MX6 (2.0L engine) diagnostic codes

No.	Indicator flashing pattern	Diagnosted circuit	Condition	Fail-safe	Memorized
34	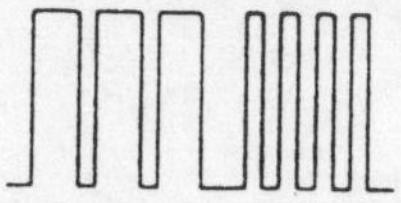	Idle air control valve	Open or short circuit	—	No
55		Vehicle speed pulse generator (ATX)	No input signal from pulse generator while driving at vehicle speed 40 km/h (25 mph) or higher in D.S or L range		
56		ATF thermosensor (ATX)			
60		Solenoid valve (1-2 shift) (ATX)			
61		Solenoid valve (2-3 shift) (ATX)			
62		Solenoid valve (3-4 shift) (ATX)		Refer to Section K	Refer to Section K
63		Solenoid valve (Lockup control) (ATX)			
64		Solenoid valve (3-2 timing) (ATX)	Open or short circuit		
65		Solenoid valve (Lockup) (ATX)			
66		Solenoid valve (Line pressure) (ATX)			
67		Coolant fan relay (No.1)		—	No
68		Coolant fan relay (No.2, No.3) (ATX)			No
69		Engine coolant temperature sensor (Fan)*		Maintains constant over 108°C {226°F} command	Yes

Fig. 39 1993 626/MX6 (2.0L engine) diagnostic codes-continued

No.	Indicator flashing pattern	Diagnosed circuit	Condition	Point	Memo-rized
02	ON  OFF	NE 2 signal, crankshaft position sensor 2	No NE 2 signal	• Crankshaft position sensor 2 connector • Wiring from crankshaft position sensor 2 to PCME • Crankshaft position sensor 2	Yes
03	ON 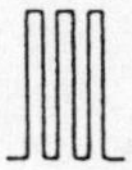 OFF	G signal, crankshaft position sensor 1	No G signal	• Distributor connector • Wiring from main relay to distributor • Wiring from distributor to PCME • Crankshaft position sensor 1	Yes
04	ON 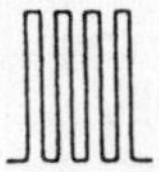 OFF	NE 1 signal, crankshaft position sensor	No NE 1 signal		Yes
05	ON 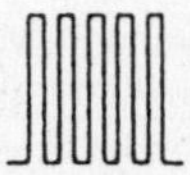 OFF	Knock sensor	Open or short circuit	• Knock sensor connector • Wiring from knock sensor to PCME • Knock sensor	Yes
08	ON 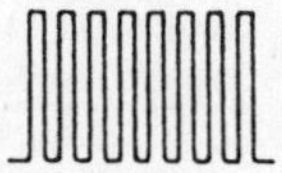 OFF	Air flow sensor	Short circuit	• Air flow sensor connector • Wiring from air flow sensor to PCME • Air flow sensor	Yes
09	ON 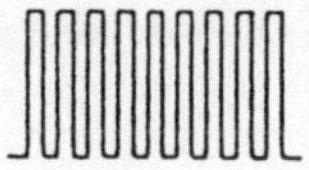 OFF	Engine coolant temperature sensor (CIS)		• Engine coolant temperature sensor connector • Wiring from engine coolant temperature sensor to PCME • Engine coolant temperature sensor resistance	Yes
10	ON 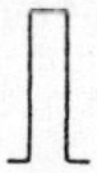 OFF	Intake air temprerature sensor (in air flow sensor)	Open or short circuit	• Air flow sensor connector • Wiring from air flow sensor to PCME • Intake air temperature sensor resistance	Yes
12	ON 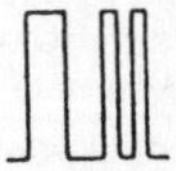 OFF	Throttle position sensor		• Throttle position sensor connector • Wiring from throttle position sensor to PCME • Throttle position sensor	Yes
14	ON  OFF	Barometric absolute pressure sensor (in PCME)		• PCME	Yes
15	ON  OFF	Heated oxygen sensor (LH)	Sensor output continues less than 0.55V 100 sec. after engine exceeds 1,500 rpm	• Heated oxygen sensor connector • Wiring from heated oxygen sensor to PCME • Heated oxygen sensor	Yes
16	ON  OFF	EGR function sensor	Open or short circuit	• EGR function sensor connector • Wiring from EGR function sensor to PCME • EGR function sensor	Yes
17	ON  OFF	Closed loop system (LH)	Sensor output not changed 50 sec. after engine exceeds 1,500 rpm	• Fuel pressure • Injection fuel leakage • Ignition system • Air leakage • PCME	Yes

Fig. 40 1993 626/MX6 (2.5L engine) diagnostic codes

No.	Indicator flashing pattern	Diagnosed circuit	Condition	Point	Memorized
23	ON / OFF 	Heated oxygen sensor (RH)	Sensor output continues less than 0.55V 100 sec. after engine exceeds 1,500 rpm	• Heated oxygen sensor connector • Wiring from heated oxygen sensor to PCME • Heated oxygen sensor	Yes
24	ON / OFF 	Closed loop system (RH)	Sensor output not changed 50 sec. after engine exceeds 1,500 rpm	• Fuel pressure • Injection fuel leakage • Ignition system • Air leakage • PCME	Yes
25	ON / OFF 	Solenoid valve (pressure regulator control)		• Solenoid valve connection • Wiring from solenoid valve to PCME • Solenoid valve continuity	No
26	ON / OFF 	Solenoid valve (purge control)		• Solenoid valve connection • Wiring from solenoid valve to PCME • Solenoid valve continuity	No
28	ON / OFF 	Solenoid valve (EGR vacuum)		• Solenoid valve connection • Wiring from solenoid valve to PCME • Solenoid valve continuity	No
29	ON / OFF 	Solenoid valve (EGR vent)		• Solenoid valve connection • Wiring from solenoid valve to PCME • Solenoid valve continuity	No
34	ON / OFF 	Idle air control valve	Open or short circuit	• Solenoid valve connector • Wiring from Solenoid valve to PCME • Solenoid valve continuity	No
41	ON / OFF 	Solenoid valve (VRIS 1)		• Solenoid valve connection • Wiring from solenoid valve to PCME • Solenoid valve continuity	No
46	ON / OFF 	Solenoid valve (VRIS 2)		• Solenoid valve connection • Wiring from solenoid valve to PCME • Solenoid valve continuity	No
67	ON / OFF 	Coolant fan relay (No.1)		• Fan relay connector • Wiring from relay to PCME • Fan relay	No
69	ON / OFF 	Engine coolant temperature sensor (fan)	Warm-up condition (above 60°C {140°F})and open or short circuit	• Engine coolant temperature sensor connector • Wiring from engine coolant temperature sensor to PCME • Engine coolant temperature sensor resistance	Yes

Fig. 41 1993 626/MX6 (2.5L engine) diagnostic codes

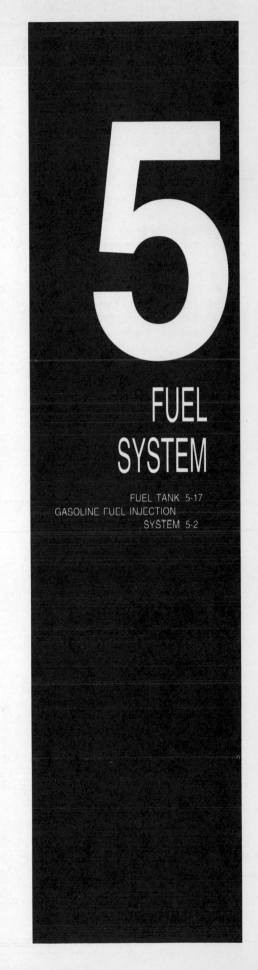

5

FUEL
SYSTEM

GASOLINE FUEL INJECTION SYSTEM

Description of System

▶ See Figures 1, 2, 3, 4, 5, 6, 7 and 8

The electronic fuel injection system on your Mazda consists of two subsystems, the fuel delivery system and the electronic control system. The fuel delivery system supplies fuel to the fuel injectors at a specified pressure. The electronic control system regulates the flow of fuel from the injectors into the engine.

The fuel delivery system consists of an electric fuel pump, fuel filters, fuel pressure regulator and fuel injectors. The electric fuel pump, mounted in the fuel tank, draws fuel through a filter screen attached to the fuel pump/sending unit assembly. The fuel is then pumped to the engine compartment, through another filter, and into the fuel injection rail. The fuel injection rail supplies fuel directly to the injectors. Constant fuel pressure is maintained by the fuel pressure regulator. The pressure regulator is mounted at the end of the fuel injection rail, downstream from the fuel injectors.

Excess fuel supplied by the fuel pump is relieved by the regulator and returned to the fuel tank through the fuel return line. The fuel injectors spray a metered quantity of fuel into the intake air stream when they are energized. The quantity of fuel is determined by the electronic control system.

The electronic control system consists of the Electronic Control Unit (ECU) and the engine sensors and switches that provide input to the ECU. The Vane Air Flow (VAF) meter monitors the amount of air flow into the engine, measures air temperature, controls the electric fuel pump and supplies this information to the ECU. Information is also supplied to the ECU regarding engine coolant temperature, engine speed, and exhaust gas oxygen content. Based on the input information, the ECU computes the required fuel flow rate and determines the needed injector pulse width, then outputs a command to the fuel injector to meter the exact quantity of fuel.

On turbocharged engines, exhaust gas energy is used to pressurize the intake air, thereby providing more than the normal amount of air into the combustion chamber. This engine has sensors and provides input to the ECU exclusive to this type of induction, otherwise the fuel injection system on the turbocharged engine operates the same as the normally aspirated engines.

Relieving Fuel System Pressure

▶ See Figures 9, 10 and 11

FUEL PRESSURE

323, Protege and MX-3

1. Remove the rear seat cushion and locate the fuel pump connector.
2. Start the engine.
3. Disconnect the fuel pump connector.
4. After the engine stalls, reconnect the fuel pump connector and turn the ignition switch **OFF**. Install the rear seat cushion.

Miata

1. Start the engine.
2. Disconnect the circuit opening relay connector, located under the left side of the instrument panel.
3. After the engine stalls, reconnect the circuit opening relay and turn the ignition switch **OFF**.

MX-6 and 626

2.0L AND 2.5L ENGINES

1. Start the engine.
2. Remove the fuel pump relay from the relay box, located in the left side of the engine compartment.
3. After the engine stalls, reinstall the relay and turn the ignition switch **OFF**.

2.2L ENGINE

1. Start the engine.
2. Disconnect the circuit opening relay connector, located under the left side of the instrument panel.
3. After the engine stalls, reconnect the circuit opening relay and turn the ignition switch **OFF**.

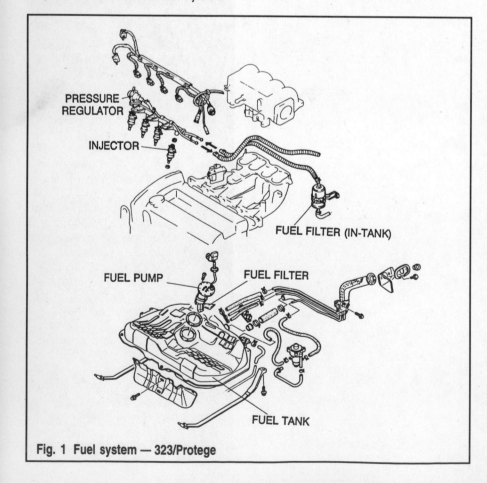

PRESSURE REGULATOR

INJECTOR

FUEL FILTER (IN-TANK)

FUEL PUMP

FUEL FILTER

FUEL TANK

Fig. 1 Fuel system — 323/Protege

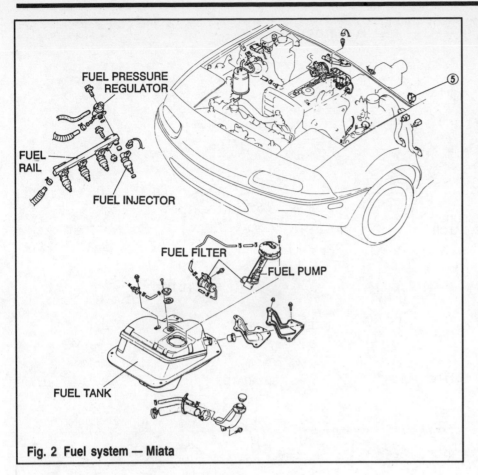

FUEL PRESSURE REGULATOR

FUEL RAIL

FUEL INJECTOR

FUEL FILTER

FUEL PUMP

FUEL TANK

Fig. 2 Fuel system — Miata

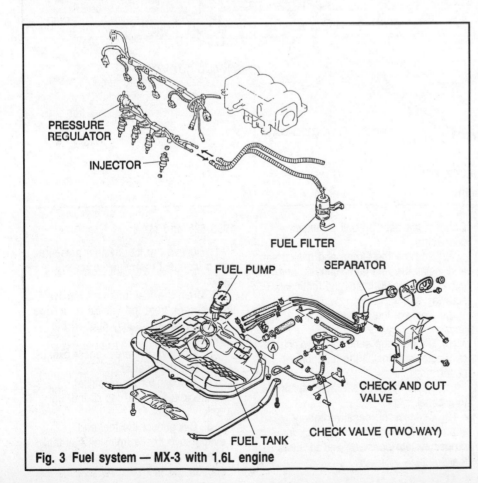

PRESSURE REGULATOR

INJECTOR

FUEL FILTER

FUEL PUMP

SEPARATOR

CHECK AND CUT VALVE

CHECK VALVE (TWO-WAY)

FUEL TANK

Fig. 3 Fuel system — MX-3 with 1.6L engine

Electric Fuel Pump

REMOVAL & INSTALLATION

▶ **See Figures 12, 13, 14, 15, 16, 17, 18 and 19**

MX-3, 323, Protege and 1990-92 626 and MX-6

1. Relieve the fuel pressure and disconnect the negative battery cable.

2. Depress the clips on each end of the rear seat cushion and remove the cushion.

3. Disconnect the electrical connector from the fuel pump/sending unit.

4. Remove the attaching screws from the fuel pump/sending unit access cover and remove the cover.

5. Disconnect the fuel supply and return hoses from the fuel pump/sending unit.

6. Remove the attaching screws and the fuel pump/sending unit from the fuel tank.

7. Disconnect the sending unit electrical connector, remove the sending unit attaching nuts and remove the sending unit from the fuel pump assembly.

To install:

8. Attach the sending unit to the fuel pump assembly and install the nuts. Connect the sending unit electrical connector.

9. Install the fuel pump/sending unit into the fuel tank with a new gasket and install the mounting screws.

10. Connect the fuel supply and return lines.

11. Install the access cover and the mounting screws.

12. Connect the sending unit electrical connector.

13. Position the rear seat cushion over the floor, making sure to align the retaining pins with the clips. Push down firmly until the 2 retaining pins are locked into the rear seat retaining clips.

14. Connect the negative battery cable, start the engine and check for proper system operation and for fuel leaks.

Miata

1. Relieve the fuel pressure and disconnect the negative battery cable.

2. Remove the inside rear package trim panels and remove the screws from the service hole cover. Remove the service hole cover.

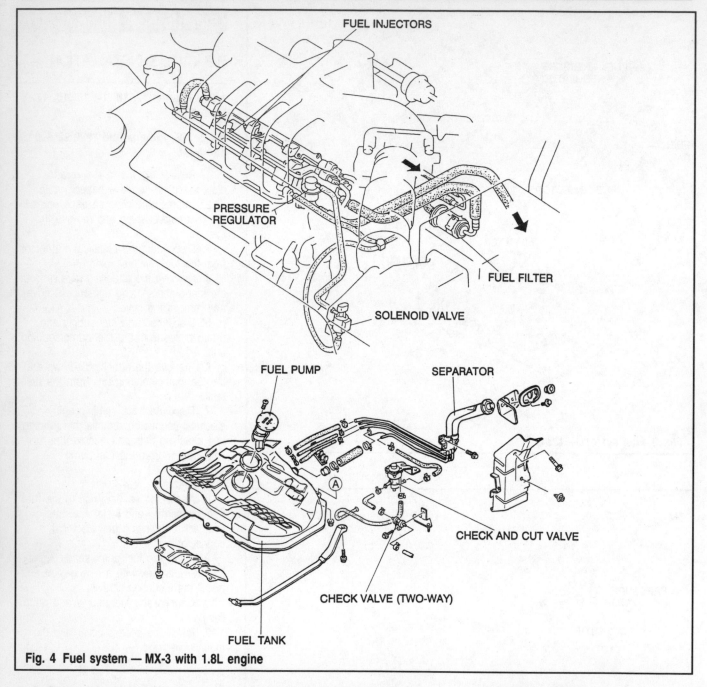

FUEL INJECTORS

PRESSURE REGULATOR

FUEL FILTER

SOLENOID VALVE

FUEL PUMP

SEPARATOR

Ⓐ

CHECK AND CUT VALVE

CHECK VALVE (TWO-WAY)

FUEL TANK

Fig. 4 Fuel system — MX-3 with 1.8L engine

3. Remove the fuel pump cover and disconnect the electrical connector from the fuel pump/sending unit.

4. Disconnect the fuel supply and return hoses from the fuel pump/sending unit.

5. Remove the attaching screws and the fuel pump/sending unit from the fuel tank.

6. Disconnect the sending unit electrical connector, remove the sending unit attaching nuts and remove the sending unit from the fuel pump assembly.

To install:

7. Attach the sending unit to the fuel pump assembly and install the nuts.

Connect the sending unit electrical connector.

8. Replace the O-ring and gasket set and install the fuel pump/sending unit into the fuel tank. Install the mounting screws.

9. Connect the fuel supply and return lines.

10. Connect the sending unit electrical connector and install the fuel pump cover.

11. Install the rear package interior trim panel.

12. Connect the negative battery cable, start the engine and check for proper system operation and for fuel leaks.

1993 626 and MX-6

1. Relieve the fuel system pressure and disconnect the negative battery cable.

2. Drain the fuel tank and remove the fuel tank from the vehicle as follows:

a. Raise and safely support the vehicle.

b. Remove the pre-silencer exhaust pipe and the heat shield.

c. Disconnect the electrical connectors from the top of the fuel tank.

d. Disconnect the fuel and evaporative hoses from the fuel tank.

e. While having an assistant support the fuel tank, remove the fuel

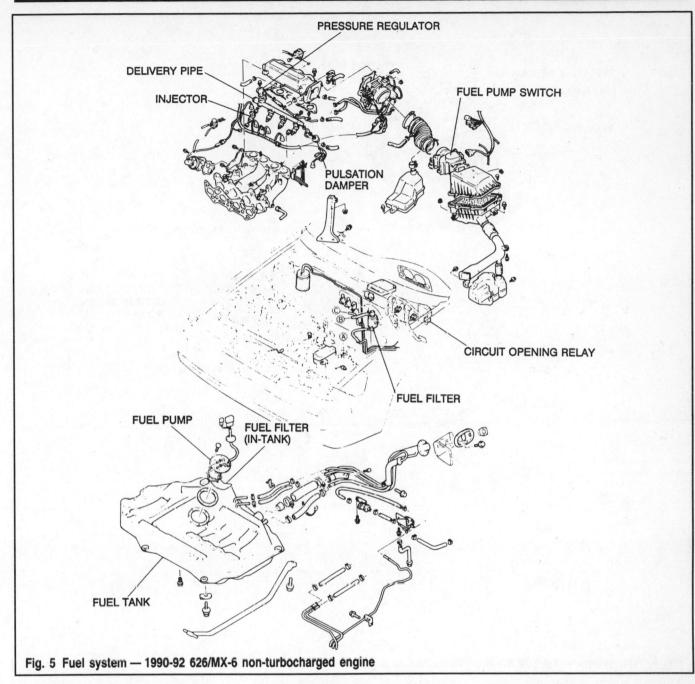

Fig. 5 Fuel system — 1990-92 626/MX-6 non-turbocharged engine

tank support straps and lower the fuel tank from the vehicle.

3. Disconnect all fuel hoses from the fuel pump unit.

4. Turn the fuel pump ring counterclockwise and remove it.

5. Remove the fuel pump and gaskets from the fuel tank.

To install:

6. Install the fuel pump with a new gasket. Turn the fuel pump ring clockwise to tighten it until the flange hits the stopper.

7. Connect the fuel hoses to the fuel pump.

8. Install the fuel tank to the vehicle as follows:

a. Have an assistant support the fuel tank in place and install the fuel tank straps. Tighten the strap bolts to 32-45 ft. lbs. (43-61 Nm).

b. Connect the fuel and evaporative hoses, making sure to push the hoses on at least 1.4 inches (35 mm).

c. Connect the fuel pump electrical connector.

d. Install the exhaust pre-silencer pipe heat shield. Tighten the bolt to 70-90 inch lbs. (7.9-10 Nm).

e. Install the exhaust pre-silencer pipe with new gaskets intact. Tighten the front nuts to 28-38 ft. lbs. (38-51

Nm). Tighten the rear bolts to 48-65 ft. lbs. (64-89 Nm).

9. Lower the vehicle and connect the negative battery cable.

TESTING

▶ **See Figures 20 and 21**

1. Relieve the pressure in the fuel system and disconnect the negative battery cable.

2. Install a suitable fuel pressure gauge between the fuel filter and the fuel rail.

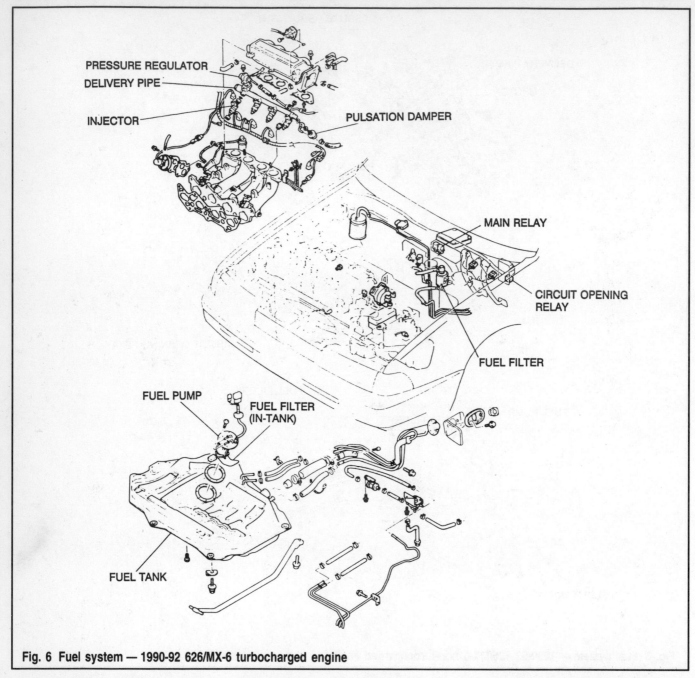

Fig. 6 Fuel system — 1990-92 626/MX-6 turbocharged engine

3. Connect a jumper wire between the **F/P** and **GRND** terminals of the fuel pump test connector.

4. Connect the negative battery cable, turn the ignition key **ON** and check the fuel pump pressure. The pressure should be as follows:

323/Protege — more than 21 psi (147 kPa)

Miata — more than 21 psi (147 kPa)

MX-3 — 37-46 psi (255-314 kPa)

1990-92 626/MX-6 — more than 21 psi (147 kPa)

1993 626/MX-6 2.0L engine — more than 50 psi (340 kPa)

1993 626/MX-6 2.5L engine — 72-92 psi (500-630 kPa)

5. If there is no fuel pressure, remove the fuel tank cap and try to hear if the fuel pump is operating. If the pump sounds like it's running, check for a restriction in the fuel line. If the pump is not running, check for power to the pump and check the pump motor ground. If there is no power to the pump, check all electrical connections and check the fuel pump relay.

6. If fuel pressure is low, check for a restriction in the fuel line or clogged fuel filters.

7. Remove the jumper wire, relieve the fuel system pressure and disconnect the negative battery cable.

8. Remove the fuel pressure gauge and reconnect the fuel line.

9. Connect the negative battery cable.

Throttle Body

REMOVAL & INSTALLATION

▶ See Figures 22, 23, 24, 25, 26, 27 and 28

323 and Protege

1. Disconnect the negative battery cable.

2. Remove the air cleaner intake duct.

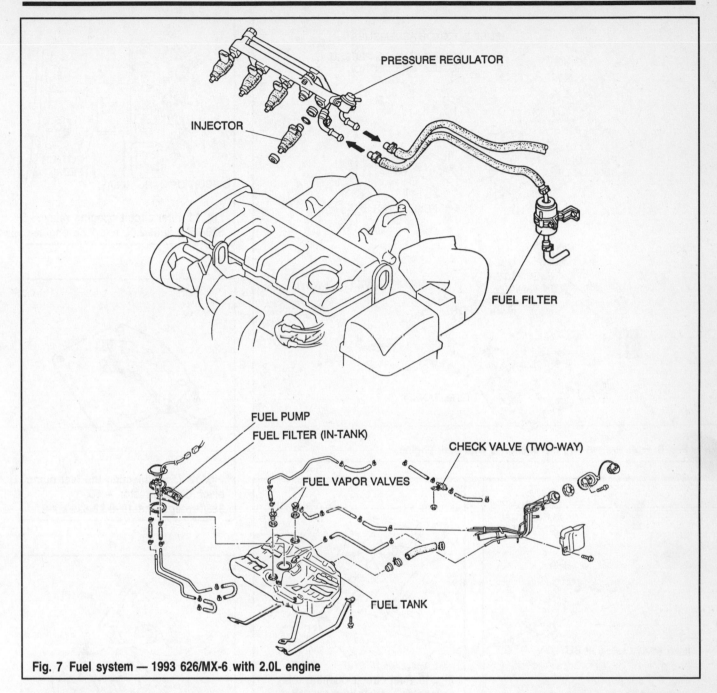

Fig. 7 Fuel system — 1993 626/MX-6 with 2.0L engine

3. Remove the air cleaner and the air cleaner element.

4. Disconnect the air flow meter connector and remove the top of the air cleaner assembly.

5. Remove the resonance chamber.

6. Remove the air hose from the throttle body.

7. Disconnect the accelerator cable from the throttle body.

8. Remove the throttle body assembly with the gasket.

To install:

9. Replace the throttle body assembly and the gasket. Tighten the bolts to 14-19 ft. lbs. (19-25 Nm.

10. Connect the accelerator cable to the throttle body and adjust as is necessary.

11. Connect the air hose to the throttle body.

12. Install the resonance chamber and connect the airflow meter connector.

13. Install the air cleaner base and install the air cleaner.

14. Install the air cleaner duct and connect the negative battery cable.

Miata

1. Disconnect the negative battery cable. Disconnect the air intake hose from the throttle body.

2. Tag and remove the hoses and electrical connectors from the throttle body. Disconnect the accelerator cable.

3. Remove the throttle body attaching bolts and remove the throttle body assembly.

4. Installation is the reverse of the removal procedure. Tighten the mounting bolts to 14-19 ft. lbs. (19-25 Nm).

MX-3

1. Disconnect the negative battery cable. Disconnect the air intake hose from the throttle body.

2. Tag and remove the hoses and electrical connectors from the throttle body. Disconnect the accelerator cable.

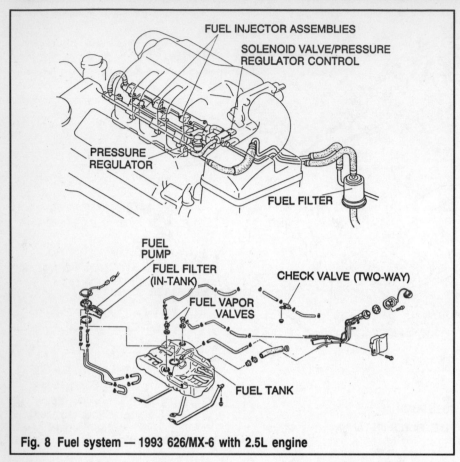

Fig. 8 Fuel system — 1993 626/MX-6 with 2.5L engine

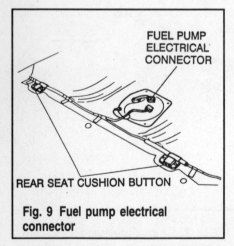

Fig. 9 Fuel pump electrical connector

Fig. 10 Fuel circuit opening relay connector — Miata and 626/MX-6 with 2.2L engine

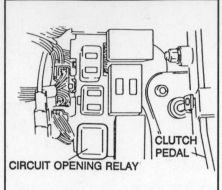

Fig. 11 Fuel circuit opening relay — 626/MX-6 with 2.0L and 2.5L engines

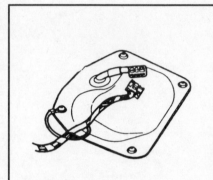

Fig. 12 Disconnecting the fuel pump electrical connector — MX-3, 323/Protege and 1990-92 626/MX-6

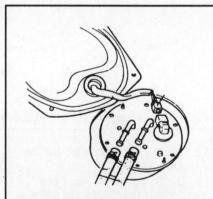

Fig. 13 Disconnecting the fuel pump electrical connector and hoses — MX-3, 323/Protege and 1990-92 626/MX-6

3. Remove the throttle body attaching bolts and remove the throttle body assembly.

4. Installation is the reverse of the removal procedure. Tighten the mounting nuts to 14-19 ft. lbs. (19-25 Nm).

1990-92 626 and MX-6

1. Disconnect the negative battery cable. Disconnect the airflow meter electrical connector.

2. Remove the air cleaner assembly and the air intake duct.

3. Mark all of the hoses and connectors that are connected to the throttle body and disconnect them. Disconnect the accelerator cable from the throttle body.

4. Remove the throttle body bolts and remove the throttle body assembly.

5. Installation is the reverse of the removal procedure. Tighten the throttle body nuts to 14-19 ft. lbs. (19-25 Nm).

1993 626 and MX-6

1. Disconnect the negative battery cable. Disconnect the air intake hose from the throttle body.

2. Tag and remove the hoses and electrical connectors from the throttle body. Disconnect the accelerator cable.

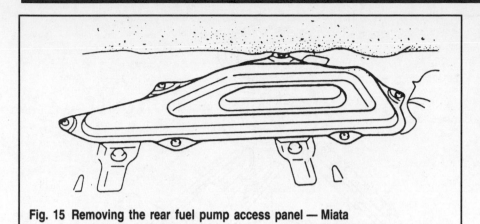

Fig. 15 Removing the rear fuel pump access panel — Miata

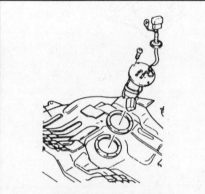

Fig. 14 Removing the fuel pump assembly — MX-3, 323/Protege and 1990-92 626/MX-6

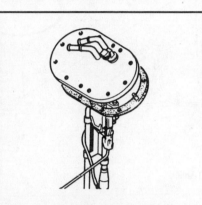

Fig. 17 Removing the fuel pump assembly with the gasket intact — Miata

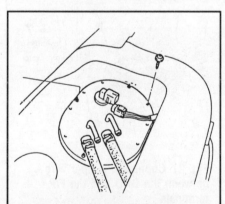

Fig. 16 Disconnecting the fuel pump electrical connector and the hoses — Miata

3. Remove the throttle body attaching bolts and remove the throttle body assembly.

4. Installation is the reverse of the removal procedure. Tighten the mounting nuts to 14-19 ft. lbs. (19-25 Nm).

Fuel Injectors

REMOVAL & INSTALLATION

▶ See Figures 29, 30, 31, 32, 33, 34 and 35

323 and Protege

1. Relieve the fuel system pressure.
2. Disconnect the negative battery cable.
3. Disconnect the electrical connectors at the injectors.
4. Remove the fuel injector harness from the fuel delivery pipe.
5. Remove the delivery pipe bolt(s) and remove the delivery pipe with the injectors and the pressure regulator.
6. Separate the injectors, grommets and the insulators from the delivery pipe assembly.
   To install:
7. Replace the fuel injector O-rings and apply a small amount of clean engine oil to the O-rings before installation.

8. Replace the fuel injector insulator seals.
9. Install the injectors to the delivery pipe and install the assembly to the engine. Tighten the delivery pipe bolt to 14-18 ft. lbs. (19-25 Nm).
10. Install the injector harness to the fuel delivery pipe and connect the injector wiring.
11. Connect the negative battery cable.

Miata

1. Relieve the fuel system pressure.
2. Disconnect the negative battery cable.
3. Drain the engine coolant and disconnect the water hoses. Remove the air valve assembly from the intake manifold.
4. Remove the PCV valve and disconnect the vacuum hoses.
5. Disconnect the fuel injector electrical connectors.
6. Remove the delivery pipe bolt(s) and remove the delivery pipe with the injectors and the pressure regulator.
7. Separate the injectors, grommets and the insulators from the delivery pipe assembly.
   To install:
8. Replace the fuel injector O-rings and apply a small amount of clean engine oil to the O-rings before installation.
9. Replace the fuel injector insulator seals.
10. Install the injectors to the delivery pipe and install the assembly to the engine. Tighten the delivery pipe bolt(s) to 14-19 ft. lbs. (19-25 Nm).
11. Connect the injector wiring and the vacuum hoses. Install the PCV valve.
12. Install the air valve to the intake manifold. Replace the gasket and tighten the bolts to 43-69 inch lbs. (5-8 Nm).
13. Connect the water hoses and refill the coolant to the proper level.
14. Connect the negative battery cable.

MX-3 with 1.6L Engine

1. Relieve the fuel system pressure.
2. Disconnect the negative battery cable.
3. Disconnect the electrical connectors at the injectors.
4. Remove the fuel injector harness from the fuel delivery pipe.
5. Remove the delivery pipe bolt(s) and remove the delivery pipe with the injectors and the pressure regulator.

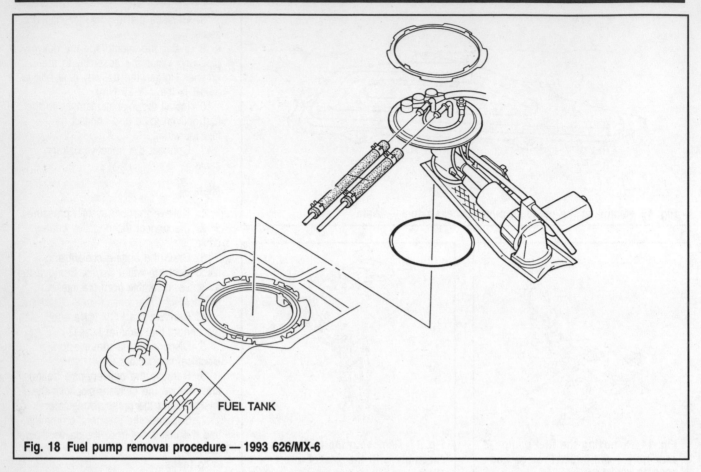

FUEL TANK

Fig. 18 Fuel pump removal procedure — 1993 626/MX-6

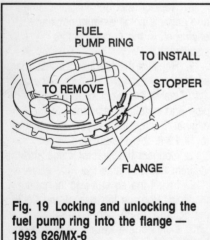

Fig. 19 Locking and unlocking the fuel pump ring into the flange — 1993 626/MX-6

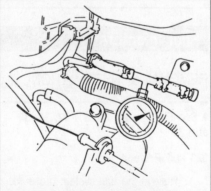

Fig. 20 Installing fuel pressure guage to check fuel pressure

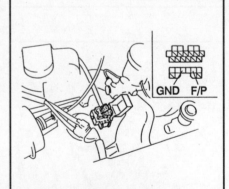

Fig. 21 Connect a jumper wire between the GND and the F/P terminals

6. Separate the injectors, grommets and the insulators from the delivery pipe assembly.

To install:

7. Replace the fuel injector O-rings and apply a small amount of clean engine oil to the O-rings before installation.

8. Replace the fuel injector insulator seals.

9. Install the injectors to the delivery pipe and install the assembly to the engine. Tighten the delivery pipe bolt to 14-18 ft. lbs. (19-25 Nm).

10. Install the injector harness to the fuel delivery pipe and connect the injector wiring.

11. Connect the negative battery cable.

MX-3 with 1.8L Engine

1. Relieve the fuel system pressure.

2. Disconnect the negative battery cable.

3. Remove the air intake hose assembly.

4. Disconnect the injector electrical connectors from the injector harness.

5. Disconnect the fuel hoses from the end of the fuel distributors.

6. Remove the fuel distributor attaching screws and remove the fuel distributor assemblies.

7. Remove the fuel injector harnesses from the fuel distributors.

8. Separate the injectors from the distributor and remove the O-ring and spacer.

To install:

9. Replace the fuel injector O-rings and apply a small amount of clean

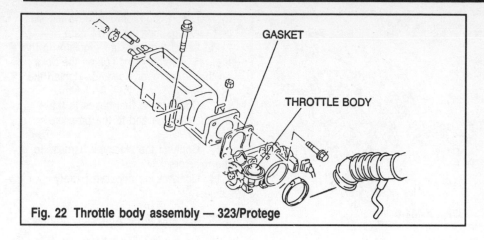

Fig. 22 Throttle body assembly — 323/Protege

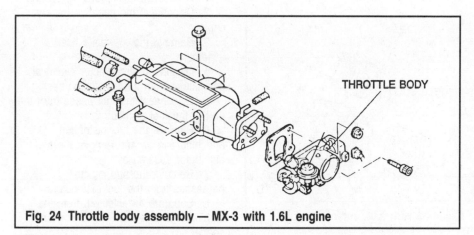

Fig. 24 Throttle body assembly — MX-3 with 1.6L engine

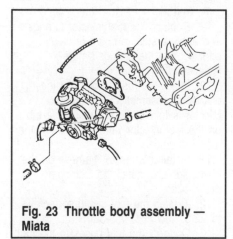

Fig. 23 Throttle body assembly — Miata

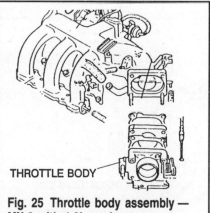

Fig. 25 Throttle body assembly — MX-3 with 1.8L engine

engine oil to the O-rings before installation.

10. Install the fuel injectors to the distributor assembly. Turn until the injector is fully seated, aligning the tab on the fuel injector with the notch in the fuel distributor.

11. Install the injector harness on the distributor and install the distributor assemblies.

12. Tighten the fuel distributor screws to 22-31 inch lbs. (2.5-3.5 Nm).

13. Connect the fuel hoses to the fuel distributors and connect the electrical connectors to the injector harness.

14. Install the air intake hose and connect the negative battery cable.

1990-92 626 and MX-6

1. Properly relieve the fuel system pressure.

2. Disconnect the negative battery cable.

3. Remove the wiring harness bracket from the end of the engine.

4. Remove the EGR modulator valve and remove the bracket.

5. Disconnect the vacuum pipe mounting bolts.

6. Remove the intake air hose from the throttle body.

7. Remove the side engine lift hook assembly.

8. Remove the dynamic chamber mounting bolts and nuts and lift the dynamic chamber away from the engine.

9. Disconnect the fuel return pipe bracket from the intake manifold.

10. Disconnect the fuel injector electrical connectors.

11. Remove the fuel delivery pipe with the pressure regulator and pulsation damper intact.

12. Separate the fuel injectors from the delivery pipe. Remove the grommets and the insulators.

To install:

13. Position the insulators and fuel injectors into the intake manifold. Position the grommets and new O-rings onto the fuel injectors. Apply a small amount of engine oil to the O-rings during installation.

14. Position the spacers and the fuel rail on the injectors. Install the attaching bolts to the fuel rail and tighten to 14-19 ft. lbs. (19-25 Nm).

15. Connect the electrical connectors to the fuel injectors.

16. Install the fuel return line bracket onto the intake manifold and install the return fuel line at the bracket. Secure with the clamp.

17. Connect the fuel return pipe bracket to the intake manifold.

18. Lower the dynamic chamber into place and tighten the mounting bolts to 14-19 ft. lbs. (19-25 Nm).

19. Install the side engine lift hook assembly and tighten the bolts to 14-19 ft. lbs. (19-25 Nm).

20. Install the intake air hose to the throttle body.

21. Install the vacuum pipe mounting bolts.

22. Install the EGR modulator valve and bracket.

23. Install the wiring harness bracket at the end of the intake manifold.

24. Connect the negative battery cable.

1993 626 and MX-6 with 2.0L Engine

1. Properly relieve the fuel system pressure.

2. Disconnect the negative battery cable.

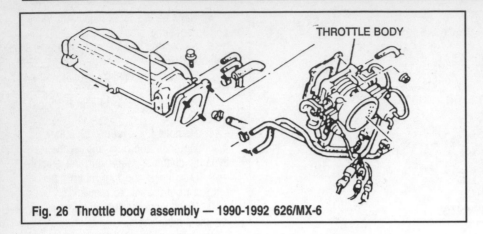

Fig. 26 Throttle body assembly — 1990-1992 626/MX-6

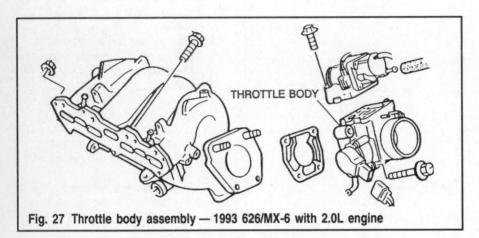

Fig. 27 Throttle body assembly — 1993 626/MX-6 with 2.0L engine

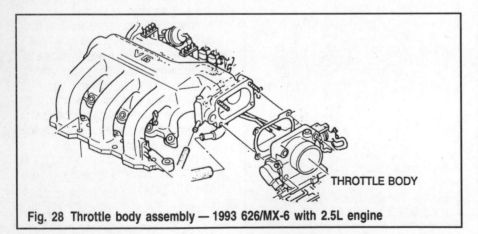

Fig. 28 Throttle body assembly — 1993 626/MX-6 with 2.5L engine

3. Disconnect the electrical connectors from the injectors and remove the wiring harness.

4. Disconnect the hose from the pressure regulator and remove the pressure regulator from the distribution pipe.

5. Disconnect the fuel hose from the distribution pipe.

6. Remove the bolts from the distribution pipe and remove the distribution pipe.

7. Remove the injectors complete with the O-rings and the insulators.

To install:

8. Replace the fuel injector O-rings and apply a small amount of clean engine oil to the O-rings before installation.

9. Replace the injector insulators and install the injectors to the intake manifold. Make sure that the injectors are properly seated and that the electrical connector points are facing upward.

10. Install the distribution pipe to the top of the injectors, making sure that it is properly seated. Tighten the top bolts

to 14-18 ft. lbs. (19-25 Nm) and the side bolt to 70-95 inch lbs. (8-11 Nm).

11. Install the pressure regulator to the fuel rail assembly and tighten the bolts so that it is properly seated. Tighten the bolts to 70-95 inch lbs. (8-11 Nm).

12. Connect the fuel hoses to the distribution pipe and to the pressure regulator.

13. Connect the electrical harness to the injectors.

14. Connect the negative battery cable.

1993 626 and MX-6 with 2.5L Engine

1. Relieve the fuel system pressure.

2. Disconnect the negative battery cable.

3. Remove the air intake hose assembly.

4. Disconnect the injector electrical connectors from the injector harness.

5. Disconnect the fuel hoses from the end of the fuel distributors.

6. Remove the fuel distributor attaching screws and remove the fuel distributor assemblies.

7. Remove the fuel injector harnesses from the fuel distributors.

8. Separate the injectors from the distributor and remove the O-ring and spacer.

To install:

9. Replace the fuel injector O-rings and apply a small amount of clean engine oil to the O-rings before installation.

10. Install the fuel injectors to the distributor assembly. Turn until the injector is fully seated, aligning the tab on the fuel injector with the notch in the fuel distributor.

11. Install the injector harness on the distributor and install the distributor assemblies.

12. Tighten the fuel distributor screws to 22-31 inch lbs. (2.5-3.5 Nm).

13. Connect the fuel hoses to the fuel distributors and connect the electrical connectors to the injector harness.

14. Install the air intake hose and connect the negative battery cable.

TESTING

◆ See Figures 36 and 37

1. Start the engine and warm it up to normal operating temperature. Allow the engine to run at idle.

2. Hold a long screwdriver against the injector and place an ear down close

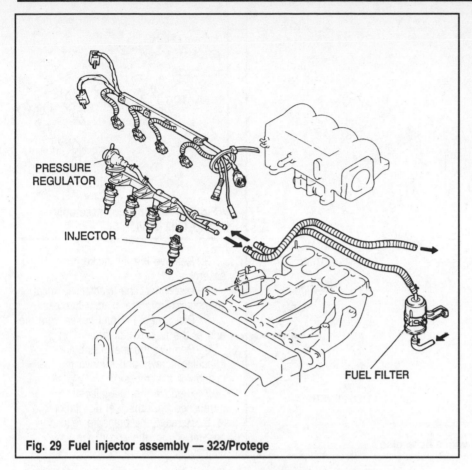

Fig. 29 Fuel injector assembly — 323/Protege

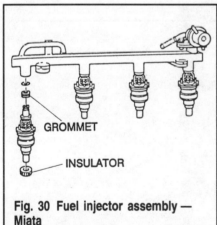

Fig. 30 Fuel injector assembly — Miata

to the screwdriver handle. Listen for injector operation noise.

3. If no sound is heard, proceed as follows:

a. Disconnect the injector harness from the injector.

b. Measure the resistance of the injector with an ohmmeter.

c. The resistance should be between 12-16 ohms.

d. If the resistance is not as specified, replace the injector.

e. If the injector resistance is as specified, inspect the wiring to the

injectors and to the control unit terminals.

Fuel Circuit Opening Relay

REMOVAL & INSTALLATION

▶ **See Figures 38 and 39**

323, Protege and MX-3

1. Remove the passenger side wall cover assembly.

2. Disconnect the relay from the connector and remove the relay from the bracket.

3. Installation is the reverse of the removal procedure.

Miata and 1990-92 626 and MX-6

1. Remove the under steering wheel cover panel.

2. Disconnect the relay from the connector and remove the relay from the bracket.

3. Installation is the reverse of the removal procedure.

TESTING

323, Protege and Miata

RESISTANCE TESTING

▶ **See Figure 40**

1. Remove the fuel circuit opening relay as previously described.

2. Using an ohmmeter, measure the resistance between terminals **STA** and **E1**. The resistance should be 21-43 ohms.

3. Measure the resistance between terminals **B** and **Fc**. The resistance should be 109-226 ohms.

4. Measure the resistance between terminals **B** and **Fp**. The resistance should be infinite.

Fuel Pressure Regulator

REMOVAL & INSTALLATION

▶ **See Figures 41, 42, 43, 44, 45 and 46**

323, Protege and Miata

1. Properly relieve the fuel system pressure.

2. Disconnect the vacuum hose from the pressure regulator.

3. Disconnect the fuel return hose from the pressure regulator.

4. Remove the pressure regulator attaching bolts and remove the fuel pressure regulator assembly.

5. Installation is the reverse of the removal procedure. Replace the O-ring and tighten the attaching bolts to 69-95 inch lbs. (8-11 Nm).

MX-3 with 1.6L Engine

1. Properly relieve the fuel system pressure.

2. Disconnect the vacuum hose from the pressure regulator.

3. Disconnect the fuel return hose from the pressure regulator.

4. Remove the pressure regulator attaching bolts and remove the fuel pressure regulator assembly.

5. Installation is the reverse of the removal procedure. Replace the O-ring and tighten the attaching bolts to 69-95 inch lbs. (8-11 Nm.)

MX-3 with 1.8L Engine

1. Relieve the fuel system pressure.

2. Disconnect the negative battery cable.

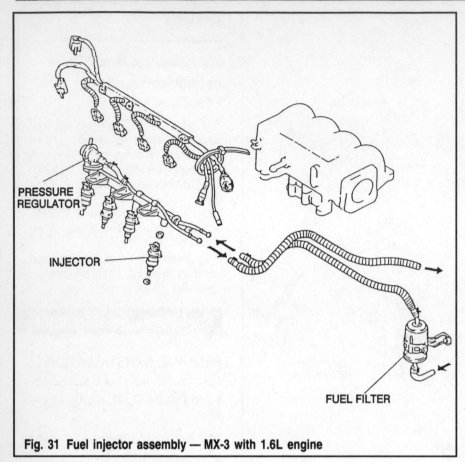

PRESSURE REGULATOR

INJECTOR

FUEL FILTER

Fig. 31 Fuel injector assembly — MX-3 with 1.6L engine

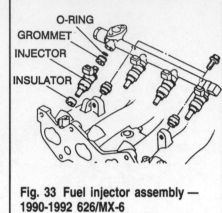

O-RING
GROMMET
INJECTOR
INSULATOR

Fig. 33 Fuel injector assembly — 1990-1992 626/MX-6

3. Remove the air intake hose assembly.
4. Disconnect the injector electrical connectors from the injector harness.
5. Disconnect the fuel hoses from the end of the fuel distributors.
6. Remove the fuel distributor attaching screws and remove the fuel distributor assemblies.
7. Remove the fuel injector harnesses from the fuel distributor.
8. Remove the pressure regulator assembly from the end of the fuel distributor.

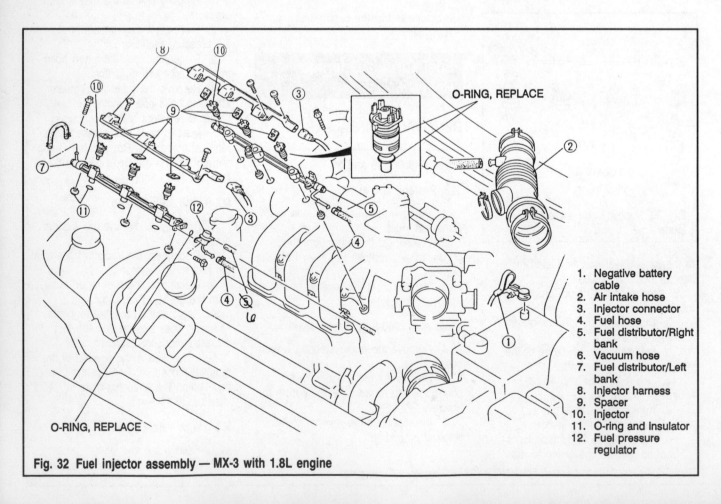

O-RING, REPLACE

O-RING, REPLACE

1. Negative battery cable
2. Air intake hose
3. Injector connector
4. Fuel hose
5. Fuel distributor/Right bank
6. Vacuum hose
7. Fuel distributor/Left bank
8. Injector harness
9. Spacer
10. Injector
11. O-ring and insulator
12. Fuel pressure regulator

Fig. 32 Fuel injector assembly — MX-3 with 1.8L engine

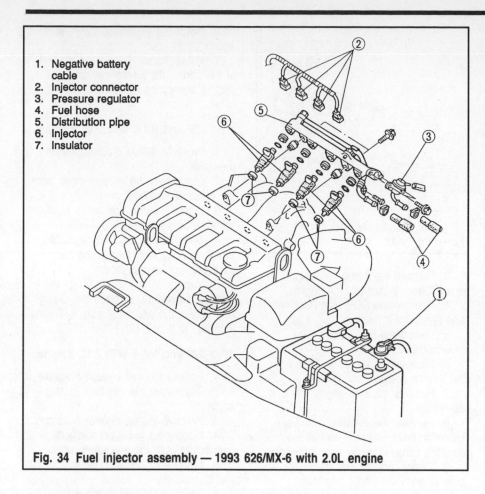

1. Negative battery cable
2. Injector connector
3. Pressure regulator
4. Fuel hose
5. Distribution pipe
6. Injector
7. Insulator

Fig. 34 Fuel injector assembly — 1993 626/MX-6 with 2.0L engine

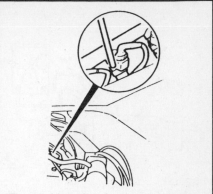

Fig. 36 Listening for fuel injection operation

To install:

9. Replace the fuel injector O-rings and apply a small amount of clean engine oil to the O-rings before installation.

10. Install the fuel pressure regulator assembly and install the fuel injectors to the fuel distributor. Turn until the injector is fully seated, aligning the tab with the notch in the fuel distributor.

11. Install the injector harness and install the distributor assemblies.

12. Tighten the fuel distributor screws to 22-31 inch lbs. (2.5-3.5 Nm).

13. Connect the fuel hoses to the ends of the fuel distributors and the

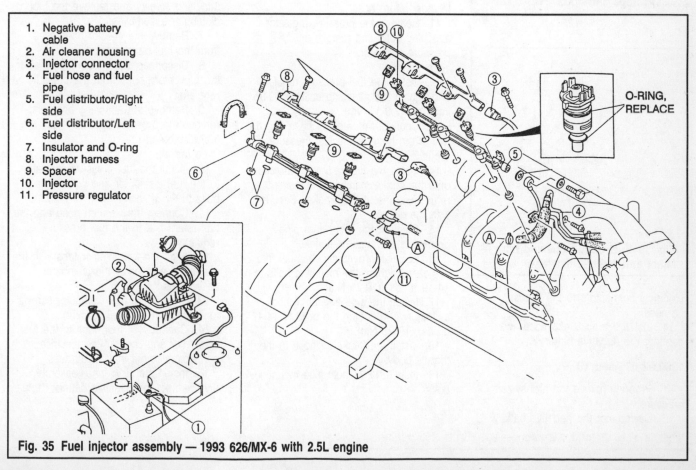

1. Negative battery cable
2. Air cleaner housing
3. Injector connector
4. Fuel hose and fuel pipe
5. Fuel distributor/Right side
6. Fuel distributor/Left side
7. Insulator and O-ring
8. Injector harness
9. Spacer
10. Injector
11. Pressure regulator

O-RING, REPLACE

Fig. 35 Fuel injector assembly — 1993 626/MX-6 with 2.5L engine

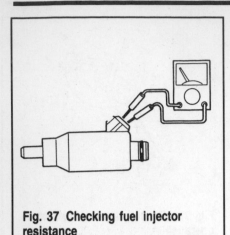

Fig. 37 Checking fuel injector resistance

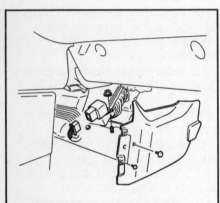

Fig. 38 Fuel circuit opening relay — 323/Protege and MX-3

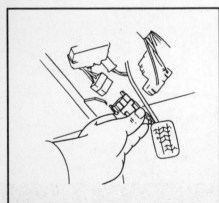

Fig. 39 Fuel circuit opening relay — Miata and 1990-92 626/MX-6

electrical connectors to the injector harness.

14. Install the air intake hose and connect the negative battery cable.

1990-92 626 and MX-6

1. Properly relieve the fuel system pressure.

2. Disconnect the negative battery cable.

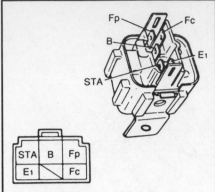

Fig. 40 Testing the fuel circuit opening relay

3. Remove the wiring harness bracket from the end of the engine.

4. Remove the EGR modulator valve and remove the bracket.

5. Disconnect the vacuum pipe mounting bolts.

6. Remove the intake air hose from the throttle body.

7. Remove the side engine lift hook assembly.

8. Remove the dynamic chamber mounting bolts and nuts and lift the dynamic chamber away from the engine.

9. Disconnect the fuel return pipe bracket from the intake manifold.

10. Disconnect the vacuum hose and the fuel return hose.

11. Remove the pressure regulator attaching bolts and remove the fuel pressure regulator.

To install:

12. Install the fuel pressure regulator and tighten the attaching bolts to 69-95 inch lbs. (7.8-11 Nm).

13. Connect the vacuum hose and the fuel return hose to the fuel pressure regulator.

14. Install the fuel return line bracket onto the intake manifold and install the return fuel line at the bracket. Secure with the clamp.

15. Connect the fuel return pipe bracket to the intake manifold.

16. Lower the dynamic chamber into place and tighten the mounting bolts to 14-19 ft. lbs. (19-25 Nm).

17. Install the side engine lift hook assembly and tighten the bolts to 14-19 ft. lbs. (19-25 Nm).

18. Install the intake air hose to the throttle body.

19. Install the vacuum pipe mounting bolts.

20. Install the EGR modulator valve and bracket.

21. Install the wiring harness bracket at the end of the intake manifold.

22. Connect the negative battery cable.

1993 626 and MX-6 with 2.0L Engine

1. Properly relieve the fuel system pressure.

2. Disconnect the vacuum hose from the pressure regulator.

3. Disconnect the fuel return hose from the pressure regulator.

4. Remove the pressure regulator attaching bolts and remove the fuel pressure regulator assembly.

5. Installation is the reverse of the removal procedure. Replace the O-ring and tighten the attaching bolts to 70-95 inch lbs. (7.8-10.7 Nm.)

1993 626 and MX-6 with 2.5L Engine

1. Relieve the fuel system pressure.

2. Disconnect the negative battery cable.

3. Remove the air cleaner assembly.

4. Disconnect the injector electrical connectors from the injector harness.

5. Disconnect the fuel hoses from the fuel distributors.

6. Remove the fuel distributor attaching screws and remove the fuel distributor assemblies.

7. Remove the injector harnesses from the fuel distributors.

8. Disconnect the vacuum hose and the fuel return hose from the pressure regulator.

9. Remove the attaching bolts and remove the pressure regulator from the fuel distributor.

To install:

10. Install the fuel pressure regulator to the fuel distributor and tighten the bolts to 61-87 inch lbs. (7-10 Nm).

11. Connect the vacuum hose and the fuel return line to the fuel pressure regulator.

12. Align the fuel injector tabs with the distributor and install the distributor assemblies.

13. Tighten the fuel distributor screws to 22-31 inch lbs. (2.5-3.5 Nm).

14. Connect the fuel hose to the fuel distributor and connect the electrical connectors to the injector harness.

15. Install the air cleaner assembly and connect the negative battery cable.

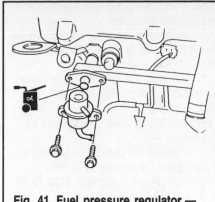

Fig. 41 Fuel pressure regulator —
323/Protege and Miata

Fig. 43 Fuel pressure regulator —
MX-3 with 1.8L engine

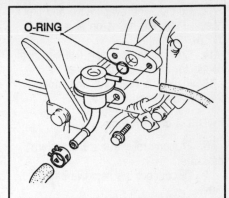

Fig. 45 Fuel pressure regulator —
1993 626/MX-6 with 2.0L engine

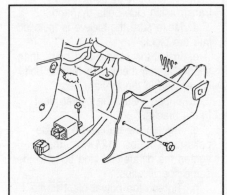

Fig. 42 Fuel pressure regulator —
MX-3 with 1.6L engine

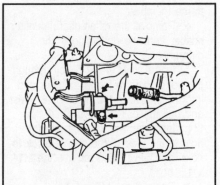

Fig. 44 Fuel pressure regulator —
1990-92 626/MX-6

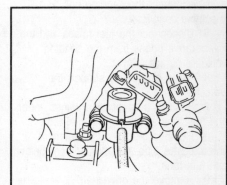

Fig. 46 Fuel pressure regulator —
1993 626/MX-6 with 2.5L engine

Pressure Regulator ControlSolenoid Valve

REMOVAL & INSTALLATION

California Emissions Equipped Vehicles

1. Disconnect the negative battery cable.

2. Disconnect the vacuum hose and the electrical connector from the pressure regulator control solenoid valve.

3. Disconnect the pressure regulator control solenoid valve from the intake manifold.

4. Installation is the reverse of the removal procedure.

FUEL TANK

Tank

REMOVAL &INSTALLATION

▶ **See Figures 47, 48, 50, 51 and ?**

323 and Protege — Except 4WD

1. Properly relieve the fuel system pressure.

2. Disconnect the negative battery cable.

3. Depress the clips on each end of the rear seat cushion and remove the cushion.

4. Disconnect the sending unit electrical connector, remove the 4 attaching screws and the sending unit access cover.

5. Raise and safely support the vehicle.

6. Disconnect the fuel hoses and the evaporative hoses from the sending unit and from the fuel tank itself.

7. Position a suitable container under the fuel tank and drain the fuel tank.

8. Remove the attaching screws and the fuel tank insulator from the front of the fuel tank.

9. Support the fuel tank and remove the 2 fuel tank straps.

10. Remove the fuel tank.

11. Position the fuel tank in place and install the 2 tank straps. Tighten the bolts to 27-38 ft. lbs. (37-52 Nm).

12. Install the fuel tank insulator and tighten the bolts to 69-95 inch lbs. (8-11 Nm).

13. Connect the evaporative and fuel hoses. Push the hoses on at least 1.4 inches (35mm).

14. Connect the sending unit electrical connector and install the cover.

15. Install the rear seat and connect the negative battery cable.

4WD 323 and Protege

1. Properly relieve the fuel system pressure.

2. Disconnect the negative battery cable.

3. Depress the clips on each end of the rear seat cushion and remove the cushion.

4. Remove both fuel pump covers and disconnect the sending unit electrical connectors.

5. Disconnect the fuel hoses and the evaporative hoses from the sending unit/fuel pumps.

6. Raise and safely support the vehicle.

7. Position a suitable container under the fuel tank and drain the fuel tank.

8. Remove the exhaust system intermediate pipe and muffler from below the fuel tank.

9. Remove the driveshaft.

10. Disconnect the fuel hoses from the fuel tank.

11. Support the fuel tank and remove the 2 fuel tank straps.

12. Remove the fuel tank.

13. Position the fuel tank in place and install the 2 tank straps. Tighten the bolts to 32-45 ft. lbs. (43-61 Nm).

14. Connect the hoses to the fuel tank.

15. Install the driveshaft. Tighten the shaft end nuts to 20-22 ft. lbs. (27-30 Nm) and the center shaft support nuts to 27-38 ft. lbs. (37-51 Nm).

16. Install the exhaust intermediate pipe/muffler with new gaskets and tighten the nuts to 30-41 ft. lbs. (40-55 Nm).

17. Connect the hoses and electrical connectors to the fuel sending unit/pump assemblies. Push the hoses on at least 1.4 inches (35mm).

18. Install the fuel pump cover assemblies and install the rear seat.

19. Connect the negative battery cable.

Miata

1. Relieve the fuel system pressure and disconnect the negative battery cable.

2. Raise and safely support the vehicle. Drain the fuel tank into a suitable container.

3. Remove the rear exhaust pipe and muffler assembly.

4. Remove the power plant frame member as follows:

   a. Mark the position of the driveshaft on the axle flange and remove the driveshaft.

   b. Disconnect the wire harness from the power plant frame member.

   c. Remove the bracket from between the frame member and transmission.

   d. Remove the differential side bolts and pry out the spacer from between the bottom of the differential and the frame member.

   e. Remove the differential mounting spacer from the underside of the differential.

   f. Insert an M14 x 1.5 bolt through the bottom of the frame member and into the sleeve in the differential. Twist and pull the bolt downward.

   g. Install an M6 x 1 bolt into the hole in the side of the sleeve block to hold the sleeve, then remove the M14 x 1.5 bolt.

   h. Remove the M6 x 1 bolt.

   i. Remove the transmission side bolts and remove the power plant frame member.

5. Label and disconnect the fuel filler hoses, fuel lines and evaporative hoses. Disconnect the fuel pump connector.

6. Remove the fuel filter cover and remove the fuel filter bolts or nuts. Remove the fuel filter with the hoses attached.

7. Remove the brake line junction nuts and remove the brake line junction with the line and hose still connected.

8. Remove the battery cable clamp and remove the battery cable.

9. Support the rear crossmember with a jack and remove the rear crossmember mounting bolts and nuts.

10. Lower the rear crossmember assembly, being careful not to damage the brake hose, brake line or fuel lines.

11. Support the fuel tank with a jack and remove the mounting bolts. Lower the fuel tank from the vehicle.

12. Raise the fuel tank into position and install the mounting bolts. Tighten to 22 ft. lbs. (30 Nm).

13. Install the rear crossmember assembly and tighten the bolts/nuts to 86 ft. lbs. (117 Nm).

14. Install the battery cable with the clamp.

15. Install the brake line junction and secure with the nuts.

16. Install the fuel filter and tighten the nuts/bolts to 95 inch lbs. (11 Nm). Install the fuel filter cover.

17. Connect the fuel pump connector, evaporative hoses, fuel lines and fuel filler hoses.

18. Install the power plant frame as follows:

   a. Install the differential mounting spacer to the underside of the differential and tighten the bolts to 38 ft. lbs. (52 Nm).

   b. Support the transmission with a jack so it is level.

   c. Position the power plant frame member and snugly tighten the transmission side bolts by hand.

   d. Make sure the sleeve is installed into the block.

   e. Install the spacer and bolts, then snugly tighten them. The reamer bolt is installed in the forward hole.

   f. Snugly install the power plant frame bracket.

   g. Tighten the transmission side bolts to 91 ft. lbs. (124 Nm), then tighten the differential side bolts to the same specification.

   h. Tighten the power plant frame bracket-to-frame member bolt to 91 ft. lbs. (124 Nm) and the power plant frame bracket-to-transmission bolts to 40 ft. lbs. (54 Nm).

   i. Measure the distance between the bottom of the power plant frame member and a straightedge laid between the floor pan channels; the distance should be 2.403-2.797 in. (61-71mm). If the distance is not as specified, reposition the power plant frame member at the transmission.

   j. Install the driveshaft, aligning the marks that were made during removal. Tighten the bolts to 22 ft. lbs. (30 Nm).

   k. Connect the wire harness to the power plant frame member.

19. Install the exhaust pipe/muffler assembly, using a new gasket. Tighten the nuts to 41 ft. lbs. (55 Nm).

20. Lower the vehicle. Fill the tank and check for leaks. Start the engine and check for leaks at all fuel line connections.

MX-3

1. Properly relieve the fuel system pressure.

2. Disconnect the negative battery cable.

3. Depress the clips on each end of the rear seat cushion and remove the cushion.

4. Disconnect the sending unit electrical connector, remove the 4 attaching screws and the sending unit access cover.

5. Raise and safely support the vehicle.

6. Disconnect the fuel hoses and the evaporative hoses from the sending unit and from the fuel tank itself.

7. Position a suitable container under the fuel tank and drain the fuel tank.

8. Remove the attaching screws and the fuel tank insulator from the front of the fuel tank.

9. Support the fuel tank and remove the 2 fuel tank straps.

10. Remove the fuel tank.

11. Position the fuel tank in place and install the 2 tank straps. Tighten the bolts to 32-45 ft. lbs. (43-62 Nm).

12. Install the fuel tank insulator and tighten the bolts to 69-95 inch lbs. (8-11 Nm).

13. Connect the evaporative and fuel hoses. Push the hoses on at least 1.4 inches (35mm).

14. Connect the sending unit electrical connector and install the cover.

15. Install the rear seat and connect the negative battery cable.

1990-2 626 and MX-6

1. Properly relieve the fuel system pressure.

2. Disconnect the negative battery cable.

3. Depress the clips on each end of the rear seat cushion and remove the cushion.

4. Disconnect the sending unit electrical connector, remove the 4 attaching screws and the sending unit access cover. Disconnect the fuel hoses from the sending unit.

5. Raise and safely support the vehicle.

6. Disconnect the fuel hoses and the evaporative hoses from the fuel tank itself.

7. Position a suitable container under the fuel tank and remove the drain plug to drain the fuel tank.

8. Support the fuel tank.

9. Remove the 2 fuel tank straps and the corner mounting bolts.

10. Remove the fuel tank.

11. Position the fuel tank in place and install the 2 tank straps. Tighten the bolts to 32-45 ft. lbs. (43-61 Nm).

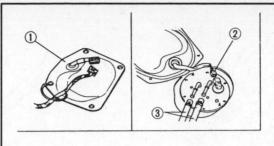

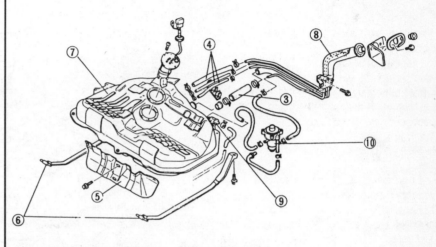

1. Fuel pump cover
2. Fuel pump connector
3. Fuel hoses
4. Evaporative hoses
5. Insulator
6. Fuel tank straps
7. Fuel tank
8. Separator
9. Check valve (two way)
10. Check and cut valve

Fig. 47 Fuel tank assembly — 2WD 323/Protege

12. Install the corner mounting bolts and tighten them to 16-22 ft. lbs. (22-30 Nm).

13. Connect the evaporative and fuel hoses. Push the hoses on at least 1.4 inches (35mm).

14. Lower the vehicle and connect the sending unit electrical connector and hoses. Install the cover.

15. Install the rear seat and connect the negative battery cable.

1993 626 and MX-6

1. Properly relieve the fuel system pressure.

2. Drain the fuel tank and disconnect the negative battery cable.

3. Raise and safely support the vehicle.

4. Remove the pre-silencer exhaust pipe.

5. Remove the exhaust pipe insulator assembly.

6. Disconnect the electrical connectors from the top of the fuel tank.

7. Disconnect the fuel and evaporative hoses from the fuel tank.

8. While having an assistant support the fuel tank, remove the fuel tank support straps and lower the fuel tank from the vehicle.

9. Lift the fuel tank into place and install the fuel tank straps. Tighten the bolts to 32-45 ft. lbs. (43-61 Nm).

10. Connect the fuel and evaporative hoses to the fuel tank, making sure to push the hose on at least 1.4 inches (35mm).

11. Connect the electrical connector to the top of the fuel tank.

12. Install the exhaust pipe insulator assembly and tighten the nut to 70-95 inch lbs. (7.9-10.7 Nm).

13. Install the pre-silencer exhaust pipe with new gaskets and tighten the rear nuts to 28-38 ft. lbs. (38-51 Nm). Tighten the front nuts to 48-65 ft. lbs. (64-89 Nm).

14. Lower the vehicle and connect the negative battery cable.

SENDING UNIT REPLACEMENT

MX-3, 323, Protege and 1990-92 626 and MX-6

1. Relieve the fuel pressure and disconnect the negative battery cable.

2. Depress the clips on each end of the rear seat cushion and remove the cushion.

3. Disconnect the electrical connector from the fuel pump/sending unit.

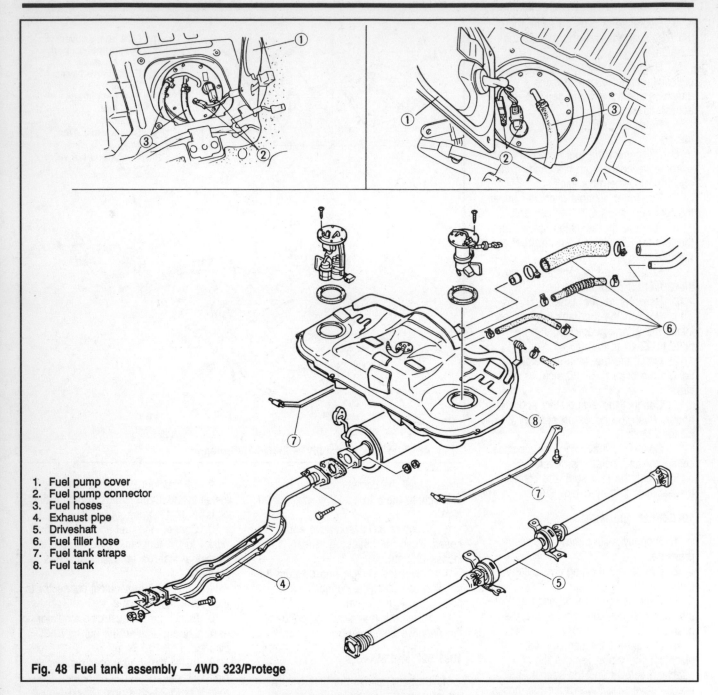

1. Fuel pump cover
2. Fuel pump connector
3. Fuel hoses
4. Exhaust pipe
5. Driveshaft
6. Fuel filler hose
7. Fuel tank straps
8. Fuel tank

Fig. 48 Fuel tank assembly — 4WD 323/Protege

4. Remove the attaching screws from the fuel pump/sending unit access cover and remove the cover.

5. Disconnect the fuel supply and return hoses from the fuel pump/sending unit.

6. Remove the attaching screws and the fuel pump/sending unit from the fuel tank.

7. Disconnect the sending unit electrical connector, remove the sending unit attaching nuts and remove the sending unit from the fuel pump assembly.

8. Attach the sending unit to the fuel pump assembly and install the nuts. Connect the sending unit electrical connector.

9. Install the fuel pump/sending unit into the fuel tank and install the mounting screws.

10. Connect the fuel supply and return lines.

11. Install the access cover and the mounting screws.

12. Connect the sending unit electrical connector.

13. Position the rear seat cushion over the floor, making sure to align the retaining pins with the clips. Push down firmly until the 2 retaining pins are locked into the rear seat retaining clips.

14. Connect the negative battery cable, start the engine and check for proper system operation and for fuel leaks.

Miata

1. Relieve the fuel pressure and disconnect the negative battery cable.

2. Remove the inside rear package trim panels and remove the screws from the service hole cover. Remove the service hole cover.

3. Remove the fuel pump cover and disconnect the electrical connector from the fuel pump/sending unit.

4. Disconnect the fuel supply and return hoses from the fuel pump/sending unit.

5. Remove the attaching screws and the fuel pump/sending unit from the fuel tank.

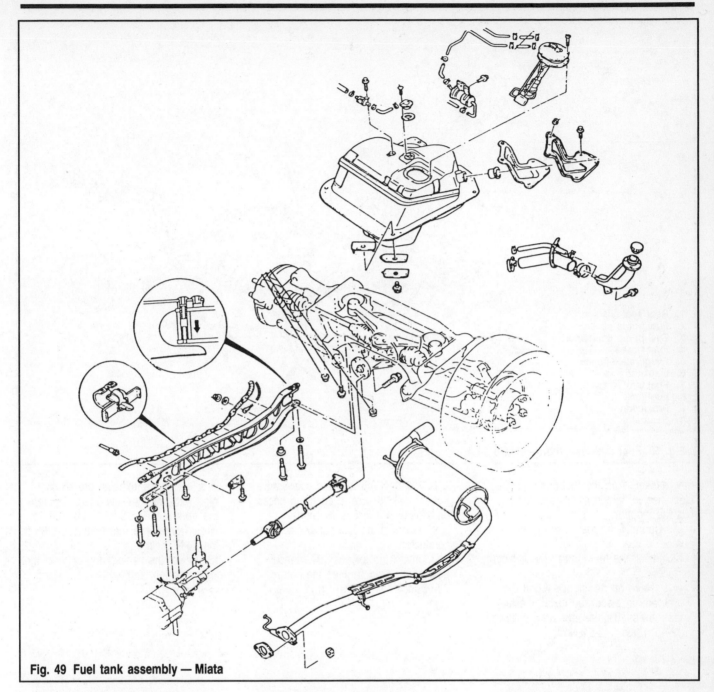

Fig. 49 Fuel tank assembly — Miata

6. Disconnect the sending unit electrical connector, remove the sending unit attaching nuts and remove the sending unit from the fuel pump assembly.

7. Attach the sending unit to the fuel pump assembly and install the nuts. Connect the sending unit electrical connector.

8. Replace the O-ring set and install the fuel pump/sending unit into the fuel tank. Install the mounting screws.

9. Connect the fuel supply and return lines.

10. Connect the sending unit electrical connector and install the fuel pump cover.

11. Install the rear package interior trim panel.

12. Connect the negative battery cable, start the engine and check for proper system operation and for fuel leaks.

1993 626 and MX-6

1. Relieve the fuel system pressure and disconnect the negative battery cable. Drain the fuel tank and remove the fuel tank from the vehicle as follows.

2. Raise and safely support the vehicle.

3. Remove the pre-silencer exhaust pipe and the heat shield.

4. Disconnect the electrical connectors from the top of the fuel tank.

5. Disconnect the fuel and evaporative hoses from the fuel tank.

6. While having an assistant support the fuel tank, remove the fuel tank support straps and lower the fuel tank from the vehicle.

7. Disconnect all fuel hoses from the fuel pump unit.

8. Turn the fuel pump ring counterclockwise and remove it.

9. Remove the fuel pump/sending unit assembly and gaskets from the fuel tank. Separate the sending unit from the fuel tank.

10. Connect the sending unit to the fuel pump. Install the fuel pump with a

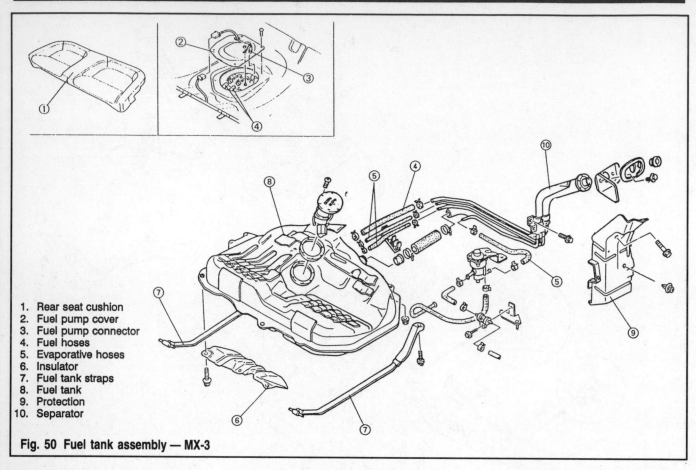

1. Rear seat cushion
2. Fuel pump cover
3. Fuel pump connector
4. Fuel hoses
5. Evaporative hoses
6. Insulator
7. Fuel tank straps
8. Fuel tank
9. Protection
10. Separator

Fig. 50 Fuel tank assembly — MX-3

new gasket. Turn the fuel pump ring clockwise to tighten it until the flange hits the stopper.

11. Connect the fuel hoses to the fuel pump.

12. Install the fuel tank to the vehicle as follows:

　a. Have an assistant support the fuel tank in place and install the fuel tank straps. Tighten the strap bolts to 32-45 ft. lbs. (43-61 Nm).

　b. Connect the fuel and evaporative hoses, making sure to push the hoses on at least 1.4 inches (35 mm).

　c. Connect the fuel pump electrical connector.

　d. Install the exhaust pre-silencer pipe heat shield. Tighten the bolt to 70-90 inch lbs. (7.9-10 Nm).

　e. Install the exhaust pre-silencer pipe with new gaskets intact. Tighten the front nuts to 28-38 ft. lbs. (38-51 Nm). Tighten the rear bolts to 48-65 ft. lbs. (64-89 Nm).

13. Lower the vehicle and connect the negative battery cable.

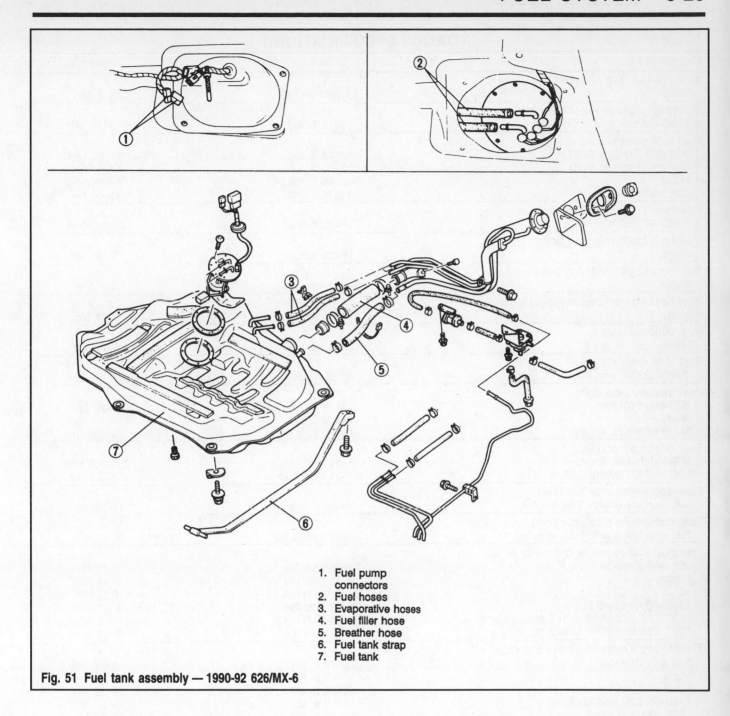

Fig. 51 Fuel tank assembly — 1990-92 626/MX-6

1. Fuel pump
   connectors
2. Fuel hoses
3. Evaporative hoses
4. Fuel filler hose
5. Breather hose
6. Fuel tank strap
7. Fuel tank

TORQUE SPECIFICATIONS

Component	U.S.	Metric
Air valve-to-intake manifold bolts/nuts		
Miata	43–69 inch lbs.	5–8 Nm
Dynamic chamber assembly bolts		
1990–92 626 and MX-6	14–19 ft. lbs.	19–25 Nm
Fuel tank strap bolts		
323 and Protege 2WD	27–38 ft. lbs.	37–52 Nm
323 and Protege 4WD	32–45 ft. lbs.	43–61 Nm
MX-3	32–45 ft. lbs.	43–61 Nm
626 and MX-6	32–45 ft. lbs.	43–61 Nm
Fuel tank corner retaining bolts		
1990–92 626 and MX-6	16–22 ft. lbs.	22–30 Nm
Fuel tank lower retaining bolts		
Miata	16–22 ft. lbs.	22–30 Nm
Fuel tank upper retaining bolts		
Miata	34–52 inch lbs.	4–6 Nm
Fuel tank side bracket retaining bolts		
Miata	69–95 inch lbs.	8–11 Nm
Fuel tank insulator		
MX-3	69–95 inch lbs.	8–11 Nm
Fuel tank drain plug		
1990–92 626 and MX-6	9–13 ft. lbs.	12–18 Nm
Fuel delivery pipe bolts		
323 and Protege	14–19 ft. lbs.	19–25 Nm
Miata	14–19 ft. lbs.	19–25 Nm
MX-3 with 1.6L engine	14–19 ft. lbs.	19–25 Nm
Fuel distributor screws		
MX-3 with 1.8L engine	22–31 inch lbs.	2.5–3.5 Nm
626 and MX-6 with 2.5L engine	22–31 inch lbs.	2.5–3.5 Nm
Fuel distribution pipe top bolts		
626 and MX-6 with 2.0L engine	14–18 ft. lbs.	19–25 Nm
Fuel distribution pipe side bolts		
626 and MX-6 with 2.0L engine	70–95 inch lbs.	8–11 Nm
Fuel pressure regulator mounting bolts		
323 and Protege	70–95 inch lbs.	8–11 Nm
Miata	70–95 inch lbs.	8–11 Nm
MX-3	70–95 inch lbs.	8–11 Nm
1990–92 626 and MX-6	70–95 inch lbs.	8–11 Nm
1993 626 and MX-6 with 2.0L engine	70–95 inch lbs.	8–11 Nm
1993 626 and MX-6 with 2.5L engine	61–87 inch lbs.	7–10 Nm
Throttle body mounting bolts and nuts		
323 and Protege	14–19 ft. lbs.	19–25 Nm
Miata	14–19 ft. lbs.	19–25 Nm
MX-3	14–19 ft. lbs.	19–25 Nm
1990–92 626 and MX-6	14–19 ft. lbs.	19–25 Nm
1993 626 and MX-6	14–19 ft. lbs.	19–25 Nm

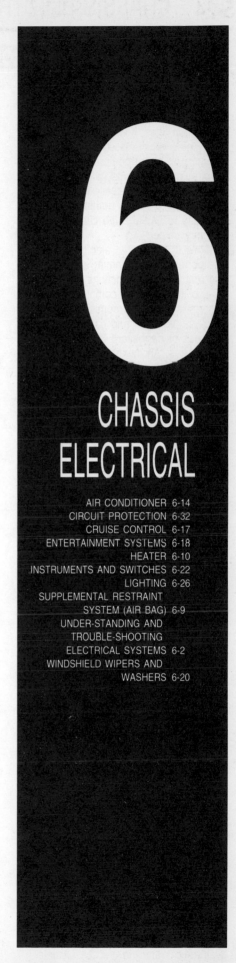

6

CHASSIS ELECTRICAL

UNDERSTANDING AND TROUBLESHOOTING ELECTRICAL SYSTEMS

With the rate at which both import and domestic manufacturers are incorporating electronic control systems into their production lines, it won't be long before every new vehicle is equipped with one or more on-board computer. These electronic components (with no moving parts) should theoretically last the life of the vehicle, provided nothing external happens to damage the circuits or memory chips.

While it is true that electronic components should never wear out, in the real world malfunctions do occur. It is also true that any computer-based system is extremely sensitive to electrical voltages and cannot tolerate careless or haphazard testing or service procedures. An inexperienced individual can literally do major damage looking for a minor problem by using the wrong kind of test equipment or connecting test leads or connectors with the ignition switch ON. When selecting test equipment, make sure the manufacturers instructions state that the tester is compatible with whatever type of electronic control system is being serviced. Read all instructions carefully and double check all test points before installing probes or making any test connections.

The following section outlines basic diagnosis techniques for dealing with computerized automotive control systems. Along with a general explanation of the various types of test equipment available to aid in servicing modern electronic automotive systems, basic repair techniques for wiring harnesses and connectors is given. Read the basic information before attempting any repairs or testing on any computerized system, to provide the background of information necessary to avoid the most common and obvious mistakes that can cost both time and money. Although the replacement and testing procedures are simple in themselves, the systems are not, and unless one has a thorough understanding of all components and their function within a particular computerized control system, the logical test sequence these systems demand cannot be followed. Minor malfunctions can make a big difference, so it is important to know how each component affects the operation of the overall electronic system to find the ultimate cause of a problem without replacing

good components unnecessarily. It is not enough to use the correct test equipment; the test equipment must be used correctly.

Safety Precautions

❊❊CAUTION

Whenever working on or around any computer based microprocessor control system, always observe these general precautions to prevent the possibility of personal injury or damage to electronic components.

• Never install or remove battery cables with the key ON or the engine running. Jumper cables should be connected with the key OFF to avoid power surges that can damage electronic control units. Engines equipped with computer controlled systems should avoid both giving and getting jump starts due to the possibility of serious damage to components from arcing in the engine compartment when connections are made with the ignition ON.

• Always remove the battery cables before charging the battery. Never use a high output charger on an installed battery or attempt to use any type of "hot shot" (24 volt) starting aid.

• Exercise care when inserting test probes into connectors to insure good connections without damaging the connector or spreading the pins. Always probe connectors from the rear (wire) side, NOT the pin side, to avoid accidental shorting of terminals during test procedures.

• Never remove or attach wiring harness connectors with the ignition switch ON, especially to an electronic control unit.

• Do not drop any components during service procedures and never apply 12 volts directly to any component (like a solenoid or relay) unless instructed specifically to do so. Some component electrical windings are designed to safely handle only 4 or 5 volts and can be destroyed in seconds if 12 volts are applied directly to the connector.

• Remove the electronic control unit if the vehicle is to be placed in an environment where temperatures exceed

approximately 176°F (80°C), such as a paint spray booth or when arc or gas welding near the control unit location in the car.

ORGANIZED TROUBLESHOOTING

When diagnosing a specific problem, organized troubleshooting is a must. The complexity of a modern automobile demands that you approach any problem in a logical, organized manner. There are certain troubleshooting techniques that are standard:

1. Establish when the problem occurs. Does the problem appear only under certain conditions? Were there any noises, odors, or other unusual symptoms?

2. Isolate the problem area. To do this, make some simple tests and observations; then eliminate the systems that are working properly. Check for obvious problems such as broken wires, dirty connections or split or disconnected vacuum hoses. Always check the obvious before assuming something complicated is the cause.

3. Test for problems systematically to determine the cause once the problem area is isolated. Are all the components functioning properly? Is there power going to electrical switches and motors? Is there vacuum at vacuum switches and/or actuators? Is there a mechanical problem such as bent linkage or loose mounting screws? Doing careful, systematic checks will often turn up most causes on the first inspection without wasting time checking components that have little or no relationship to the problem.

4. Test all repairs after the work is done to make sure that the problem is fixed. Some causes can be traced to more than one component, so a careful verification of repair work is important to pick up additional malfunctions that may cause a problem to reappear or a different problem to arise. A blown fuse, for example, is a simple problem that may require more than another fuse to repair. If you don't look for a problem that caused a fuse to blow, for example, a shorted wire may go undetected.

Experience has shown that most problems tend to be the result of a fairly simple and obvious cause, such as loose or corroded connectors or air leaks in the intake system; making careful inspection of components during testing essential to quick and accurate troubleshooting. Special, hand held computerized testers designed specifically for diagnosing the EEC-IV system are available from a variety of aftermarket sources, as well as from the vehicle manufacturer, but care should be taken that any test equipment being used is designed to diagnose that particular computer controlled system accurately without damaging the control unit (ECU) or components being tested.

➡Pinpointing the exact cause of trouble in an electrical system can sometimes only be accomplished by the use of special test equipment. The following describes commonly used test equipment and explains how to put it to best use in diagnosis. In addition to the information covered below, the manufacturer's instructions booklet provided with the tester should be read and clearly understood before attempting any test procedures.

TEST EQUIPMENT

Jumper Wires

Jumper wires are simple, yet extremely valuable, pieces of test equipment. Jumper wires are merely wires that are used to bypass sections of a circuit. The simplest type of jumper wire is merely a length of multistrand wire with an alligator clip at each end. Jumper wires are usually fabricated from lengths of standard automotive wire and whatever type of connector (alligator clip, spade connector or pin connector) that is required for the particular vehicle being tested. The well equipped tool box will have several different styles of jumper wires in several different lengths. Some jumper wires are made with three or more terminals coming from a common splice for special purpose testing. In cramped, hard-to-reach areas it is advisable to have insulated boots over the jumper wire terminals in order to prevent accidental grounding, sparks, and possible fire, especially when testing fuel system components.

Jumper wires are used primarily to locate open electrical circuits, on either the ground (-) side of the circuit or on the hot (+) side. If an electrical component fails to operate, connect the jumper wire between the component and a good ground. If the component operates only with the jumper installed, the ground circuit is open. If the ground circuit is good, but the component does not operate, the circuit between the power feed and component is open. You can sometimes connect the jumper wire directly from the battery to the hot terminal of the component, but first make sure the component uses 12 volts in operation. Some electrical components, such as fuel injectors, are designed to operate on about 4 volts and running 12 volts directly to the injector terminals can burn out the wiring. By inserting an inline fuseholder between a set of test leads, a fused jumper wire can be used for bypassing open circuits. Use a 5 amp fuse to provide protection against voltage spikes. When in doubt, use a volt meter to check the voltage input to the component and measure how much voltage is being applied normally. By moving the jumper wire successively back from the lamp toward the power source, you can isolate the area of the circuit where the open is located. When the component stops functioning, or the power is cut off, the open is in the segment of wire between the jumper and the point previously tested.

✳✳CAUTION

Never use jumpers made from wire that is of lighter gauge than used in the circuit under test. If the jumper wire is of too small gauge, it may overheat and possibly melt. Never use jumpers to bypass high resistance loads (such as motors) in a circuit. Bypassing resistances, in effect, creates a short circuit which may, in turn, cause damage and fire. Never use a jumper for anything other than temporary bypassing of components in a circuit.

12 Volt Test Light

The 12 volt test light is used to check circuits and components while electrical current is flowing through them. It is used for voltage and ground tests. Twelve volt test lights come in different styles but all have three main parts; a ground clip, a probe, and a light. The most commonly used 12 volt test lights have pick-type probes. To use a 12 volt test light, connect the ground clip to a good ground and probe wherever necessary with the pick. The pick should be sharp so that it can penetrate wire insulation to make contact with the wire, without making a large hole in the insulation. The wrap-around light is handy in hard to reach areas or where it is difficult to support a wire to push a probe pick into it. To use the wrap around light, hook the wire to probed with the hook and pull the trigger. A small pick will be forced through the wire insulation into the wire core.

✳✳CAUTION

Do not use a test light to probe electronic ignition spark plug or coil wires. Never use a pick-type test light to probe wiring on computer controlled systems unless specifically instructed to do so. Any wire insulation that is pierced by the test light probe should be taped and sealed with silicone after testing.

Like the jumper wire, the 12 volt test light is used to isolate opens in circuits. But, whereas the jumper wire is used to bypass the open to operate the load, the 12 volt test light is used to locate the presence of voltage in a circuit. If the test light glows, you know that there is power up to that point; if the 12 volt test light does not glow when its probe is inserted into the wire or connector, you know that there is an open circuit (no power). Move the test light in successive steps back toward the power source until the light in the handle does glow. When it does glow, the open is between the probe and point previously probed.

➡The test light does not detect that 12 volts (or any particular amount of voltage) is present; it only detects that some voltage is present. It is advisable before using the test light to touch its terminals across the battery posts to make sure the light is operating properly.

Self-Powered Test Light

The self-powered test light usually contains a 1.5 volt penlight battery. One type of self-powered test light is similar in design to the 12 volt test light. This type has both the battery and the light in the handle and pick-type probe tip. The second type has the light toward the open tip, so that the light illuminates the contact point. The self-powered test light is dual purpose piece of test equipment. It can be used to test for either open or short circuits when power is isolated from the circuit (continuity test). A powered test light should not be used on any computer controlled system or component unless specifically instructed to do so. Many engine sensors can be destroyed by even this small amount of voltage applied directly to the terminals.

Open Circuit Testing

To use the self-powered test light to check for open circuits, first isolate the circuit from the vehicle's 12 volt power source by disconnecting the battery or wiring harness connector. Connect the test light ground clip to a good ground and probe sections of the circuit sequentially with the test light. (start from either end of the circuit). If the light is out, the open is between the probe and the circuit ground. If the light is on, the open is between the probe and end of the circuit toward the power source.

Short Circuit Testing

By isolating the circuit both from power and from ground, and using a self-powered test light, you can check for shorts to ground in the circuit. Isolate the circuit from power and ground. Connect the test light ground clip to a good ground and probe any easy-to-reach test point in the circuit. If the light comes on, there is a short somewhere in the circuit. To isolate the short, probe a test point at either end of the isolated circuit (the light should be on). Leave the test light probe connected and open connectors, switches, remove parts, etc., sequentially, until the light goes out. When the light goes out, the short is between the last circuit component opened and the previous circuit opened.

➡ **The 1.5 volt battery in the test light does not provide much current. A weak battery may not provide enough power to illuminate the test light even when a complete circuit is made (especially if there are high resistances in the circuit). Always make sure that the test battery is strong. To check the battery, briefly touch the ground clip to the probe; if the light glows brightly the battery is strong enough for testing. Never use a self-powered test light to perform checks for opens or shorts when power is applied to the electrical system under test. The 12 volt vehicle power will quickly burn out the 1.5 volt light bulb in the test light.**

Voltmeter

A voltmeter is used to measure voltage at any point in a circuit, or to measure the voltage drop across any part of a circuit. It can also be used to check continuity in a wire or circuit by indicating current flow from one end to the other. Voltmeters usually have various scales on the meter dial and a selector switch to allow the selection of different voltages. The voltmeter has a positive and a negative lead. To avoid damage to the meter, always connect the negative lead to the negative (-) side of circuit (to ground or nearest the ground side of the circuit) and connect the positive lead to the positive (+) side of the circuit (to the power source or the nearest power source). Note that the negative voltmeter lead will always be black and that the positive voltmeter will always be some color other than black (usually red). Depending on how the voltmeter is connected into the circuit, it has several uses.

A voltmeter can be connected either in parallel or in series with a circuit and it has a very high resistance to current flow. When connected in parallel, only a small amount of current will flow through the voltmeter current path; the rest will flow through the normal circuit current path and the circuit will work normally. When the voltmeter is connected in series with a circuit, only a small amount of current can flow through the circuit. The circuit will not work properly, but the voltmeter reading will show if the circuit is complete or not.

Available Voltage Measurement

Set the voltmeter selector switch to the 20V position and connect the meter negative lead to the negative post of the battery. Connect the positive meter lead to the positive post of the battery and turn the ignition switch ON to provide a load. Read the voltage on the meter or digital display. A well charged battery should register over 12 volts. If the meter reads below 11.5 volts, the battery power may be insufficient to operate the electrical system properly. This test determines voltage available from the battery and should be the first step in any electrical trouble diagnosis procedure. Many electrical problems, especially on computer controlled systems, can be caused by a low state of charge in the battery. Excessive corrosion at the battery cable terminals can cause a poor contact that will prevent proper charging and full battery current flow.

Normal battery voltage is 12 volts when fully charged. When the battery is supplying current to one or more circuits it is said to be "under load". When everything is off the electrical system is under a "no-load" condition. A fully charged battery may show about 12.5 volts at no load; will drop to 12 volts under medium load; and will drop even lower under heavy load. If the battery is partially discharged the voltage decrease under heavy load may be excessive, even though the battery shows 12 volts or more at no load. When allowed to discharge further, the battery's available voltage under load will decrease more severely. For this reason, it is important that the battery be fully charged during all testing procedures to avoid errors in diagnosis and incorrect test results.

Voltage Drop

When current flows through a resistance, the voltage beyond the resistance is reduced (the larger the current, the greater the reduction in voltage). When no current is flowing, there is no voltage drop because there is no current flow. All points in the circuit which are connected to the power source are at the same voltage as the power source. The total voltage drop always equals the total source voltage. In a long circuit with many connectors, a series of small, unwanted voltage drops due to corrosion at the connectors can add up to a total loss of voltage which impairs the operation of the normal loads in the circuit.

INDIRECT COMPUTATION OF VOLTAGE DROPS

1. Set the voltmeter selector switch to the 20 volt position.
2. Connect the meter negative lead to a good ground.
3. Probe all resistances in the circuit with the positive meter lead.
4. Operate the circuit in all modes and observe the voltage readings.

DIRECT MEASUREMENT OF VOLTAGE DROPS

1. Set the voltmeter switch to the 20 volt position.
2. Connect the voltmeter negative lead to the ground side of the resistance load to be measured.
3. Connect the positive lead to the positive side of the resistance or load to be measured.
4. Read the voltage drop directly on the 20 volt scale.

Too high a voltage indicates too high a resistance. If, for example, a blower motor runs too slowly, you can determine if there is too high a resistance in the resistor pack. By taking voltage drop readings in all parts of the circuit, you can isolate the problem. Too low a voltage drop indicates too low a resistance. If, for example, a blower motor runs too fast in the MED and/or LOW position, the problem can be isolated in the resistor pack by taking voltage drop readings in all parts of the circuit to locate a possibly shorted resistor. The maximum allowable voltage drop under load is critical, especially if there is more than one high resistance problem in a circuit because all voltage drops are cumulative. A small drop is normal due to the resistance of the conductors.

HIGH RESISTANCE TESTING

1. Set the voltmeter selector switch to the 4 volt position.
2. Connect the voltmeter positive lead to the positive post of the battery.
3. Turn on the headlights and heater blower to provide a load.
4. Probe various points in the circuit with the negative voltmeter lead.
5. Read the voltage drop on the 4 volt scale. Some average maximum allowable voltage drops are:

FUSE PANEL — 7 volts
IGNITION SWITCH — 5 volts
HEADLIGHT SWITCH — 7 volts
IGNITION COIL (+) — 5 volts
ANY OTHER LOAD — 1.3 volts

➡**Voltage drops are all measured while a load is operating; without current flow, there will be no voltage drop.**

Ohmmeter

The ohmmeter is designed to read resistance (ohms) in a circuit or component. Although there are several different styles of ohmmeters, all will usually have a selector switch which permits the measurement of different ranges of resistance (usually the selector switch allows the multiplication of the meter reading by 10, 100, 1000, and 10,000). A calibration knob allows the meter to be set at zero for accurate measurement. Since all ohmmeters are powered by an internal battery (usually 9 volts), the ohmmeter can be used as a self-powered test light. When the ohmmeter is connected, current from the ohmmeter flows through the circuit or component being tested. Since the ohmmeter's internal resistance and voltage are known values, the amount of current flow through the meter depends on the resistance of the circuit or component being tested.

The ohmmeter can be used to perform continuity test for opens or shorts (either by observation of the meter needle or as a self-powered test light), and to read actual resistance in a circuit. It should be noted that the ohmmeter is used to check the resistance of a component or wire while there is no voltage applied to the circuit. Current flow from an outside voltage source (such as the vehicle battery) can damage the ohmmeter, so the circuit or component should be isolated from the vehicle electrical system before any testing is done. Since the ohmmeter uses its own voltage source, either lead can be connected to any test point.

➡**When checking diodes or other solid state components, the ohmmeter leads can only be connected one way in order to measure current flow in a single direction. Make sure the positive (+) and negative (-) terminal connections are as described in the test procedures to verify the one-way diode operation.**

In using the meter for making continuity checks, do not be concerned with the actual resistance readings. Zero resistance, or any resistance readings, indicate continuity in the circuit. Infinite resistance indicates an open in the circuit. A high resistance reading where there should be none indicates a problem in the circuit. Checks for short circuits are made in the same manner as checks for open circuits except that the circuit must be isolated from both power and normal ground. Infinite resistance indicates no continuity to ground, while zero resistance indicates a dead short to ground.

RESISTANCE MEASUREMENT

The batteries in an ohmmeter will weaken with age and temperature, so the ohmmeter must be calibrated or "zeroed" before taking measurements. To zero the meter, place the selector switch in its lowest range and touch the two ohmmeter leads together. Turn the calibration knob until the meter needle is exactly on zero.

➡**All analog (needle) type ohmmeters must be zeroed before use, but some digital ohmmeter models are automatically calibrated when the switch is turned on. Self-calibrating digital ohmmeters do not have an adjusting knob, but its a good idea to check for a zero readout before use by touching the leads together. All**

computer controlled systems require the use of a digital ohmmeter with at least 10 megohms impedance for testing. Before any test procedures are attempted, make sure the ohmmeter used is compatible with the 8electrical system or damage to the on-board computer could result.

To measure resistance, first isolate the circuit from the vehicle power source by disconnecting the battery cables or the harness connector. Make sure the key is OFF when disconnecting any components or the battery. Where necessary, also isolate at least one side of the circuit to be checked to avoid reading parallel resistances. Parallel circuit resistances will always give a lower reading than the actual resistance of either of the branches. When measuring the resistance of parallel circuits, the total resistance will always be lower than the smallest resistance in the circuit. Connect the meter leads to both sides of the circuit (wire or component) and read the actual measured ohms on the meter scale. Make sure the selector switch is set to the proper ohm scale for the circuit being tested to avoid misreading the ohmmeter test value.

✳✳CAUTION

Never use an ohmmeter with power applied to the circuit. Like the self-powered test light, the ohmmeter is designed to operate on its own power supply. The normal 12 volt automotive electrical system current could damage the meter.

Ammeters

An ammeter measures the amount of current flowing through a circuit in units called amperes or amps. Amperes are units of electron flow which indicate how fast the electrons are flowing through the circuit. Since Ohms Law dictates that current flow in a circuit is equal to the circuit voltage divided by the total circuit resistance, increasing voltage also increases the current level (amps). Likewise, any decrease in resistance will increase the amount of amps in a circuit. At normal operating voltage, most circuits have a characteristic amount of amperes, called "current draw" which can be measured using an ammeter. By referring to a specified current draw rating, measuring the amperes, and comparing the two values, one can determine what is happening within the circuit to aid in diagnosis. An open circuit, for example, will not allow any current to flow so the ammeter reading will be zero. More current flows through a heavily loaded circuit or when the charging system is operating.

An ammeter is always connected in series with the circuit being tested. All of the current that normally flows through the circuit must also flow through the ammeter; if there is any other path for the current to follow, the ammeter reading will not be accurate. The ammeter itself has very little resistance to current flow and therefore will not affect the circuit, but it will measure current draw only when the circuit is closed and electricity is flowing. Excessive current draw can blow fuses and drain the battery, while a reduced current draw can cause motors to run slowly, lights to dim and other components to not operate properly. The ammeter can help diagnose these conditions by locating the cause of the high or low reading.

Multimeters

Different combinations of test meters can be built into a single unit designed for specific tests. Some of the more common combination test devices are known as Volt/Amp testers, Tach/Dwell meters, or Digital Multimeters. The Volt/Amp tester is used for charging system, starting system or battery tests and consists of a voltmeter, an ammeter and a variable resistance carbon pile. The voltmeter will usually have at least two ranges for use with 6, 12 and 24 volt systems. The ammeter also has more than one range for testing various levels of battery loads and starter current draw and the carbon pile can be adjusted to offer different amounts of resistance. The Volt/Amp tester has heavy leads to carry large amounts of current and many later models have an inductive ammeter pickup that clamps around the wire to simplify test connections. On some models, the ammeter also has a zero-center scale to allow testing of charging and starting systems without switching leads or polarity. A digital multimeter i s a voltmeter, ammeter and ohmmeter combined in an instrument which gives a digital readout. These are often used when testing solid state circuits because of their high input impedance (usually 10 megohms or more).

The tach/dwell meter combines a tachometer and a dwell (cam angle) meter and is a specialized kind of

voltmeter. The tachometer scale is marked to show engine speed in rpm and the dwell scale is marked to show degrees of distributor shaft rotation. In most electronic ignition systems, dwell is determined by the control unit, but the dwell meter can also be used to check the duty cycle (operation) of some electronic engine control systems. Some tach/dwell meters are powered by an internal battery, while others take their power from the car battery in use. The battery powered testers usually require calibration much like an ohmmeter before testing.

Special Test Equipment

A variety of diagnostic tools are available to help troubleshoot and repair computerized engine control systems. The most sophisticated of these devices are the console type engine analyzers that usually occupy a garage service bay, but there are several types of aftermarket electronic testers available that will allow quick circuit tests of the engine control system by plugging directly into a special connector located in the engine compartment or under the dashboard. Several tool and equipment manufacturers offer simple, hand held testers that measure various circuit voltage levels on command to check all system components for proper operation. Although these testers usually cost about $300-$500, consider that the average computer control unit (or ECM) can cost just as much and the money saved by not replacing perfectly good sensors or components in an attempt to correct a problem could justify the purchase price of a special diagnostic tester the first time it's used.

These computerized testers can allow quick and easy test measurements while the engine is operating or while the car is being driven. In addition, the on-board computer memory can be read to access any stored trouble codes; in effect allowing the computer to tell you where it hurts and aid trouble diagnosis by pinpointing exactly which circuit or component is malfunctioning. In the same manner, repairs can be tested to make sure the problem has been corrected. The biggest advantage these special testers have is their relatively easy hookups that minimize or eliminate the chances of making the wrong connections and getting false voltage

readings or damaging the computer accidentally.

➡️**It should be remembered that these testers check voltage levels in circuits; they don't detect mechanical problems or failed components if the circuit voltage falls within the preprogrammed limits stored in the tester PROM unit. Also, most of the hand held testes are designed to work only on one or two systems made by a specific manufacturer.**

A variety of aftermarket testers are available to help diagnose different computerized control systems. Owatonna Tool Company (OTC), for example, markets a device called the OTC Monitor which plugs directly into the assembly line diagnostic link (ALDL). The OTC tester makes diagnosis a simple matter of pressing the correct buttons and, by changing the internal PROM or inserting a different diagnosis cartridge, it will work on any model from full size to subcompact, over a wide range of years. An adapter is supplied with the tester to allow connection to all types of ALDL links, regardless of the number of pin terminals used. By inserting an updated PROM into the OTC tester, it can be easily updated to diagnose any new modifications of computerized control systems.

Wiring Harnesses

INFORMATION

The average automobile contains about ½mile of wiring, with hundreds of individual connections. To protect the many wires from damage and to keep them from becoming a confusing tangle, they are organized into bundles, enclosed in plastic or taped together and called wire harnesses. Different wiring harnesses serve different parts of the vehicle. Individual wires are color coded to help trace them through a harness where sections are hidden from view.

A loose or corroded connection or a replacement wire that is too small for the circuit will add extra resistance and an additional voltage drop to the circuit. A ten percent voltage drop can result in slow or erratic motor operation, for example, even though the circuit is complete. Automotive wiring or circuit conductors can be in any one of three forms:

1. Single strand wire

2. Multistrand wire
3. Printed circuitry

Single strand wire has a solid metal core and is usually used inside such components as alternators, motors, relays and other devices. Multistrand wire has a core made of many small strands of wire twisted together into a single conductor. Most of the wiring in an automotive electrical system is made up of multistrand wire, either as a single conductor or grouped together in a harness. All wiring is color coded on the insulator, either as a solid color or as a colored wire with an identification stripe. A printed circuit is a thin film of copper or other conductor that is printed on an insulator backing. Occasionally, a printed circuit is sandwiched between two sheets of plastic for more protection and flexibility. A complete printed circuit, consisting of conductors, insulating material and connectors for lamps or other components is called a printed circuit board. Printed circuitry is used in place of individual wires or harnesses in places where space is limited, such as behind instrument panels.

Wire Gauge

Since computer controlled automotive electrical systems are very sensitive to changes in resistance, the selection of properly sized wires is critical when systems are repaired. The wire gauge number is an expression of the cross section area of the conductor. The most common system for expressing wire size is the American Wire Gauge (AWG) system.

Wire cross section area is measured in circular mils. A mil is 0.001 in.; a circular mil is the area of a circle one mil in diameter. For example, a conductor 1/4 inch in diameter is 0.250 in. or 250 mils. The circular mil cross section area of the wire is 250 squared or 62,500 circular mils. Imported car models usually use metric wire gauge designations, which is simply the cross section area of the conductor in square millimeters.

Gauge numbers are assigned to conductors of various cross section areas. As gauge number increases, area decreases and the conductor becomes smaller. A 5 gauge conductor is smaller than a 1 gauge conductor and a 10 gauge is smaller than a 5 gauge. As the cross section area of a conductor decreases, resistance increases and so does the gauge number. A conductor with a higher gauge number will carry less current than a conductor with a lower gauge number.

➡**Gauge wire size refers to the size of the conductor, not the size of the complete wire. It is possible to have two wires of the same gauge with different diameters because one may have thicker insulation than the other.**

12 volt automotive electrical systems generally use 10, 12, 14, 16 and 18 gauge wire. Main power distribution circuits and larger accessories usually use 10 and 12 gauge wire. Battery cables are usually 4 or 6 gauge, although 1 and 2 gauge wires are occasionally used. Wire length must also be considered when making repairs to a circuit. As conductor length increases, so does resistance. An 18 gauge wire, for example, can carry a 10 amp load for 10 feet without excessive voltage drop; however if a 15 foot wire is required for the same 10 amp load, it must be a 16 gauge wire.

An electrical schematic shows the electrical current paths when a circuit is operating properly. It is essential to understand how a circuit works before trying to figure out why it doesn't. Schematics break the entire electrical system down into individual circuits and show only one particular circuit. In a schematic, no attempt is made to represent wiring and components as they physically appear on the vehicle; switches and other components are shown as simply as possible. Face views of harness connectors show the cavity or terminal locations in all multi-pin connectors to help locate test points.

If you need to backprobe a connector while it is on the component, the order of the terminals must be mentally reversed. The wire color code can help in this situation, as well as a keyway, lock tab or other reference mark.

WIRING REPAIR

Soldering is a quick, efficient method of joining metals permanently. Everyone who has the occasion to make wiring repairs should know how to solder. Electrical connections that are soldered are far less likely to come apart and will conduct electricity much better than connections that are only "pig-tailed" together. The most popular (and preferred) method of soldering is with an electrical soldering gun. Soldering irons are available in many sizes and wattage ratings. Irons with higher wattage ratings deliver higher temperatures and recover lost heat faster. A small soldering iron rated for no more than 50 watts is recommended, especially on electrical systems where excess heat can damage the components being soldered.

There are three ingredients necessary for successful soldering; proper flux, good solder and sufficient heat. A soldering flux is necessary to clean the metal of tarnish, prepare it for soldering and to enable the solder to spread into tiny crevices. When soldering, always use a resin flux or resin core solder which is non-corrosive and will not attract moisture once the job is finished. Other types of flux (acid core) will leave a residue that will attract moisture and cause the wires to corrode. Tin is a unique metal with a low melting point. In a molten state, it dissolves and alloys easily with many metals. Solder is made by mixing tin with lead. The most common proportions are 40/60, 50/50 and 60/40, with the percentage of tin listed first. Low priced solders usually contain less tin, making them very difficult for a beginner to use because more heat is required to melt the solder. A common solder is 40/60 which is well suited for all-around general use, but 60/40 melts easier, has more tin f or a better joint and is preferred for electrical work.

Soldering Techniques

Successful soldering requires that the metals to be joined be heated to a temperature that will melt the solder — usually 360-460°F (182-238°C). Contrary to popular belief, the purpose of the soldering iron is not to melt the solder itself, but to heat the parts being soldered to a temperature high enough to melt the solder when it is touched to the work. Melting flux-cored solder on the soldering iron will usually destroy the effectiveness of the flux.

➡**Soldering tips are made of copper for good heat conductivity, but must be "tinned" regularly for quick transference of heat to the project and to prevent the solder from sticking to the iron. To "tin" the iron, simply heat it and touch the flux-cored solder to the tip; the solder will flow over the hot tip. Wipe the excess off with a clean rag, but be careful as the iron will be hot.**

After some use, the tip may become pitted. If so, simply dress the tip smooth with a smooth file and "tin" the tip again. An old saying holds that "metals well cleaned are half soldered." Flux-cored solder will remove oxides but rust, bits of insulation and oil or grease must be removed with a wire brush or emery cloth. For maximum strength in soldered parts, the joint must start off clean and tight. Weak joints will result in gaps too wide for the solder to bridge.

If a separate soldering flux is used, it should be brushed or swabbed on only those areas that are to be soldered. Most solders contain a core of flux and separate fluxing is unnecessary. Hold the work to be soldered firmly. It is best to solder on a wooden board, because a metal vise will only rob the piece to be soldered of heat and make it difficult to melt the solder. Hold the soldering tip with the broadest face against the work to be soldered. Apply solder under the tip close to the work, using enough solder to give a heavy film between the iron and the piece being soldered, while moving slowly and making sure the solder melts properly. Keep the work level or the solder will run to the lowest part and favor the thicker parts, because these require more heat to melt the solder. If the soldering tip overheats (the solder coating on the face of the tip burns up), it should be retinned. Once the soldering is completed, let the soldered joint stand until cool. Tape and seal all soldered wire spli ces after the repair has cooled.

Wire Harness and Connectors

The on-board computer (ECA) wire harness electrically connects the control unit to the various solenoids, switches and sensors used by the control system. Most connectors in the engine compartment or otherwise exposed to the elements are protected against moisture and dirt which could create oxidation and deposits on the terminals. This protection is important because of the very low voltage and current levels used by the computer and sensors. All connectors have a lock which secures the male and female terminals together, with a secondary lock holding the seal and terminal into the connector. Both terminal locks must be released when disconnecting ECA connectors.

These special connectors are weatherproof and all repairs require the use of a special terminal and the tool required to service it. This tool is used to remove the pin and sleeve terminals. If removal is attempted with an ordinary pick, there is a good chance that the terminal will be bent or deformed. Unlike standard blade type terminals, these terminals cannot be straightened once they are bent. Make certain that the connectors are properly seated and all of the sealing rings in place when connecting leads. On some models, a hinge-type flap provides a backup or secondary locking feature for the terminals. Most secondary locks are used to improve the connector reliability by retaining the terminals if the small terminal lock tangs are not positioned properly.

Molded-on connectors require complete replacement of the connection. This means splicing a new connector assembly into the harness. All splices in on-board computer systems should be soldered to insure proper contact. Use care when probing the connections or replacing terminals in them as it is possible to short between opposite terminals. If this happens to the wrong terminal pair, it is possible to damage certain components. Always use jumper wires between connectors for circuit checking and never probe through weatherproof seals.

Open circuits are often difficult to locate by sight because corrosion or terminal misalignment are hidden by the connectors. Merely wiggling a connector on a sensor or in the wiring harness may correct the open circuit condition. This should always be considered when an open circuit or a failed sensor is indicated. Intermittent problems may also be caused by oxidized or loose connections. When using a circuit tester for diagnosis, always probe connections from the wire side. Be careful not to damage sealed connectors with test probes.

All wiring harnesses should be replaced with identical parts, using the same gauge wire and connectors. When signal wires are spliced into a harness, use wire with high temperature insulation only. With the low voltage and current levels found in the system, it is important that the best possible connection at all wire splices be made by soldering the splices together. It is seldom necessary to replace a complete harness. If replacement is necessary, pay close attention to insure proper harness routing. Secure the harness with suitable plastic wire clamps to prevent vibrations from causing the harness to wear in spots or contact any hot components.

➡ **Weatherproof connectors cannot be replaced with standard connectors. Instructions are provided with replacement connector and terminal packages. Some wire harnesses have mounting indicators (usually pieces of colored tape) to mark where the harness is to be secured.**

In making wiring repairs, it's important that you always replace damaged wires with wires that are the same gauge as the wire being replaced. The heavier the wire, the smaller the gauge number. Wires are color-coded to aid in identification and whenever possible the same color coded wire should be used for replacement. A wire stripping and crimping tool is necessary to install solderless terminal connectors. Test all crimps by pulling on the wires; it should not be possible to pull the wires out of a good crimp.

Wires which are open, exposed or otherwise damaged are repaired by simple splicing. Where possible, if the wiring harness is accessible and the damaged place in the wire can be located, it is best to open the harness and check for all possible damage. In an inaccessible harness, the wire must be bypassed with a new insert, usually taped to the outside of the old harness.

When replacing fusible links, be sure to use fusible link wire, NOT ordinary automotive wire. Make sure the fusible segment is of the same gauge and construction as the one being replaced and double the stripped end when crimping the terminal connector for a good contact. The melted (open) fusible link segment of the wiring harness should be cut off as close to the harness as possible, then a new segment spliced in as described. In the case of a damaged fusible link that feeds two harness wires, the harness connections should be replaced with two fusible link wires so that each circuit will have its own separate protection.

➡ **Most of the problems caused in the wiring harness are due to bad ground connections. Always check all vehicle ground connections for corrosion or looseness before performing any power feed checks to eliminate the chance of a bad ground affecting the circuit.**

Repairing Hard Shell Connectors

Unlike molded connectors, the terminal contacts in hard shell connectors can be replaced. Weatherproof hard-shell connectors with the leads molded into the shell have non-replaceable terminal ends. Replacement usually involves the use of a special terminal removal tool that depress the locking tangs (barbs) on the connector terminal and allow the connector to be removed from the rear of the shell. The connector shell should be replaced if it shows any evidence of burning, melting, cracks, or breaks. Replace individual terminals that are burnt, corroded, distorted or loose.

➡**The insulation crimp must be tight to prevent the insulation from sliding back on the wire when the wire is pulled. The insulation must be visibly compressed under the crimp tabs, and the ends of the crimp should be turned in for a firm grip on the insulation.**

The wire crimp must be made with all wire strands inside the crimp. The terminal must be fully compressed on the wire strands with the ends of the crimp tabs turned in to make a firm grip on the wire. Check all connections with an ohmmeter to insure a good contact. There should be no measurable resistance between the wire and the terminal when connected.

Mechanical Test Equipment

INFORMATION

Vacuum Gauge

Most gauges are graduated in inches of mercury (in.Hg), although a device called a manometer reads vacuum in inches of water (in. H_2O). The normal vacuum reading usually varies between 18 and 22 in.Hg at sea level. To test engine vacuum, the vacuum gauge must be connected to a source of manifold vacuum. Many engines have a plug in the intake manifold which can be removed and replaced with an adapter fitting. Connect the vacuum gauge to the fitting with a suitable rubber hose or, if no manifold plug is available, connect the vacuum gauge to any device using manifold vacuum, such as EGR valves, etc. The vacuum gauge can be used to determine if enough vacuum is reaching a component to allow its actuation.

Hand Vacuum Pump

Small, hand-held vacuum pumps come in a variety of designs. Most have a built-in vacuum gauge and allow the component to be tested without removing it from the vehicle. Operate the pump lever or plunger to apply the correct amount of vacuum required for the test specified in the diagnosis routines. The level of vacuum in inches of Mercury (in.Hg) is indicated on the pump gauge. For some testing, an additional vacuum gauge may be necessary.

Intake manifold vacuum is used to operate various systems and devices on late model vehicles. To correctly diagnose and solve problems in vacuum control systems, a vacuum source is necessary for testing. In some cases, vacuum can be taken from the intake manifold when the engine is running, but vacuum is normally provided by a hand vacuum pump. These hand vacuum pumps have a built-in vacuum gauge that allow testing while the device is still attached to the component. For some tests, an additional vacuum gauge may be necessary.

SUPPLEMENTAL RESTRAINT SYSTEM (AIR BAG)

General Information

SYSTEM OPERATION

There are 3 crash sensors mounted in the front of the vehicle. There is another sensor mounted in the passenger compartment of the vehicle which monitors the deceleration rate of the vehicle upon collision. When any of the crash sensors and the deceleration sensor are simultaneously activated, the air bag will be deployed. The air bag system does contain a warning lamp which will illuminate and stay lit if there is a problem within the system. The complete air bag system is controlled by the diagnostic module unit. The module unit contains a diagnostic feature which will display a coded warning lamp display when trouble does exist.

SYSTEM COMPONENTS

The air bag system consists of an air bag module, clock spring, the 3 crash

sensors, the deceleration sensor, the warning lamp and the diagnostic module unit.

SYSTEM PRECAUTIONS

1. Before replacing any air bag component, disconnect the negative battery cable and disconnect the orange and blue clockspring electrical connector, located below the steering wheel.
2. The air bag components are not intended to be disassembled. They should be replaced if they are defective.
3. The air bag wiring harness should never be repaired, if it is defective it must be replaced.
4. Never use an ohmmeter to test the air bag module. Doing so could accidently deploy the air bag.
5. When carrying a live undeployed air bag module, carry it so that the trim

cover is pointing away from your body at all times.
6. When placing a live undeployed air bag on a flat surface, make certain to face the trim cover upward at all times.
7. In the event that the air bag has been deployed, always wear gloves and safety glasses to handle the air bag assembly. The air bag may contain caustic material deposits.
8. Because of the content of the air bag assembly, a deployed unit must be properly disposed of.
9. The position of the crash sensors in the front end is very important, if the front end ever suffers any damage of any type, the sensors must be inspected.
10. If the steering wheel is ever removed, the air bag clockspring connector must be adjusted.

HEATER

Blower Motor

REMOVAL & INSTALLATION

▶ **See Figure 1**

323/Protege

1. Disconnect the negative battery cable.

2. Open the glove box and remove the glove box retaining screws. Remove the glove box assembly.

3. Remove the inner glove box assembly screws and remove the inner glove box.

4. Unclip and remove the heater blower seal plate.

5. Remove the 3 heater blower mounting nuts and remove the blower unit case.

6. Remove the screws and separate the two halves of the blower unit case.

7. Remove the blower fan from the blower motor. Remove the mounting screws and separate the blower motor from the case.

To install:

8. Install the blower motor to the case and install the screws.

9. Install the blower fan to the blower motor.

10. Connect the 2 halves of the blower unit case and install the screws.

11. Install the heater blower unit case to the vehicle and tighten the mounting nuts.

12. Install the heater blower seal plate.

13. Install the inner glove box assembly.

14. Install the glove box door.

15. Connect the negative battery cable.

Miata

▶ **See Figure 2**

1. Disconnect the negative battery cable.

2. Remove the glove box assembly.

3. Remove the blower unit mounting bolt and nuts.

4. Installation is the reverse of the removal procedure. Tighten the bolt and nuts to 69-95 inch lbs. (8-11 Nm).

1990-92 626 and MX-6

1. Disconnect the negative battery cable.

2. Remove the glove box and the underdash cover.

3. Remove the blower unit attaching bolts and remove the blower unit assembly.

4. Installation is the reverse of the removal procedure.

1993 626 and MX-6

1. Disconnect the negative battery cable.

2. Remove the sound deadening panel from the passenger side.

3. Remove the glove box assembly and the brace.

4. Remove the cooling hose from the blower motor assembly.

5. Disconnect the electrical connector from the blower motor.

6. Remove the 3 blower motor-to-blower motor housing screws and blower motor.

7. If necessary, remove the blower wheel-to-blower motor clip and the wheel.

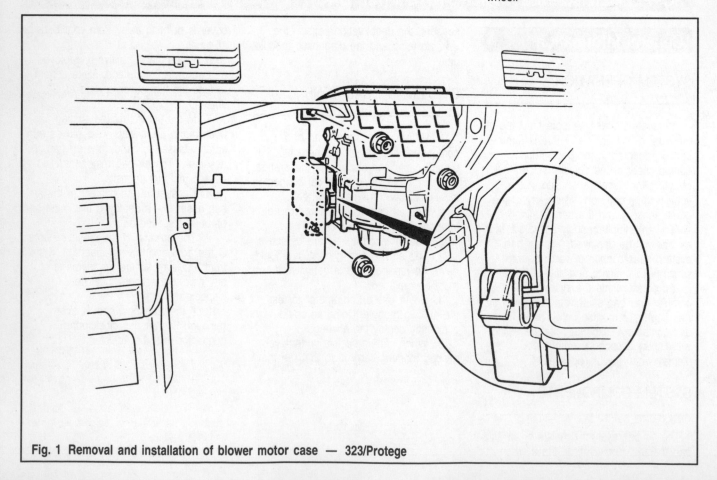

Fig. 1 Removal and installation of blower motor case — 323/Protege

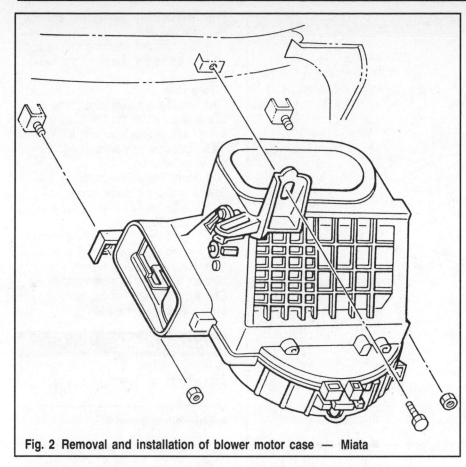

Fig. 2 Removal and installation of blower motor case — Miata

8. To install, reverse the removal procedure and check the blower motor operation.

Heater Core

REMOVAL & INSTALLATION

▶ See Figures 3 and 4

323/Protege

1. Disconnect the negative battery cable.
2. Drain the engine coolant.
3. Remove the instrument panel/dash assembly from the vehicle. Refer to Section 10.
4. Remove the seal plate from between the heater unit and the blower unit.
5. Unlock the heater hose connector at the heater core side and disconnect the hose(s).
6. Remove the heater hose(s) and cap the hose(s).
7. Remove the attaching nuts and remove the heater unit assembly.
8. Remove the heater core attaching screw and remove the heater core.

To install:

9. Install the heater core to the heater case and install the mounting screws.
10. Install the heater unit to the vehicle and install the mounting nuts.
11. Install and connect the heater hose(s). Make sure that they are secure.
12. Install the seal plate to between the heater case and the blower case.
13. Install the instrument panel/dash assembly. Refer to Section 10.
14. Refill the coolant to the proper level and connect the negative battery cable.

Miata

1. Disconnect the negative battery cable.
2. Remove the dash panel assembly. Refer to Section 10.
3. Drain the coolant.
4. Disconnect the heater hoses from the heater core and cap the hoses.
5. Remove the heater unit attaching nuts and remove the heater unit from the vehicle.
6. Remove the heater core attaching screws and remove the heater core from the heater case.

To install:

7. Install the heater core to the heater case and install the attaching screws.
8. Install the heater case to the vehicle and tighten the nuts to 69-95 inch lbs. (8-11 Nm).
9. Connect the heater hoses to the heater core. Make sure the hoses are secure.
10. Refill the coolant to the proper level.
11. Install the dash panel assembly. Refer to Section 10.
12. Connect the negative battery cable.

1990-92 626/MX-6

1. Disconnect the negative battery cable.
2. Drain the engine coolant.
3. Remove the instrument panel/dash assembly from the vehicle. Refer to Section 10.
4. Remove the heater hose(s) and cap the hose(s).
5. Remove the attaching nuts and remove the heater unit assembly.
6. Remove the heater core attaching screw and remove the heater core.

To install:

7. Install the heater core to the heater case and install the mounting screws.
8. Install the heater unit to the vehicle and install the mounting nuts.
9. Install and connect the heater hose(s). Make sure that they are secure.
10. Install the instrument panel/dash assembly. Refer to section 10.
11. Refill the coolant to the proper level and connect the negative battery cable.

1993 626/MX-6

1. Disconnect the negative battery cable. Drain the cooling system into a suitable container.
2. Remove the instrument panel assembly. Refer to Section 10.
3. Properly remove the air conditioner cooling unit. Refer to Section 6.
4. Disconnect the heater hoses from the heater core extension tubes and cap the extension tubes to prevent spilling coolant into the passenger compartment.
5. Remove the nuts and remove the heater unit case.
6. Remove the airflow mode actuator attaching screws amd remove the airflow mode actuator.
7. Remove the airflow mode door assembly.

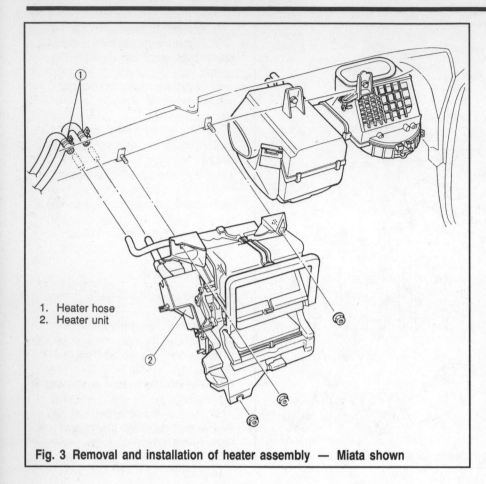

1. Heater hose
2. Heater unit

Fig. 3 Removal and installation of heater assembly — Miata shown

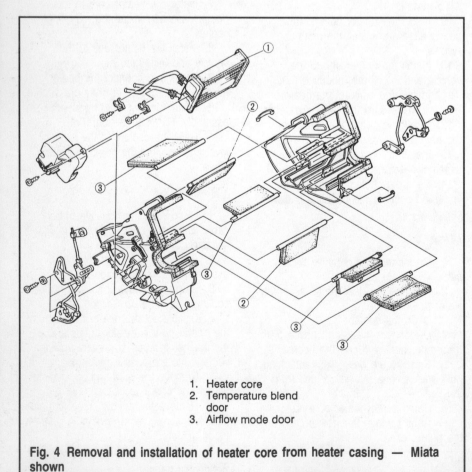

1. Heater core
2. Temperature blend door
3. Airflow mode door

Fig. 4 Removal and installation of heater core from heater casing — Miata shown

8. Remove the mix actuator and the mix door assembly.

9. Remove the attaching screws and remove the heater core form the heater unit.

To install:

10. Install the heater core in the heater case. Install the heater core tube braces and secure them with the screws.

11. Install the mix actuator and the mix door assembly.

12. Install the airflow mode door assembly and the mode actuator.

13. Install the heater unit case and tighten the nuts.

14. Install the air conditioning cooling unit and the instrument panel assembly.

15. Refill the cooling system and connect the negative battery cable. Check the operation of the heater system and check for leaks.

Control Cables

REMOVAL & INSTALLATION

▶ **See Figures 5 and 6**

1. Disconnect the negative battery cable.

2. Remove the control panel assembly. Refer to the procedure in this Section.

3. Remove the applicable housing brace and remove the cable.

To install:

4. Insert the cable end into the hole of the control lever.

5. Position the cable housing into its seat.

6. Install the cable housing brace.

7. Install the control panel assembly.

8. Check the operation of the control cable.

ADJUSTMENT

Airflow Mode Cable

323/PROTEGE

1. Position the mode lever to the **DEFROST** position.

2. From under the dash at the control linkage on the heater unit side, remove the cable from the retaining clip.

3. Align the set pin hole with the matching hole of the heater unit and insert a pin in the holes to hold in place.

4. Make certain that the mode lever is in the **DEFROST** position.

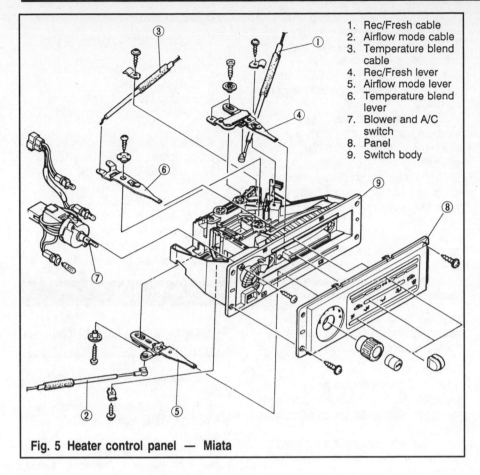

1. Rec/Fresh cable
2. Airflow mode cable
3. Temperature blend cable
4. Rec/Fresh lever
5. Airflow mode lever
6. Temperature blend lever
7. Blower and A/C switch
8. Panel
9. Switch body

Fig. 5 Heater control panel — Miata

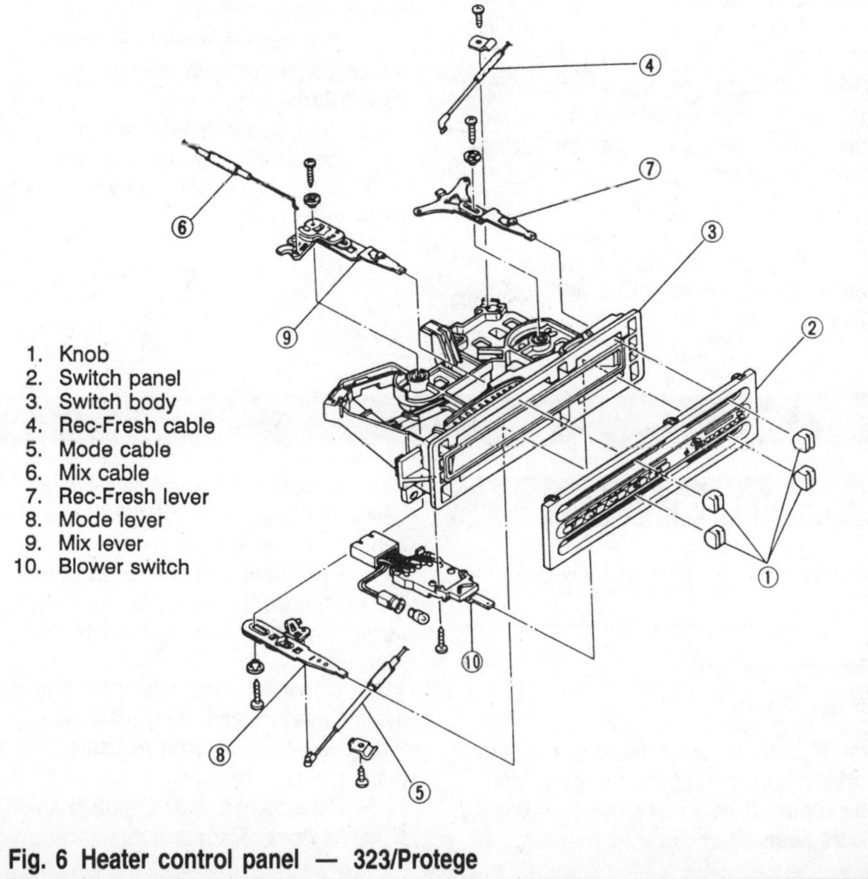

1. Knob
2. Switch panel
3. Switch body
4. Rec-Fresh cable
5. Mode cable
6. Mix cable
7. Rec-Fresh lever
8. Mode lever
9. Mix lever
10. Blower switch

Fig. 6 Heater control panel — 323/Protege

5. Connect the mode cable to the retaining clip. Keep tension on the wire when installing the clip.

6. Check the function of the mode lever. If the lever functions properly, remove the set pin.

MIATA

1. Position the mode control lever to the **VENT** position.

2. At the control linkage, located on the side of the heater assembly, adjust the shutter lever so that it is as close as can be to the heater unit. Clamp the wire tight at that point.

3. Check the mode control lever for proper operation.

1990-92 626/MX-6 WITH CABLE TYPE CONTROLS

1. Position the mode control lever to the **DEFROST** position.

2. At the control linkage, located on the side of the heater assembly, adjust the shutter lever so that it is as close as can be to the heater unit. Clamp the wire tight at that point.

3. Check the mode control lever for proper operation.

MIX/Temperature Blend Cable

323/PROTEGE

1. At the the heater assembly, disconnect the MIX cable from the heater unit.

2. Set the MIX lever to the **COLD** position.

3. Set the door to the **COLD** position and tighten the clamp to the cable in place.

4. Check the operation of the mix lever.

REC/FRESH Control Cable

323/PROTEGE

1. Position the REC/FRESH control lever in the fresh air position.

2. Remove the passenger's side sound deadening panel.

3. Remove the cable located on the left side of the blower case from the cable housing brace.

4. Installation is the reverse of the removal procedure. With the cable end on the door lever pin, push the door lever forward to its extreme stop.

5. Secure the cable into the cable housing brace.

6. Check the air door control lever for proper operation.

7. Install the passenger's side sound deadening panel.

Control Panel

REMOVAL & INSTALLATION

323 and Protege

1. Disconnect the negative battery cable.

2. From the right side of the dash, remove the side trim panel.

3. From directly below the glovebox, remove the trim panel.

4. Remove the center trim panel.

5. Remove the upper and lower instrument cluster assemblies. Disconnect the electrical connectors from the top assembly.

6. Remove the glove box and the inside glove box lining.

7. Remove the control panel retaining screws and disconnect the control cable wires from the control panel. Remove the control panel from the vehicle.

   To install:

8. Connect the control cable wires to the control panel and install the panel assembly.

9. Install the glove box and the inside glove box lining.

10. Install the instrument cluster upper and lower assemblies. Make sure to connect all of the electrical connectors.

11. Install the center trim panel assembly.

12. Install the trim panel below the glovebox and install the side trim panel.

13. Connect the negative battery cable.

1990-92 626/MX-6

1. Disconnect the negative battery cable.

2. Remove the bezel cover from the control assembly face.

3. Remove the 4 attaching screws from the control assembly housing.

4. Remove the passenger and driver side sound deadening panels.

5. Remove the REC/FRESH control cable at the REC/FRESH selector door assembly.

6. Disconnect the blower switch electrical connector and the control assembly illumination electrical connector.

7. Remove the temperature control cable from the temperature blend door assembly at the right-hand side of the heater case.

8. Remove the function selector cable from the function control door assembly at the left-hand side of the heater case.

9. Remove the control assembly and control cables as an assembly.

➡**While removing the control panel assembly, notice how the cables are routed for proper installation**

   To install:

10. Position the control panel assembly into the instrument panel while routing the control cables as noted during removal.

11. Connect the blower switch and control assembly illumination electrical connectors.

12. Secure the control assembly with the 4 attaching screws.

13. Install the plastic bezel cover onto the face of the control assembly.

14. Install and adjust all control cables to their respective control and selector door assemblies and adjust the cables. Refer to the procedures in this Section.

15. Install both sound deadening panels.

16. Connect the negative battery cable. Check for proper control assembly operation.

1993 626/MX-6

1. Disconnect the negative battery cable.

2. Remove the upper and lower steering wheel panels.

3. Remove the lower dash panel. Make sure to disconnect the switch connectors.

4. Remove the heater control unit mounting screws and pull the unit out.

5. Disconnect the electrical connectors from the control unit and remove the control unit.

6. Installation is the reverse of the removal procedure. Make sure to connect all of the electrical connectors and test all accesories when done.

Blower Switch

REMOVAL & INSTALLATION

1. Disconnect the negative battery cable.

2. Remove the control assembly from the vehicle. Refer to the procedure in this Section.

3. Remove the blower switch knob by pulling it straight off of the blower switch shaft.

4. Remove the attaching nut from the blower switch shaft.

5. Remove the male side blower switch connector from the control assembly housing.

6. Remove the blower switch assembly from the control assembly.

7. Installation is the reverse of the removal procedure.

AIR CONDITIONER

➡**Refer to Section 1 for discharging, charging, etc. of the air conditioning system.**

Compressor

REMOVAL & INSTALLATION

323/Protege

▶ See Figure 7

➡**The suction accumulator/drier and orifice tube (liquid line) should also be replaced whenever the compressor is replaced.**

1. Disconnect the negative battery cable and properly discharge the air conditioning refrigerant system.

2. Remove the engine undercover.

3. Remove the drive belt from the pulleys by first loosening the belt tensioner.

4. Disconnect the suction hose from the compressor and immediately plug the open fittings to keep moisture out of the system.

5. Disconnect the discharge hose from the compressor and immediately

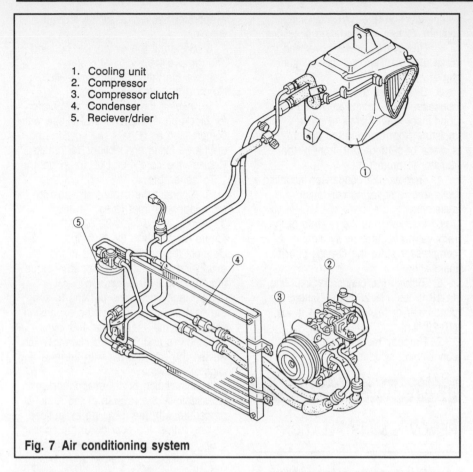

1. Cooling unit
2. Compressor
3. Compressor clutch
4. Condenser
5. Reciever/drier

Fig. 7 Air conditioning system

plug the open fittings to keep moisture out of the system.

6. Remove the 2 compressor mounting bolts and remove the compressor from the bracket.

To install:

7. Install the compressor to the bracket and tighten the mounting bolts to 17-26 ft. lbs. (24-35 Nm).

8. Apply clean oil to the compressor O-rings and install in place. Connect the hoses to the compressor and tighten the inlet and outlet line mounting bolts to 8-11 ft. lbs. (10-16 Nm).

9. Install the drive belt and adjust the tension as necessary.

10. Recharge the air conditioning system.

11. Install the engine undercover and connect the negative battery cable.

Miata

1. Raise and safely support the vehicle.

2. Properly discharge the air conditioning system.

3. Remove the splash shield and air guide from under the engine.

4. Disconnect the suction hose from the compressor.

5. Disconnect the discharge hose from the compressor.

6. Remove the compressor mounting bolts and remove the compressor from the vehicle.

7. Installation is the reverse of the removal procedure. Tighten the compressor mounting bolts to 10-16 ft. lbs. (15-22 Nm). Connect the compressor lines to the compressor and tighten the bolts to 7-12 ft. lbs. (10-16 Nm).

1990-92 626/MX-6

1. Raise and safely support the vehicle.

2. Properly discharge the air conditioning system.

3. Remove the engine under cover.

4. Disconnect the suction hose from the compressor.

5. Disconnect the discharge hose from the compressor.

6. Remove the compressor mounting bolts and remove the compressor from the vehicle.

7. Installation is the reverse of the removal procedure. Tighten the compressor mounting bolts to 17-26 ft. lbs. (24-35 Nm). Connect the compressor lines to the compressor and tighten the bolts.

1993 626/MX-6

1. Raise and safely support the vehicle.

2. Properly discharge the air conditioning system.

3. Remove the drive belt as follows:

a. FS engine-Loosen the idle pulley lock nut and then loosen the adjuster bolt. Remove the belt.

b. KL engine-Loosen the upper power steering pump bolt. Loosen the lower power steering pump bolt and then loosen the adjuster bolt. Remove the drive bolt.

4. Remove the engine under cover.

5. Disconnect the flexible hoses from the compressor.

6. Remove the compressor mounting bolts and remove the compressor from the vehicle.

7. Installation is the reverse of the removal procedure. Tighten the compressor mounting bolts as follows:

a. On the KL engine, adjust the belt adjustment by turning the adjuster bolt. When the belt is properly adjusted, tighten the locknut to 23-34 ft. lbs.

b. On the FS engine, adjust the belt by turning the adjusting bolt until the belt is in proper adjustment. Tighten the upper bolt to 32-45 ft. lbs. and the lower bolt to 28-38 ft. lbs.

8. Connect the compressor lines to the compressor and tighten the bolts.

Condenser and Reciever/Drier

REMOVAL & INSTALLATION

323/Protege

1. Disconnect the negative battery cable and properly discharge the refrigerant from the air conditioning system. Observe all safety precautions.

2. Remove the grille and remove the reciever/drier assembly.

3. Remove the upper radiator brackets.

4. Remove the condenser mounting bolts and remove the condenser assembly. Immediately plug the condenser open fittings to prevent moisture from entering.

5. Installation is the reverse of the removal procedure. Apply clean compressor oil to the O-rings prior to installation.

6. Tighten the condenser inlet line to 11-18 ft. lbs. (15-25 Nm) and the outlet line to 87-174 inch lbs. (10-20 Nm).

7. Properly recharge the air conditioning system.

Miata

1. Disconnect the negative battery cable and properly discharge the refrigerant from the air conditioning system. Observe all safety precautions.

2. Raise and safely support the vehicle. Remove the splash shield and air guide from under the vehicle.

3. Disconnect the air conditioner lines from the reciever/drier.

4. Remove the condenser mounting bolts and nuts and remove the condenser and reciever/drier as an assembly. Immediately plug the open fittings to prevent moisture from entering.

5. Installation is the reverse of the removal procedure. Apply clean compressor oil to the O-rings prior to installation.

6. Tighten the condenser inlet line to 11-18 ft. lbs. (15-25 Nm) and the reciever/drier inlet and outlet lines to 7-14 ft. lbs. (10-20 Nm).

7. Properly recharge the air conditioning system.

1990-92 626/MX-6

1. Disconnect the negative battery cable and properly discharge the refrigerant from the air conditioning system. Observe all safety precautions.

2. Remove the grille and remove the reciever/drier assembly.

3. Remove the upper radiator brackets and lift up on the radiator. Push the radiator towards the engine. Place a piece of cardboard in front of the radiator to protect it.

4. Remove the condenser mounting bolts and remove the condenser assembly. Immediately plug the condenser open fittings to prevent moisture from entering.

5. Installation is the reverse of the removal procedure. Apply clean compressor oil to the O-rings prior to installation.

6. Tighten the flexible hose and liquid pipe connectors to 11-18 ft. lbs. (15-25 Nm).

7. Properly recharge the air conditioning system.

1993 626/MX-6 and MX-3

1. Disconnect the negative battery cable and properly discharge the

refrigerant from the air conditioning system. Observe all safety precautions.

2. Remove the lower cover and the fresh air duct. Remove the radiator upper mount.

3. Disconnect the lines from the condenser and immediately plug the condenser open fittings to prevent moisture from entering the system. Place a piece of cardboard in front of the radiator to protect it.

4. Remove the condenser mounting bolts and remove the condenser assembly.

5. Installation is the reverse of the removal procedure. Apply clean compressor oil to the O-rings prior to installation.

6. Tighten the condenser inlet line to 11-18 ft. lbs. (15-25 Nm). Tighten the condenser outlet lines to 8-14 ft. lbs. (10-20 Nm).

7. Properly recharge the air conditioning system.

Evaporator Core

REMOVAL & INSTALLATION

1. Disconnect the negative battery cable. Discharge the refrigerant system as described in Section 1. On the 626 and MX-6, remove the under cover, glove box and glove box stay at this time.

2. Disconnect and plug the evaporator suction and discharge lines from their respective fittings. On the 1993 626/MX-6 disconnect the A/C amplifier connector. Plug the fitings immediately to prevent the entry of dirt and moisture into the system.

3. On the 323/Protege and 1990-92 626/MX-6, remove the grommets from the suction and discharge lines. On 323/Protege, remove the glove box at this time.

4. Remove the drain hose from the evaporator housing. Remove the lower duct.

5. Remove the sealing plates from both sides of the evaporator housing.

6. Disconnect the electrical and vacuum connections from the evaporator housing. On 323/Protege, remove the air duct bands.

7. Remove the evaporator unit retaining bolts or nuts. Remove the

evaporator housing assembly from the vehicle.

8. Separate the evaporator housing and remove the evaporator core. Remove the thermostat/thermoswitch. Remove the expansion valve.

9. Inspect the fins of the evaporator for blockage. Remove any blockage with compressed air. Check the suction and discharge fitting connections for cracks. Replace the core if cracks are evident.

To assemble:

10. Connect the expansion valve to the evaporator inlet fitting. On the 323/Protege and 1990-92 626/MX-6, torque the fitting to 22-25 ft. lbs. Connect the discharge fitting to the expansion valve, if so equipped. Torque the fitting to 9-10 ft. lbs. On 323/Protege, install the packing to seal the heat sensitive tube of the expansion valve. Assemble the upper and lower case halves and install the thermoswitch. Fasten the case halves with the retaining clips or screws.

11. Installation of the evaporator unit is essentially the reverse of the removal procedure with the following exceptions:

a. Adjust the position of the cooling unit that its connections are aligned with those on the heater and blower units.

b. On 323/Protege, torque the discharge tube fitting to 9-10 ft. lbs. and the suction tube fitting to 22-25 ft. lbs. On 1990-92 626/MX-6, torque both tube fittings to 11-18 ft. lbs. On the 1993 626/MX-6 torque the outlet pipe fitting to 15-21 ft. lbs. and the inlet pipe fitting to 87-174 inch lbs.

c. If the evaporator was replaced, add approximately 50cc of new compressor oil to the compressor.

d. Evacuate, charge and leak test the system as described in Section 1 and check the system for proper operation.st

Control Panel

REMOVAL & INSTALLATION

For removal and installation of the control panel, and control cable adjustment, refer to the procedures under HEATER, in this Section.

A/C Amplifier

REMOVAL & INSTALLATION

1993 626/MX-6

1. Disconnect the negative battery cable.
2. Remove the glove box, the under cover, the side cover and the side console unit.
3. Disconnect the A/C amplifier connector.
4. Remove the evaporator case as previously described. Remove the A/C compressor from the evaporator case.
5. Installation is the reverse of the removal procedure.

Blower Switch

REMOVAL & INSTALLATION

1. Disconnect the negative battery cable.
2. Remove the control assembly from the vehicle. Refer to the procedure in this Section.
3. Remove the A/C push-button knob by pulling it straight off the blower switch shaft.
4. Remove the blower switch knob by pulling it straight off the blower switch shaft.
5. Remove the attaching nut from the blower switch shaft.
6. Remove the A/C indicator light from the blower switch housing.
7. Remove the male side blower switch connector from the control assembly housing.
8. Remove the blower switch assembly from the control assembly.
9. Installation is the reverse of the removal procedure. Check the blower switch for proper operation.

Refrigerant Lines

QUICK-CONNECT COUPLINGS

The refrigerant lines on Mazda vehicles are connected to the various air conditioning system components (except compressor) with spring lock couplings. These couplings require the use of special tools to connect and disconnect them. Do not attempt to disconnect a refrigerant line using any other type of tool, or the line may be damaged.

CRUISE CONTROL

Control Switches

REMOVAL & INSTALLATION

Main Control Switch

1. Disconnect the negative battery cable.
2. Pull the main switch out of the dash and disconnect the electrical connector.
3. Installation is the reverse of the removal procedure.

Clutch and Brake Switches

➡**The removal and installation procedures are the same for both the clutch and the brake switch.**

1. Disconnect the negative battery cable.
2. Disconnect the electrical connectors from the rear of the switch.
3. Remove the locknut and the switch.
   To install:
4. Install the adjuster nut onto the switch and install the switch into the bracket. Install the locknut onto the switch.
5. Adjust the switch so the pedal height is 8.42 in. (214mm), then tighten the locknut.

6. Connect the electrical connectors to the rear of the switch. Connect the negative battery cable.

Set/Coast and Resume/Accel switch
323/PROTEGE

1. Disconnect the negative battery cable.
2. Remove the steering wheel cap/pad bolts and separate the cap/pad assembly from the steering wheel.
3. Remove the switch mounting bolts and disconnect the electrical connectors. Separate the switch assembly from the cap/pad assembly.
4. Installation is the reverse of the removal procedure.

Control Unit

REMOVAL & INSTALLATION

323/PROTEGE

1. Disconnect the negative battery cable.
2. Remove the blower unit from under the dash as described earlier in this Section.
3. Remove the attaching bolts and disconnect the electrical connector from the cruise control unit. Remove the unit from the vehicle.
4. Installation is the reverse of the removal procedure.

1990-92 626/MX-6

1. Disconnect the negative battery cable.
2. Remove the passenger side kick panel.
3. Disconnect the electrical connector from the control unit.
4. Remove the control unit mounting nut and remove the control unit from the vehicle.
5. Installation is the reverse of the removal procedure.

1993 626/MX-6

1. Disconnect the negative battery cable.
2. From under the steering wheel, disconnect the electrical connector from the control unit.
3. Remove the control unit mounting nuts and remove the control unit from the vehicle.
4. Installation is the reverse of the removal procedure.

Actuator

REMOVAL & INSTALLATION

1. Disconnect the negative battery cable.

2. Disconnect the actuator electrical connector.

3. Tag the position of the vacuum hoses on the actuator. Remove the routing clip from the actuating cable. Remove the 2 vacuum lines from the actuator.

4. Loosen the adjusting nut and locknut.

5. Pull the dust boot to gain access to the actuator rod. Remove the actuator cable from the actuator rod and bracket.

6. Remove the actuator mounting nuts and remove the actuator.

7. Installation is the reverse of the removal procedure. Adjust the actuator

cable according to the procedure in this Section.

Actuator Cable

REMOVAL & INSTALLATION

1. Disconnect the negative battery cable.

2. On the non-turbocharged engine, pull the dust boot out of the actuator. On the turbocharged engine, remove the plastic cover.

3. Loosen the adjusting nut and locknut.

4. Remove the actuator cable from the bracket (spool and bracket on turbocharged engine) and 3 routing clips.

5. Squeeze the lock tabs and remove the cable end from the pedal assembly.

6. Squeeze the lock tabs securing the cable housing to the bulkhead.

Remove the actuator cable through the engine compartment.

7. Installation is the reverse of the removal procedure. Adjust the actuator cable according to the procedure in this Section.

ADJUSTMENT

1. Remove the clip from the actuator cable.

2. Press a finger against the cable to check the free-play. There should be approximately 0.0039-0.197 inch (1-5 mm) of free-play for the 323/Protege and 0.039-0.118 in. (1-3mm) for the 626/MX6 and the MX3.

3. If the free-play is not as specified, loosen the adjusting nut and adjust as is necessary.

ENTERTAINMENT SYSTEMS

Radio, Tape Player and Compact Disc Player

REMOVAL & INSTALLATION

323/Protege
▶ See Figure 8

1. Disconnect the negative battery cable.

2. Remove the trim panel from around the radio. Be careful not to break the trim panel clips.

3. Remove the radio mounting screws and remove the radio. Disconnect the connectors at the back of the radio.

4. Installation is the reverse of the removal procedure.

Miata
▶ See Figure 9

1. Disconnect the negative battery cable.

2. Remove the center 2 vents and remove the center trim panel. Be careful not to break the trim panel clips.

3. Remove the radio mounting screws and remove the radio. Disconnect the connectors at the back of the radio.

4. Installation is the reverse of the removal procedure.

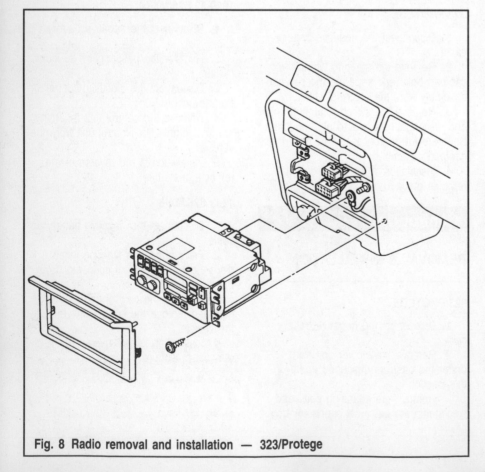

Fig. 8 Radio removal and installation — 323/Protege

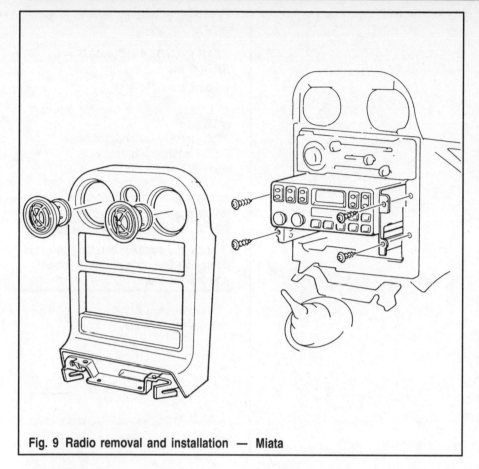

Fig. 9 Radio removal and installation — Miata

1990-92 626/MX-6

1. Disconnect the negative battery cable and remove the ash tray.

2. Remove the center storage pocket from below the radio.

3. Remove the trim panel from around the radio. Be careful not to break the trim panel clips.

4. Remove the radio mounting screws and remove the radio. Disconnect the connectors at the back of the radio.

5. Installation is the reverse of removal procedure.

1993 626/MX-6

▶ See Figures 10 and 11

1. Using a protected screwdriver, pry out the hole covers on the radio unit.

2. Use Mazda special radio puller tools 49 UN01 050 or equivalent and pull the radio out. Disconnect the elevctrical connectors.

3. Installation is the reverse of the removal procedure. The anti-theft code must be entered to the radio to reset it once the power has been disconnected from the radio. Consult with the original owners manual for this code.

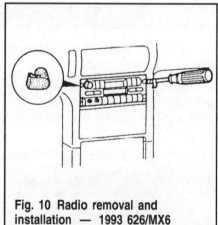

Fig. 10 Radio removal and installation — 1993 626/MX6

Speakers

REMOVAL & INSTALLATION

Front Door Speakers

▶ See Figure 12

1. Disconnect the negative battery cable.

2. Remove the inner door trim panel. Refer to the procedure in Section 10.

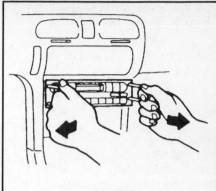

Fig. 11 Radio removal and installation — 1993 626/MX6

3. Remove the speaker retaining screws.

4. Pull out the speaker and disconnect the electrical connector.

5. Remove the speaker.

✳✳WARNING

Handle the speaker carefully to avoid damaging the cone during removal and installation.

6. Installation is the reverse of the removal procedure.

Headrest Mounted Speakers

MIATA

▶ See Figure 13

1. Disconnect the negative battery cable.

2. Unzip the headrest zippers.

3. Disconnect the speaker wire connectors and remove the speakers.

4. Installation is the reverse of the removal procedure.

Rear Speakers

REAR SHELF MOUNTED SPEAKERS

▶ See Figure 14

1. Disconnect the negative battery cable.

2. Remove the rear package trim panel. Refer to the procedure in Section 10.

3. Disconnect the electrical connector.

4. Remove the speaker retaining screws and remove the speaker.

✳✳WARNING

Handle the speaker carefully to avoid damaging the cone during removal and installation.

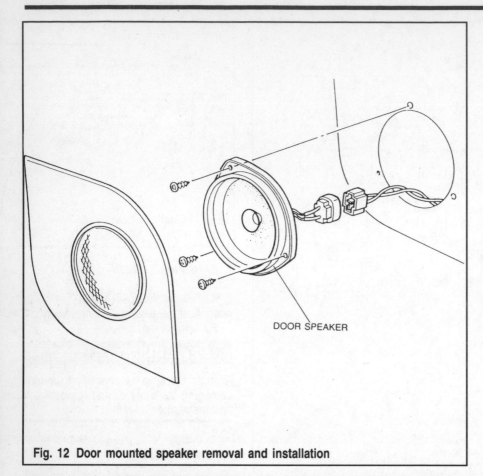

Fig. 12 Door mounted speaker removal and installation

DOOR SPEAKER

5. Installation is the reverse of the removal procedure.

REAR QUARTER MOUNTED SPEAKERS

▶ **See Figure 15**

1. Disconnect the negative battery cable.
2. Remove the speaker cover.
3. Disconnect the electrical connector.
4. Remove the speaker retaining screws and remove the speaker.

> ✳✳**WARNING**

Handle the speaker carefully to avoid damaging the cone during removal and installation.

5. Installation is the reverse of the removal procedure.

WINDSHIELD WIPERS AND WASHERS

Windshield Wiper Blade and Arm

REMOVAL & INSTALLATION

▶ **See Figures 16 and 17**

1. Unscrew the retaining nut and remove the arm and blade assembly from the pivot shaft.
2. Remove the wiper blade from the wiper arm. Refer to Section 1.
   To install:
3. Install the wiper blade on the wiper arm.
4. Turn the wiper switch **ON** and allow the motor to move the pivot shafts through 3-4 cycles. Turn the wiper switch **OFF** .
5. Install the arm and blade assembly so the tip of the wiper blade is 0.79-1.18 in. (20-30mm) from the bottom of the windshield.
6. Install the retaining nut and tighten to 7-10 ft. lbs. (10-14 Nm).

7. Cycle the wipers several times and retorque the retaining nut.

➡**Make sure the windshield wiper arm is horizontal to the pivot shaft so the pivot shaft splines are fully seated in the wiper arm.**

Rear Window Wiper Blade and Arm

REMOVAL & INSTALLATION

1. Lift the cover and remove the retaining nut.
2. Remove the arm and blade assembly.
3. Remove the wiper blade from the wiper arm. Refer to Section 1.
   To install:
4. Install the wiper blade on the wiper arm.
5. Turn the wiper switch **ON** and allow the motor to move the pivot shafts through 3-4 cycles. Turn the wiper switch **OFF** .

6. Install the arm and blade assembly so the tip of the wiper blade is 0.79-1.18 in. (20-30mm) from the bottom of the rear window.
7. Install and tighten the retaining nut.

Windshield Wiper Motor

REMOVAL & INSTALLATION

▶ **See Figures 18 and 19**

1. Disconnect the negative battery cable.
2. Remove the windshield wiper arm and blades assemblies. Refer to the procedure in this Section.
3. Disconnect the hose from the wiper washer jet nozzle.
4. Remove the lower cowl molding.
5. Remove the wiper linkage cover.
6. Disconnect the wiper linkage by pulling off the wiper motor output arm. Disconnect the electrical connectors.
7. Remove the wiper motor mounting bolts and remove the wiper motor.

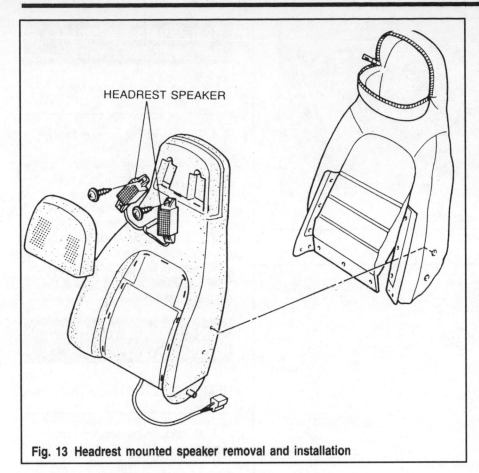

Fig. 13 Headrest mounted speaker removal and installation

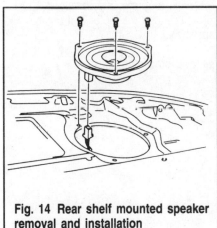

Fig. 14 Rear shelf mounted speaker removal and installation

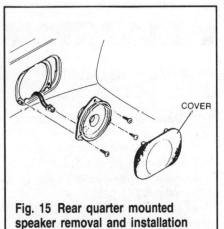

Fig. 15 Rear quarter mounted speaker removal and installation

To install:
8. Install the wiper motor and mounting bolts.
9. Connect the electrical connectors.
10. Attach the wiper linkage to the motor output arm.
11. Install the wiper linkage cover and the lower molding.
12. Connect the washer nozzles and connect the negative battery cable.
13. Install the wiper arm and blade assemblies.

Rear Window Wiper Motor

REMOVAL & INSTALLATION

1. Disconnect the negative battery cable.
2. Remove the arm and blade assembly. Refer to the procedure in this Section.
3. Remove the boot, nut, and the mount from the rear wiper motor pivot.

4. Remove the liftgate interior trim panel. Refer to Section 10.
5. Disconnect the wiper motor electrical connector.
6. Remove the rear wiper motor mounting bolts, and remove the motor.
To install:
7. Install the rear wiper motor and attaching bolts. Make sure the ground wire is connected tightly.
8. Connect the motor electrical connector.
9. Install the liftgate trim panel.
10. Install the mount, nut and boot to the motor pivot shaft.
11. Connect the negative battery cable. Install the rear wiper arm and blade assembly.

Wiper Linkage

REMOVAL & INSTALLATION

▶ **See Figure 20**

1. Remove the arm and blade assemblies. Refer to the procedure in this Section.
2. Remove the lower moulding and wiper linkage cover.
3. Disconnect the wiper linkage by disconnecting it from the wiper motor output arm.
4. Remove the pivot shaft retaining caps and remove the pivot shafts and wiper linkage.
5. Installation is the reverse of the removal procedure.

Windshield Washer Fluid Reservoir

REMOVAL & INSTALLATION

1. Disconnect the negative battery cable.
2. If necessary, remove the radiator coolant reservoir.
3. Remove the washer reservoir retaining bolts.
4. Disconnect the electrical connector and the hose from the washer reservoir.
5. Remove the washer reservoir assembly.
6. Installation is the reverse of the removal procedure.

Fig. 16 Front wiper arm removal and installation

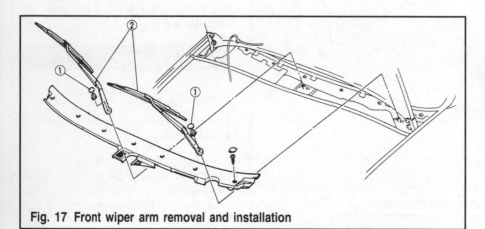

Fig. 17 Front wiper arm removal and installation

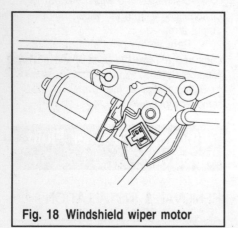

Fig. 18 Windshield wiper motor

Rear Window Washer Reservoir

REMOVAL & INSTALLATION

1. Disconnect the negative battery cable.
2. Remove the left-hand lower trunk side trim panel. Refer to Section 10.
3. Remove the refill cap and disengage the support. Remove the support from the refill hose.
4. Disconnect the electrical connector and remove the hose.
5. Remove the rear washer reservoir.
6. Installation is the reverse of the removal procedure.

Rear Window Washer Motor

REMOVAL & INSTALLATION

1. Disconnect the negative battery cable.
2. Remove the rear window washer reservoir, as previously described.
3. Remove the motor and pump assembly.
4. Installation is the reverse of the removal procedure.

Windshield Washer Motor

REMOVAL & INSTALLATION

1. Disconnect the negative battery cable.
2. Remove the windshield washer fluid reservoir, as previously described.
3. Pry off the washer motor and pump assembly.
4. Installation is the reverse of the removal procedure.

INSTRUMENTS AND SWITCHES

Instrument Cluster

REMOVAL & INSTALLATION

323/Protege
▶ See Figures 21 and 22

1. Disconnect the negative battery cable.

2. Remove the steering wheel. Refer to Section 8.
3. Remove the 2 column cover screws and remove the cover.
4. Remove the meter hood assembly and remove the instrument cluster screws.
5. Carefully pull the cluster module outward and disconnect the electrical connectors and the speedometer cable connector from the instrument cluster.

6. Remove the instrument cluster.
7. Installation is the reverse of the removal procedure. Check all gauges for proper operation.

Miata
▶ See Figures 23 and 24

1. Disconnect the negative battery cable.
2. Lower the steering column.

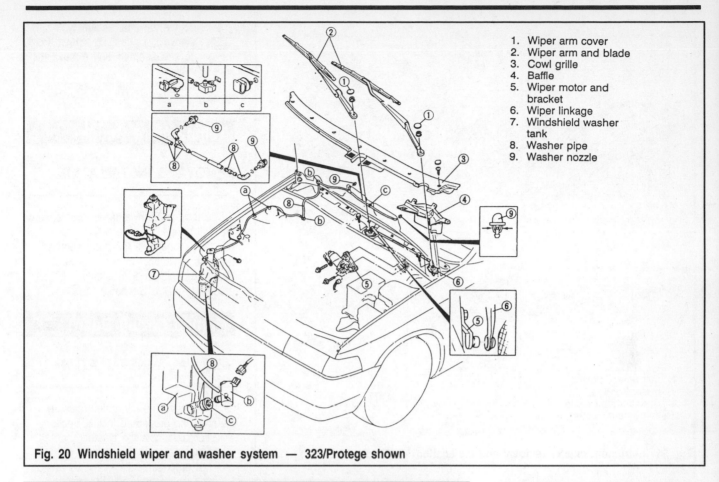

Fig. 20 Windshield wiper and washer system — 323/Protege shown

1. Wiper arm cover
2. Wiper arm and blade
3. Cowl grille
4. Baffle
5. Wiper motor and bracket
6. Wiper linkage
7. Windshield washer tank
8. Washer pipe
9. Washer nozzle

Fig. 19 Windshield wiper motor

3. Remove the instrument cluster cover.

4. Remove the meter hood assembly and remove the instrument cluster screws.

5. Carefully pull the cluster module outward and disconnect the electrical connectors and the speedometer cable connector from the instrument cluster.

6. Remove the instrument cluster.

7. Installation is the reverse of the removal procedure. Check all gauges for proper operation.

626/MX6

▶ **See Figures 25, 26 and 27**

1. Disconnect the negative battery cable.

2. Lower the steering column.

3. Remove the instrument cluster cover.

4. Remove the meter hood assembly and remove the instrument cluster screws.

5. Carefully pull the cluster module outward and disconnect the electrical connectors and the speedometer cable connector from the instrument cluster.

6. Remove the instrument cluster.

7. Installation is the reverse of the removal procedure. Check all gauges for proper operation.

Speedometer

REMOVAL & INSTALLATION

1. Remove the instrument cluster. Refer to the procedure in this Section.

2. Remove the cluster lens.

3. Remove the attaching screws and the speedometer.

4. Installation is the reverse of the removal procedure.

Tachometer

REMOVAL & INSTALLATION

1. Remove the instrument cluster. Refer to the procedure in this Section.

2. Remove the cluster lens.

3. Remove the attaching screws and the tachometer.

4. Installation is the reverse of the removal procedure.

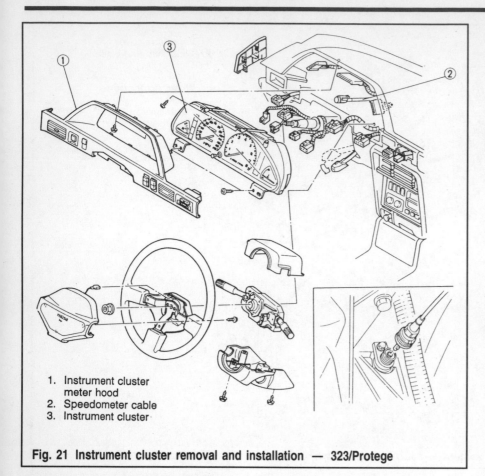

1. Instrument cluster meter hood
2. Speedometer cable
3. Instrument cluster

Fig. 21 Instrument cluster removal and installation — 323/Protege

Speedometer Cable

REMOVAL & INSTALLATION

1. Disconnect the negative battery cable.

2. Remove the upper and lower instrument cluster cover panels. (Do not remove the instrument cluster).

3. Reach behind the instrument cluster, depress the lock tab and pull the speedometer cable out of the instrument cluster.

4. Open the hood and locate the speedometer cable connector. Unscrew the connector and separate the upper and lower cables.

5. Slide the rubber dust boot back from the lower cable-to-transaxle connector. Unscrew the speedometer cable from the speedometer driven gear on the transaxle.

6. Remove the rubber grommet from the firewall and slide the grommet down the cable. Gently pry the retaining ring from the firewall and pull the speedometer cable out through the firewall.

To install:

7. Insert the upper speedometer cable through the firewall into the lower instrument panel.

8. Install the retaining ring and grommet into the firewall.

9. Connect the lower speedometer cable to the speedometer driven gear. Slide the boot into position.

10. Join both cables and tighten the connector.

11. Connect the upper speedometer cable to the rear of the speedometer. Make sure the locking tab is secured onto the back of the speedometer head.

12. Install the upper and lower instrument cluster covers.

13. Connect the negative battery cable. Check speedometer operation.

Fuel Gauge

REMOVAL & INSTALLATION

Electronic Instrument Cluster

1. Remove the instrument cluster. Refer to the procedure in this Section.

2. Remove the lens assembly.

3. Remove the attaching screws from the gauge subassembly and remove the subassembly.

4. Installation is the reverse of the removal procedure.

Temperature Gauge

REMOVAL & INSTALLATION

The temperature gauge is integral with the fuel gauge subassembly. If the gauge malfunctions, the subassembly must be replaced. Refer to the Fuel Gauge removal and installation procedure in this Section.

Printed Circuit Board

REMOVAL & INSTALLATION

1. Remove the instrument cluster. Refer to the procedure in this Section.

2. Disassemble the cluster.

3. Installation is the reverse of the removal procedure.

Combination Switch

REMOVAL & INSTALLATION

▶ See Figures 28, 29, 30 and 31

❈❈CAUTION

Before removing the steering wheel or horn pad, the air bag system connectors, Orange and Blue, must be disconnected under the steering wheel.

1. Disconnect the negative battery cable.

2. Remove the horn cap.

3. Remove the steering wheel.

4. Remove the 2 column cover screws and remove the cover.

5. Disconnect the electrical connections from the combination switch.

6. Remove the combination switch as an assembly.

7. Installation is the reverse of the removal procedure. Check the switch operation.

WITH TACHOMETER

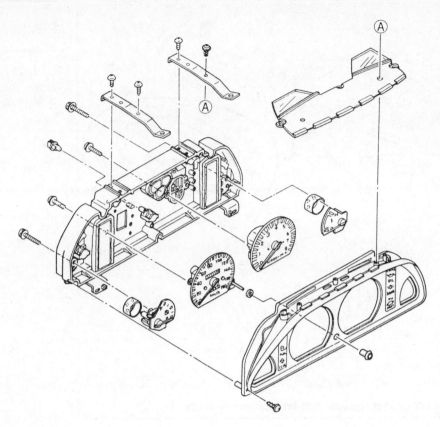

WITHOUT TACHOMETER

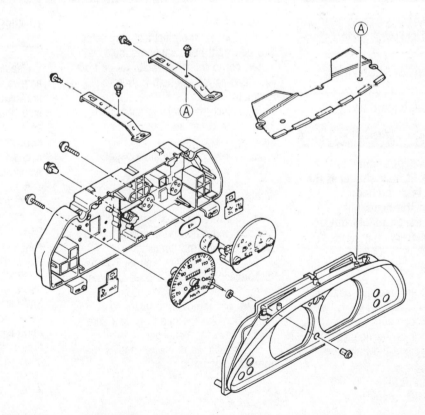

Fig. 22 Instrument cluster disassembly — 323/Protege

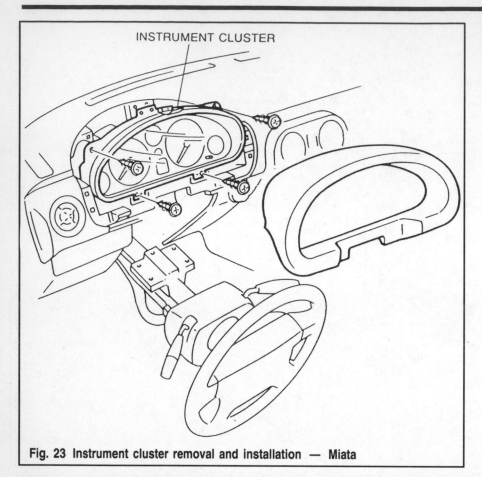

INSTRUMENT CLUSTER

Fig. 23 Instrument cluster removal and installation — Miata

Clock

REMOVAL & INSTALLATION

The clock is built-in to the electronic radios. If the clock malfunctions, the radio must be repaired or replaced.

LIGHTING

Headlights

REMOVAL & INSTALLATION

▶ **See Figures 32, 33 and 34**

✲✲CAUTION

The halogen headlight contains pressurized gas. It may shatter if the glass envelope is scratched or dropped. Handle the headlight carefully. Keep the headlight out of the reach of children.

All except Miata

1. Disconnect the negative battery cable.
2. Turn the plastic surrounding ring, located in the back of the headlight lens assembly, and remove the bulb from the headlight housing.
3. Disconnect the bulb from the electrical connector.

To install:

4. Connect the electrical connector to the headlight bulb, caution should be taken not to touch the bulb, as oil from skin can cause the bulb to burn out prematurely.
5. Install the retaining collar and secure the collar and bulb to the headlight housing.
6. Connect the negative battery cable.

Miata

1. Turn the ignition key to the ON position and push the headlight up button to raise the headlights.
2. Turn the ignition key OFF and disconnect the negative battery cable.
3. Remove the headlight bezel screws and remove the bezel.
4. Remove the headlight ring screws and remove the headlight.
5. Installation is the reverse of the removal procedure.

AIMING

Headlight aim is adjusted with the screws located at the bottom center and the middle left-hand side of the driver side headlight or the bottom center and center outside of the passenger side headlight. The adjusting screws are accessible with the headlights in the extended position.

A rough adjustment can be made while shining the headlights on a wall or on the rear of another vehicle, but headlight adjustment should really be made using proper headlight aiming equipment.

Headlight aim adjustment should be made with the fuel tank approximately half full, the vehicle unloaded and the trunk empty, except for the spare tire and jacking equipment. Make sure all tires are inflated to the proper pressure.

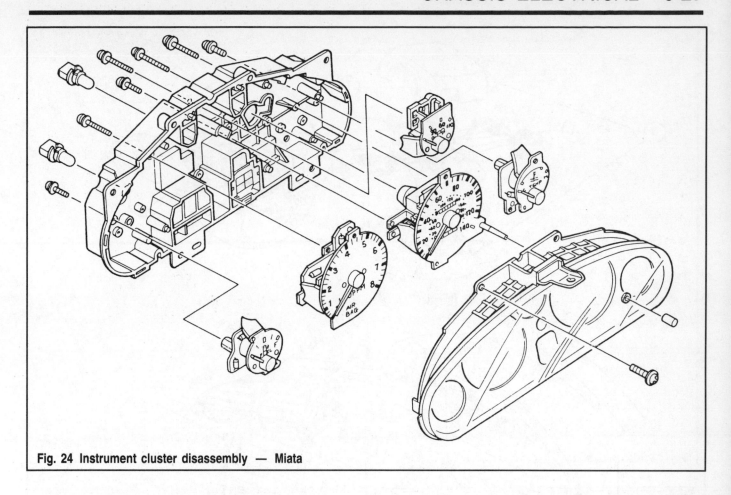

Fig. 24 Instrument cluster disassembly — Miata

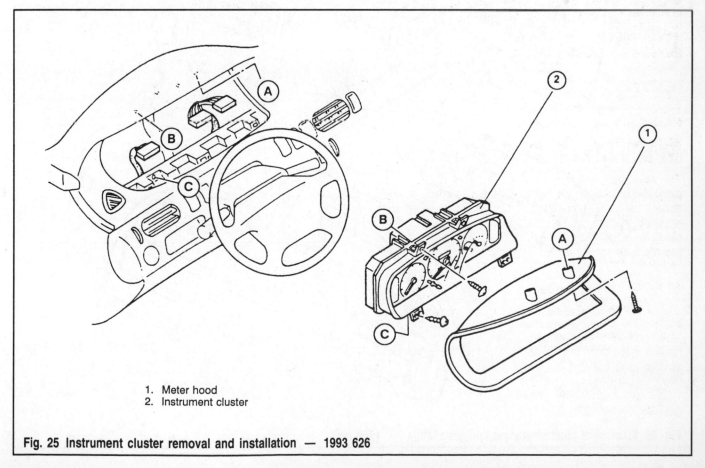

1. Meter hood
2. Instrument cluster

Fig. 25 Instrument cluster removal and installation — 1993 626

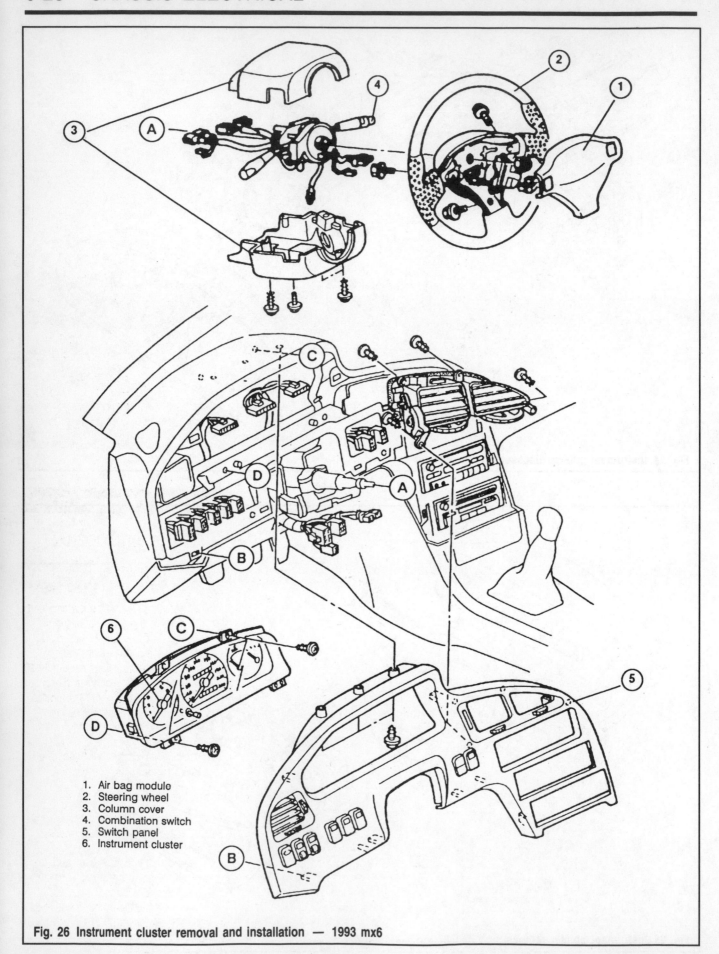

1. Air bag module
2. Steering wheel
3. Column cover
4. Combination switch
5. Switch panel
6. Instrument cluster

Fig. 26 Instrument cluster removal and installation — 1993 mx6

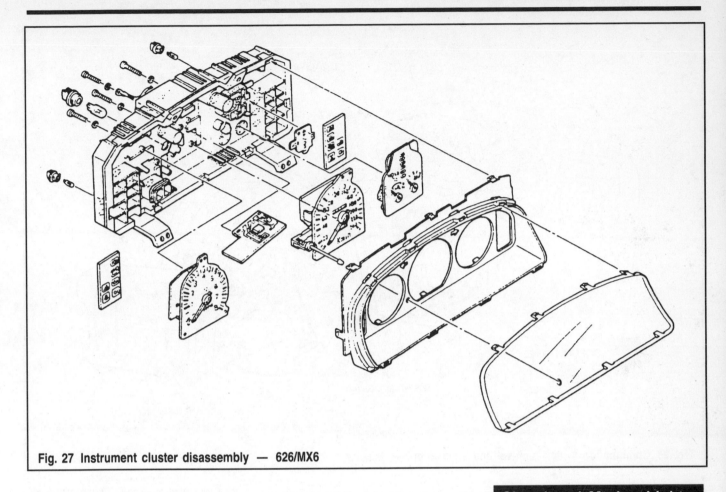

Fig. 27 Instrument cluster disassembly — 626/MX6

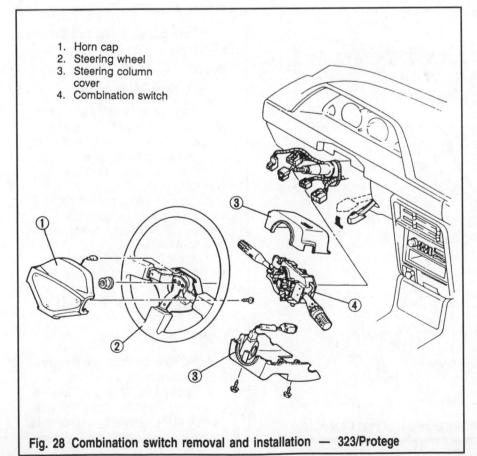

1. Horn cap
2. Steering wheel
3. Steering column cover
4. Combination switch

Fig. 28 Combination switch removal and installation — 323/Protege

Signal and Marker Lights

REMOVAL & INSTALLATION

Front Turn Signal and Parking Lights

1. Remove the attaching screws and partially remove the front parking light lens.

2. Remove the bulb socket and rubber gasket from the lens assembly by turning it in a counterclockwise direction.

3. Remove the bulb from the socket by carefully pushing it in to clear the socket slots and twisting it counterclockwise.

4. Installation is the reverse of the removal procedure.

Front Side Marker Lights

1. Remove the attaching screws and partially remove the front side marker light lens.

2. Remove the bulb socket and rubber gasket from the lens by turning it in a clockwise direction.

3. Remove the bulb from the socket by carefully pushing it in to clear the socket slots and twisting it counterclockwise.

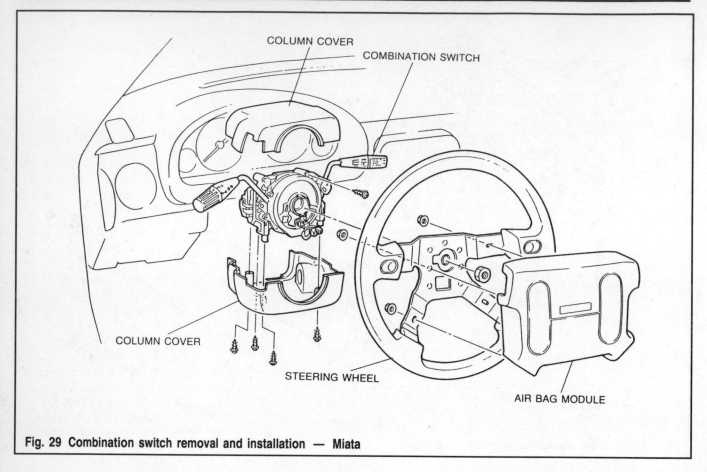

Fig. 29 Combination switch removal and installation — Miata

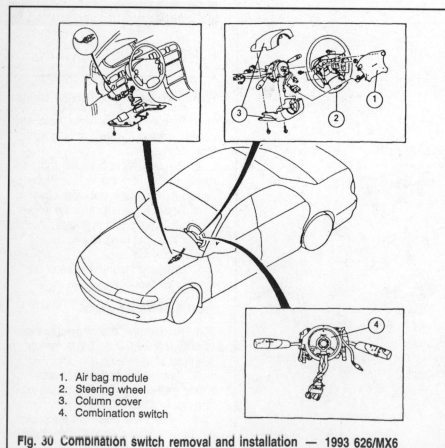

1. Air bag module
2. Steering wheel
3. Column cover
4. Combination switch

Fig. 30 Combination switch removal and installation — 1993 626/MX6

4. Installation is the reverse of the removal procedure.

Rear Turn Signal, Brake and Parking Lights

BULBS

▶ See Figures 35, 36 and 37

1. Remove the plastic fasteners securing the trunk end trim panel and remove the panel (Refer to Section 10). Remove the right side upper trunk side garnish to gain access to the far right side bulb.

2. Carefully remove the desired socket wiring from its respective retaining clip and turn it counterclockwise to remove the socket.

3. Carefully push the bulb in far enough to clear the socket slots, turn it counterclockwise and remove.

4. Installation is the reverse of the removal procedure.

LENS

1. Remove the trunk end trim panel. Refer to Section 10.

2. Remove the upper trunk side garnish and lower trunk side trim from the side of the vehicle that needs to be removed.

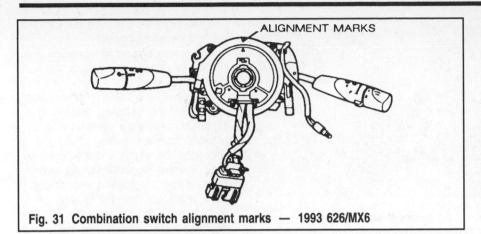

Fig. 31 Combination switch alignment marks — 1993 626/MX6

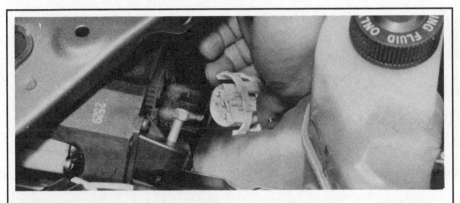

Fig. 32 Disconnecting the headlight bulb electrical connector — All except Miata

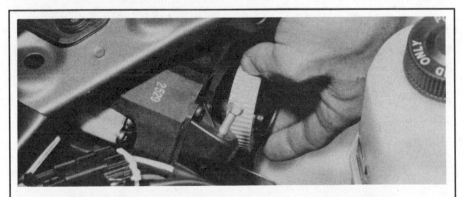

Fig. 33 Removal of headlight bulb retaining ring — All except Miata

3. Disconnect the rear light electrical connector.

4. Remove the attaching nuts from the light assembly.

5. Remove the light assembly and rubber gaskets from the vehicle. The light bulb sockets remain with the light housing during removal.

6. Installation is the reverse of the removal procedure.

High Mount Brake Light

BULB

1. Remove the service window cover from the lower liftgate trim panel.

2. Disconnect the high mount brake light electrical connector.

3. Turn the service arm counterclockwise and remove the bulb/socket assembly.

4. Remove the bulb from the socket by pulling it straight out.

5. Installation is the reverse of the removal procedure.

HOUSING

1. Remove the liftgate side trim panels and the lower liftgate trim panel. Refer to Section 10.

2. Remove the attaching nuts from the light housing and carefully push in on the housing assembly.

3. Remove the housing and gasket assembly through the passenger side of the lift gate.

4. Disconnect the electrical connector.

5. Turn the service arm counterclockwise and remove the bulb/socket assembly.

6. Installation is the reverse of the removal procedure.

Dome Light

1. Disconnect the negative battery cable.

2. Grasp the dome light lens and pull down until the lens is removed.

3. Carefully pull the bulb from its holder. If the bulb is difficult to remove, carefully pry it out with a small piece of wood or equivalent.

4. Check the bulb holder for bent tangs and adjust them, if necessary.

To install:

5. Push the bulb into its holder until it is firmly secured.

6. Position the dome light lens into the holder, then push up on the lens until it snaps into position.

7. Connect the negative battery cable.

Cargo Area Light

1. Disconnect the negative battery cable.

2. Carefully remove the cargo light lens from its housing.

3. Carefully pull the bulb from its holder. If the bulb is difficult to remove, carefully pry it out with a small piece of wood or equivalent.

4. Check the bulb holder for bent tangs and adjust them, if necessary.

To install:

5. Push the bulb into its holder until it is firmly secured.

6. Position the cargo lens onto its housing and fasten the lens to the housing.

7. Connect the negative battery cable.

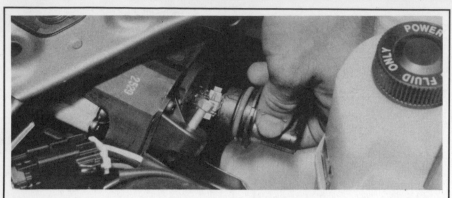

Fig. 34 Removal of the headlight bulb — All except Miata

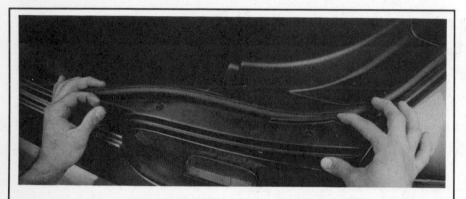

Fig. 35 Removal and installation of rear lens bulb access panel — MX-3

Rear Console Light

1. Disconnect the negative battery cable.

2. Carefully remove the rear console light lens.

3. Remove the bulb by pulling it straight out of the socket.

4. Installation is the reverse of the removal procedure.

License Plate Lights

1. Loosen, but do not completely remove the attaching screws on the light lens. Remove the license plate lens assembly.

2. Remove the bulb by pulling it straight down and away from the socket.

3. Installation is the reverse of the removal procedure.

Fog Lights

REMOVAL & INSTALLATION

1. Disconnect the negative battery cable.

2. Remove the mounting nut from the fog light mounting bracket.

3. Remove the fog light housing and bracket as an assembly through the front fascia of the vehicle.

4. Remove the attaching screws from the fog light lens retaining brackets at the housing. Carefully remove the lens assembly from the housing, then disconnect the electrical connectors.

5. Remove the wire retaining rubber grommet from the housing and remove the wire harness from the housing.

6. Remove the mounting nut from the mounting bracket and remove the bracket from the fog light housing.

7. Remove the bulb as follows:

    a. Carefully remove the rubber grommet from the lens assembly.

    b. Release the bulb retaining bracket by pushing in on the release tabs and pulling up.

    c. Remove the bulb assembly from the housing by pulling it straight out of the lens.

8. Installation is the reverse of the removal procedure. Make sure the bulb is correctly piloted into the lens assembly.

❋❋CAUTION

The halogen fog light bulb contains gas under pressure. The bulb may shatter if the glass envelope is scratched or the bulb is dropped. Handle the bulb carefully. Grasp the bulb only by its base. Avoid touching the glass envelope. Keep the bulb out of the reach of children.

CIRCUIT PROTECTION

Fuses

▶ **See Figures 38, 39 and 40**

The main fuse block is located inside the left side of the engine compartment near the battery. There is also an interior fuse panel located just above the left side kick panel.

REPLACEMENT

Main Fuse Block

1. Disconnect the negative battery cable.

2. Unhook the lock tab from the main fuse block cover and open the cover.

3. Pull the fuse from the main fuse holder.

4. Installation is the reverse of the removal procedure.

Interior Fuse Panel

The interior fuses simply unplug from the fuse panel. Use the fuse puller tool provided with your car to remove fuses from the panel. The tool is located on the back of the interior fuse panel cover.

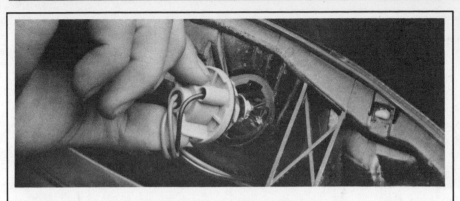

Fig. 36 Removal and installation of rear light bulb — MX-3

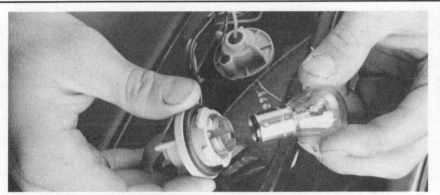

Fig. 37 Disconnecting rear light bulb — MX-3

Circuit Breaker

A bimetal circuit breaker is located in the joint box, which is just above the interior fuse panel. This circuit breaker protects the rear window defrost circuit and is the plug-in type.

Relays

The main relay box is located on the upper left-hand side of the firewall (bulkhead). There is also a relay box mounted inside the vehicle under the left side of the instrument panel.

REPLACEMENT

1. Disconnect the negative battery cable.
2. If replacing a relay at the main relay box, disconnect the electrical connector and slide the relay from its mounting bracket.
3. If replacing a relay at the interior relay box, simply unplug the relay.
4. Installation is the reverse of the removal procedure.

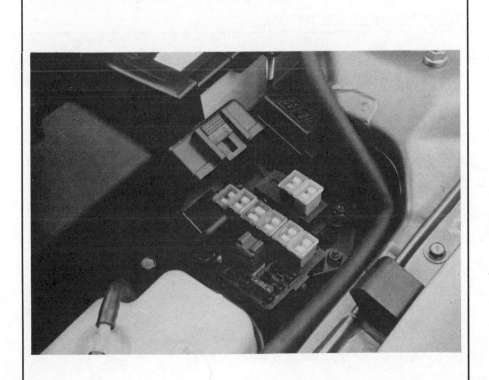

Fig. 39 Underhood fuse/relay box

Fig. 38 Underhood fuse/relay box

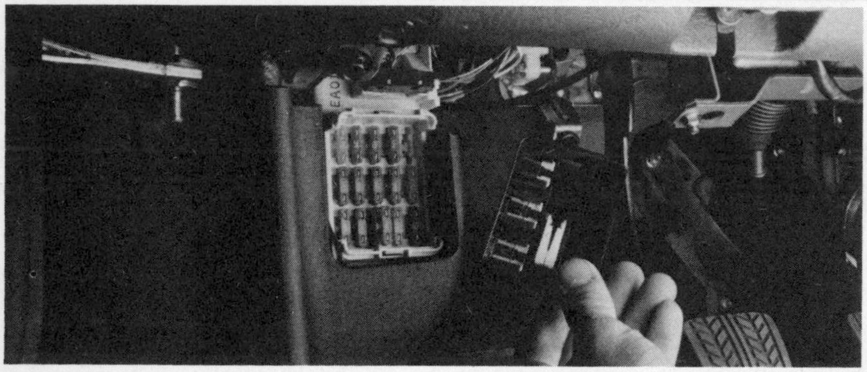

Fig. 40 Underdash fuse box

TORQUE SPECIFICATIONS

Component	U.S.	Metric
Air conditioner compressor-to-bracket bolts;		
323/Protege and MX-3	17–26 ft. lbs.	24–35 Nm
Miata	10–16 ft. lbs.	15–22 Nm
1990–92 626/MX-6	17–26 ft. lbs.	24–35 Nm
1993 626/MX-6 with KL engine	23–34 ft. lbs.	31–46 Nm
1993 626/MX-6 with FS engine upper bolt	32–45 ft. lbs.	44–61 Nm
1993 626/MX-6 with FS engine lower bolt	28–38 ft. lbs.	38–52 Nm
Compressor inlet and outlet lines	8–11 ft. lbs.	10–16 Nm
Expansion valve-to-evaporator inlet fitting;		
323/Protege and 1990–92 626/MX-6	22–25 ft. lbs.	30–34 Nm
Discharge fitting-to-expansion valve;		
323/Protege	9–10 ft. lbs.	12–14 Nm
Air conditioner suction tube fitting;		
323/Protege	9–10 ft. lbs.	12–14 Nm

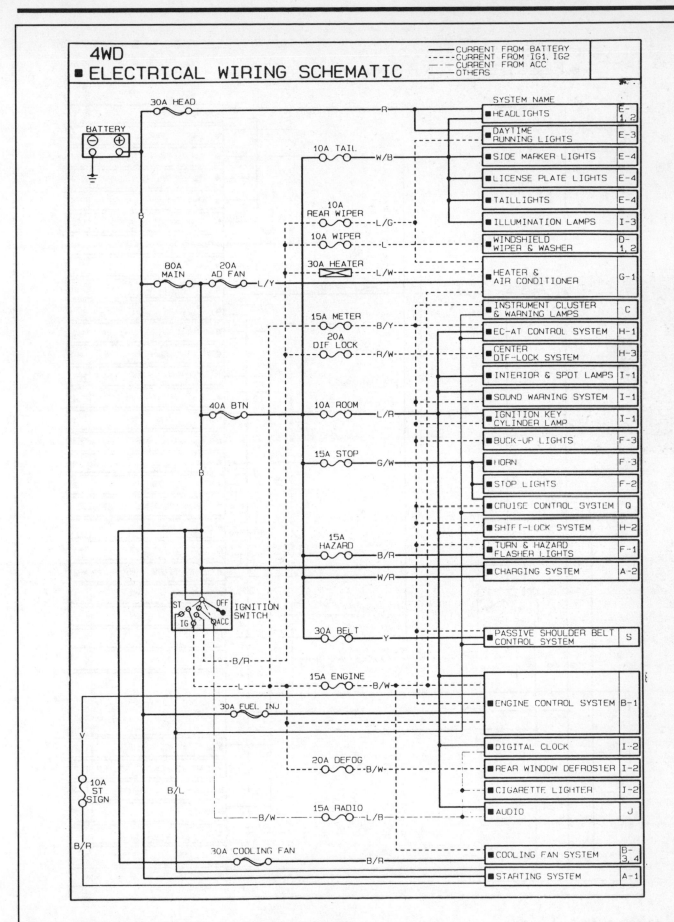

Fig. 41 1990-91 323/Protege 4WD electrcial wiring schematic

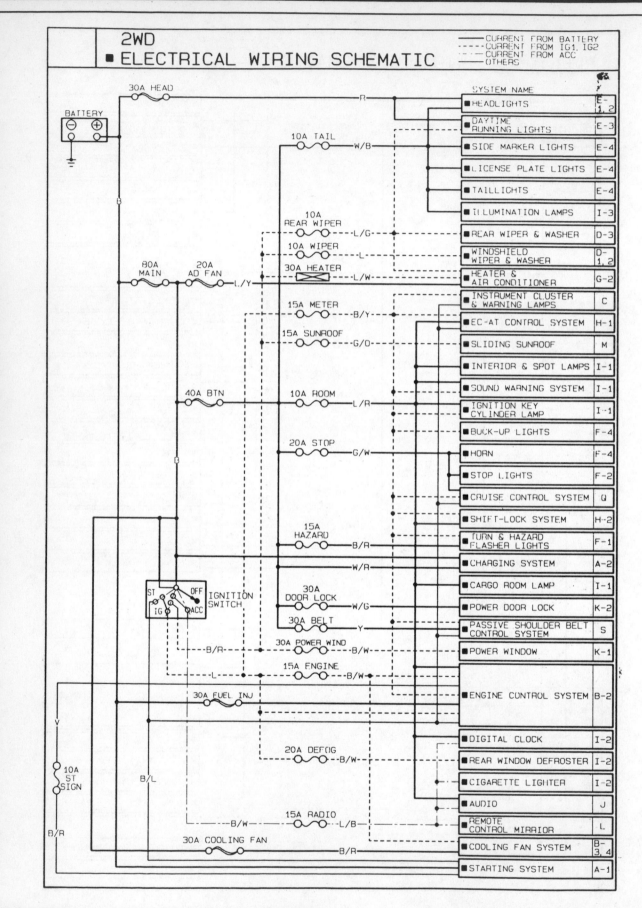

Fig. 42 1990-91 323/Protege 2WD electrical wiring schematic

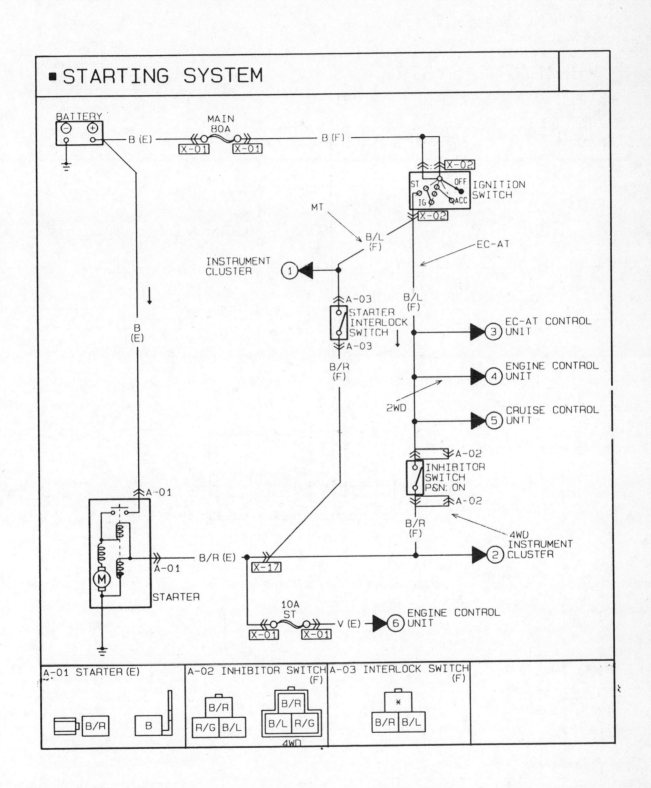

Fig. 43 Starting system — 1990-91 323/Protege

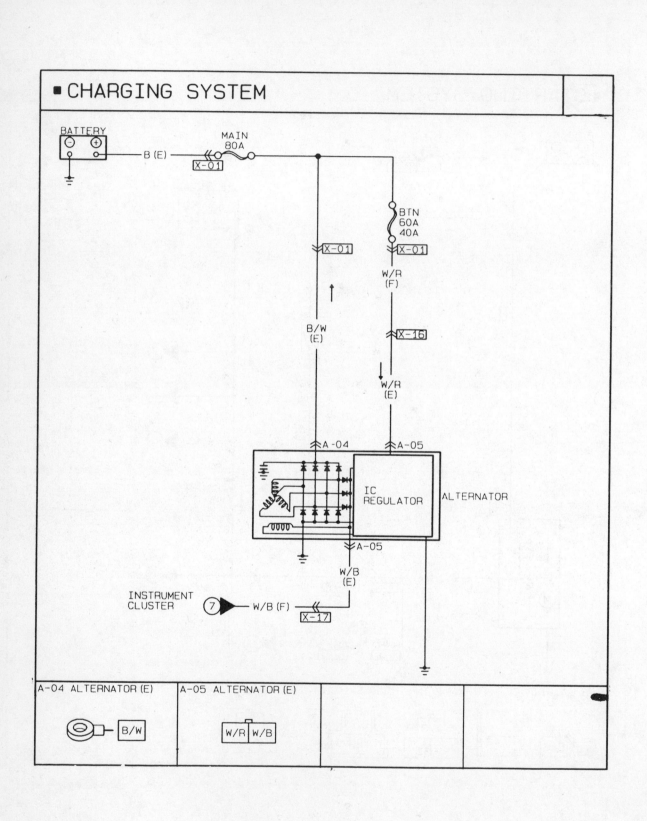

Fig. 44 Charging system — 1990-91 323/Protege

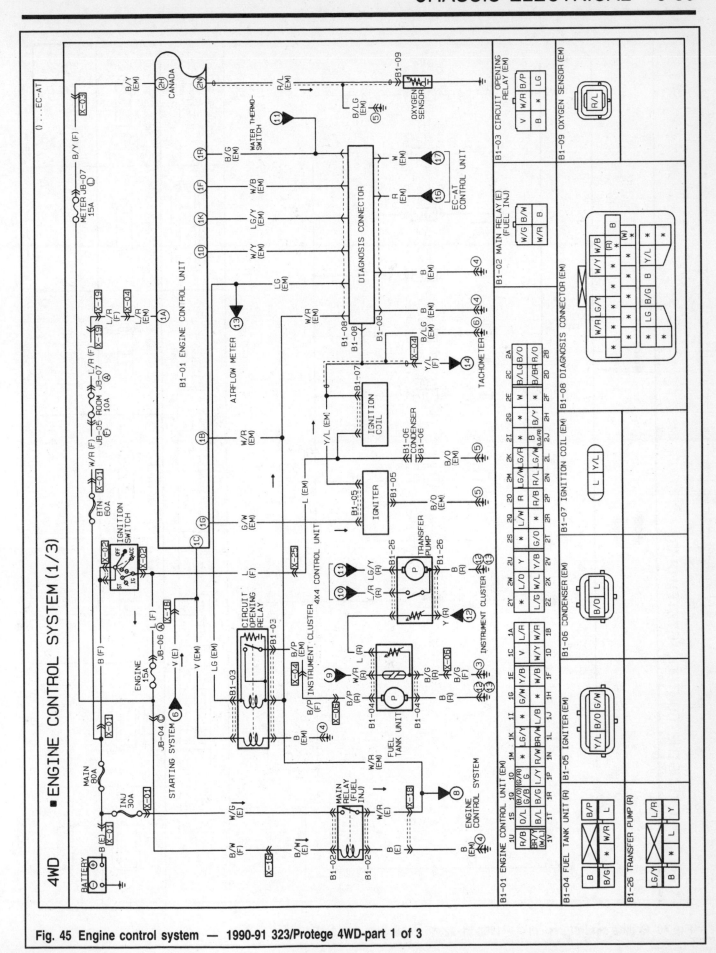

Fig. 45 Engine control system — 1990-91 323/Protege 4WD-part 1 of 3

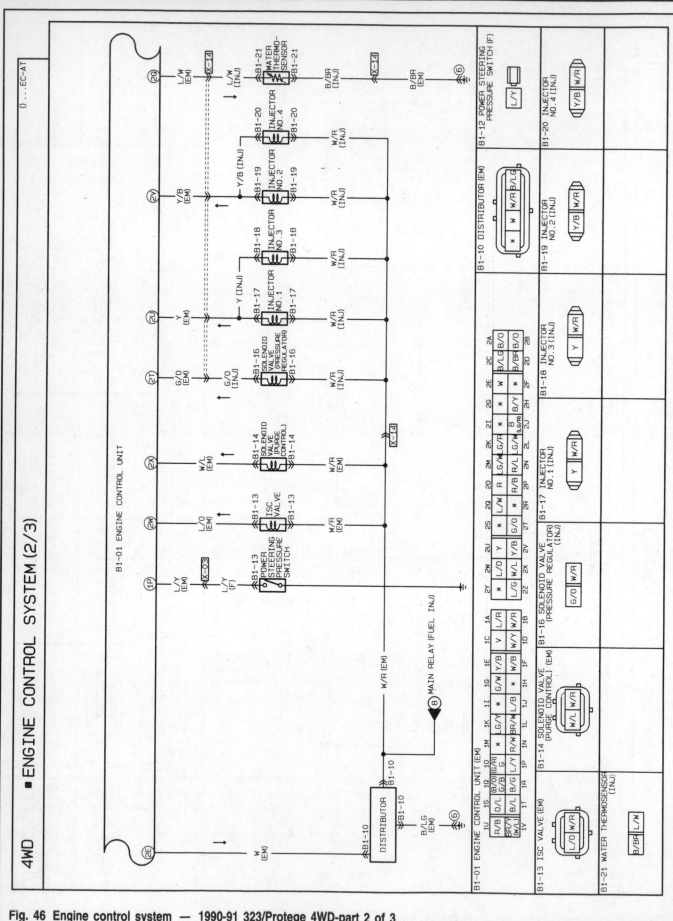

Fig. 46 Engine control system — 1990-91 323/Protege 4WD-part 2 of 3

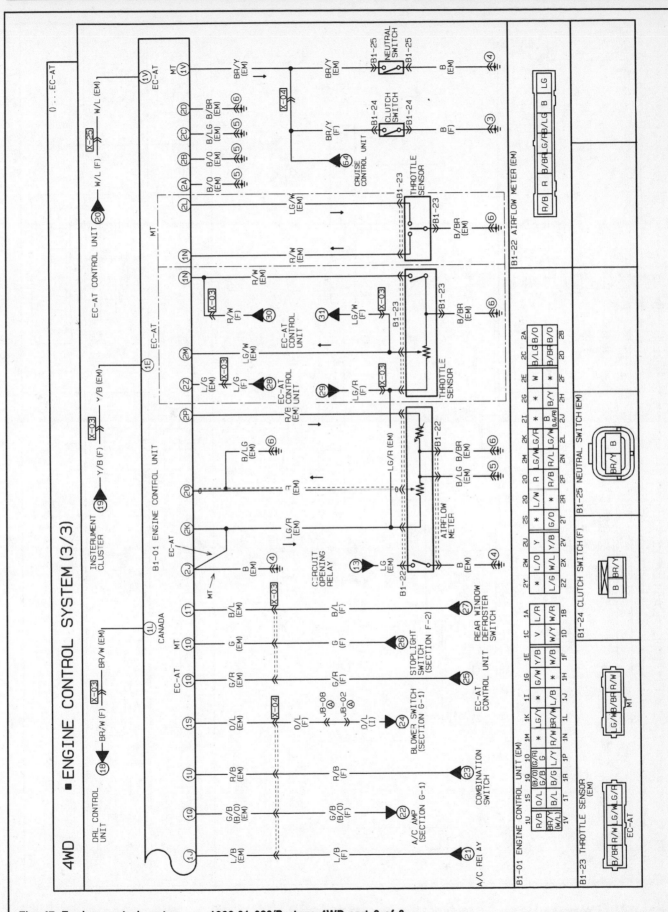

Fig. 47 Engine control system — 1990-91 323/Protege 4WD-part 3 of 3

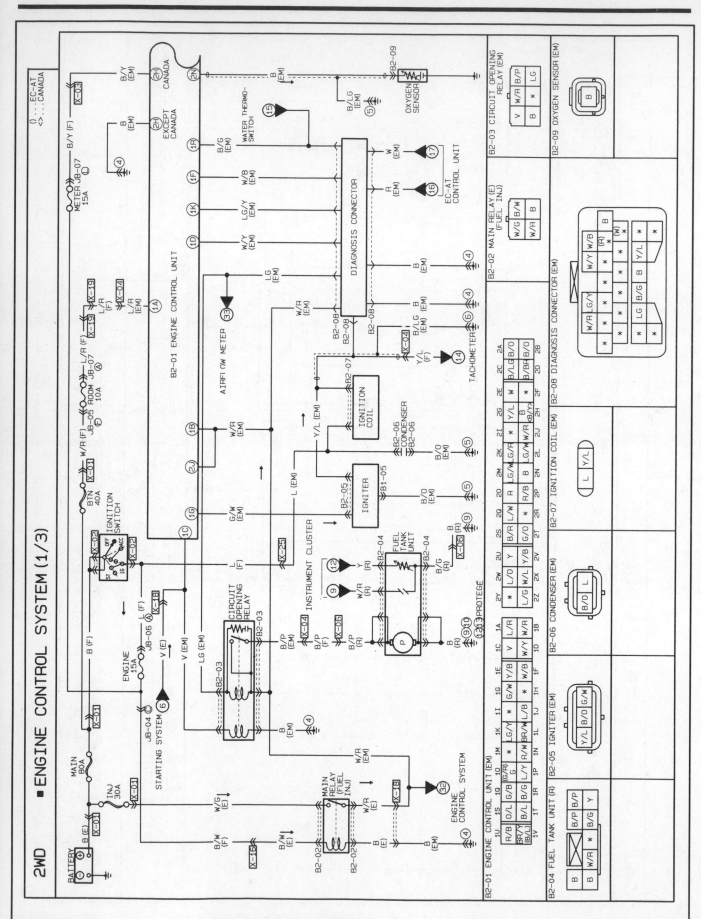

Fig. 48 Engine control system — 1990-91 323/Protege 2WD-part 1 of 3

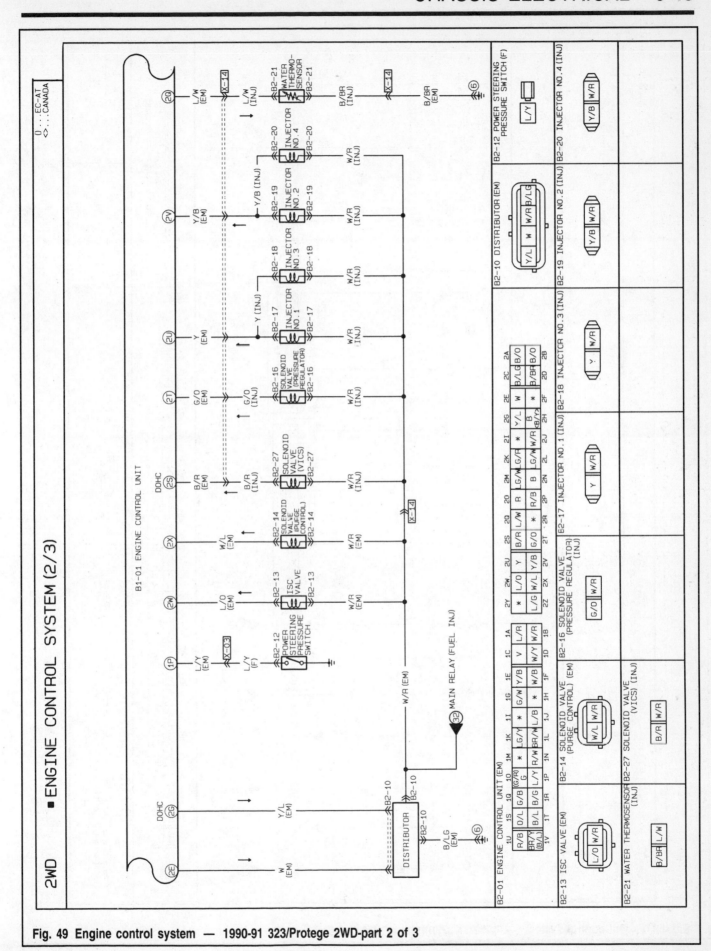

Fig. 49 Engine control system — 1990-91 323/Protege 2WD-part 2 of 3

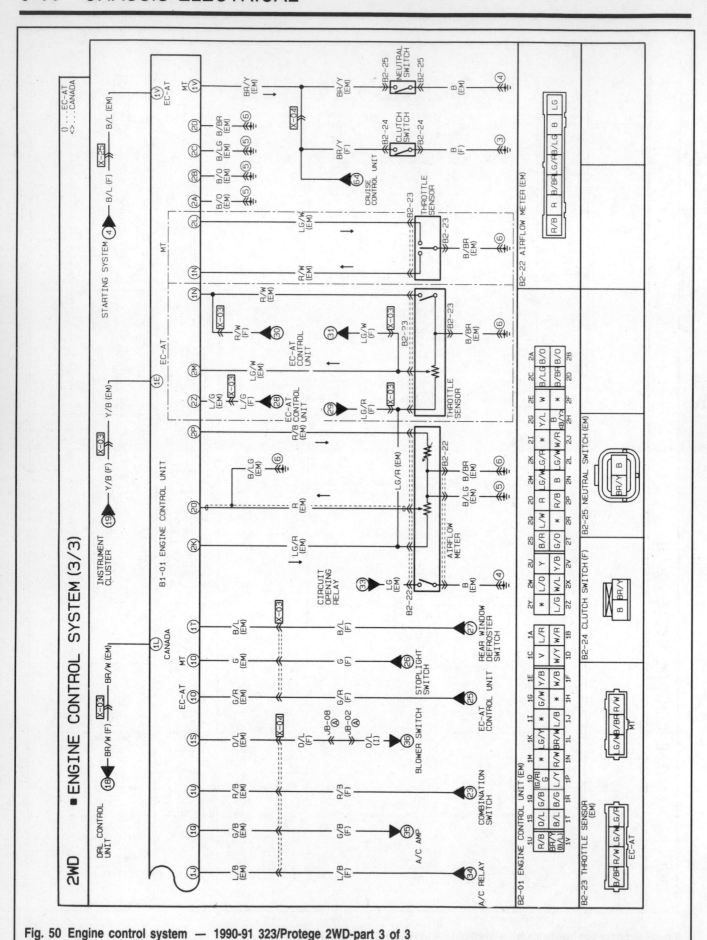

Fig. 50 Engine control system — 1990-91 323/Protege 2WD-part 3 of 3

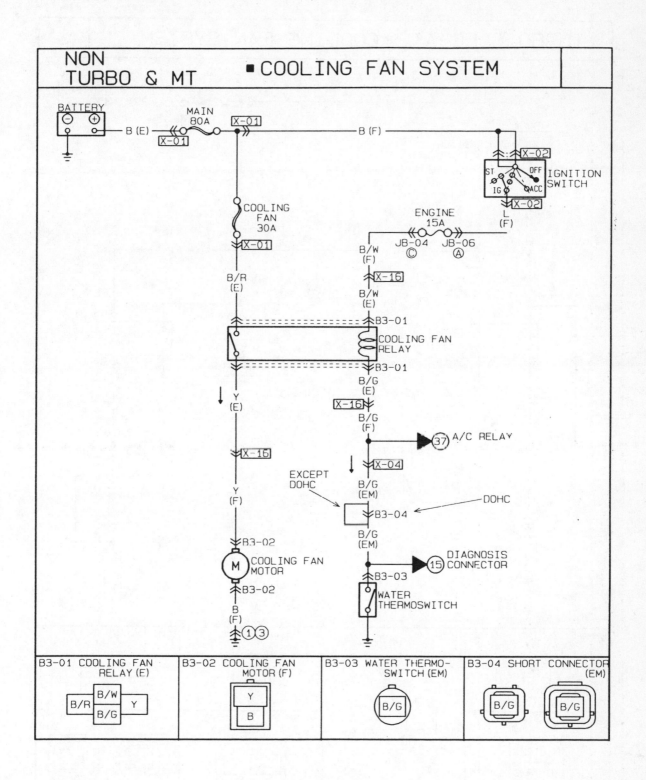

Fig. 51 Cooling fan system wiring diagram — 1990-91 323/Protege Non-turbo and M/T

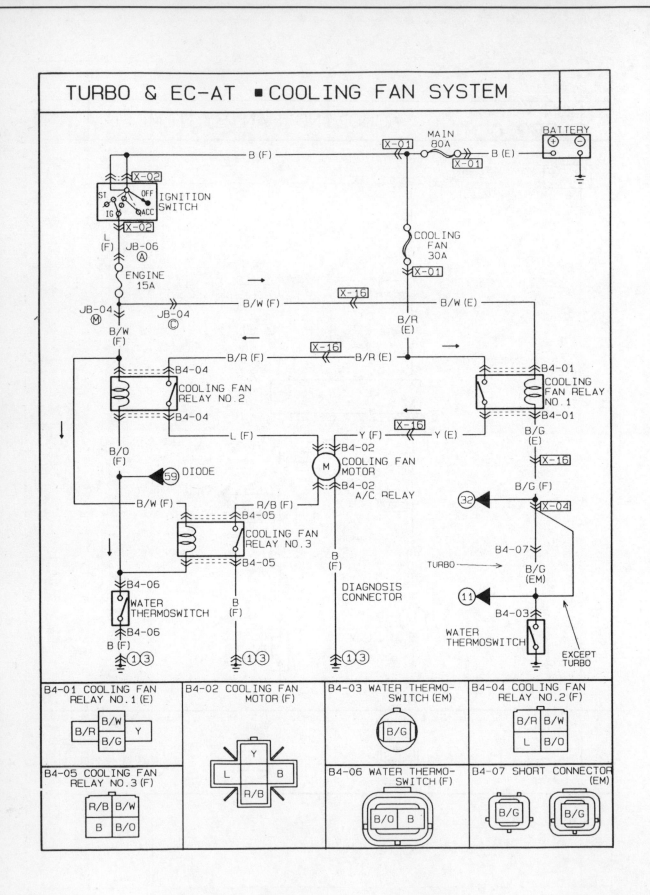

Fig. 52 Cooling fan system wiring diagram — 1990-91 323/Protege Turbo and EC-A/T

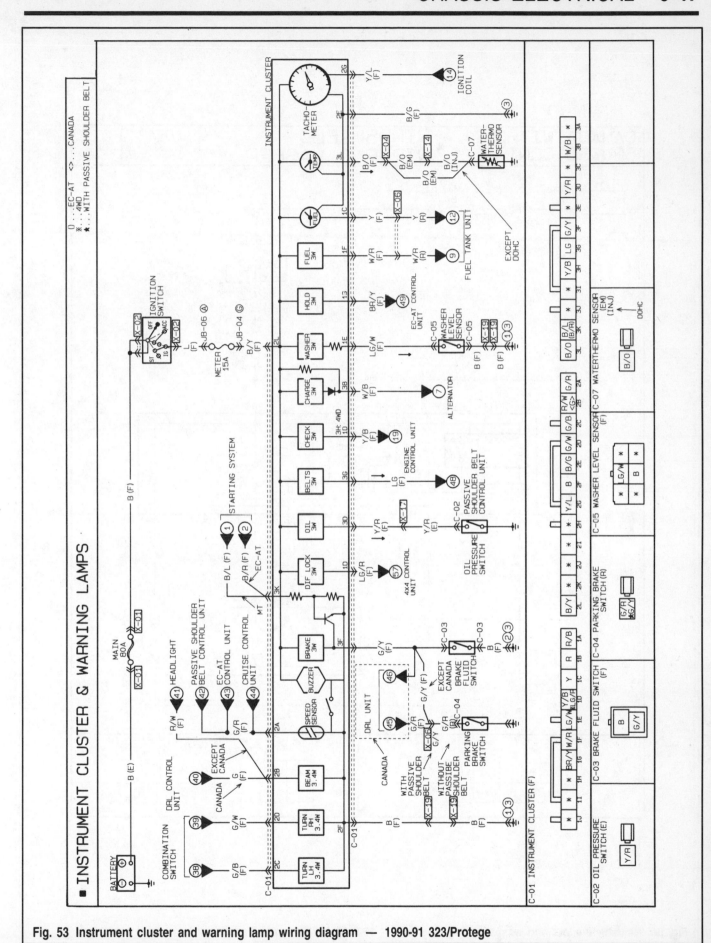

Fig. 53 Instrument cluster and warning lamp wiring diagram — 1990-91 323/Protege

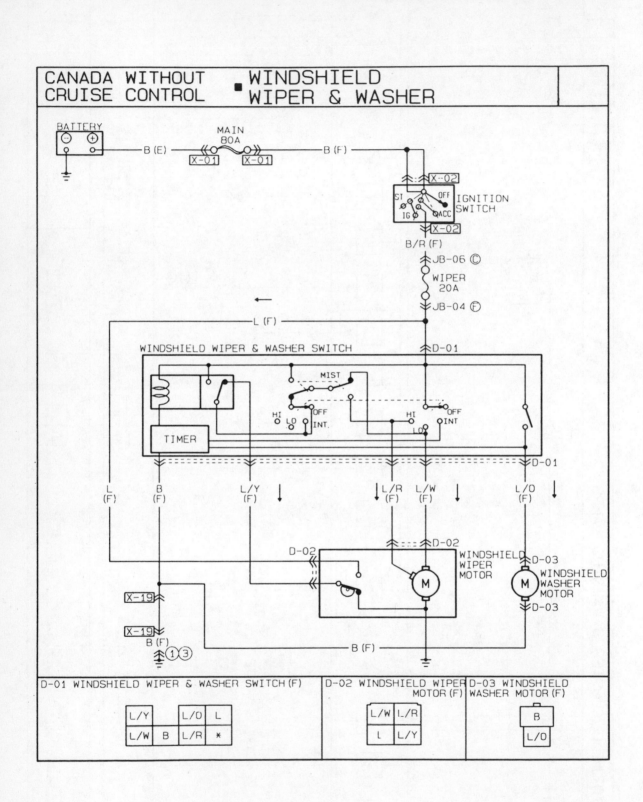

Fig. 54 Windshield wiper and washer wiring diagram — 1990-91 323/Protege - Canada without cruise control

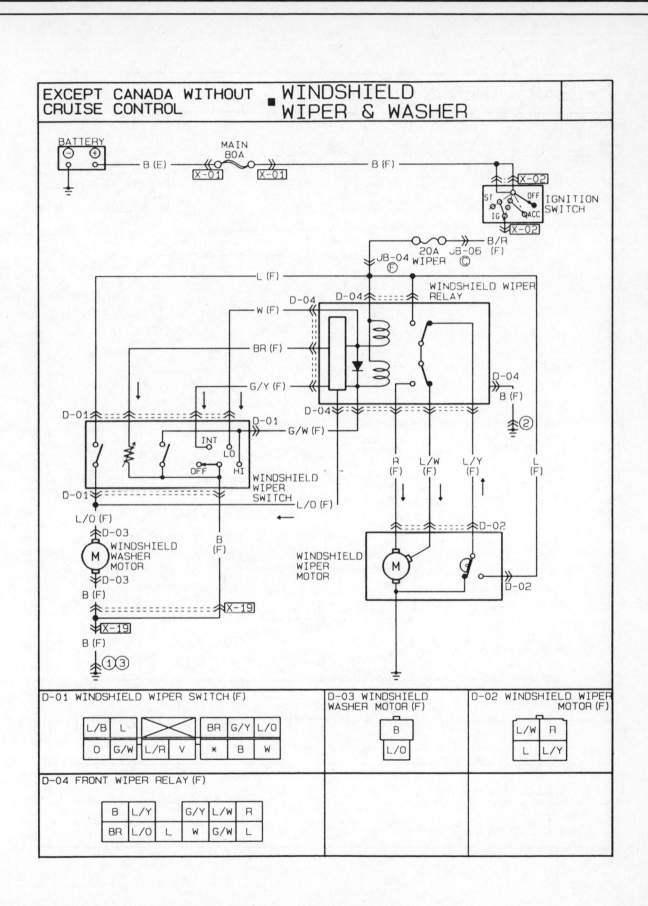

Fig. 55 Windshield wiper and washer wiring diagram — 1990-91 323/Protege

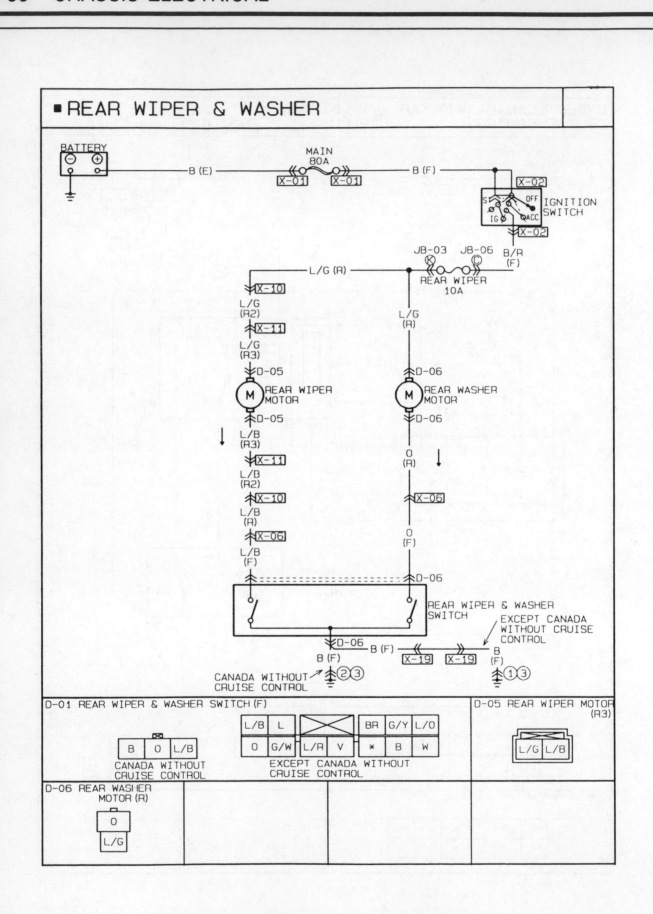

Fig. 56 Rear windshield wiper and washer wiring diagram — 1990-91 323/Protege

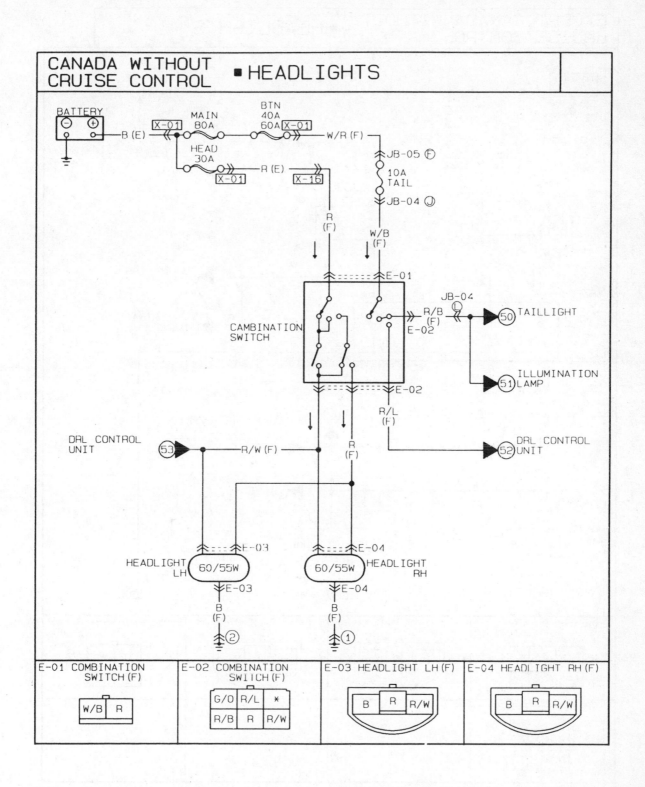

Fig. 57 Headlights wiring diagram — 1990-91 323/Protege - Canada without cruise control

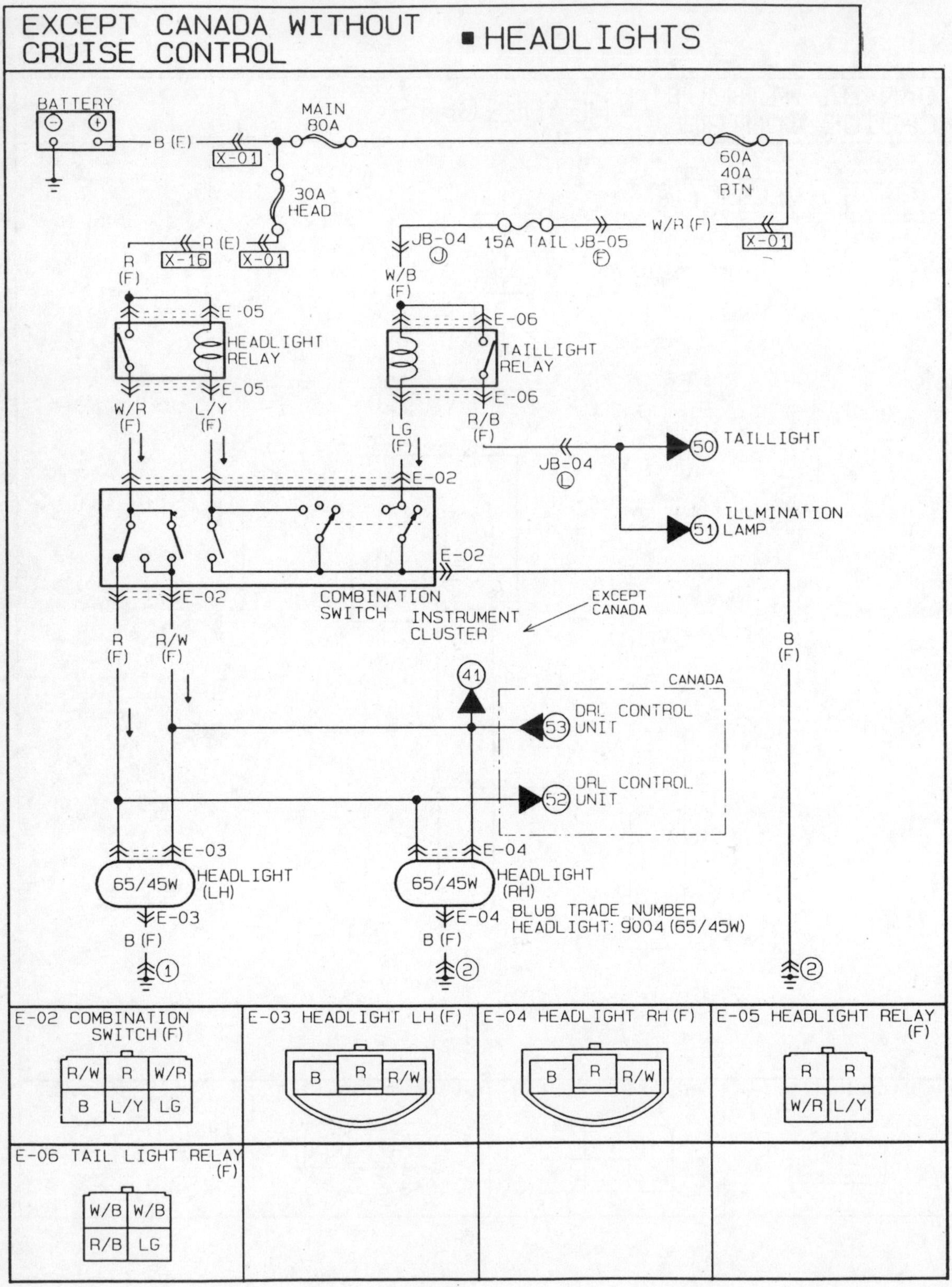

Fig. 58 Headlights wiring diagram — 1990-91 323/Protege

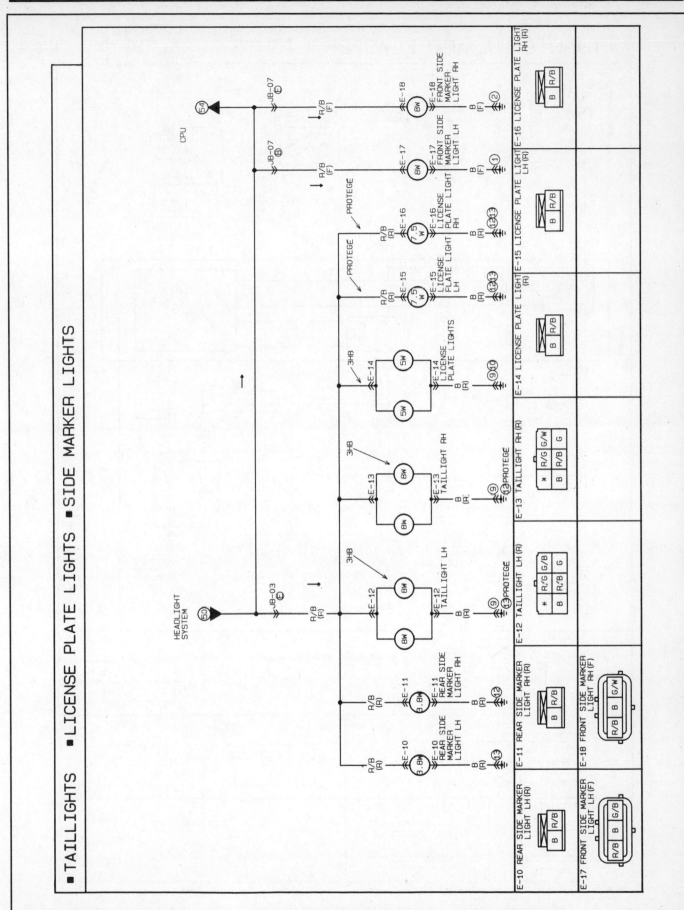

Fig. 59 Taillights, License plate lights and Side marker lights wiring diagram — 1990-91 323/Protege

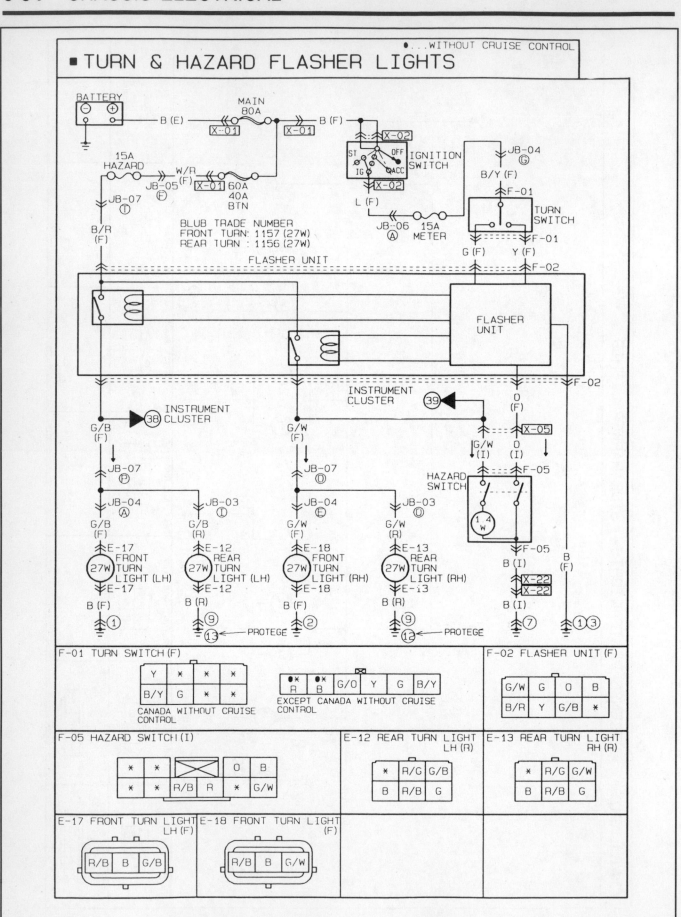

Fig. 60 Turn signal and hazard flasher lights wiring diagram — 1990-91 323/Protege

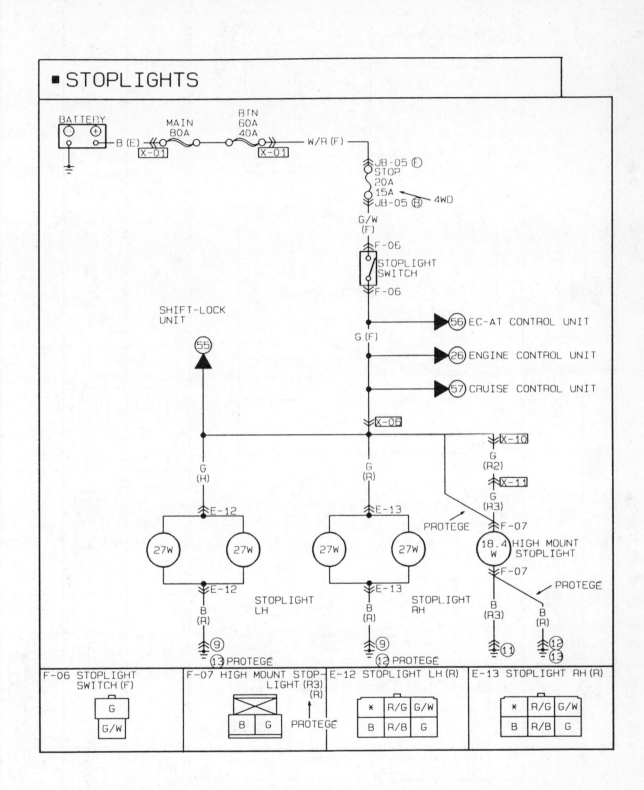

Fig. 61 Stoplights wiring diagram — 1990-91 323/Protege

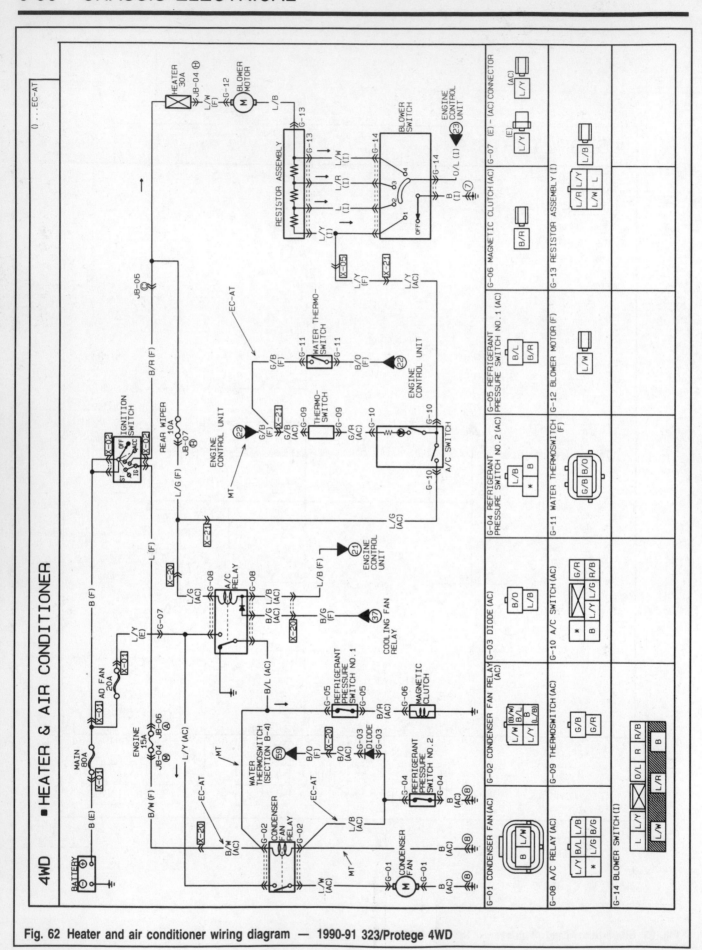

Fig. 62 Heater and air conditioner wiring diagram — 1990-91 323/Protege 4WD

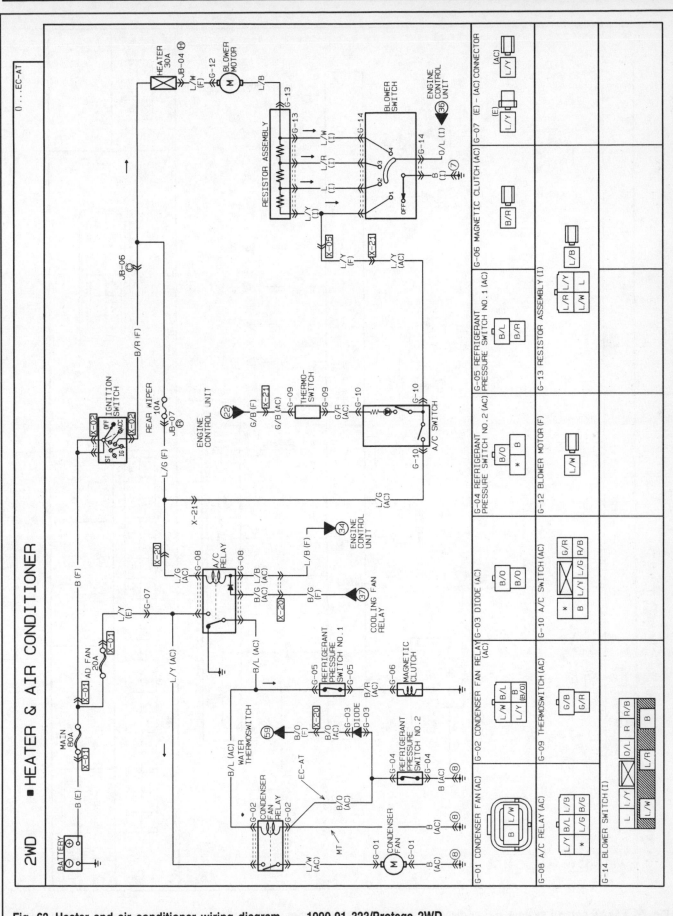

Fig. 63 Heater and air conditioner wiring diagram — 1990-91 323/Protege 2WD

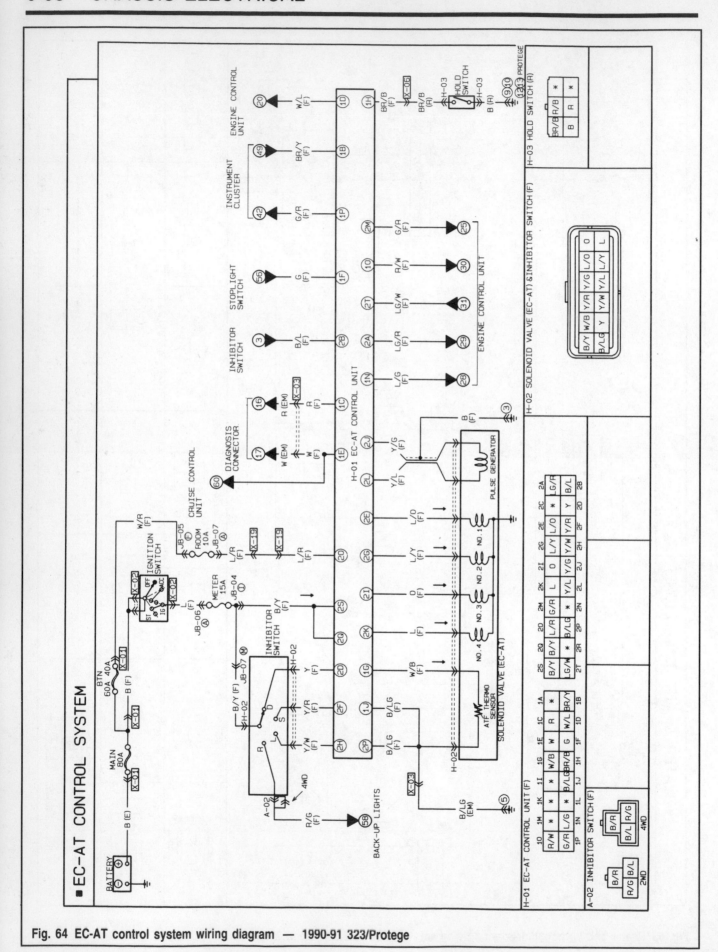

Fig. 64 EC-AT control system wiring diagram — 1990-91 323/Protege

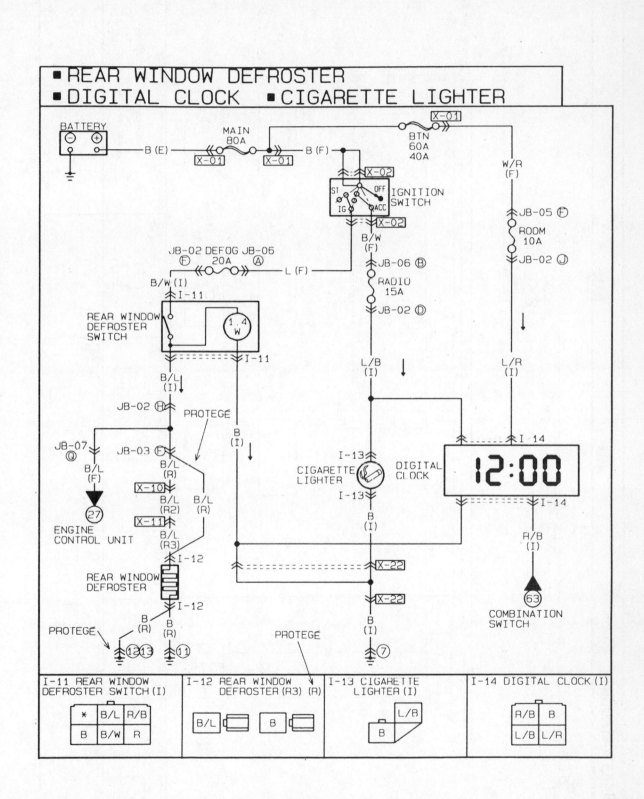

Fig. 65 Rear window defroster/Clock/Lighter wiring diagram — 1990-91 323/Protege

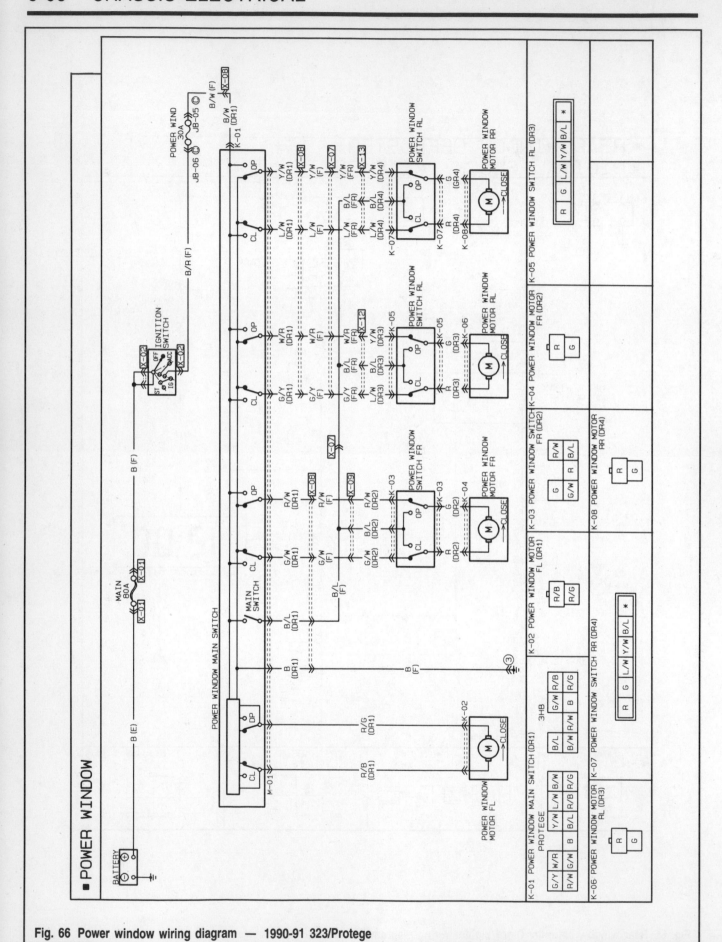

Fig. 66 Power window wiring diagram — 1990-91 323/Protege

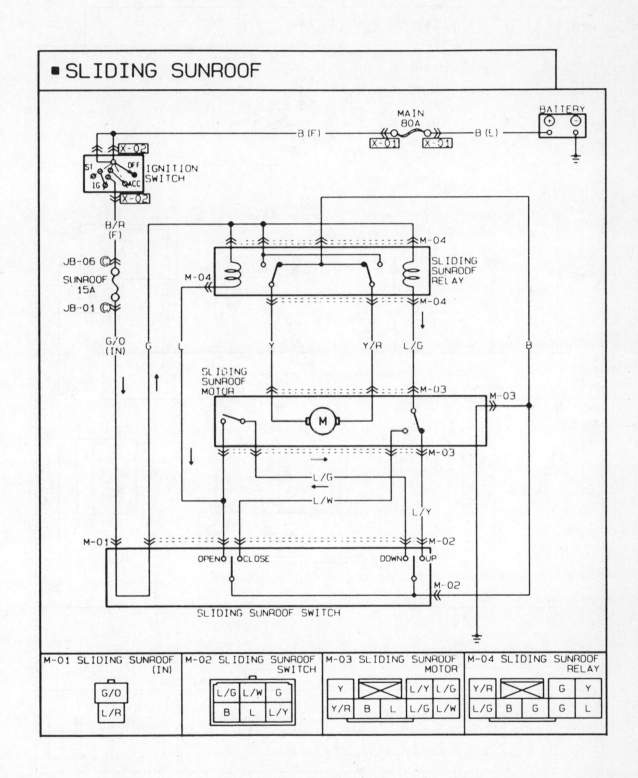

Fig. 67 Power sunroof wirng diagram — 1990-91 323/Protege

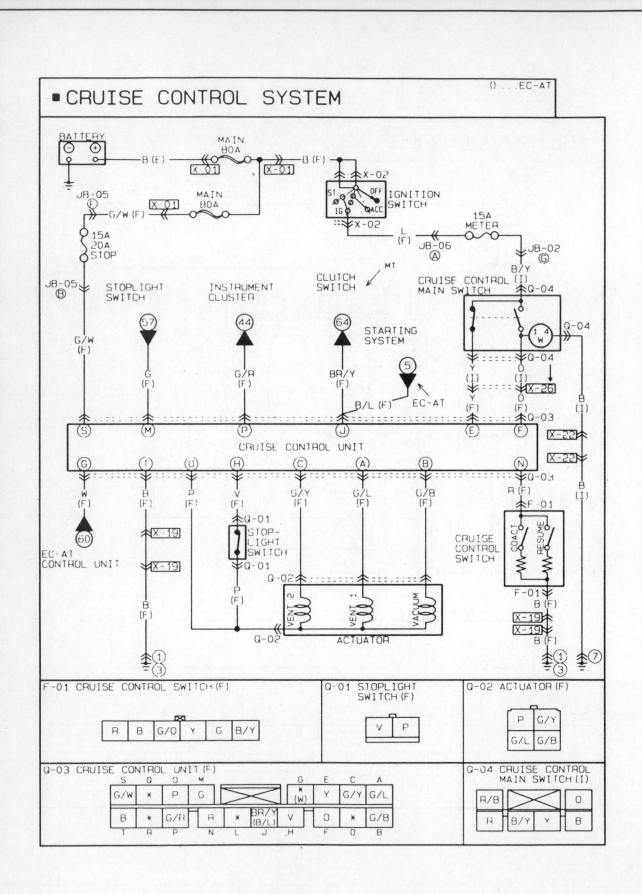

Fig. 68 Cruise control system wiring diagram — 1990-91 323/Protege

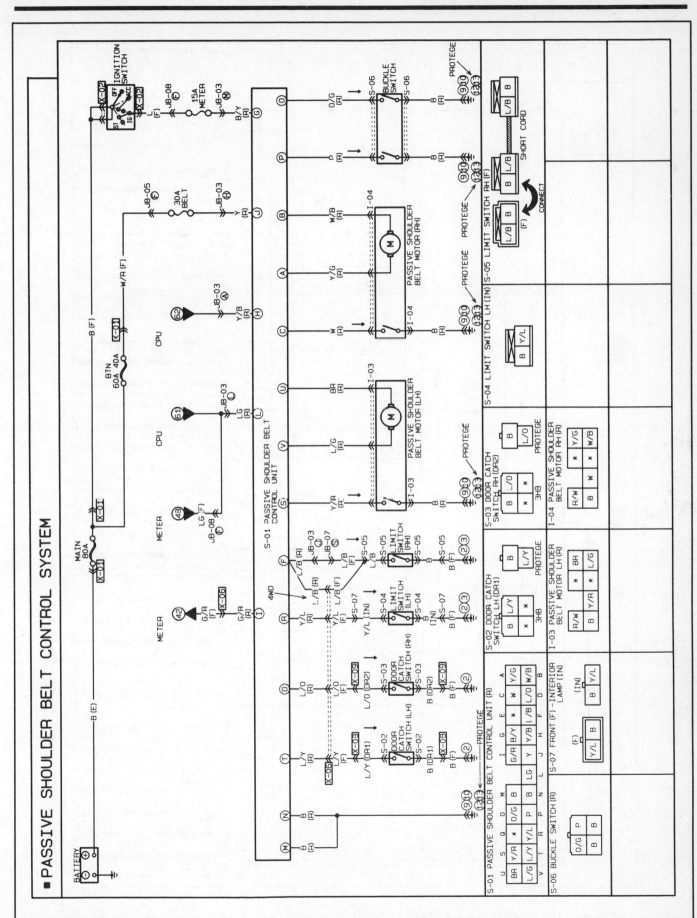

Fig. 69 Passive shoulder seatbelt control system wiring diagram — 1990-91 323/Protege

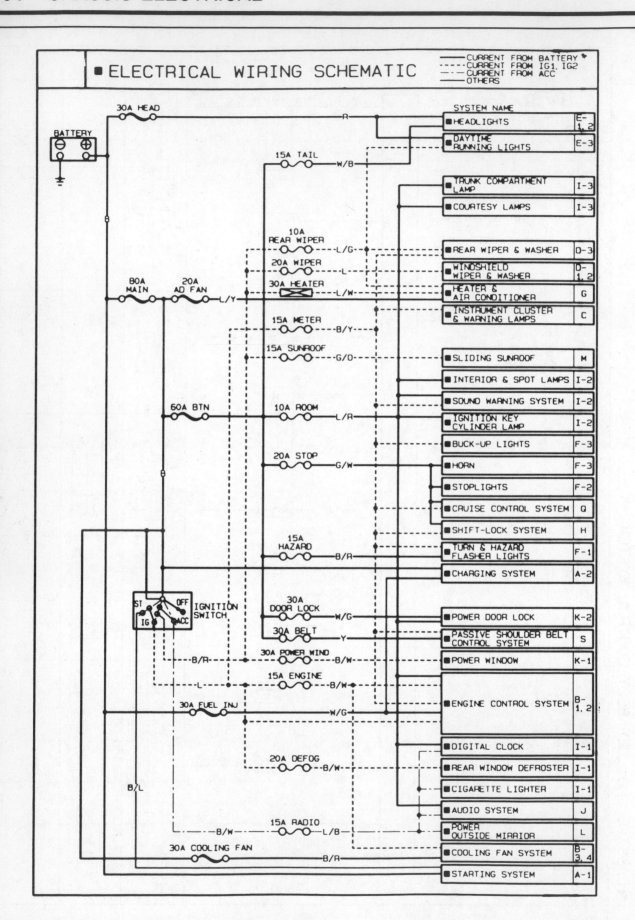

Fig. 70 1992 323/Protege electrical wiring schematic

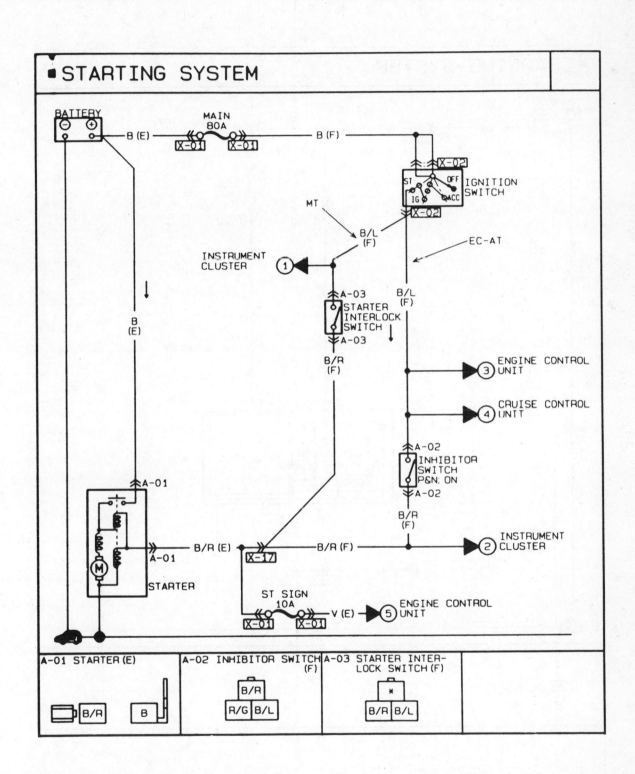

Fig. 71 Starting system — 1992 323/Protege

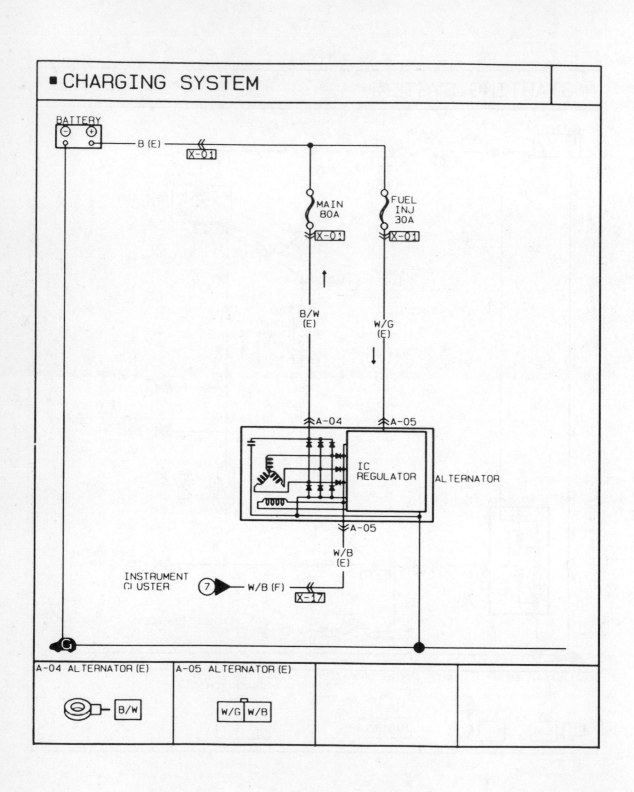

Fig. 72 Charging system — 1992 323/Protege

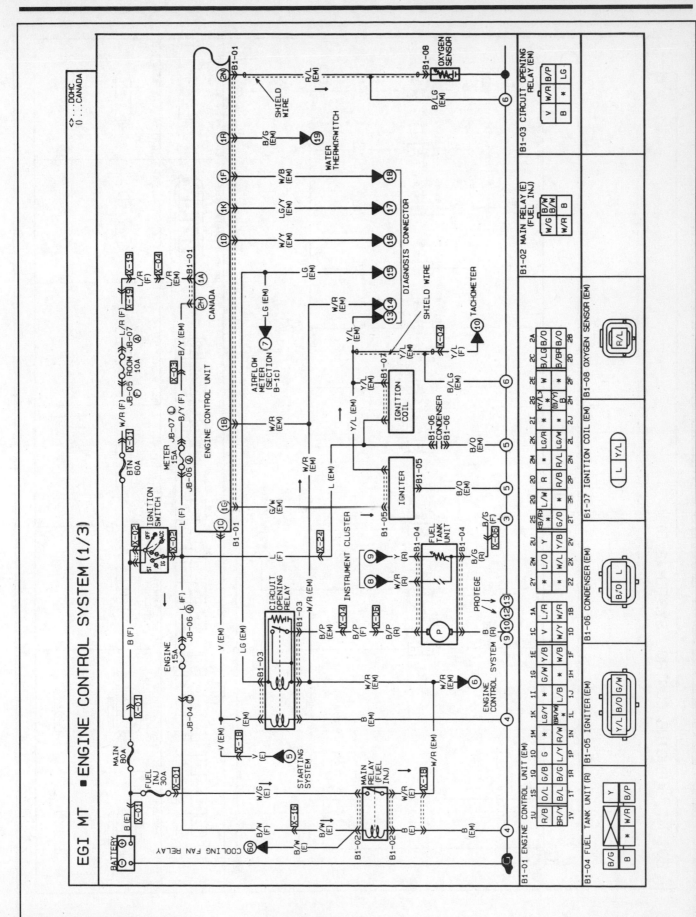

Fig. 73 Engine control system — 1992 323/Protege-part 1 of 3

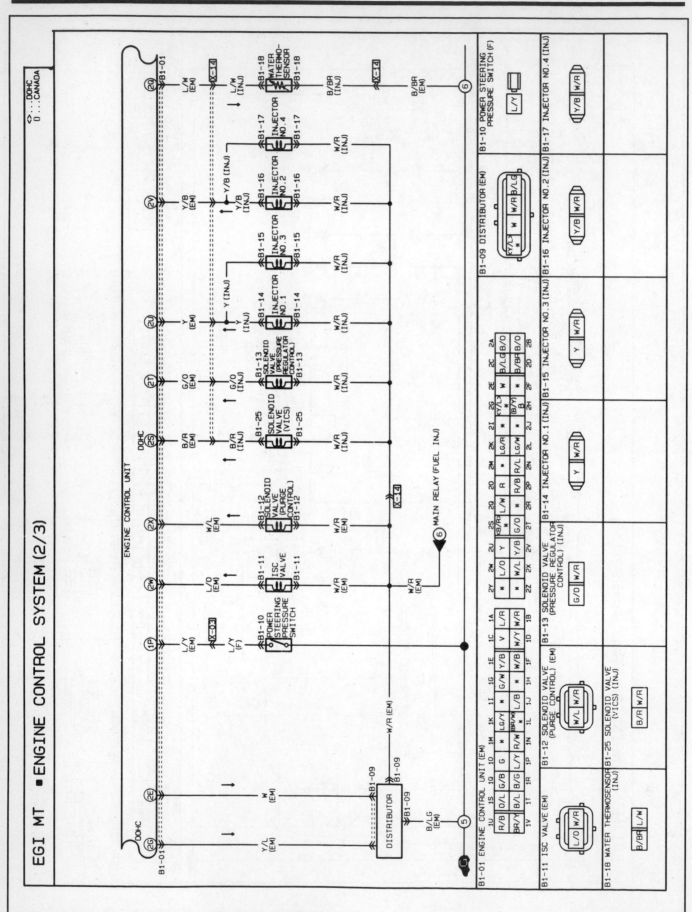

Fig. 74 Engine control system — 1992 323/Protege-part 2 of 3

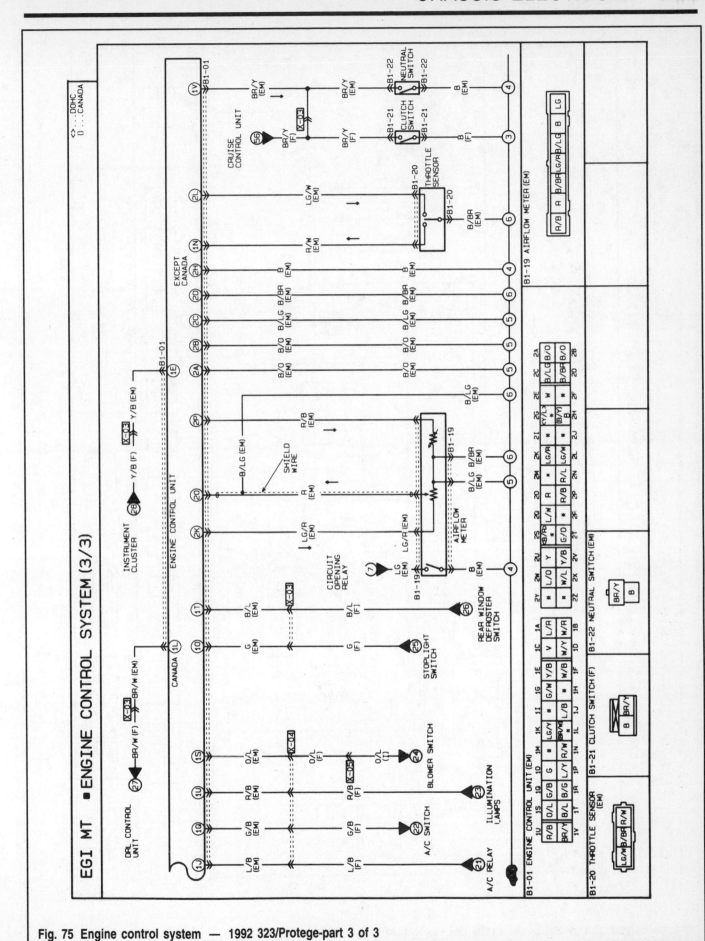

Fig. 75 Engine control system — 1992 323/Protege-part 3 of 3

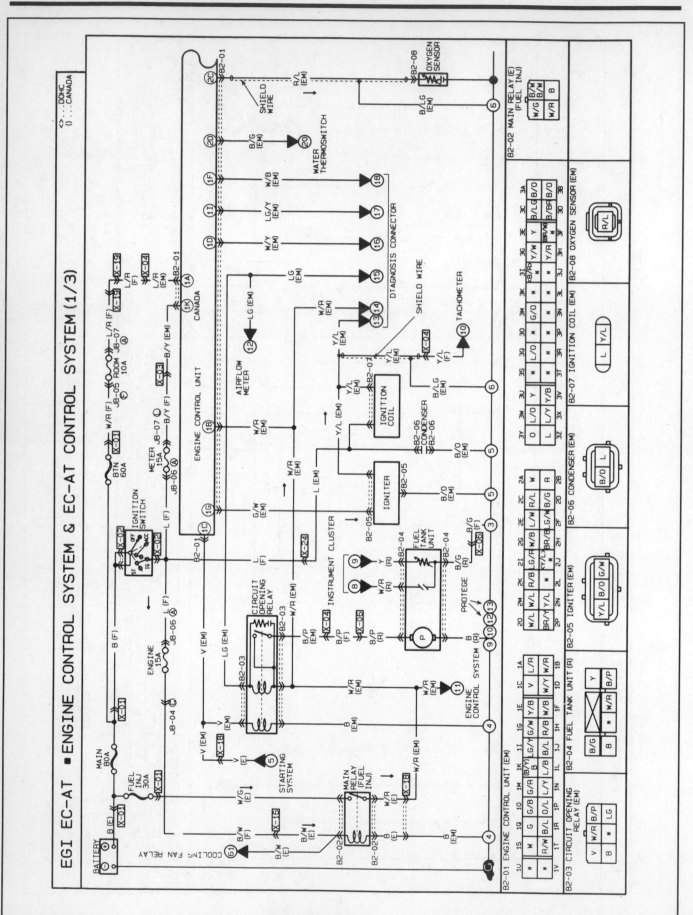

Fig. 76 Engine control and EC-AT system — 1992 323/Protege part 1 of 3

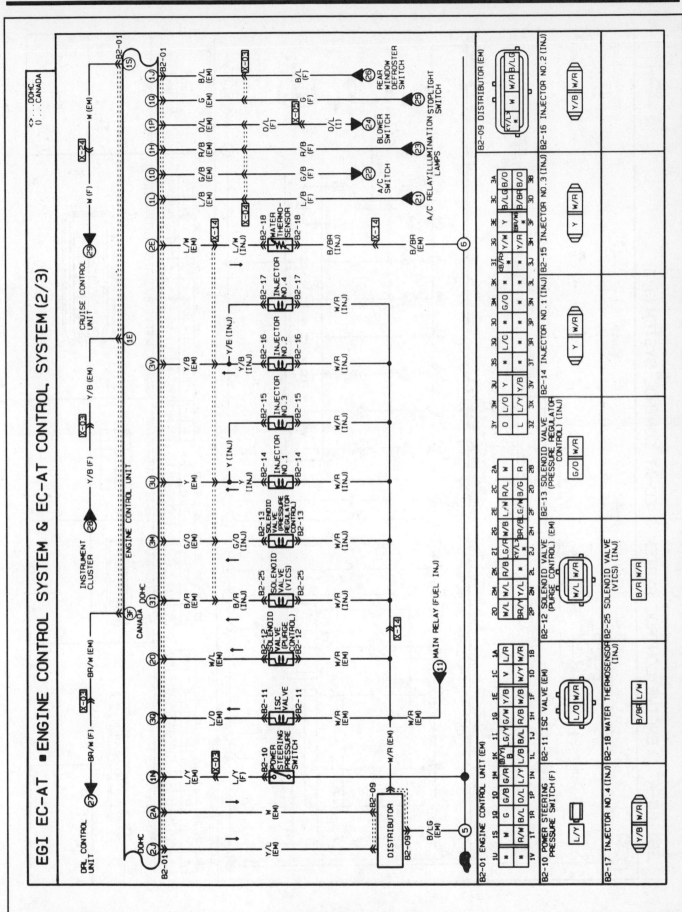

Fig. 77 Engine control and EC-AT system — 1992 323/Protege-part 2 of 3

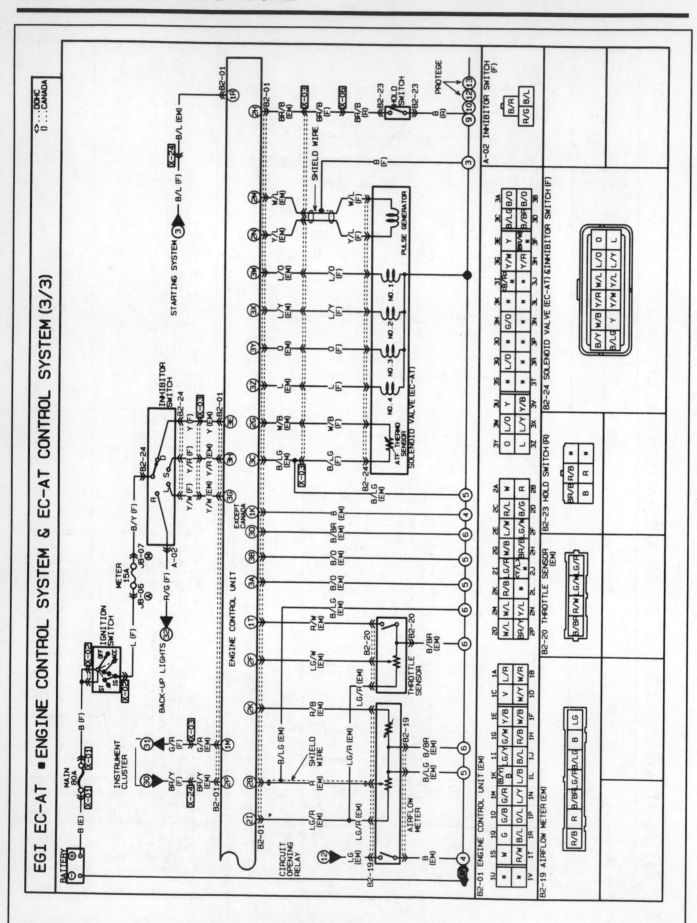

Fig. 78 Engine control and EC-AT system — 1992 323/Protege-part 3 of 3

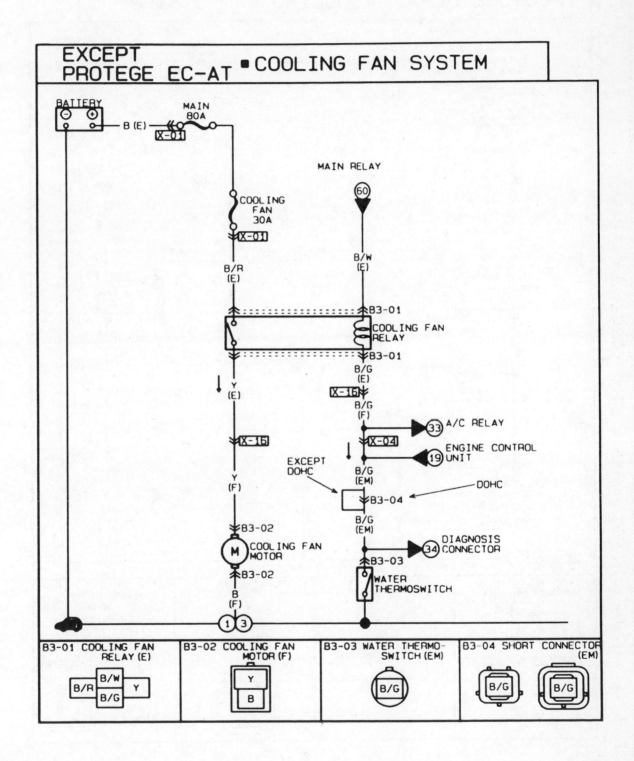

Fig. 79 Cooling fan system wiring schematic — 1992 323/Protege except EC-AT

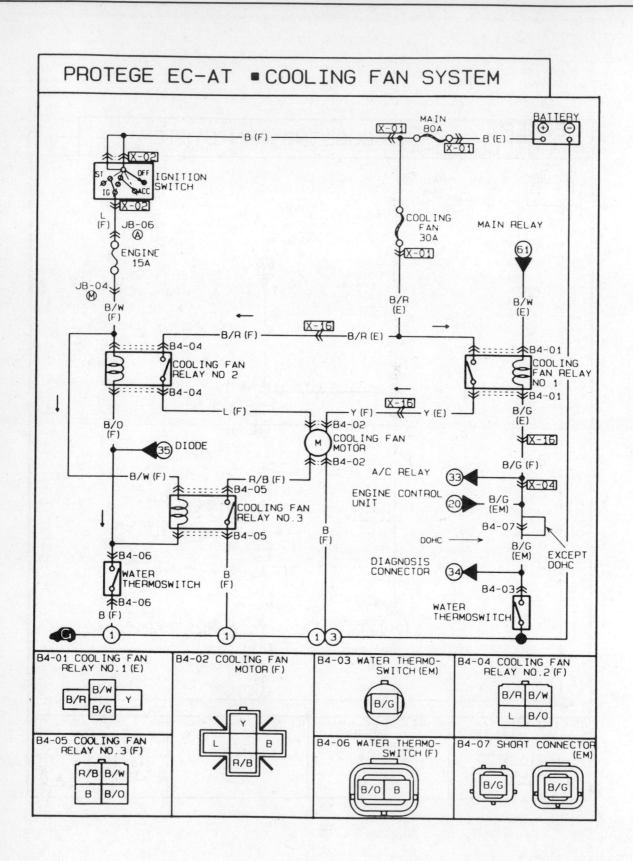

Fig. 80 Cooling fan system wiring schematic — 1992 323/Protege EC-AT

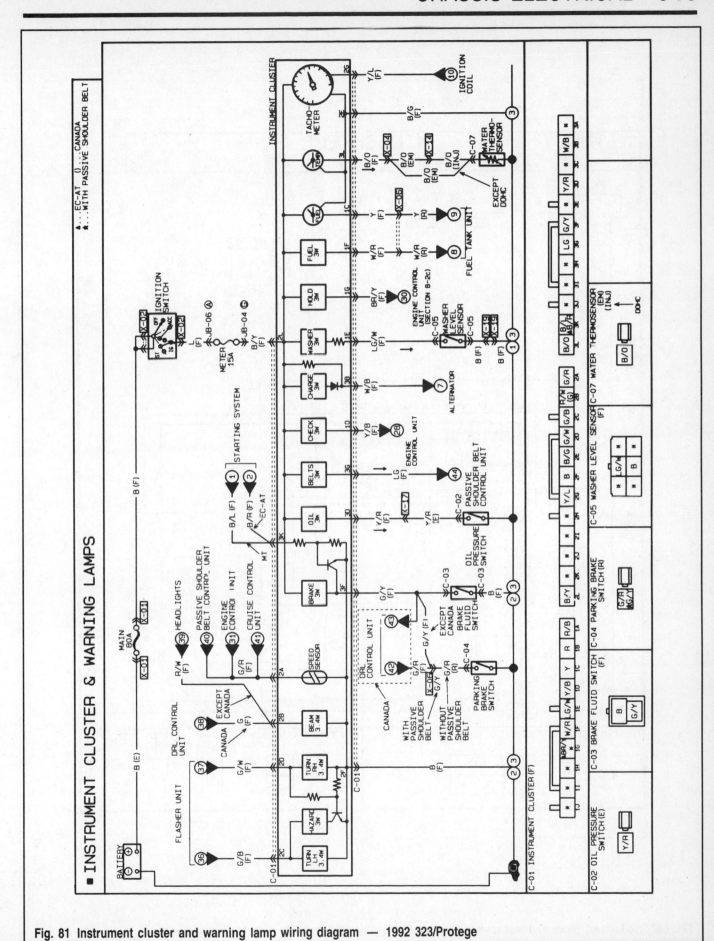

Fig. 81 Instrument cluster and warning lamp wiring diagram — 1992 323/Protege

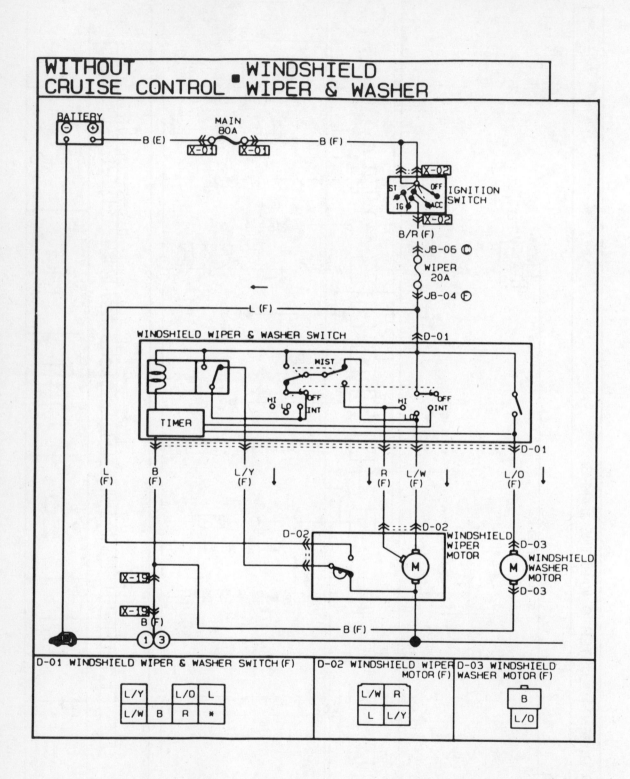

Fig. 82 Windshield wiper and washer wiring diagram — 1992 323/Protege - without cruise control

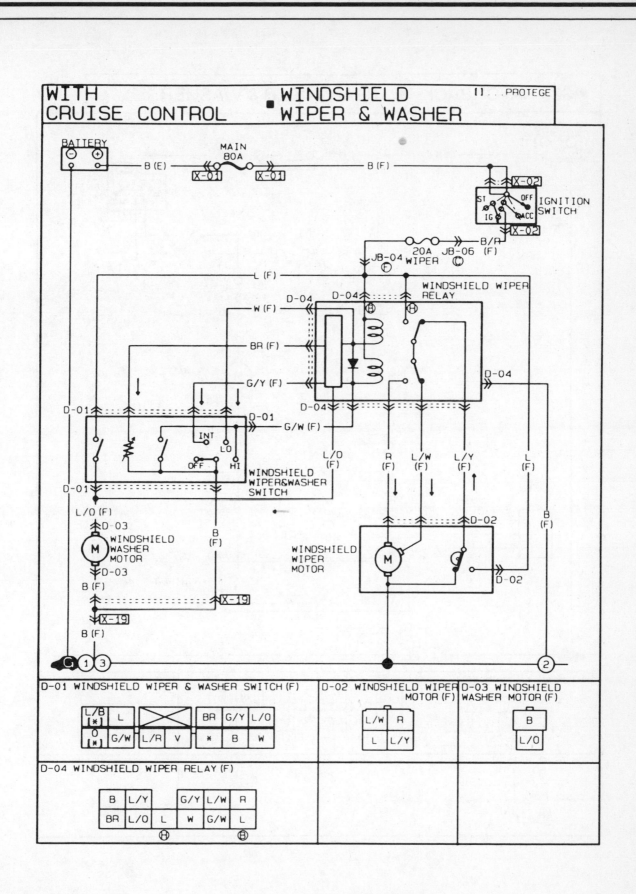

Fig. 83 Windshield wiper and washer wiring diagram — 1990-91 323/Protege with cruise control

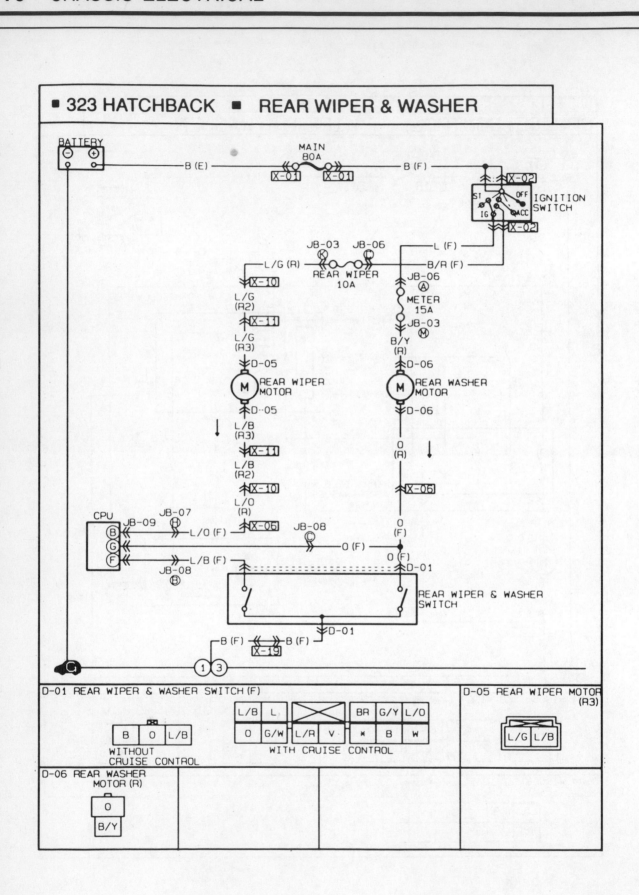

Fig. 84 Rear windshield wiper and washer wiring diagram — 1992 323 hatchback

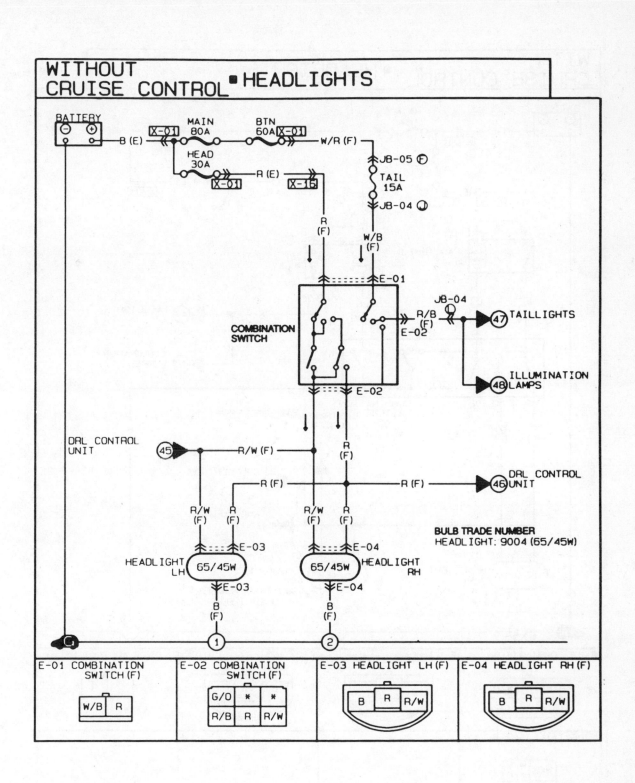

Fig. 85 Headlights wiring diagram — 1992 323/Protege without cruise control

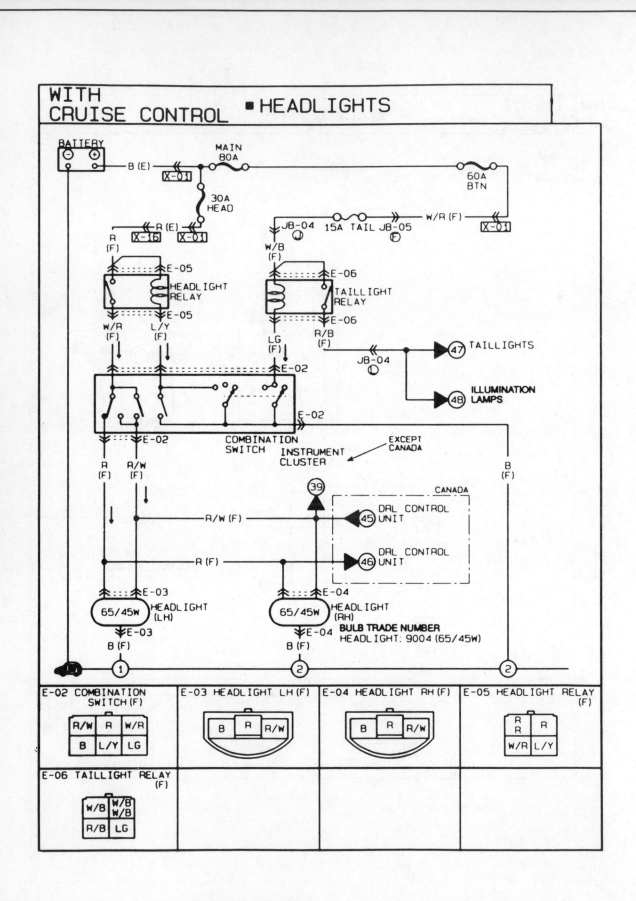

Fig. 86 Headlights wiring diagram — 1992 323/Protege with cruise control

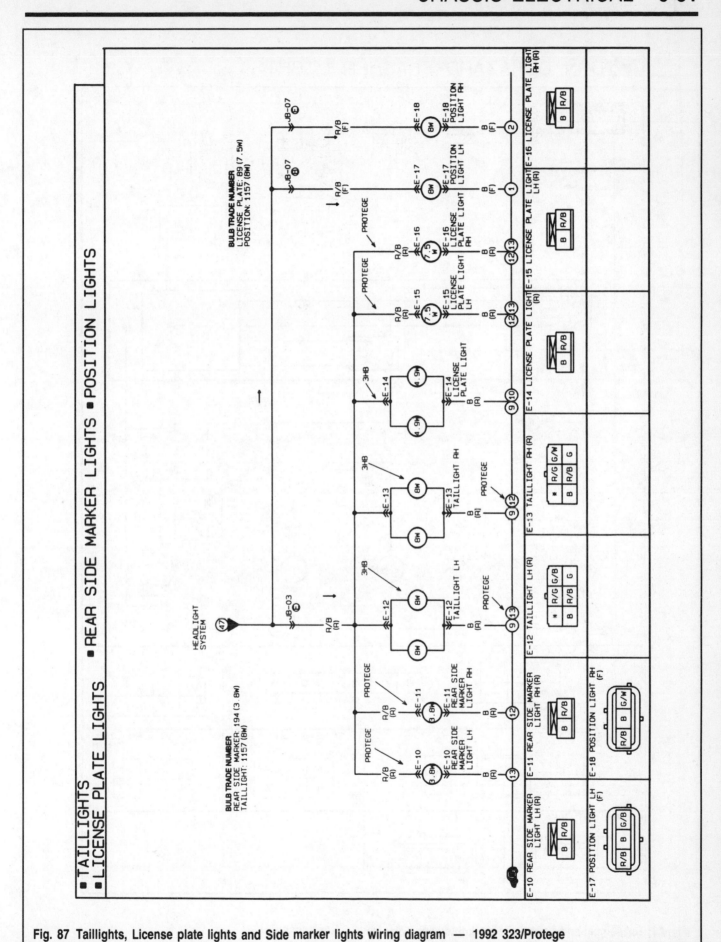

Fig. 87 Taillights, License plate lights and Side marker lights wiring diagram — 1992 323/Protege

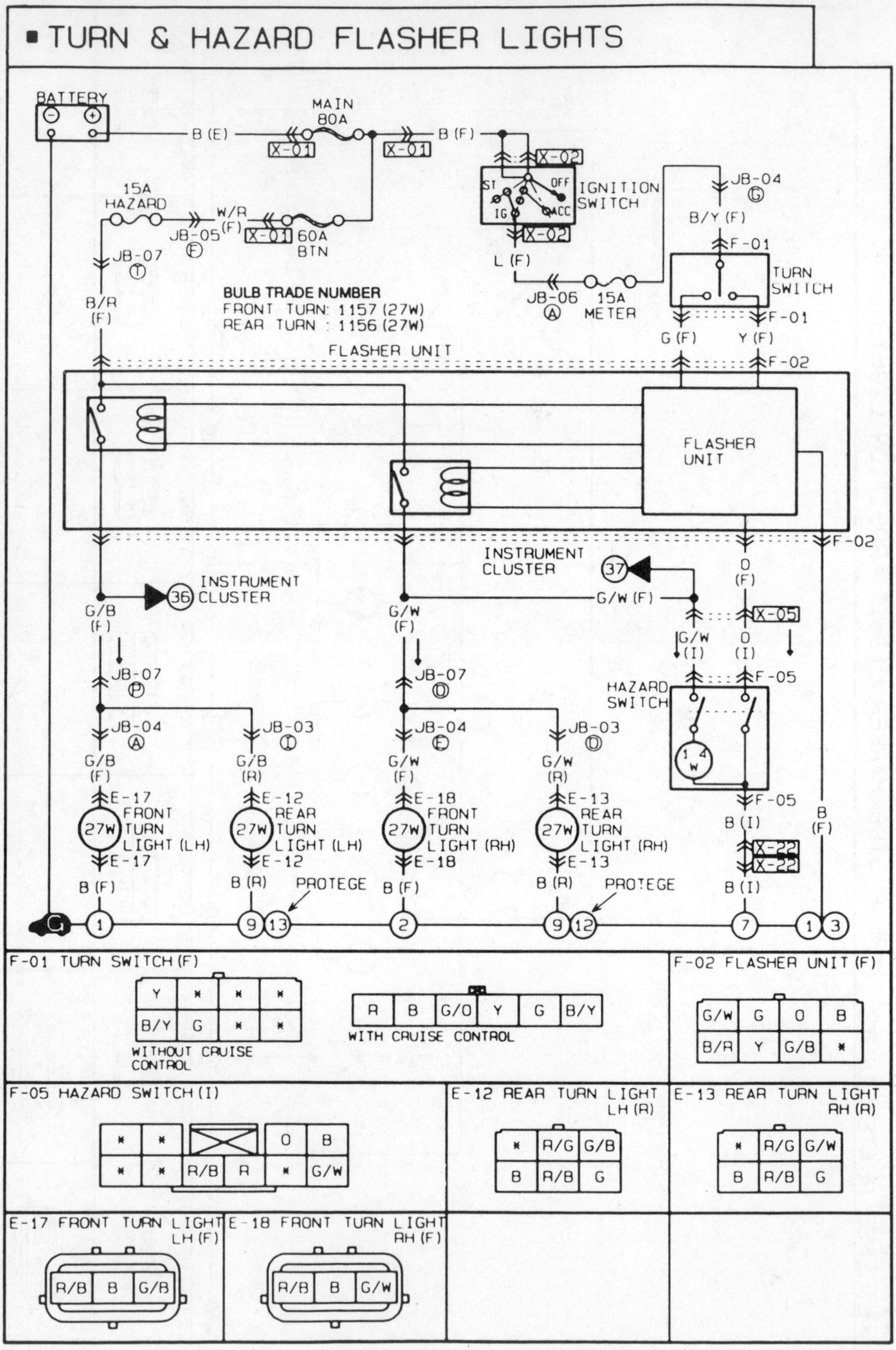

■ TURN & HAZARD FLASHER LIGHTS

BULB TRADE NUMBER
FRONT TURN : 1157 (27W)
REAR TURN : 1156 (27W)

Fig. 88 Turn signal and hazard flasher lights wiring diagram — 1992 323/Protege

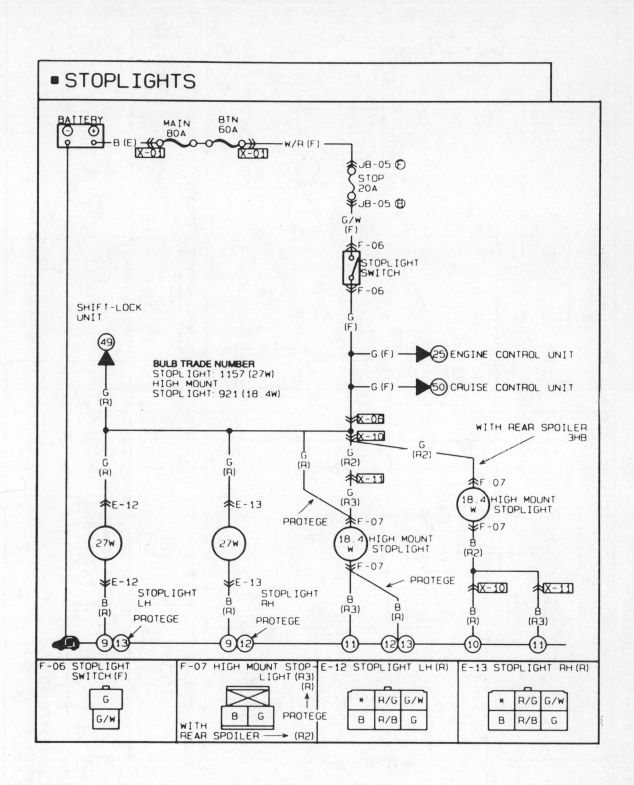

Fig. 89 Stoplights wiring diagram — 1992 323/Protege

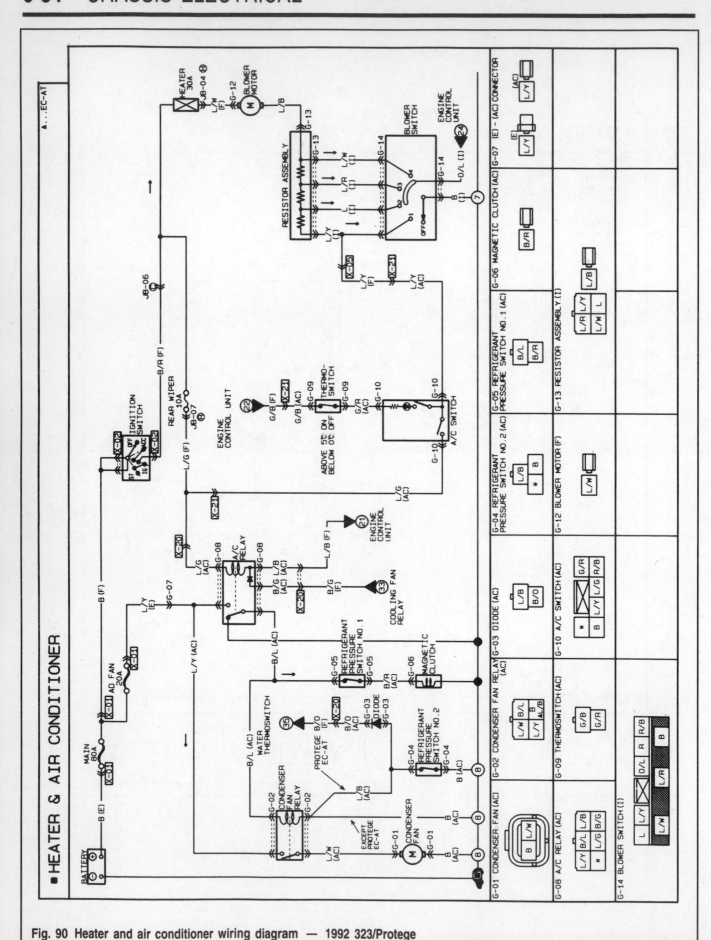

Fig. 90 Heater and air conditioner wiring diagram — 1992 323/Protege

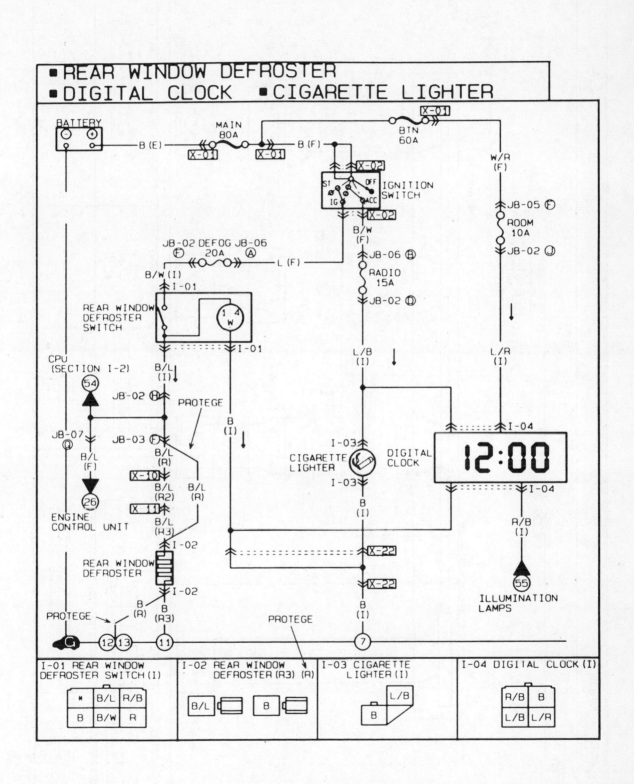

Fig. 91 Rear window defroster/Clock/Lighter wiring diagram — 1992 323/Protege

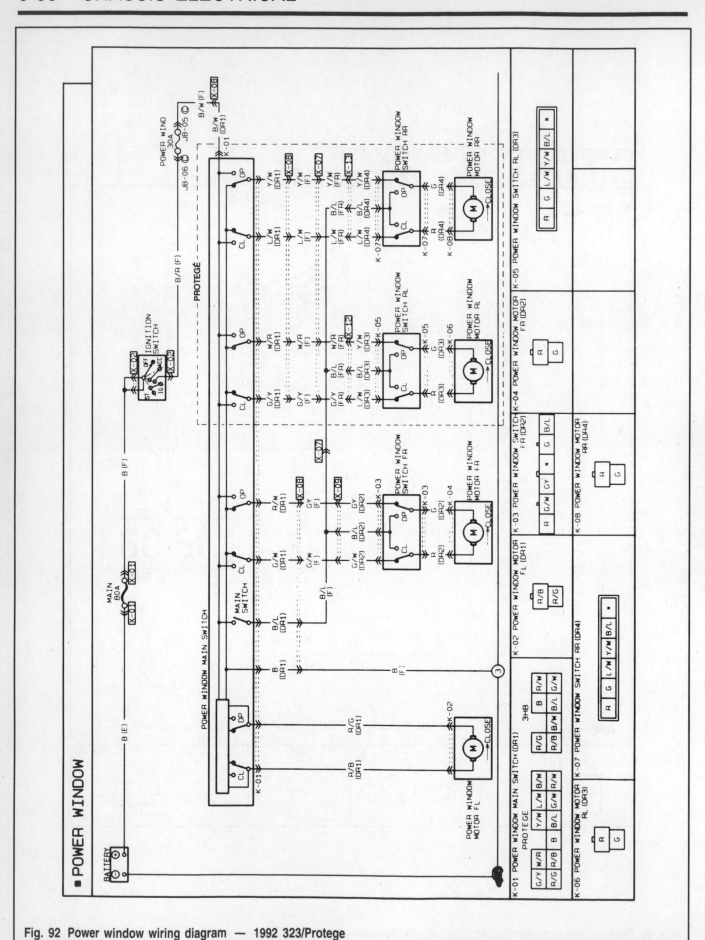

Fig. 92 Power window wiring diagram — 1992 323/Protege

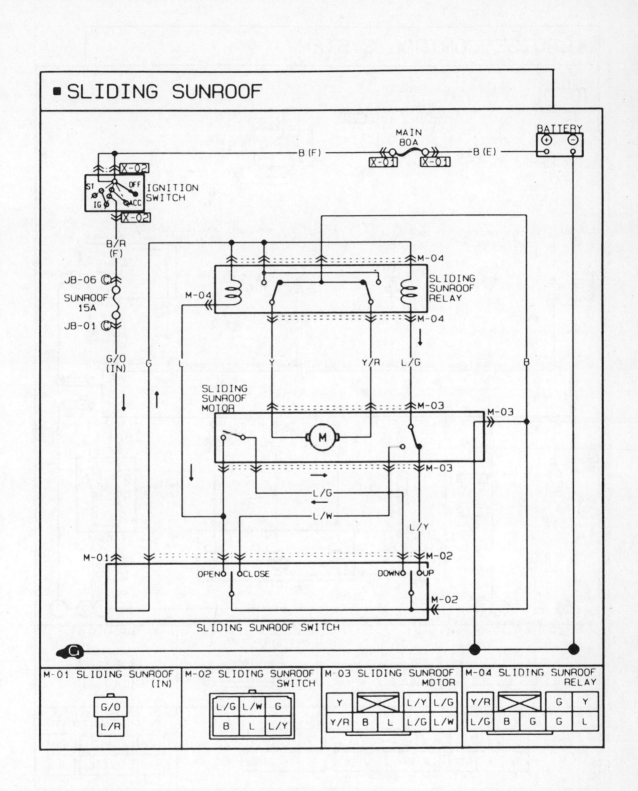

Fig. 93 Power sunroof wirng diagram — 1992 323/Protege

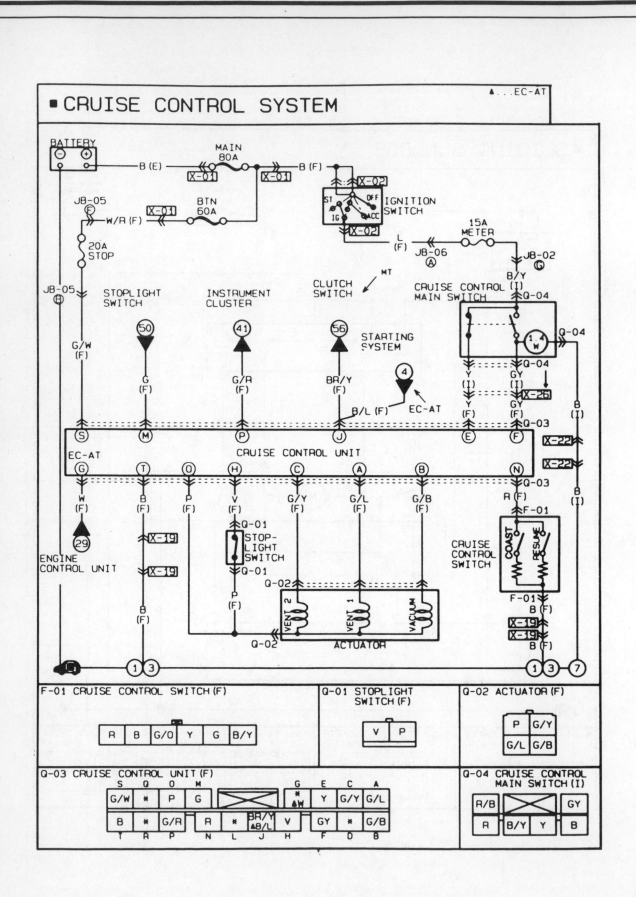

Fig. 94 Cruise control system wiring diagram — 1992 323/Protege

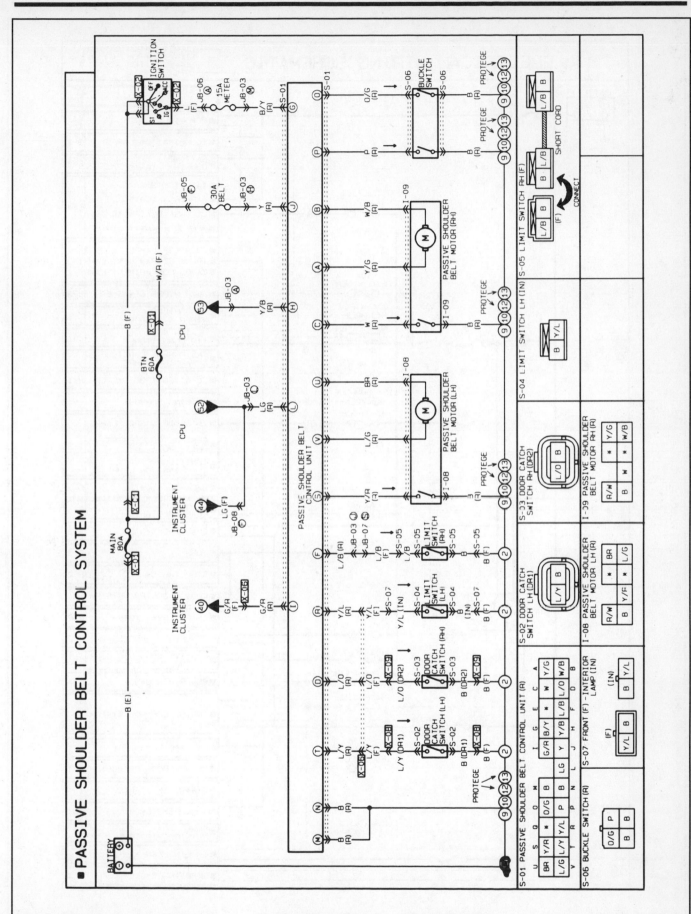

Fig. 95 Passive shoulder seatbelt control system wiring diagram — 1992 323/Protege

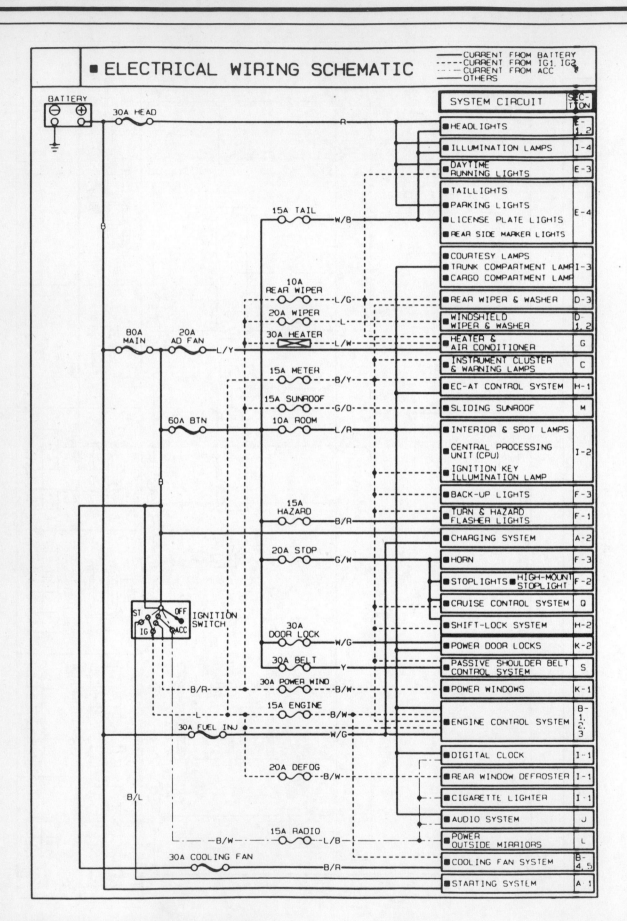

Fig. 96 1993 323/Protege electrical wiring schematic

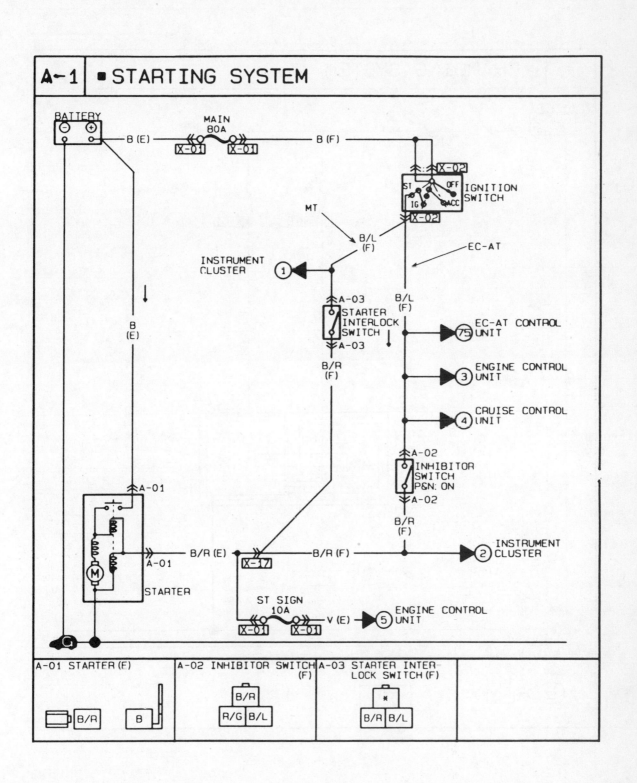

Fig. 97 Starting system — 1993 323/Protege

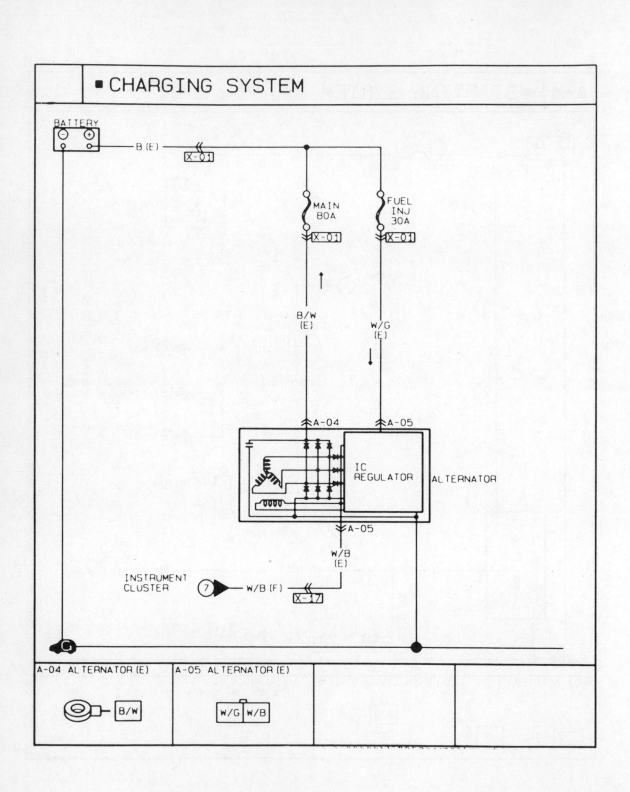

Fig. 98 Charging system — 1993 323/Protege

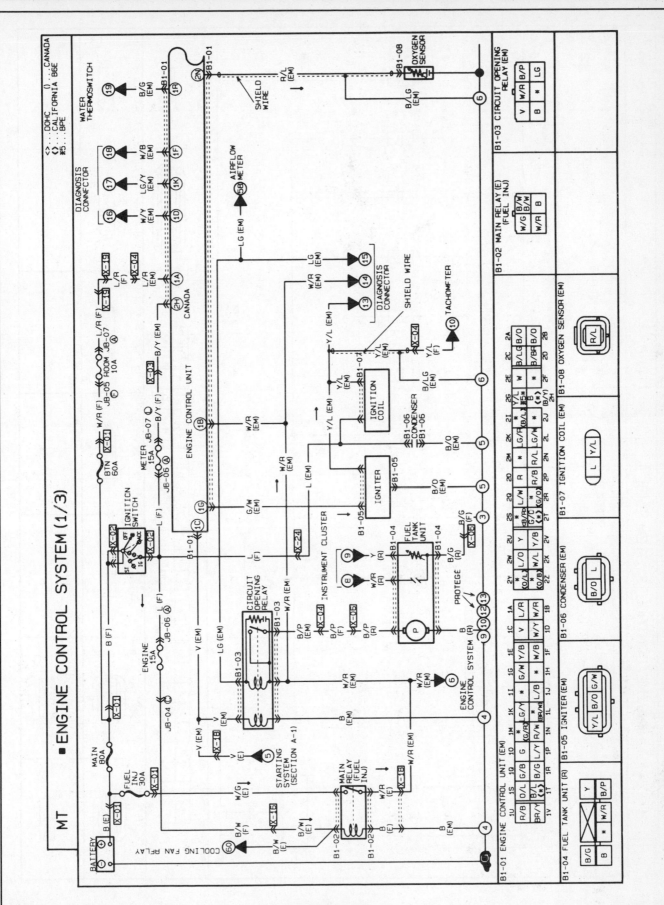

Fig. 99 Engine control system — 1993 323/Protege M/T-part 1 of 3

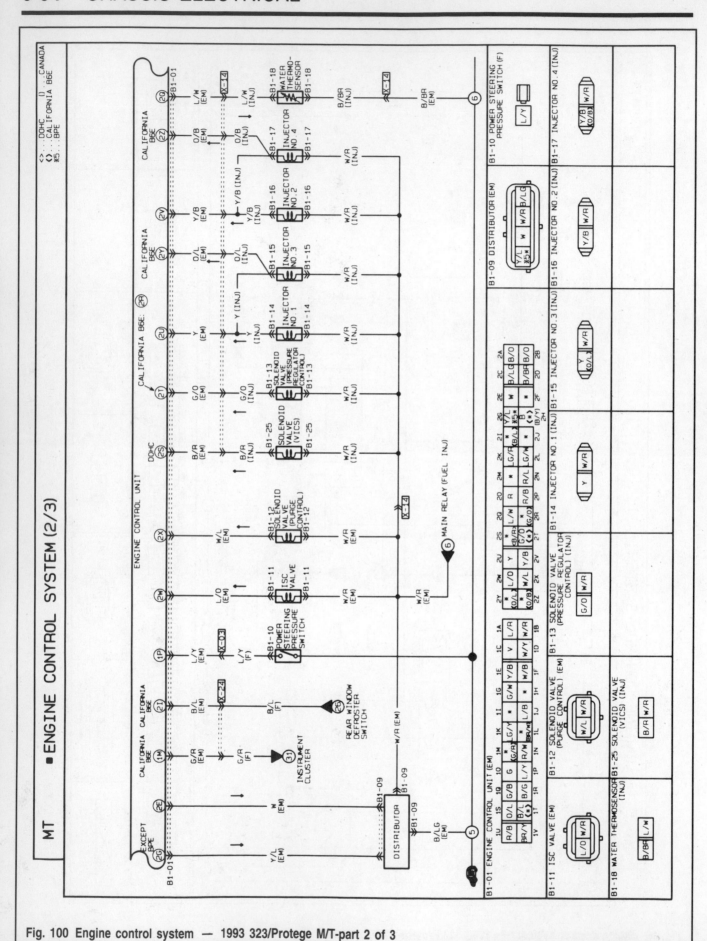

Fig. 100 Engine control system — 1993 323/Protege M/T-part 2 of 3

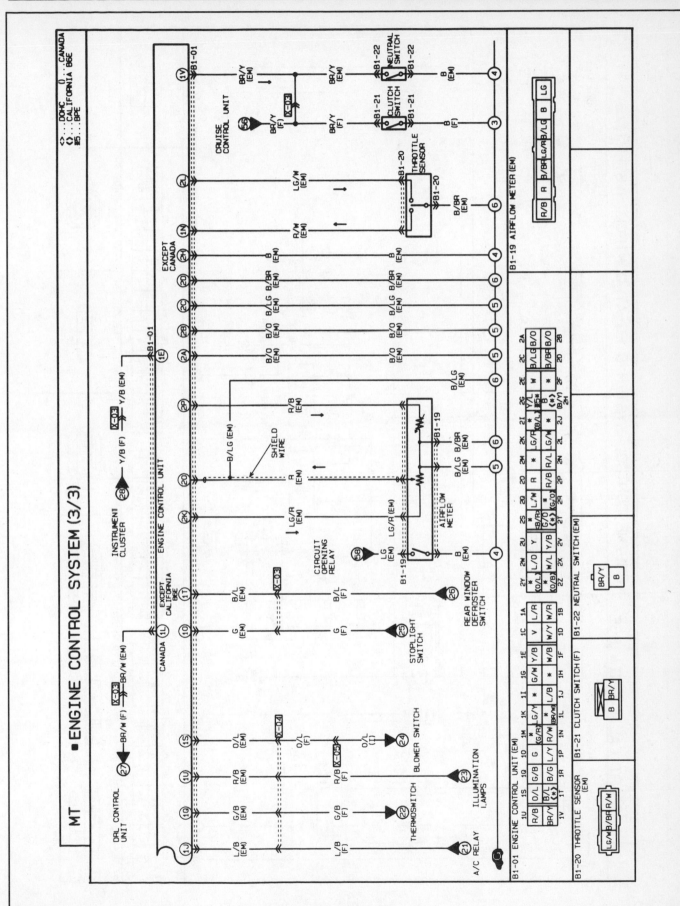

Fig. 101 Engine control system — 1993 323/Protege M/T-part 3 of 3

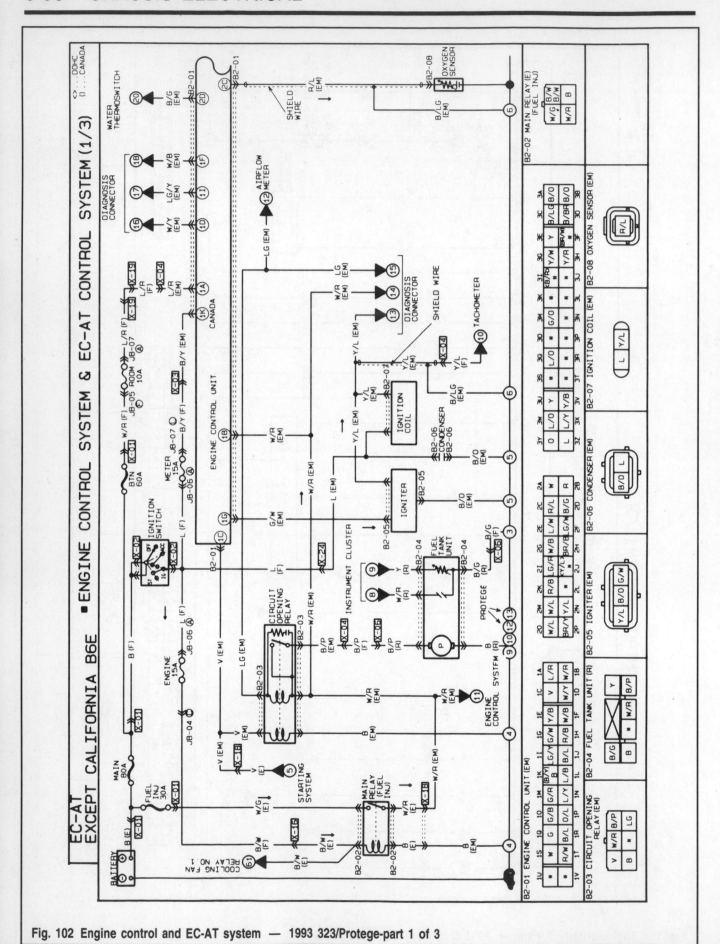

Fig. 102 Engine control and EC-AT system — 1993 323/Protege-part 1 of 3

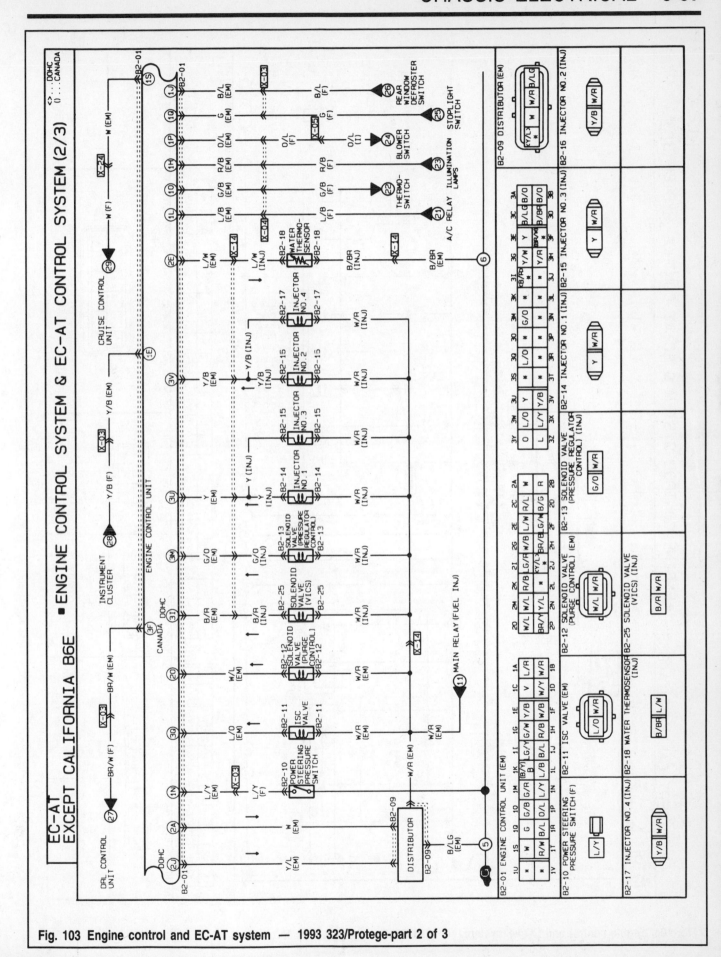

Fig. 103 Engine control and EC-AT system — 1993 323/Protege-part 2 of 3

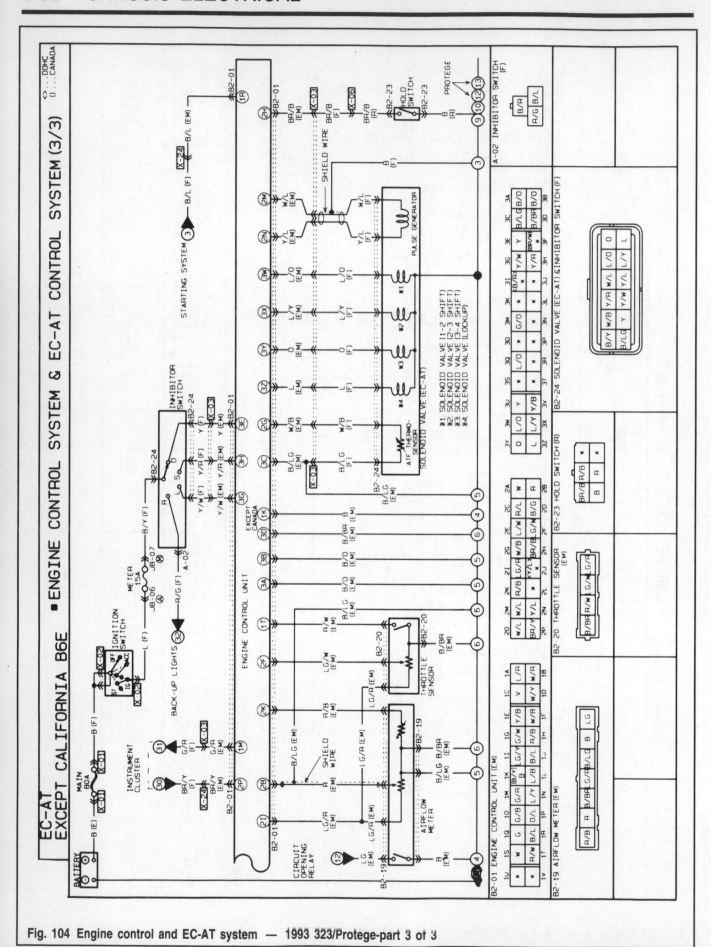

Fig. 104 Engine control and EC-AT system — 1993 323/Protege-part 3 of 3

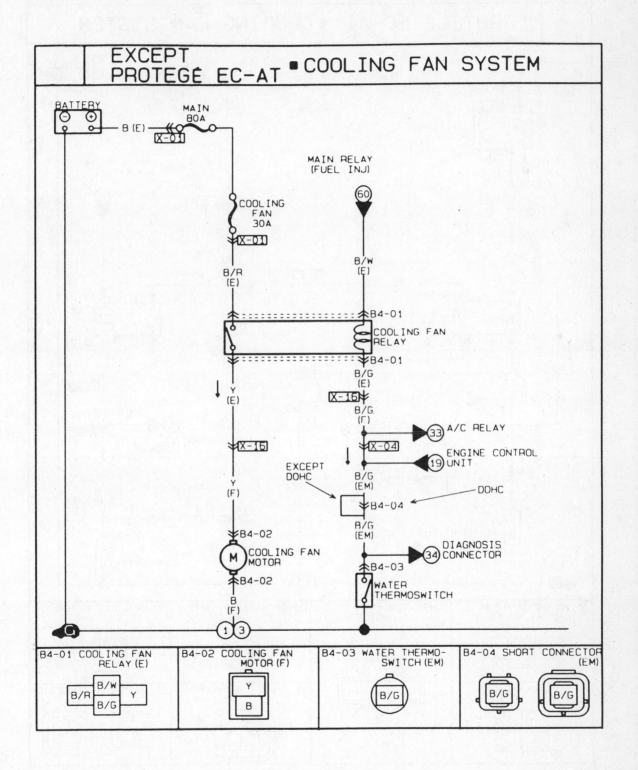

Fig. 105 Cooling fan system wiring schematic — 1993 323/Protege except EC-AT

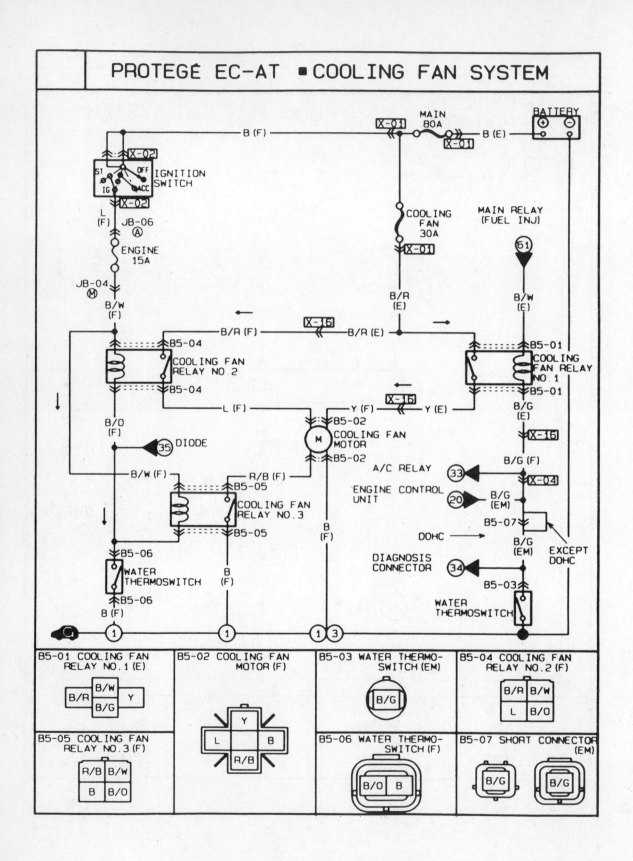

Fig. 106 Cooling fan system wiring schematic — 1993 323/Protege EC-AT

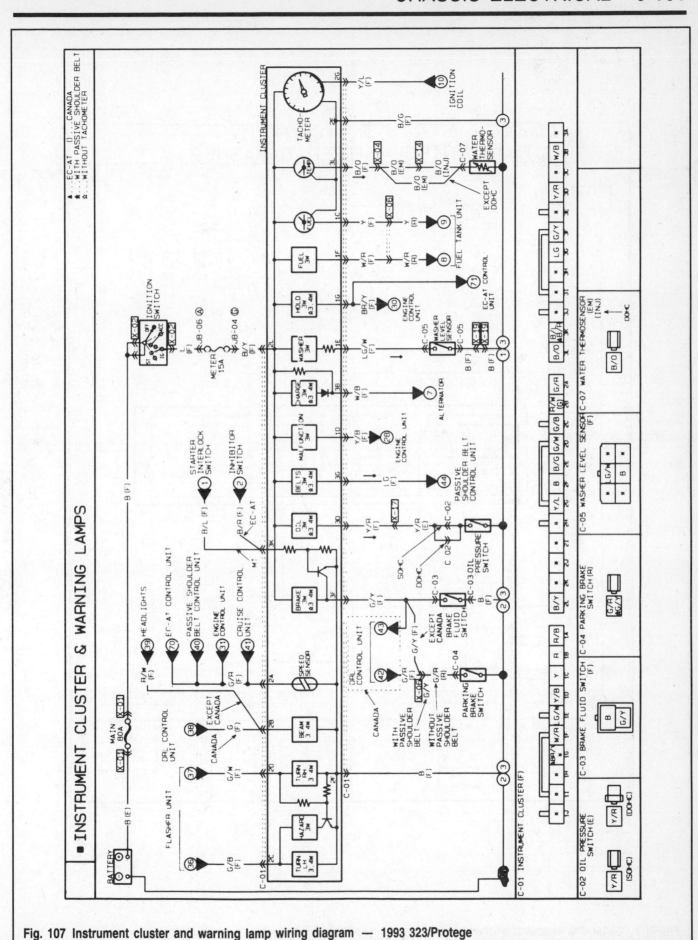

Fig. 107 Instrument cluster and warning lamp wiring diagram — 1993 323/Protege

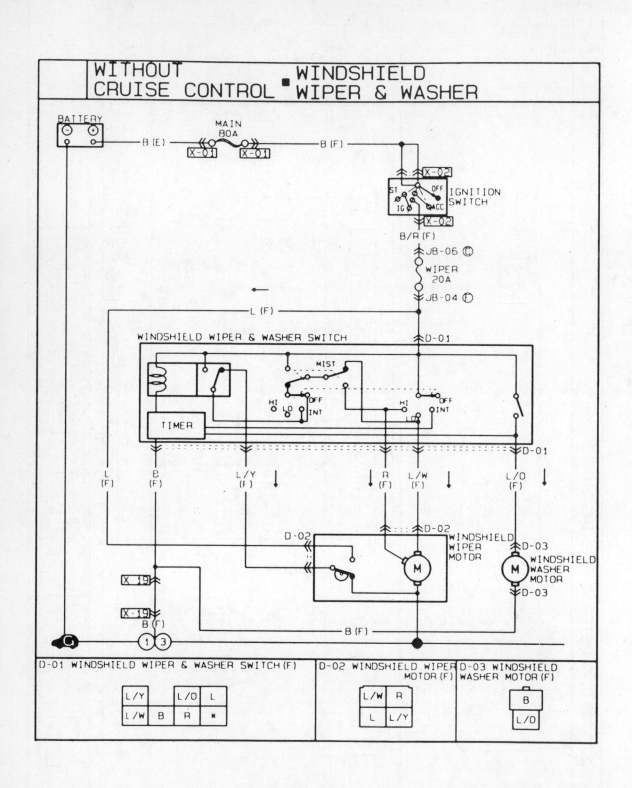

Fig. 108 Windshield wiper and washer wiring diagram — 1993 323/Protege - without cruise control

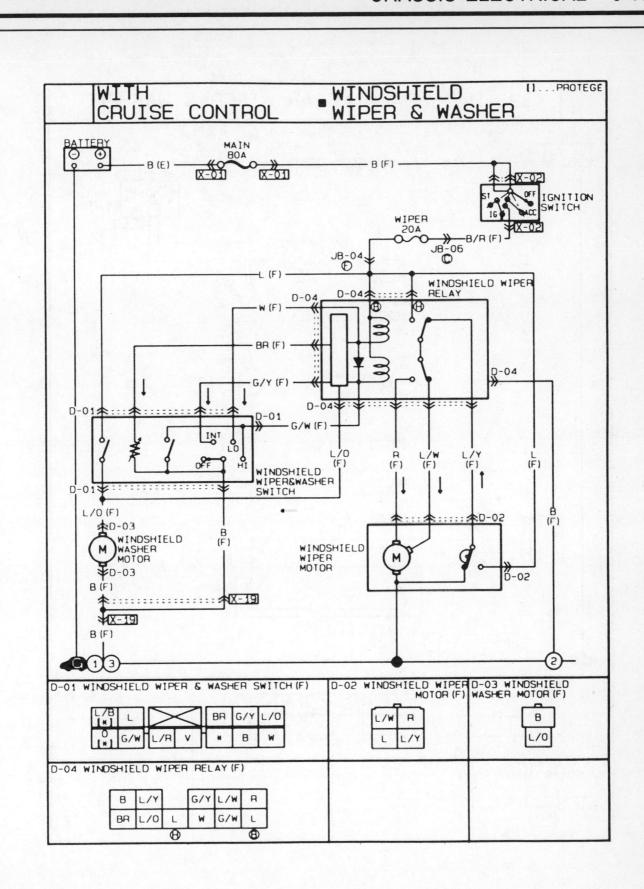

Fig. 109 Windshield wiper and washer wiring diagram — 1990-91 323/Protege with cruise control

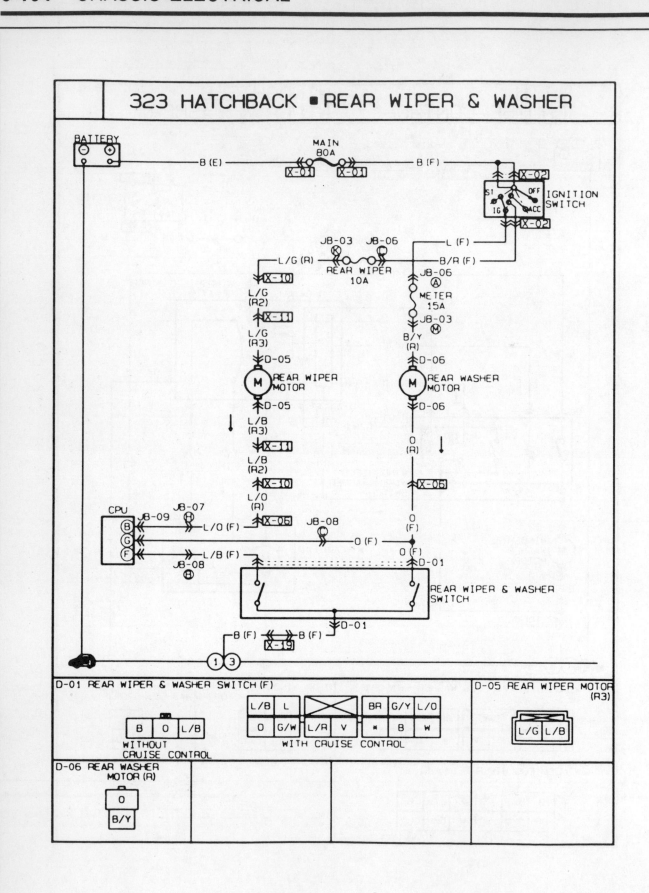

Fig. 110 Rear windshield wiper and washer wiring diagram — 1993 323 hatchback

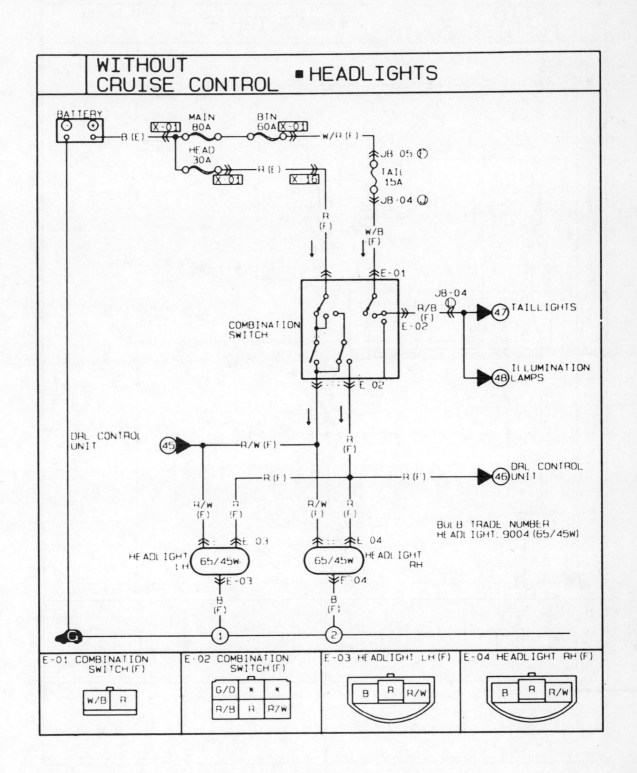

Fig. 111 Headlights wiring diagram — 1993 323/Protege without cruise control

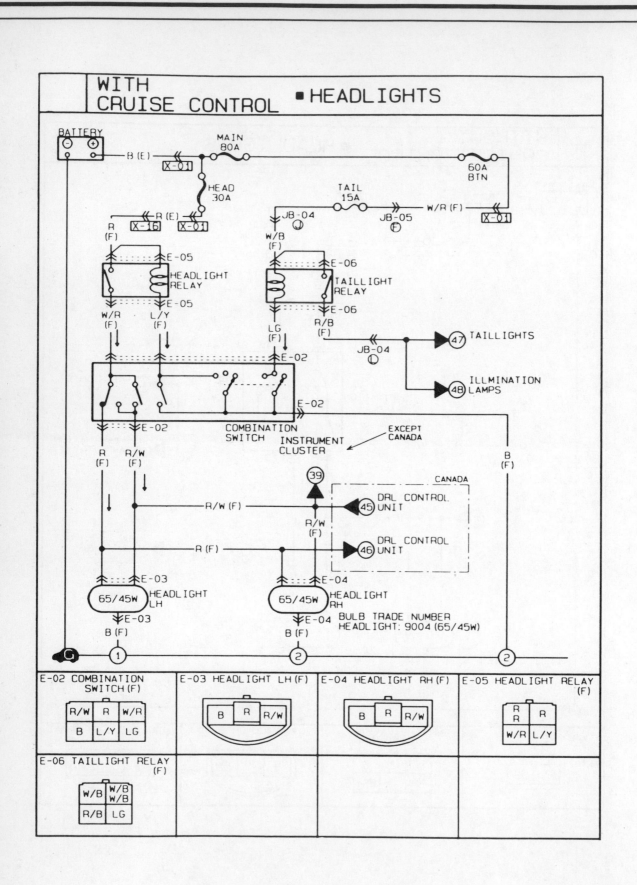

Fig. 112 Headlights wiring diagram — 1993 323/Protege with cruise control

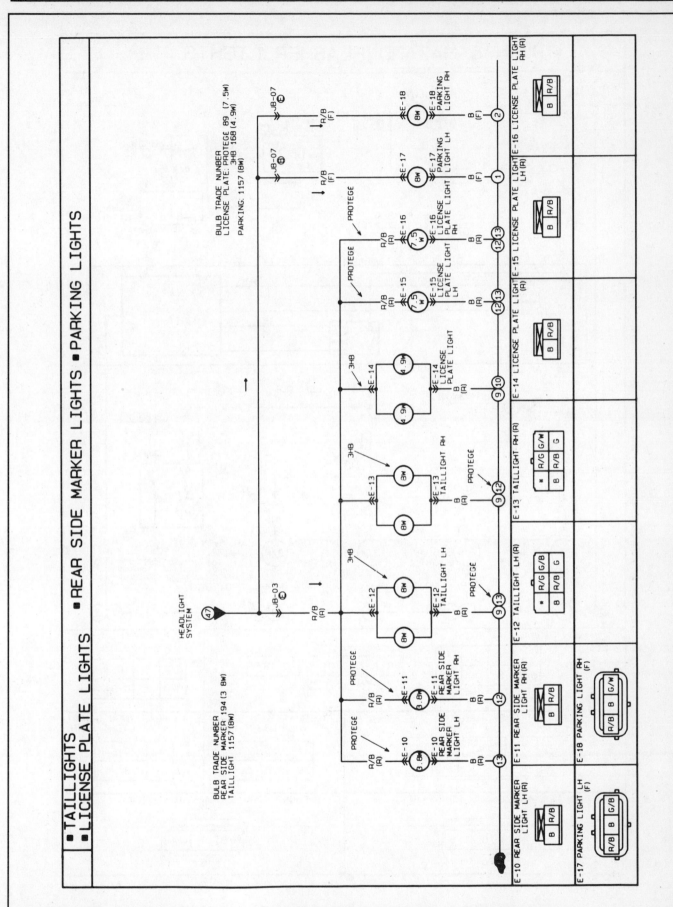

Fig. 113 Taillights, License plate lights and Side marker lights wiring diagram — 1993 323/Protege

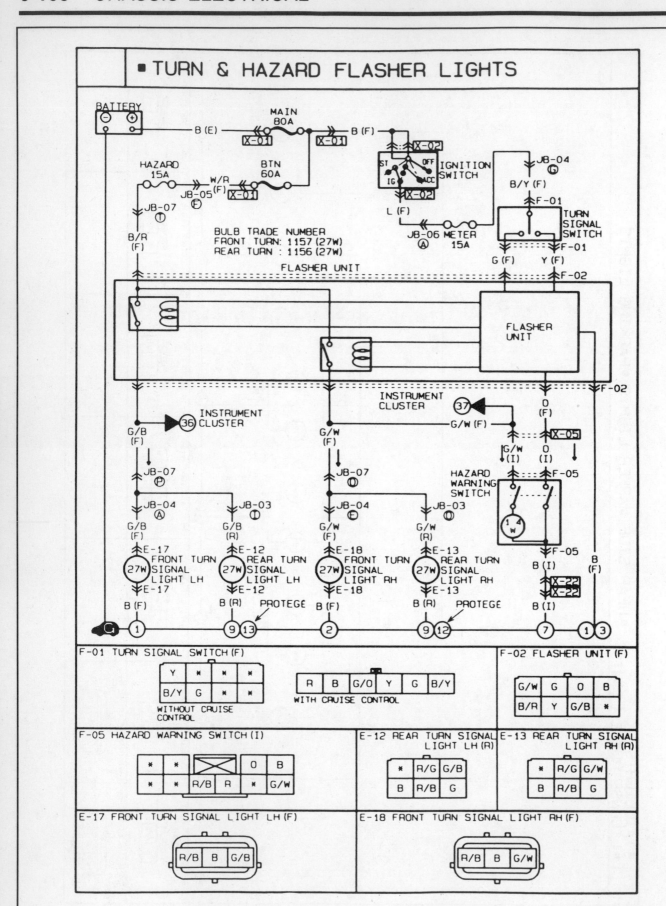

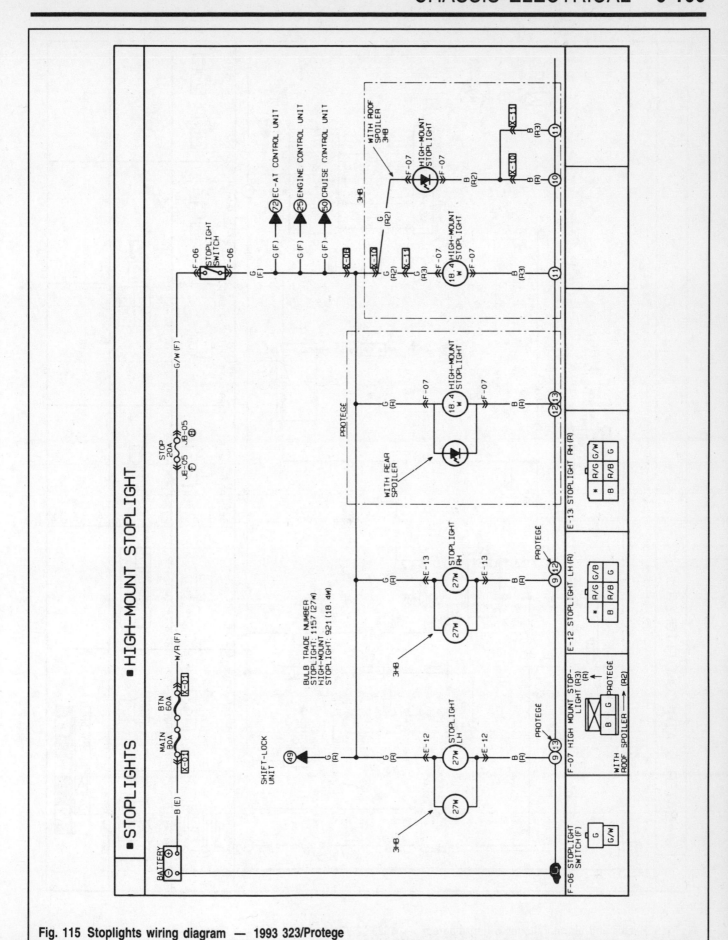

Fig. 115 Stoplights wiring diagram — 1993 323/Protege

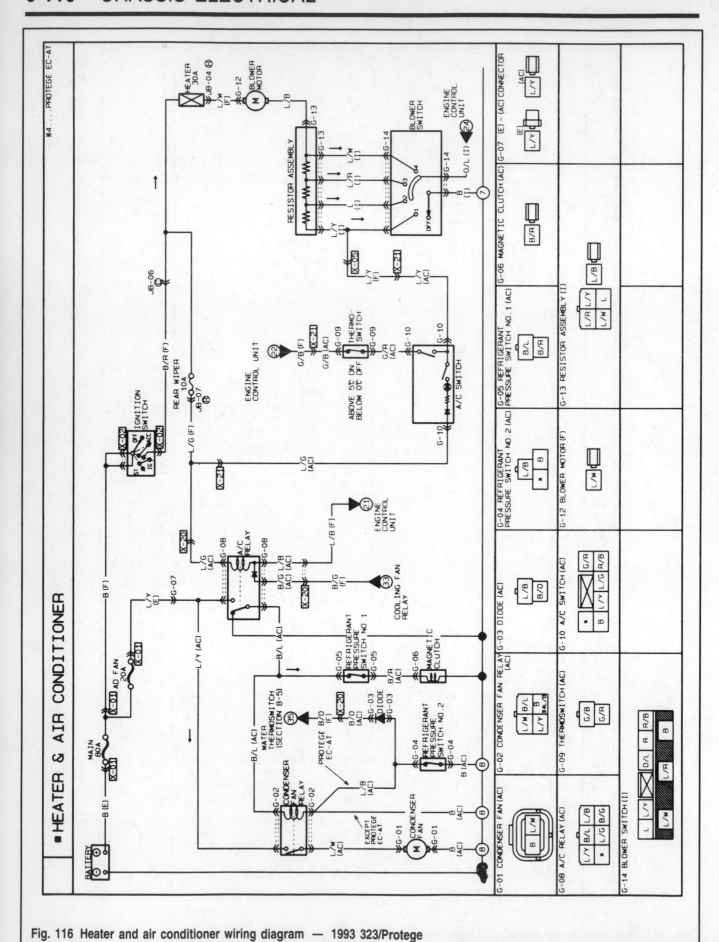

Fig. 116 Heater and air conditioner wiring diagram — 1993 323/Protege

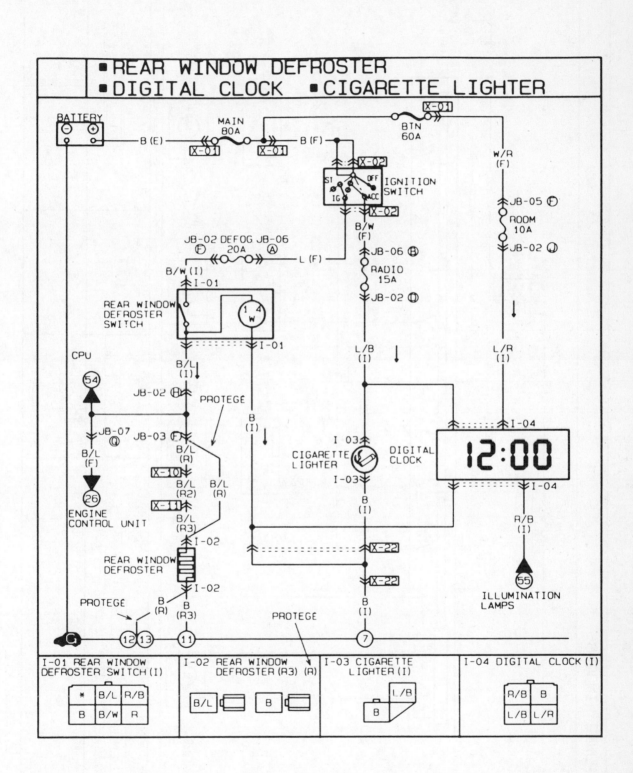

Fig. 117 Rear window defroster/Clock/Lighter wiring diagram — 1993 323/Protege

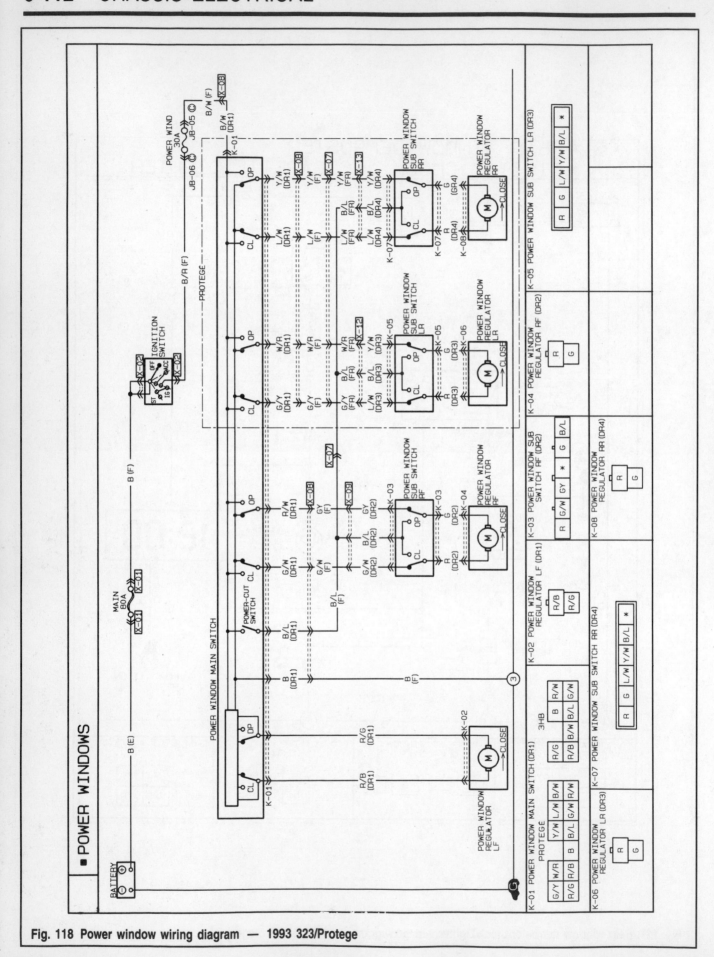

Fig. 118 Power window wiring diagram — 1993 323/Protege

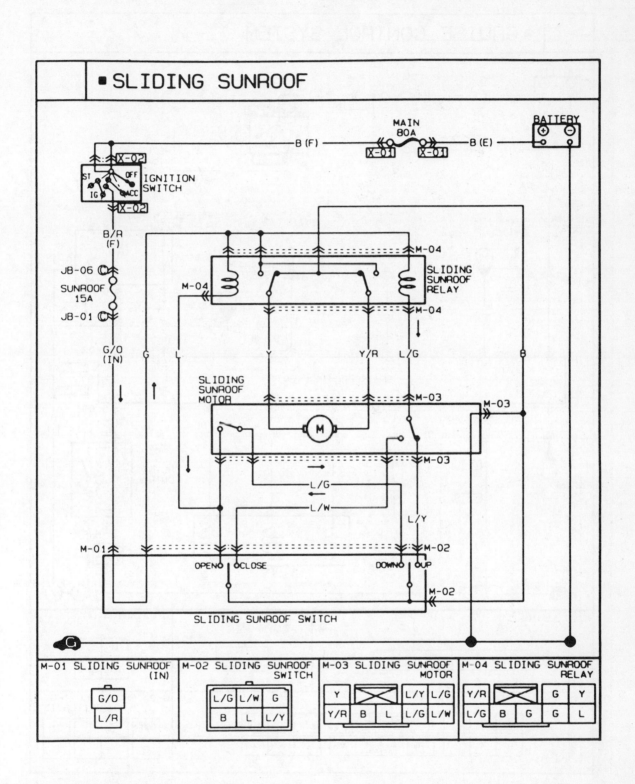

Fig. 119 Power sunroof wiring diagram — 1993 323/Protege

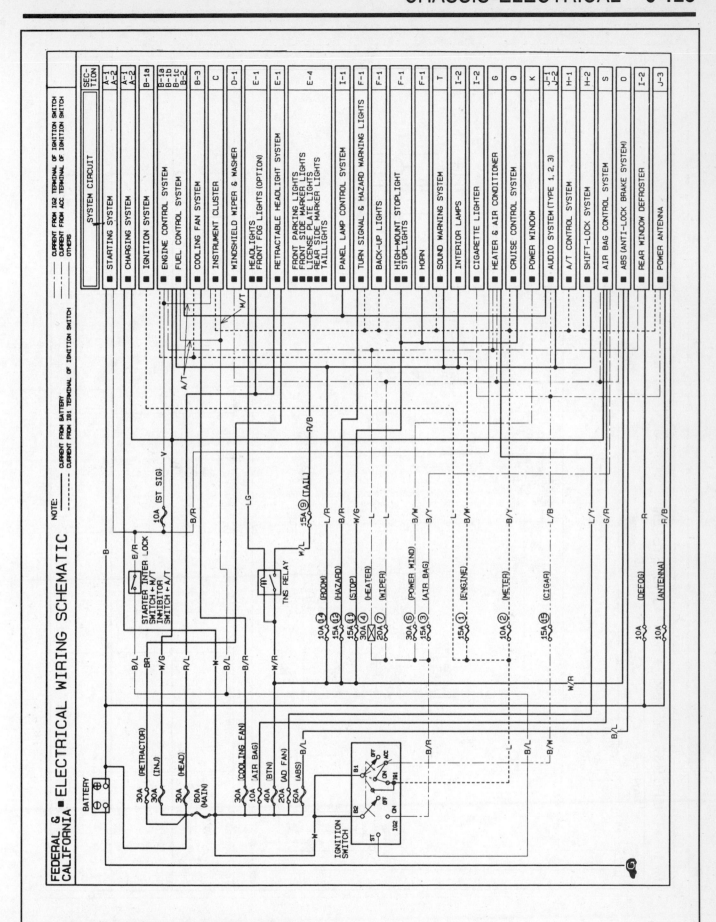

Fig. 129 1992-93 Miata electrical wiring schematic

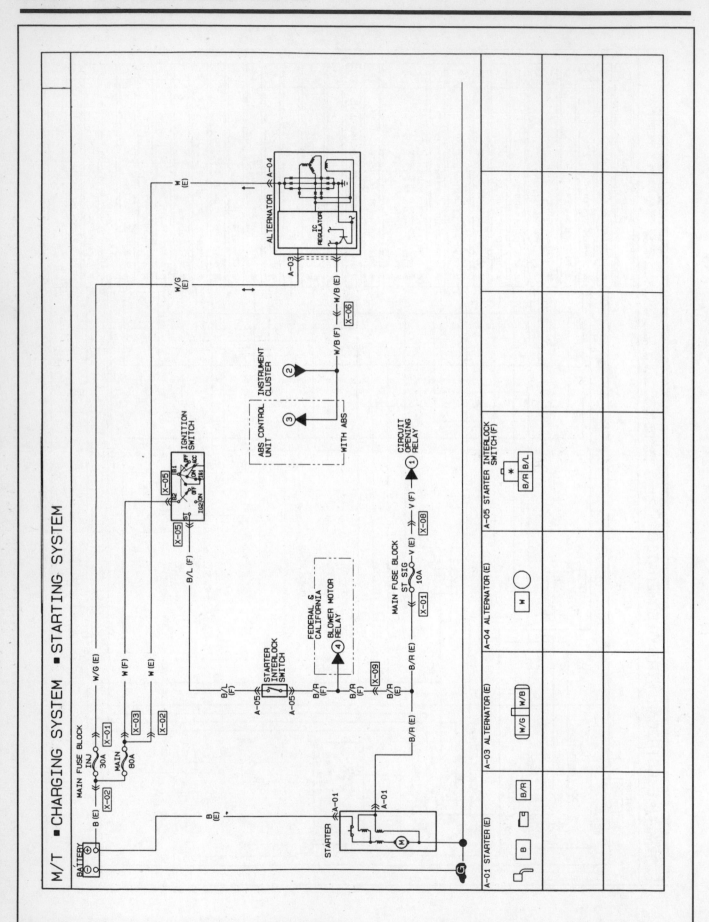

Fig. 130 Starting and charging system — 1992-93 Miata M/T

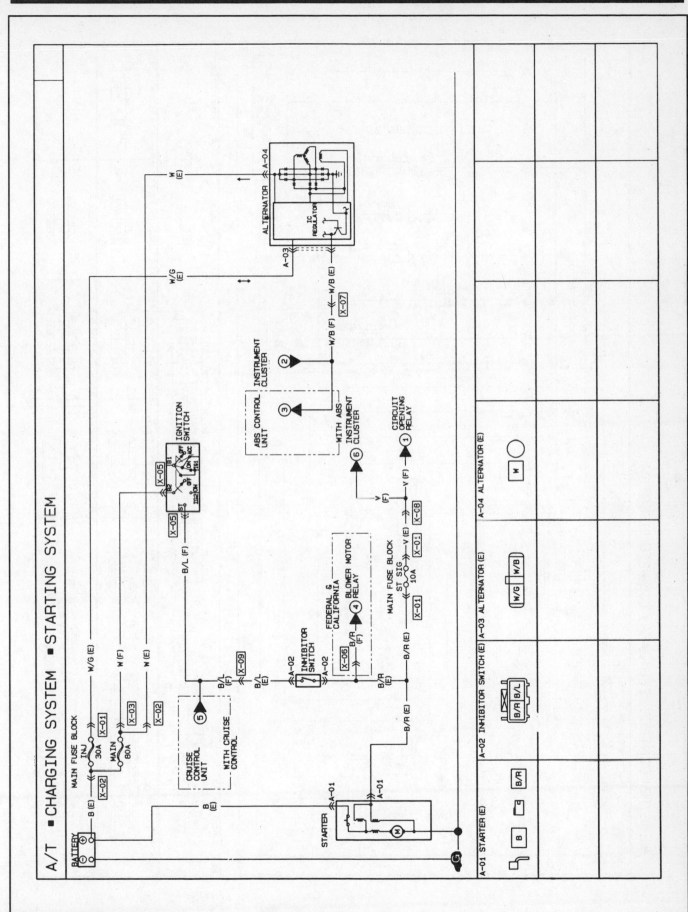

Fig. 131 Starting and charging system — 1992-93 Miata A/T

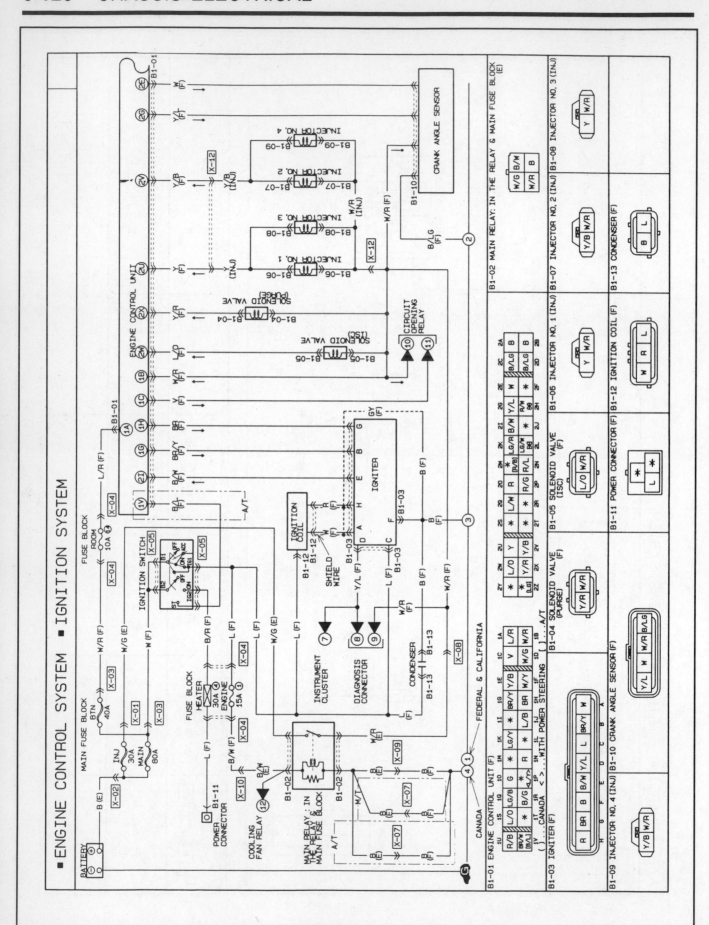

Fig. 132 Engine control and ignition system — 1992-93 Miata-part 1 of 3

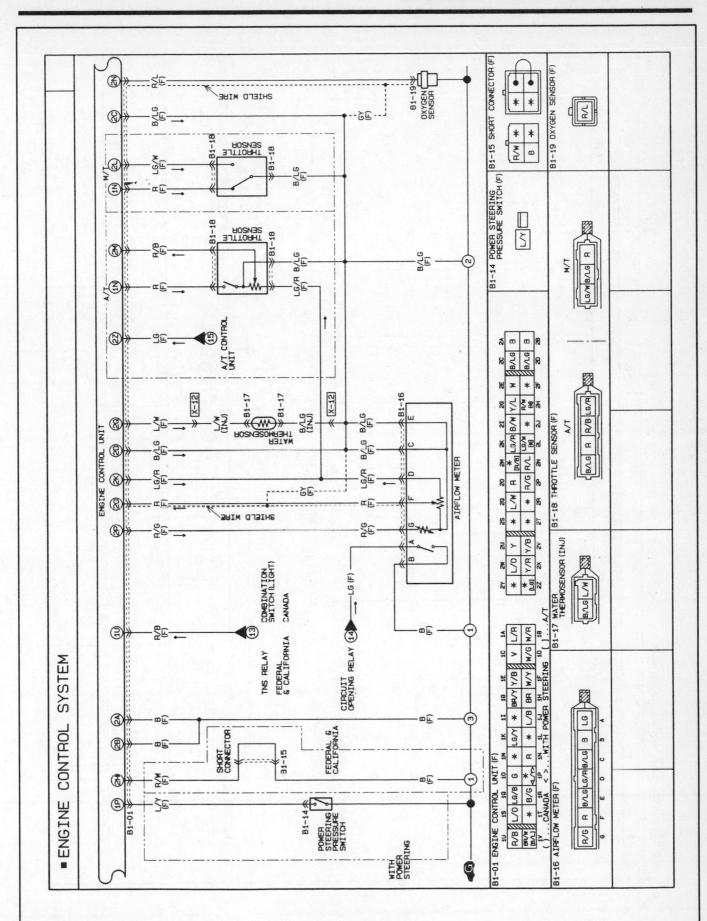

Fig. 133 Engine control and ignition system — 1992-93 Miata-part 2 of 3

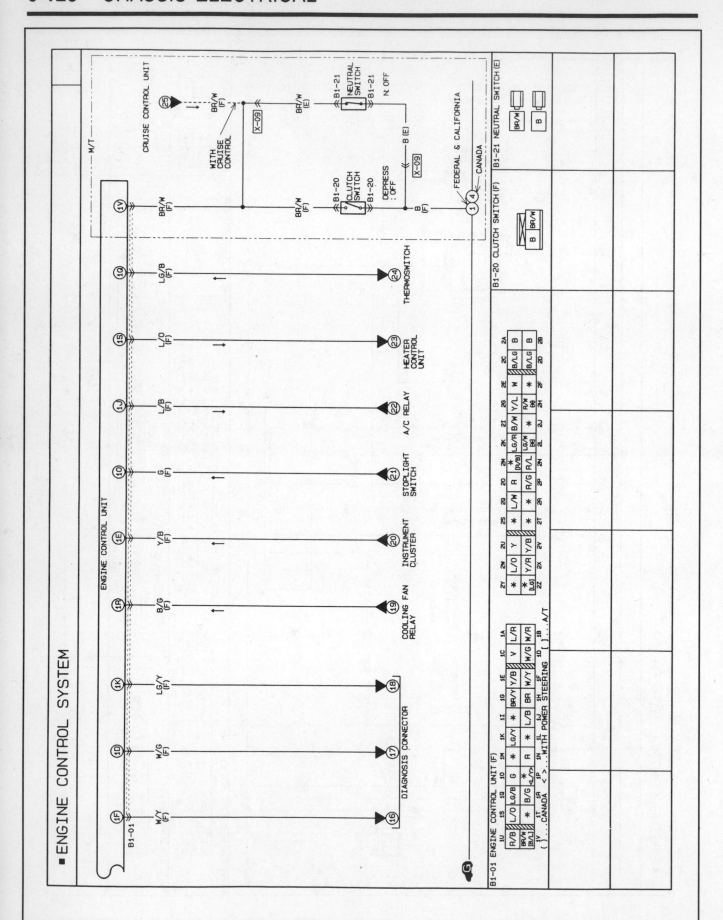

Fig. 134 Engine control and ignition system — 1992-93 Miata-part 3 of 3

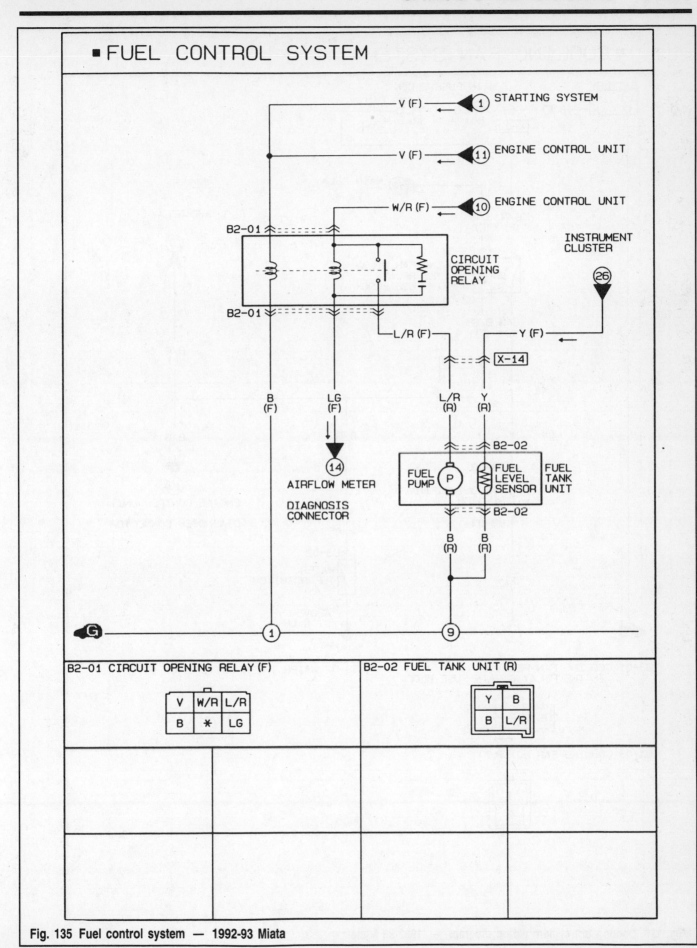

Fig. 135 Fuel control system — 1992-93 Miata

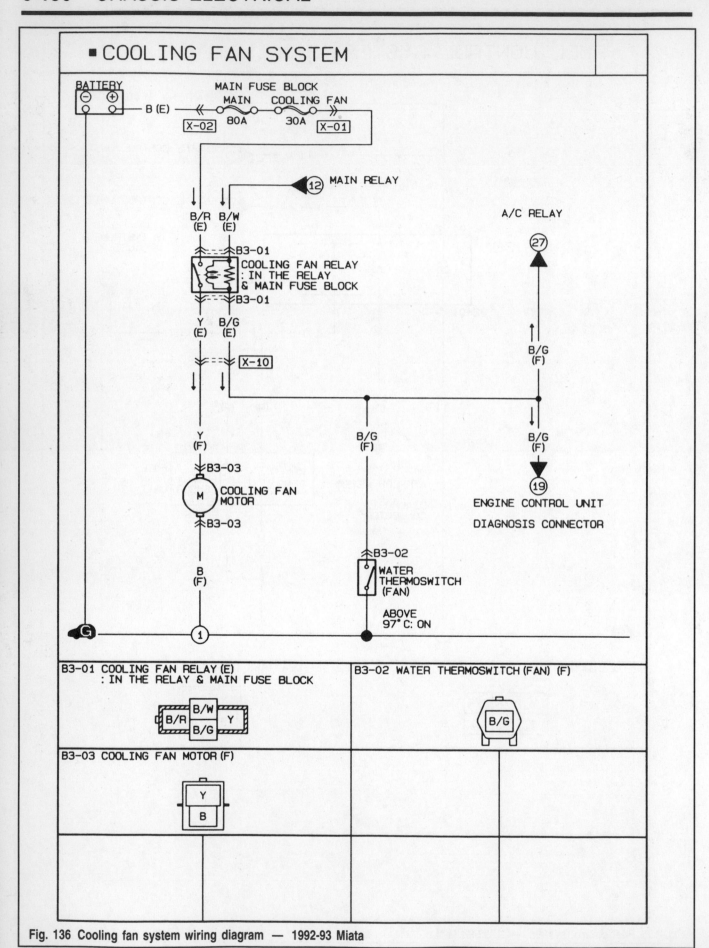

Fig. 136 Cooling fan system wiring diagram — 1992-93 Miata

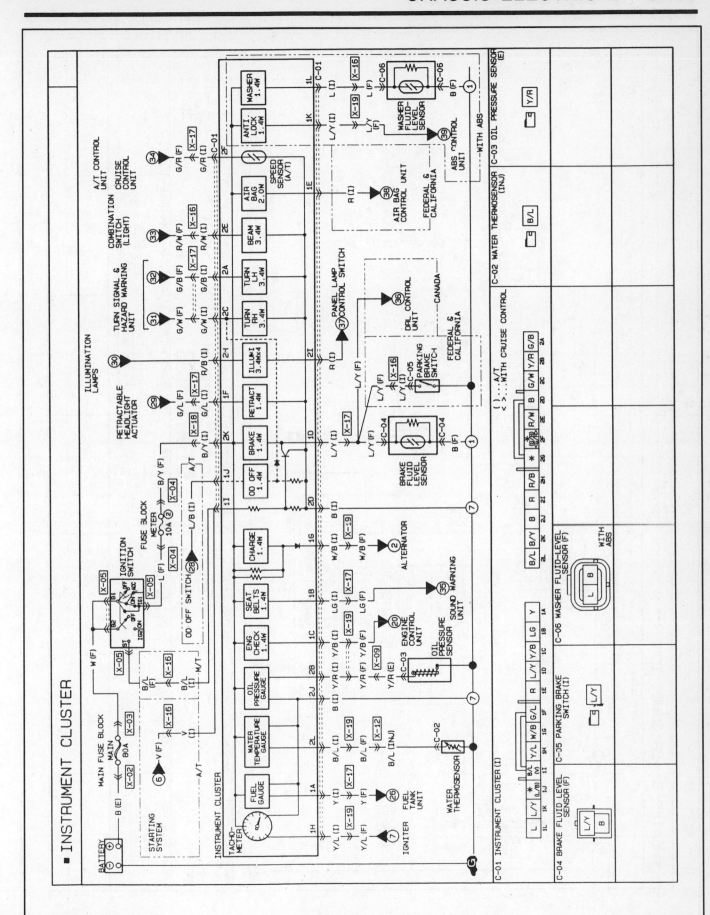

Fig. 137 Instrument cluster wiring diagram — 1992-93 Miata

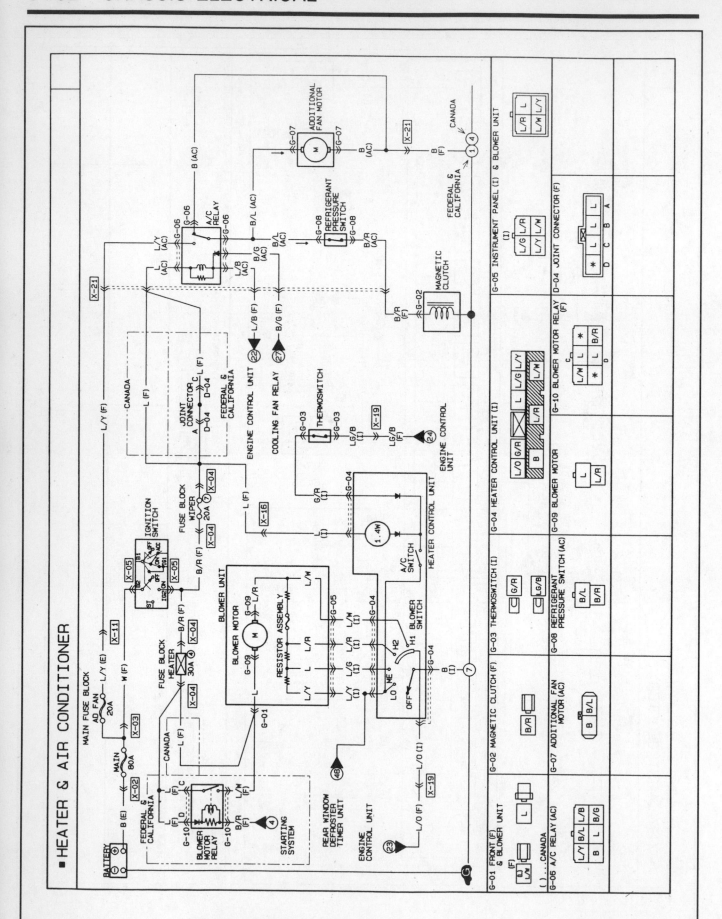

Fig. 138 Heater and air conditioner wiring diagram — 1992-93 Miata

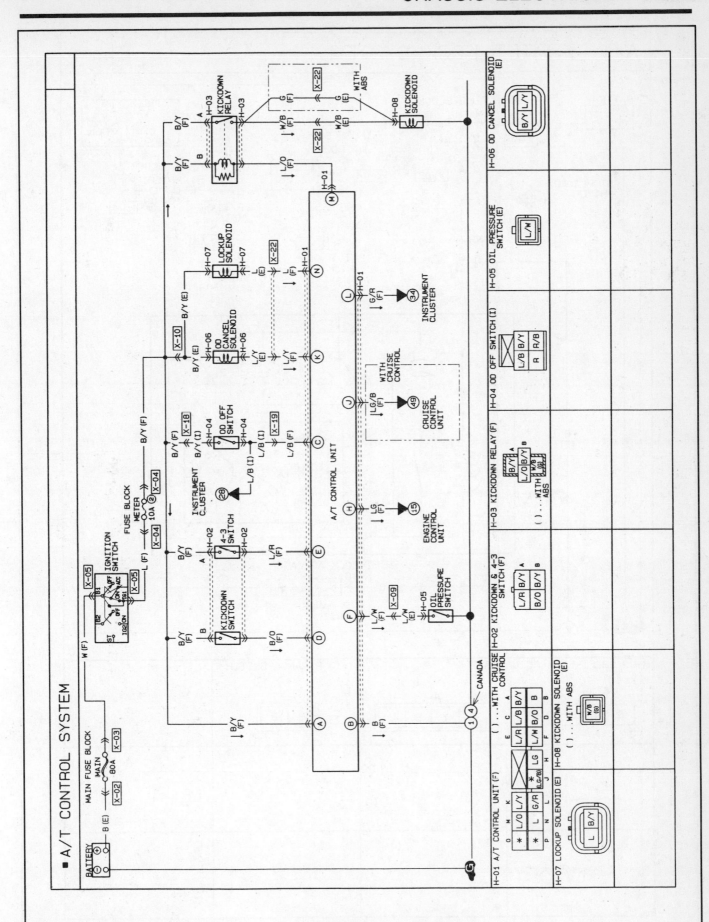

Fig. 139 Automatic transmission control system wiring diagram — 1992-93 Miata

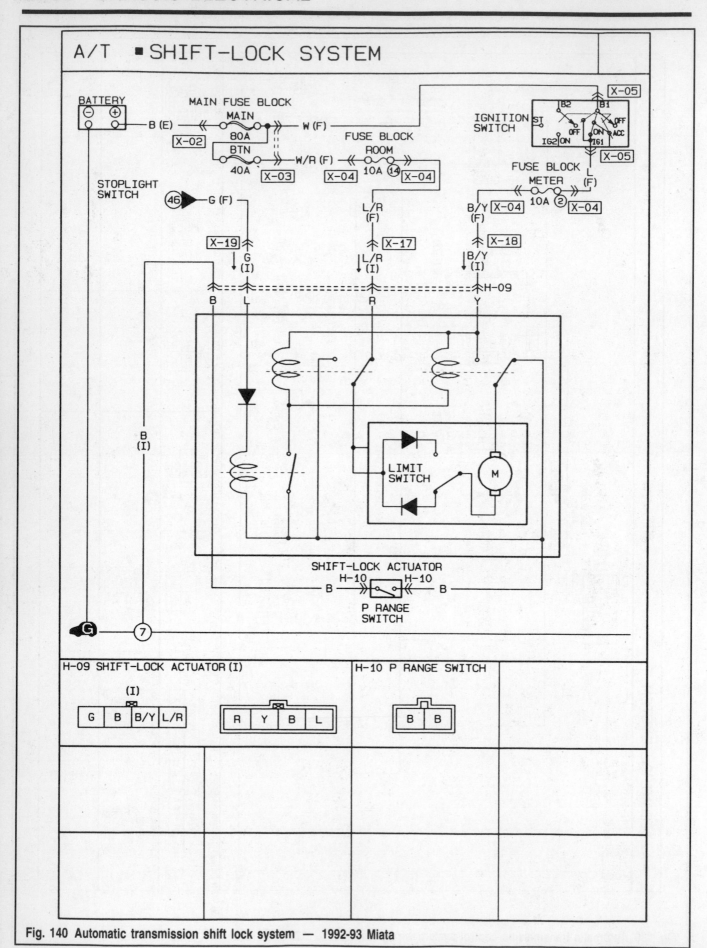

Fig. 140 Automatic transmission shift lock system — 1992-93 Miata

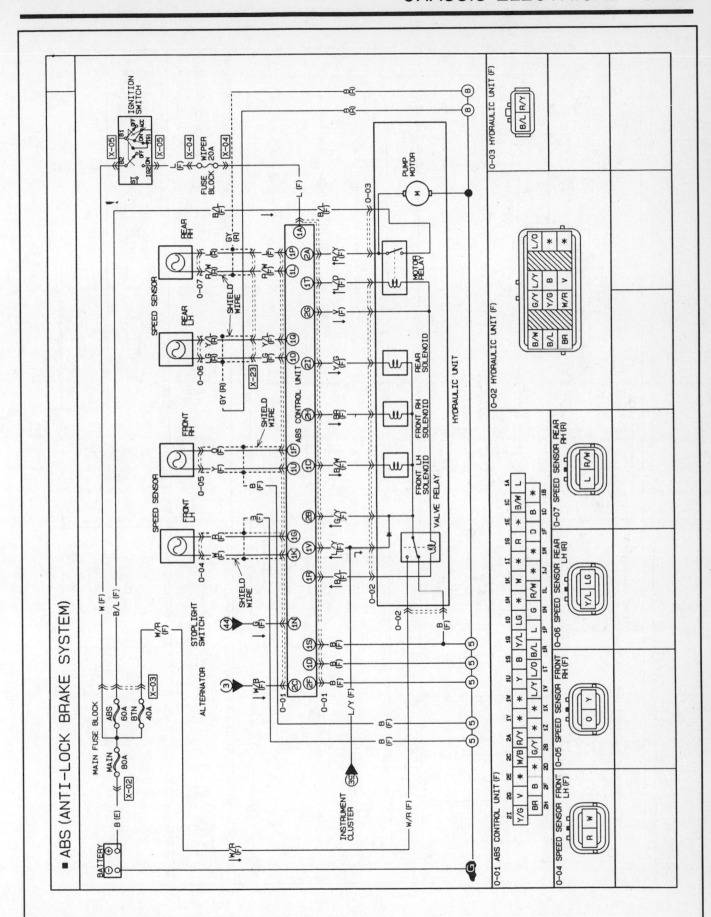

Fig. 141 ABS system wiring diagram — 1992-93 Miata

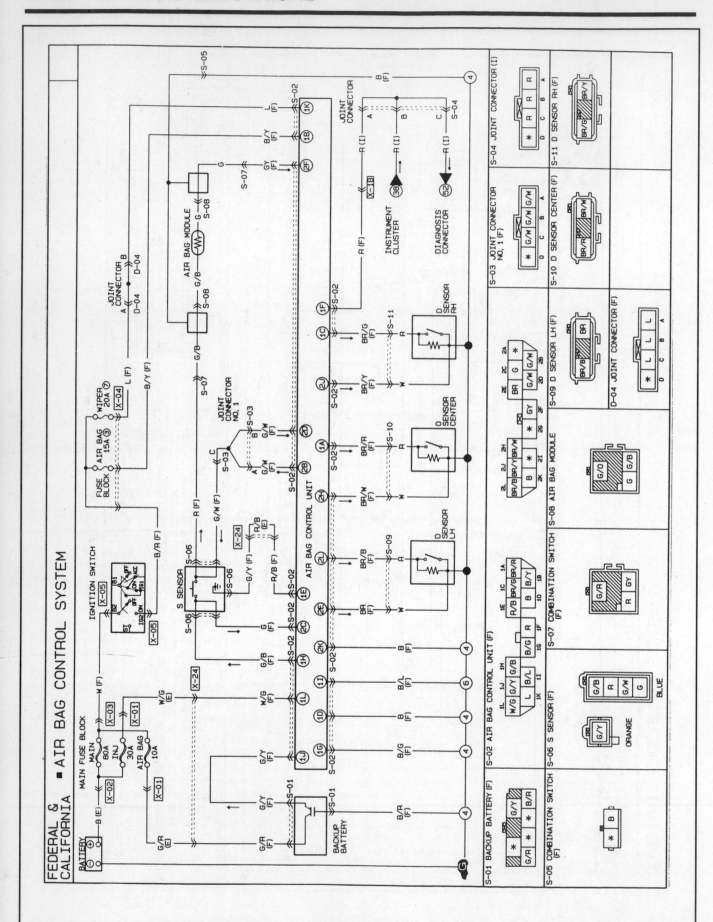

Fig. 142 Air bag control system wiring diagram — 1992-93 Miata

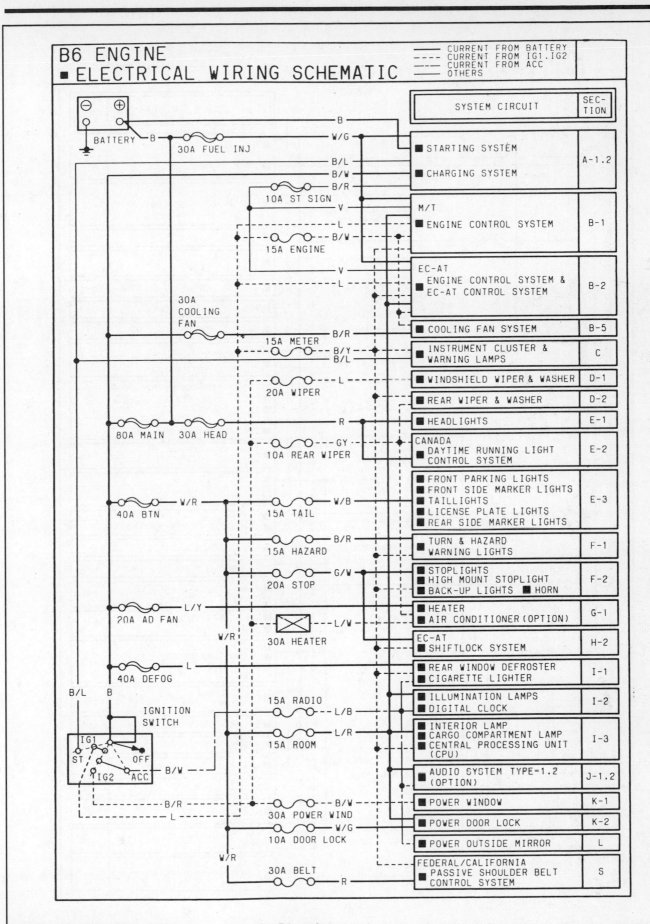

Fig. 143 Engine wiring schematic — MX3 with B6 engine

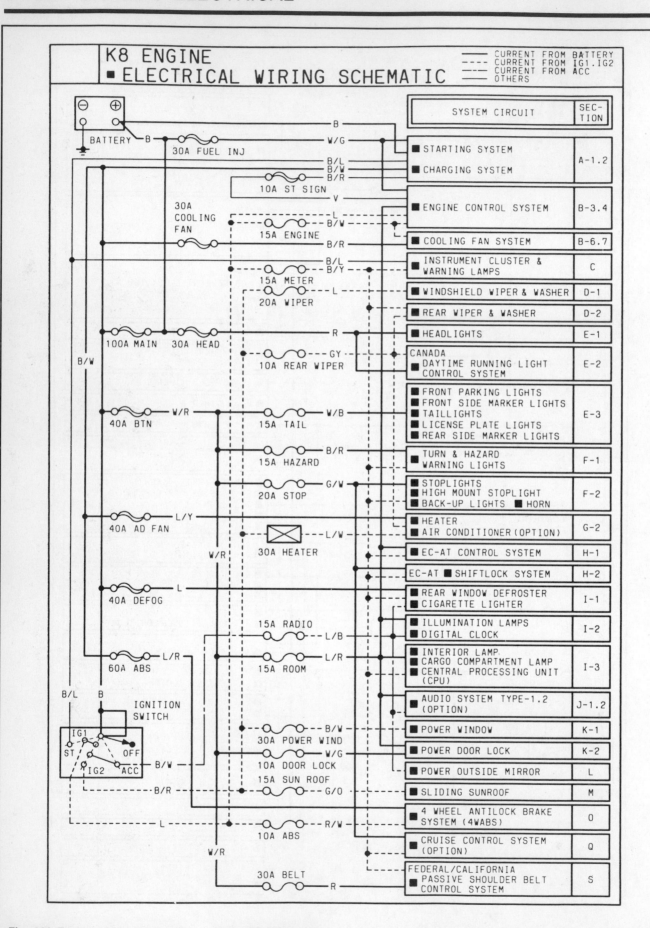

Fig. 144 Engine wiring schematic — MX3 with K8 engine

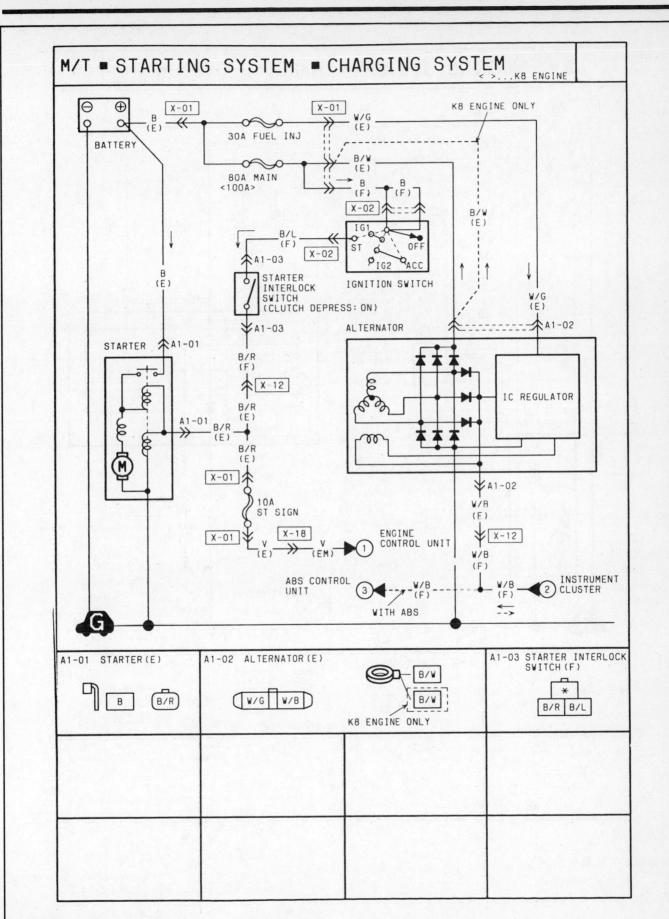

Fig. 145 Starting and charging system — MX3 with M/T

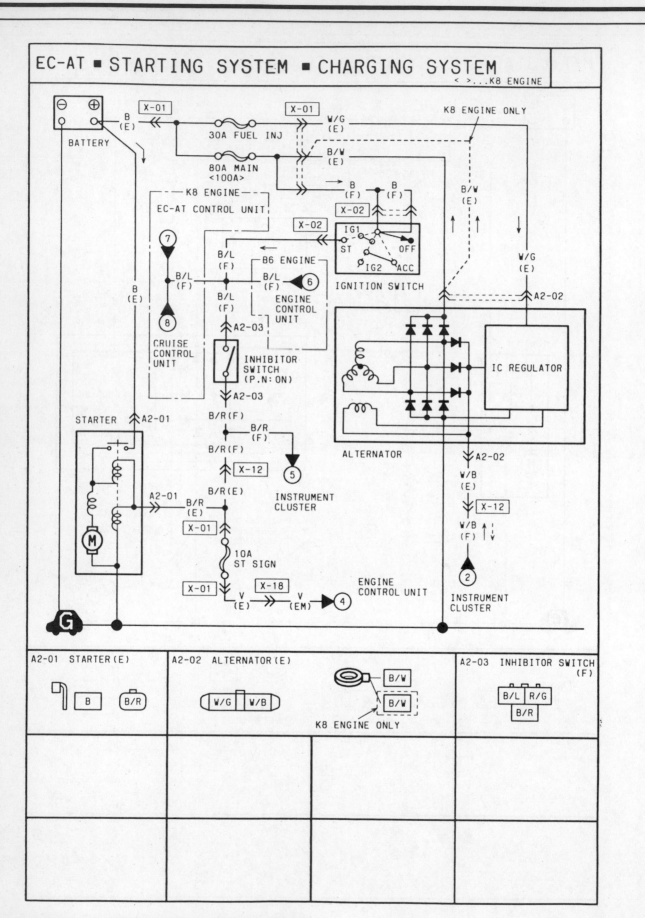

Fig. 146 Starting and charging system — MX3 with EC-A/T

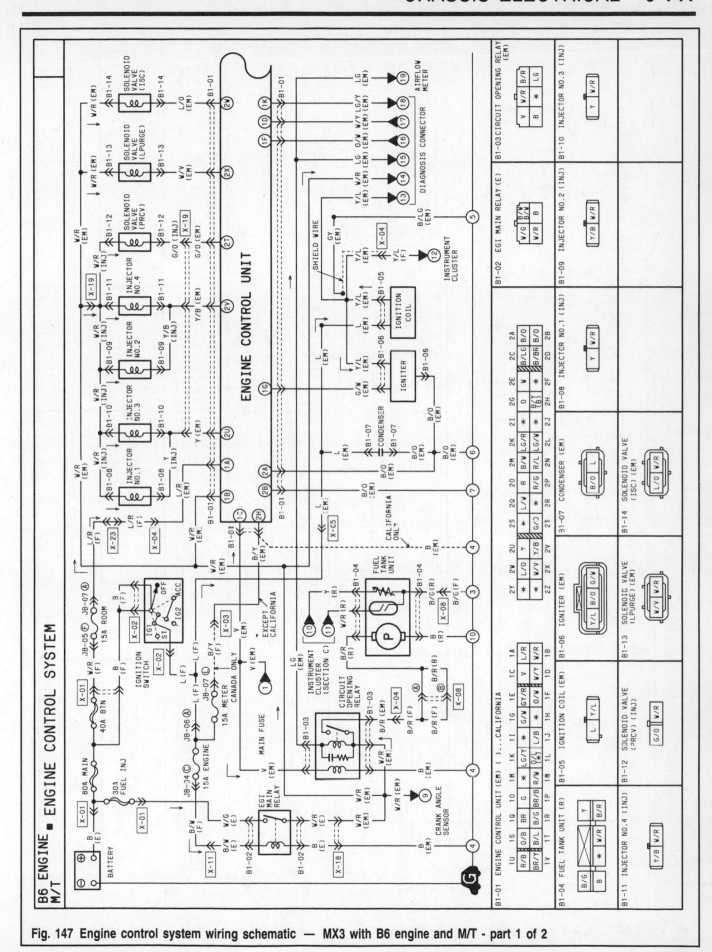

Fig. 147 Engine control system wiring schematic — MX3 with B6 engine and M/T - part 1 of 2

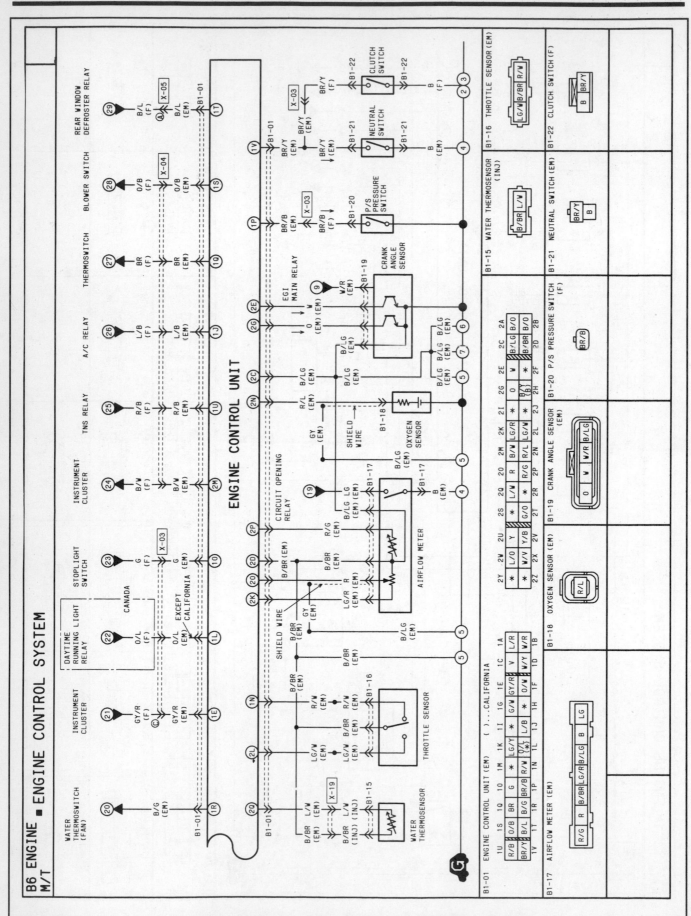

Fig. 148 Engine control system wiring schematic — MX3 with B6 engine and M/T - part 2 of 2

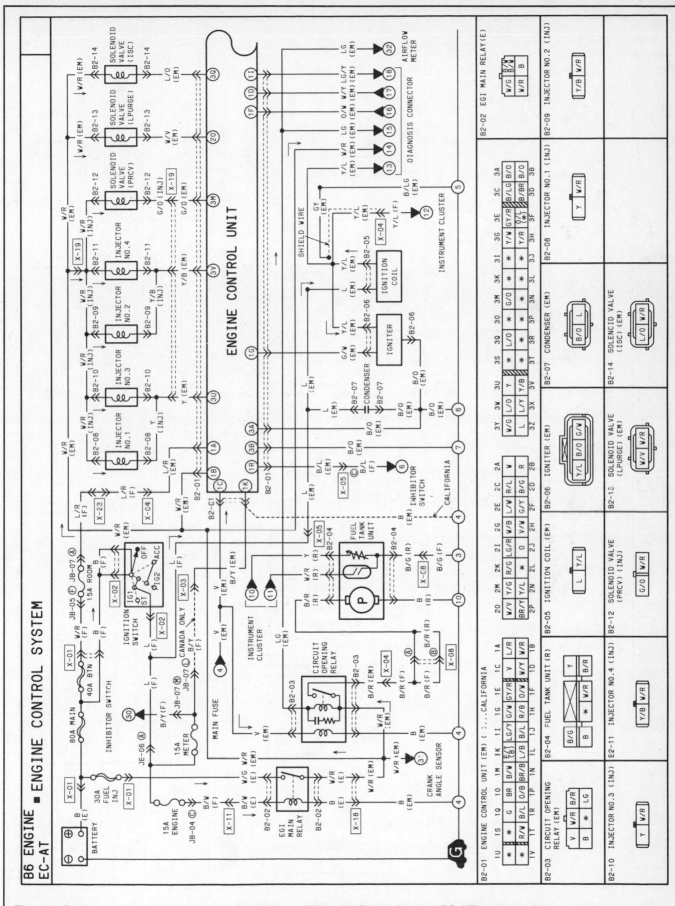

Fig. 149 Engine control system wiring schematic — MX3 with B6 engine and EC-A/T - part 1 of 2

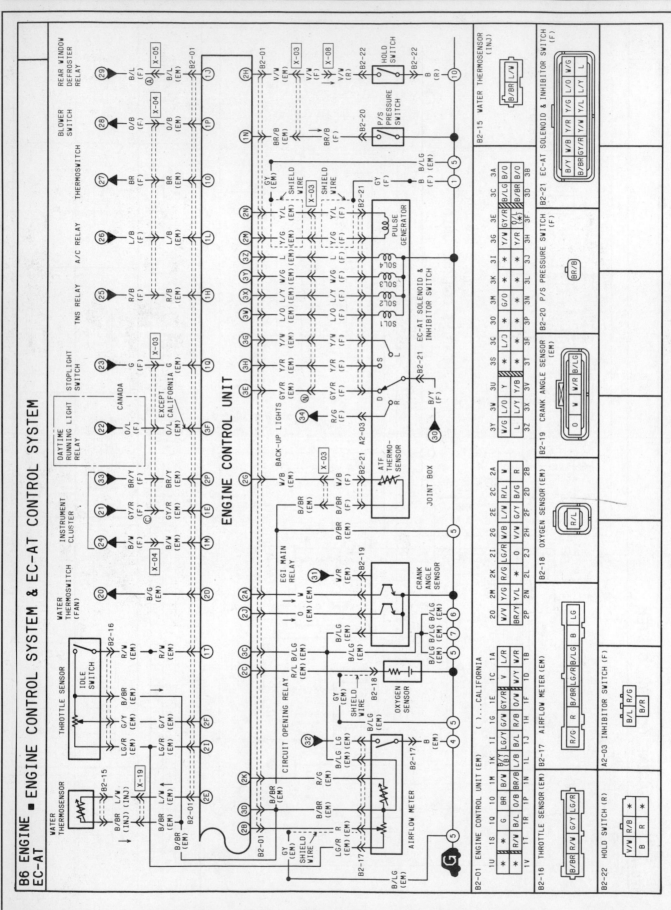

Fig. 150 Engine control system wiring schematic — MX3 with B6 engine and EC-A/T - part 2 of 2

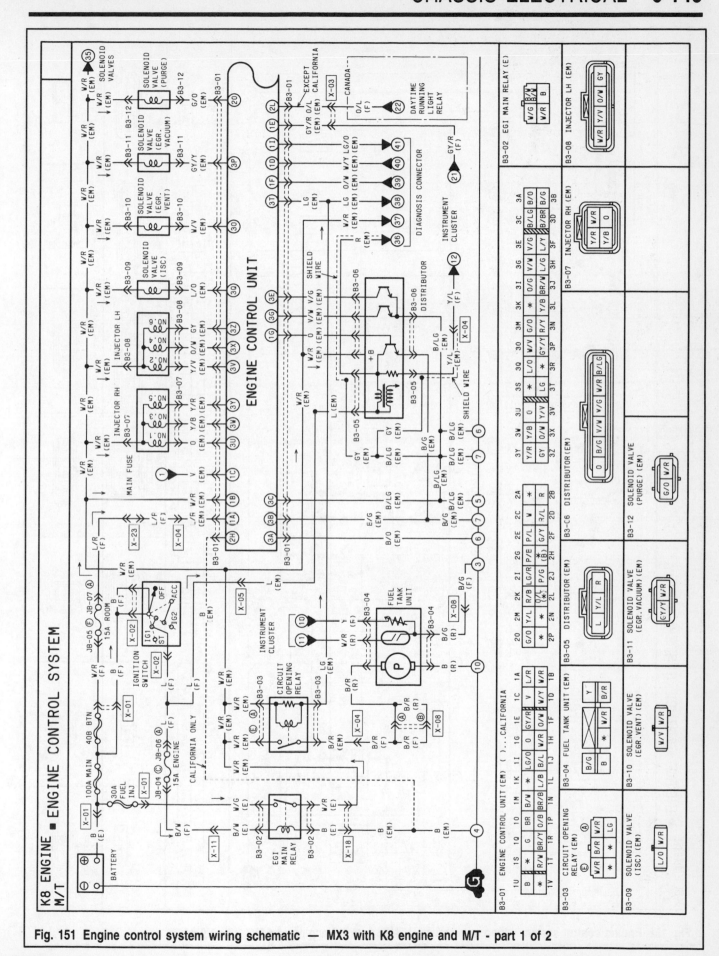

Fig. 151 Engine control system wiring schematic — MX3 with K8 engine and M/T - part 1 of 2

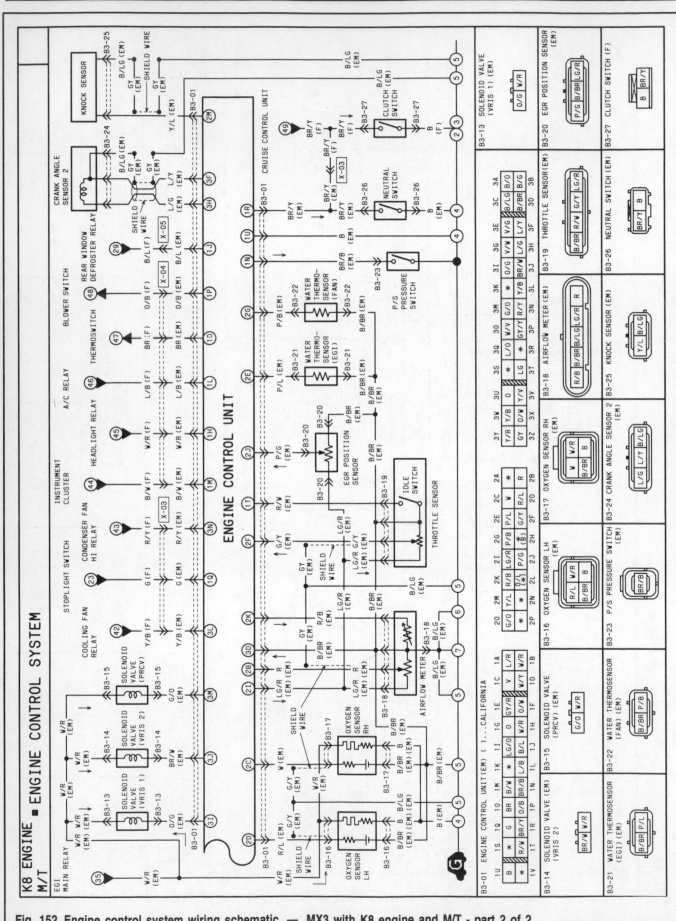

Fig. 152 Engine control system wiring schematic — MX3 with K8 engine and M/T - part 2 of 2

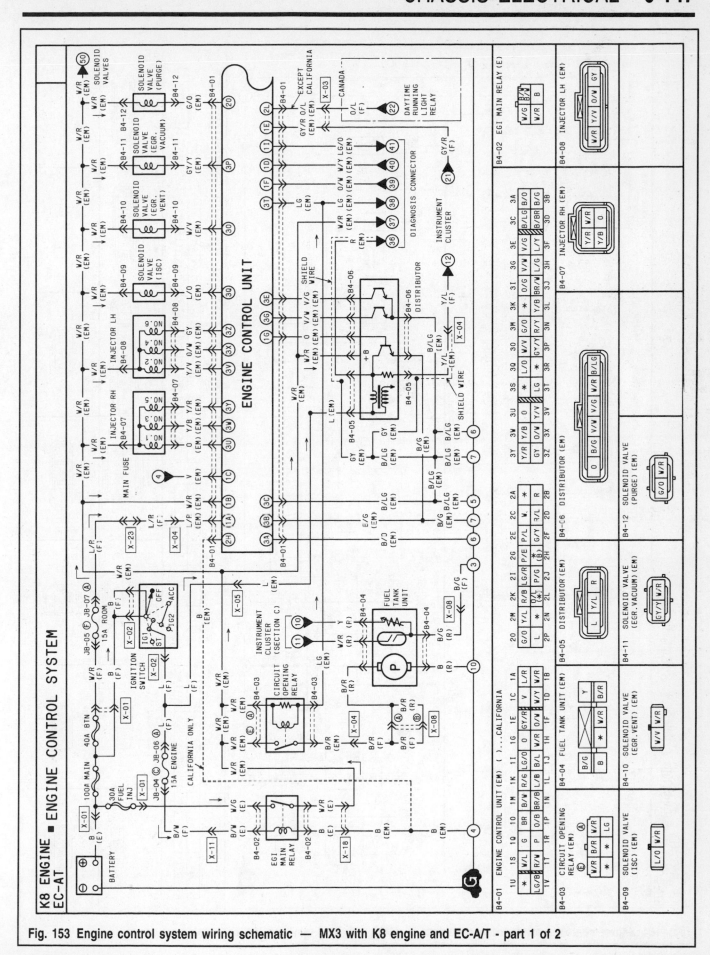

Fig. 153 Engine control system wiring schematic — MX3 with K8 engine and EC-A/T - part 1 of 2

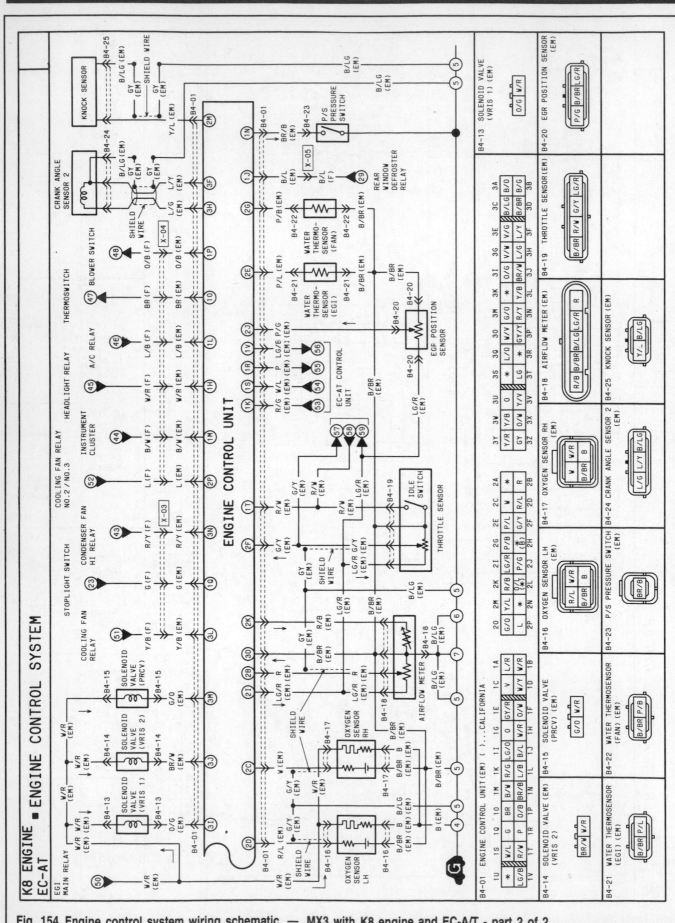

Fig. 154 Engine control system wiring schematic — MX3 with K8 engine and EC-A/T - part 2 of 2

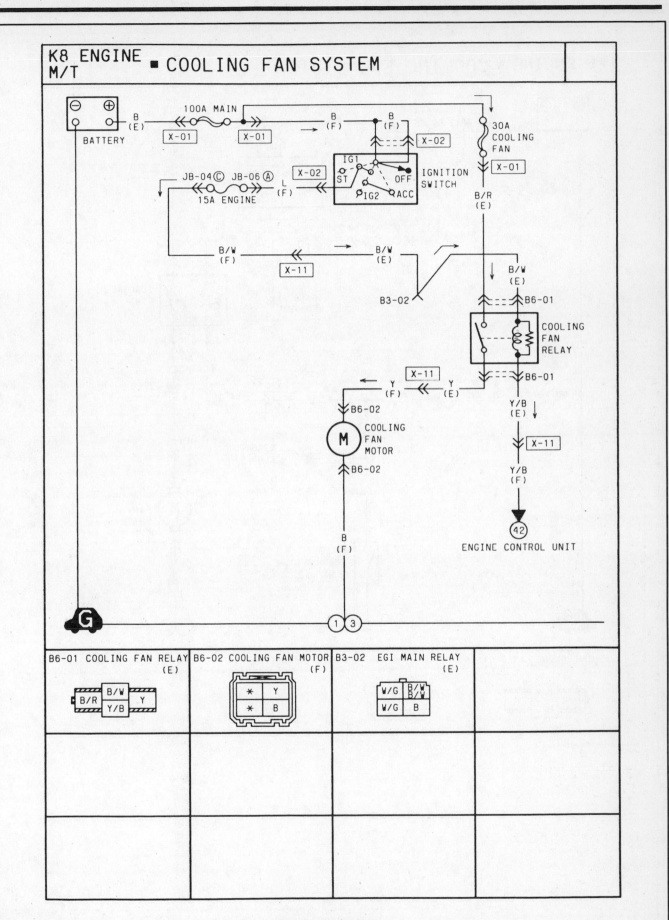

Fig. 155 Cooling fan system wiring schematic — MX3 with B6 engine

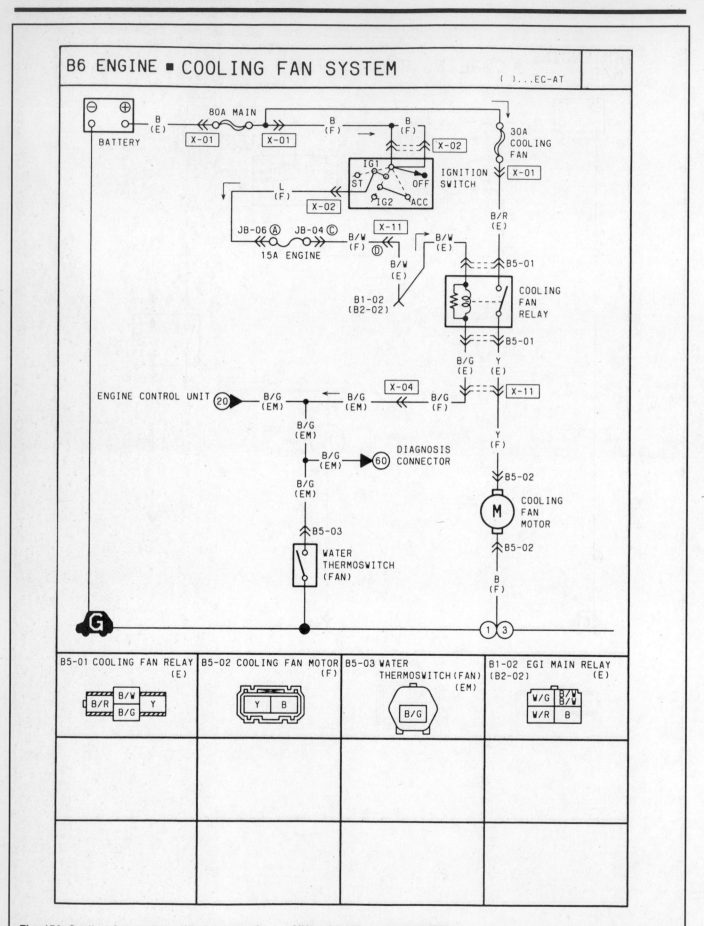

Fig. 156 Cooling fan system wiring schematic — MX3 with K8 engine and M/T

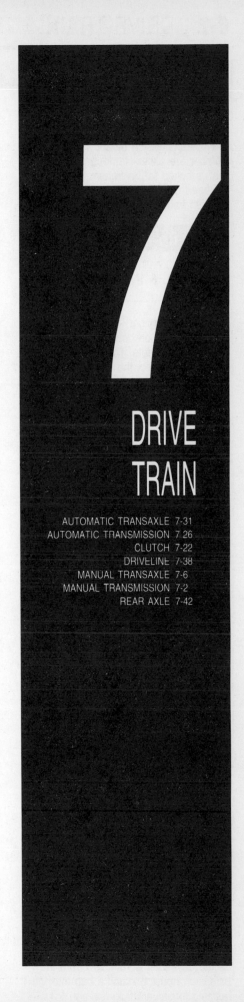

7

DRIVE
TRAIN

MANUAL TRANSMISSION

Identification

The transmission model and serial number are either stamped on a plate that is bolted to the transmission case or stamped directly on the case itself. The location varies from model to model.

Back-up Light Switch

REMOVAL & INSTALLATION

The back-up light switch is threaded into the extension housing near the speedometer cable. To remove the switch, disconnect the electrical wiring connectors making a note of which goes to which. Loosen and remove the switch from the extension housing. Remove the metal gasket from the switch and install a new one. To install the switch, thread it into the extension housing and tighten it just enough to crush the gasket. Connect the wiring and check the switch operates properly.

Transmission

REMOVAL & INSTALLATION

Miata

▶ **See Figures 1, 2, 3 and 4**

1. Disconnect the negative battery cable.
2. Raise and safely support the vehicle.
3. Remove the transmission drain plug and drain the transmission fluid.
4. From inside the vehicle, remove the gear shift knob.
5. Remove the rear console unit.
6. Remove the shift lever bolts and remove the shift lever assembly.
7. From under the vehicle, remove the under engine splash shield.
8. Disconnect the exhaust pipe from the manifold and remove the exhaust pipe and muffler assembly.
9. Place marks on the driveshaft flanges for installation purposes and remove the driveshaft by removing the bolts at the flange and sliding the shaft out of the extension housing. As soon as the driveshaft is removed from the extension housing install a cap into the housing to prevent fluid leakage.

10. Remove the clutch release cylinder from the side of the transmission housing
11. Disconnect the starter electrical connections and remove the starter.
12. Disconnect the speedometer cable from the transmission and feed it through the power plant frame member.
13. Remove the power plant frame as follows:
    a. Disconnect the wire harness from the power plant frame assembly.
    b. Install a transmission jack under the transmission and support it.
    c. Remove the bracket from between the power plant frame and the transmission extension.
    d. Remove the differential side bolts and pry out the spacer.
    e. Remove the differential mounting spacer.
    f. Install a M14 X 1.5 bolt into the mounting block sleeve as shown and scew the bolt in. Pull down on the bolt and install a M6 X 1 bolt into the side hole.
    g. Remove the long bolt and then the shorter bolt. Remove the transmission side bolts and remove the power plant frame assembly.
14. Remove the transmission mounting bolts and remove the transmission from the vehicle.

To install the transmission:

15. Raise and safely support the vehicle.
16. Install the transmission to the vehicle. It may be necessary to tilt the engine up by pushing up on the oil pan with a wooden block. Tighten the mounting bolts to 47-66 ft. lbs. (64-89 Nm).
17. Install the power plant frame as follows:
    a. Install the differential mounting spacer. Tighten the bolts to 27-38 ft. lbs. (37-52 Nm).
    b. Support the transmission so that it is level.
    c. Install the power plant frame and tighten the transmission side bolts by hand.
    d. Make sure that the sleeve is installed to the block of the power plant frame and install the spacer and the bolts.
    e. Install the power plant frame bracket and tighten the side bolts to 77-91 ft. lbs. (104-124 Nm).
    f. Tighten the differential side bolts to 77-91 ft. lbs. (104-124 Nm).

g. Install the power plant frame bracket and tighten the lower bolt to 77-91 ft. lbs. (104-124 Nm). Tighten the upper 2 bolts to 27-40 ft. lbs. (36-54 Nm).
    h. Remove the trnsmission jack and connect the transmission wire harness.
18. Connect the speedometer cable to the transmission and install the starter.
19. Install the clutch release cylinder and tighten the bolts to 12-17 ft. lbs. (16-23 Nm).
20. Install the driveshaft to the transmission extension and align the driveshaft flange marks.
21. Install the exhaust pipe to the manifold and tighten the mounting nuts to 23-34 ft. lbs. (31-46 Nm).
22. Install the engine under engine splash shield.
23. If the transmission has been overhauled or the extension housing has been removed, refill the transmission change control case. The capacity of the change control case is 4.9 — 5.8 cubic inches (80-95 cc).
24. Apply oil to the shift control lever and install the shift control lever. Tighten the bolts to 69-95 inch lbs. (7.8-11 Nm).
25. Install the rear console assembly and the shifter knob.
26. Refill the transmission to the proper level and connect the negative battery cable.
27. Start the engine and allow it to warm up. Inspect for any oil leakage.

DISASSEMBLY

▶ **See Figures 5, 6, 7 and 8**

Miata

TRANSMISSION HOUSING ASSEMBLY

1. Remove the transmission from the vehicle as previously described.
2. Remove the release bearing, release fork and boot from the transmission.
3. From inside the housing remove the front cover assembly and the gasket.
4. Remove the front oil seal, the adjustment shim and the snap ring.
5. Remove the speedometer drive gear from the side of the transmission.
6. Remove the neutral switch from the side of the transmission.
7. Remove the back-up light switch from the side of the transmission.

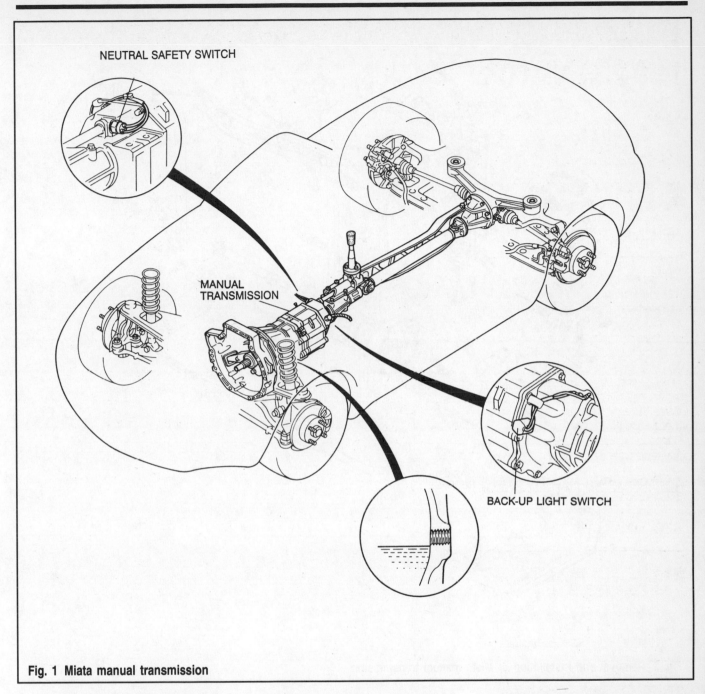

NEUTRAL SAFETY SWITCH

MANUAL
TRANSMISSION

BACK-UP LIGHT SWITCH

Fig. 1 Miata manual transmission

8. Remove the extension housing bolts and twist the housing to remove it.

9. Using Mazda special tool 49 0305 430, remove the transmission case from the intermediate housing and the gear assembly.

10. From inside the transmission housing, remove the snap rings and the speedometer gear.

11. Remove the steel ball from the shaft.

12. Remove the rear oil seal and replace if necessary.

SHIFT FORK AND ROD ASSEMBLY

1. Remove the roll pins from the 1st/2nd shift rod end, the 3rd/4th shift rod end and the 5th/reverse shift rod

end. Replace the roll pins, they cannot be reused.

2. Remove the 3 shift rod ends.

3. Remove the intermediate housing and inspect as follows:

 a. Measure the housing pin height.

 b. The pin height must be 0.354-0.394 inch (9.0-10.0 mm).

4. Remove the roll pins from the shift forks. All roll pins must be replaced, they cannot be used again.

5. Remove the cap plugs, the ball springs and the balls.

6. Remove the C-clip from the 1st/2nd shift rod and remove the interlock pin.

7. Remove the C-clip from the 3rd/4th shift rod and remove the shift rod and the 3rd/4th shift rod fork.

8. Remove the 1st/2nd shift fork and remove the interlock pin.

9. Remove the clip, spacer and spring assembly from the bearing housing assembly.

10. Remove the 5th/Reverse shift rod and fork and remove the corresponding spring and ball.

MAINSHAFT AND COUNTERSHAFT ASSEMBLIES

1. From the mainshaft assembly, remove the snap ring, the washer, the retainer ring and the C-washer.

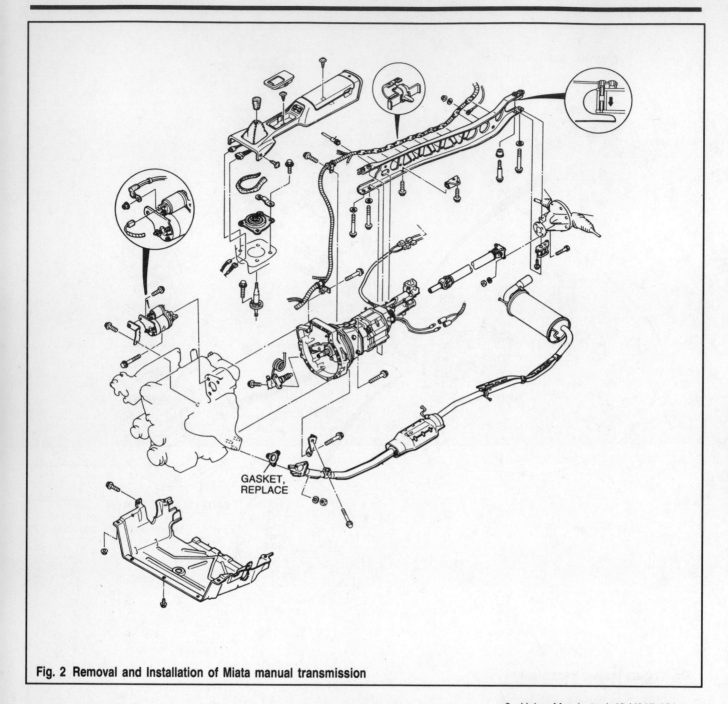

Fig. 2 Removal and Installation of Miata manual transmission

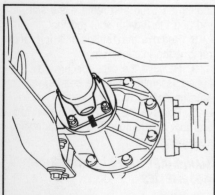

Fig. 3 Matchmarking drive shaft to the rear-Miata

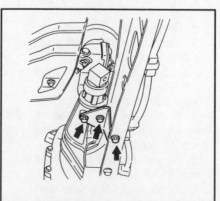

Fig. 4 Removing the power plant frame from the transmission-Miata

2. Using Mazda tool 49-H017-101 and 49-0839-425C or equivalent, remove the mainshaft rear bearing. Inspect the bearing, and replace if necessary.

3. Remove the retaining ring, the C-washer, the thrust lock washer and the steel ball from the mainshaft.

4. Remove the locknut from the countershaft as follows:

a. Shift the clutch hub sleeves to 1st and reverse gear to double-engage the gears.

b. Uncrimp the tabs on the locknut.

c. Install Mazda special tool 49-0259-440 to the main shaft end and tighten the mainshaft in a vise.

d. Remove the locknut.

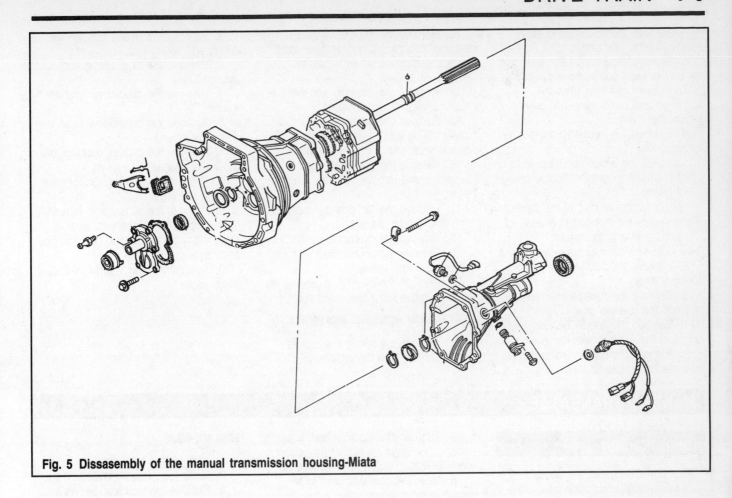

Fig. 5 Dissasembly of the manual transmission housing-Miata

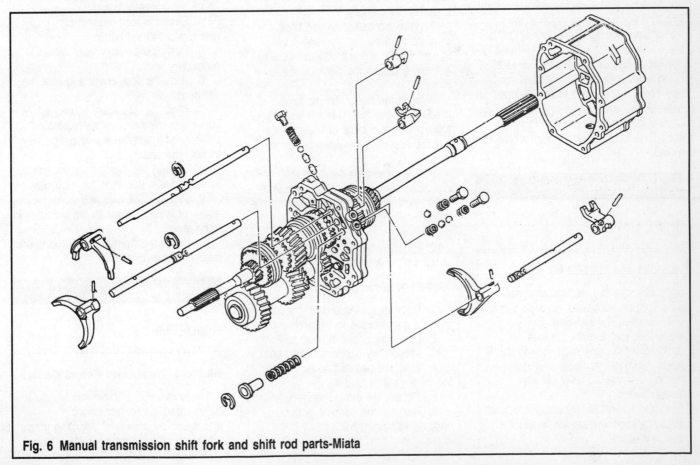

Fig. 6 Manual transmission shift fork and shift rod parts-Miata

5. Remove the countershaft rear bearing with a gear puller.

6. Remove the counter 5th gear from the countershaft and remove the spacer.

7. Remove 5th gear from the mainshaft and remove the 5th gear synchronizer ring.

8. Remove the mainshaft locknut as follows:

a. Shift the clutch hub sleeves to 1st and reverse gear to double-engage the gears.

b. Uncrimp the tabs of the locknut and secure the housing in a vise.

c. Use Mazda special tool 49-1243-465A and remove the locknut.

9. Remove the 5th/Reverse clutch hub assembly.

10. Remove the reverse synchronizer ring and the reverse gear.

11. Remove the needle bearing, inner race and the washer from the mainshaft.

12. Remove the counter reverse gear from the countershaft.

13. Remove the main drive gear bearing from the main drive gear using Mazda special tool 49-0710-520 or equivalent.

14. Remove the snapring and remove the countershaft front bearing.

15. Remove the bearing housing assembly by lightly tapping on the countershaft with a copper hammer.

16. Remove the mainshaft gear assembly and remove the main drive gear.

17. Remove the 4th gear synchonizer ring and needle bearing.

18. Remove the mainshaft washer.

19. Remove the countershaft and the syncronizer key spring.

20. Remove the clutch hub sleeve, the syncronizer key and the clutch hub.

EXTENSION HOUSING ASSEMBLY

1. Remove the spring cap, spring and steel ball from the assembly.

2. Remove the Select lock spindle, spring and spring cap.

3. Remove the plug, spring and pushpin.

4. Remove the blind cover and the roll pin.

5. Remove the control lever and the control lever end.

6. Remove the change bushing and the wave washer.

7. Remove the change control case and the rod cover.

8. Remove the oil passage assembly.

9. Inspect all components and replace any that appear to be damaged or defective.

10. Assembly is the reverse of the steps above.

MANUAL TRANSAXLE

Identification

Most transaxle codes are available from the vehicle information code plate on the cowl in the engine compartment. The first portion of the code is the transmission designation; following this, there is a blank box; at the right end of the line is the axle or final drive ratio.

On other models the transaxle model and serial number are either stamped on a plate that is bolted to the transmission case or stamped directly on the case itself. The location varies from model to model.

Adjustments

SHIFT LINKAGE

1989 323 and 1989-92 MX-6/626

1. Remove the necessary console parts to gain access to the shift cable.

2. Loosen the locknuts. On MX-6/626, also loosen the lock bolt.

3. Move the gearshift lever to the **P** range. Shift the transaxle to **P** by moving the manual lever on the transaxle.

4. On MX-6/626, tighten the lockbolt while holding the gearshift lever in **P**.

5. Turn the front locknut until it just touches the lever on 323 or the spacer on MX-6/626. Tighten the rear locknut.

6. Move the gearshift lever to **N**. Attach a suitable pull scale to the gearshift lever knob.

7. With the botton on the knob pressed in, push the gearshift lever toward **R** with a force of approximately 4.4 lbs. Measure the distance the lever moves.

8. With the botton on the knob pressed in, pull the gearshift lever toward **D** with a force of approximately 4.4 lbs. Measure the distance the lever moves.

9. The difference between the distances measured in Steps 7 and 8 must not exceed 0.315 in. (8mm). If the difference is greater, repeat the procedure.

10. Reinstall the console parts and check shifter operation.

1990-93 323/Protege and MX-3

1. Remove the necessary console parts to gain access to the shift cable.

2. Move the gearshift lever to **P**.

3. Loosen the cable mounting bolts.

4. Push the gearshift lever against the **P** range and hold it.

5. Tighten the cable mounting bolts.

6. Reinstall the console parts and check shifter operation.

1993 MX-6/626

1. Remove the front console.

2. Move the gearshift lever to **P**.

3. Remove the indicator screws and lift up the indicator panel.

4. Slide the lock cover and disconnect the set button.

5. Push the selector lever adjust **P** range.

6. Slide the lock cover and lock the set button.

7. Align the alignment screws in the slider with the holes in the indicator panel. Install suitable heavy gauge wire to hold the slider.

8. Tighten the indicator panel screw, in sequence, to 26 inch lbs. (2.9 Nm).

9. Remove the wire and verify the gearshift lever aligns with the indicator in each range.

10. Install the front console and check gearshift lever operation.

Shift Lever

ADJUSTMENT

All Front Wheel Drive Except Below

The shift lever on most models may be adjusted during transmission installation by means of adjusting shims on the three bolts between the cover plate and the packing. The force

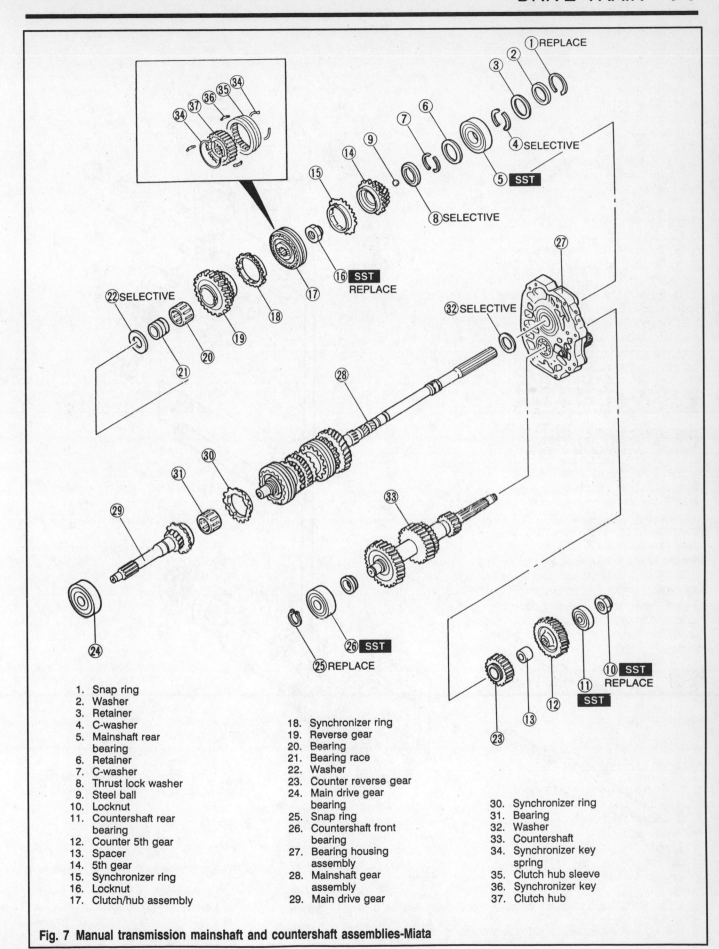

1. Snap ring
2. Washer
3. Retainer
4. C-washer
5. Mainshaft rear bearing
6. Retainer
7. C-washer
8. Thrust lock washer
9. Steel ball
10. Locknut
11. Countershaft rear bearing
12. Counter 5th gear
13. Spacer
14. 5th gear
15. Synchronizer ring
16. Locknut
17. Clutch/hub assembly
18. Synchronizer ring
19. Reverse gear
20. Bearing
21. Bearing race
22. Washer
23. Counter reverse gear
24. Main drive gear bearing
25. Snap ring
26. Countershaft front bearing
27. Bearing housing assembly
28. Mainshaft gear assembly
29. Main drive gear
30. Synchronizer ring
31. Bearing
32. Washer
33. Countershaft
34. Synchronizer key spring
35. Clutch hub sleeve
36. Synchronizer key
37. Clutch hub

Fig. 7 Manual transmission mainshaft and countershaft assemblies-Miata

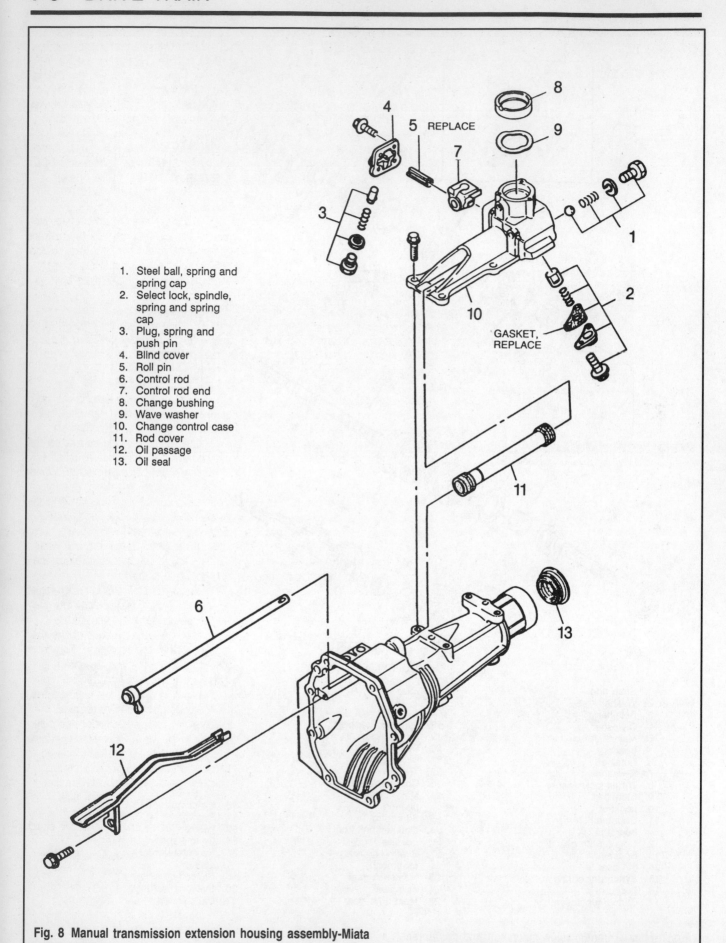

1. Steel ball, spring and spring cap
2. Select lock, spindle, spring and spring cap
3. Plug, spring and push pin
4. Blind cover
5. Roll pin
6. Control rod
7. Control rod end
8. Change bushing
9. Wave washer
10. Change control case
11. Rod cover
12. Oil passage
13. Oil seal

REPLACE

GASKET, REPLACE

Fig. 8 Manual transmission extension housing assembly-Miata

required to move the shift knob should be 4.4-8.8 lbs.

1990 323 With 4WD Only

1. Set the transaxle shift lever to the Neutral position.

2. On the transaxle make sure the shift and select levers are also in the Neutral position.

3. Remove the shift lever console.

4. Disconnect the shift and select cables from the control levers by remvong the pins, flatwashers and spring clips. The clips must be replaced.

5. Make sure the select cable end hole aligns with the select lever pin. If not aligned, loosen cable adjusting nut **A** and rotate the cable end until the holes are aligned.

6. Place the shift lever at the center of its front-to-rear stoke.

7. Make sure the select cable end hole aligns with the select lever pin. If not aligned, loosen cable adjusting nut **B** and rotate the cable end until the holes are aligned.

8. Connect the cables.

Back-up Light Switch

The back-up light switch is threaded into the transaxle case. To remove the switch, first remove the wire clamp from the transxle case that secures the switch wire. Next, disconnect the electrical wiring multi-connector. Loosen and remove the switch from the transaxle case. Remove the metal gasket from the switch and install a new one. To install the swItch, thread it into the transaxle case and tighten just enough to crush the gasket. Connect the wiring, install the wire clamp and check that the switch operates properly.

Transaxle

REMOVAL & INSTALLATION

323/Protege without 4WD

◗ See Figures 9 and 10

1. Disconnect the negative battery cable. Remove the air cleaner. Loosen the front wheel lug nuts.

2. Disconnect the speedometer from the transaxle. Disconnect the clutch cable from the release lever and remove the clutch cable bracket mounting bolts.

3. Remove the ground wire installation boot. Remove the water pipe bracket. Remove the secondary air pipe and the EGR pipe bracket.

4. Remove the wire harness clip. Disconnect the coupler for the neutral switch and back-up lamp switch. Disconnect the body ground connector.

5. Remove the two upper transaxle mounting bolts. Mount the engine support tool 49-ER301-025A or equivalent to the engine hanger.

6. Raise and support the vehicle safely. Drain the transaxle oil into a suitable container and remove the front wheels.

7. Remove the engine under cover and side covers. Remove the front stabilizer.

8. Remove the lower arm ball joints and the knuckle clinch bolts, pull the lower arm downward and separate the lower arms from the knuckles.

9. Separate the driveshaft by pulling the front hub outward. Make sure not to use too much force at once, increase the force gradually. Be sure the driveshaft's ball joint is bent to its maximum extent. Do not allow the axleshafts to drop. Damage may occur to the ball and socket joints and to the rubber boots. Wire the shafts to the vehicle body when released from the differential.

10. Remove the transaxle crossmember. Separate the change control rod from the transaxle. Remove the extension bar from the transaxle. Remove the wiring and the starter motor.

11. Remove the end plates. Lean the engine toward the transaxle side to lower the transaxle by loosening the engine support hook bolt. Support the transaxle with a suitable transaxle jack.

12. Remove the necessary engine brackets. Remove the remaining transaxle mounting bolt and No. 2 engine bracket. Lower the jack and slide the transaxle out from under the vehicle.

To install the transaxle:

13. Before installing the transaxle, coat the splines of the primary shaft gear with molybdenum disulfide grease.

14. Attach a thick rope to two places on the transaxle. Place a board on the jack and lower the tranaxle onto the board. Using the jack, lift the transaxle into postion and throw the end of the rope over the support fixture bar. Tension the rope to guide the transaxle onto its mounts while lifting the transxle with the jack. Once the transaxle is in place, have an assistant install all the transaxle-to-engine mounting bolts. Torque the bolts to to 47-66 ft. lbs.

15. Install the end plates and the starter motor. Install the extension bar and control rod. Torque the extension bar nuts to 23-34 ft. lbs. and the change control rod nuts to 12-17 ft. lbs.

16. Attach the No. 2 mounting bracket to the trasaxle and torque the bracket bolts to 27-38 ft. lbs. Install the crossmember and left side lower control arm assembly. Torque bolts **A** to 47-66 ft. lbs. and bolts **B** to 20-34 ft. lbs.

17. Remove the jack and rope. Remove the support fixture.

18. Install the starter and connect the wiring. Attach the surge tank bracket and gusset plate. Install the end plate, clutch release cylinder and remaining gusset plates. Torque the gusset plate bolts to 27-38 ft. lbs.

19. Replace the clips at the inner ends of the driveshaft and cross-shaft back into the transaxle, first turn the differential side gear by inserting your finger into the shaft hole so the shaft splines and gear recesses will fit into one another. Force the shaft in so the spring clip will lock. After the shaft is installed, connect it to the driveshaft. Then, pull the front disc-caliper assembly outward to make sure the driveshaft will not come out of the transmission. When installing the other driveshaft, use the same general technique to first force the spring clip to lock and then check that It has locked in a similar manner.

20. Connect the lower arm ball joints to the steering knuckles and torque the nuts to 32-40 ft. lbs.

21. Install the stabilizer bar and adjust as follows: Tighen the locknuts and the adjusting nuts so that 11mm of the through-bolt threads protrude above the top of nut **B** in the illustration. This is dimension **C** . Once this dimension is obtained, tighen nut **B** to 23-33 ft. lbs. and bolts **A** to 9-13 ft. lbs. Connect the tie rod ends using new cotter pins.

22. Install the engine under and side covers. Install the front wheels and lower the vehicle. Connect the body ground wire and neutral and back-up switch coupler. Install the EGR plpe bracket, secondary air pipe and water pipe bracket. Attach the clutch cable mounting bracket and connect the clutch cable to the release lever.

23. Connect the speedometer cable, then install the air cleaner assembly. Connect the negative battery cable. Adjust clutch and shift linkage as required. Refill the transaxle with the proper grade of gear oil.

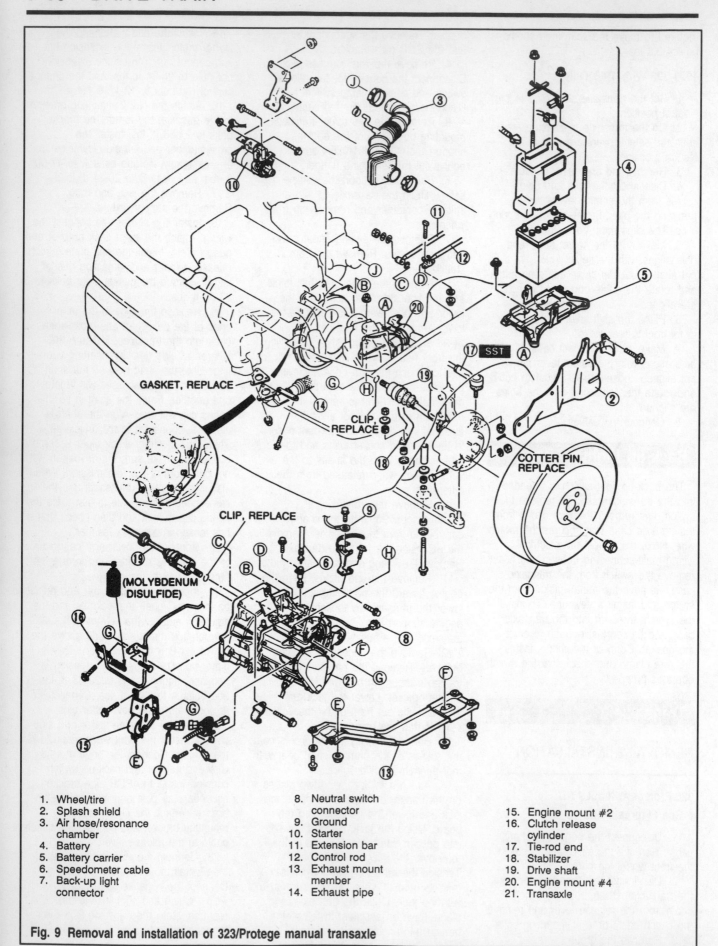

GASKET, REPLACE

CLIP,
REPLACE

(MOLYBDENUM
DISULFIDE)

CLIP, REPLACE

COTTER PIN,
REPLACE

1. Wheel/tire
2. Splash shield
3. Air hose/resonance chamber
4. Battery
5. Battery carrier
6. Speedometer cable
7. Back-up light connector
8. Neutral switch connector
9. Ground
10. Starter
11. Extension bar
12. Control rod
13. Exhaust mount member
14. Exhaust pipe
15. Engine mount #2
16. Clutch release cylinder
17. Tie-rod end
18. Stabilizer
19. Drive shaft
20. Engine mount #4
21. Transaxle

Fig. 9 Removal and installation of 323/Protege manual transaxle

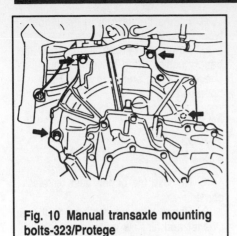

Fig. 10 Manual transaxle mounting bolts-323/Protege

323/Protege with 4WD

1. Remove the battery and the air cleaner assembly. Disconnect the speedometer cable in the center. Remove the clutch release cylinder retaining bolt and clip and remove the clutch release cylinder. Raise and support the vehicle safely and drain the tranaxle and engine oil.

2. Disconnect the neutral safety switch, back-up lamp switch, differential lock sensor switch and differential lock motor electrical connectors. Disconnect the transaxle shift and select control cables from the transaxle by removing the pins and cable retaining clips. Route the cables off to the side and out of the way.

3. Mount the engine support fixture 49-8017-5A0 or equivalent to the engine strut mounting blocks. To mount the support fixture, first the nuts must be removed from the mounting blocks. Remove the No. 4 engine mount bracket and remove the the front wheel.

4. Remove the side cover and under cover. Remove the propeller shaft and crossmember. Remove the oil filter and differential lock assembly (the differential lock assembly is fastened with three bolts). Disconnect the starter wiring and remove the starter and stabilizer bar.

5. Disconnect the tie rod end from the lower control arm. Insert a small pry bar between the driveshaft and the transaxle case and tap the end of the lever to uncouple the driveshaft from the differential side gear. Remove the remaining driveshaft in the same manner. Insert differential side gear holder 49-B027-001 or its equivalent to hold the side gears in place and prevent misalignment.

6. Remove the end plate bolts and connect a suitable hoist and lifting strap to the transaxle. Lift the transaxle and

transfer carrier assembly out of the engine.

To install the transaxle:

7. Attach a thick rope to two places on the transaxle. Place a board on the jack and lower the tranaxle onto the board. Using the jack, lift the transaxle into postion and throw the end of the rope over the support fixture bar. Tension the rope to guide the transaxle onto its mounts while lifting the transxle with the jack. Once the transaxle is in place, have an assistant install all the transaxle-to-engine and transfer mounting bolts. Torque the bolts to 66-86 ft. lbs.

8. Install the end plates.

9. Replace the clips at the inner ends of the driveshaft and cross-shaft back into the transaxle, first turn the differential side gear by inserting your finger into the shaft hole so the shaft splines and gear recesses will fit into one another. Force the shaft in so the spring clip will lock. After the shaft is installed, connect It to the driveshaft. Then, pull the front disc-caliper assembly outward to make sure the driveshaft will not come out of the transmission. When installing the other driveshaft, use the same general technique to first force the spring clip to lock and then check that it has locked in a similar manner. When installing the joint shaft, torque mounting bolts to 31-46 ft. lbs.

10. Connect the tie rods to the lower arm and torque the pinch bolts to 32-40 ft. lbs. Install and adjust the stabilizer bar as described in Step 19 for 2WD 323s in the above procedure. Dimension **C** for 4WD vehicles is 8.5mm and the torque specs are the same.

11. Install the starter, differential lock assembly, oil filter, propeller shaft, side covers and under covers. Install the front wheels and lower the vehicle.

12. Install the No. 4 mounting bracket. Torque nuts **A** to 37-45 ft. lbs. and nuts **B** to 14-19 ft. lbs.

13. Remove the support fixture and replace the strut mounting block nuts. Torque the nuts to 17-22 ft. lbs. Connect the shift and select control cables using new retaining clips. Connect all the electrical and sensor wiring. Fill the transaxle to the proper level through the speedometer drive gear opening. Fill the crankcase. Adjust the shift and select control cables as described above.

MX-3

1.6L ENGINE
♦ See Figure 11

1. Disconnect the negative battery cable. Raise and safely support the vehicle. Drain the fluid from the transaxle.

2. Remove the wheel and tire assemblies and the splash shield.

3. Remove the resonance duct and the air cleaner assembly.

4. Disconnect the positive battery cable and remove the battery and battery tray. Label and disconnect the neutral switch and backup light connectors and the ground wire.

5. Disconnect the extension bar and shift control rod from the transaxle.

6. Remove the cotter pins and nuts and separate the tie rod ends from the knuckles. Disconnect the stabilizer links from the lower control arms.

7. Remove the halfshafts.

8. Remove the intake manifold support bracket and the starter.

9. Support the engine using engine support tool 49 G017 5A0 or equivalent. Remove the bolts/nuts and remove the engine mount member.

10. Remove the mounting bolts and line clip and position the clutch slave cylinder aside, without disconnecting the hydraulic line.

11. Remove the front and left side transaxle mounts.

12. Loosen the engine support tool and lean the engine toward the transaxle. Support the transaxle with a jack. Remove the transaxle mounting bolts and carefully remove the transaxle.

To install:

13. Raise the transaxle into position and install the transaxle-to-engine bolts. Tighten to 66 ft. lbs. (89 Nm). Install the oil pan-to-transaxle bolts and tighten to 38 ft. lbs. (52 Nm).

14. Loosely tighten the left side transaxle mount bolts. Install the front transaxle mount and tighten to 38 ft. lbs. (52 Nm).

15. Install the clutch slave cylinder and tighten the bolts to 17 ft. lbs. (23 Nm).

16. Install the engine mount member, aligning the front and rear transaxle mount stud bolts. Install the mount member-to-mount nuts and tighten to 38 ft. lbs. (52 Nm) and the mount member-to-body bolts/nuts and tighten to 66 ft. lbs. (89 Nm).

17. Tighten the left side transaxle mount-to-transaxle bolts to 69 ft. lbs. (93 Nm). Remove the engine support tool.

18. Install the starter and intake manifold support bracket. Tighten the bolts/nuts to 38 ft. lbs. (52 Nm).

19. Install the halfshafts.

20. Connect the stabilizer bar link to the lower control arm and tighten the nut to 45 ft. lbs. (61 Nm). Connect the tie rod end to the steering knuckle and tighten the nut to 42 ft. lbs. (57 Nm). Install a new cotter pin.

21. Connect the extension bar to the transaxle and tighten the bolt to 38 ft. lbs. (52 Nm). Connect the shift control rod and tighten the bolt to 17 ft. lbs. (23 Nm).

22. Remove the speedometer driven gear and add the proper type and quantity of oil. Install the driven gear and tighten the bolt to 100 inch lbs. (11 Nm). Connect the speedometer cable.

23. Connect the electrical connectors and ground wire. Install the battery tray and battery.

24. Install the air cleaner assembly and the resonance duct. Install the splash shield and the wheel and tire assemblies.

25. Lower the vehicle and connect the battery cables. Start the engine and check for leaks and proper transaxle operation.

1.8L ENGINE

▶ See Figure 12

1. Relieve the fuel system pressure and disconnect the negative battery cable. Raise and safely support the vehicle and drain the fluid from the transaxle.

2. Remove the wheel and tire assemblies and the splash shield.

3. Remove the resonance duct and the air cleaner assembly.

4. Disconnect the positive battery cable and remove the battery and battery tray.

5. Remove the starter and the wiring harness bracket. Disconnect the fuel lines and remove the fuel filter.

6. Label and disconnect the connectors for the neutral switch, backup light switch and speedometer sensor.

7. Remove the mounting bolts and line clip and position the clutch slave cylinder aside, without disconnecting the hydraulic line.

8. Remove the transverse member and the front exhaust pipe/converter assembly.

9. Disconnect the extension bar and shift control rod from the transaxle.

10. Remove the cotter pins and nuts and separate the tie rod ends from the

knuckles. Disconnect the stabilizer links from the lower control arms.

11. Remove the halfshafts and the intermediate shaft.

12. Support the engine using engine support tool 49 G017 5A0 or equivalent. Remove the bolts/nuts and remove the engine mount member.

13. Remove the left side transaxle mount and the transaxle inspection plate.

14. Loosen the engine support tool and lean the engine toward the transaxle. Support the transaxle with a jack. Remove the transaxle mounting bolts and carefully remove the transaxle.

To install:

15. Raise the transaxle into position and install the transaxle-to-engine bolts. Tighten to 73 ft. lbs. (99 Nm).

16. Install the transmission inspection plate and tighten the bolts to 38 ft. lbs. (52 Nm).

17. Loosely tighten the left side transaxle mount bolts.

18. Install the engine mount member, aligning the front and rear transaxle mount stud bolts. Install the mount member-to-mount nuts and tighten to 38 ft. lbs. (52 Nm) and the mount member-to-body bolts/nuts and tighten to 66 ft. lbs. (89 Nm).

19. Tighten left side transaxle mount-to-transaxle nut **A** to 69 ft. lbs. (93 Nm) and nuts **B** to 30 ft. lbs. (40 Nm). Remove the engine support tool.

20. Install the halfshafts and joint shaft.

21. Connect the stabilizer bar link to the lower control arm and tighten the nut to 45 ft. lbs. (61 Nm). Connect the tie rod end to the steering knuckle and tighten the nut to 42 ft. lbs. (57 Nm). Install a new cotter pin.

22. Connect the extension bar to the transaxle and tighten the bolt to 38 ft. lbs. (52 Nm). Connect the shift control rod and tighten the bolt to 17 ft. lbs. (23 Nm).

23. Install the exhaust pipe, using new gaskets. Tighten the manifold flange nuts to 38 ft. lbs. (52 Nm).

24. Install the transverse member and tighten the bolts to 93 ft. lbs. (127 Nm).

25. Connect the electrical connectors. Install the fuel filter and connect the fuel lines.

26. Install the starter and the wiring harness bracket.

27. Install the battery tray and battery.

28. Install the air cleaner assembly and the resonance duct. Install the splash shield and the wheel and tire assemblies.

29. Fill the transaxle with the proper type and quantity of oil.

30. Lower the vehicle and connect the battery cables. Start the engine and check for leaks and proper transaxle operation.

MX-6/626

1989-92

▶ See Figure 13

1. Remove the battery and battery carrier.

2. Remove the air ducting and the air cleaner and air flow meter assembly.

3. Unplug the wiring and remove the fuse block.

4. Disconnect the speedometer cable and the transaxle grounds.

5. Raise and support the vehicle safely and remove the front wheels and splash shield. Drain the transaxle oil.

6. Remove the clutch release cylinder and disconnect the tie rod ends.

7. Remove the stabilizer control links. Remove the nuts and bolts from the lower control arm ball joints and pull the lower control arms downward to separate them from the steering knuckles. Be careful not to damage the ball joint dust boots.

8. Insert a small prybar between the left driveshaft and the transaxle case and tap the end of the lever to uncouple the driveshaft from the differential side gear. Pull the front hub forward and separate the driveshaft from the transaxle. Remove the left joint shaft bracket. Separate the right driveshaft and joint shaft in the same manner as the left.

➡**Do not insert the lever too deeply between the shaft and the case or the oil seal lip could be damaged. To avoid damage to the oil seal, hold the CV-joint at the differential and pull the driveshaft straight out.**

9. Once both drive and joint shafts are removed, install differential side gear holders 49-G030-455 (turbo), 49-G027-003 or their equivalents, in the differential side gears to hold them in place and prevent misalignment.

10. Remove the engine-to-transaxle gusset plates and under cover. Remove the extension bar and the control rod. Remove the manifold bracket and the starter.

11. Suspend the engine from the engine hanger with a suitable lifting device or engine support fixture.

12. Remove the front and left engine mounts and bracket. Disconnect the

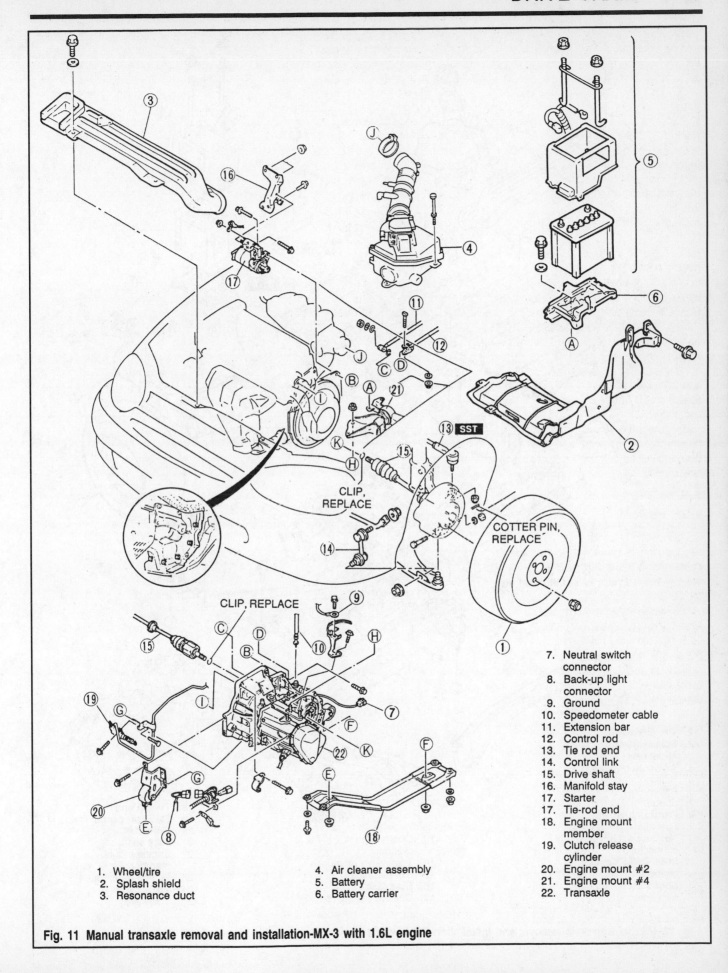

CLIP, REPLACE

COTTER PIN, REPLACE

CLIP, REPLACE

SST

7. Neutral switch connector
8. Back-up light connector
9. Ground
10. Speedometer cable
11. Extension bar
12. Control rod
13. Tie rod end
14. Control link
15. Drive shaft
16. Manifold stay
17. Starter
17. Tie-rod end
18. Engine mount member
19. Clutch release cylinder
20. Engine mount #2
21. Engine mount #4
22. Transaxle

1. Wheel/tire
2. Splash shield
3. Resonance duct

4. Air cleaner assembly
5. Battery
6. Battery carrier

Fig. 11 Manual transaxle removal and installation-MX-3 with 1.6L engine

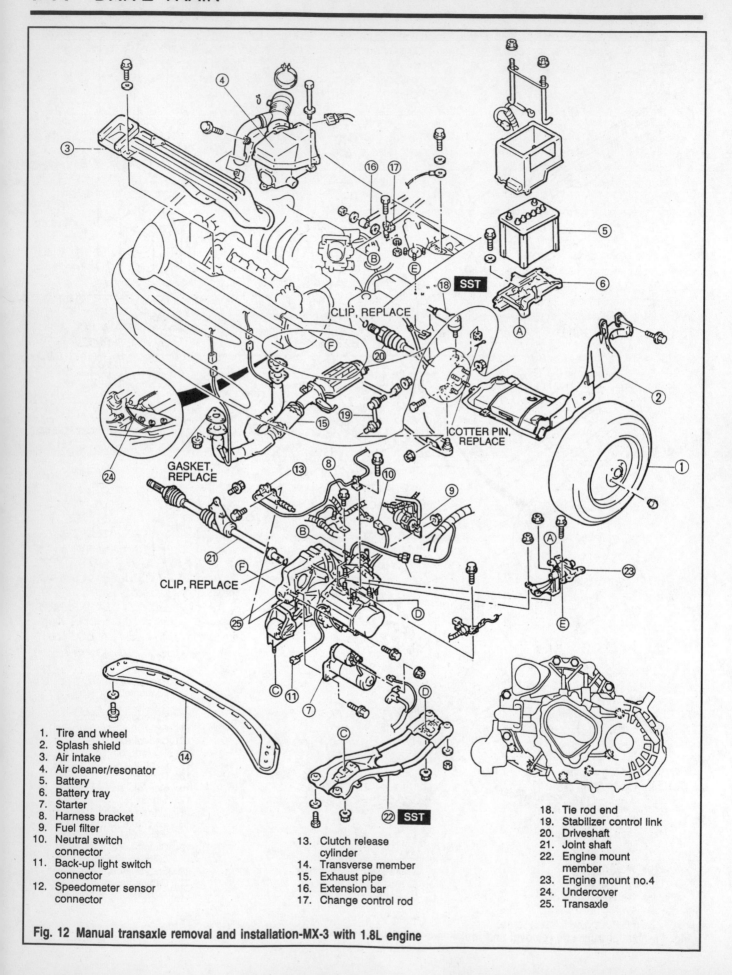

CLIP, REPLACE

COTTER PIN, REPLACE

GASKET, REPLACE

CLIP, REPLACE

SST

SST

1. Tire and wheel
2. Splash shield
3. Air intake
4. Air cleaner/resonator
5. Battery
6. Battery tray
7. Starter
8. Harness bracket
9. Fuel filter
10. Neutral switch connector
11. Back-up light switch connector
12. Speedometer sensor connector

13. Clutch release cylinder
14. Transverse member
15. Exhaust pipe
16. Extension bar
17. Change control rod

18. Tie rod end
19. Stabilizer control link
20. Driveshaft
21. Joint shaft
22. Engine mount member
23. Engine mount no.4
24. Undercover
25. Transaxle

Fig. 12 Manual transaxle removal and installation-MX-3 with 1.8L engine

rubber hanger from the crossmember, then remove the crossmember and left side lower control arm as an assembly.

13. Lean the engine towards the transaxle and support the transaxle with a jack. Remove the transaxle-to-engine bolts and slide the transaxle back and out from under the vehicle.

To install:

14. Lightly lubricate the main shaft spline and the release bearing fork contact points with molybdenum grease and install the release bearing.

15. Carefully guide the transaxle into place, making sure the main shaft spline fits properly into the clutch disc. Start all the transaxle-to-engine bolts, then torque them to 86 ft. lbs. (117 Nm).

16. Install the front mount and torque nuts and bolts to 66 ft. lbs. (89 Nm).

17. Install the left mount crossmember and torque the mount-to-transaxle bolts to 38 ft. lbs. (52 Nm). Torque the crossmember bolts to 40 ft. lbs. (54 Nm), the nuts to 69 ft. lbs. (93 Nm).

18. Install the starter and bracket and torque the bolts to 38 ft. lbs. (52 Nm). Connect the wiring

19. Connect the shift linkage and the extension bar. Install the transaxle-to-engine gusset plates and torque the bolts to 38 ft. lbs. (52 Nm).

20. Install the halfshafts. When assembling the suspension pieces, torque the ball joint pinch bolts and the tie rod ends to 40 ft. lbs. (54 Nm). Install new cotter pins.

21. Assemble the stabilizer bar links and adjust them so that 0.8 in. (20mm) of thread protrudes above the locknut.

22. Install the clutch release cylinder and the splash shields.

23. Connect all wiring and the speedometer cable. Install the air flow meter and air cleaner assembly and the fuse box.

24. Fill the transaxle with the proper amount of oil and install the air ducting and battery.

1993

▶ **See Figures 14 and 15**

1. Disconnect the battery cables and remove the battery and battery tray. Raise and safely support the vehicle. Drain the transaxle fluid.

2. Remove the ducts and the air cleaner assembly.

3. If equipped with 2.5L engine, remove the starter.

4. Label and disconnect the electrical connectors for the park/neutral switch,

backup light switch and vehicle speed sensor. Disconnect the ground wires.

5. Remove the fuel filter mounting nuts and position the filter aside, leaving the fuel lines attached. Remove the wiring harness bracket.

6. Remove the mounting bolts and the hydraulic line clips, then position the clutch slave cylinder aside, leaving the hydraulic line attached.

7. Remove the wheel and tire assemblies and the splash shields. Remove the transverse member.

8. If equipped with 2.5L engine, disconnect the oxygen sensor connectors and remove the front exhaust pipe/catalytic converter assembly.

9. Disconnect the extension bar and shift control rod from the transaxle.

10. Remove the cotter pins and nuts and separate the tie rod ends from the knuckles. Disconnect the stabilizer bar from the lower control arms.

11. Remove the halfshafts and the intermediate shaft.

12. If equipped with 2.0L engine, remove the starter.

13. Remove the engine mount rubber at the right side of the engine mount member. Remove the rear transaxle mount.

14. Support the engine using engine support tool 49 G017 5A0 or equivalent. Remove the nuts and bolts and remove the engine mount member.

15. If equipped with 2.5L engine, remove the transaxle housing inspection plate.

16. Remove the left side transaxle mount.

17. Loosen the engine support tool and lean the engine toward the transaxle. Support the transaxle on a jack and remove the transaxle mounting bolts. Carefully remove the transaxle from the vehicle.

18. Remove the front transaxle mount.

To install:

19. Install the front transaxle mount and tighten the mount-to-transaxle bolts to 44 ft. lbs. (60 Nm). Loosely tighten the mount through bolt and nut.

20. Raise the transaxle into position and install the transaxle mounting bolts. If equipped with 2.5L engine, install inspection cover. Tighten the mounting bolts to the proper torque values.

21. Loosely tighten the left side transaxle mount bolts and nuts.

22. Use the engine support tool to make sure the transaxle bolt holes and the rear transaxle mount are aligned. Install the bolts and tighten to 68 ft. lbs. (93 Nm).

23. Install the engine mount member, making sure the engine mount rubbers are properly installed. Tighten the mount member-to-body bolts/nuts to 68 ft. lbs. (93 Nm) and the front transaxle mount nuts to 77 ft. lbs. (104 Nm).

24. Tighten the front transaxle mount through bolt and nut to 86 ft. lbs. (116 Nm).

25. Tighten the left side transaxle mount bolts and nut to 68 ft. lbs. (93 Nm) and remove the engine support tool.

26. Install the engine mount rubber on the right side of the mount member and tighten the bolts to 44 ft. lbs. (60 Nm).

27. If equipped with 2.0L engine, install the starter.

28. Install the intermediate shaft and halfshafts.

29. Connect the stabilizer bar link to the lower control arm and tighten to 39 ft. lbs. (53 Nm). Install the tie rod end to the steering knuckle and tighten the nut to 32 ft. lbs. (44 Nm).

30. Connect the shift control rod to the transaxle and tighten the bolt to 18 ft. lbs. (25 Nm). Connect the extension bar and tighten the nut to 38 ft. lbs. (51 Nm).

31. If equipped with 2.5L engine, install the exhaust pipe, using new gaskets. Tighten the exhaust manifold flange nuts to 38 ft. lbs. (51 Nm). Connect the oxygen sensor connectors.

32. Install the transverse member and tighten the bolts to 96 ft. lbs. (131 Nm).

33. Install the splash shields and the wheel and tire assemblies.

34. Install the clutch slave cylinder and tighten the bolts to 16 ft. lbs. (22 Nm). Install the wiring harness bracket and tighten the bolts to 130 inch lbs. (14 Nm).

35. Install the fuel filter mounting nuts and tighten to 95 inch lbs. (11 Nm). Connect the grounds and electrical connectors.

36. If equipped with 2.5L engine, install the starter.

37. Install the air cleaner assembly and air ducts. Install the battery tray and battery.

38. Fill the transaxle with the proper type and quantity of fluid and lower the vehicle.

39. Connect the battery cables and start the engine. Check for leaks and for proper transaxle operation.

OVERHAUL

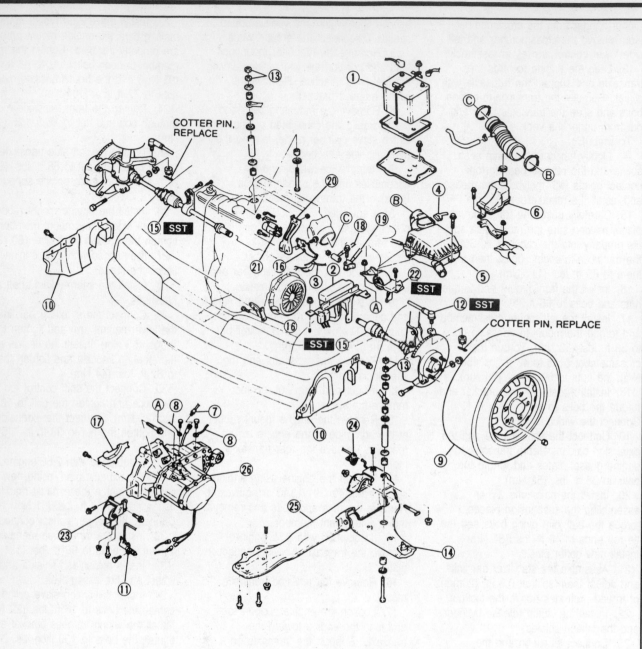

COTTER PIN, REPLACE

SST

COTTER PIN, REPLACE

1. Battery
2. Main fuse block
3. Distributor lead
4. Airflow meter connector
5. Air cleaner assembly
6. Resonance chamber
7. Speedometer cable
8. Ground
9. Wheels
10. Splash sheilds
11. Clutch release cylinder
12. Tie rod end
13. Nuts

14. Lower arm ball joint
15. Driveshaft
16. Gusset plate
17. Under cover
18. Extension bar
19. Control rod
20. Surge tank bracket
21. Starter
21. Joint shaft bracket
22. Engine mount no.4
23. Engine mount no.2
24. Hanger rubber
25. Crossmember
26. Transaxle

Fig. 13 Manual transaxle removal and installation-1989-92 626/MX-6

FS ENGINE

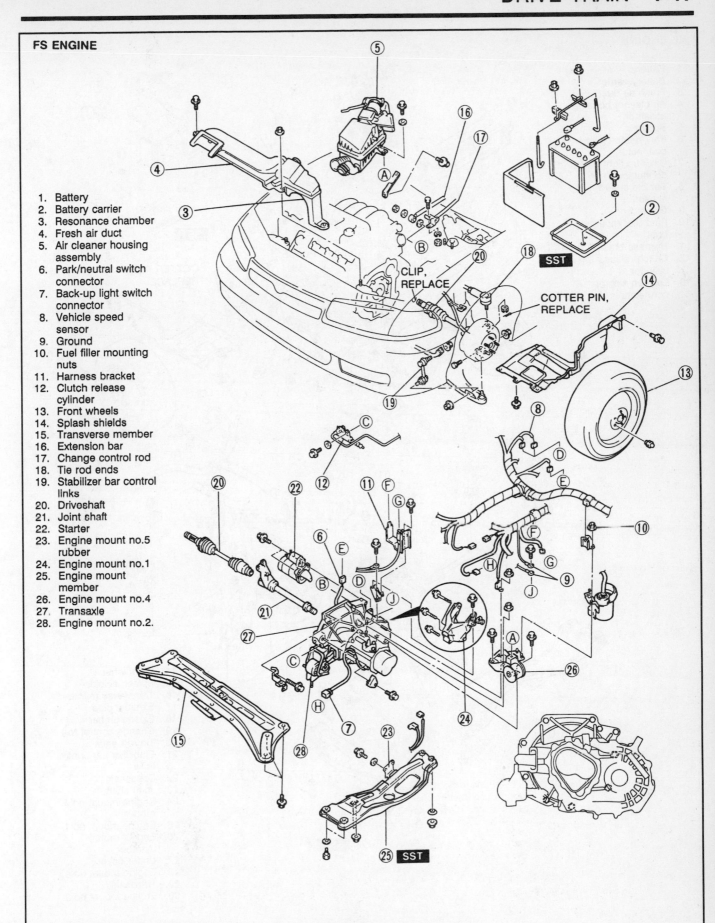

1. Battery
2. Battery carrier
3. Resonance chamber
4. Fresh air duct
5. Air cleaner housing assembly
6. Park/neutral switch connector
7. Back-up light switch connector
8. Vehicle speed sensor
9. Ground
10. Fuel filler mounting nuts
11. Harness bracket
12. Clutch release cylinder
13. Front wheels
14. Splash shields
15. Transverse member
16. Extension bar
17. Change control rod
18. Tie rod ends
19. Stabilizer bar control links
20. Driveshaft
21. Joint shaft
22. Starter
23. Engine mount no.5 rubber
24. Engine mount no.1
25. Engine mount member
26. Engine mount no.4
27. Transaxle
28. Engine mount no.2.

CLIP, REPLACE

SST

COTTER PIN, REPLACE

SST

Fig. 14 Manual transaxle removal and installation-1993 626/MX-6 with 2.0L engine

KL ENGINE

1. Battery
2. Battery carrier
3. Fresh air duct
4. Air cleaner housing assembly
5. Starter
6. Park/neutral switch connector
7. Back-up light switch connector
8. Vehicle speed sensor
9. Ground
10. Fuel filler mounting nuts
11. Harness bracket
12. Clutch release cylinder
13. Oxygen sensor connector

14. Front wheels
15. Splash shields
16. Transverse member
17. Exhaust pipe
18. Extension bar
19. Change control rod
20. Tie rod ends
21. Stabilizer bar control links
22. Driveshaft
23. Joint shaft
24. Engine mount no.5 rubber
25. Engine mount no.1
26. Engine mount member
27. Under cover
28. Engine mount no.4
29. Transaxle
30. Engine mount no.2.

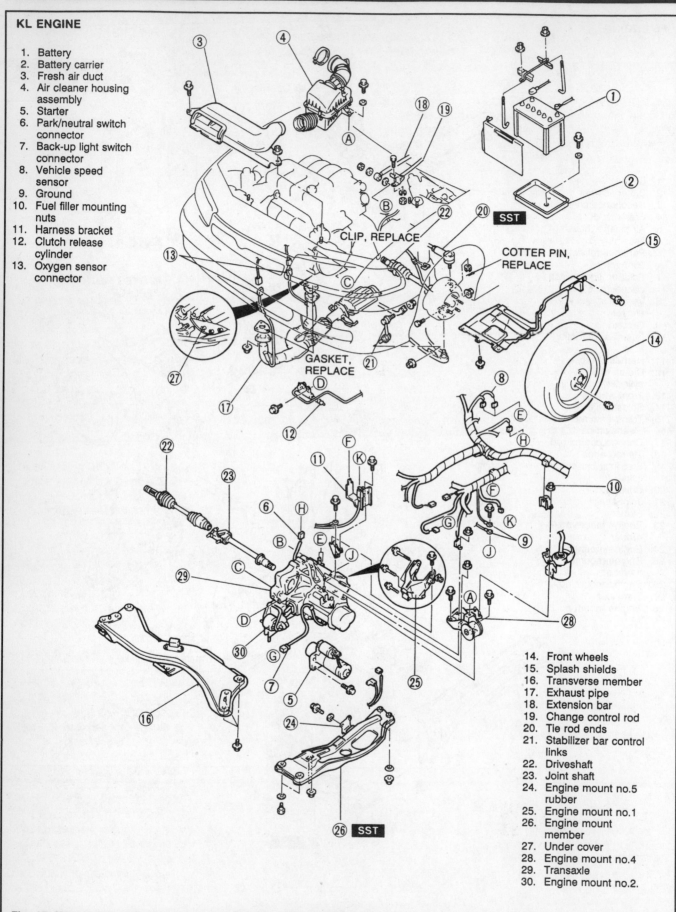

Fig. 15 Manual transaxle removal and installation-1993 626/MX-6 with 2.5L engine

MAJOR COMPONENT DISASSEMBLY AND ASSEMBLY

▶ **See Figure 16**

➡The procedures described are for both the 4-speed and the 5-speed transaxle. The 5-speed unit has a rear cover which easily distinguishes it from the other unit.

5th Gear

1. Remove the rear cover. Remove the roll pin that secures the 5th gear shift fork to the selector shaft. Shift the transaxle unit into either 1st or 2nd gear.

➡**Do not shift into 4th gear or you may cause damage to the gears.**

2. Move the 5th gear clutch sleeve, to engage 5th gear and double lock the transmission.
3. Straighten the tab of the locknut on both the primary and secondary shafts. Remove the locknuts from the shafts.
4. Pull the 5th gear clutch hub assembly out along with the 5th fork.

➡**Remove the fork to gain access to the primary shaft locknut.**

5. Reinstall the 5th gear clutch hub and move the sleeve to the 5th gear position in order to lock the transmission.
6. Remove the primary shaft locknut and remove the 5th gear from the transmission case.
7. Install the 5th gear on the primary shaft. Be sure that the marked boss is facing toward the locknut. Install the bushing and the 5th gear on the secondary shaft.
8. Install the synchronizer ring and clutch hub and the selector fork. Do not install the shift fork pin.

➡**The stop washer or plate for the clutch hub must be installed between the locknut and clutch hub to prevent overtravel of the clutch when shifting into reverse gear to prevent the synchronizer keys from falling out.**

9. Install the locknuts on both shafts and tighten them slightly.
10. Shift into 1st or 2nd gear only, using the control rod. Shift into 5th gear to double lock the transmission.
11. Tighten the primary shaft locknut and lock the hub.

➡**Do not tighten the secondary shaft locknut until the selector fork is installed. Remove the locknut and**

clutch hub from the secondary gear shaft and reassemble it with the selector fork. **Do not insert the drive pin at this time.**

12. Move the 5th gear selector clutch to engage the 5th gear in order to lock the transmission.
13. Shift the unit into either 1st or 2nd gear.
14. Install the roll pin securing the 5th gear shift fork to the selector shaft. Install the cover.

Primary Shaft

The Mazda manual transaxle uses two types of primary shafts, 1 for the 4-speed transaxle and 1 for the 5-speed transaxle. Both shafts are made as a cluster with reverse, 1st, 2nd, 3rd and 4th gears integral. The 5th gear (when equipped) is splined into the end of the shaft, thus distinguishing between the 4- and 5-speed unit.

Secondary Shaft

The secondary shaft assembly consists of the secondary shaft, gears, clutch hub and sleeve assemblies, synchro rings and bearings. The secondary shaft is manufactured integrally with the final drive gear.

There are three different types of secondary shafts used in the 4-speed transaxle and 2 different types used in the 5-speed transaxle. All of these shafts vary by the number of gear teeth on the final drive gears.

➡**The combination of the final drive gear on the secondary shaft and ring gear are identified by the groove provided in the construction of each individual gear.**

Secondary Gears

1. Install a suitable bearing puller in the grooves between the gear and the gear spline of 4th gear. Remove the bearing and the 4th gear from the assembly.
2. Remove the snapring on the 3rd and 4th clutch hub. Slide out the clutch hub and the sleeve assembly.
3. Remove the 3rd gear, the thrust washer and the 2nd gear.
4. Remove the snapring and slide out the clutch hub and reverse gear assembly and 1st gear.
5. Install the bearing remover tool under the rollers and press out the shaft.
6. Assembly is the reverse of disassembly.

Synchronizer Rings

Bridge type synchronizer rings are used in the Mazda transaxle. There are three different synchronizer rings; 1 for 2nd, 3rd and 4th speed, another for 1st and 3rd speed and 1 for 5th speed if the vehicle is so equipped. The 1st speed synchro ring can be identified from the other two because it has less teeth.

Thrust Clearance

The thrust clearance of each gear is checked by using a feeler gauge. The specification for thrust clearance is 0.5mm.

Reverse Idler Shaft and Shift Rod

The reverse idler shaft has an integral mounting post which is secured to the case with a bolt. When installing the idler shaft, align the holes of the shaft with the notch in the transaxle case. When installing reverse shift rod to the shift gate, be sure that the screw holes are aligned ad that the hole of the shift rod is not 180 degrees out of phase.

Bearing Preload Adjustment

➡**When the clutch housing, transaxle case, primary shaft, secondary shaft, bearings or differential case are replaced the bearing preload should be checked and adjusted.**

1. Remove the oil seal and the differential bearing outer race. Adjust the shim from the transaxle case.
2. Remove the bearing outer races from the primary and secondary shafts. Adjust the shims from the transaxle case and the clutch housing.
3. Reinstall the outer races to the transaxle case.
4. Install the outer races to (removed in Step 2) to their respective selectors. Install the selectors, primary shaft assembly and the secondary shaft assembly to the clutch housing.
5. Install the transaxle case and place the ten collars between the transaxle case and the clutch housing.
6. To properly settle each bearing, using the tool, turn the selector in a direction where the gap is widened until it cannot be turned by hand. Then turn the selector in the opposite direction until the gap is eliminated. Manually turn the selector to a direction where the gap

becomes wider until the selector cannot be turned.

➡ **Make sure that the shaft turns smoothly.**

7. Measure the gap of the selector with a feeler gauge.

➡ **This measurement should be taken at 90 degree intervals along the circumference of the selector**

8. Take the maximum reading and determine the shim to be used as follows.

9. For the primary shaft bearing, 1st subtract 1.00mm (thickness of the diaphram spring) from the gap (determined in Step 7).

(Example) Measurement 1.39mm minus 1.00mm equals 0.39mm, select the next larger and close shim which would be 0.40mm.

➡ **Do not use more than 2 shims.**

10. For the secondary shaft bearing, select a shim which has a thickness that is larger and closer to the gap (determined in Step 7).

(Example) Measurement 0.42mm, select the next larger and closer shim which would be 0.45mm.

➡ **Do not use more than 2 shims to accomplish this task.**

11. For the differential bearing, set the preload adapters (tool 49-00180-510A and 49-FT01-515 or equivalent) to the pinion shaft through the hole for the driveshaft of the transaxle case. Hook a spring scale to the adapter and check the bearing preload.

➡ **While checking the preload, turn the selector until the reading of the spring scale becomes 1.1-1.5 lbs.**

12. Then measure the gap of the selector on the differential using a feeler gauge.

➡ **This measurement should be taken at 90 degree intervals along the circumference of the selector.**

13. Select a shim that has a thickness larger and closer to the maximum reading that was taken in the previous step.

(Example) Measurement 0.54mm, select the next larger and closer shim which would be 0.60mm.

➡ **Do not use more than 3 shims to accomplish this task.**

14. Remove the shim selectors and each bearing outer race. Install the shims selected in previous steps between the transaxle case and bearing outer race.

15. A diaphram spring is used to keep the bearing preload as specified and also to maintain low level gear noise. So when installing the diaphram spring, be sure it is in the proper direction.

16. When installing the oil funnel on the clutch housing, be sure that it is in the proper position.

17. After assembly the treansaxle, recheck the preloads of the differential bearing and the primary shaft bearing.

18. The differential bearing preload should be 0.3-6.6 inch lbs. and the reading on the spring scale should be 0.07-1.7 lbs.

19. The primary shaft preload should be 1.7-3.5 inch lbs. and the reading on the spring scale should be 0.4-0.9 lbs.

Differential

The final gear is helical cut with the same tooth design as that used in the transmission. No adjustments are required.

There are three different ring gears in numbers of gear teeth on the manual transaxle. They are indicated by the marks (grooves) provided on the gear outer surface.

The backlash between the differential side gear and pinion gear is adjusted by the thrust washer installed behind the side gear teeth. There are 3 different thicknesses of thrust washers available.

When checking the backlash, insert both driveshafts into the side gears.

Halfshafts

REMOVAL & INSTALLATION

Front

1. Raise and safely support the vehicle. Remove the wheel and tire assemblies.

2. Remove the splash shield, if equipped, and drain the transaxle.

3. Raise the staked portion of the hub locknut with a hammer and chisel. Lock the hub by applying the brakes and remove the nut.

4. Disconnect the stabilizer bar from the lower control arm.

5. Remove the cotter pin and nut from the tie rod end ball stud. Use a

suitable tool to separate the tie rod end from the knuckle.

6. On 1993 MX-6/626, remove the transverse member.

7. Remove the lower ball joint pinch bolt and nut. Use a prybar to pry down the lower control arm and separate the ball joint from the knuckle.

8. If removing the left side shaft on MX-3 and 1993 MX-6/626 with automatic transaxle, proceed as follows:

a. Suspend the engine using engine support tool 49 G017 5A0 or equivalent.

b. Remove the bolts and nuts and remove the engine mount member.

9. Position a prybar between the inner CV-joint and transaxle case. Carefully pry the halfshaft from the transaxle being careful not damage the oil seal. If equipped with a right side intermediate shaft, insert the prybar between the halfshaft and intermediate shaft and tap on the bar to uncouple them.

10. Pull outward on the hub/knuckle assembly, push the outer CV-joint stub shaft through the hub, and remove the halfshaft. If the halfshaft is stuck in the hub, install the old hub nut to protect the stub shaft threads. Tap on the nut, using only a soft mallet, to remove the halfshaft.

➡ **Install plug tool 49 G030 455 or equivalent, into the transaxle after removing the halfshaft, to keep the differential side gear in position. If the gear becomes mispositioned, the differential may have to be removed to realign the gear.**

11. Remove the intermediate shaft, if necessary, by removing the support bearing bolts and pulling the shaft from the transaxle.

To install:

12. If removed, install a new circlip on the end of the intermediate shaft, with the end gap facing upward.

13. Install the intermediate shaft in the transaxle, being careful not to damage the oil seals. Install the support bearing bolts and tighten, in sequence, to 45 ft. lbs. (61 Nm).

14. Install a new circlip on the end of the halfshaft, with the end gap facing upward. Insert the halfshaft into the transaxle, being careful not to damage the oil seal. If equipped, push the halfshaft into the intermediate shaft.

15. Insert the other end of the halfshaft through the hub. loosely install a new locknut.

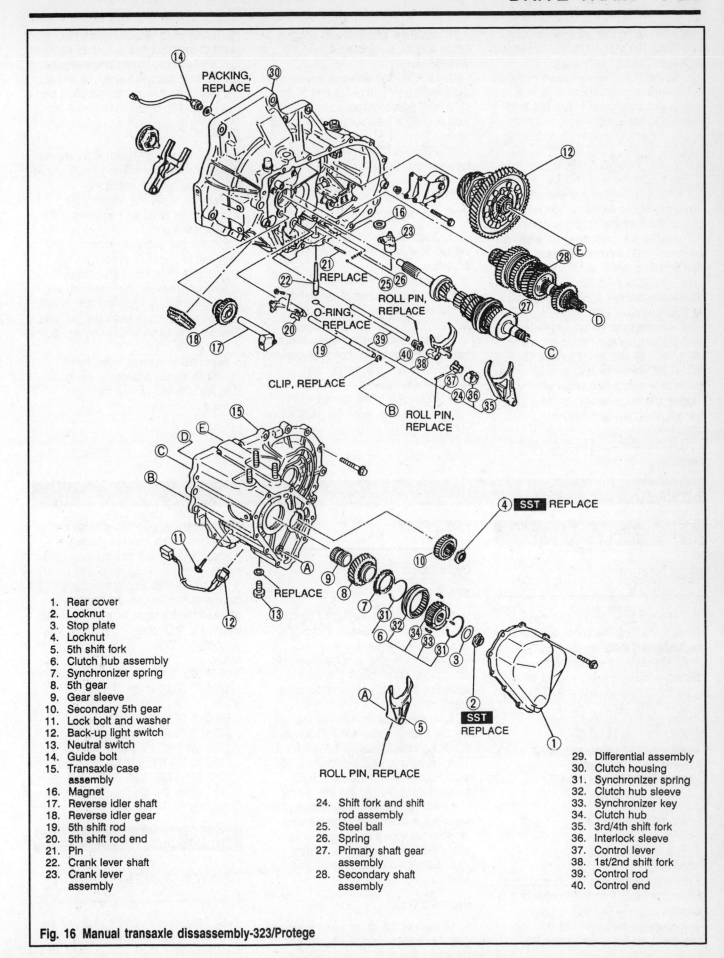

1. Rear cover
2. Locknut
3. Stop plate
4. Locknut
5. 5th shift fork
6. Clutch hub assembly
7. Synchronizer spring
8. 5th gear
9. Gear sleeve
10. Secondary 5th gear
11. Lock bolt and washer
12. Back-up light switch
13. Neutral switch
14. Guide bolt
15. Transaxle case assembly
16. Magnet
17. Reverse idler shaft
18. Reverse idler gear
19. 5th shift rod
20. 5th shift rod end
21. Pin
22. Crank lever shaft
23. Crank lever assembly

24. Shift fork and shift rod assembly
25. Steel ball
26. Spring
27. Primary shaft gear assembly
28. Secondary shaft assembly

29. Differential assembly
30. Clutch housing
31. Synchronizer spring
32. Clutch hub sleeve
33. Synchronizer key
34. Clutch hub
35. 3rd/4th shift fork
36. Interlock sleeve
37. Control lever
38. 1st/2nd shift fork
39. Control rod
40. Control end

Fig. 16 Manual transaxle dissassembly-323/Protege

16. If installing the left side shaft on MX-3 and 1993 MX-6/626 with automatic transaxle, proceed as follows:

a. Install the engine mount member. Tighten the mount member-to-body nuts and bolts to 66 ft. lbs. (89 Nm).

b. On MX-3, tighten the mount-to-mount member nuts to 38 ft. lbs. (52 Nm).

c. On 1993 MX-6/626, tighten the front mount-to-mount member nuts to 77 ft. lbs. (104 Nm) and the side mount bolts to 44 ft. lbs. (60 Nm).

d. Remove the engine support tool.

17. Install the lower ball joint into the knuckle. Install the pinch bolt and nut and tighten to 40 ft. lbs. (54 Nm).

18. On 1993 MX-6/626, install the transverse member and tighten the bolts to 96 ft. lbs. (132 Nm).

19. Connect the tie rod end to the steering knuckle and tighten the nut to 42 ft. lbs. (57 Nm) on all except 1993 MX-6/626, where the torque is 32 ft. lbs. (44 Nm). Install a new cotter pin. Tighten the nut, if necessary, to align the ball stud hole with the nut castellation.

20. Connect the stabilizer bar to the lower control arm.

21. Install the splash shield and the wheel and tire assemblies. Lower the vehicle.

22. Lock the hub with the brakes. Tighten the new hub nut to 235 ft. lbs. (318 Nm). After torquing, stake the locknut using a hammer and dull bladed chisel.

23. Fill the transaxle with the proper type and quantity of fluid.

Rear

4WD 323/Protege

1. Raise and safely support the vehicle. Remove the wheel and tire assembly.

2. Remove the wheel hub nut.

3. Mark the position of the halfshaft on the output flange and remove the nuts.

4. Remove the trailing link-to-knuckle bolt and the lateral link bolt. Pull outward on the knuckle/hub assembly and remove the halfshaft.

5. Installation is the reverse of the removal procedure. Align the halfshaft on the output shaft flange. Tighten the halfshaft-to-output flange nuts to 47 ft. lbs. (64 Nm), the trailing link-to-knuckle bolt to 87 ft. lbs. (117 Nm), the lateral link bolt to 93 ft. lbs. (126 Nm) and the hub nut to 235 ft. lbs. (318 Nm).

CV-JOINT OVERHAUL

Disassemble the driveshaft as shown in the exploded view. The clip (2) should be removed with an ordinary screwdriver, while the snapring (4) should be removed with snapring pliers or a similar tool.

Pull the ball bearings, inner ring and cage out of the shaft while still assembled. Then insert an ordinary screwdriver between the inner ring and cage to gently pry each ball out. Finally, matchmark the cage and inner ring and then turn the cage 30 degrees and pull it off the inner ring.

Assemble in reverse order, being careful to repack bearings in the grease supplied with the kit in a thorough manner.

CLUTCH

Adjustments

PEDAL HEIGHT

1. Remove the carpet and measure the distance from the upper surface of the pedal pad to the firewall.

2. The distance should be as follows:

1989 323 with cable clutch: 8.44-8.64 in. (214.5-219.5mm)

1989 323 with hydraulic clutch: 9.02-9.22 in. (229-234mm)

1990-93 323/Protege and MX-3: 7.72-8.03 in. (196-204mm)

Miata: 6.89-7.28 in. (175-185mm)

1989 MX-6/626: 8.52-8.72 in. (216.5-221.5mm)

1990-92 MX-6/626: 6.73-7.13 in. (171-181mm)

1993 MX-6/626: 7.32-8.31 in. (186-211mm)

3. If the distance is not as specified, loosen the locknut on the stopper bolt or switch.

4. Turn the switch or bolt until the distance is correct, then tighten the locknut.

FREE PLAY

Cable Clutch

323

1. Depress the pedal lightly by hand and measure the free-play; it should be 0.35-0.59 in. (9-15mm).

2. If the free-play is not as specified, depress the clutch pedal 7 times and straighten the clutch cable in the cable bracket.

3. At the transaxle, depress the release lever by hand and pull the slack out of the cable. Measure the gap at **A**. Turn the adjusting nut until there is about 0.080 in. (2mm) clearance between the cable pin and the lever.

4. After adjustment, ensure that when the clutch is disengaged, the distance between the floor and the upper center of the pedal is about 3.3 in. (85mm).

5. Recheck the pedal height and adjust, if necessary.

Hydraulic Clutch

1. Depress the clutch pedal by hand until resistance is felt. The free-play should be 0.04-0.12 in. (1-3mm).

2. If the free-play is not correct, loosen the clutch master cylinder pushrod locknut and turn the pushrod to adjust.

3. After adjustment, check the disengagement height; the distance between the upper surface of the pedal pad to the floor when the clutch is fully disengaged. Disengagement height is as follows:

1989 323: 3.23 in. (82mm)

1990-93 323/Protege: 1.61 in. (41mm)

MX-3: 2.17 in. (55mm)

Miata: 2.68 in. (68mm)

1989 MX-6/626: 2.7 in. (68mm)

1990-92 MX-6/626: 1.54 in. (39mm)

1993 MX-6/626: 2.64 in. (67mm)

4. Tighten the locknut. Recheck pedal height.

Clutch Cable

REMOVAL & INSTALLATION

1. Remove the adjusting nut and pin.

2. Unbolt and remove the clutch cable bracket.

3. Disconnect the cable from the clutch pedal.

4. Withdraw the cable from the engine compartment.

5. Installation is the reverse of the removal procedure. Coat the pedal cable hook and the joint between the release lever and pin with lithium grease.

Driven Disc and Pressure Plate

REMOVAL & INSTALLATION

▶ See Figures 17, 18, 19, 20 and 21

1. Disconnect the negative battery cable. Raise and safely support the vehicle.

2. Remove the transmission or transaxle.

3. Gradually loosen the clutch pressure plate bolts, in a criss-cross pattern. Support the pressure plate and remove the bolts. Remove the pressure plate and clutch disc.

4. Inspect the pilot bearing. If it is worn or damaged and does not turn easily by hand, remove it using a puller/slide hammer.

5. Check the flywheel surface for scoring, cracks or burning and machine or replace, as necessary.

6. Install holder tool 49 E011 1A0 or equivalent, to keep the flyeheel from turning. Loosen the flywheel bolts evenly and gradually in a criss-cross pattern. Remove the flywheel.

7. Install holder tool 49 F011 101 or equivalent, to keep the flyeheel from turning. Remove the locknut. Remove the flywheel, using a suitable puller and remove the key from the eccentric shaft.

8. Inspect the clutch release bearing for wear. Replace it if it sticks or does not run easily.

9. Inspect the release fork for wear or damage and replace as necessary.

To install:

10. Lubricate the release fork fingers and pivot with molybdenum grease and install in the release fork boot.

11. Install the clutch release bearing on the release fork.

12. If removed, install a new pilot bearing in the flywheel, using a suitable installation tool.

13. Make sure the flywheel mounting surface and the crankshaft or eccentric shaft mounting surfaces are clean. Remove any old sealant from the

flywheel bolt hole threads and the flywheel bolts.

14. Install the flywheel.

15. Apply sealant to the flywheel bolt threads and install them hand tight. Install the flywheel holding tool. Tighten the bolts, in a criss-cross pattern, to 76 ft. lbs. (102 Nm) on all except MX-3 1.8L engine and MX-6/626 2.5L engine. On MX-3 1.8L engine and MX-6/626 2.5L engine, tighten the bolts to 49 ft. lbs. (67 Nm).

16. Apply a small amount of molbdenum grease to the clutch disc splines and install the clutch disc on the flywheel, spring side toward the transmission or transaxle. Install a suitable alignment tool in the pilot bearing to position the clutch disc.

17. Install the clutch pressure plate, aligning the dowel holes with the flywheel dowels. Install the pressure plate bolts and gradually tighten, in a criss-cross pattern to 20 ft. lbs. (26 Nm). Remove the alignment tool.

18. Install the transmission or transaxle and lower the vehicle.

Clutch Master Cylinder

REMOVAL & INSTALLATION

1. Disconnect the negative battery cable.

2. On 1990-93 323/Protege and MX-3, remove the battery and the diagnostic connector.

3. On 1993 MX-6/626, remove the evaporative canister.

4. On 1990-93 323/Protege, MX-3 and 1993 MX-6/626, disconnect the hose from the brake master cylinder reservoir and plug the reservoir port.

5. Remove the hydraulic line from the master cylinder using a tubing wrench.

6. Remove the mounting nuts and remove the master cylinder and gasket.

To install:

7. Install the master cylinder with a new gasket. Tighten the nuts to 18 ft. lbs. (25 Nm) on all except MX-3. On MX-3, tighten the nuts to 8.7 ft. lbs. (12 Nm).

8. Attach the hydraulic line and tighten the fitting with the tubing wrench.

9. If equipped, remove the plug from the brake master cylinder reservoir and connect the hose.

10. Install the remaining components in the reverse of removal. Bleed the air from the system.

OVERHAUL

1. Thoroughly clean the outside of the master cylinder.

2. Drain the hydraulic fluid from the cylinder. Unbolt the reservoir from the cylinder body. If equipped with banjo fittings, loosen the union bolt and remove the fitting and gaskets from the body of the master cylinder. Discard the gaskets and purchase new ones.

3. Remove the boot from the cylinder.

4. Release the wire piston stop with a screwdriver and withdraw the stop washer.

5. Withdraw the piston, piston cups, and return spring from the cylinder bore.

6. Wash all the parts in clean hydraulic (brake) fluid.

7. Examine the piston cups. If they are damaged, softened, or swollen, replace them with new ones.

8. Check the piston and bore for scoring or roughness.

9. Use a wire gauge to check the clearance between the piston and its bore. Replace either the piston or the cylinder if the clearance is greater than 0.15mm.

10. Be sure that the compensating port in the cylinder is not clogged.

To assemble the master cylinder:

1. Dip the piston and cups in clean hydraulic (brake) fluid.

2. Bolt the reservoir up to the cylinder body.

3. Fit the return spring into the cylinder.

4. Insert the primary cup into the bore so that its flat side is facing the piston.

5. Place the secondary cup on the piston and insert them in the cylinder bore.

6. Install the stop washer and the wire piston stop.

7. Fill the reservoir half-full of hydraulic fluid. Operate the piston with a screwdriver until fluid spurts out of the cylinder outlet. Install the banjo fittings with new gaskets. Leave the union bolt snug until such time as the master cylinder is in place on the firewall this way you can move the fitting up and down to align fluid line.

8. Fit the boot on the cylinder.

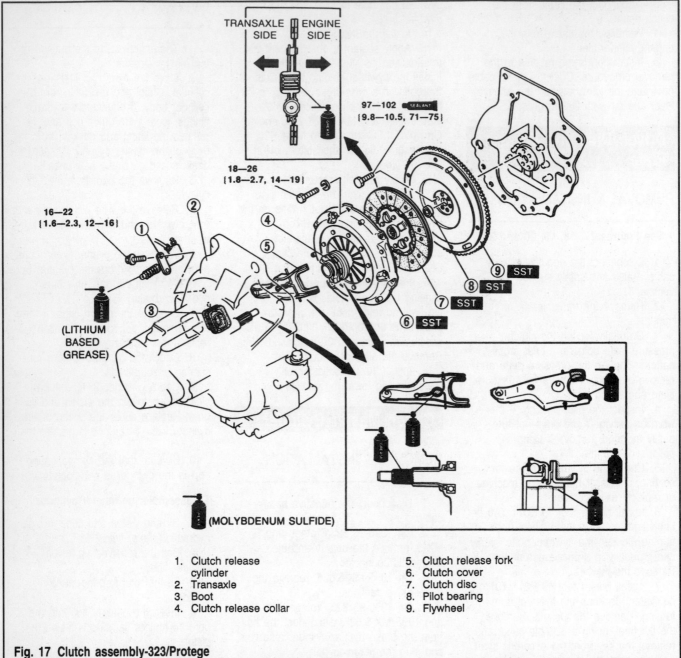

TRANSAXLE □ ENGINE
SIDE □ SIDE

97—102 SEALANT
[9.8—10.5, 71—75]

18—26
[1.8—2.7, 14—19]

16—22
[1.6—2.3, 12—16]

(LITHIUM
BASED
GREASE)

9 SST
8 SST
7 SST
6 SST

(MOLYBDENUM SULFIDE)

1. Clutch release
   cylinder
2. Transaxle
3. Boot
4. Clutch release collar
5. Clutch release fork
6. Clutch cover
7. Clutch disc
8. Pilot bearing
9. Flywheel

Fig. 17 Clutch assembly-323/Protege

Clutch Slave Cylinder

REMOVAL & INSTALLATION

1. Disconnect the negative battery cable.

2. If equipped with a flexible hydraulic line connecting the slave cylinder, loosen the fitting at the hose-tube junction and remove the clip from the bracket. Remove the hose from the slave cylinder using a tubing wrench and plug the hydraulic line.

3. On all other vehicles, loosen the hydraulic line fitting at the slave cylinder. Disconnect and plug the line.

4. Remove the slave cylinder mounting bolts and remove the slave cylinder.

To install:

5. Install the slave cylinder and tighten the bolts to 16 ft. lbs. (22 Nm).

6. Connect the hydraulic line and tighten with a tubing wrench.

7. If equipped with a flexible hose, connect the hose and tighten with a tubing wrench. Attch the hose to the bracket and install the clip. Connect hydraulic line and tighten the fitting with a tubing wrench.

8. Bleed the air from the system.

OVERHAUL

1. Thoroughly clean the outside of the cylinder body.

2. Drain the hydraulic fluid from the cylinder.

3. Remove the boot from the cylinder.

4. Release the wire piston stop with a screwdriver and withdraw the stop washer.

5. Withdraw the piston, piston cups, and return spring from the cylinder bore.

6. Wash all the parts in clean hydraulic (brake) fluid.

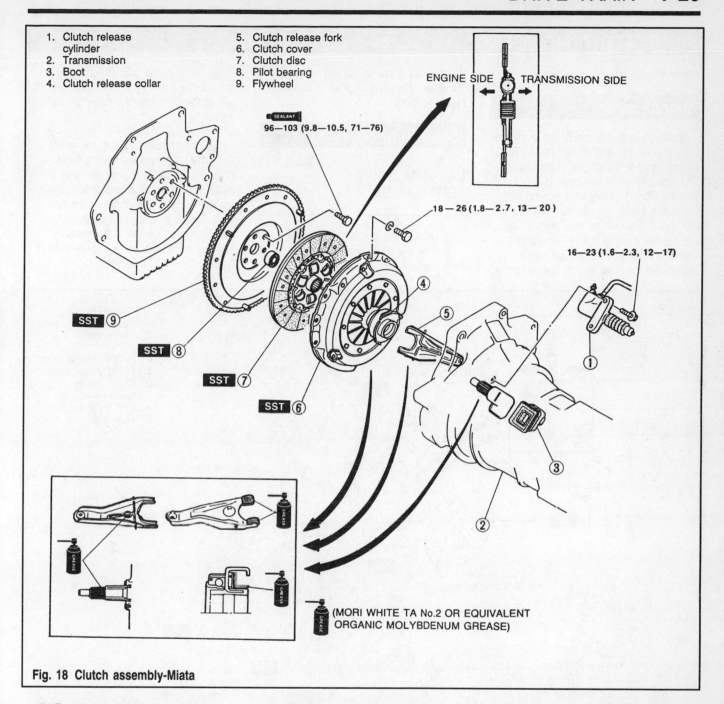

1. Clutch release cylinder
2. Transmission
3. Boot
4. Clutch release collar
5. Clutch release fork
6. Clutch cover
7. Clutch disc
8. Pilot bearing
9. Flywheel

ENGINE SIDE ← → TRANSMISSION SIDE

SEALANT 96—103 (9.8—10.5, 71—76)

18—26 (1.8—2.7, 13—20)

16—23 (1.6—2.3, 12—17)

SST 9
SST 8
SST 7
SST 6

(MORI WHITE TA No.2 OR EQUIVALENT ORGANIC MOLYBDENUM GREASE)

Fig. 18 Clutch assembly-Miata

7. Examine the piston cups. If they are damaged, softened, or swollen, replace them with new ones.

8. Check the piston and bore for scoring or roughness.

9. Use a wire gauge to check the clearance between the piston and its bore. Replace either the piston or the cylinder if the clearance is greater than 0.15mm.

To assemble:

10. Dip the piston and cups in clean hydraulic (brake) fluid.

11. Fit the return spring into the cylinder.

12. Insert the primary cup into the bore so that its flat side is facing the piston.

13. Place the secondary cup on the piston and insert them in the cylinder bore.

14. Install the stop washer and the wire piston stop.

15. Fit the boot on the cylinder.

HYDRAULIC SYSTEM BLEEDING

1. Remove the rubber cap from the bleeder screw on the release cylinder.

2. Place a bleeder tube over the end of the bleeder screw.

3. Submerge the other end of the tube in a jar half filled with hydraulic brake fluid.

4. Slowly pump the clutch pedal fully and allow it to return slowly, several times.

5. While pressing the clutch pedal to the floor, loosen the bleeder screw until the fluid starts to run out. Then close the bleeder screw. Keep repeating this Step, while watching the hydraulic fluid in the jar. As soon as the air bubbles disappear, close the bleeder screw.

6. During the bleeding procedure the reservoir must be kept at least ¾full.

AUTOMATIC TRANSMISSION

▶ See Figure 22

Identification

Most transmission codes are available from the vehicle information code plate on the cowl in the engine compartment. The first portion of the code is the transmission designation; following this, there is a blank box; at the right end of the line is the axle or final drive ratio.

On other models the transmission model and serial number are either stamped on a plate that is bolted to the transmission case or stamped directly on the case itself. The location varies from model to model.

Fluid Pan

PAN REMOVAL & INSTALLATION

1. Raise and support the vehicle.
2. Place a drain pan under the transmission pan.

3. Remove the pan attaching bolts (except the two at the front). Loosen the two at the front slightly. Allow the fluid to drain.
4. Remove the pan.
5. Remove and discard the gasket.
6. Clean all gasket mating surfaces. Wipe the inside of the oil pan with a clean rag. Remove any deposits with solvent and dry the inside of the pan.
7. Install a new pan gasket and install the pan on the transmission. Tighten the pan bolts in a criss-cross pattern. DO NOT overtighten.

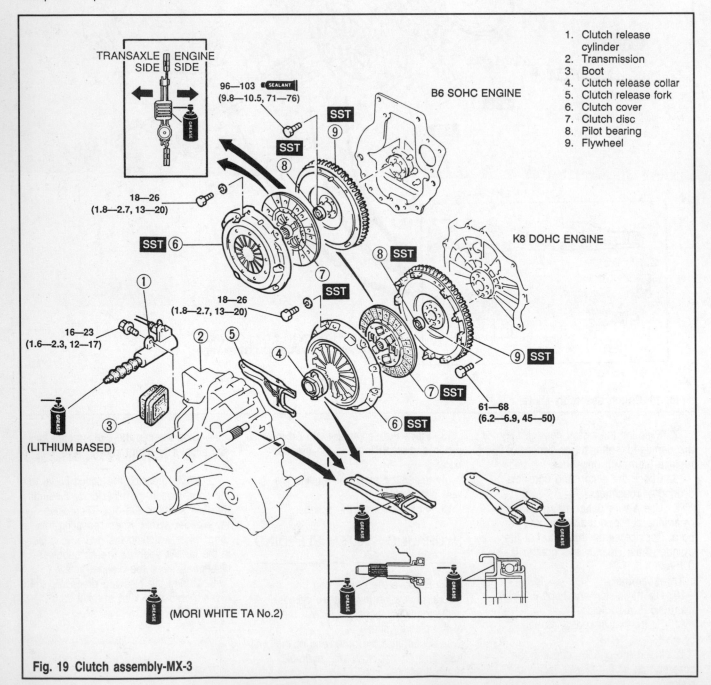

1. Clutch release cylinder
2. Transmission
3. Boot
4. Clutch release collar
5. Clutch release fork
6. Clutch cover
7. Clutch disc
8. Pilot bearing
9. Flywheel

Fig. 19 Clutch assembly-MX-3

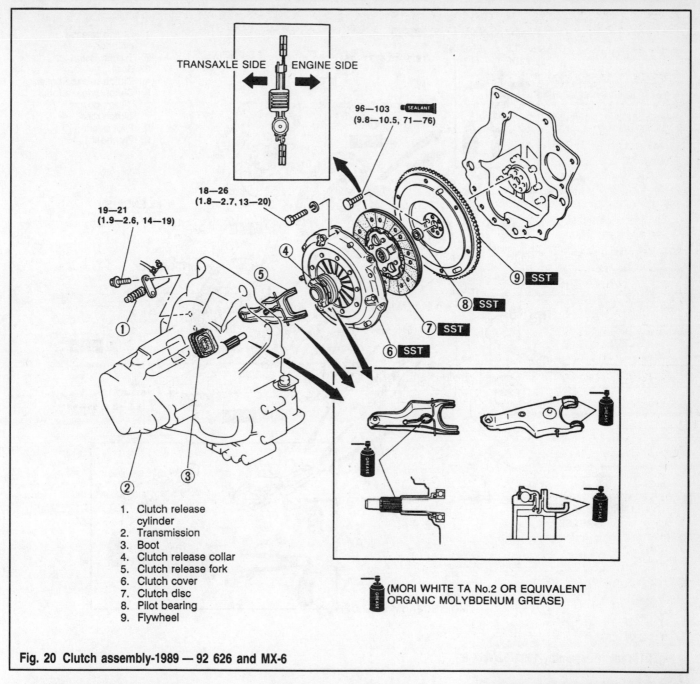

1. Clutch release cylinder
2. Transmission
3. Boot
4. Clutch release collar
5. Clutch release fork
6. Clutch cover
7. Clutch disc
8. Pilot bearing
9. Flywheel

18—26 (1.8—2.7, 13—20)
19—21 (1.9—2.6, 14—19)
96—103 (9.8—10.5, 71—76) SEALANT

TRANSAXLE SIDE ← → ENGINE SIDE

(MORI WHITE TA No.2 OR EQUIVALENT ORGANIC MOLYBDENUM GREASE)

Fig. 20 Clutch assembly-1989 — 92 626 and MX-6

8. Lower the vehicle and fill the transmission with fluid. Check the transmission operation.

Adjustments

SELECTOR LEVER

1. Disconnect the negative battery cable.
2. Remove the rear console, shifter knob, selector knob, selector sleeve and the indicator panel.
3. Loosen the shift rod locknut.

4. Shift the transmission into P by pushing the lower adjustment lever forward.
5. Adjust the lever as is required and tighten the locknut to 13-18 ft. lbs. (18-25 Nm).
6. Move the selector through the normal positions and make sure the operation is proper.
7. Assemble the shifter panel and the rear console.
8. Connect the negative battery cable.

Transaxle

REMOVAL & INSTALLATION

♦ See Figure 23

1. Disconnect the negative battery cable. Raise and safely support the vehicle and drain the transmission fluid.
2. Remove the engine under cover and disconnect the shift rod. Remove the exhaust system.
3. Mark the position of the driveshaft to the rear axle flange and remove the driveshaft.

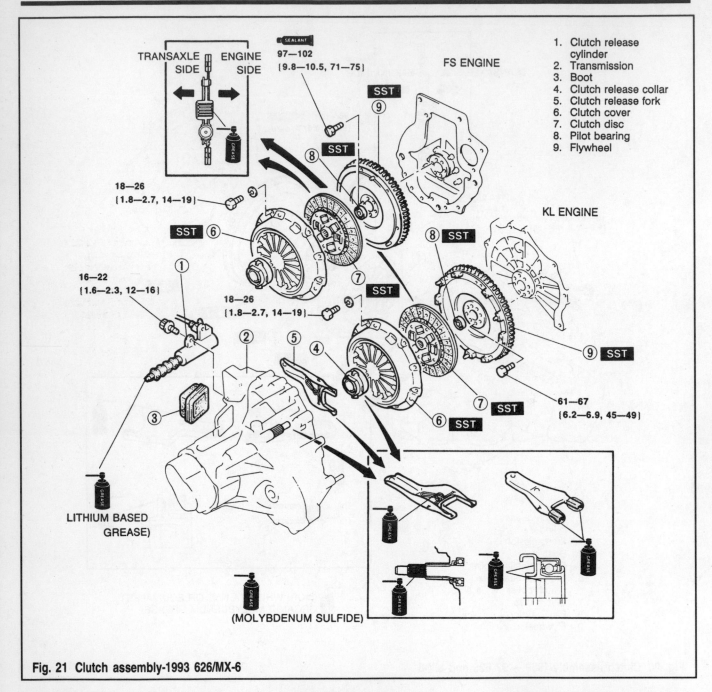

SEALANT
97—102
{9.8—10.5, 71—75}

TRANSAXLE SIDE | ENGINE SIDE

GREASE

FS ENGINE

1. Clutch release cylinder
2. Transmission
3. Boot
4. Clutch release collar
5. Clutch release fork
6. Clutch cover
7. Clutch disc
8. Pilot bearing
9. Flywheel

SST

18—26
{1.8—2.7, 14—19}

SST 6

SST

KL ENGINE

16—22
{1.6—2.3, 12—16}

18—26
{1.8—2.7, 14—19}

SST

SST

9 SST

61—67
{6.2—6.9, 45—49}

SST

SST

LITHIUM BASED GREASE)

GREASE

GREASE

GREASE

GREASE

GREASE

GREASE

(MOLYBDENUM SULFIDE)

Fig. 21 Clutch assembly-1993 626/MX-6

4. Disconnect the speedometer cable and disconnect the vacuum hose from the vacuum diaphragm.

5. Label and disconnect the electrical connections from the transmission assembly.

6. Remove the dipstick and the dipstick tube. Disconnect the oil cooler lines.

7. Support the transmission and differential with jacks.

8. Remove the power plant frame as follows:

a. Disconnect the wire harness from the power plant frame assembly.

b. Install a transmission jack under the transmission and support it.

c. Remove the bracket from between the power plant frame and the transmission extension.

d. Remove the differential side bolts and pry out the spacer.

e. Remove the differential mounting spacer.

f. Install a M14 X 1.5 bolt into the mounting block sleeve as shown and scew the bolt in. Pull down on the bolt and install a M6 X 1 bolt into the side hole.

g. Remove the long bolt and then the shorter bolt. Remove the transmission side bolts and remove the power plant frame assembly.

9. Remove the transmission mounting bolts and remove the transmission from the vehicle.

To install the transmission:

10. Raise and safely support the vehicle.

11. Install the transmission to the vehicle. It may be necessary to tilt the engine up by pushing up on the oil pan with a wooden block. Tighten the mounting bolts to 47-66 ft. lbs. (64-89 Nm).

12. Install the power plant frame as follows:

a. Install the differential mounting spacer. Tighten the bolts to 27-38 ft. lbs. (37-52 Nm).

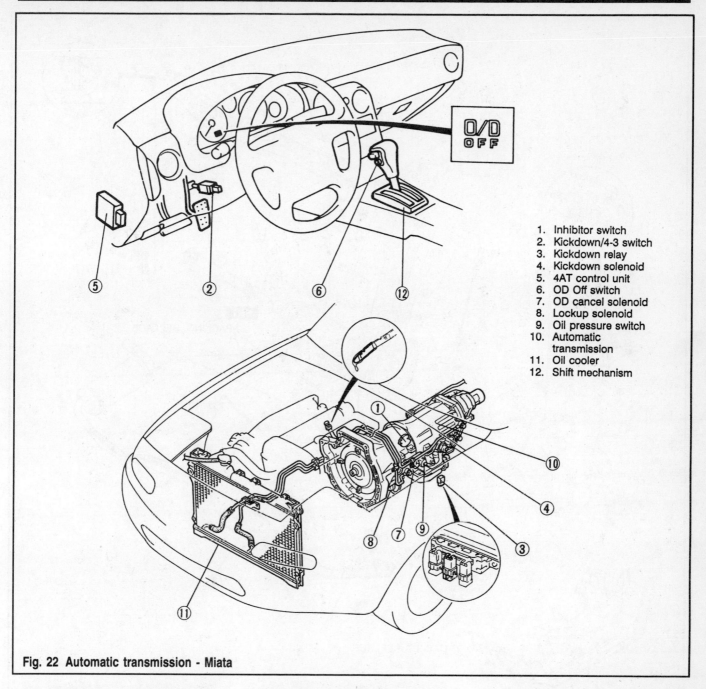

1. Inhibitor switch
2. Kickdown/4-3 switch
3. Kickdown relay
4. Kickdown solenoid
5. 4AT control unit
6. OD Off switch
7. OD cancel solenoid
8. Lockup solenoid
9. Oil pressure switch
10. Automatic transmission
11. Oil cooler
12. Shift mechanism

Fig. 22 Automatic transmission - Miata

b. Support the transmission so that it is level.

c. Install the power plant frame and tighten the transmission side bolts by hand.

d. Make sure that the sleeve is installed to the block of the power plant frame and install the spacer and the bolts.

e. Install the power plant frame bracket and tighten the side bolts to 77-91 ft. lbs. (104-124 Nm).

f. Tighten the differential side bolts to 77-91 ft. lbs. (104-124 Nm).

g. Install the power plant frame bracket and tighten the lower bolt to

77-91 ft. lbs. (104-124 Nm). Tighten the upper 2 bolts to 27-40 ft. lbs. (36-54 Nm).

h. Remove the trnsmission jack and connect the transmission wire harness.

13. Connect the speedometer cable to the transmission and install the starter.

14. Connect the oil cooler lines using new gaskets.

15. Install the dipstick tube and the dipstick.

16. Connet the electrical connectors, the vacuum hose and the speedometer cable.

17. Install the driveshaft, making sure to align the marks that were made during removal. Tighten the bolts to 22 ft. lbs. (30 Nm).

18. Install the exhaust system.

19. Install the engine under cover and connect the shift rod.

20. Lower the vehicle and connect the negative battery cable. Fill the transmission with the proper type and quantity of fluid. Start the engine and check for leakage and proper operation.

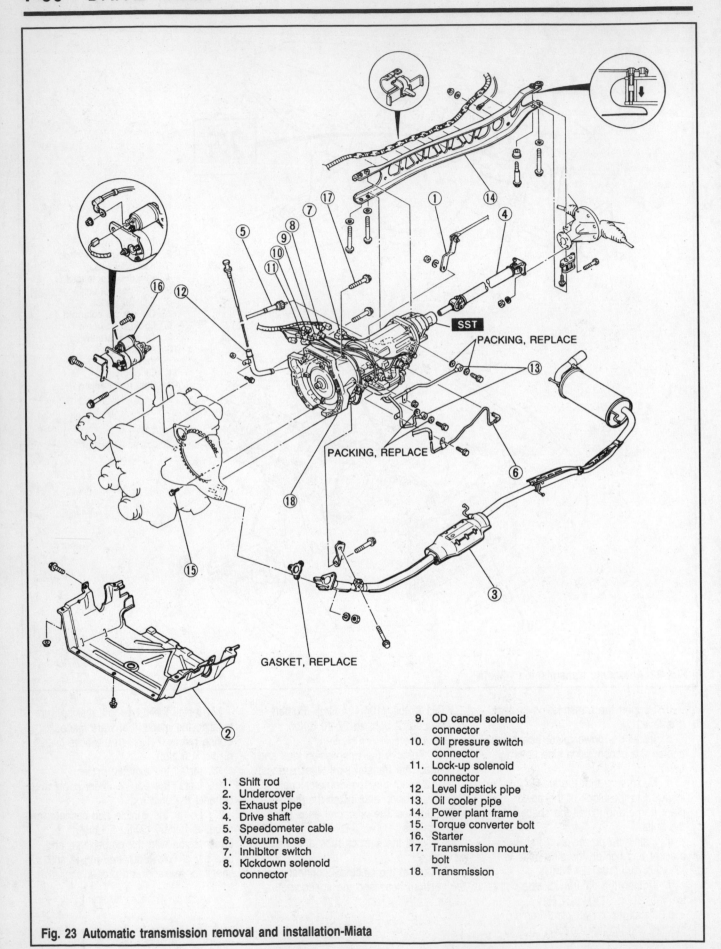

PACKING, REPLACE

SST

PACKING, REPLACE

GASKET, REPLACE

1. Shift rod
2. Undercover
3. Exhaust pipe
4. Drive shaft
5. Speedometer cable
6. Vacuum hose
7. Inhibitor switch
8. Kickdown solenoid connector

9. OD cancel solenoid connector
10. Oil pressure switch connector
11. Lock-up solenoid connector
12. Level dipstick pipe
13. Oil cooler pipe
14. Power plant frame
15. Torque converter bolt
16. Starter
17. Transmission mount bolt
18. Transmission

Fig. 23 Automatic transmission removal and installation-Miata

AUTOMATIC TRANSAXLE

Identification

On all models, the Vehicle Information Code Plate mounted on the firewall in the engine compartment lists the transmission or transaxle type. On the third line, labeled Transaxle the transaxle model is listed, preceding a space. The serial number is stamped following the space.

Fluid Pan

REMOVAL & INSTALLATION

1. Raise and support the vehicle.
2. Place a drain pan under the transmission pan.
3. Remove the pan attaching bolts (except the two at the front). Loosen the two at the front slightly. Allow the fluid to drain.
4. Remove the pan.
5. Remove and discard the gasket.
6. Clean all gasket mating surfaces. Wipe the inside of the oil pan with a clean rag. Remove any deposits with solvent and dry the inside of the pan.
7. Install a new pan gasket and install the pan on the transmission. Tighten the pan bolts in a criss-cross pattern. DO NOT overtighten.
8. Lower the vehicle and fill the transmission with fluid. Check the transmission operation.

FILTER SERVICE

1. Remove the transmission oil pan as described above.
2. Remove the attaching bolts and remove the filter assembly.
3. Install the filter and torque the bolts alternately (diagonally) is several stages to 4-5 ft. lbs.

Adjustments

BAND ADJUSTMENT

➡On the 323/Protege this adjustment can be made by removing the cover located on the lower right front of the transmission (three bolts). On the 626/MX-6, the transmission pan must be removed; the servo piston stem and locknut are visible at the left front.

Loosen the locknut and then torque the servo piston stem to 9-11 ft.lb. Then, back off exactly two turns. Hold the stem stationary and tighten the locknut to 11-29 ft.lb.

KICKDOWN SWITCH AND DOWNSHIFT SOLENOID ADJUSTMENT

➡The kickdown switch is located on the accelerator linkage above the accelerator pedal.

1. Check the accelerator linkage for smooth operation.
2. Turn the ignition ON, but do not start the engine.
3. Depress the accelerator pedal fully to the floor. As the pedal nears the end of its travel, a light click should be heard from the downshift solenoid.
4. If the kickdown switch operates too soon, loosen the locknut on the switch shaft. Adjust the shaft so that the accelerator linkage makes contact with it when the pedal is depressed approximately 7/8 of the way to the floor. Tighten the locknut.
5. If no noise comes from the solenoid at all, check the wiring for the solenoid and the switch.
6. If the wiring is in good condition, remove the wire from the solenoid and connect it to a 12V power source. If the solenoid does not click when connected, it is defective and should be replaced.

➡When the solenoid is removed, about two pints of transmission fluid will leak out; have a container ready to catch it. Remember to add more fluid to the transmission after installing the new solenoid.

1989-92 626

1. Disconnect the wiring connectors from the kickdown switch.
2. Screw out the kick-down switch a few turns.
3. Dully depress the accelerator pedal.
4. Gradually screw in the kick-down switch until you hear a clicking sound then screw it in 1/2 turn more.
5. Tighten the locknut and connect the wiring connectors.

Neutral Safety (Inhibitor) Switch/Back-up Light Switch

REMOVAL & INSTALLATION

1. Disconnect the linkage from the gear selector lever on the switch.
2. Unbolt and remove the switch from the transmission.
3. Place the new switch onto the transmission and bolt it in place.
4. Connect the selector lever linakge and adjust the switch as described immediately below.

ADJUSTMENT

1. Place the transmission selector lever in the neutral position.
2. Loosen the switch mounting bolts.
3. Remove the screw on the switch body and move the switch so that the screw hole is aligned with the small hole inside of the switch. Check the alignment by inserting a small pin in the hole.
4. Tighten the mounting bolts and remove the pin.
5. Install the screw to the switch body and tighten.
6. Check the adjustment by trying to start the engine in all gears. It should only start in Park and Neutral.

Transaxle

REMOVAL & INSTALLATION

323 and Protege
▸ See Figure 24

1. Raise and safely support the vehicle and remove the front wheels. Remove the battery and battery box and the air cleaner and ducting.
2. Remove the splash shield and drain the transaxle oil.
3. Disconnect the speedometer cable, throttle cable, shift cable and the wiring from the transaxle.
4. Disconnect the wiring and remove the starter.
5. On 4WD models, matchmark the flanges and remove the driveshaft.

6. Disconnect the exhaust pipe from the manifold and the catalytic converter and remove the pipe.

7. Disconnect the tie rod ends and lower ball joints and remove the halfhsafts. Use special tool 49 G030 455 or equivalent to hold the differential side gears in place when the halfshafts are removed.

8. On 4WD models, to remove the differential lock motor, remove the sensor switch. Insert a small screwdriver into the hole and turn the rod ½ turn counterclockwise. Remove the bolts and remove the motor.

9. If equipped, remove the torque converter-to-flywheel nuts.

10. Disconnect the oil cooler hoses and plug them to prevent leakage.

11. Install the necessary lifting equipment and support the engine from above. Remove the lower mounting frame and support the transaxle from below with a jack.

12. Remove the front and left rear mounts and allow the engine/transaxle to tilt towards the left.

13. Remove the bolts and slide the transaxle away from the engine to lower it out of the vehicle. Do not let the torque converter fall out.

To install:

14. Make sure the torque converter is properly placed and carefully guide the transaxle into place. Start all the transaxle-to-engine bolts, then torque them to 59 ft. lbs. (80 Nm).

15. Install the left rear mount but do not torque the bolts yet.

16. Install the torque converter-to-flywheel nuts and torque to 25 ft. lbs. (34 Nm).

17. On 4WD models, install the differential lock motor.

18. Install the halfshafts, making sure the inner joint is firmly seated into place. Torque the extension shaft bracket bolts to 46 ft. lbs. (62 Nm).

19. Assemble the suspension. Torque the lower ball joint pinch bolt and the tie rod end nuts to 43 ft. lbs. (59 Nm). If equipped with a stabilizer bar, adjust the link with ¾ in. (19mm) of thread showing above the locknut.

20. Install the front mount to the transaxle and torque the bolts to 38 ft. lbs. (52 Nm).

21. Install the lower mounting frame and torque the frame-to-body nuts and bolts to 66 ft. lbs. (89 Nm). Torque the mount-to-frame nuts and bolts to 38 ft. lbs. (52 Nm).

22. Connect the cooler hoses, making sure the clamp does not interfere with other parts.

23. Connect the shift cable, speedometer cable, throttle cable and the wiring.

24. Install the starter and connect the wiring.

25. On 4WD models, install the driveshaft, making sure to align the matchmarks. Torque the nuts to 22 ft. lbs. (30 Nm).

26. Install the splash shields and wheels.

27. Install the air cleaner and battery.

MX-3

▶ **See Figures 25 and 26**

1. If equipped with 1.8L engine, relieve the fuel system pressure. Disconnect the negative battery cable. Raise and safely support the vehicle. Drain the transaxle fluid.

2. Remove the wheel and tire assemblies and the splash shields.

3. Disconnect the air flow meter connector and remove the resonance duct and air cleaner assembly.

4. If equipped with 1.8L engine, remove the strut bar from between the strut towers.

5. Disconnect the positive battery cable and disconnect the wiring harness from the battery tray. Remove the battery and battery tray.

6. If equipped with 1.6L engine, disconnect the speedometer cable. If equipped with 1.8L engine, disconnect the speed sensor connector.

7. Remove the clip from the cable housing and the spring clip from the transaxle lever, then remove the shift cable.

8. Label and disconnect the electrical connectors for the inhibitor switch and solenoid valve. Remove the bolt from the harness bracket and position the harness aside.

9. Remove the throttle cable at the throttle body and routing brackets. Disconnect and plug the oil cooler hoses.

10. If equipped with 1.8L engine, disconnect the oxygen sensor connectors and remove the fuel filter and the transverse member. If equipped with 1.6L engine, remove the intake manifold support bracket.

11. Remove the starter and remove the front exhaust pipe.

12. Remove the pinch bolt and separate the lower ball joint from the steering knuckle. Remove the cotter pin

and nuts and separate the tie rod ends from the knuckles.

13. Disconnect the stabilizer bar from the lower control arms. Remove the brake hose and ABS sensor cable clips.

14. Support the engine using engine support tool 49 G017 5A0 or equivalent. Remove the nuts and bolt and remove the engine mount member.

15. Remove the halfshafts and intermediate shaft, if equipped. Remove the left side transaxle mount.

16. On 1.8L engine, remove the lower converter housing cover. Hold the flexplate with a small prybar and remove the torque converter nuts.

17. On 1.6L engine, insert a small prybar through the converter housing service hole and hold the flexplate. Remove the cover from the oil pan side service hole and remove the torque converter nuts.

18. Remove the front transaxle mount.

19. Loosen the engine support tool to lean the engine toward the transaxle. Support the transaxle with a jack and remove the transaxle mounting bolts. Carefully lower the transaxle from the vehicle, being careful not to drop the torque converter.

To install:

20. Make sure the torque converter is completely installed in the transaxle. Lay a straightedge across the bellhousing and measure the distance to the torque converter (not the stud); it should be 0.535 in. (13.6mm). If the distance is less than specification, push the converter into the pump while rotating it, to properly engage the pump drive.

21. Raise the transaxle into position, making sure the converter studs align with the flexplate holes, and install the transaxle-to-engine bolts. Tighten to 59 ft. lbs. (80 Nm).

22. Install the front transaxle mount and tighten the bolt(s) to 38 ft. lbs. (52 Nm).

23. Hold the flexplate with a small prybar and tighten the converter nuts, gradually and evenly, to 25-36 ft. lbs. (34-49 Nm). On 1.6L engine, install the service hole cover. On 1.8L engine, install the access plate.

24. Install the left side transaxle mount. Tighten the mount-to-body bolts to 45 ft. lbs. (61 Nm) and the mount-to-transaxle nuts to 69 ft. lbs. (93 Nm).

25. Install the halfshafts.

26. Install the engine mount member. Tighten the mount member-to-mount nuts to 38 ft. lbs. (52 Nm) and the mount member-to-body nuts/bolts to 66

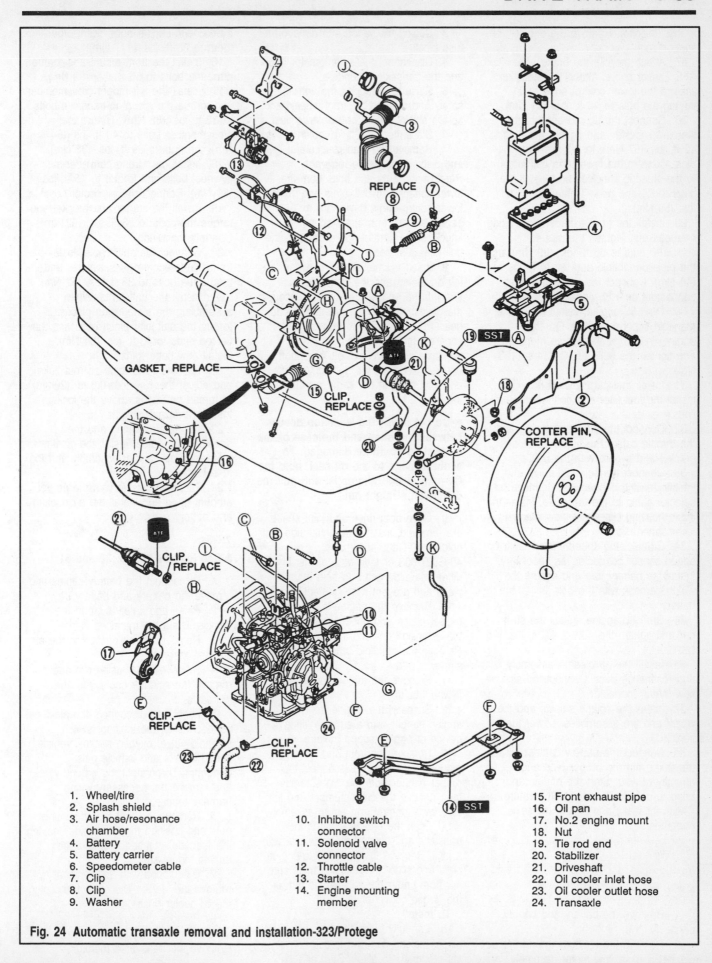

1. Wheel/tire
2. Splash shield
3. Air hose/resonance chamber
4. Battery
5. Battery carrier
6. Speedometer cable
7. Clip
8. Clip
9. Washer
10. Inhibitor switch connector
11. Solenoid valve connector
12. Throttle cable
13. Starter
14. Engine mounting member
15. Front exhaust pipe
16. Oil pan
17. No.2 engine mount
18. Nut
19. Tie rod end
20. Stabilizer
21. Driveshaft
22. Oil cooler inlet hose
23. Oil cooler outlet hose
24. Transaxle

Fig. 24 Automatic transaxle removal and installation-323/Protege

ft. lbs. (89 Nm). Remove the engine support tool.

27. Attach the clip the brake hose and ABS sensor cable. Attach the stabilizer links to the lower control arms and tighten the nuts to 45 ft. lbs. (61 Nm).

28. Connect the tie rod ends to the steering knuckles and tighten the nuts to 42 ft. lbs. (57 Nm). Install new cotter pins. Connect the lower arm ball joints to the steering knuckles and install the pinch bolts and nuts. Tighten to 43 ft. lbs. (59 Nm).

29. Install the front exhaust pipe, using new gaskets. Tighten the pipe-to-converter nuts to 66 ft. lbs. (89 Nm) and the pipe-to-manifold nuts to 34 ft. lbs. (46 Nm). Connect the oxygen sensor connectors on 1.8L engine.

30. On 1.6L engine, install the intake manifold support bracket. On 1.8L engine, install the transverse member and tighten the bolts to 90 ft. lbs. (123 Nm).

31. Install the starter. On 1.8L engine, install the fuel filter and connect the fuel lines.

32. Connect the oil cooler hoses and the throttle cable. Position the harness bracket and secure with the bolt.

33. Connect the solenoid valve and inhibitor switch connectors. Connect the selector cable to the transaxle. Install the cable housing clip and a new manual lever spring clip.

34. Connect the speedometer cable or speed sensor connector, as necessary. Install the battery tray and secure the wiring harness with the bolt. Install the battery.

35. On 1.8L engine, install the strut bar and tighten the nuts to 20 ft. lbs. (26 Nm).

36. Install the air cleaner assembly and resonance duct. Connect the air flow meter connector.

37. Install the splash shields and the wheel and tire assemblies. Lower the vehicle.

38. Connect the battery cables. Fill the transaxle with the proper type and quantity of fluid. Start the engine and bring to normal operating temperature. Check for leaks and proper transaxle operation.

MX-6/626

1989-92

▶ See Figure 27

1. Remove the battery and battery carrier.

2. Remove the air ducting and the air cleaner and air flow meter assembly.

3. Unplug the wiring and remove the fuse block.

4. Disconnect the speedometer cable and the transaxle grounds.

5. Raise and support the vehicle safely and remove the front wheels and splash shield. Drain the transaxle fluid.

6. Disconnect the fluid cooler hoses.

7. Remove the stabilizer control links and disconnect the tie rod ends. Remove the nuts and bolts from the lower control arm ball joints and pull the lower control arms downward to separate them from the steering knuckles. Be careful not to damage the ball joint dust boots.

8. Insert a small prybar between the left driveshaft and the transaxle case and tap the end of the lever to uncouple the driveshaft from the differential side gear. Pull the front hub forward and separate the driveshaft from the transaxle. Remove the left joint shaft bracket. Separate the right driveshaft and joint shaft in the same manner as the left.

➡**Do not insert the lever too deeply between the shaft and the case or the oil seal lip could be damaged. To avoid damage to the oil seal, hold the CV-joint at the differential and pull the driveshaft straight out.**

9. Once both drive and joint shafts are removed, install differential side gear holders 49-G030-455 (turbo), 49-G027-003 or their equivalents, in the differential side gears to hold them in place and prevent misalignment.

10. Remove the engine-to-transaxle gusset plates and under cover. Remove the extension bar and the control rod. Remove the manifold bracket and the starter.

11. Remove the torque converter-to-flywheel bolts.

12. Suspend the engine from the engine hanger with a suitable lifting device or engine support fixture.

13. Remove the front and left engine mounts and bracket. Disconnect the rubber hanger from the crossmember, then remove the crossmember and left side lower control arm as an assembly.

14. Lean the engine towards the transaxle and support the transaxle with a jack. Remove the transaxle-to-engine bolts and slide the transaxle back and out from under the vehicle. Do not let the torque converter fall out.

To install:

15. Carefully guide the transaxle into place, making sure the torque converter fits properly into place. Start all the

transaxle-to-engine bolts, then torque them to 86 ft. lbs. (117 Nm).

16. Install the front mount and torque nuts and bolts to 66 ft. lbs. (89 Nm).

17. Install the left mount crossmember and torque the mount-to-transaxle bolts to 38 ft. lbs. (52 Nm). Torque the crossmember bolts to 40 ft. lbs. (54 Nm), the nuts to 69 ft. lbs. (93 Nm).

18. Install the torque converter-to-flywheel bolts and torque to 45 ft. lbs. (61 Nm). Connect the oil cooler hoses.

19. Install the starter and bracket and torque the bolts to 38 ft. lbs. (52 Nm). Connect the wiring

20. Connect the shift cable. Install the transaxle-to-engine gusset plates and torque the bolts to 38 ft. lbs. (52 Nm).

21. Install the halfshafts. When assembling the suspension pieces, torque the ball joint pinch bolts and the tie rod ends to 40 ft. lbs. (54 Nm). Install new cotter pins.

22. Assemble the stabilizer bar links and adjust them so that 0.8 in. (20mm) of thread protrudes above the locknut. Install the splash shields.

23. Connect all wiring and the speedometer cable. Install the air flow meter and air cleaner assembly and the fuse box.

24. Fill the transaxle with the proper amount of oil and install the air ducting and battery.

1993

▶ See Figures 28, 29, 30 and 31

1. Disconnect the battery cables and remove the battery and battery tray.

2. Raise and safely support the vehicle. Drain the transaxle fluid.

3. Remove the air ducts and the air cleaner assembly.

4. Remove the housing clip and remove the selector cable from the transaxle.

5. Label and disconnect the electrical connectors for the inhibitor switch, solenoid valve, oxygen sensor, vehicle speed sensor and vehicle pulse generator. Disconnect the ground wires and remove the necessary wiring harness brackets.

6. Remove the fuel filter mounting nuts and position the filter aside, leaving the fuel line attached. Remove the engine mount stay.

7. If equipped with 2.5L engine, remove the starter. Disconnect and plug the oil cooler hoses.

8. Remove the wheel and tire assemblies and the splash shields. Remove the transverse member.

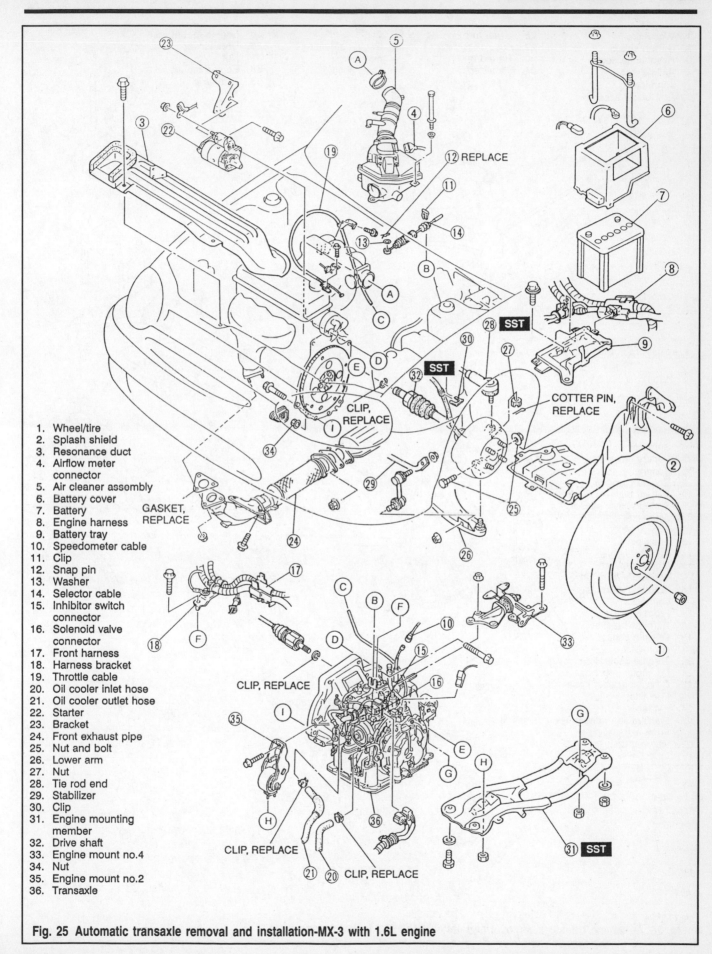

1. Wheel/tire
2. Splash shield
3. Resonance duct
4. Airflow meter connector
5. Air cleaner assembly
6. Battery cover
7. Battery
8. Engine harness
9. Battery tray
10. Speedometer cable
11. Clip
12. Snap pin
13. Washer
14. Selector cable
15. Inhibitor switch connector
16. Solenoid valve connector
17. Front harness
18. Harness bracket
19. Throttle cable
20. Oil cooler inlet hose
21. Oil cooler outlet hose
22. Starter
23. Bracket
24. Front exhaust pipe
25. Nut and bolt
26. Lower arm
27. Nut
28. Tie rod end
29. Stabilizer
30. Clip
31. Engine mounting member
32. Drive shaft
33. Engine mount no.4
34. Nut
35. Engine mount no.2
36. Transaxle

REPLACE

CLIP, REPLACE

SST

SST

SST

COTTER PIN, REPLACE

GASKET, REPLACE

CLIP, REPLACE

CLIP, REPLACE

CLIP, REPLACE

SST

Fig. 25 Automatic transaxle removal and installation-MX-3 with 1.6L engine

1. Wheel/tire
2. Splash shield
3. Resonance duct
4. Airflow meter connector
5. Air cleaner assembly

28. Lower arm
29. Nut
30. Tie rod end
31. Stabilizer

32. Clip
33. Engine mounting member
34. Drive shaft

35. Engine mount no.4
36. Undercover
37. Nut
38. Engine mount no.2
39. Transaxle

6. Strut bar
7. Battery cover
8. Battery
9. Engine harness
10. Battery tray
11. Speedometer sensor connector
12. Clip
13. Snap pin
14. Selector cable
15. Inhibitor switch connector
16. Solenoid valve connector
17. Front harness
18. Harness bracket
19. Oxygen sensor connector
20. Throttle cable
21. Oil cooler inlet hose
22. Oil cooler outlet hose
23. Fuel filter
24. Starter
25. Transverse member
26. Front exhaust pipe
27. Nut and bolt

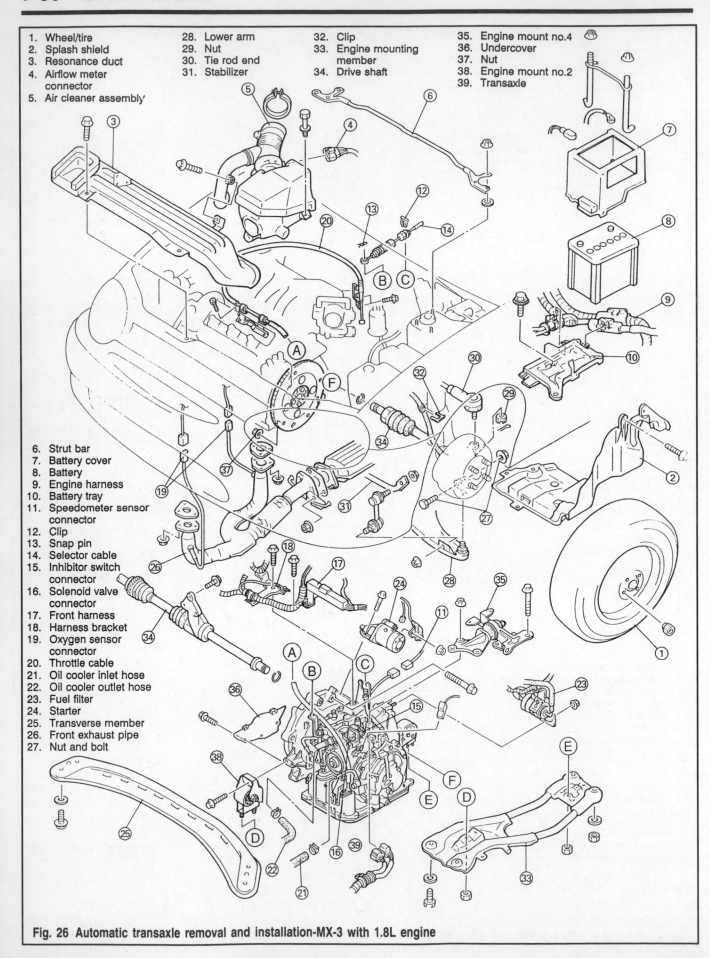

Fig. 26 Automatic transaxle removal and installation-MX-3 with 1.8L engine

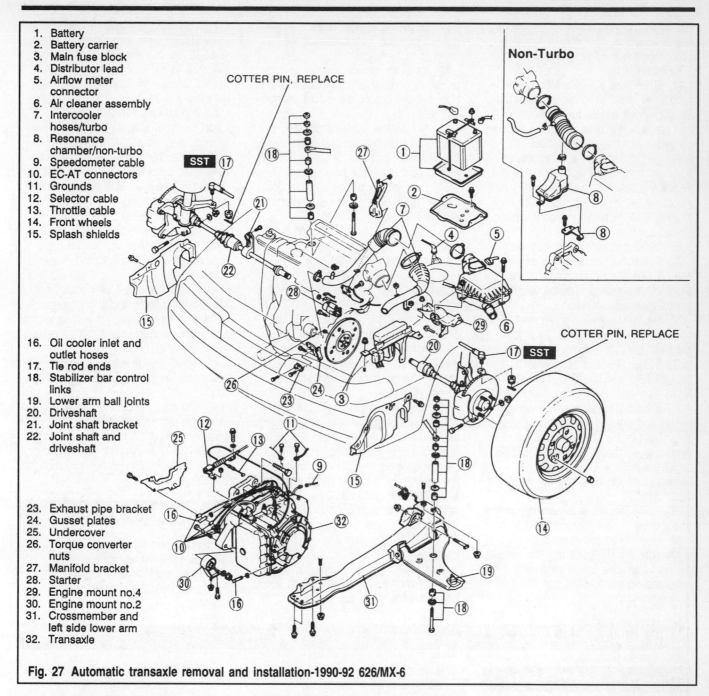

1. Battery
2. Battery carrier
3. Main fuse block
4. Distributor lead
5. Airflow meter connector
6. Air cleaner assembly
7. Intercooler hoses/turbo
8. Resonance chamber/non-turbo
9. Speedometer cable
10. EC-AT connectors
11. Grounds
12. Selector cable
13. Throttle cable
14. Front wheels
15. Splash shields

16. Oil cooler inlet and outlet hoses
17. Tie rod ends
18. Stabilizer bar control links
19. Lower arm ball joints
20. Driveshaft
21. Joint shaft bracket
22. Joint shaft and driveshaft

23. Exhaust pipe bracket
24. Gusset plates
25. Undercover
26. Torque converter nuts
27. Manifold bracket
28. Starter
29. Engine mount no.4
30. Engine mount no.2
31. Crossmember and left side lower arm
32. Transaxle

COTTER PIN, REPLACE

SST

Non-Turbo

COTTER PIN, REPLACE

SST

Fig. 27 Automatic transaxle removal and installation-1990-92 626/MX-6

9. If equipped with 2.5L engine, remove the front exhaust pipe.

10. Remove the pinch bolts from the steering knuckles. Pry the lower control arms down to separate the ball joints from the knuckles.

11. Remove the cotter pins and nuts and separate the tie rod ends from the knuckles. Remove the nuts and disconnect the stabilizer links from the lower control arms.

12. Remove the brake hose clips from the struts and remove the ABS speed sensor harness mounting nuts.

13. Separate the right side halfshaft from the intermediate shaft using a hammer and brass drift. Pry the left side shaft from the transaxle using a prybar

inserted between the transaxle and the inner CV-joint. Be careful not to damage the oil seal.

14. Suspend the halfshafts with rope, in a level position. Insert plug tools 49 G030 455 or equivalent into the differential side gears to keep them from becoming mispositioned.

15. Remove the intermediate shaft.

16. If equipped with 2.0L engine, remove the intake manifold support bracket and remove the starter.

17. Remove the engine mount rubber from the right side of the engine mount member. Remove the mount-to-transaxle bolts from the rear transaxle mount.

18. Support the engine using engine support tool 49 G017 5A0 or equivalent.

Remove the engine mount member nuts and bolts and remove the engine mount member.

19. If equipped with 2.5L engine, remove the torque converter access plate. On 2.0L engine, remove the seal rubber from the transaxle case near the starter mounting hole.

20. Hold the flexplate with a small prybar and remove the torque converter nuts.

21. Remove the left side transaxle mount.

22. Loosen the engine support tool and lean the engine toward the transaxle. Support the transaxle with a jack and remove the transaxle mounting bolts. Carefully lower the transaxle from

the vehicle, being careful not to drop the torque converter.

23. Remove the front transaxle mount.

To install:

24. Make sure the torque converter is completely installed in the transaxle. Lay a straightedge across the bellhousing and measure the distance to the torque converter (not the stud); it should be 0.602 in. (15.3mm) on 2.0L engine or 0.551 in. (14mm) on 2.5L engine. If the distance is less than specification, push the converter into the pump while rotating it, to properly engage the pump drive.

25. Install the front transaxle mount.

26. Raise the transaxle into position, making sure the torque converter studs align with the flex plate holes, and install the transaxle mountin bolts.

27. On 2.5L engine, tighten the transaxle mounting bolts to 73 ft. lbs. (99 Nm). On 2.0L engine, tighten bolts **A** to 73 ft. lbs. (99 Nm), bolts **B** to 38 ft. lbs. (51 Nm) and bolt **C** to 18 ft. lbs. (25 Nm).

28. Hold the flexplate with the small prybar and install the torque converter nuts. Tighten the bolts, gradually and evenly, to 45 ft. lbs. (60 Nm). On 2.5L engine, install the torque converter access plate. On 2.0L engine, install the seal rubber.

29. Install the left side transaxle mount and loosely tighten the bolts and nuts.

30. Use the engine support tool to make sure the transaxle bolt holes and the rear transaxle mount align. Install the bolts and tighten to 68 ft. lbs. (93 Nm).

31. Install the engine mount member, making sure the mount rubbers are installed properly.

32. Install the mount member-to-body bolts/nuts and tighten to 68 ft. lbs. (93 Nm). Loosely tighten the mount member-to-mount nuts.

33. Tighten the left transaxle mount mount-to-transaxle nuts and bolt to 68 ft. lbs. (93 Nm). Tighten the mount through bolt to 86 ft. lbs. (116 Nm).

34. Remove the engine support tool. Tighten the mount member-to-mount nuts to 77 ft. lbs. (104 Nm).

35. Install the mount rubber on the right side of the mount member. Tighten the bolts to 68 ft. lbs. (93 Nm).

36. If equipped with 2.0L engine, install the starter and the intake manifold support bracket.

37. Remove the plug tool from the differential side gear. Install the intermediate shaft into the transaxle. Install the support bearing to the engine and tighten the bolts, in sequence, to 45 ft. lbs. (61 Nm).

38. Remove the plug from the other differential side gear. Install a new circlip on the halfshaft with end gap facing upward. Install the halfshaft into the transaxle, being careful not to damage the seal. Make sure the circlip seats in the differential side gear, by pulling out on the shaft; it must not pull out.

39. Install a new circlip on the end of the other halfshaft and connect it to the intermediate shaft.

40. Connect the lower ball joints to the steering knuckles. Install the pinch bolts and tighten to 43 ft. lbs. (58 Nm).

41. Connect the stabilizer links to the lower control arms and tighten the nuts to 39 ft. lbs. (53 Nm). Connect the tie rod ends to the steering knuckles and tighten the nuts to 32 ft. lbs. (44 Nm). Install new cotter pins.

42. If equipped with 2.5L engine, install the front exhaust pipe, using new gaskets, and install the starter.

43. Install the transverse member and tighten the bolts to 96 ft. lbs. (131 Nm). Install the splash shields and the wheel and tire assemblies.

44. Connect the oil cooler hoses. Install the engine mount stay.

45. Install the harness brackets and the ground wires. Connect the electrical connectors.

46. Position the fuel filter and install the mounting bolts. Install the selector cable to the cable bracket and install the clip. Connect the cable to the transaxle lever.

47. Install the air cleaner assembly and ducts. Install the battery and battery tray.

48. Connect the battery cables. Fill the transaxle with the proper type and quantity of fluid. Start the engine and bring to normal operating temperature. Check for leaks and proper transaxle operation.

Halfshafts

Halfshaft removal, installation and overhaul proecedures for automatic transaxles are the same for manual transaxles described earlier in this Section.

DRIVELINE

Driveshaft and U-Joints

REMOVAL & INSTALLATION

Miata and 323 W/4WD

1. Matchmark the rear U-joint with the rear companion flange. Remove the bolts attaching the driveshaft to the rear companion flange.

2. Remove the center support bearing bracket from the underbody.

3. Pull the driveshaft rearward and out of the transmission. Plug the rear seal opening.

4. Installation is the reverse of removal. Make sure that you align the matchmarks. Torque the rear companion flange bolts to 22 ft. lbs.

U-JOINT OVERHAUL

Perform this procedure with the driveshaft removed from the car.

1. Matchmark both the yoke and the driveshaft so that they can be returned to their original balancing position during assembly.

2. Remove the bearing snaprings from the yoke.

3. Use a hammer and a brass drift to drive in one of the bearing cups. Remove the cup which is protruding from the other side of the yoke.

4. Remove the other bearing cups by pressing them from the spider.

5. Withdraw the spider from the yoke.

6. Examine the spider journals for rusting or wear. Check the bearing for smoothness or pitting.

➡ **The spider and bearing are replace as a complete assembly only.**

7. Check the seals and rollers for wear or damage.

To assemble the U-joint:

8. Pack the bearing cups with grease.

9. Fit the rollers into the cups and install the dust seals.

10. Place the spider in the yoke and them fit one of the bearing cups into its bore in the yoke.

11. Press the bearing cup home, while guiding the spider into it, so that a snapring can be installed.

1. Battery
2. Battery carrier
3. Resonance chamber
4. Fresh air duct
5. Air cleaner assembly
6. Resonance chamber
7. Clip
8. Selector cable
9. Inhibitor switch
   connector
10. Solenoid valve
    connector
11. Oxygen sensor
    connector
12. Ground
13. Bolt
14. Vehicle speed
    sensor connector

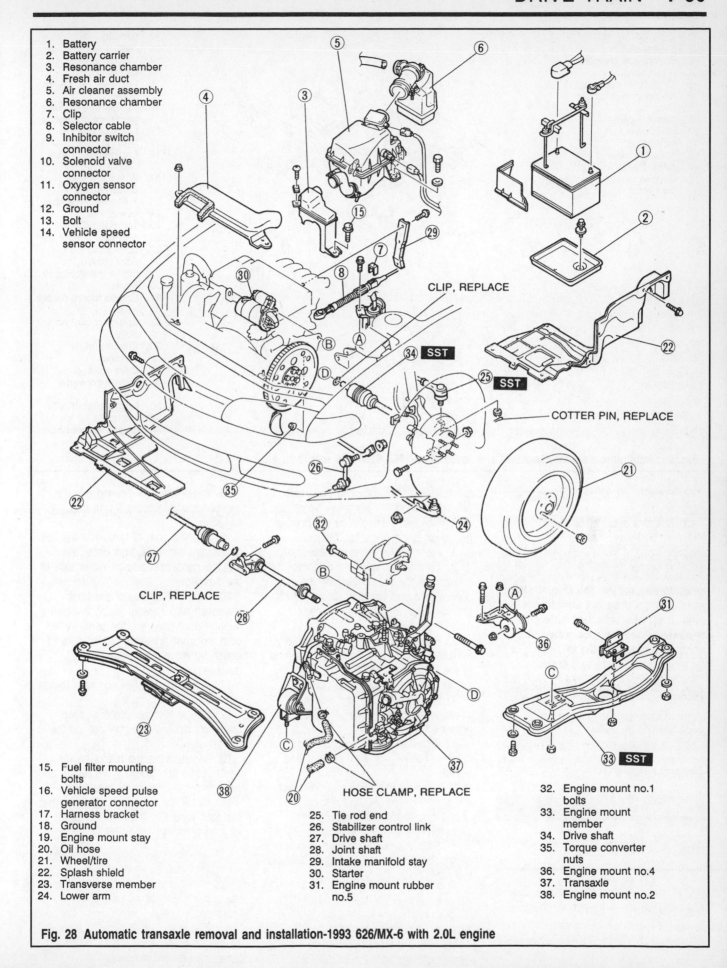

CLIP, REPLACE

SST

COTTER PIN, REPLACE

CLIP, REPLACE

SST

HOSE CLAMP, REPLACE

15. Fuel filter mounting
    bolts
16. Vehicle speed pulse
    generator connector
17. Harness bracket
18. Ground
19. Engine mount stay
20. Oil hose
21. Wheel/tire
22. Splash shield
23. Transverse member
24. Lower arm

25. Tie rod end
26. Stabilizer control link
27. Drive shaft
28. Joint shaft
29. Intake manifold stay
30. Starter
31. Engine mount rubber
    no.5

32. Engine mount no.1
    bolts
33. Engine mount
    member
34. Drive shaft
35. Torque converter
    nuts
36. Engine mount no.4
37. Transaxle
38. Engine mount no.2

Fig. 28 Automatic transaxle removal and installation-1993 626/MX-6 with 2.0L engine

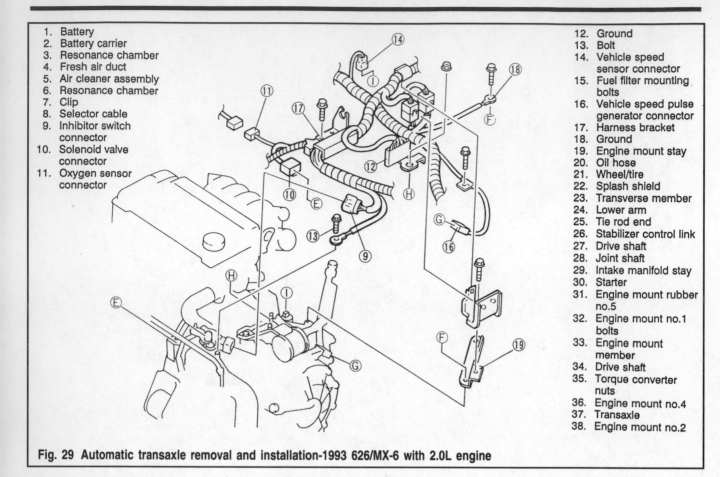

1. Battery
2. Battery carrier
3. Resonance chamber
4. Fresh air duct
5. Air cleaner assembly
6. Resonance chamber
7. Clip
8. Selector cable
9. Inhibitor switch connector
10. Solenoid valve connector
11. Oxygen sensor connector

12. Ground
13. Bolt
14. Vehicle speed sensor connector
15. Fuel filter mounting bolts
16. Vehicle speed pulse generator connector
17. Harness bracket
18. Ground
19. Engine mount stay
20. Oil hose
21. Wheel/tire
22. Splash shield
23. Transverse member
24. Lower arm
25. Tie rod end
26. Stabilizer control link
27. Drive shaft
28. Joint shaft
29. Intake manifold stay
30. Starter
31. Engine mount rubber no.5
32. Engine mount no.1 bolts
33. Engine mount member
34. Drive shaft
35. Torque converter nuts
36. Engine mount no.4
37. Transaxle
38. Engine mount no.2

Fig. 29 Automatic transaxle removal and installation-1993 626/MX-6 with 2.0L engine

12. Press-fit the other bearings into the yoke.

13. Select a snapring to obtain minimum end-play of the spider. Use snaprings of the same thickness on both sides to center the spider.

➡**When assembled, the U-joint should have a slight drag but should not bind. If it does bind, use different thickness snaprings. Selective fit snaprings are available in sizes ranging from 1.2mm to 1.4mm.**

14. Install the spider/yoke assembly and bearings into the driveshaft in the same manner as the spider was assembled to the yoke.

15. Test the operation of the U-joint assembly. The spider should move freely with no binding.

Center Bearing

REPLACEMENT

The center support bearing is a sealed unit which requires no periodic maintenance. The following procedure should be used if it becomes necessary to replace the bearing. You will need a pair of snapring pliers for this job.

1. Remove the driveshaft assembly.

2. To maintain driveline balance, matchmark the rear driveshaft, the center yoke and the front driveshaft so that they may be installed in their original positions.

3. Remove the center universal joint from the center yoke, leaving it attached to the rear driveshaft. See the following section for the correct procedure.

4. Remove the nut and washer securing the center yoke to the front driveshaft.

5. Slide the center yoke off the splines. The rear oil seal should slide off with it.

6. If the oil has remained on top of the snapring, remove and discard the seal. Remove the snapring from its groove. Remove the bearing.

7. Slide the center support and front oil seal from the front driveshaft. Discard the seal.

8. Install the new bearing into the center support. Secure it with the snapring.

9. Apply a coat of grease to the lips of the new oil seals, and install them into the center support on either side of the bearing.

10. Coat the splines of the front driveshaft with grease. Install the center support assembly and the center yoke onto the front driveshaft, being sure to match up the marks made during disassembly.

11. Install the washer and nut. Torque the nut to 116-130 ft. lbs.

12. Check that the center support assembly rotates smoothly around the driveshaft.

13. Align the mating marks on the center yoke and the rear driveshaft, and assemble the center universal joint.

14. Install the driveshaft. Be sure that the rear yoke and the axle flange re aligned properly.

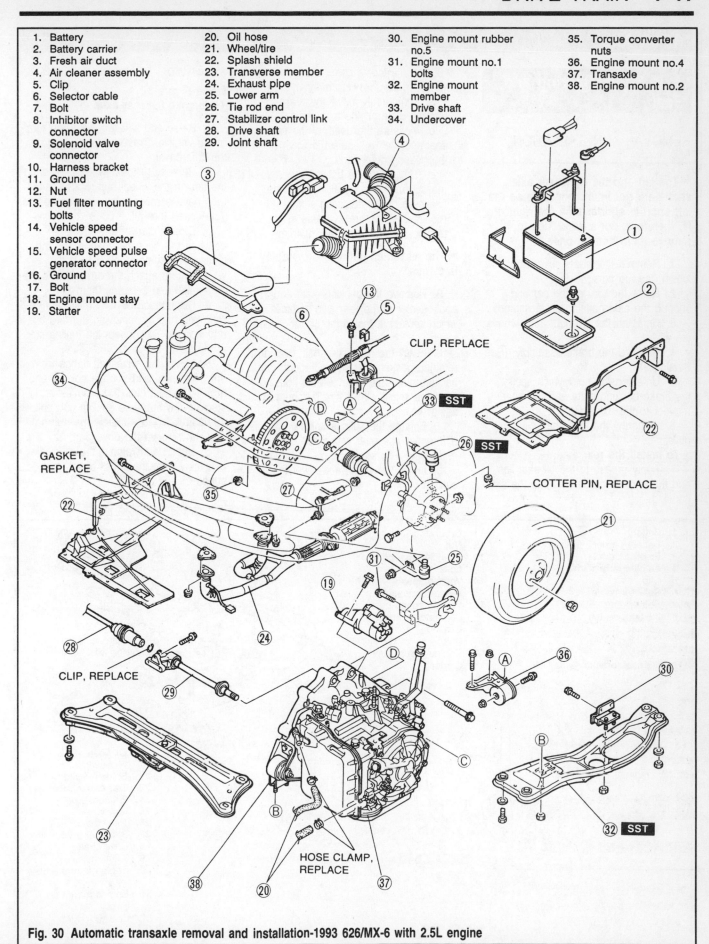

1. Battery
2. Battery carrier
3. Fresh air duct
4. Air cleaner assembly
5. Clip
6. Selector cable
7. Bolt
8. Inhibitor switch connector
9. Solenoid valve connector
10. Harness bracket
11. Ground
12. Nut
13. Fuel filter mounting bolts
14. Vehicle speed sensor connector
15. Vehicle speed pulse generator connector
16. Ground
17. Bolt
18. Engine mount stay
19. Starter
20. Oil hose
21. Wheel/tire
22. Splash shield
23. Transverse member
24. Exhaust pipe
25. Lower arm
26. Tie rod end
27. Stabilizer control link
28. Drive shaft
29. Joint shaft
30. Engine mount rubber no.5
31. Engine mount no.1 bolts
32. Engine mount member
33. Drive shaft
34. Undercover
35. Torque converter nuts
36. Engine mount no.4
37. Transaxle
38. Engine mount no.2

CLIP, REPLACE

GASKET, REPLACE

COTTER PIN, REPLACE

CLIP, REPLACE

HOSE CLAMP, REPLACE

Fig. 30 Automatic transaxle removal and installation-1993 626/MX-6 with 2.5L engine

REAR AXLE

Axle Shaft, Bearing and Seal

REMOVAL & INSTALLATION

➡The left and the right rear axle shafts are not interchangeable as the left shaft is shorter than the right. It is, therefore, not a good idea to remove them both at once.

1. Remove the wheel cover and loosen the lug nuts.
2. Raise the rear of the car and support the axle housing on jackstands.
3. Unfasten the lug nuts and remove the wheel.
4. Remove the brake assembly. (See Section 9).
5. Unfasten the nuts which secure the brake backing plate and the bearing retainer to the axle housing.
6. Withdraw the axle shaft with a puller.
   To install the rear axle:
7. Apply grease to the oil seal lips and then insert the oil seal into the axle housing.

8. On all models check the axle shaft end-play in the following manner:
   a. Temporarily install the brake backing plate on the axle shaft.
   b. Measure the depth of the bearing seal and then measure the width of the bearing outer race.
   c. The difference between the two measurements is equal to the overall thickness of the adjusting shims required. Shims are available in thicknesses of 0.1mm and 0.4mm.

➡**The maximum permissible endplay is 0.1mm.**

9. Remove the backing plate and apply sealer to the rear axle surfaces which contact it. Install the backing plate again.
10. Install the rear axle shaft, bearing retainer, gasket, and shims through the backing plate and into the axle housing. Coat the shims with a small amount of sealer first.
11. Engage the splines on the differential side gear with those on the end of the axle shaft.
12. Install the wheel and lower the car.

323 w/4WD

▶ **See Figure 32**
To remove the rear axle:

1. Raise and safely support the rear of the vehicle. Drain the lubricant from the differential.
2. Remove the rear wheels. Raise the tab on the wheel hub locknut, and then have someone apply the brakes as you loosen the nut.
3. Clearly mark the relationship between the driveshaft flange and the differential. Remove the nuts and washers that attach the driveshaft to the differential and separate them.
4. Disconnect the lateral link from the rear axle hub by removing the thru bolt and washer. Disconnect the trailing link in the same manner.
5. Lower the driveshaft flange from the differential and pull the splined end from the wheel hub. If the driveshaft is stuck in the hub, use special hub puller 49-0839-425C to withdraw the hub so you can remove the driveshaft.
6. Unbolt and remove the rear axle assembly from the shock absorber support.

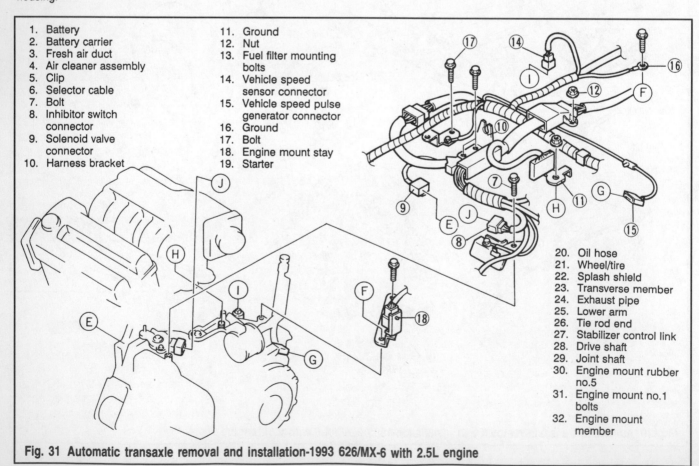

1. Battery
2. Battery carrier
3. Fresh air duct
4. Air cleaner assembly
5. Clip
6. Selector cable
7. Bolt
8. Inhibitor switch connector
9. Solenoid valve connector
10. Harness bracket
11. Ground
12. Nut
13. Fuel filter mounting bolts
14. Vehicle speed sensor connector
15. Vehicle speed pulse generator connector
16. Ground
17. Bolt
18. Engine mount stay
19. Starter
20. Oil hose
21. Wheel/tire
22. Splash shield
23. Transverse member
24. Exhaust pipe
25. Lower arm
26. Tie rod end
27. Stabilizer control link
28. Drive shaft
29. Joint shaft
30. Engine mount rubber no.5
31. Engine mount no.1 bolts
32. Engine mount member

Fig. 31 Automatic transaxle removal and installation-1993 626/MX-6 with 2.5L engine

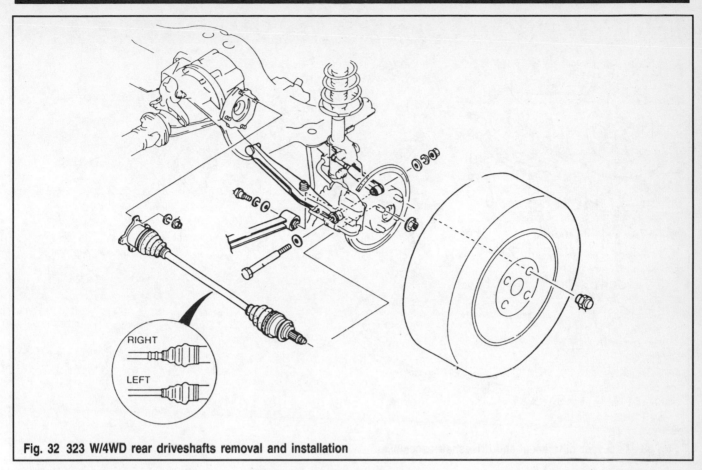

Fig. 32 323 W/4WD rear driveshafts removal and installation

To replace the bearings and oil seals:

7. Press the wheel hub and disc plate from the knuckle using and arbor press and special attachments 49-B026-102, 49-G033-102 and 49-G030-727. Support the wheel hub and disc plate to keep it fram falling.

8. Matchmark the wheel hub and the disc plate and remove wheel hub.

9. Support the wheel hub on V-blocks with the bolts facing down. Place special tool 49-0636-145 between the oil seal and the hub. Press the outer bearing and oil seal from the hub. Save the spacer.

10. Pry the inner oil seal from the wheel hub with a screwdriver and drive the inner and outer bearing races out of the hub using a brass drift punch and a hammmer.

11. Install the new inner and outer bearing races and seat them in the knuckle by tapping alternately and evenly using the brass drift and hammer.

12. Install the inner bearing, original spacer and outer bearing and place special preload adjustment tool 49-B001-727 on top of the outer bearing. Torque the special tool to 17 in. lbs. Mount the knuckle in a protected jaw vise so that the jaws are clamped on the wheel hub shaft. Hook a spring scale to the knuckle and measure the preload. The preload is correct at 1.74-6.94 on the scale. If not as specified, adjust the preload by selecting the appropriate spacer. If the bearing preload is greater than the specified amount go to thicker spacer and vice versa if less than specified. If the preload is within the specified value, use the old spacer.

13. Install the inner bearing into the knuckle. Coat the lip of the inner oil seal with a good quality lithium based grease and install the seal using special seal installer tool 49-B001-795. This tool may be substituted for a piece of pipe or socket that closely approximates the diameter of the seal. Install the outer bearing and outer oil seal in the same manner as the inner. Pack the inner and outer bearings with lithium based grease.

14. Place the disc plate onot the wheel hub so that the matchmarks are aligned and install the wheel hub retaining bolts. Torque the bolts to 33-40 ft. lbs.

15. Press the hub into the knuckle.

To install the rear axle:

16. Attach the knuckle assembly to the shock absorber support and torque the retaining bolts to 58-86 ft. lbs.

17. Insert the splined end of the driveshaft into the wheel hub and connect the trailing and lateral links. Torque the trailing link bolt to 58-56 ft. lbs. and the lateral link bolt to 46-55 ft. lbs.

18. Attach the driveshaft flange to the differential by aligning the matchmarks. Torque the flange nuts to 36-43 ft. lbs.

19. Install a new locknut and torque it to 116-174 ft. lbs. Stake the locknut tab into the groove of the spridle using a small cold chisel.

20. Install the rear wheels and lower the vehicle.

Differential Carrier

REMOVAL & INSTALLATION

Miata

▶ **See Figure 33**

1. Raise the vehicle and support it safely with jackstands.

2. Using wrench 49 0259 730, remove the differential drain plug and drain the lubricant from the differential. Install the plug after all of the fluid has drained.

3. Remove the axle shafts.

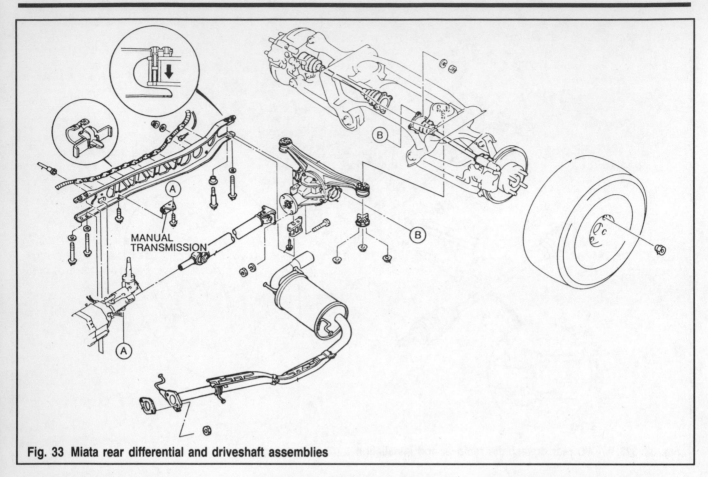

Fig. 33 Miata rear differential and driveshaft assemblies

4. Remove the driveshaft.

5. Remove the carrier-to-differential housing retaining fasteners and remove the carrier assembly from the housing.

6. Clean the carrier and axle housing mating surfaces.

7. If the differential originally used a gasket between the carrier and the differential housing, replace the gasket. If the unit had no gasket, apply a thin film of oil-resistant silicone sealer to the mating surfaces of both the carrier and the housing and allow the sealer to set according to the manufacturer's instructions.

8. Place the carrier assembly onto the housing and install the carrier-to-housing fasteners. Torque the fasteners to 12-17 ft. lb.

9. Install the driveshaft(s) and axle shafts as previously outlined.

10. Install the brake drums and wheels.

11. Fill the differential with the proper amount of SAE 80W-90 fluid (see the Capacities Chart).

323 w/4WD

1. Drain the differential fluid into a suitable drain pan.

2. Remove the propeller shaft.

3. Raise the rear of the vehicle and support safely.

4. Mark the relationship between the driveshaft and output flanges and separate the driveshafts from the differential.

5. Have an assistant apply the brakes and remove the axle nut.

6. Disconnect the stabilizer from the crossmember.

❊❊CAUTION

Never remove both ends of the stabilizer.

7. Disconnect the lateral and trailing links.

8. Grasp the wheel hub by the rotor disc and pull it out until the driveshaft can be disconnected from the spline.

9. Support the differential with a jack and remove the mounting hardware from the front and rear attachment points. Lower the differntial to the floor.

To install the differential:

10. Raise the differential up into the frame and install the front and rear fasteners. Torque the front fasteners to 3-50 ft. lbs. and the rear fasteners to 80-97 ft. lbs.

11. Insert the driveshaft spline into the wheel hub and align the matchmarks on

the driveshaft with the output shaft. Install the flange fasteners and torque them to 36-43 ft. lbs.

12. Connect the lateral link and torque the mounting bolt to 69-86 ft. lbs. Connect the trailing link to the crosmember and torque the mounting bolt to 9-13 ft. lbs.

13. Install the propeller shaft and torque the flange bolts to 20-22 ft. lbs.

14. Mount the wheels and lower the vehcicle.

15. Fill the differential to the proper level (see Capacities Chart) and install the drain plug.

Axle Housing

REMOVAL & INSTALLATION

Miata

1. Raise the vehicle on a hoist and support the axle assembly with a suitable lifting device. Drain the lubricant from the axle housing and remove the driveshaft.

2. Remove the wheel, the brake drum and the drum assembly.

3. Disconnect the parking brake cable from the lever and at the brake flange plate.

4. Disconnect the hydraulic brake lines from the connectors.

5. Disconnect the shock absorbers from the axle brackets.

6. Remove the nuts and washers from the U-bolts.

7. Remove the U-bolts, spring plates and spacers from the axle assembly.

8. Lower the jack and remove the axle assembly.

To install the axle housing:

9. Raise the axle housing into place and install the spacers, spring plates and U-bolts.

10. Install the U-bolt nuts and washers. Remove the jack.

11. Connect the shock absorbers to the axle brackets.

12. Connect and tighten the brake lines.

13. Connnect the parking brake cable to the lever on the brake flange lever plate.

14. Install the rear brakes, brake drum and rear wheels.

15. Connect the driveshaft and fill the axle housing to the proper level.

Pinion Seal

REMOVAL & INSTALLATION

1. Raise and support the front end on jackstands.

2. Matchmark and remove the driveshaft.

3. Remove the wheels and brake calipers.

4. Using an in. lbs. torque wrench on the companion flange nut, measure the rotational torque of the differential and note the reading.

5. Hold the companion flange from turning and remove the locknut.

6. Using a puller, remove the companion flange.

7. Using a center punch to deform the seal and pry it out of the bore.

8. Coat the outer edge of the new seal with sealer and drive it into place with a seal driver.

9. Coat the seal lip with clean gear oil.

10. Coat the companion flange with chassis lube and install it.

11. Install the nut and tighten it until the previously noted rotational torque is achieved. Torque on the nut should not exceed 130 ft. lbs.

12. Install the driveshaft.

13. Replace any lost gear oil.

TORQUE SPECIFICATIONS

Component	U.S.	Metric
Manual Transaxle:		
323/Protege;		
Clutch release cylinder and clutch pipe bolt:	12–17 ft. lbs.	16–23 Nm
Speedometer driven gear bolt:	69–104 inch lbs.	8–12 Nm
Drain plug:	36 ft. lbs.	49 Nm
Transaxle case to clutch housing bolts:	14–19 ft. lbs.	19–26 Nm
Neutral switch:	14–18 ft. lbs.	20–25 Nm
Rear bearing retainer:	15 ft. lbs.	21 Nm
Primary and secondary shaft locknuts:	94–152 ft. lbs.	128–206 Nm
5th gear shift rod end bolts:	10 ft. lbs.	14 Nm
Transaxle to engine mounting bolts:	47–66 ft. lbs.	64–89 Nm
Wheel nut:	87 ft. lbs.	118 Nm
MX3 and 626/MX6 F5M-R transaxle;		
Speedometer driven gear:	69–100 inch lbs.	8–11 Nm
Drain plug:	29–43 ft. lbs.	39–59 Nm
Change rod bolt:	10–14 ft. lbs.	14–19 Nm
Change arm bolt:	9–10 ft. lbs.	12–14 Nm
Primary and secondary shaft locknuts:	94–152 ft. lbs.	128–206 Nm
5th gear shift rod end bolts:	10 ft. lbs.	14 Nm
Transaxle to engine mounting bolts:	47–66 ft. lbs.	64–89 Nm
Wheel nut:	87 ft. lbs.	118 Nm
MX3 G5M-R and 626/MX6 transaxle;		
Drain plug:	29–43 ft. lbs.	39–59 Nm
Change rod bolt:	10–14 ft. lbs.	14–19 Nm
Change arm bolt:	9–10 ft. lbs.	12–14 Nm
Primary and secondary shaft locknuts:	94–145 ft. lbs.	128–196 Nm
5th gear shift rod end bolts:	10 ft. lbs.	14 Nm
Transaxle to engine mounting bolts:	47–66 ft. lbs.	64–89 Nm
Wheel nut:	87 ft. lbs.	118 Nm
Manual Transmission:		
Miata;		
Extension housing oil passage bolt:	69–95 inch lbs.	8–11 Nm
Shifter select lock spindle bolt:	69–95 inch lbs.	8–11 Nm
Extension housing-to-change control case:	69–95 inch lbs.	8–11 Nm
Bearing cover to bearing housing bolts	69–95 inch lbs.	8–11 Nm
Mainshaft and countershaft locknuts:	94–145 ft. lbs.	128–196 Nm
Intermediate cap plugs:	14–19 ft. lbs.	19–26 Nm
Extension housing-to-transmission case bolts:	13–20 ft. lbs.	18–26 Nm
Transmission-to-engine bolts:	47–66 ft. lbs.	64–89 Nm
Shift lever shaft assembly-to-transmission case:	95 inch lbs.	11 Nm
Automatic Transaxle;		
Control valve body cover:	74–95 inch lbs.	8–11 Nm
Pulse generator:	69–95 inch lbs.	8–11 Nm
ATF thermoswitch:	22–29 inch lbs.	29–39 Nm
Oil cooler:	69–95 inch lbs.	8–11 Nm
Transaxle to engine bolts:	66–86 ft. lbs.	89–117 Nm

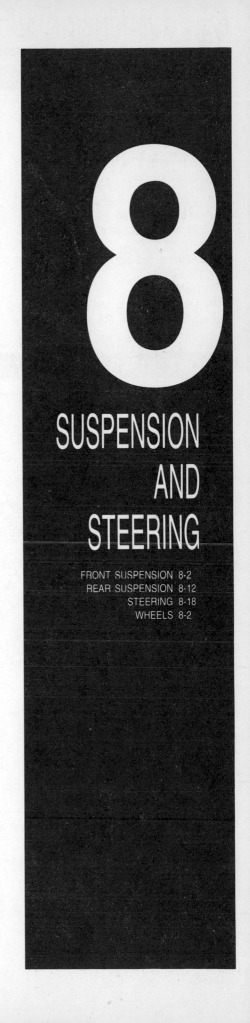

8

SUSPENSION AND STEERING

WHEELS

Wheels

REMOVAL & INSTALLATION

1. If using a lug wrench, loosen the lug nuts before raising the vehicle.
2. Raise the vehicle and support safely.
3. Remove the lug nuts and wheel from the vehicle.

To install:

4. Install the wheel and hand tighten the lug nuts until they are snug.

5. Lower the vehicle and torque the lug nuts EVENLY to 65-87 ft. lbs (88-118 Nm) in a criss-cross pattern.

INSPECTION

Before putting on wheels, check for any cracks on wheels or enlarged mounting holes, remove any corrosion on the mounting surfaces with a wire brush. Installation of wheels without a good metal-to-metal contact at the mounting surface can cause wheel nuts to loosen. Recheck the wheel nuts after 1,000 miles of driving.

Wheel Lug Studs

REPLACEMENT

Wheel lug studs can be replaced only after the hub assembly is removed. Refer to Steering Knuckle, Hub and Bearing removal & installation procedure later in this Section, to do this. After the hub and bearing assembly the wheel lug stud must pe pressed out and a new one pressed in place.

FRONT SUSPENSION

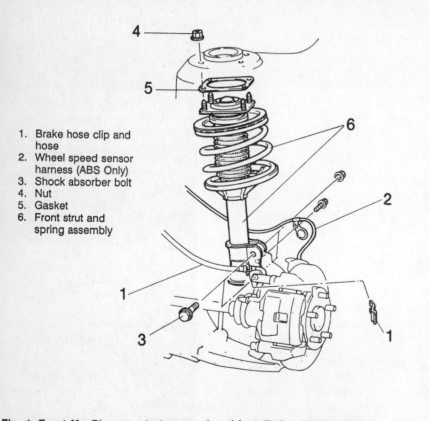

1. Brake hose clip and hose
2. Wheel speed sensor harness (ABS Only)
3. Shock absorber bolt
4. Nut
5. Gasket
6. Front strut and spring assembly

Fig. 1 Front MacPherson strut removal and installation-1993 626/MX-6

MacPherson Struts

REMOVAL & INSTALLATION

▶ **See Figure 1**

Except Miata

1. Raise and safely support the vehicle. Remove the wheel and tire assembly.
2. Support the lower control arm with a jack.
3. Remove the bolt or clip attaching the brake hose and/or ABS sensor harness to the strut.
4. On 323 and MX-6/626 with automatic adjusting suspension, disconnect the electrical connector and remove the actuator from the top of the strut.
5. On MX-6/626, if removing the left side strut, remove the ignition coil bracket.
6. Pain alignment marks on the strut mounting block and strut tower, so the strut can be reinstalled in the same position.
7. Remove the upper strut mounting block nuts and the strut-to-knuckle bolts and remove the strut assembly.

To install:

8. Install the strut into the strut tower, aligning the paint marks made during removal. Install the mounting nuts and tighten to 27 ft. lbs. (36 Nm) on 323/Protege or 46 ft. lbs. (63 Nm) on MX-3 and MX-6/626.
9. Install the strut-to-knuckle bolts and tighten to 86 ft. lbs. (117 Nm).

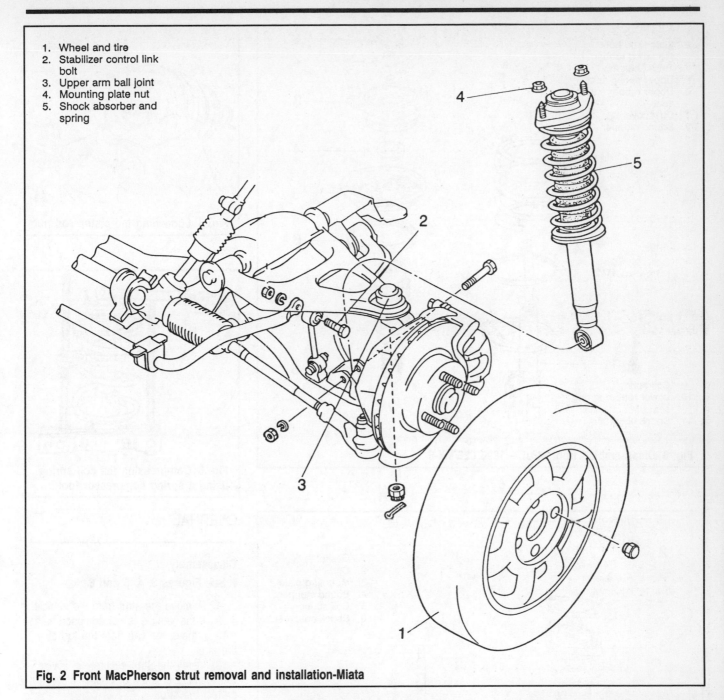

1. Wheel and tire
2. Stabilizer control link bolt
3. Upper arm ball joint
4. Mounting plate nut
5. Shock absorber and spring

Fig. 2 Front MacPherson strut removal and installation-Miata

10. If equipped with automatic adjusting suspension, install the actautor and connect the electrical connector.

11. Install the clip or bolt attaching the brake hose and/or ABS sensor harness.

12. Install the wheel and tire assembly and lower the vehicle. Check the front end alignment.

Miata

▶ See Figure 2

1. Raise and safely support the vehicle. Remove the wheel and tire assembly.

2. Remove the engine undercover. Remove the band for the wheel speed sensor harness.

3. Remove the bolt and disconnect the stabilizer bar from the link.

4. Pain alignment marks on the upper strut mounting block and the strut tower, so the strut can be reinstalled in the same position.

5. Remove the nuts from the strut mounting block. Remove the lower strut mounting bolt and nut.

6. Loosen the lower control arm bolts and pull down on the hub/knuckle assembly. Remove the strut up through the upper control arm.

To install:

7. Position the strut sund install the lower bolt and nut. Tighten to 69 ft. lbs. (93 Nm).

8. Install the strut in the strut tower, making sure the paint marks made during removal are aligned, and install the upper mounting block nuts. Tighten to 27 ft. lbs. (36 Nm).

9. Connect the stabilizer bar to the link and tighten the bolt to 40 ft. lbs. (54 Nm).

10. Tighten the lower control arm bolts and nuts to 83 ft. lbs. (113 Nm).

11. Install the engine undercover and the band for the wheel speed sensor harness. Install the wheel and tire assembly and lower the vehicle.

12. Check the front wheel alignment.

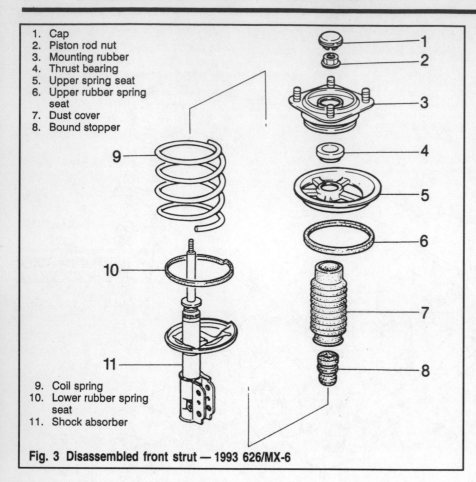

1. Cap
2. Piston rod nut
3. Mounting rubber
4. Thrust bearing
5. Upper spring seat
6. Upper rubber spring seat
7. Dust cover
8. Bound stopper

9. Coil spring
10. Lower rubber spring seat
11. Shock absorber

Fig. 3 Disassembled front strut — 1993 626/MX-6

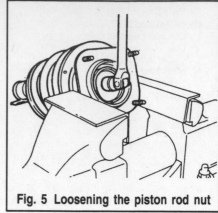

Fig. 5 Loosening the piston rod nut

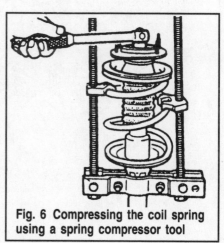

Fig. 6 Compressing the coil spring using a spring compressor tool

OVERHAUL

Disassembly

▶ See Figures 3, 4, 5 and 6

1. Remove the strut from the vehicle.

2. If the vehicle is not equipped with AAS, remove the cap from the top of the strut.

3. Install the strut securely in a vise with either aluminum or copper plates to protect the strut.

4. Loosen the piston rod upper nut several turns but do not remove it.

5. Install the lower end of the strut in the vise and install a coil spring compressor. Compress the coil spring and remove the upper nut.

✳✳CAUTION

Failure to fully compress the spring and hold it securely can be extremely dangerous.

6. Slowly release the coil spring tension.

7. Remove the suspension support, dust seal, spring seat, spring insulators, coil spring and bumper.

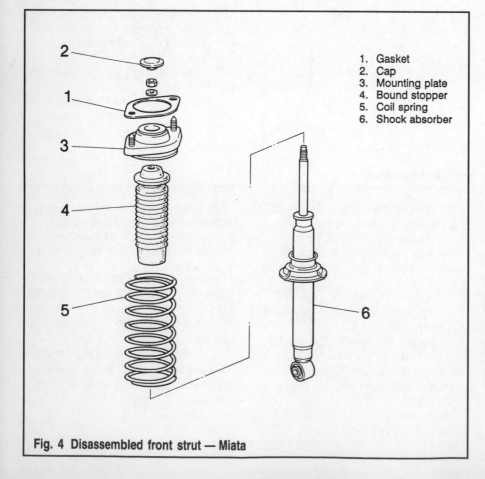

1. Gasket
2. Cap
3. Mounting plate
4. Bound stopper
5. Coil spring
6. Shock absorber

Fig. 4 Disassembled front strut — Miata

8. While pushing on the piston rod, make sure that the pull stroke is even and that there is no unusual noise or resistance.

9. Push the piston rod in and then release it. Make sure that the return rate is constant.

10. If the shock absorber does not operate as described, replace it.

Assembly

1. Install the strut assembly into a vise.

2. Install the bound stopper and dust boot onto the piston rod.

3. Install the coil spring and compress the coil spring with the spring compressor.

4. Install the rubber seat, the spring upper seat, the bearing and the mounting block. Make sure that the spring upper seat notched portion is facing inward and tighten the piston rod upper nut.

5. Remove the spring compressor from the strut. Secure the upper mounting block in the vise. Tighten the nut to 47-59 ft. lbs. (64-80 Nm).

6. Make sure that the spring is well seated in the upper seats.

7. Install the strut to the vehicle.

Upper Ball Joints

INSPECTION

1. Disconnect the upper ball joint from the spindle.

2. Shake and rotate the ball stud several times.

3. Install the stud nut and measure the force required to rotate the stud in the socket, using an inch pound torque wrench.

4. Specifications for rotation torque are as follows:
   Miata: 3.5-15.6 inch lbs. (0.4-1.8 Nm)

5. If the torque is not within specification, replace the upper control arm.

REMOVAL & INSTALLATION

The upper ball joint is an integral part of the upper control arm and cannot be replaced separately. If the upper ball joint is defective, the entire upper control arm must be replaced.

Lower Ball Joints

INSPECTION

1. Disconnect the lower ball joint from the knuckle or spindle.

2. Shake and rotate the ball joint stud several times.

3. Attach a suitable pull scale to the ball joint stud and measure the preload.

4. While the ball stud is rotating, the pull scale reading should be as follows:
   323, Protege, MX-3 and 1989-92 MX-6/626: 4.4-7.7 lbs.
   Miata: 0.9-4.0 lbs.
   1993 MX-6/626: 2.2-11.0 lbs.

5. If the pull scale reading is not as specified, replace the ball joint or lower control arm, as required.

REMOVAL & INSTALLATION

Except 323/Protege, MX-3 and Miata

The lower ball joint is an integral part of the lower control and cannot be replaced separately. If the lower ball joint is defective, the entire lower control arm must be replaced.

323/Protege and MX-3
▶ See Figure 7

1. Raise and safely support the vehicle. Remove the wheel and tire assembly.

2. Remove the ball joint stud pinch bolt and nut from the steering knuckle. Pry the lower control arm down from the knuckle, and separate the ball joint from the knuckle.

3. Remove the bolt and nut and remove the ball joint from the lower control arm.

4. Installation is the reverse of the removal procedure. Tighten the ball joint-to-lower control arm bolt and nut to 86 ft. lbs. (117 Nm). Tighten the ball joint pinch bolt and nut to 43 ft. lbs. (59 Nm). Check the front wheel alignment.

Miata
▶ See Figure 8

1. Raise and safely support the vehicle. Remove the wheel and tire assembly.

2. Remove the cotter pin and loosen the nut on the lower ball joint. With the nut protecting the ball joint stud, press the stud from the knuckle using press tool 49 0727 575 or equivalent. Remove the nut from the ball stud.

3. Remove the ball joint-to-lower control arm bolts and nut and remove the lower ball joint.

4. Installation is the reverse of the removal procedure. Tighten the ball joint-to-lower control arm bolts to 69 ft. lbs. (93 Nm). Tighten the ball joint stud nut to 57 ft. lbs. (77 Nm) and install a new cotter pin.

Upper Control Arms

REMOVAL & INSTALLATION

Miata
▶ See Figure 9

1. Raise and safely support the vehicle. Remove the wheel and tire assembly.

2. Remove the undercover and remove the band for the wheel speed sensor harness. Support the lower control arm with a jack.

3. Remove the cotter pin and loosen the upper ball joint nut. Press the ball joint stud from the knuckle using press tool 49 0118 850C or equivalent. Remove the nut.

4. Remove the lower strut mounting bolt.

5. Remove the upper control arm bolt and nut and remove the upper control arm.

   To install:

6. Install the upper control arm and loosely tighten the bolt and nut.

7. Loosely install the lower strut mounting bolt.

8. Connect the ball joint to the spindle and tighten to 45 ft. lbs. (61 Nm). Install a new cotter pin.

9. Install the band for the wheel speed sensor and install the undercover.

10. Install the wheel and tire assembly and lower the vehicle. When the vehicle is on the ground, tighten the upper control arm bolt and nut to 101 ft. lbs. (137 Nm) and the lower strut mounting bolt to 69 ft. lbs. (93 Nm).

11. Check the front wheel alignment.

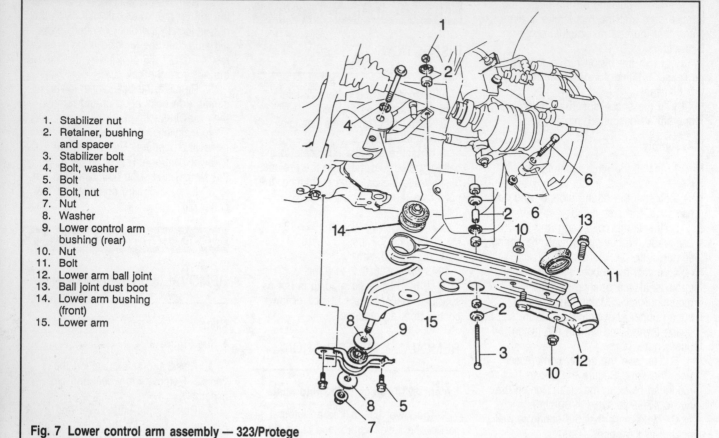

1. Stabilizer nut
2. Retainer, bushing and spacer
3. Stabilizer bolt
4. Bolt, washer
5. Bolt
6. Bolt, nut
7. Nut
8. Washer
9. Lower control arm bushing (rear)
10. Nut
11. Bolt
12. Lower arm ball joint
13. Ball joint dust boot
14. Lower arm bushing (front)
15. Lower arm

Fig. 7 Lower control arm assembly — 323/Protege

Stabilizer Bar

REMOVAL & INSTALLATION

All except MX-3 and 1993 626/MX-6
▶ **See Figures 10, 11 and 12**

1. Raise and support the vehicle safely. Remove the front wheels.
2. Remove the 2 stabilizer nuts and remove the upper bushing.
3. Remove the stabilizer bolt, bushing and retainer.
4. Remove the bushing, retainer and spacer.
5. Remove the stabilizer center bushings and bracket and remove the stabilizer bar from the vehicle. Examine the insulators (bushings) carefully for any sign of wear and replace them if necessary.

➡**Check the bushings inside the brackets for wear or deformation. A worn bushing can cause a distinct noise as the bar twists during cornering operation.**

To install:
6. Install stabilizer bar bushings in the correct position.

7. Temporarily install stabilizer bar brackets. Install the stabilizer bar center bracket bolts and tighten to 27-40 ft. lbs. (38-54 Nm).
8. Install the bushing retainers and spacers. Install the bolt retainer and bushing.
9. Install the upper link nuts. Tighten the link nuts so that there is 0.71-0.87 inches (18.1-22.1mm) of thread exposed.
10. Torque the top link nut to 12-17 ft. lbs. (16-23 Nm).
11. Install front wheels and lower the vehicle.
12. Check front wheel alignment.

MX-3 AND 1993 626/MX-6
▶ **See Figures 13 and 14**

1. Raise and safely support the vehicle. Remove the front tire/wheels.
2. Remove the engine undercover.
3. Install an engine support device, such as Mazda tool number 49 G017 5A0 or equivalent, to the vehicle.
4. Remove the tie rod end /steering knuckle assembly.
5. Remove the transverse member from under the engine.
6. Remove the engine mount member.

7. Disconnect the oxygen sensor connectors and remove the front exhaust pipe from the manifold.
8. Remove the stabilizer nuts and insulator pad.
9. Disconnect the steering lines and plug. Remove the steering gear and linkage assembly.
10. Remove the lower arm and front crossmember assembly bolts and remove the assembly from the vehicle.
11. Remove the remaining stabilizer bar bolts and remove the stabilizer bar.

To install:
12. Install the stabilizer bar to the vehicle and install the mounting bolts. If the mounting bushings were removed, make sure that they are replaced to the original positions and that the bushings are aligned with the marks on the bar. Tighten the stabilizer bar bolts to 32-43 ft. lbs. (43-59 Nm).
13. Install the lower arm and front crossmember assembly to the vehicle. Tighten the mounting bolts to 69-93 ft. lbs. (93-127 Nm).
14. Install the steering gear and linkage. Tighten the mounting nuts to 27-38 ft. lbs. (37-52 Nm) and connect the lines to the steering gear and linkage.

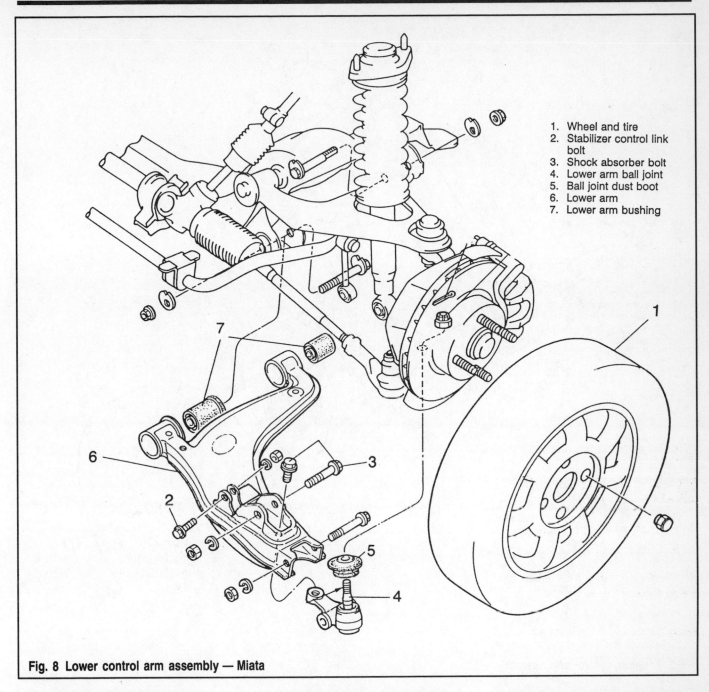

1. Wheel and tire
2. Stabilizer control link bolt
3. Shock absorber bolt
4. Lower arm ball joint
5. Ball joint dust boot
6. Lower arm
7. Lower arm bushing

Fig. 8 Lower control arm assembly — Miata

15. Install the insulator plate and install the stabilizer nuts. Tighten the stabilizer nuts to 32-45 ft. lbs. (43-61 Nm).

16. Replace the exhaust pipe gaskets and tighten the nuts to 27-38 ft. lbs. (37-52 Nm).

17. Install the engine mount member. Tighten the mounting bolts to 47-66 ft. lbs. (64-89 Nm) and the nuts to 27-38 ft. lbs. (37-52 Nm).

18. Install the transverse member and tighten the bolts to 69-93 ft. lbs. (93-127 Nm).

19. Connect the tie rod end to the stering knuckle. Replace the cotter pin.

20. Remove the engine support device and install the under engine cover.

21. Install the wheels and lower the vehicle.

Lower Control Arms

REMOVAL & INSTALLATION

▶ See Figure 15

Except Miata

1. Raise and safely support the vehicle. Remove the wheel and tire assembly.

2. Disconnect the stabilizer bar link from the lower control arm.

3. Remove the lower ball joint pinch bolt from the steering knuckle.

4. Remove the lower control arm bolts and nuts and remove the lower control arm.

To install:

5. Install the lower control arm and loosely tighten the mounting nuts and bolts.

6. Connect the lower ball joint to the steering knuckle. Install the pinch bolt and tighten to 40 ft. lbs. (54 Nm).

7. On 323, Protege and 1989-92 MX-6/626, assemble the stabilizer bar link. Tighten the top nut until ³⁄₄in. of threads are exposed.

8. On MX-3 and 1993 MX-6/626, connect the stabilizer link to the lower

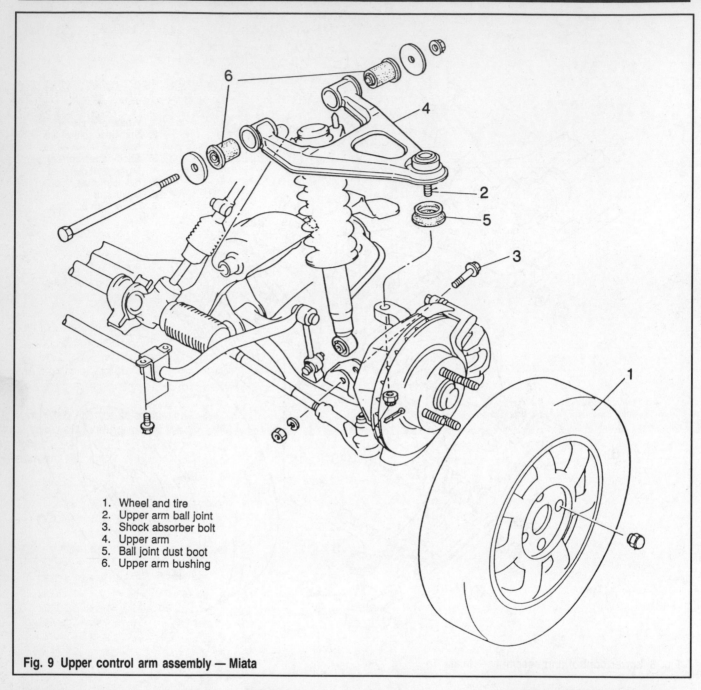

1. Wheel and tire
2. Upper arm ball joint
3. Shock absorber bolt
4. Upper arm
5. Ball joint dust boot
6. Upper arm bushing

Fig. 9 Upper control arm assembly — Miata

control arm and tighten the nut to 39 ft. lbs. (53 Nm).

9. Install the wheel and tire assembly and lower the vehicle. With the vehicle at normal ride height, tighten the lower control arm mounting bolts.

10. On 323, Protege and MX-3, tighten the front bushing through bolt and the rear bushing strap bolts to 93 ft. lbs. (127 Nm).

11. On 1989-92 MX-6/626, tighten the bushing through bolts to 78 ft. lbs. (106 Nm).

12. On 1993 MX-6/626, tighten the front bushing through bolt to 78 ft. lbs. (106 Nm) and the rear bushing strap bolts to 96 ft. lbs. (131 Nm).

13. Check the front wheel alignment.

Miata

1. Raise and safely support the vehicle. Remove the wheel and tire assembly. Remove the undercover.

2. Remove the stabilizer bar link bolt and the lower strut mounting bolt.

3. Remove the cotter pin and loosen the nut on the lower ball joint. With the nut protecting the ball joint stud, press the stud from the knuckle using press tool 49 0727 575 or equivalent. Remove the nut.

4. Paint alignment marks on the adjusting cams and the chassis for assembly reference. Remove the bolts, nuts and adjusting cams and lower control arm.

5. Install the lower control arm and loosely tighten the bolts and nuts.

6. Connect the lower ball joint to the knuckle and tighten the nut to 57 ft. lbs. (77 Nm). Install a new cotter pin.

7. Loosely install the lower strut mounting bolt and stabilizer link bolt.

8. Install the wheel and tire assembly and the undercover. Lower the vehicle.

9. With the vehicle at normal ride height, tighten the lower control arm bolts and nuts to 83 ft. lbs. (113 Nm), being sure to align the marks on the cam plates and chassis made during removal.

10. Tighten the lower strut mounting bolt to 69 ft. lbs. (93 Nm) and the stabilizer link bolt to 40 ft. lbs. (54 Nm).

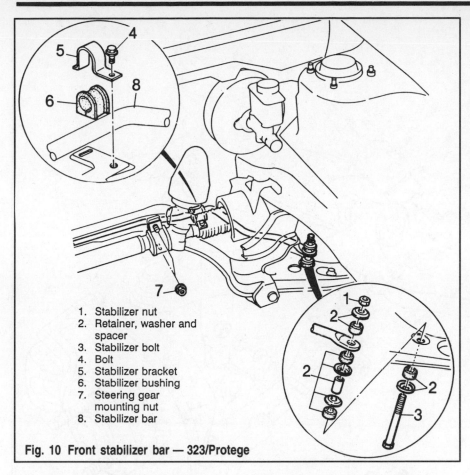

1. Stabilizer nut
2. Retainer, washer and spacer
3. Stabilizer bolt
4. Bolt
5. Stabilizer bracket
6. Stabilizer bushing
7. Steering gear mounting nut
8. Stabilizer bar

Fig. 10 Front stabilizer bar — 323/Protege

11. Check the front wheel alignment.

CONTROL ARM BUSHING REPLACEMENT

1. For the front bushing, cut away the projecting rubber portion of the bushing with a knife.

2. Install the control arm in a vise and install Mazda bushing removal tool 49 G034 2A0 or equivalent to the control arm. Remove the old bushing by tightening the nut on the tool.

3. To install a new bushing, apply soapy water to the new bushing and use Mazda tool 49 G034 2A0 or equivalent and pull the new bushing into place.

Front Wheel Bearings

ADJUSTMENT

Miata

The wheel bearings on these vehicles are not adjustable. To check if the bearing is serviceable, remove the wheel and tire assembly, brake caliper and disc brake rotor. Install a dial indicator with the indicator foot resting on the wheel hub. Try to move the hub in and out. If there is more than 0.002 in. (0.05mm) bearing play on Miata, check the wheel hub nut torque or replace the hub and bearing assembly, if necessary.

REMOVAL & INSTALLATION

Miata

1. Remove the dust cap. Unstake and loosen the locknut.

2. Raise and safely support the vehicle. Remove the wheel and tire assembly.

3. Remove the brake caliper and suspend it from the coil spring.

4. Remove the disc brake rotor.

5. Remove and discard the hub nut. Remove the wheel hub and bearing assembly.

6. On Miata, the wheel hub and bearing cannot be disassembled.

To install:

7. Install the hub over the spindle. Loosely install a new hub nut.

8. Install the brake rotor and the disc brake caliper. Install the wheel and tire assembly and lower the vehicle.

9. When the vehicle is on the ground, tighten the hub nut. Tighten to 159 ft. lbs. (216 Nm) on Miata.

10. Install a new dust cap.

Steering Knuckle, Hub And Bearing

REMOVAL & INSTALLATION

▶ See Figure 16

All Except Miata

1. Raise and safely support the vehicle. Remove the front wheel and tire assemblies.

2. Uncrimp the tab on the center locknut and remove the locknut. Discard the old locknut.

3. Remove the caliper assembly from the knuckle. Do not diconnect the brake lines. Support the caliper with a piece of wire. Do not allow the caliper to hang by the hose at any time. Remove the brake disc.

4. Remove the tie rod end cotter pin and remove the tie rod end nut. Using Mazda tool 49 0118 850C or equivalent, press the tie rod end out of the knuckle assembly.

5. Remove the stabilizer upper nuts and remove the stabilizer link bolt.

6. Remove the outer lower arm to ball joint mounting bolt and nut. Separate the lower arm from the knuckle assembly.

7. Remove the ABS speed sensor if so equipped.

8. Using a plastic mallet, tap the driveshaft free of the knuckle assembly. Remove the knuckle assembly.

9. Clamp the knuckle in a vise with protected jaws.

10. Remove the inner oil seal from the knuckle.

11. Use Mazda hub puller tools 49 G033 102, 49 G033 104 and 49 G033 105 or equivalent, and remove the front wheel hub from the knuckle assembly.

12. Remove the bearing inner race from the front wheel hub.

13. Remove the retaining ring from within the knuckle and using the hub puller tools, press the front wheel bearing from the knuckle.

14. Remove the brake dust shield.

15. Clean and inspect all parts but do not wash or clean the wheel bearing. The bearing must be replaced.

16. Using Mazda press tools 49 G033 107 and 49 H026 103 or equivalent,

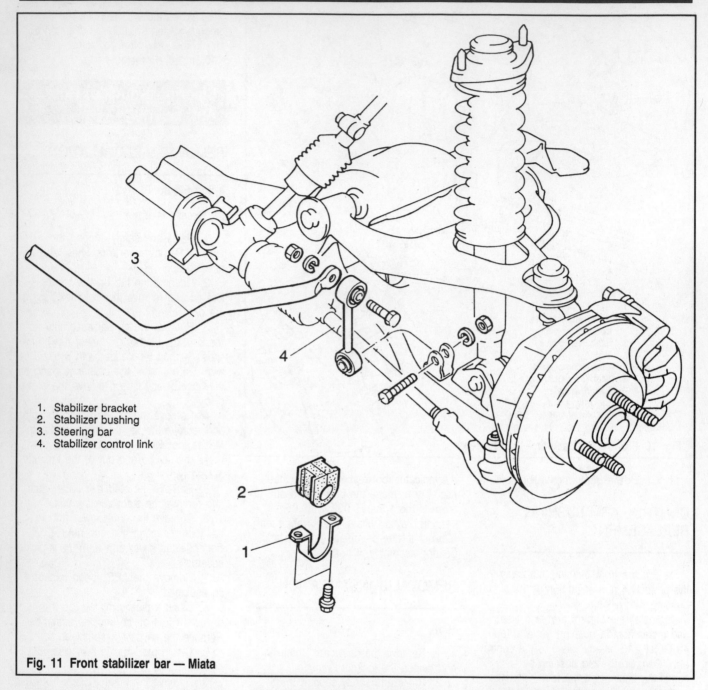

1. Stabilizer bracket
2. Stabilizer bushing
3. Steering bar
4. Stabilizer control link

Fig. 11 Front stabilizer bar — Miata

install a new dust shield cover assembly to the knuckle.

17. Using the press tools, press a new wheel bearing into the knuckle assembly.

18. Install the wheel bearing retaining ring, and install a new oil seal using installation tool 49 V001 795.

19. Install the front wheel hub by using the Mazda press tools or equivalent.

20. Install the bearing/hub and knuckle assembly in place. Loosely tighten the knuckle to shock absorber bolt.

21. Install the lower arm ball joint to the knuckle and tighten the nut to 27-40 ft. lbs. (36-54 Nm).

22. Install the driveshaft to the knuckle assembly.

23. Install the stabilizer control link and tighten the nuts so that there is 0.71-0.87 inches (18.1-22.1mm) of thread exposed. Torque the top link nut to 12-17 ft. lbs. (16-23 Nm).

24. If equipped with ABS, install the wheel speed sensor and tighten the bolts to 12-17 ft. lbs. (16-23Nm).

25. Connect the tie rod ends to the knuckle and tighten the nuts to 31-42 ft. lbs. (42-57 Nm). Replace the cotter pins.

26. Install a new wheel hub lock nut and tighten the locknut to 174-235 ft. lbs. (235-319 Nm).

27. Check the end play of the wheel bearing by installing a dial indicator

against the wheel hub and trie to move the brake disc back and forth. There should be no more than 0.0079 inch (0.2mm) of free play present.

28. Stake the locknut into place by bending it into the groove.

29. Install the brake caliper(s) and tighten the bolts to 58-72 ft. lbs. (78-98 Nm).

30. Install the front wheels and lower the vehicle.

31. With the vehicle lowered check all of the bolts and re-torque as is necessary.

32. Inspect the front end alignment and adjust as is necessary.

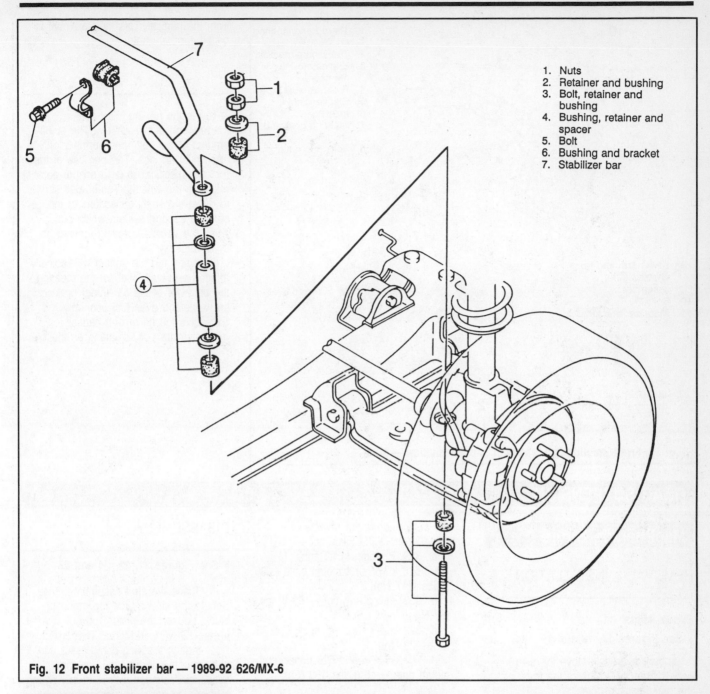

1. Nuts
2. Retainer and bushing
3. Bolt, retainer and bushing
4. Bushing, retainer and spacer
5. Bolt
6. Bushing and bracket
7. Stabilizer bar

Fig. 12 Front stabilizer bar — 1989-92 626/MX-6

Front End Alignment

Alignment of the front wheels is essential if your car is to go, stop and turn as designed. Alignment can be altered by collision, overloading, poor repair or bent components.

If you are diagnosing bad handling and/or poor road manners, the first place to check is the tires. Although the tires may wear as a result of an alignment problem, worn or poorly inflated tires can make you search for alignment problems which don't exist.

Once you have eliminated all other causes (always check and repair front end parts BEFORE wheel alignment),

unload everything from the trunk except the spare tire, set the tire pressures to the correct level and take the car to a reputable alignment facility. Since the alignment settings are measured in very small increments, it is almost impossible for the home mechanic to accurately determine the settings. The explanations that follow will help you understand the three dimensions of alignment: caster, camber and toe.

CASTER

Caster is the tilting of the steering axis either forward or backward from the

vertical, when viewed from the side of the vehicle. A backward tilt is said to be positive and a forward tilt is said to be negative.

CAMBER

Camber is the tilting of the wheels from the vertical (leaning in or out) when viewed from the front of the vehicle. When the wheels tilt outward at the top, the camber is said to be positive. When the wheels tilt inward at the top the camber is said to be negative. The amount of tilt is measured in degrees

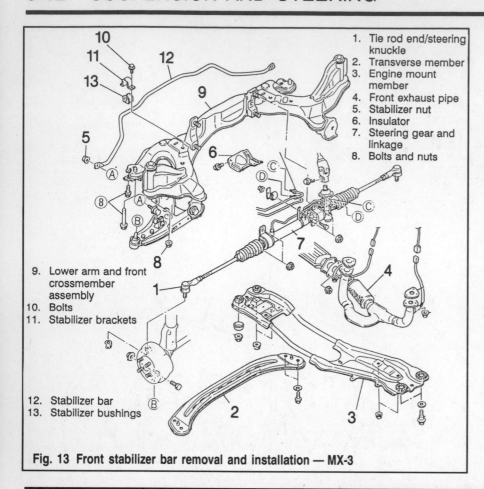

1. Tie rod end/steering knuckle
2. Transverse member
3. Engine mount member
4. Front exhaust pipe
5. Stabilizer nut
6. Insulator
7. Steering gear and linkage
8. Bolts and nuts
9. Lower arm and front crossmember assembly
10. Bolts
11. Stabilizer brackets
12. Stabilizer bar
13. Stabilizer bushings

Fig. 13 Front stabilizer bar removal and installation — MX-3

from the vertical. This measurement is called camber angle.

TOE

Toe is the turning in or out (parallelism) of the wheels. The actual amount of toe setting is normally only a fraction of an inch. The purpose of toe-in (or out) specification is to ensure parallel rolling of the wheels. Toe-in also serves to offset the small deflections of the steering support system which occur when the vehicle is rolling forward or under braking.

Changing the toe setting will radically affect the overall "feel" of the steering, the behavior of the car under braking, tire wear and even fuel economy. Excessive toe (in or out) causes excessive drag or scrubbing on the tires.

REAR SUSPENSION

MacPherson Struts

REMOVAL & INSTALLATION

Except Miata
▶ **See Figures 17, 18 and 19**

1. As required, remove the side trim panels from the inside of the trunk or the rear seat and trim.

2. If equipped with Adjustable Shock Absorber (ASA) system, disconnect the wiring and remove the cap. Loosen and remove the top mounting nuts from the strut mounting block assembly.

3. Raise and safely support the vehicle and remove the rear wheels. The suspension will drop when the weight lifts off the wheels.

4. On 1989 323 with 2WD, remove the long bolt connecting the trailing arm to the bottom of the strut.

5. Unclip the brake line or wiring retainers as required and unbolt the bottom strut mount. Remove the strut.

6. Installation is the reverse of removal. Torque the following:
   a. 323, Protege, MX-3 and MX-6/626 lower strut mount bolts — 86 ft. lbs (117 Nm).
   b. 323 trailing arm bolt — 50 ft. lbs. (68 Nm).
   c. 323 upper strut mount nuts — 22 ft. lbs.(29 Nm).
   d. MX-3, MX-6 and 626 upper strut mount nuts — 46 ft. lbs. (63 Nm).

Miata
▶ **See Figure 20**

1. Raise and safely support the vehicle and remove the rear wheels.

2. On the left side, remove the fuel filler pipe protector panel.

3. Remove the bolt from the lower stabilzer bar connecting link.

4. Remove the upper mount nuts and lower mount bolt and lift the spring and shock absorber out as an assembly.

5. Installation is the reverse of removal. Torque the upper mount nuts to 27 ft. lbs. (36 Nm), the lower mount bolt to 69 ft. lbs. (93 Nm) and the stabilizer link bolt to 40 ft. lbs. (54 Nm).

DISASSEMBLY

▶ **See Figures 21, 22, 24 and 25**

1. Place the strut assembly in vise. Secure the strut by the top mounting block. Loosen the piston rod nut several turns. DO NOT REMOVE THE NUT.

2. Attach a spring compressor and compress the spring until the upper suspension support is free of any spring tension. Do not over-compress the spring.

3. Hold the upper support and then remove the nut on the end of the shock piston rod.

4. Remove the support, coil spring, insulator and bumper.

INSPECTION

Check the shock absorber by moving the piston shaft through its full range of travel. It should move smoothly and evenly throughout its entire travel without any trace of binding or notching. Use a small straightedge to check the piston

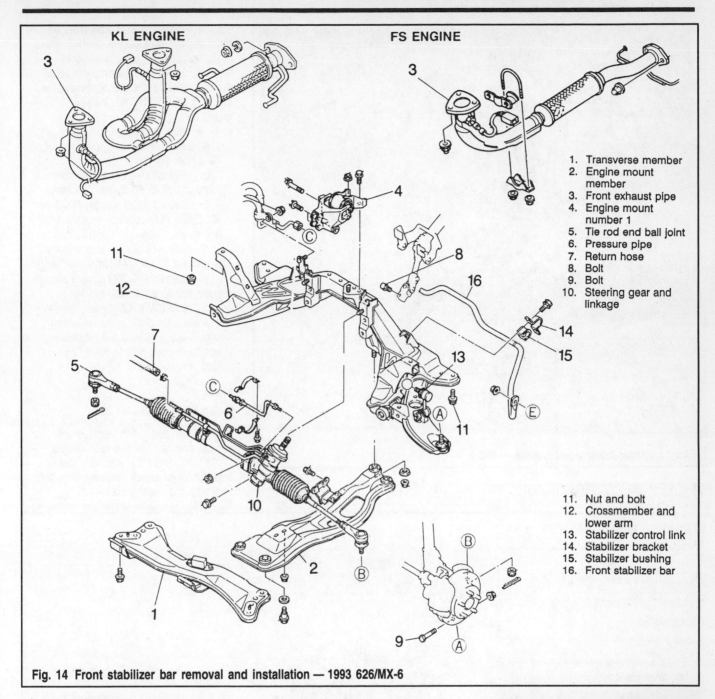

KL ENGINE

FS ENGINE

1. Transverse member
2. Engine mount member
3. Front exhaust pipe
4. Engine mount number 1
5. Tie rod end ball joint
6. Pressure pipe
7. Return hose
8. Bolt
9. Bolt
10. Steering gear and linkage

11. Nut and bolt
12. Crossmember and lower arm
13. Stabilizer control link
14. Stabilizer bracket
15. Stabilizer bushing
16. Front stabilizer bar

Fig. 14 Front stabilizer bar removal and installation — 1993 626/MX-6

shaft for any bending or deformation. If a shock absorber is replaced, the old one should be drilled at the center to vent the internal gas. Wear safety goggles and drill a small hole (2-3mm) into the center of the shock absorber. The gas within the strut is colorless, odorless and non-toxic, but should be vented to make the unit safe for disposal.

ASSEMBLY

1. Install the spring to the strut lower assembly. Make sure the spring end aligns with the step in the lower seat.

2. Install the spring compressor to the spring and comptress the spring.

3. Install the rubber stopper, the stopper seat and the seal to the strut rod.

4. Install the rubber seat and the mounting block. Align the rubber seat so that the tab faces inward. Install the mounting block nut.

5. Secure the strut mounting block in a vise and tighten the mounting block nut to the specified torque.

6. Install the cap to the top of the strut.

7. Install the strut as outlined under MacPherson Strut Removal & Installation, outlined earlier in this Section.

Rear Control Arms

REMOVAL & INSTALLATION

323/Protege, MX-3 and 1989-92 MX6/626

▶ See Figures 25, 26 and 27

1. Raise and safely support the vehicle and remove the wheels.

2. Before disconnecting the stabilizer bar link, on all except MX-3, measure the length of the threads protruding above the locknut. Remove the nuts and through bolt to disconnect the stabilizer bar.

Fig. 15 Rear lower control arms — MX-3

3. Remove the nuts and bolts as required and remove the control arms.

4. Installation is the reverse of removal. Make sure to properly adjust the stabilizer bar before tightening the locknuts and check rear wheel alignment.

5. Torque the following:

a. Inner control arm through bolt to 70 ft. lbs. (95 Nm).

b. 1989 323 outer control arm through bolt to 55 ft. lbs. (75 Nm).

c. 1990-93 323/Protege, MX-3 and MX-6/626 outer control arm through bolt to 86 ft. lbs. (117 Nm).

d. 1989 323 trailing arm-to-body bolt to 54 ft. lbs. (74 Nm).

e. Except 1989 323 trailing arm-to-body bolt to 69 ft. lbs. (93 Nm).

f. 1989 2WD 323 trailing arm-to-knuckle bolt to 50 ft. lbs. (68 Nm).

g. Except 1989 2WD 323 trailing arm-to-knuckle bolt to 86 ft. lbs. (117 Nm).

Miata

▶ **See Figures 28 and 29**

1. Raise and safely support the vehicle and remove the rear wheels.

2. Disconnect the stabilizer bar link and the lower shock absorber mounting bolt from the lower arm.

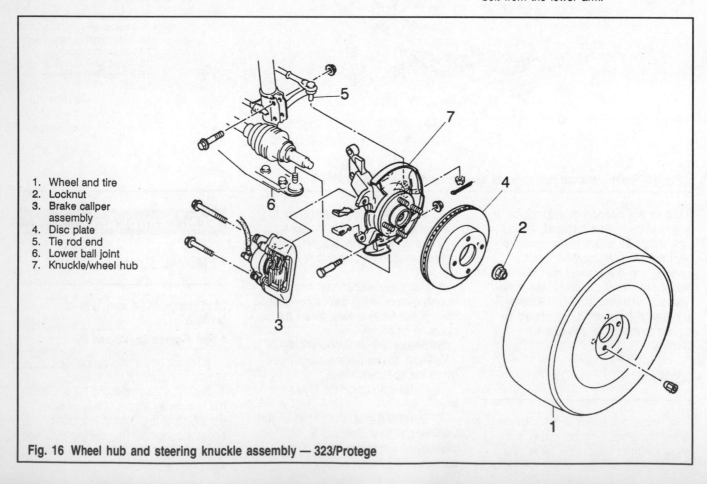

1. Wheel and tire
2. Locknut
3. Brake caliper assembly
4. Disc plate
5. Tie rod end
6. Lower ball joint
7. Knuckle/wheel hub

Fig. 16 Wheel hub and steering knuckle assembly — 323/Protege

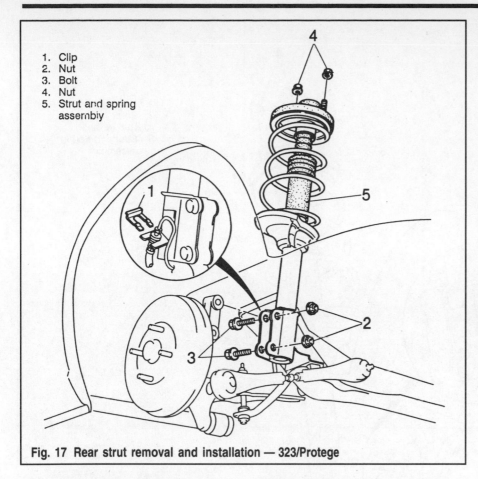

1. Clip
2. Nut
3. Bolt
4. Nut
5. Strut and spring assembly

Fig. 17 Rear strut removal and installation — 323/Protege

3. Remove the nuts and eccentric bolts and the outer through bolt and remove the lower control arm. The bushings can be replaced separately.

4. To remove the upper control arm, either re-install the lower control arm or remove the brake caliper, halfshaft and hub carrier. Do not allow the carrier to be supported only by the halfshaft.

5. Installation is the reverse of removal. Torque the upper arm through bolts ot 49 ft. lbs. (67 Nm). Torque the lower arm outer through bolt to 55 ft. lbs. (75 Nm). After aligning the rear wheels, torque the eccentric bolts to 70 ft. lbs. (95 Nm).

1993 MX-6/626
▶ **See Figure 30**

1. Raise and safely support the vehicle. Remove the wheel and tire assemblies.

2. Remove the access cap from the underside of the rear crossmember.

3. Remove the bolts and nuts and remove the lateral links and trailing link. If removing the rear lateral link, paint and alignment mark on the cam plate and crossmember for assembly reference.

4. Installation is the reverse of removal procedure. Tighten the inner and outer lateral link bolts/nuts to 86 ft. lbs. (116 Nm). Tighten the trailing link-to-body bolt to 68 ft. lbs. (93 Nm) and the trailing link-to-knuckle bolt to 86 ft. lbs. (116 Nm).

5. Do not final tighten the bolts until the vehicle is on the ground and at normal ride height.

Rear Stabilizer Bar

REMOVAL & INSTALLATION

323/Protege

1. Raise and safely support the rear of the vehicle.

2. Remove the rear wheels from the vehicle.

3. Remove the upper stabilizer nut, bushing, retainer and spacer.

4. Remove the stabilizer bolt and the remaining bushings, retainers and spacers.

5. Remove the stabilzer bracket bolts and remove the stabilizer bar.

6. Installation is the reverse of the removal procedure. Align the stabilizer bushing with the marks painted on the bar.

7. Tighten the stabilizer bracket bolts to 32-43 ft. lbs. (43-59 Nm). Tighten the top stabilizer nut so that there is 0.64-0.72 inch (16.2-18.2mm) of thread exposed at the end of the bolt.

Miata

1. Raise and safely support the rear of the vehicle.

2. Remove the rear wheels from the vehicle.

3. Remove the stabilizer bracket and the stabilizer bushing, inspect the bushing for deterioration or wear and replace if necessary.

4. Remove the stabilizer to control link bolt and remove the stabilizer bar.

5. Installation is the reverse of the removal procedure. Tighten the control link to stabilizer bar bolts to 27-40 ft. lbs. (36-54Nm).

6. Align the bushing on the stabilizer bar with the painted marking. Tighten the stabilizer bracket bolts to 14-21 ft. lbs. (20-28Nm).

MX-3

1. Raise and safely support the rear of the vehicle.

2. Remove the rear wheels from the vehicle.

3. Remove the stabilizer bar to link mounting nut and protectors.

4. Remove the stabilizer bracket and remove the stabilizer bar. Remove the stabilizer bushings and inspect the bushing for deterioration or wear. Replace if necessary.

5. Installation is the reverse of the removal procedure. Tighten the stabilizer bar to link nuts to 32-45 ft. lbs. (43-61 Nm).

1989-92 626/MX-6

1. Raise and safely support the rear of the vehicle.

2. Remove the rear wheels from the vehicle.

3. Remove the upper stabilizer nut, bushing, retainer and spacer.

4. Remove the stabilizer bolt and the remaining bushings, retainers and spacers.

5. Remove the stabilzer bracket bolts and remove the stabilizer bar.

6. Installation is the reverse of the removal procedure. Align the stabilizer bushing with the marks painted on the bar.

7. Tighten the stabilizer bracket bolts to 27-40 ft. lbs. (36-54 Nm). Tighten the top stabilizer nut so that there is

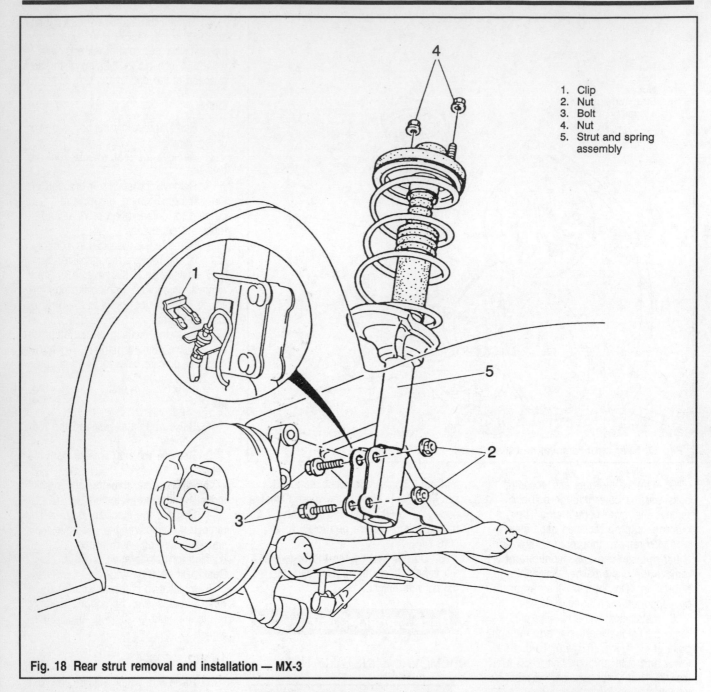

1. Clip
2. Nut
3. Bolt
4. Nut
5. Strut and spring assembly

Fig. 18 Rear strut removal and installation — MX-3

approximately 0.41 inch (10.4mm) of thread exposed at the end of the bolt.

1993 626/MX-6

1. Raise and safely support the rear of the vehicle.
2. Remove the rear wheels from the vehicle.
3. Remove the stabilizer bar to link mounting nut and protectors.
4. Remove the stabilizer bracket and remove the stabilizer bar. Remove the stabilizer bushings and inspect the bushing for deterioration or wear. Replace if necessary.
5. Installation is the reverse of the removal procedure. Tighten the stabilizer

bar to link nuts to 27-39 ft. lbs. (37-53 Nm).

Rear Axle Shaft, Bearing and Seal

REMOVAL & INSTALLATION

4WD 323/Protege

1. Loosen the axle nut, then raise and safely support the vehicle.
2. Remove the wheel and tire assembly and the axle nut.
3. To remove just the halfshaft, matchmark the inner drive flanges so the

shaft can be installed the same position. Remove the trailing link bolt and the lower control arm bolt. Remove the drive flange nuts and pull the rear strut out far enough to disengage the flanges. Slide the shaft out of the hub spline. If stuck, use a plastic hammer to avoid damaging the axle threads.
4. Remove the brake caliper assembly and hang it from the body. Do not let it hang by the hose.
5. To remove the knuckle, remove the bolts from the bottom of the strut and pull the knuckle off strut.
6. Be careful not to distort the back plate. If damaged or removed, a new one must be pressed onto the knuckle.

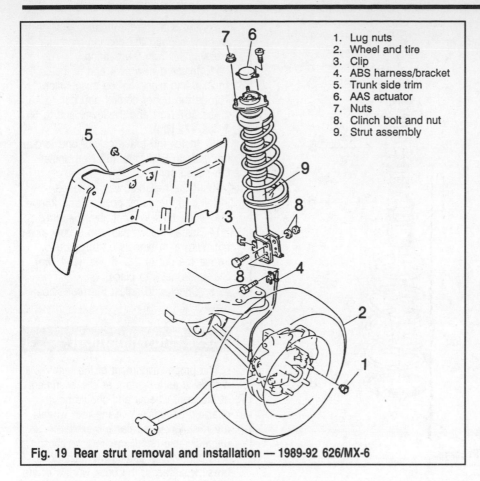

1. Lug nuts
2. Wheel and tire
3. Clip
4. ABS harness/bracket
5. Trunk side trim
6. AAS actuator
7. Nuts
8. Clinch bolt and nut
9. Strut assembly

Fig. 19 Rear strut removal and installation — 1989-92 626/MX-6

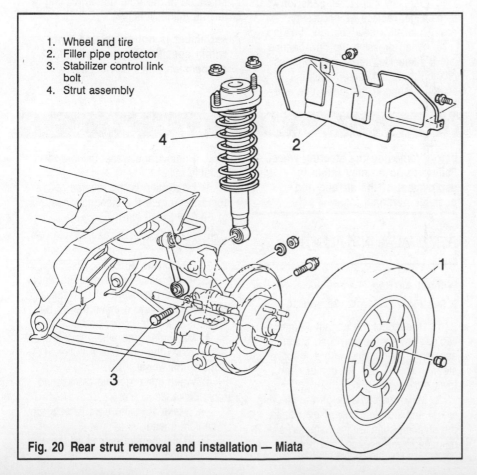

1. Wheel and tire
2. Filler pipe protector
3. Stabilizer control link bolt
4. Strut assembly

Fig. 20 Rear strut removal and installation — Miata

7. To remove the hub, remove the seal and properly support the assembly to press the hub out from the back. If the inner bearing race stays on the hub, use a chisel to move it far enough to grab it with a bearing puller.

8. Remove the snapring and press the bearing out of the knuckle.

To install:

9. Carefully inspect all parts for wear or damage, replace as necessary. Always install a new seal and bearing.

10. When pressing the new bearing into the knuckle, make sure to press only on the outer race. Install the snapring, support the inner race and press the hub into the bearing. Failure to properly support the bearing races for pressing will ruin the bearing.

11. Install a new seal and fit the knuckle into place on the strut. Install all the bolts before tightening any of them. Torque the knuckle-to-strut and the trailing link bolts to 93 ft. lbs. (127 Nm). Torque the lower control arm bolt to 86 ft. lbs. (117 Nm).

12. Install the brake caliper and torque the bolts to 44 ft. lbs. (60 Nm).

13. If the halfshaft was removed, install it in the same position and torque the flange nuts to 47 ft. lbs. (64 Nm).

14. Install the washer and a new axle nut. With all 4 wheels on the ground, torque the nut to 235 ft. lbs. (318 Nm). Stake the nut into place.

15. Check and adjust the rear wheel alignment.

Miata

1. Loosen the axle nut, then raise and safely support the vehicle.

2. Remove the wheel and tire assembly and the axle nut.

3. To remove just the halfshaft, matchmark the inner drive flanges so the shaft can be installed the same position. Remove the nuts, pull the halfshaft flange off the differential flange and slide the shaft out of the hub spline. If stuck, use a plastic hammer to avoid damaging the axle threads.

4. Remove the brake caliper assembly and hang it from the body. Do not let it hang by the hose. Remove the disc and the ABS speed sensor.

5. Remove the lower and upper control arm bolts and remove the knuckle and hub assembly from the vehicle.

6. Be careful not to distort the back plate. If damaged or removed, a new one must be pressed onto the knuckle.

7. To remove the hub, remove the seal and properly support the assembly

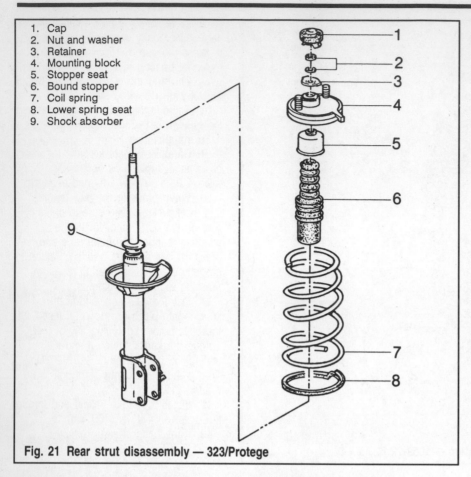

1. Cap
2. Nut and washer
3. Retainer
4. Mounting block
5. Stopper seat
6. Bound stopper
7. Coil spring
8. Lower spring seat
9. Shock absorber

Fig. 21 Rear strut disassembly — 323/Protege

to press the hub out from the back. If the inner bearing race stays on the hub, use a chisel to move it far enough to grab it with a bearing puller.

8. Remove the snapring and press the bearing out of the knuckle.

To install:

9. Carefully inspect all parts for wear or damage, replace as necessary. Always install a new seal and bearing.

10. When pressing the new bearing into the knuckle, make sure to press only on the outer race. Install the snapring, support the inner race and

press the hub into the bearing. Failure to properly support the bearing races for pressing will ruin the bearing.

11. Install a new seal and fit the knuckle into place on the suspension. Torque the upper control arm bolt to 49 ft. lbs. (67 Nm) and the lower bolt to 55 ft. lbs. (75 Nm).

12. Install the brake caliper and torque the bolts to 51 ft. lbs. (69 Nm). Install the speed sensor.

13. If the halfshaft was removed, install it in the same position and torque the flange nuts to 47 ft. lbs. (64 Nm).

14. Install the washer and a new axle nut. With all 4 wheels on the ground, torque the nut to 217 ft. lbs. (294 Nm). Stake the nut into place.

15. Check and adjust the rear wheel alignment.

Rear End Alignment

The proper alignment of the rear wheels is as important as the alignment of the front wheels and should be checked periodically. If the rear wheels are misaligned the car will exhibit unpredictable handling characteristics. This behavior is particularly hazardous on slick surfaces; the back wheels of the car may attempt to go in directions unrelated to the front during braking or turning maneuvers.

➡**Camber is not adjustable-if not within specifications replace the suspension parts as necessary.**

STEERING

Air Bag

DISARMING THE AIR BAG SYSTEM

On models with an airbag, wait at least 90 seconds from the time that the ignition switch is turned to the LOCK position and the battery is disconnected before performing any further work.

Steering Wheel

✳✳CAUTION

If equipped with an air bag, the vehicle battery and the system's own back-up battery must be disconnected

before removing the steering wheel. Failure to do so may result in deployment of the air bag and possible personal injury.

REMOVAL & INSTALLATION

Without Air Bag
▶ **See Figures 31, 32, 33 and 34**

1. Disconnect the negative battery cable. Remove the horn pad button assembly. If equipped with a 4 spoke steering wheel, pull the center cap toward the wheel top.

2. Make matchmarks on the steering wheel and steering shaft. Never strike the steering shaft with a hammer, as damage to the column may result.

3. Remove the wheel using a suitable puller.

4. Installation is the reverse of removal. Torque the steering wheel nut to 36 ft. lbs. (49 Nm).

With Air Bag

1. Disarm the air bag.

2. At the back of the steering wheel hub, remove the nuts that hold the air bag assembly and remove the air bag. Place it in a safe place, pad side up.

3. Matchmark the wheel to the shaft and remove the nut. Use a puller to remove the wheel.

4. When installing, the clockspring must be reset.

　a. Make sure the front wheels are straight-ahead.

　b. Turn the clockspring all the way to the right.

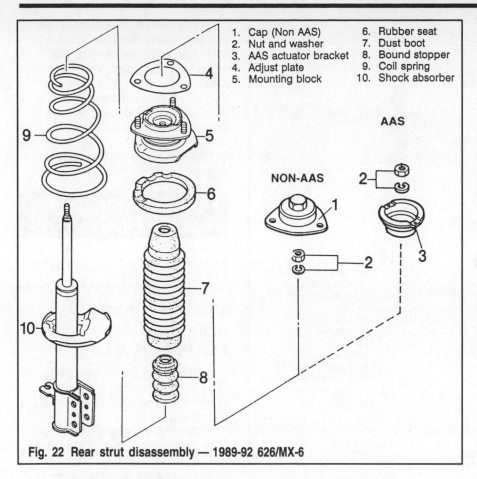

1. Cap (Non AAS)
2. Nut and washer
3. AAS actuator bracket
4. Adjust plate
5. Mounting block
6. Rubber seat
7. Dust boot
8. Bound stopper
9. Coil spring
10. Shock absorber

Fig. 22 Rear strut disassembly — 1989-92 626/MX-6

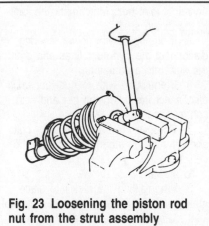

Fig. 23 Loosening the piston rod nut from the strut assembly

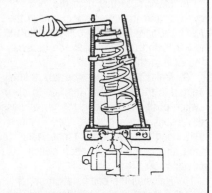

Fig. 24 Removing the piston rod nut from the strut

c. Turn the clockspring back about 2 ³/₄ turns and align the marks.

d. Connect the wiring and install the steering wheel.

5. Torque the steering wheel nut to 36 ft. lbs. (49 Nm). Install the air bag unit.

Combination Switch

REMOVAL & INSTALLATION

Without Airbag System

1. Disconnect the negative battery cable.

2. Remove the lower dash cover and the air duct.

3. Remove the upper and lower steering column covers.

4. Remove the steering wheel. Refer to the necessary service procedure.

5. Disconnect the wiring at the connector.

6. Unscrew the mounting screws and remove the switch.

7. When reinstalling, place the switch in correct position and tighten the bolts.

8. Connect the wiring harness and reinstall the steering wheel.

9. Reinstall the column cover(s).

10. Install the lower dash trim panel.

11. Connect the negative battery cable. Check system for proper operation.

With Airbag System

1. Disconnect the negative battery cable. Wait at least 90 seconds before working on the vehicle.

2. Remove (matchmark before removal) the steering wheel, as outlined in this Section.

3. Remove the instrument lower finish panel (as required), air duct and upper and lower column covers.

4. Disconnect the combination switch connector.

5. Disconnect the cable connectors, remove the spiral cable housing attaching screws and slide the cable assembly from the front of the combination switch.

6. Remove the screws that attach the combination switch to its mounting brackets and remove the combination switch from the vehicle.

To install:

7. Position the combination switch onto the mounting bracket and install the retaining screws.

8. Connect the electrical connector.

9. Install the upper/lower column covers, air duct and instrument lower finish panel.

10. Turn the spiral cable on the combination switch counterclockwise by hand until it becomes harder to turn. Then rotate the cable clockwise about 3 turns to align the alignment mark. The connector should be straight up.

11. Install the steering wheel (align matchmarks) onto the shaft and torque nut to 26 ft. lbs. (35 Nm).

12. Connect the air bag connector and install the steering pad.

13. Connect the battery cable, check operation and the steering wheel center point.

14. Connect the negative battery cable. Check all combination switch functions for proper operation. Check the steering wheel center point.

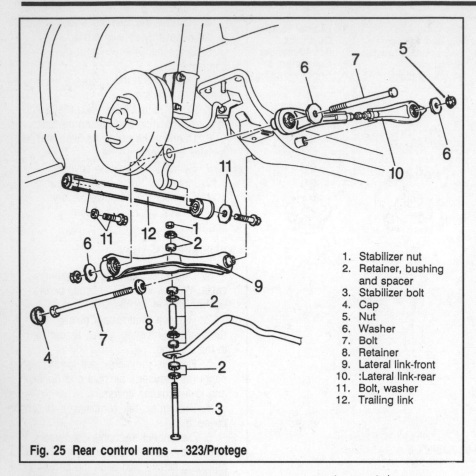

1. Stabilizer nut
2. Retainer, bushing and spacer
3. Stabilizer bolt
4. Cap
5. Nut
6. Washer
7. Bolt
8. Retainer
9. Lateral link-front
10. :Lateral link-rear
11. Bolt, washer
12. Trailing link

Fig. 25 Rear control arms — 323/Protege

Ignition Switch/Ignition Lock Cylinder

REMOVAL & INSTALLATION

1. Disconnect the negative battery cable.

2. Unscrew the retaining screws and remove the upper and lower steering column covers.

3. Remove the retaining screws and remove the steering column trim.

4. Turn the ignition key to the **ACC** position.

5. Push the lock cylinder stop in with a small, round object (cotter pin, punch, etc.) and pull out the ignition key and the lock cylinder.

➡You may find that removing the steering wheel and the combination switch makes the job easier.

6. Loosen the mounting screw and withdraw the ignition switch from the lock housing.

To install:

7. Position the ignition switch so that the recess and the bracket tab are properly aligned. Install the retaining screw.

8. Make sure that both the lock cylinder and the column lock are in the ACC position. Slide the cylinder into the lock housing until the stop tab engages the hole in the lock.

9. Make certain the stop tab is firmly seated in the slot. Turn the key to each switch position, checking for smoothness of motions and a positive feel. Remove and insert the key a few times, each time turning the key to each switch position.

10. Reinstall the combination switch and the steering wheel if they were removed.

11. Install the steering column trim and the upper and lower column covers.

12. Connect the negative battery cable.

Steering Column

REMOVAL & INSTALLATION

1. Disconnect the negative battery cable and remove the steering wheel.

2. Remove the upper and lower column covers and the combination switch.

3. Remove the dash board panels and air ducts as required.

4. Disconnect the universal joint where the column passes through the floor.

5. Disconnect the automatic transmission interlock cable from the ignition switch and unbolt the column from the vehicle.

6. Installation is the reverse of removal.

Front Wheel Steering Rack and Pinion

REMOVAL & INSTALLATION

323, Protege, Miata and MX-3

WITHOUT 4WD

▶ **See Figures 35, 36 and 37**

1. Disconnect the negative battery cable. Raise and safely support the vehicle and remove the wheel and tire assemblies.

2. Remove the engine undercover.

3. Remove the cotter pins and nuts and disconnect the tie rod ends.

4. Remove the steering column universal joint bolt. Matchmark the joint to the pinion shaft.

5. If equipped with power steering, disconnect the hydraulic lines and drain the fluid into a container.

6. If equipped with manual transaxle, disconnect the extension bar and shift control rod from the transaxle.

7. Remove the bracket nuts or bolts and remove the steering rack from the vehicle.

To install:

8. When fitting the rack into place, make sure the pinion shaft and universal joint matchmarks are correctly aligned. Fit the shaft into the joint and start the steering rack bracket nuts or bolts.

9. Tighten the bracket nuts or bolts to 34 ft. lbs. (46 Nm) on 1989 323, 38 ft. lbs. (52 Nm) on 1990-93 323/Protege and MX-3 or 43 ft. lbs. (59 Nm) on Miata. Install the universal joint bolt and torque it to 20 ft. lbs. (26 Nm).

10. Connect the tie rod ends and torque the nuts to 33 ft. lbs. (44 Nm) on 1989 323 and Miata or 42 ft. lbs. (57 Nm) on 1990-93 323/Protege and MX-3, then tighten as required to install a new cotter pin.

11. If equipped, connect the power steering hydraulic lines and install the undercover.

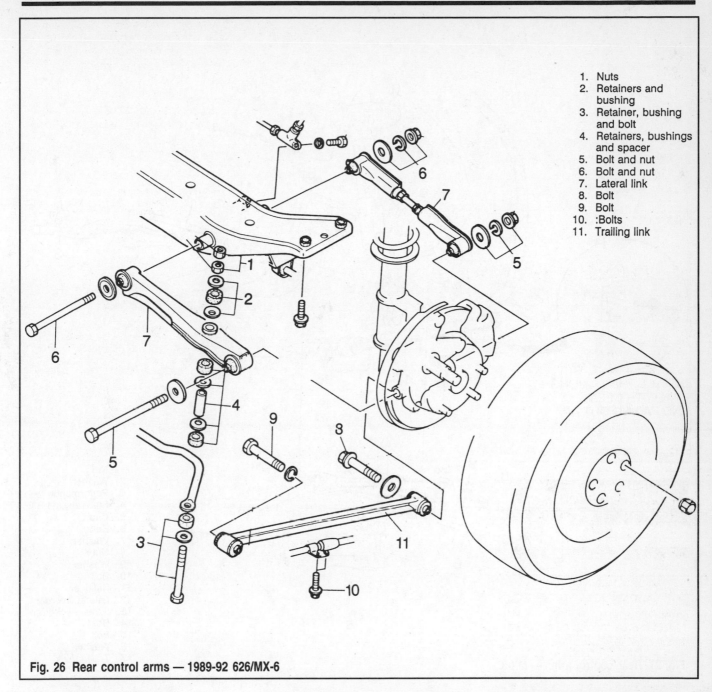

1. Nuts
2. Retainers and bushing
3. Retainer, bushing and bolt
4. Retainers, bushings and spacer
5. Bolt and nut
6. Bolt and nut
7. Lateral link
8. Bolt
9. Bolt
10. :Bolts
11. Trailing link

Fig. 26 Rear control arms — 1989-92 626/MX-6

12. Install the wheel and tire assemblies and lower the vehicle. If equipped with power steering, fill the system with the proper fluid and bleed the air from the system.

WITH 4WD

1. Remove the battery and battery tray. Raise and safely support the vehicle and remove the front wheels and front crossmember.

2. Disconnect the tie rod ends and remove the bolt from the steering column universal joint. Matchmark the universal joint to the pinion shaft.

3. Disconnect the hydraulic lines and drain the fluid into a container.

4. To remove the steering rack, the front-to-rear engine mount member must be removed:

   a. Use the proper lifting equipment and support the engine from above.

   b. Disconnect the front and rear engine mounts from the mount member and remove the mount member.

   c. Remove the rear mount from the engine.

5. Remove the exhaust pipe and catalytic converter.

6. Matchmark the flanges and remove the driveshaft.

7. Lower the engine gradually until the lower left rack mounting bolt can be reached. Do not lower too far or the halfshaft joints will be damaged.

8. Remove the mount bolts and move the rack to the left to remove the steering rack.

   To install:

9. When fitting the rack into place, make sure the pinion shaft and universal joint matchmarks are correctly aligned. Fit the shaft into the joint and start the steering rack bracket bolts. Torque the nuts and bolts to 38 ft. lbs. (52 Nm).

10. Use new gaskets and install the exhaust pipe. Torque the flange nuts to 34 ft. lbs. (46 Nm).

11. Install the driveshaft and torque the flange nuts to 22 ft. lbs. (30 Nm).

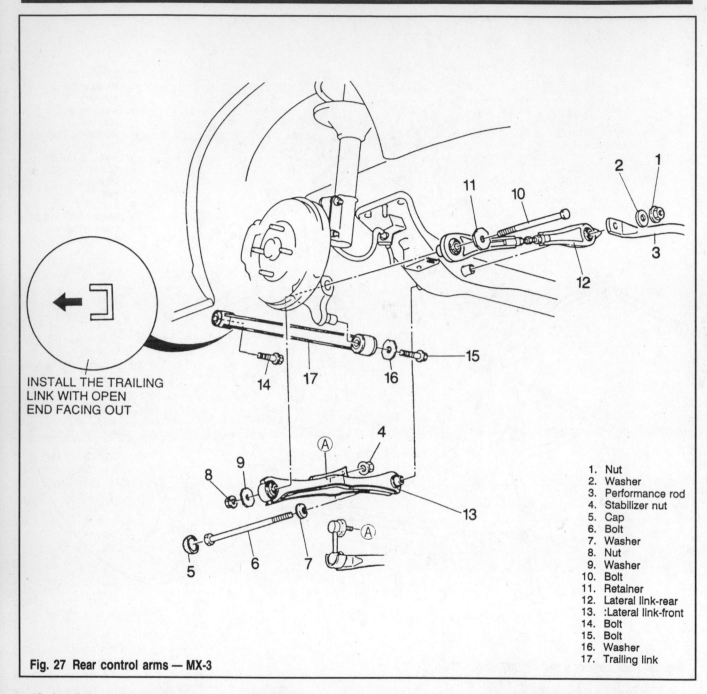

INSTALL THE TRAILING
LINK WITH OPEN
END FACING OUT

1. Nut
2. Washer
3. Performance rod
4. Stabilizer nut
5. Cap
6. Bolt
7. Washer
8. Nut
9. Washer
10. Bolt
11. Retainer
12. Lateral link-rear
13. :Lateral link-front
14. Bolt
15. Bolt
16. Washer
17. Trailing link

Fig. 27 Rear control arms — MX-3

12. Install the engine mount and mount member. Torque the mount member nuts to 66 ft. lbs. (89 Nm), the mount-to-engine nuts to 38 ft. lbs. (52 Nm).

13. Connect the fluid lines. Install the universal joint bolt and torque it to 20 ft. lbs. (27 Nm).

14. Connect the tie rod ends and torque the nuts to 42 ft. lbs. (57 Nm) and tighten as required to install a new cotter pin.

15. Install the front crossmember and torque the bolts to 86 ft. lbs. (117 Nm).

16. Fill the pump with fluid and bleed the air from the system.

MX6/626

2-WEEL STEERING
2-WHEEL STEERING

▶ **See Figure 38**

1. Disconnect the negative battery cable. Raise and safely support the vehicle.

2. Remove the wheel and tire assemblies. If equipped, remove the mud flaps on 1989-92 vehicles.

3. Remove the cotter pins and nuts and separate the tie rod ends from the knuckles.

4. If equipped with 2.5L engine, remove the transverse member and the front exhaust pipe. On 1993 vehicles, support the engine with engine support

tool 49 G017 502 or equivalent, and remove the rear transaxle mount.

5. Disconnect the power steering pressure and return lines. Disconnect the oil pressure switch conector, if equipped.

6. Mark the position of the steering shaft in the column universal joint. Remove the universal joint pinch bolt.

7. Remove the mounting bolts and remove the steering gear.

To install:

8. Position the steering gear, making sure the marks made on the universal joint and steering gear shaft align, and install the mounting nuts and bolts. Tighten to 40 ft. lbs. (54 Nm). On 1993 vehicles, the bolts and nuts must be torqued in sequence.

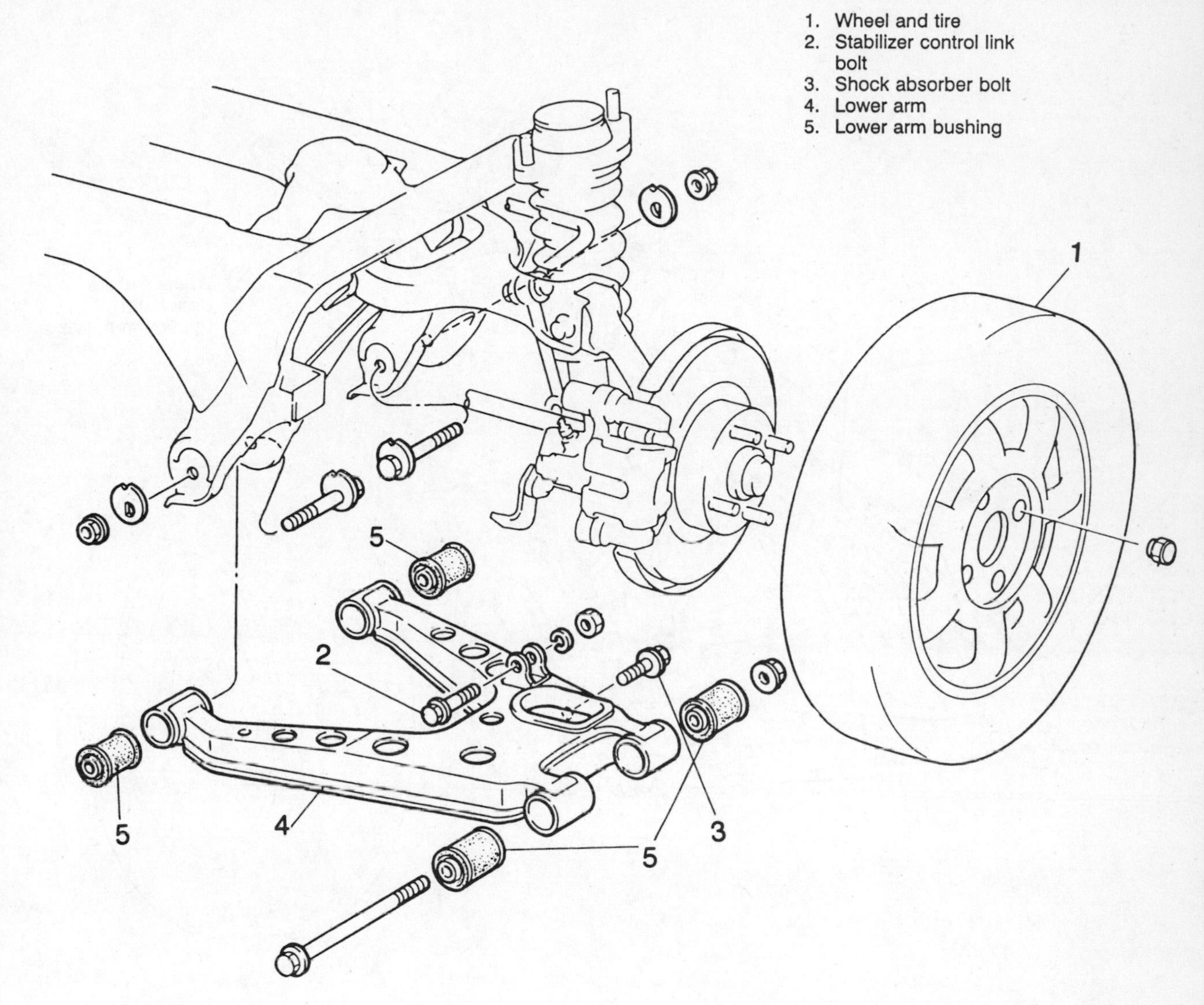

1. Wheel and tire
2. Stabilizer control link bolt
3. Shock absorber bolt
4. Lower arm
5. Lower arm bushing

Fig. 28 Lower control arm — Miata

9. Install the universal joint pinch bolt and tighten to 20 ft. lbs. (26 Nm).

10. Connect the power steering lines and the oil pressure switch, if equipped.

11. On 1993 vehicles, install the rear transaxle mount. Tighten the mounting bolts and nut to 69 ft. lbs. (93 Nm). Remove the engine support tool.

12. If equipped with 2.5L engine, install the front exhaust pipe, using new gaskets. Tighten the pipe-to-catalytic converter nuts to 66 ft. lbs. (89 Nm) and the pipe-to-exhaust manifold nuts to 38 ft. lbs. (89 Nm). Connect the oxygen sensors.

13. If equipped with 2.5L engine, install the transverse member and tighten the bolts to 97 ft. lbs. (131 Nm).

14. Connect the tie rod ends to the knuckles. On 1989-92 vehicles, tighten the nuts to 42 ft. lbs. (57 Nm). On 1993 vehicles, tighten the nuts to 33 ft. lbs. (44 Nm). Install new cotter pins.

15. Install the wheel and tire assemblies and lower the vehicle. Fill the power steering system with the proper fluid and bleed the air from the system.

16. Check the front wheel alignment.

4-WHEEL STEERING

1. Remove the battery and battery tray. Raise and safely support the vehicle and remove the front wheels and front crossmember.

2. Disconnect the tie rod ends and remove the bolt from the steering column universal joint. Matchmark the universal joint to the pinion shaft.

3. Disconnect the hydraulic lines and drain the fluid into a container.

4. Remove the exhaust pipe and catalytic converter.

5. Disconnect the front-to-rear steering angle transfer shaft.

6. Remove the left engine mount.

7. Remove the nuts and bolts from the sub-frames and allow the frame members to hang down.

8. Remove the stabilizer bar.

9. Remove the mounting bolts and remove the steering rack.

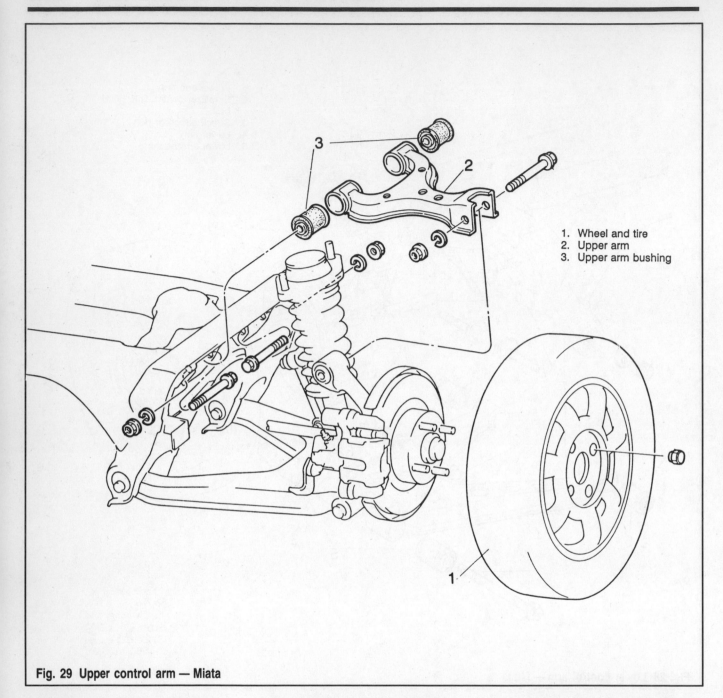

1. Wheel and tire
2. Upper arm
3. Upper arm bushing

Fig. 29 Upper control arm — Miata

To install:

10. When fitting the rack into place, make sure the pinion shaft and universal joint matchmarks are correctly aligned. Fit the shaft into the joint and start the steering rack bracket bolts. Torque the nuts and bolts to 38 ft. lbs. (52 Nm).

11. Install the stabilizer bar and adjust the links.

12. Attach the sub-frames and torque the bolts to 40 ft. lbs. (54 Nm).

13. Install the engine mount.

14. Connect the front-to-rear steering shaft.

15. Use new gaskets and install the exhaust pipe and catalytic converter.

16. Connect the hydraulic lines and install the front crossmember.

17. Connect the tie rod ends. Torque the nuts to 33 ft. lbs. (44 Nm) and tighten as required to install a new cotter pin.

18. With all parts installed, fill and bleed the system and adjust the rear steering angle transfer shaft.

Tie Rod Ends

REMOVAL & INSTALLATION

1. Raise and support the vehicle safely. Remove the wheel and tire assembly.

2. Remove the cotter pin and loosen the nut on the tie rod end ball stud. With the nut protecting the ball stud, press the stud from the knuckle using press tool 49 0118 850C or equivalent. Remove the nut and the tie rod end from the knuckle.

3. Paint a reference mark across the tie rod, jam nut and shaft.

4. Loosen the jam nut and unscrew the tie rod end from the shaft.

To install:

5. Thread the tie rod onto the shaft and align the marks made during removal. If installing a new tie rod end, try to assemble it in the same position as the old one.

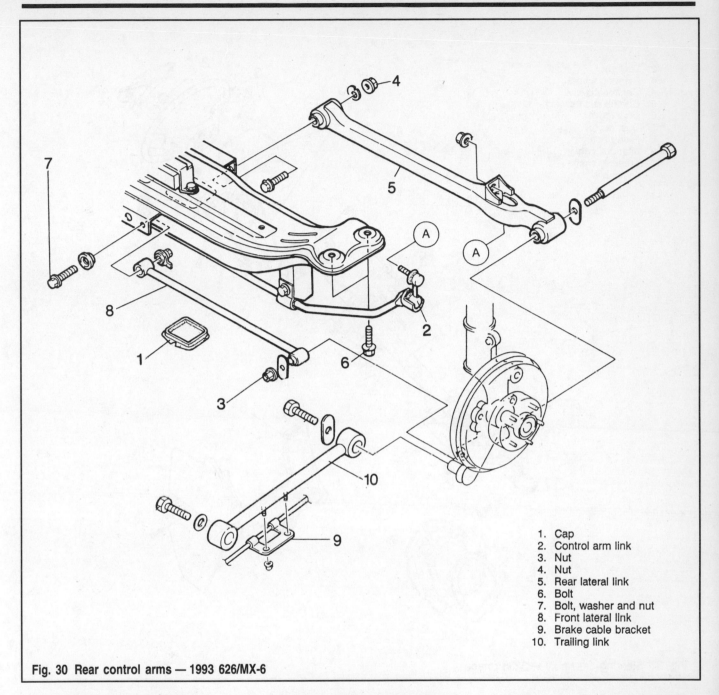

1. Cap
2. Control arm link
3. Nut
4. Nut
5. Rear lateral link
6. Bolt
7. Bolt, washer and nut
8. Front lateral link
9. Brake cable bracket
10. Trailing link

Fig. 30 Rear control arms — 1993 626/MX-6

6. Install the tie rod end into the knuckle. Install the nut and tighten to 32 ft. lbs. (44 Nm) on 1989 323, Miata, 1989-91 929, RX-7 and 1993 MX-6/626, 42 ft. lbs. (57 Nm) on 1990-93 323/Protege, MX-3 and 1989-92 MX-6/626 or 47 ft. lbs. (64 Nm) on 1992-93 929.

7. Install a new cotter pin. If the cotter pin cannot be installed because the ball stud hole and the nut castellation do not align, tighten the nut further until the cotter pin can be installed. Never loosen the nut to install the cotter pin.

8. Tighten the jam nut.

9. Install the wheel and tire asembly and lower the vehicle. Check the front wheel alignment.

Manual Steering Gear and Linkage

REMOVAL & INSTALLATION

323/Protege

1. Raise and safely support the vehicle. Disconnect the negative battery cable and remove the front wheels.

2. Remove the cotter pins from both steering tie rod ends and remove the nuts.

3. Use Mazda special tie rod press tool 49 0118 850C or equivalent and press the tie rod out of the knuckle arm.

4. Remove the set plate from the firewall.

5. Remove the fixing bolt from the steering shaft to steering gear pinion shaft and seperate the shaft from the steering gear.

6. Remove the steering gear mounting nuts and remove the steering gear to the right of the vehicle.

To install:

7. Install the steering gear to the vehicle and install the mounting nuts in

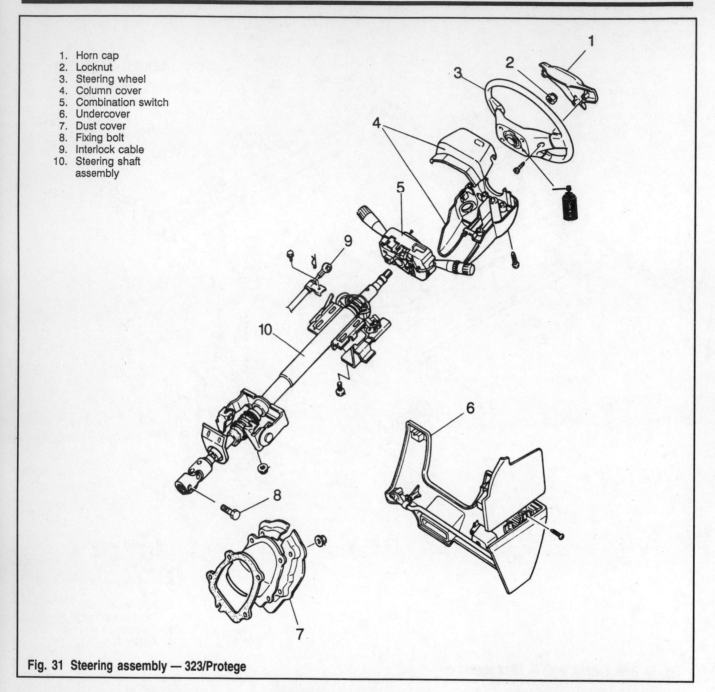

1. Horn cap
2. Locknut
3. Steering wheel
4. Column cover
5. Combination switch
6. Undercover
7. Dust cover
8. Fixing bolt
9. Interlock cable
10. Steering shaft assembly

Fig. 31 Steering assembly — 323/Protege

the order shown. Tighten the nuts to 28-38 ft. lbs. (37-52Nm).

8. Connect the steering shaft to the steering gear pinion shaft. Tighten the bolt/nut to 13-20 ft. lbs. (18-27Nm).

9. Install the set plate to the firewall.

10. Install the tie rod ends to the knuckle arm and tighten the nuts to 31-42 ft. lbs. (42-57Nm). Install the cotter pins.

11. Install the wheels to the vehicle, lower the vehicle and connect the negative battery cable. Check the front end alignment.

OVERHAUL

1. Remove the manual steering gear as described above.

2. Paint a mark on the matching mark of the tie rod end and threads for reassembly purposes.

3. Remove the tie rod ends and remove the tie rod boots.

4. Uncrimp the tie rod locking washer and remove the tie rod assembly.

5. Remove the locknut, the adjustment cover, the spring, the pressure pad plate and the pressure pad from the pinion connection point.

6. Remove the pinion protector by gently tapping on it with a plastic hammer.

7. Remove the oil seal, the snap ring cap and the snap ring from the pinion assembly.

8. Remove the pinion by grasping the serrated portion and pulling straight out.

9. Remove the rack portion by pulling it out in the direction shown.

10. Remove the mounting rubber from the housing.

To assemble:

11. Inspect the rubber boots for cracking, damage or deterioration and replace if necessary.

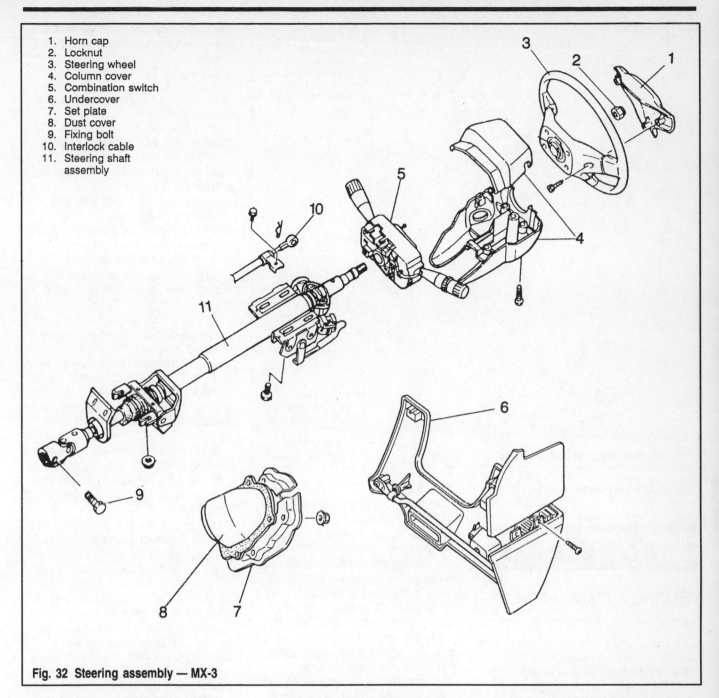

1. Horn cap
2. Locknut
3. Steering wheel
4. Column cover
5. Combination switch
6. Undercover
7. Set plate
8. Dust cover
9. Fixing bolt
10. Interlock cable
11. Steering shaft assembly

Fig. 32 Steering assembly — MX-3

12. Check for cracking, worn teeth or damage to the rack and pinion. Replace any component that appears damaged.

13. Check for looseness, abnormal noise, poor bearing operation such as binding or sticking inside the gear housing. Replace any component that is damaged.

14. Inspect the rack bushing inside the gear housing for excessive wear. Replace if necessary.

15. Inspect the pressure pad where it contacts the rack for excessive wear. Replace if necessary.

16. Check the tie rods and tie rod ends. Replace if necessary.

17. Fill and coat the pinion gear and gear housing with lithium based grease.

18. Install the mounting rubber to the housing, until it contacts the end.

19. Install the rack to the housing in the opposite direction of removal.

20. Install the pinion gear, the snap ring, the snap ring cap and the oil seal. Press the oil seal into place with Mazda tool 49 F032 308 or equivalent.

21. Install the pinion protector to the housing. Press the pinion protector into place with Mazda tool 49 F032 308 or equivalent.

22. Install the pressure pad and adjustment cover to the housing. Make sure that the pressure pad contacts the rack. Tighten the adjustment cover to 39-56 inch lbs. (4-6 Nm) and then loosen it 5°-35°. Tighten the locknut

securely against the adjustment cover. Tighten the locknut to 29-36 ft. lbs. (39-49 Nm).

23. Using a pull-scale, measure the pinion torque. From the neutral position (±90°), it should be 31.8-45.9 ounces (900-1300g).

24. Install new washers to the tie rods and screw the tie rods onto the rack. Tighten the tie rods to the specified torque.

25. Align the lock washer with the rack groove and crimp it into place.

26. Install the boots and secure with new wire.

27. Install the tie rod ends and align them with the marks made prior to disassembly.

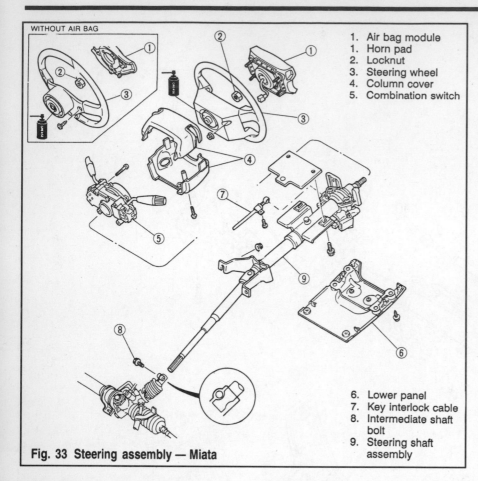

WITHOUT AIR BAG

1. Air bag module
1. Horn pad
2. Locknut
3. Steering wheel
4. Column cover
5. Combination switch

6. Lower panel
7. Key interlock cable
8. Intermediate shaft bolt
9. Steering shaft assembly

Fig. 33 Steering assembly — Miata

28. Install the steering gear to the vehicle.

Power Steering Gear and Linkage

REMOVAL & INSTALLATION

1. Raise and safely support the vehicle. Disconnect the negative battery cable and remove the front wheels.

2. Remove the cotter pins from both steering tie rod ends and remove the nuts.

3. Use Mazda special tie rod press tool 49 0118 850C or equivalent and press the tie rod out of the knuckle arm.

4. Disconnect the pressure line and return pipe from the steering gear. Remove the set plate from the firewall.

5. Remove the fixing bolt from the steering shaft to steering gear pinion shaft and seperate the shaft from the steering gear.

6. Disconnect the manual trans shifter linkage if necessary.

7. Remove the steering gear mounting nuts and remove the steering gear to the right of the vehicle.

To install:

8. Install the steering gear to the vehicle and install the mounting nuts/bolts. Tighten the nuts to 28-38 ft. lbs. (37-52Nm).

9. Connect the steering shaft to the steering gear pinion shaft. Tighten the bolt/nut to the specified torque.

10. Connect the manual trans shift linkage if disconnected. Install the set plate to the firewall.

11. Connect the pressure line and return hose to the steering gear.

12. Install the tie rod ends to the knuckle arm and tighten the nuts to 31-42 ft. lbs. (42-57Nm). Install the cotter pins.

13. Install the wheels to the vehicle, lower the vehicle and connect the negative battery cable. Bleed the power steering system and check the front end alignment.

OVERHAUL

➡**Overhauling a Mazda power steering gear assembly is very complex and involved. Don not attempt the overhaul procedure without the proper tools. There are many special tools required and all of**

these are available from either a Mazda dealer or a reputable tool dealer.

▶ **See Figure 39**

1. Remove the power steering gear as described above.

2. Disconnect the oil pipe from the steering gear. Plug all open ports.

3. Paint a mark on the matching mark of the tie rod end and threads for reassembly purposes.

4. Remove the tie rod ends and remove the tie rod boots.

5. Uncrimp the tie rod locking washer and remove the tie rod assembly.

6. Remove the locknut, the adjustment cover, the spring and the support yoke from the pinion housing cover.

7. Use a 0.06 inch drill and drill out the crimped portion of the housing cover threaded portion.

8. Using Mazda special wrench 49 B032 306 or equivalent, remove the pinion shaft plug. Remove the O-ring, oil seal and the bearing, using Mazda tools 49 B032 317 and 49 B032 316 or equivalent.

9. Remove the pinion by grasping the serrated portion and pulling straight out.

10. Remove the outer box assembly from the rack, using tool 49 B032 307 or equivalent.

11. Remove the O-ring, U-gasket and steering rack from the housing.

To assemble:

12. Check for cracking, worn teeth or damage to the rack and pinion. Replace any component that appears damaged.

13. Check for looseness, abnormal noise, poor bearing operation such as binding or sticking inside the gear housing. Replace any component that is damaged.

14. Inspect the rack bushing inside the gear housing for excessive wear. Replace if necessary.

15. Inspect the support yoke/pressure pad where it contacts the rack for excessive wear. Replace if necessary.

16. Check the tie rods and tie rod ends. Replace if necessary.

17. Fill and coat the pinion gear and gear housing with lithium based grease.

18. Install the mounting rubber to the housing, until it contacts the end.

19. Install a new oil seal and new seal ring to the rack's piston using Mazda special press tool 49 B032 319 or equivalent.

20. Install the outer box assembly to the rack using special tool 49 B032 313

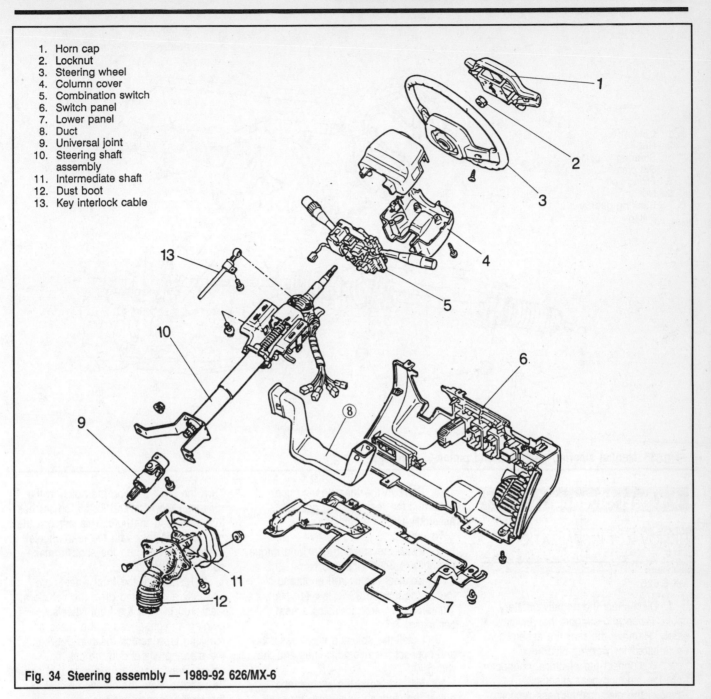

1. Horn cap
2. Locknut
3. Steering wheel
4. Column cover
5. Combination switch
6. Switch panel
7. Lower panel
8. Duct
9. Universal joint
10. Steering shaft assembly
11. Intermediate shaft
12. Dust boot
13. Key interlock cable

Fig. 34 Steering assembly — 1989-92 626/MX-6

and tighten the unit with special wrench 49 B032 307.

21. Using Mazda oil seal installation tools 49 G032 797, 49 B032 309 and 49 B032 310 install the oil seal to the pinion port.

22. Install a new seal ring to the pinion shaft using Mazda installation tool 49 B032 312 or equivalent. Install the pinion shaft to the gear housing, using Mazda special tool 49 B032 311 or equivalent.

23. Use Mazda special tool 49 B032 315 or equivalent and press a new oil seal into place in the pinion port. Use Mazda special wrench 49 B032 306 or

equivalent and tighten the plug in the housing.

24. Apply sealant to the adjusting cover and install the cover to the gear housing. Tighten the cover to 95 inch lbs. (11Nm) and move the rack back and forth at least 3 times.

25. Loosen the adjusting cover and then immediately retorque the cover to 39-48 inch lbs. (4.4-5.4Nm). Loosen the adjusting cover 0-40 degrees.

26. Using a pull-scale, measure the pinion torque. From the neutral (straight ahead) position (+/- 90°), it should be 2.2-3.1 lbs. (1.0-1.4 kg).

27. Install new washers to the tie rods and screw the tie rods onto the rack. Tighten the tie rods to the specified torque.

28. Align the lock washer with the rack groove and crimp it into place.

29. Install the boots and secure with new wire.

30. Install the tie rod ends and align them with the marks made prior to disassembly.

31. Install the steering gear to the vehicle.

1. Cotter pin
2. Nut
3. Steering knuckle
4. Set plate
5. Fixing bolt
6. Nut
7. Steering gear and linkage

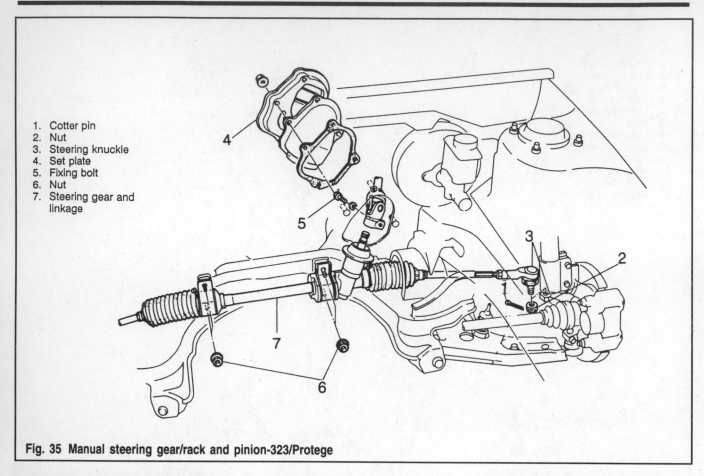

Fig. 35 Manual steering gear/rack and pinion-323/Protege

4 Wheel Steering Gear

REMOVAL & INSTALLATION

MX-6/626

1. Disconnect the negative battery cable. Raise and support the vehicle safely. Remove the rear tire assemblies, as required for working clearance.

2. Disconnect the electrical connector from the steering gear assembly. Remove the electrical harness retaining bolts.

3. Remove the steering angle transfer shaft cover. Disconnect the universal joint and bolts from the steering angle transfer shaft assembly. Remove the lower cover and the brake line joint block.

4. Disconnect and cap all required fluid lines. Disconnect the lower spring link retaining bolts. Remove the solenoid valve, which is mounted on the steering gear assembly.

5. Using the proper tool, disconnect the tie rod ends from the knuckles. Remove the mounting bolts from the left and right sub-frames. Allow the components to hang freely.

6. Remove the rear steering gear bolts and the rear steering gear assembly from the vehicle.

To install:

7. Install the steering gear and torque the bolts to 34 ft. lbs. (46 Nm).

8. Connect the tie rod ends and torque the nuts to 33 ft. lbs. (44 Nm). Tighten as required to install a new cotter pin.

9. Install the solenoid valve assembly and connect the hydraulic lines and the wiring.

10. Fill and bleed the system and adjust the steering angle transfer shaft.

Adjustment

➡**The shaft connecting the front and rear steering racks must be adjusted any time it is disconnected or the wheels are aligned. Failure to properly adjust the steering angle transfer shaft will make the vehicle hard to control.**

1. Raise and safely support the vehicle. Remove the steering angle transfer shaft covers.

2. Disconnect the shaft joint at the rear by removing the bolt from the universal joint.

3. At the rear rack, remove the plug at the center and look into the hole.

Turn the shaft to align the notch in the rack with the hole and install the set bolt that is next to the hole. This will lock the rear steering rack with the rear wheels centered. Try to turn the shaft to make sure it really is locked.

4. Make sure the front wheels are correctly aligned and drive the vehicle at least 100 ft. With the front wheels pointed straight-ahead, put a piece of masking tape across the gap between the steering wheel and the column cover. Draw a line on the tape that can be used to align the steering wheel in the straight-ahead position.

5. Raise and support the vehicle again and put the steering wheel in the straight-ahead position.

6. Install the steering angle transfer shaft joint bolt and torque it to 20 ft. lbs. (27 Nm). Remove the lock bolt from the rear rack and install the plug.

Power Steering Pump

REMOVAL & INSTALLATION

1. Disconnect the negative battery cable. Disconnect and plug the hoses at

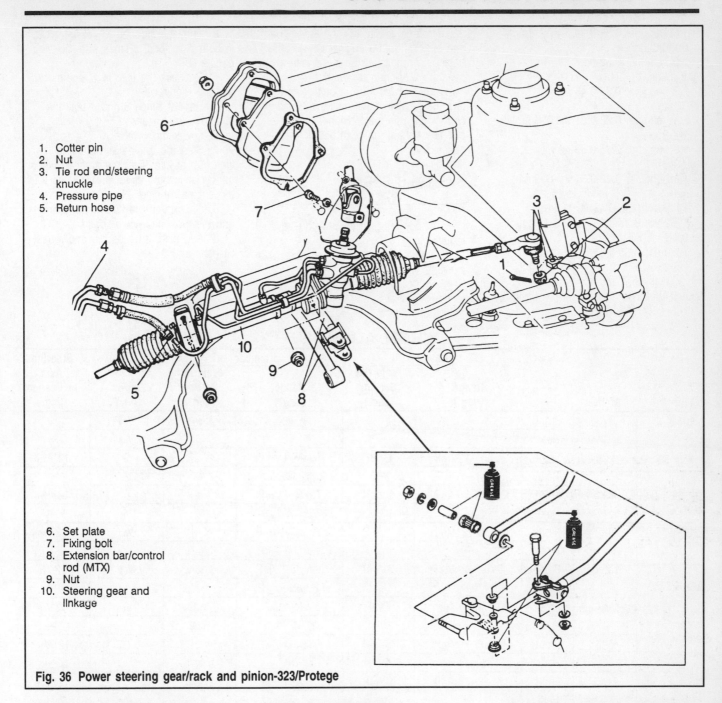

1. Cotter pin
2. Nut
3. Tie rod end/steering knuckle
4. Pressure pipe
5. Return hose

6. Set plate
7. Fixing bolt
8. Extension bar/control rod (MTX)
9. Nut
10. Steering gear and linkage

Fig. 36 Power steering gear/rack and pinion-323/Protege

the pump. If equipped, disconnect the pressure switch connector.

2. Remove the pump drive belt.

3. On all except 323, Protege, MX-3 and Miata, it is necessary to remove the pump pulley before removing the pump. Hold the pulley with tool 49 W023 585A or equivalent, or if possible, insert a small prybar through 1 of the holes in the pulley to hold it. Remove the pulley nut and pulley.

4. Support the pump, remove the mounting bolts and lift out the pump.

5. Installation is the reverse of removal. Tighten the pulley nut to 43 ft. lbs. (58 Nm). Adjust the belt tension and fill and bleed the system.

BELT ADJUSTMENT

1. Apply approximately 22 lbs. pressure to the drive belt at a point midway between the pulleys. A new belt should deflect as follows:
323
1.6L engine: 0.31-0.35 in. (8-9mm)
Protege
1.6L engine: 0.31-0.35 in. (8-9mm)
Miata
1.6L engine: 0.31-0.35 in. (8-9mm)
MX-6/626
2.0L engine: 0.30-0.35 in. (7.5-9.0mm)
2.2L engine: 0.31-0.39 in. (8-10mm)

2.5L engine: 0.24-0.28 in. (6-7mm)
MX-3
1.6L engine: 0.31-0.35 in. (8-9mm)
1.8L engine: 0.24-0.28 in. (6-7mm)
929
1989-91: 0.28-0.35 in. (7-9mm)
1992-93: 0.31-0.37 in. (8.0-9.5mm)
RX-7
1989-91: 0.43-0.51 in. (11-13mm)
1993: 0.14-0.15 in. (3.5-4.0mm)

2. A used belt should deflect as follows:
323
1.6L engine: 0.35-0.39 in. (9-10mm)
Protege
1.6L engine: 0.35-0.39 in. (9-10mm)
Miata

1.6L engine: 0.35-0.39 in. (9-10mm)
MX-6/626
2.0L engine: 0.32-0.37
(8.0-9.5mm)
2.2L engine: 0.35-0.43 in.
(9-11mm)
2.5L engine: 0.28-0.31 in. (7-8mm)
MX-3
1.6L engine: 0.35-0.39 in.
(9-10mm)
1.8L engine: 0.28-0.31 in. (7-8mm)
929
1989-91: 0.35-0.43 in. (9-11mm)
1992-93: 0.37-0.43 in. (9.5-11.0mm)
RX-7
1989-91: 0.55-0.63 in. (14-16mm)
1993: 0.18-0.19 in. (4.5-5.0mm)
3. If the belt tension is not as specified, loosen the pump pivot bolt on 323, Protege, Miata, MX-3 1.6L engine and MX-6/626 2.0L engine. On all other engines the belt tension is set with a separate tensioner assembly.
4. Loosen the locknut or bolt and turn the tensioner bolt until the tension is correct. Tighten the tensioner locknut or bolt and tighten the pivot bolt, if necessary.

SYSTEM BLEEDING

1. Check the fluid level. Add fluid, as required.
2. Raise and safely support the vehicle.
3. Turn the steering wheel full cycle, in both directions, 5 times with the engine **OFF** .
4. Recheck the fluid level again and add, as required.
5. Repeat Steps 3 and 4 until the fluid level stabilizes.
6. Lower the vehicle.
7. Start the engine and allow to warm up at idle. Turn the steering wheel full cycle, in both directions, 5 times with the engine running.
8. Check that the fluid is not foamy and the level has not dropped.
9. Add fluid, if necessary and repeat Steps 7 and 8.

WHEEL ALIGNMENT

			Caster		Camber			Steering Axis Inclination (deg.)
Year	Model		Range (deg.)	Preferred Setting (deg.)	Range (deg.)	Preferred Setting (deg.)	Toe-in (in.)	
1989	323	Front	①	②	③	④	$5/64$	⑤
		Rear	—	—	⑥	⑦	$5/64$	—
	626	Front	$7/16$P-$1^{15}/16$P	$1^3/16$P	$7/16$N-$1^1/16$P	$5/16$P	0	$12^{13}/16$
		Rear	—	—	⑧	⑨	$1/8$	—
	MX6	Front	$7/16$P-$1^{15}/16$P	$1^3/16$P	$7/16$N-$1^1/16$P	$5/16$P	0	$12^{13}/16$
		Rear	—	—	⑧	⑨	$1/8$	—
1990	323	Front	$1^5/16$P-$2^{13}/16$P	$2^1/16$P	$1^3/16$N-$1^1/16$P	$1/16$N	$3/32$	$12^7/16$
		Rear	—	—	$1^1/16$N-$7/16$P	$5/16$N	$3/32$	—
	Protege	Front	$1^5/16$P-$2^{13}/16$P	$2^1/16$P	$1^3/16$N-$1^1/16$P	$1/16$N	$3/32$	$12^7/16$
		Rear	—	—	$1^1/16$N-$7/16$P	$5/16$N	$3/32$	—
	Miata	Front	$3^3/4$P-$5^1/4$P	$4^1/2$P	$3/8$N-$1^1/8$P	$3/8$P	$1/8$	$11^5/16$
		Rear	—	—	$1^1/4$N-$1/4$N	$3/4$N	$1/8$	—
	626	Front	$7/16$P-$1^{15}/16$P	$1^3/16$P	$7/16$N-$1^1/16$P	$5/16$P	0	$12^{13}/16$
		Rear	—	—	⑧	⑨	$1/8$	—
	MX6	Front	$7/16$P-$1^{15}/16$P	$1^3/16$P	$7/16$N-$1^1/16$P	$5/16$P	0	$12^{13}/16$
		Rear	—	—	⑧	⑨	$1/8$	—
1991	323	Front	1P-$2^7/8$P	$1^{15}/16$P	$27/32$N-$21/32$P	$3/32$N	$3/32$	$12^7/16$
		Rear	—	—	$1^1/16$N-$7/16$P	$5/16$N	$3/32$	—
	Protege	Front	⑩	⑪	⑫	⑬	$3/32$	⑭
		Rear	—	—	$1^1/16$N-$7/16$P	$5/16$N	$3/32$	—
	Miata	Front	$3^{11}/16$P-$5^3/16$P	$4^7/16$P	$3/8$N-$1^1/8$P	$3/8$P	$1/8$	$11^5/16$
		Rear	—	—	$1^1/4$N-$1/4$N	$3/4$N	$1/8$	—
	626	Front	$15/16$P-$2^7/16$P	$1^{11}/16$P	$7/16$N-$1^1/16$P	$5/16$P	0	$12^{13}/16$
		Rear	—	—	$1^1/4$N-$1/4$P	$1/2$N	$1/8$	—
	MX6	Front	$15/16$P-$2^7/16$P	$1^{11}/16$P	$7/16$N-$1^1/16$P	$5/16$P	0	$12^{13}/16$
		Rear	—	—	$1^1/4$N-$1/4$P	$1/2$N	$1/8$	—

WHEEL ALIGNMENT

Year	Model		Caster Range (deg.)	Caster Preferred Setting (deg.)	Camber Range (deg.)	Camber Preferred Setting (deg.)	Toe-in (in.)	Steering Axis Inclination (deg.)
1992	323	Front	$1P$–$2\frac{7}{8}P$	$1\frac{15}{16}P$	$\frac{27}{32}N$–$\frac{21}{32}P$	$\frac{3}{32}N$	$\frac{3}{32}$	$12\frac{7}{16}$
		Rear	—	—	$1\frac{1}{16}N$–$\frac{7}{16}P$	$\frac{5}{16}N$	$\frac{3}{32}$	—
	Protege	Front	$1P$–$2\frac{7}{8}P$	$1\frac{15}{16}P$	$\frac{27}{32}N$–$\frac{21}{32}P$	$\frac{3}{32}N$	$\frac{3}{32}$	$12\frac{7}{16}$
		Rear	—	—	$1\frac{1}{16}N$–$\frac{7}{16}P$	$\frac{5}{16}N$	$\frac{3}{32}$	—
	Miata	Front	$3\frac{11}{16}P$–$5\frac{3}{16}P$	$4\frac{7}{16}P$	$\frac{3}{8}N$–$1\frac{1}{8}P$	$\frac{3}{8}P$	$\frac{1}{8}$	$11\frac{5}{16}$
		Rear	—	—	$1\frac{1}{4}N$–$\frac{1}{4}N$	$\frac{3}{4}N$	$\frac{1}{8}$	—
	MX3	Front	$1\frac{7}{8}P$–$3\frac{3}{8}P$	$2\frac{5}{8}P$	$1\frac{9}{16}N$–$\frac{1}{16}N$	$\frac{13}{16}N$	$\frac{1}{8}$	$13\frac{3}{4}$
		Rear	—	—	$1\frac{11}{16}N$–$\frac{3}{16}N$	$\frac{15}{16}N$	$\frac{3}{32}$	—
	626	Front	$\frac{15}{16}P$–$2\frac{7}{16}P$	$1\frac{11}{16}P$	$\frac{7}{16}N$–$1\frac{1}{16}P$	$\frac{5}{16}P$	0	$12\frac{13}{16}$
		Rear	—	—	$1\frac{1}{4}N$–$\frac{1}{4}P$	$\frac{1}{2}N$	$\frac{1}{8}$	—
	MX6	Front	$\frac{15}{16}P$–$2\frac{7}{16}P$	$1\frac{11}{16}P$	$\frac{7}{16}N$–$1\frac{1}{16}P$	$\frac{5}{16}P$	0	$12\frac{13}{16}$
		Rear	—	—	$1\frac{1}{4}N$–$\frac{1}{4}P$	$\frac{1}{2}N$	$\frac{1}{8}$	—
1993	323	Front	$1P$–$2\frac{7}{8}P$	$1\frac{15}{16}P$	$\frac{27}{32}N$–$\frac{21}{32}P$	$\frac{3}{32}N$	$\frac{3}{32}$	$12\frac{7}{16}$
		Rear	—	—	$1\frac{1}{16}N$–$\frac{7}{16}P$	$\frac{5}{16}N$	$\frac{3}{32}$	—
	Protege	Front	$1P$–$2\frac{7}{8}P$	$1\frac{15}{16}P$	$\frac{27}{32}N$–$\frac{21}{32}P$	$\frac{3}{32}N$	$\frac{3}{32}$	$12\frac{7}{16}$
		Rear	—	—	$1\frac{1}{16}N$–$\frac{7}{16}P$	$\frac{5}{16}N$	$\frac{3}{32}$	—
	Miata	Front	$3\frac{11}{16}P$–$5\frac{3}{16}P$	$4\frac{7}{16}P$	$\frac{3}{8}N$–$1\frac{1}{8}P$	$\frac{3}{8}P$	$\frac{1}{8}$	$11\frac{5}{16}$
		Rear	—	—	$1\frac{1}{4}N$–$\frac{1}{4}N$	$\frac{3}{4}N$	$\frac{1}{8}$	—
	MX3	Front	$1\frac{7}{8}P$–$3\frac{3}{8}P$	$2\frac{5}{8}P$	$1\frac{9}{16}N$–$\frac{1}{16}N$	$\frac{13}{16}N$	$\frac{1}{8}$	$13\frac{3}{4}$
		Rear	—	—	$1\frac{11}{16}N$–$\frac{3}{16}N$	$\frac{15}{16}N$	$\frac{3}{32}$	—
	626	Front	$1\frac{7}{8}P$–$3\frac{3}{8}P$	$2\frac{5}{8}P$	$1\frac{3}{8}N$–$\frac{5}{32}P$	$\frac{19}{32}N$	$\frac{1}{8}$	$15\frac{1}{16}$
		Rear	—	—	$\frac{29}{32}N$–$\frac{19}{32}P$	$\frac{5}{32}N$	$\frac{1}{8}$	—
	MX6	Front	$2\frac{1}{4}P$–$3\frac{3}{4}P$	$3P$	$1\frac{7}{16}N$–$\frac{1}{16}P$	$\frac{11}{16}N$	$\frac{1}{8}$	$15\frac{1}{4}N$
		Rear	—	—	$1\frac{1}{8}N$–$\frac{3}{8}P$	$\frac{5}{8}N$	$\frac{1}{8}$	—

N—Negative
P—Positive

① 2WD: $1\frac{1}{16}P$–$2\frac{1}{16}P$
  4WD: $1\frac{1}{16}P$–$2\frac{9}{16}P$
② 2WD: $1\frac{9}{16}P$
  4WD: $1\frac{13}{16}P$
③ 2WD: $\frac{5}{16}P$–$1\frac{5}{16}P$
  4WD: $\frac{17}{32}P$–$1\frac{17}{32}P$
④ 2WD: $1\frac{13}{16}P$
  4WD: $1\frac{1}{32}P$

⑤ 2WD: $12\frac{3}{8}$
  4WD: 12
⑥ 2WD: $\frac{5}{32}N$–$1\frac{3}{32}P$
  4WD: $\frac{13}{16}N$–$\frac{5}{16}P$
⑦ 2WD: 0
  4WD: $\frac{7}{16}N$
⑧ 2WD: $1\frac{1}{4}N$–$\frac{1}{4}P$
  4WD: $\frac{3}{4}N$–$\frac{3}{4}P$
⑨ 2WD: $\frac{1}{2}N$
  4WD: 0

⑩ 2WD: $1P$–$2\frac{7}{8}P$
  4WD: $1\frac{5}{8}P$–$3\frac{1}{2}P$
⑪ 2WD: $1\frac{15}{16}P$
  4WD: $2\frac{9}{16}P$
⑫ 2WD: $\frac{27}{32}N$–$\frac{21}{32}P$
  4WD: $1\frac{1}{2}N$–0
⑬ 2WD: $\frac{3}{32}N$
  4WD: $\frac{3}{4}N$
⑭ 2WD: $12\frac{7}{16}$
  4WD: $12\frac{3}{16}$

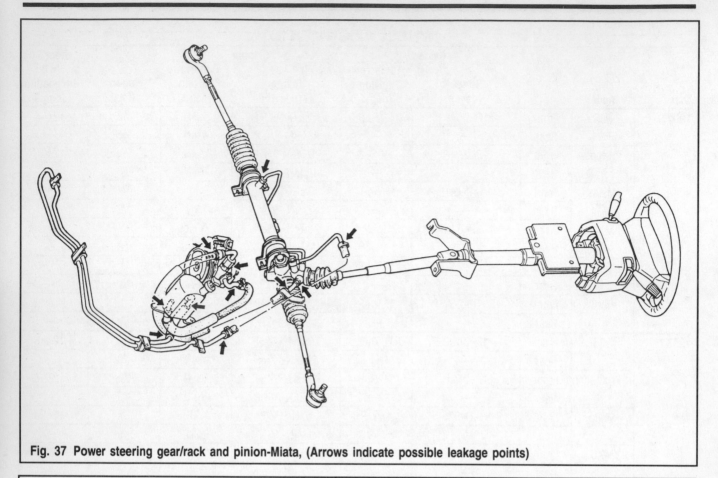

Fig. 37 Power steering gear/rack and pinion-Miata, (Arrows indicate possible leakage points)

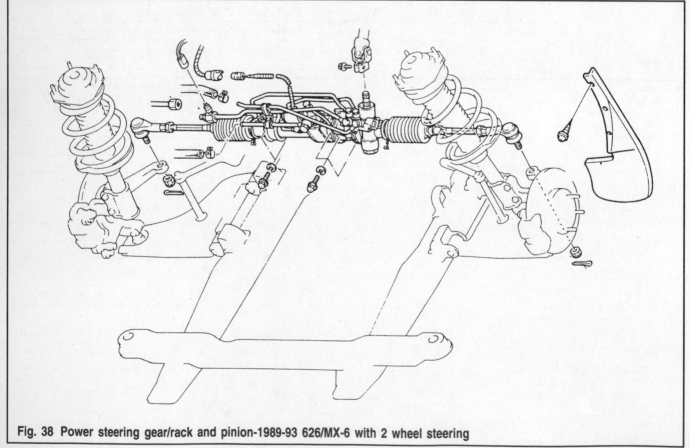

Fig. 38 Power steering gear/rack and pinion-1989-93 626/MX-6 with 2 wheel steering

1. Oil pipe
2. Tie rod end
3. Locknut
4. Boot clamp
5. Boot wire
6. Boot
7. Housing cover
8. Locknut
9. Tie rod
10. Washer
11. Locknut
12. Adjusting cover
13. Plate
14. Yoke spring
15. Support yoke
16. Dust cover
17. Retaining ring
18. Pinion shaft assembly
19. Plug assembly
20. Upper bearing
21. Oil seal
22. O-ring
23. Plug

24. Snap ring
25. Control valve
26. Seal ring
27. O-ring
28. Seal ring
29. Pinion shaft
30. Mounting bracket and rubber
31. Stop ring
32. Steering rack assembly
33. Holder
34. O-ring
35. Y-packing
36. Seal ring
37. O-ring
38. Steering rack
39. Oil seal
40. Backup ring
41. Lower bearing
42. Oil seal
43. Spacer
44. Center bearing
45. Mounting bracket
46. Mounting rubber
47. Gear housing

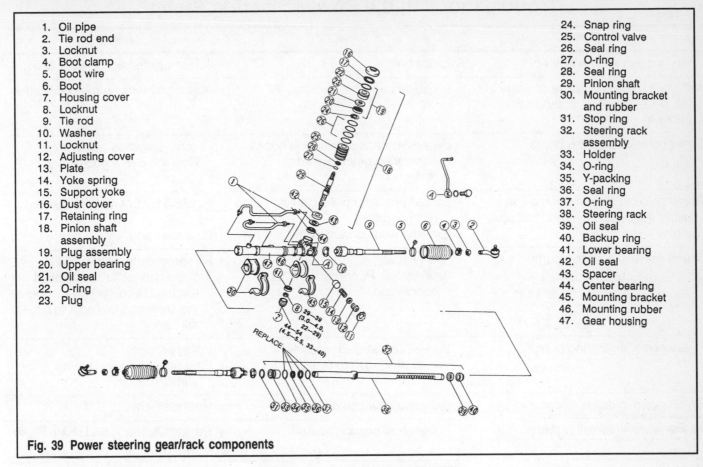

Fig. 39 Power steering gear/rack components

TORQUE SPECIFICATIONS

Component	U.S.	Metric
Tie rod lock nut	41 ft. lbs.	56 Nm
Front shock absorber to steering knuckle	203 ft. lbs.	275 Nm
Tie rod end to steering knuckle	36 ft. lbs.	49 Nm
Ball joint to lower arm	105 ft. lbs.	142 Nm
Hub bearing lock nut	137 ft. lbs.	186 Nm
2WD rear axle bearing lock nut	90 ft. lbs.	123 Nm
2WD rear axle carrier to shock absorber	105 ft. lbs.	142 Nm
2WD No. 1 suspension arm to body	65 ft. lbs.	88 Nm
2WD No. 2 suspension arm to body	80 ft. lbs.	108 Nm
2WD strut rod to body	65 ft. lbs.	88 Nm
4WD shock absorber to body	18 ft. lbs.	25 Nm
4WD shock absorber to rear axle housing	27 ft. lbs.	37 Nm
4WD lateral control rod to body	72 ft. lbs.	98 Nm
4WD upper and lower control arms to body	72 ft. lbs.	98 Nm
4WD upper and lower control arms to rear axle housing	72 ft. lbs.	98 Nm
Steering joint set bolt	26 ft. lbs.	35 Nm
Stabilizer bar to lower arm	13 ft. lbs.	18 Nm
Power steering pump pulley nut: 4A—FE and 7A-FE engines	32 ft. lbs.	43 Nm
4A-GE engine	28 ft. lbs.	38 Nm
Power steering gear bracket to body	43 ft. lbs.	59 Nm
Manual steering gear bracket to body	43 ft. lbs.	59 Nm

Troubleshooting the Power Steering Pump

Problem	Cause	Solution
Chirp noise in steering pump	• Loose belt	• Adjust belt tension to specification
Belt squeal (particularly noticeable at full wheel travel and stand still parking)	• Loose belt	• Adjust belt tension to specification
Growl noise in steering pump	• Excessive back pressure in hoses or steering gear caused by restriction	• Locate restriction and correct. Replace part if necessary.
Growl noise in steering pump (particularly noticeable at stand still parking)	• Scored pressure plates, thrust plate or rotor • Extreme wear of cam ring	• Replace parts and flush system • Replace parts
Groan noise in steering pump	• Low oil level • Air in the oil. Poor pressure hose connection.	• Fill reservoir to proper level • Tighten connector to specified torque. Bleed system by operating steering from right to left—full turn.
Rattle noise in steering pump	• Vanes not installed properly • Vanes sticking in rotor slots	• Install properly • Free up by removing burrs, varnish, or dirt
Swish noise in steering pump	• Defective flow control valve	• Replace part
Whine noise in steering pump	• Pump shaft bearing scored	• Replace housing and shaft. Flush system.
Hard steering or lack of assist	• Loose pump belt • Low oil level in reservoir **NOTE:** Low oil level will also result in excessive pump noise • Steering gear to column misalignment • Lower coupling flange rubbing against steering gear adjuster plug • Tires not properly inflated	• Adjust belt tension to specification • Fill to proper level. If excessively low, check all lines and joints for evidence of external leakage. Tighten loose connectors. • Align steering column • Loosen pinch bolt and assemble properly • Inflate to recommended pressure
Foaming milky power steering fluid, low fluid level and possible low pressure	• Air in the fluid, and loss of fluid due to internal pump leakage causing overflow	• Check for leaks and correct. Bleed system. Extremely cold temperatures will cause system aeriation should the oil level be low. If oil level is correct and pump still foams, remove pump from vehicle and separate reservoir from body. Check welsh plug and body for cracks. If plug is loose or body is cracked, replace body.

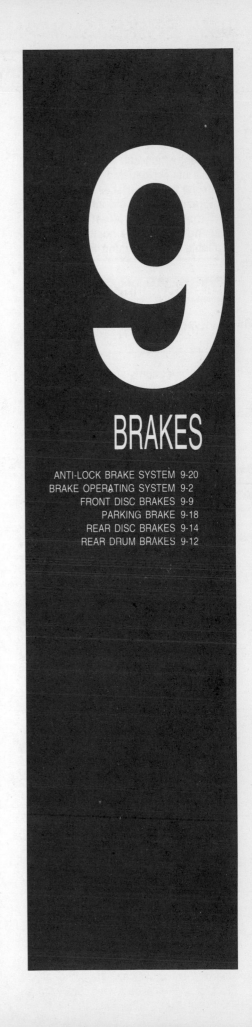

9

BRAKES

BRAKE OPERATING SYSTEM

❋❋CAUTION

Brake pads and shoes contain asbestos, which has been determined to be a cancer causing agent. Never clean the brake surfaces with compressed air! Avoid inhaling any dust from brake surfaces! When cleaning brakes, use commercially available brake cleaning fluids.

Basic System Operation

HYDRAULIC SYSTEM

Hydraulic systems are used to actuate the brakes of all modern automobiles. A hydraulic system rather than a mechanical system is used for two reasons. First, fluid under pressure can be carried to all parts of an automobile by small hoses — some of which are flexible — without taking up a significant amount of room or posing routing problems. Second, hydraulics can offer a great deal of mechanical advantage, producing a great deal of pressure at the wheels generated by little pressure at the pedal.

The master cylinder consists of a fluid reservoir and a single or double cylinder and piston assembly. Double (or dual) master cylinders are designed to separate the front and rear braking systems hydraulically in case of a leak. The master cylinder coverts mechanical motion from the pedal into hydraulic pressure within the lines. This pressure is translated back into mechanical motion at the wheels by either the wheel cylinder (drum brakes) or the caliper (disc brakes).

Steel lines carry the brake fluid to a point on the vehicle's frame near each of the vehicle's wheels. The fluid is then carried to the calipers and wheel cylinders (if equipped with drum brakes) by flexible tubes. Flexible tubes allow for suspension and steering movements.

In drum brake systems, wheel cylinders are used to apply the brakes. Each wheel cylinder contains two pistons, one at either end, which push outward in opposite directions and force the brake shoe into contact with the drum.

In disc brake systems, the cylinders are part of the calipers. One, two or four cylinders are used to force the brake pads against the disc, but all cylinders contain one piston only.

All brake cylinder (master cylinder, wheel cylinder or caliper) pistons employ some type of seal, usually made of rubber, to minimize the leak age of fluid around the piston. A rubber dust boot seals the outer end of the cylinder against dust and dirt. The boot fits around the outer end of either the piston or the brake actuating rod.

When at rest the entire hydraulic system, from the piston(s) in the master cylinder to those in the wheel cylinders or calipers, is full of brake fluid. Upon application of the brake pedal, fluid trapped in front of the master cylinder piston(s) is forced through the lines to the caliper or wheel cylinders. Here it applies pressure on the pistons, which forces the brake linings against the rotors or drums.

Upon release of the brake pedal, a spring located inside the master cylinder immediately returns the master cylinder pistons to the normal position. The pistons contain check valves and the master cylinder has compensating ports drilled in it. These are uncovered as the pistons reach their normal position. The piston check valves allow fluid to flow toward the wheel cylinders or calipers as the pistons withdraw. Then, as the return springs force the brake pads or shoes into the released position, the excess fluid reservoir through the compensating ports. It is during the time the pedal is in the released position that any fluid that has leaked out of the system will be replaced through the compensating ports.

Dual circuit master cylinders employ two pistons, located one behind the other, in the same cylinder. The primary piston is actuated directly by mechanical linkage from the brake pedal through the power booster. The secondary piston is actuated by fluid trapped between the two pistons. If a leak develops in front of the secondary piston, it moves forward until it bottoms against the front of the master cylinder, and the fluid trapped between the pistons will operate the rear brakes. If the rear brakes develop a leak, the primary piston will move forward until direct contact with the secondary piston takes place, and it will force the secondary piston to actuate the front brakes. In either case, the brake pedal moves farther when the brakes

are applied, and less braking power is available.

All dual-circuit systems incorporate a switch which senses either line pressure or fluid level. This system will warn the driver when only half of the brake system is operational.

Disc brake systems also contain a metering valve and a proportioning valve. The metering valve keeps pressure from traveling to the disc brakes on the front wheels until the brake shoes on the rear wheels have contacted the drum, ensuring that the front brakes will never be used alone. The proportioning valve controls the pressure to the rear brakes avoiding rear wheel lock-up during braking.

DISC BRAKES

Instead of the traditional expanding brakes that press out ward against a circular drum, disc brake systems employ a cast iron disc with brake pads positioned on either side of it. Braking is achieved in a way similar to the braking of a bicycle using hand brakes. On the bicycle, the brake pads squeeze onto the rim of the wheel, slowing its motion. Automobile disc brakes use the same principal but apply the braking effort to a separate disc, normally called the rotor.

The disc or rotor is a one-piece casting mounted just inside the wheel. Some rotors are one solid piece while others have cooling fins between the two braking surfaces. These vented rotors enable air to circulate between the braking surfaces cooling them quicker and making them less sensitive to heat buildup, warpage and fade. Disc brakes are only slightly affected by dirt and water, contaminants are thrown off of the braking surface by centrifugal force. Secondly, since disc pads are constantly in contact with the rotors they tend to clean dirt and contaminants from the braking surface during vehicle movement. The equal clamping action of the two brake pads, present in a properly operation system, tend to deliver uniform, straight-line stops. Unequal application of the pads between the left and right wheels can cause a vicious pull during braking. All disc brakes are inherently self-adjusting.

There are three general types of disc brake:

1. A fixed caliper.

2. A floating caliper.

3. A sliding caliper.

The sliding and floating designs are quite similar. In fact, these two types are often lumped together. In both designs, the pad on the inside of the rotor is moved into contact with the rotor by hydraulic force. The caliper, which is not held in a fixed position, moves slightly on its mount, bringing the other pad into contact with the rotor. There are various methods of attaching floating calipers. Some pivot at the bottom or top, and some slide on mounting bolts. Many uneven brake wear problems can be caused by dirty or seized slides and pivots.

DRUM BRAKES

Drum brakes employ two brake shoes mounted on a stationary backing plate. These shoes are positioned inside a circular cast iron drum which rotates with the wheel. The shoes are held in place by springs; this allows them to slide toward the drum (when they are applied) while keeping the linings in alignment.

The shoes are actuated by a wheel cylinder which is mounted at the top of the backing plate. When the brakes are applied, hydraulic pressure forces the wheel cylinder's two actuating links outward. Since these links bear directly against the top of the brake shoe webbing, the tops of the shoes are then forced outward against the inside of the drum. This action forces the bottoms of the two shoes to contact the brake drum by rotating the entire assembly slightly. When the pressure within the wheel cylinder is relaxed, return springs pull the shoes away from the drum.

Most drum brakes are designed to self-adjust during application of the brakes while the vehicle is moving in reverse. This causes both shoes to rotate very slightly with the drum, moving an adjusting lever or cable and thereby causing rotation of the adjusting screw via a star wheel. This automatic adjustment system reduces the need for maintenance adjustments but in most cases, periodic adjustment is still required.

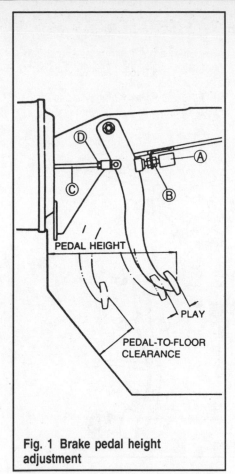

Fig. 1 Brake pedal height adjustment

Adjustment

DISC BRAKES

Mazda disc brakes are self adjusting. Periodic adjustment of disc brakes is not required. When new disc brake pads have been installed, the brake pedal must be pumped to seat the pads against the rotors, prior to moving the vehicle. If the pads are not seated before the vehicle is put into gear or driving the vehicle, the brake pedal will have to be applied a number of times before any braking action will be achieved.

BRAKE PEDAL HEIGHT

▶ **See Figure 1**

Measure the brake pedal height from the floor of the vehicle to the upper surface of the brake pedal. The distance should be 6.73-7.13 in. (171-181mm). If the brake pedal height is incorrect, adjust as follows:

1. Disconnect the stop lamp switch connector.

2. Loosen the locknut on the base of the stop light switch and move the switch to a position where it does not contact the brake pedal .

a. Loosen the operating rod locknut. Adjust the height of the brake pedal by turning the operating rod using pliers. Once the desired pedal height is obtained, tighten the locknut on the operating rod.

b. Screw the stop light switch until the it contacts the brake pedal stopper. Turn switch in until the brake pedal just starts to move. At this point, return (loosen) the stoplight switch ½-1 turn and secure in this position by tightening the locknut.

c. Connect the electrical connector to the stop light switch.

d. Check to be sure that the stop lights are not illuminated with no pressure on the brake pedal.

e. Without starting the vehicle, depress the brake pedal. If the brake light switch is properly connected, the brake lights will illuminate.

BRAKE PEDAL FREEPLAY

1. With the engine OFF, depress the brake pedal fully several times to evacuate the vacuum in the booster.

2. Once all the vacuum assist has been eliminated, press the brake pedal down by hand and confirm that the amount of movement before resistance is felt is within 0.16-0.28 in. (4-7mm).

3. If the freeplay is less than desired, confirm that the brake light switch is in proper adjustment.

4. If there is excessive freeplay, look for wear or play in the clevis pin and brake pedal arm. Replace worn parts as required and recheck brake pedal freeplay.

Brake Light Switch

REMOVAL & INSTALLATION

1. Disconnect the negative battery cable.

2. Disconnect the stop lamp switch electrical harness connector.

3. Loosen the locknut holding the switch to the bracket. Remove the locknut and the switch.

To install:

4. Install the new switch and install the locknut, tightening it just snug.

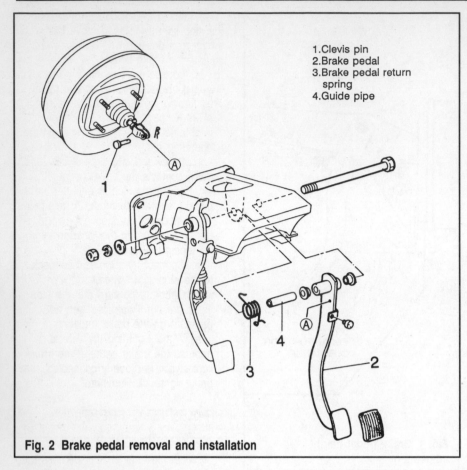

1. Clevis pin
2. Brake pedal
3. Brake pedal return spring
4. Guide pipe

Fig. 2 Brake pedal removal and installation

Brake Pedal

REMOVAL & INSTALLATION

▶ See Figure 2

1. Disconnect the negative battery cable.

2. Remove the cotter pin and clevis pin from the master cylinder.

3. Remove the brake pedal assembly bolt and remove the brake pedal.

4. Carefully remove the washers, bushings and lever from the end of the pedal rod. Keep all components in order of removal to aid in installation.

To install:

5. Install the pedal(s) in position with new bushing as required. Lubricate bushing with grease prior to installation. Guide the pedal rod bolt through the bushings and the brake pedal until the completely installed. Install the bushings and lever to the ends of the pedal rod bolt and install mounting nut. Tighten mounting nut to 14-15 ft. lbs. (20 — 34 Nm).

6. Install the return spring to the pedal.

5. Reposition the brake light switch so that the distance between the outer case of the switch and the pedal is 0.02-0.04 in. (0.5-1.0mm). Note that the switch plunger must press against the pedal to keep the brake lights off. As the pedal moves away from the switch, the plunger extends and closes the switch, which turns on the stop lights.

6. Hold the switch in the correct position and tighten the locknut.

7. Connect the wiring to the switch.

8. Check the operation of the switch. Turn the ignition key to the ON position but do not start the engine. Have an assistant observe the brake lights at the rear of the vehicle while you push on the brake pedal. The lights should come on just as the brake pedal passes the point of free play.

9. Adjust the brake light switch as necessary. The small amount of free play in the pedal should not trigger the brake lights; if the switch is set incorrectly, the brake lights will flicker due to pedal vibration on road bumps.

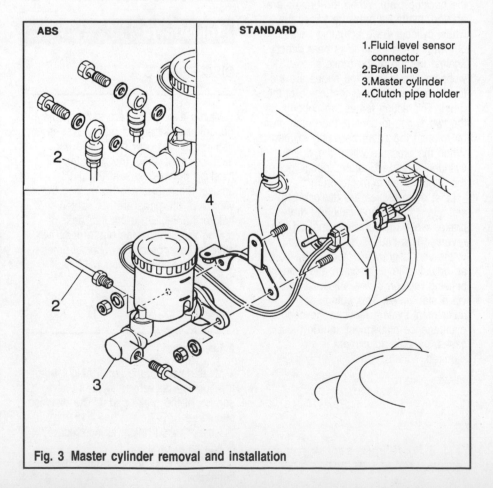

1. Fluid level sensor connector
2. Brake line
3. Master cylinder
4. Clutch pipe holder

Fig. 3 Master cylinder removal and installation

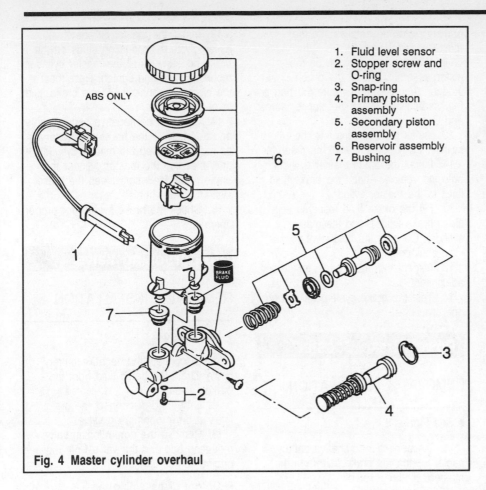

1. Fluid level sensor
2. Stopper screw and O-ring
3. Snap-ring
4. Primary piston assembly
5. Secondary piston assembly
6. Reservoir assembly
7. Bushing

Fig. 4 Master cylinder overhaul

7. Install clevis pin and washers through operating rod and brake pedal. Install new cotter pin.

8. Adjust the brake pedal and the brake light switch as necessary.

Master Cylinder

REMOVAL & INSTALLATION

▶ **See Figure 3**

1. Disconnect the negative battery cable.

2. Disconnect the fluid level sensor connector, if equipped.

3. Disconnect the brake lines from the master cylinder. A special wrench, Mazda number 49-0259-770B must be used to do this. Wrap the lines with a rag and plug the lines to prevent drainage.

4. Remove the 2 nuts securing the master cylinder to the brake booster and remove the master cylinder.

To install:

5. Install master cylinder to the mounting studs and install the mounting nuts. Tighten mounting nuts to 7-12 ft. lbs. (10-16 Nm).

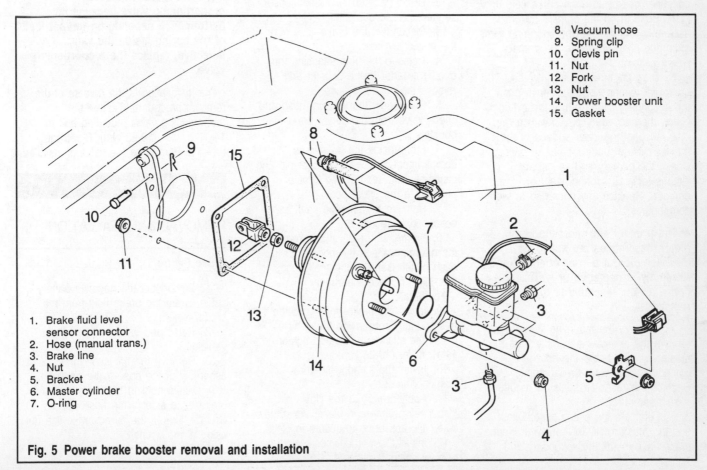

8. Vacuum hose
9. Spring clip
10. Clevis pin
11. Nut
12. Fork
13. Nut
14. Power booster unit
15. Gasket

1. Brake fluid level sensor connector
2. Hose (manual trans.)
3. Brake line
4. Nut
5. Bracket
6. Master cylinder
7. O-ring

Fig. 5 Power brake booster removal and installation

6. Fill the reservoir to the proper level with clean DOT 3 brake fluid. Bleed the master cylinder.

7. Install the brake lines to the master cylinder and tighten to 9-16 ft. lbs. (13-22 Nm) on non-ABS equipped models. On ABS equipped models, tighten the line bolts to 14-22 ft. lbs. (20-29 Nm).

8. Apply the brake pedal and check for firmness. If the pedal is spongy, air is present in the system. If air remains in the system, the entire system must be bled.

9. Connect the negative battery cable and the fluid level sensor connector. Check the brakes for proper operation and leaks.

OVERHAUL

▶ See Figure 4

1. Drain the brake fluid from the master cylinder reservoir. Remove the master cylinder from the vehicle.

2. If equipped with a fluid level sensor, remove it from the reservoir.

3. Remove the piston stopper screw and O-ring from it's position below the master cylinder. Have a suitable container nearby to drain brake fluid into.

4. Push in on the primary piston assembly and remove the snap-ring with snap-ring pliers. Remove the primary piston assembly.

5. Blow compressed air into the brake line connection in order to push the secondary piston out of the cylinder. Catch the secondary piston with a rag.

6. Inspect the inner surface of the master cylinder body for rust or pitting. Check the primary and secondary pistons for rust, scoring, wear or damage. Replace any damaged or worn components.

➡**The primary and the secondary piston assemblies are not to be disassembled. If a component on the assembly is damaged or worn, the entire piston assembly is to be replaced.**

7. Remove the mounting screw and remove the reservoir assembly from the master cylinder body. Inspect the components for wear or damage. Replace the reservoir seals as required.

To assemble:

8. Lubricate the piston assemblies and the master cylinder bore with clean brake fluid. Install the secondary and primary piston assemblies into the master cylinder body.

9. While pushing inward on the piston assembly, install the piston stopper snap-ring. Make sure the ring is fully seated and install the stopper screw and O-ring.

10. Install the bushings into the cylinder body bores. Install the reservoir.

11. Install the brake master cylinder onto the vehicle. Attach the brake fluid lines to the master cylinder.

12. Fill the brake fluid reservoir with clean brake fluid. Bleed the master cylinder. Connect the fluid level sensor, if so equipped.

13. Inspect the brake pedal for proper adjustment.

14. Test the brake system for proper operation.

Power Brake Booster

REMOVAL & INSTALLATION

▶ See Figure 5

1. Disconnect the negative battery cable. Siphon the brake fluid from the master cylinder reservoir.

2. Disconnect the fluid level sensor connector, if so equipped.

3. Disconnect the brake lines from the master cylinder.

4. Remove the nuts attaching the master cylinder to the booster and remove the master cylinder.

5. Disconnect the vacuum hose and check valve from the power brake booster.

6. From inside the passenger compartment, remove the cotter pin and clevis pin that secures the booster pushrod to the brake pedal.

7. Remove the steering shaft as described in section 8.

8. From inside the vehicle, remove the nuts that attach the booster to the dash panel. Remove the brake booster from the engine compartment.

To install:

9. Install the brake booster to the dash panel. From inside the vehicle, install the attaching nuts and tighten to 14-19 ft. lbs.(19-25 Nm).

10. Install the steering shaft as described in section 8.

11. Apply grease to the clevis pin and install with washers in place. Install new cotter pin and bend to secure in place.

12. Install the vacuum hose to the booster fitting.

13. Install the master cylinder assembly to the mounting studs on the brake booster. Install the master cylinder mounting nuts and tighten. Reconnect the electrical connector to the brake fluid level sensor.

14. Connect the negative battery cable and add fluid to the brake fluid reservoir as required. Bleed the master cylinder. If after bleeding the master cylinder the brake pedal feels soft, bleed the brake system at all wheels.

15. Check the brake system for proper operation.

Proportioning Valve

REMOVAL & INSTALLATION

▶ See Figure 6

1. Disconnect the negative battery cable. Drain the brake fluid from the brake system.

2. Label and disconnect the brake lines at the proportioning valve.

3. Remove the proportioning valve mounting bolt and the valve from the engine compartment.

➡**Do not disassemble the proportioning valve because its performance depends on the set load of the spring inside the valve. If defective, replace the proportioning valve.**

4. Installation is the reverse of the removal procedure. Tighten the proportioning valve mounting bolt to 14-17 ft. lbs. (19-23 Nm). Bleed the brake system once the valve is installed.

Brake Hose

REMOVAL & INSTALLATION

▶ See Figure 7

1. Disconnect the negative battery cable. Drain the brake fluid from the brake system.

2. Raise and safely support the vehicle.

3. Remove the tire and wheel assembly of the hose to be replaced.

4. While holding the locknut on the brake hose side of the hose with a wrench, loosen the flared brake line nut using a line wrench.

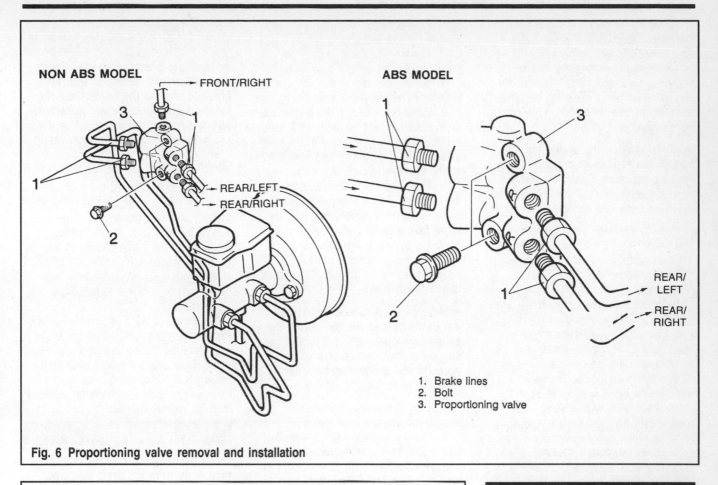

NON ABS MODEL — FRONT/RIGHT, REAR/LEFT, REAR/RIGHT

ABS MODEL — REAR/LEFT, REAR/RIGHT

1. Brake lines
2. Bolt
3. Proportioning valve

Fig. 6 Proportioning valve removal and installation

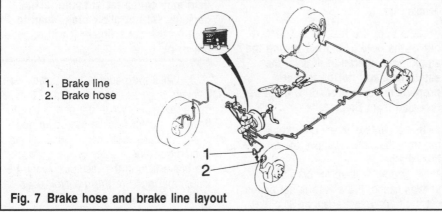

1. Brake line
2. Brake hose

Fig. 7 Brake hose and brake line layout

Brake Line

REMOVAL & INSTALLATION

✳✳CAUTION

When replacing a steel brake pipe, always use steel tubing of the same pressure rating and diameter. The replacement pipe should be of the same length. Copper tubing or lines must never be used as a replacement for steel brake lines.

5. Pull off the brake hose clip and remove the brake hose from the mounting bracket.

6. Remove the brake hose retainer bolt and washer from the caliper, if equipped. Remove the hose from the vehicle.

To install:

7. Install the brake hose retainer bolt and new washer through the end of the brake hose, if equipped. Install onto caliper and tighten to 10-16 ft. lbs. (13-22 Nm). If not equipped with hose mounting bolt, thread hose into caliper. In both cases, make sure the hose is not twisted or kinked once installed.

8. Install the other end of the brake hose through the mounting bracket and thread the brake line into the fitting. Be careful not to cross-thread the fittings.

9. While holding the locknut on the brake hose side of the hose with a wrench, tighten the flared brake line nut to 10-16 ft. lbs. (13-22 Nm). Once tightened, install the hose retainer clip into the groove in the brake hose.

10. Fill the system with clean brake fluid. Bleed the brake system.

11. Install the tire and wheel assembly. Check the brake system for proper operation.

1. Drain the brake fluid from the master cylinder reservoir.

2. Clean all dirt from the brake tube connections before loosening. Unscrew the connection at both ends of the steel pipe, using a back-up wrench when ever possible.

3. Once the tube is disconnected, cap all brake system openings to prevent contamination.

To install:

4. Try to obtain a pre-manufactured steel replacement line that is approximately the same size as the line being replaced.

5. Match the new line against the line being replaced. Using a suitable tube bender, make the necessary bends in the replacement line so it the same shape as the original line. Work slowly and carefully; try to make the bends as close as possible to those on the line being replaced.

➡**When bending the brake line, be careful not to kink or crack the line. If the line becomes kinked or cracked, it must be replaced. Do not try to bend the steel lines too sharply.**

6. Before installing the replacement brake line, flush it with clean brake fluid. This will remove any foreign material in the line, preventing brake system contamination.

7. Install the replacement brake line onto the vehicle and connect all fittings. Install new sealing washers where used. Make sure to attach the brake lines to the retainer clips, as provided.

8. Inspect the positioning of the replacement brake line. Make sure the brake line will not contact any components that could rub a hole in the line and cause a leak.

9. Bleed the brake system.

10. Inspect the system for leaks and proper operation.

BRAKE LINE FLARING

Use only brake line tubing approved for automotive use; never use copper tubing. Whenever possible, try to work with manufactured brake lines. These lines are available at most parts stores and have machine made flares, the quality of which is hard to duplicate with most of the available inexpensive flaring kits.

When the brakes are applied, there is a great amount of pressure developed in the hydraulic system. An improperly formed or cracked flare can leak with resultant loss of braking power. If you have never made a double-flare, take the time to familiarize yourself with the flaring kit components and there operation. Practice forming double-flares on scrap tubing until you are satisfied with the results. The flare should be uniform in thickness around the total circumference of the tubing. Carefully inspect the side walls of the tubing for cracks. Discard the tubing if deformed or cracked.

The following procedure applies to most commercially available double-flaring kits. If these instructions differ

from those provided with your kit, follow the instructions in the kit.

1. Cut the brake line to the necessary length using a tube cutter.

2. Square the end of the tubing with a file and chamfer the edges.

3. Insert the tubing in the proper size hole in the bar until the end of the tube sticks out the thickness of a single flare adapter. Tighten the bar wing nuts tightly so the tube can not move.

4. Place the single flare adapter into the tube and slide the bar into the yoke.

5. Position the yoke screw over the single flare adapter and tighten it until the bar is locked in the yoke. Continue tightening the yoke screw until the adapter bottoms on the bar. This should form a single flare.

➡**Make sure the tube is not forced out of the hole in the bar during the single flare operation. If it is, the single flare will not be formed properly and the procedure must be repeated from Step 1.**

6. Loosen the yoke screw and remove the single flare adapter.

7. Position the yoke screw over the tube and tighten until the taper contacts the single flare and the bar is locked in the yoke. Continue tightening to form the double-flare.

➡**Make sure the tube is not forced out of the hole in the bar during the single flare operation. If it is, the single flare will not be formed properly and the procedure must be repeated from Step 1.**

8. Loosen the screw and remove the bar from the yoke. Remove the tubing from the bar.

9. Check the flare for cracks or uneven flaring. If the flare is not perfect, cut it off and begin again at Step 1.

Brake System Bleeding

Bleeding the brake system is required anytime the normally closed system has been opened to the atmosphere. When bleeding the system, keep the brake fluid level in the master cylinder reservoir above ½full. If the reservoir is empty, air will be pushed through the system. If equipped with ABS, refer to the ABS portion of Section 5 for bleeding procedure.

PROCEDURE

➡**If using a pressure bleeder, follow the instructions furnished with the unit and choose the correct adaptor for the application. Do not substitute an adapter that "almost fits" as it will not work and could be dangerous.**

Master Cylinder

Due to the location of the fluid reservoir, bench bleeding of the master cylinder is not recommended. The master cylinder is to be bled while mounted on the brake booster. If the fluid reservoir runs dry, bleeding of the entire system will be necessary. Two people will be required to bleed the brake system.

1. Fill the brake fluid reservoir with clean brake fluid. Disconnect the brake tube from the master cylinder.

2. Have a helper slowly depress the brake pedal. Once depressed, hold it in that position. Brake fluid will be expelled from the master cylinder.

✳✳CAUTION

When bleeding the brakes, keep your face away from the area. Spraying fluid may cause facial and/or visual damage. Do not allow brake fluid to spill on the car's finish; it will remove the paint.

3. While the pedal is held down, use a finger to close the outlet port of the master cylinder. While the port is closed, have the helper release the brake pedal.

4. Repeat this procedure until all air is bled from the master cylinder. Check the brake fluid in the reservoir every 4-5 times, making sure the reservoir does not run dry. Add clean DOT 3 brake fluid to the reservoir as needed. All air is bled from the master cylinder when the fluid expelled from the port is free of bubbles.

5. Connect the brake tube to the port on the master cylinder. Add clean fluid to fill the reservoir to the appropriate level.

Calipers

1. Fill the master cylinder with fresh brake fluid. Check the level often during this procedure. Raise and safely support the vehicle.

2. Starting with the wheel furthest from the master cylinder, remove the protective cap from the bleeder and

place where it will not be lost. Clean the bleeder screw.

3. Start the engine and run at idle.

✳✳CAUTION

When bleeding the brakes, keep face away from the brake area. Spewing fluid may cause physical and/or visual damage. Do not allow brake fluid to spill on the car's finish; it will remove the paint.

4. If the system is empty, the most efficient way to get fluid down to the wheel is to loosen the bleeder about 1/2-3/4 turn, place a finger firmly over the bleeder and have a helper pump the brakes slowly until fluid comes out the bleeder. Once fluid is at the bleeder,

close it before the pedal is released inside the vehicle.

➡ If the pedal is pumped rapidly, the fluid will churn and create small air bubbles, which are almost impossible to remove from the system. These air bubbles will accumulate and a spongy pedal will result.

5. Once fluid has been pumped to the caliper, open the bleed screw again, have the helper press the brake pedal to the floor, lock the bleeder and have the helper slowly release the pedal. Wait 15 seconds and repeat the procedure (including the 15 second wait) until no more air comes out of the bleeder upon application of the brake pedal. Remember to close the bleeder before the pedal is released inside the vehicle each time the bleeder is opened. If not, air will be introduced into the system.

6. If a helper is not available, connect a small hose to the bleeder, place the end in a container of brake fluid and proceed to pump the pedal from inside the vehicle until no more air comes out the bleeder. The hose will prevent air from entering the system.

7. Repeat the procedure on the remaining calipers in the following order:
   a. Left front caliper
   b. Left rear caliper
   c. Right front caliper

8. Hydraulic brake systems must be totally flushed if the fluid becomes contaminated with water, dirt or other corrosive chemicals. To flush, bleed the entire system until all fluid has been replaced with the correct type of new fluid.

9. Install the bleeder cap on the bleeder to keep dirt out. Always road test the vehicle after brake work of any kind is done.

FRONT DISC BRAKES

✳✳CAUTION

Brake pads and shoes may contain asbestos, which has been determined to be a cancer causing agent. Never

clean the brake surfaces with compressed air! Avoid inhaling any dust from brake surfaces! When cleaning brakes, use commercially available brake cleaning fluids.

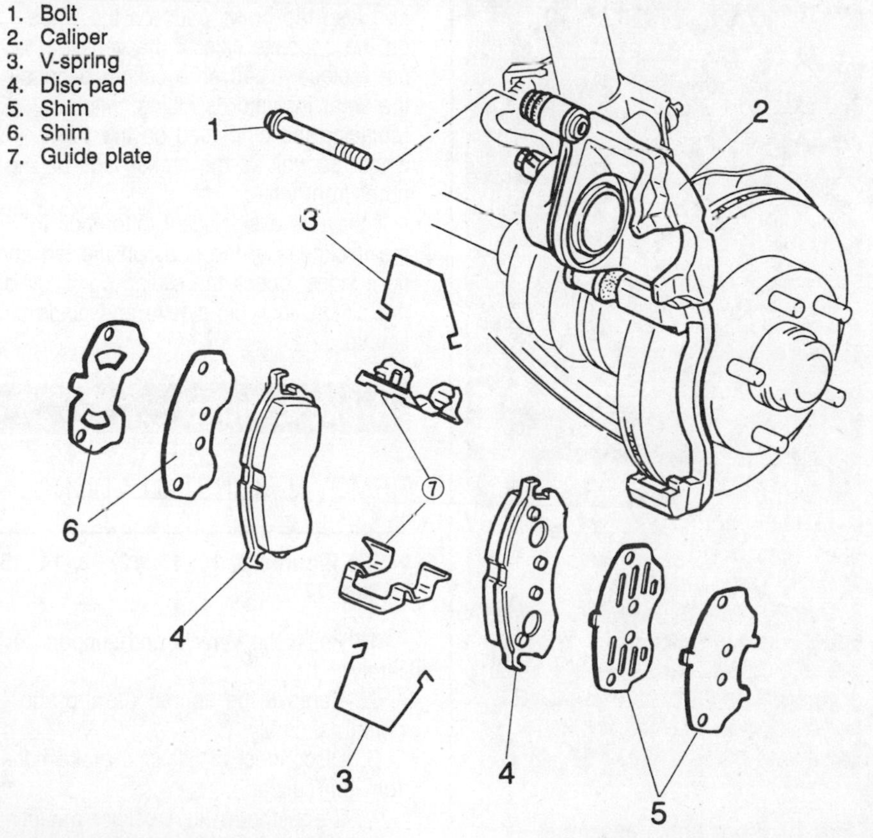

Brake Pads

REMOVAL & INSTALLATION

▸ See Figure 8

1. Disconnect the negative battery cable.

2. Remove some of the brake fluid from the master cylinder reservoir. The reservoir should be no more than 1/2 full. When the pistons are depressed into the calipers, excess fluid will flow up into the reservoir.

3. Raise the vehicle and support safely.

4. Remove the appropriate tire and wheel assemblies.

5. If equipped with 1 lower caliper mounting bolt, remove the caliper lower mounting bolt and pivot the caliper up and support it. If equipped with 2 caliper mounting bolts, remove both and support the caliper with mechanics wire. Do not kink the brake line or allow the caliper to hang by the brake line.

6. Remove the brake pads, shims and if so equipped, pins. Take note of positioning to aid installation.

7. If the caliper is single piston design, push the caliper back into the bore with a C-clamp or other suitable tool. If the caliper is a 4 piston type caliper, use Mazda tool 49-0221-600C or equivalent and the old inner brake pad,

1. Bolt
2. Caliper
3. V-spring
4. Disc pad
5. Shim
6. Shim
7. Guide plate

Fig. 8 Front brake pad assembly

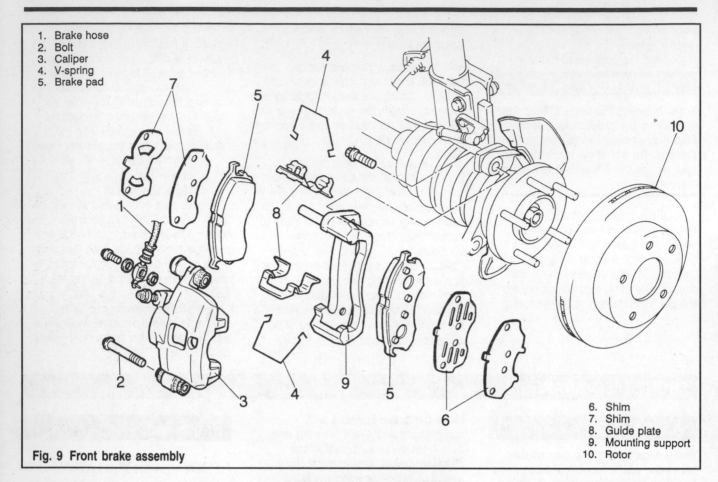

1. Brake hose
2. Bolt
3. Caliper
4. V-spring
5. Brake pad

6. Shim
7. Shim
8. Guide plate
9. Mounting support
10. Rotor

Fig. 9 Front brake assembly

push the caliper piston(s) into the caliper bore.

To install:

8. Install the brake pads and shims to the caliper support. Install the caliper over the brake pads.

➡**Be careful that the piston boot does not become caught when lowering the caliper onto the support. Do not twist the brake hose during caliper installation.**

9. Install the caliper mounting bolt(s).
10. Install the tire and wheel assemblies. Connect the negative battery cable.
11. Lower the vehicle and test the brakes for proper operation.

INSPECTION

The front brake pads have built in wear indicators that contact the brake disc when the brake pad thickness becomes 0.08 in. (2.0mm) and emit a squealing sound to warn the driver.

Inspect the thickness of the brake linings by looking through the brake caliper body check port. The thickness limit of the lining is 0.08 in. (2.0mm).

Fig. 10 Front brake assembly — MX-3

When the limit is exceeded, replace the pads on both sides of the brake disc and also the brake pads on the wheel on the opposite side of the vehicle. Do not replace 1 pad on a caliper because the wear indicator is hitting, without replacing the other pad on the same wheel as well as the brake pads on the other front wheel.

If there is a significant difference in the thickness of the pads on the left and right sides, check the sliding condition of the piston, lock pin sleeve and guide pin sleeve.

Brake Caliper

REMOVAL & INSTALLATION

◗ **See Figures 9, 10, 11, 12, 13, 14, 15, 16 and 17**

1. Raise the vehicle and support safely.
2. Remove the appropriate tire and wheel assembly.
3. Disconnect the flexible brake hose from the caliper.
4. If equipped with 1 caliper mounting bolt, remove the lower caliper bolt and pivot the caliper upward. Slide the top of

Fig. 11 Removing the clip from the front brakes — MX-3

the caliper off of the top pin and remove it from the vehicle. If equipped with 2 caliper mounting bolts, remove both bolts and remove the caliper.

5. Installation is the reverse of the removal procedure. Tighten the bolts to the required torque.

6. Bleed the brake system.

OVERHAUL

1. Remove the caliper from the vehicle.

2. Drain the remaining fluid from the caliper.

3. Remove the snap ring from inside the caliper piston chamber. Remove the dust seal from inside the chamber.

4. Place a strip of wood in the caliper where the brake pads normally are. Insert an air nozzle into the hose connection hole of the caliper and blow compressed air into the hole. Doing this will force the caliper piston out of the caliper.

❊❊CAUTION

Do not place fingers near the open area of the caliper. The piston can be blown out of the caliper bore with great force, causing personal injury.

5. Remove the piston from the caliper. Use Mazda tool 49-0208-701A or equivalent and remove the piston seal from the caliper.

6. Check the inside of the caliper for rust, pitting, deterioration or cracking. If deep pitting or corrosion is present, do not recondition the caliper. Replacement will be required.

7. Using crocus cloth, very lightly sand the sides of the caliper bore to remove rust or minor pitting.

8. Clean the components to be reused with an aerosol brake cleaner and dry them thoroughly using compressed

To assemble:

9. Obtain a caliper kit and new piston to be used during caliper assembly. Lubricate the inside of the caliper bore with clean DOT 3 brake fluid.

10. Install the piston seal into the bore groove. Lubricate the piston with clean brake fluid. Install new piston into the bore by pushing it straight in.

11. Lubricate the edges of the piston with brake fluid. Install the piston dust boot and snap-ring.

12. Install the guide pin boot and lock pin boot, if removed.

13. Position the caliper onto the guide pin. Pivot the caliper into place and install the lower bolt. Tighten the lower bolt to 23-30 ft. lbs. (31-41 Nm).

14. Install the remaining components and bleed the brake system.

Brake Disc (Rotor)

REMOVAL & INSTALLATION

1. Raise the vehicle and support safely. Remove appropriate wheel assembly.

2. Remove the caliper and brake pads. Support the caliper out of the way using wire.

3. The rotor on most models is held to the hub by 2 small threaded screws. Remove screws, if equipped, and pull off the rotor.

4. Installation is the reverse of the removal process.

Fig. 12 Removing front brake pins — MX-3

Fig. 13 Removing front brake pad retaining clip — MX-3

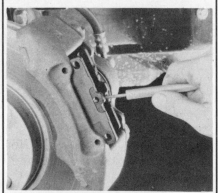

Fig. 14 Removing front brake pads — MX-3

INSPECTION

Using a micrometer, measure the disc thickness in at least eight positions, approximately 45 degrees apart and 0.39 in. (10mm) in from the outer edge of the disc. The minimum thickness is 0.87 in. (22mm), with a maximum thickness variation of 0.0006 in. (0.015mm).

If the disc is below limits for thickness, remove it and install a new one. If the thickness variation exceeds the specifications, replace the disc or turn rotor with on the car type brake lathe.

REAR DRUM BRAKES

✳✳CAUTION

Brake pads and shoes may contain asbestos, which has been determined to be a cancer causing agent. Never clean the brake surfaces with compressed air! Avoid inhaling any dust from brake surfaces! When cleaning brakes, use commercially available brake cleaning fluids.

Brake Drums

REMOVAL & INSTALLATION

▶ **See Figure 18**

1. Disconnect the negative battery cable.

2. Loosen the rear wheel lug nuts. Raise and safely suport the vehicle.

3. Remove the rear wheel and remove the center hub cap. Uncrimp the locknut and remove it.

4. Pull the brake drum outward to remove. If the brake drum is difficult to remove, push the operating lever stopper at the backing plate upward to release the operating lever and to increase the shoe clearance.

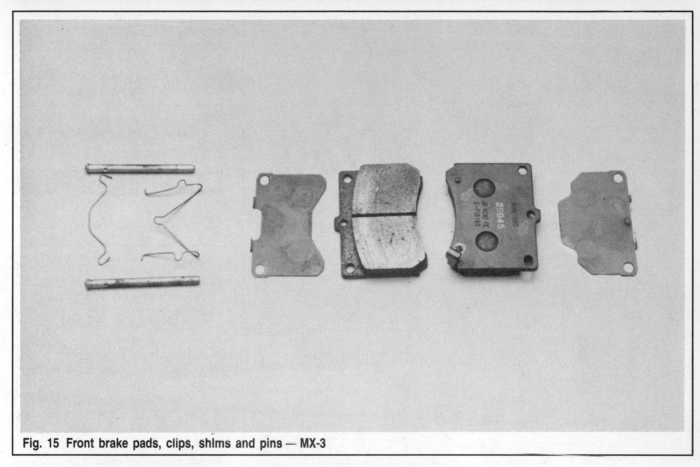

Fig. 15 Front brake pads, clips, shims and pins — MX-3

Fig. 16 Compressing the front brake caliper piston — MX-3

5. Installation is the reverse of the removal procedure. Install a new locknut and tighten it to 72-130 ft. lbs. (98-177Nm). Crimp the locknut.

INSPECTION

Inpect the brake drum for any abnormal scratches, uneven or abnormal wear. Minor items may be corrected by sanding lightly. The maximum drum inner diameter is 9.06 inch (230.1 mm).

Brake Shoes

INSPECTION

Inspect the brake shoes for peeling, cracking or extremely uneven wear of the brake shoe lining. Measure the brake shoe lining thickness. The minimum thickness is 0.04 inch (1.0 mm).

REMOVAL & INSTALLATION

1. Remove the brake drum as previously described.
2. Disconnect the parking brake cable from the backside of the brake backing plate.
3. From the brake shoe side of the backing plate remove the upper return spring.
4. From the lower (leading side) brake shoe, remove the hold pin and the spring.
5. Remove the lower (leading side) brake shoe and lower return spring and the anti-rattle spring.
6. Remove the upper (trailing side) brake shoe hold pin and spring and remove the upper brake shoe.

To install:

7. Install the upper (trailing side) brake shoe to the operating lever and then to the wheel cylinder and backing plate. Install the brake shoe hold spring and hold pin.
8. Install the anti-rattle spring.
9. Install the lower return spring to both brake shoes.
10. Install the leading side brake shoe to the operating lever and then to the wheel cylinder and anchor plate.
11. Install the hold spring and hold pin to the leading side brake shoe.
12. Install the upper return spring.
13. Install the brake drum as previously described.

Wheel Cylinders

REMOVAL & INSTALLATION

▶ See Figure 19

1. Remove the brake drum(s) and brake shoes as previously described.
2. Disconnect the brake line from the back of the backing plate with a line type wrench.

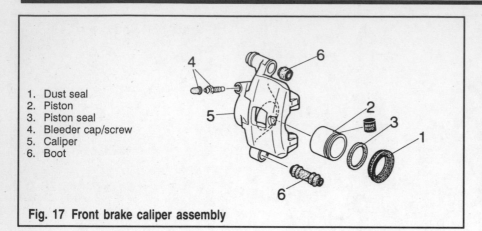

1. Dust seal
2. Piston
3. Piston seal
4. Bleeder cap/screw
5. Caliper
6. Boot

Fig. 17 Front brake caliper assembly

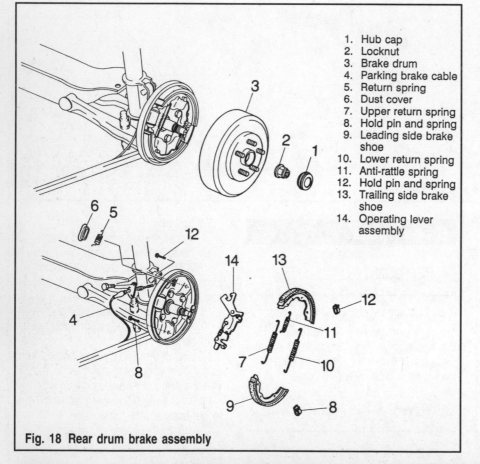

1. Hub cap
2. Locknut
3. Brake drum
4. Parking brake cable
5. Return spring
6. Dust cover
7. Upper return spring
8. Hold pin and spring
9. Leading side brake shoe
10. Lower return spring
11. Anti-rattle spring
12. Hold pin and spring
13. Trailing side brake shoe
14. Operating lever assembly

Fig. 18 Rear drum brake assembly

3. Remove the wheel cylinder mounting bolt(s) and remove the wheel cylinder from the backing plate.

4. Installation is the reverse of the removal procedure. Replace the wheel cylinder to backing plate gasket. Tighten the wheel cylinder bolt(s) to 7-9 ft. lbs. (10-13 Nm).

5. Bleed the brake system and check operation.

Brake Backing Plate

REMOVAL & INSTALLATION

1. Remove the brake drum as previously described.
2. Remove the brake shoes as previously described.
3. Remove the wheel cylinder as previously described.
4. Remove the backing plate mounting bolts and remove the backing plate.
5. Installation is the reverse of the removal procedure. Tighten the mounting bolts to 33-44 ft. lbs. (45-59 Nm).

REAR DISC BRAKES

❊❊CAUTION

Brake pads and shoes may contain asbestos, which has been determined to be a cancer causing agent. Never clean the brake surfaces with compressed air! Avoid inhaling any dust from brake surfaces! When cleaning brakes, use commercially available brake cleaning fluids.

Brake Pads

REMOVAL & INSTALLATION

▶ See Figure 20

1. Disconnect the battery negative cable.
2. Remove some of the brake fluid from the master cylinder reservoir. The reservoir should be no more than ½ full. When the pistons are depressed into the calipers, excess fluid will flow up into the reservoir.
3. Raise the vehicle and support safely.
4. Remove the appropriate tire and wheel assemblies. Loosen the parking brake cable adjustment from inside the vehicle.

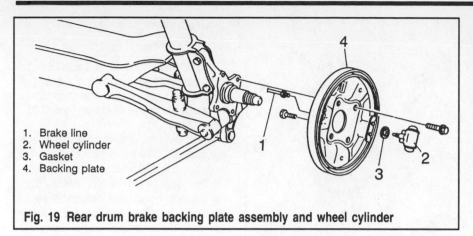

1. Brake line
2. Wheel cylinder
3. Gasket
4. Backing plate

Fig. 19 Rear drum brake backing plate assembly and wheel cylinder

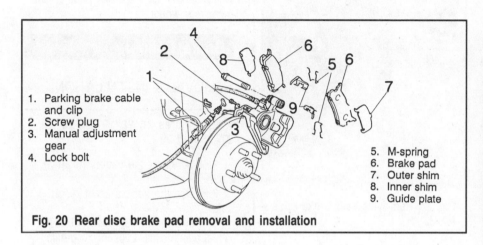

1. Parking brake cable and clip
2. Screw plug
3. Manual adjustment gear
4. Lock bolt

5. M-spring
6. Brake pad
7. Outer shim
8. Inner shim
9. Guide plate

Fig. 20 Rear disc brake pad removal and installation

1. Parking brake cable and clip
2. Connecting bolt
3. Brake hose
4. Screw plug
5. Manual adjustment gear
6. Lock bolt
7. Caliper
8. M-spring
9. Disc pad
10. Outer shim
11. Inner shim
12. Guide plate
13. Bolt
14. Mounting support
15. Rotor

Fig. 21 Rear disc brake assembly

Fig. 22 Removing the rear brake caliper — MX-3

Fig. 23 Supporting rear brake caliper — MX-3

5. Disconnect the parking brake cable from the cable bracket and the operating lever.

6. Remove the upper caliper mounting bolt and pivot the caliper downward off of the pads. Do not allow the caliper to hang by the brake line.

7. Remove the brake pads and spring clips from the caliper support. Take note of positioning of each to aid in installation.

To install:

8. Install the brake pads, shims and spring clips to the caliper support. Pivot the caliper over the brake pads.

➡**Be careful that the piston boot does not become caught when pivoting the caliper onto the support. Do not twist the brake hose during caliper installation.**

9. Lubricate and install the top caliper mounting bolt. Tighten the bolt to 12-17 ft. lbs. (16-23 Nm). Attach the parking brake cable to the operating lever and tighten the locknut to 12-17 ft. lbs. (16-23 Nm).

10. Start the engine and forcefully depress the brake pedal 5-6 times. Apply the parking brake and make sure the adjustment is within specifications. Adjust the parking brake cable, as required.

11. Check the disc brake drag by applying the brakes several times and then rotating the wheels to check for excessive dragging.

12. Install the tire and wheel assemblies. Lower the vehicle.

13. Test the brakes for proper operation.

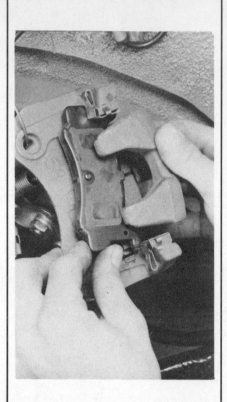

Fig. 24 Removing rear brake pads — MX-3

INSPECTION

Inspect the thickness of the brake linings by looking through the brake caliper body check port. The minimum allowable thickness of the lining is 0.08 in. (2.0mm).

When the limit is exceeded, replace the pads on both sides of the brake disc and also the brake pads on the wheel on the opposite side of the vehicle. Do not replace 1 pad on a caliper because the lining is below specifications, without replacing the other pad on the same wheel as well as the brake pads on the other rear wheel.

Brake Caliper

REMOVAL & INSTALLATION

▸ **See Figures 21, 22, 23, 24, 25, 26, 27, 28 and 29**

1. Disconnect the battery negative cable.

2. Raise the vehicle and support safely.

3. Remove the appropriate tire and wheel assemblies. Loosen the parking

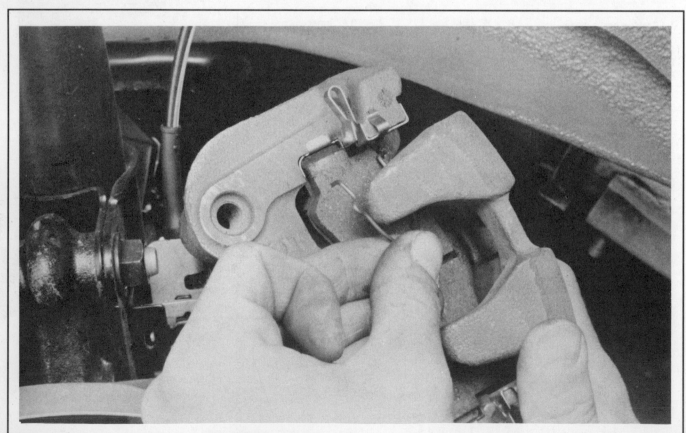

Fig. 25 Removing rear brake pad clips — MX-3

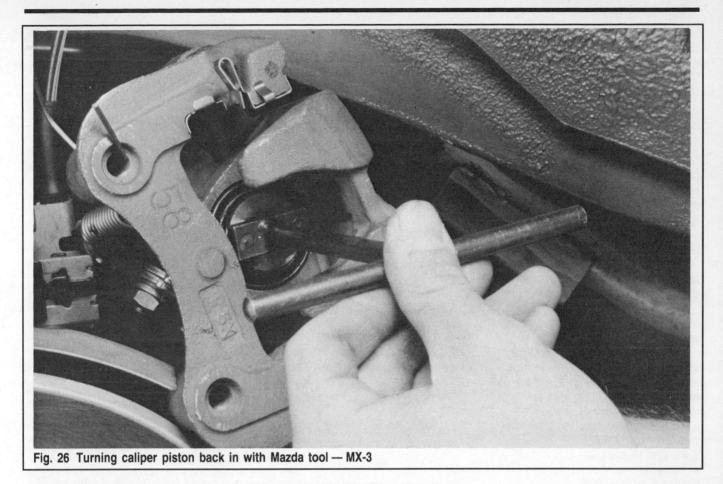

Fig. 26 Turning caliper piston back in with Mazda tool — MX-3

Fig. 27 Turning caliper piston back in with needlenose pliers — MX-3

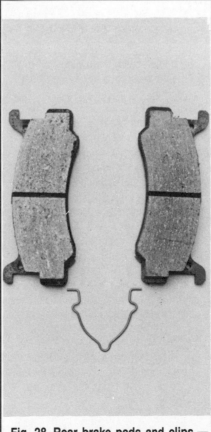

Fig. 28 Rear brake pads and clips — MX-3

brake cable adjustment from inside the vehicle.

4. Disconnect the parking brake cable from the cable bracket and the operating lever.

5. Disconnect the flexible brake line from the caliper assembly.

6. Remove the caliper upper mounting bolt and pivot the claiper downward. Slide the caliper off of the guide pin. Remove the caliper from the vehicle.

To install:

7. Lubricate the caliper pin and slide the caliper onto the guide pin. Pivot the caliper over the brake pads.

8. Connect the brake hose to the caliper and tighten the hose nut to 16-20 ft. lbs. (22-26 Nm).

9. Install the upper caliper mounting bolt and tighten the bolt to 33-49 ft. lbs. (45-67 Nm).

10. Bleed the brake system and inspect the brake system for proper operation.

11. Install the wheel and lower the vehicle. Connect the negative battery cable.

OVERHAUL

1. Remove the caliper from the vehicle.

2. Remove the guide pin and boot from the caliper, if still installed.

3. Remove the retaining ring and dust seal from the piston bore.

4. Using Mazda rear disc brake piston driver tool 49-FA18-602 or equivalent, twist the piston out of the caliper bore, making certain to turn the tool counterclockwise.

5. Remove the piston seal using Mazda tool 49-0208-701A or an equivalent seal removal hook tool. Be careful removing the seal, the side of the bore may be damaged.

6. From within the caliper bore, remove the snap ring and the adjuster spindle.

7. Remove the stopper, the O-ring and the connecting link from the bore.

8. Place the caliper in a vise and remove the return spring from the underside of the caliper.

9. Remove the operating lever, the boot and the boot clip.

10. Use Mazda puller tool 49-1285-071 or equivalent and remove the needle bearing from the caliper.

To assemble:

11. Install a new needle bearing with the needle bearing hole facing the caliper cylinder. Press the needle bearing into the caliper with tool 49-B043-002 or equivalent until the tool bottoms out against the caliper.

12. Install the connecting link into the operating lever.

13. Assemble the adjuster spindle and the stopper and install the adjuster and stopper into the caliper cylinder. Make sure that the 2 stopper pins fit into the caliper.

14. Install the snap ring into the caliper and make sure the adjuster spindle moves smoothly.

15. Install the dust seal into the caliper piston groove. Install the piston to the caliper and turn the piston into the caliper cylinder by turning it in clockwise with Mazda tool 49-FA18-602 or equivalent. Turn the piston in fully and align the piston grooves in a 12 oclock/6 oclock position.

16. Fit the dust seal into the caliper cylinder.

17. Install the caliper to the vehicle.

Brake Disc (Rotor)

REMOVAL & INSTALLATION

1. Raise the vehicle and support safely. Remove appropriate wheel assembly.

2. Disconnect the parking brake cable from the rear caliper assembly.

3. Remove the caliper and brake pads. Support the caliper out of the way using wire.

4. Remove the brake rotor (disc) from the rear hub assembly.

5. Installation is the reverse of the removal procedure.

INSPECTION

Using a micrometer, measure the disc thickness at eight positions, approximately 45 degrees apart and 0.39 in. (10mm) in from the outer edge of the disc. The minimum thickness is 0.31 in. (8mm). If the disc is beyond limits for thickness, remove it and install a new one.

PARKING BRAKE

Cables

REMOVAL & INSTALLATION

▶ **See Figure 30**

1. Disconnect the negative battery cable.

2. If the vehicle is equipped with a rear center console, remove it as follows:

   a. Remove the screw plugs in the side covers. Remove the retainer screws and the side covers from the vehicle.

   b. Remove the mounting bolts and the floor console from the vehicle.

3. Loosen the cable adjusting nut at the parking brake handle. Disconnect the brake cable from the handle and remove the retaining spring.

4. Raise the vehicle and support safely. Remove the parking brake cable mounting bolts. Disconnect the cable end from the parking brake assembly.

5. Unfasten any remaining frame retainers and remove the cables from the vehicle.

To install:

6. Install the cable to the rear actuator. Secure in place with the parking brake cable mounting bolts.

7. Reattach the parking brake cables to the parking brake handle inside the vehicle. Tighten the adjusting nut until the proper tension is placed on the cable.

8. Secure all cable retainers. Apply and release the parking brake a number of times once all adjustments have been made. With the rear wheels raised, make sure the parking brake is not causing excess drag on the rear wheels.

9. Install the rear center console assembly.

10. Road test the vehicle and check for proper brake operation. Check that the parking brake holds the vehicle on an incline.

ADJUSTMENT

1. Make sure the parking brake cable is free and is not frozen or sticking. With the engine running, forcefully depress the brake pedal 5-6 times.

2. Apply the parking brake while counting the number of notches. Check desired parking brake stroke should be 5-7 notches.

3. If adjustment is required, remove the adjusting nut clip and turn the adjusting nut which is located at the front of the parking brake cable.

4. After adjustment, check there is no looseness between the adjusting nut and the parking brake lever, then tighten the locknut.

➡ **Do not adjust the parking brake too tight. If the number of notches is less than specification, the cable has been pulled too much and the automatic adjuster will fail or the brakes will drag.**

5. After adjusting the lever stroke, raise the rear of the vehicle and safely

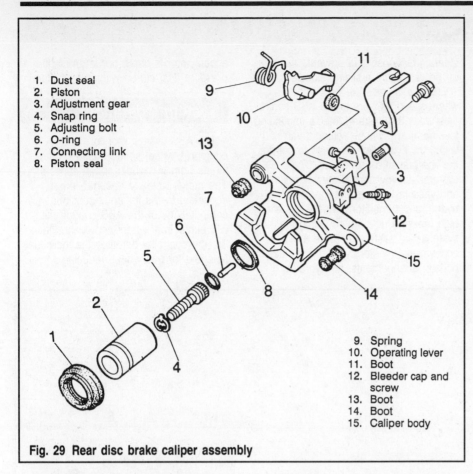

1. Dust seal
2. Piston
3. Adjustment gear
4. Snap ring
5. Adjusting bolt
6. O-ring
7. Connecting link
8. Piston seal

9. Spring
10. Operating lever
11. Boot
12. Bleeder cap and screw
13. Boot
14. Boot
15. Caliper body

Fig. 29 Rear disc brake caliper assembly

support. With the parking brake lever in the released position, turn the rear wheels to confirm that the rear brakes are not dragging.

6. Check that the parking brake holds the vehicle on an incline.

Brake Lever

REMOVAL & INSTALLATION

▶ See Figure 31

1. Disconnect the negative battery cable.

2. Remove the rear center console, if so equipped, from the vehicle as follows:

   a. Remove the screw plugs in the side covers. Remove the retainer screws and the side covers from the vehicle.

   b. Remove the mounting bolts and the console from the vehicle.

3. Loosen the cable adjusting nut and disconnect the parking brake cable from the parking brake lever.

4. Remove the parking brake switch from the parking brake lever. Remove the switch.

5. Remove the mounting bolts and the parking brake lever.

To install:

6. Lubricate the sliding parts of the ratchet plate and the ratchet pawl on the parking brake lever assembly. Install assembly into the vehicle.

7. Install the parking brake switch to the lever assembly and secure in position.

8. Lubricate and install the bushing and the parking brake stay.

9. Install the cable if removed. Install the parking brake cable rod and adjusting nut in position. Tighten the adjusting nut until the proper tension is obtained. Adjust the parking brake stroke, as required.

10. Apply and release the parking brake a number of times once all adjustments have been made. With the rear wheels raised, make sure the parking brake is not causing excess drag on the rear wheels.

11. Install the center console assembly.

12. Road test the vehicle and check for proper brake operation. Check that the parking brake holds the vehicle on an incline.

ANTI-LOCK BRAKE SYSTEM

General Description

Anti-lock braking systems are designed to prevent locked-wheel skidding during hard braking or during braking on slippery surfaces. The front wheels of a vehicle cannot apply steering force if they are locked and sliding; the vehicle will continue in its previous direction of travel. The four wheel anti-lock brake systems found on Mazda vehicles holds the individual wheels just below the point of locking, which inturn allows some

steering response and prevents the rear of the vehicle from sliding sideways.

Electrical signals are sent from the wheel speed sensors to the ABS control unit; when the system detects impending lock-up at any wheel, solenoid valves within the hydraulic unit cycle to control the line pressure as needed. The systems employ normal master cylinder and vacuum booster arrangements; no hydraulic accumulator is used, nor is any high pressure fluid stored within the system. The system employs a conventional master cylinder and vacuum booster arrangements; no hydraulic

accumulator is used, nor is any high pressure fluid stored within the system.

System Operation

The ABS system monitors and compares wheel speed based on the inputs from the wheel speed sensors. The brake pressure is controlled according to the impending lock-up computations of the ABS control unit.

If either front wheel approaches lock-up, the controller actuates the individual solenoid for that wheel, reducing

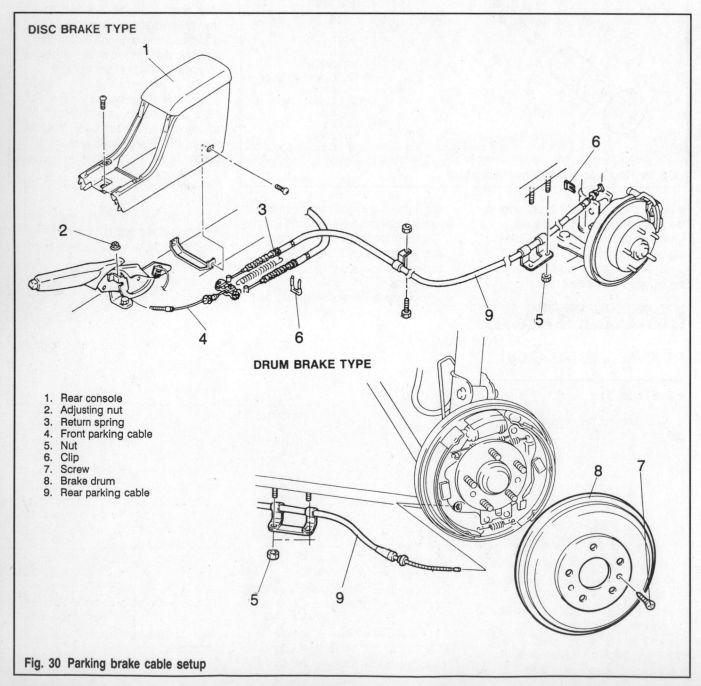

DISC BRAKE TYPE

DRUM BRAKE TYPE

1. Rear console
2. Adjusting nut
3. Return spring
4. Front parking cable
5. Nut
6. Clip
7. Screw
8. Brake drum
9. Rear parking cable

Fig. 30 Parking brake cable setup

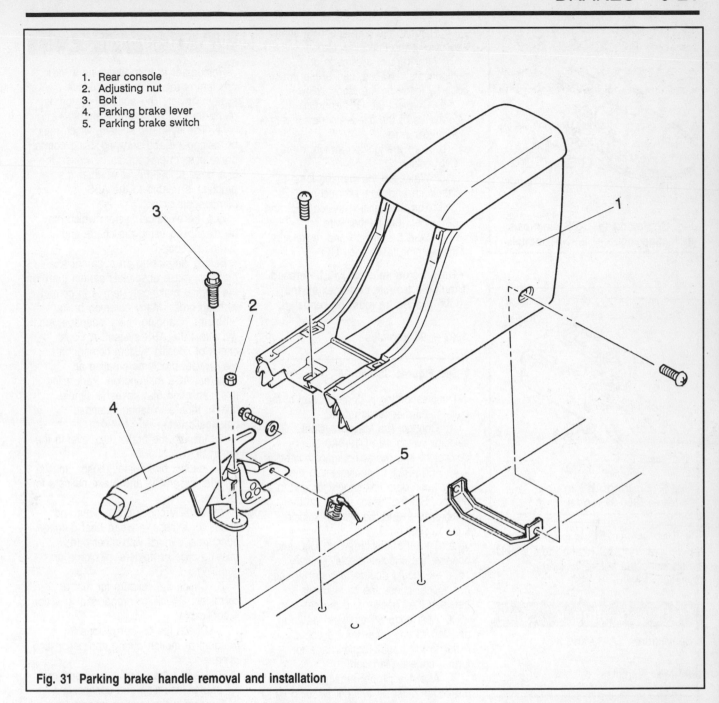

1. Rear console
2. Adjusting nut
3. Bolt
4. Parking brake lever
5. Parking brake switch

Fig. 31 Parking brake handle removal and installation

pressure in the line. Impending lock-up at either rear wheel will engage the rear control solenoid; hydraulic pressure is reduced equally to both rear wheels, reducing the tendency of the rear to skid sideways under braking.

System Precautions

• Certain components within the ABS system are not intended to be serviced or repaired individually. Only those components with removal and installation procedures should be serviced.

• Do not use rubber hoses or other parts not specifically specified for the ABS system. When using repair kits,

replace all parts included in the kit. Partial or incorrect repair may lead to functional problems and require the replacement of components.

• Lubricate rubber parts with clean, fresh brake fluid to ease assembly. Do not use lubricated shop air to clean parts; damage to rubber components may result.

• Use only DOT 3 brake fluid from an unopened container.

• If any hydraulic component or line is removed or replaced, it may be necessary to bleed the entire system.

• A clean repair area is essential. Always clean the reservoir and cap thoroughly before removing the cap. The

slightest amount of dirt in the fluid may plug an orifice and impair the system function. Perform repairs after components have been thoroughly cleaned; use only denatured alcohol to clean components. Do not allow ABS components to come into contact with any substance containing mineral oil; this includes used shop rags.

• The Anti-Lock control unit is a microprocessor similar to other computer units in the vehicle. Ensure that the ignition switch is **OFF** before removing or installing controller harnesses. Avoid static electricity discharge at or near the controller.

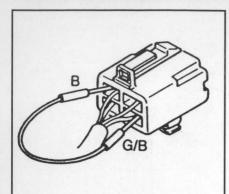

Fig. 32 Setting the ABS diagnosis indication mode — 1990-91 models

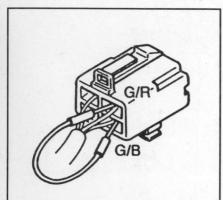

Fig. 33 Clearing ABS trouble codes — 1990-91 models

• If any arc welding is to be done on the vehicle, the ALCU connectors should be disconnected before welding operations begin.

Troubleshooting

▶ **See Figures 32, 33 and 34**

1990 — 91 Vehicles

1. Turn the ignition switch ON and OFF several times and observe the ABS warning lamp.
2. If the ABS warning lamp illuminates constantly, set the system to the diagnosis indication mode as follows:
   a. Remove the drivers seat.
   b. Disconnect the check connector from the under seat control unit.
   c. Connect terminal wires G/B and B at the check connector with a jumper wire.
   d. Start the engine. The system is now in the diagnosis mode.
3. Observe the ABS warning lamp. Count the flashes of the lamp.

4. Refer to the corresponding chart and correct the indicated item.
5. After repairs are made or components replaced, cancel the trouble code by following the steps below:
   a. Connect the G/R and G/B terminals of the check connector with a jumper wire.
   b. Turn the ignition switch to the ON position.
   c. Watch for the warning lamp to illuminate and wait 1-2 seconds.
   d. Turn the ignition switch OFF and disconnect the jumper wire.
   e. Start the engine and make sure the warning lamp goes OFF.

➥**Only 1 trouble code will be erased, if multiple trouble codes exist, the above procedure must be repeated.**

1992 — 93 Vehicles

▶ **See Figures 35 and 36**

Troubleshooting is done by way of the built-in self diagnostic mode.
1. Connect the Mazda system selector switch 49-BO19-9A0 or equivalent and the self-diagnosis checker # 49-HO18-9A1 or equivalent to the under hood data link connector and to a ground. Set the select switch on the checker to A and the system selector knob to position 3.
2. Turn the ignition switch **ON** and observe the checker display. Initially, code 88 should appear. If code 88 does not appear check the connections between the checker and the selector.
3. After code 88 appears, watch for and record any other trouble codes. Refer to the trouble code charts for further code explanation.
4. After the proper repairs are made, the codes must be erased by doing the following:
   a. At the data link connector under the hood, connect the TBS terminal to GND.
   b. Turn the ignition switch to the **ON** position.
   c. Output all of the memorized trouble codes.
   d. After the first trouble code repeats itself, depress the brake pedal 10 times at intervals of less than 1 second. This will clear all trouble codes.

Visual Inspection

Remember to first determine if the problem is related to the anti-lock system or not. The anti-lock system is made up of 2 basic sub-systems:
1. The hydraulic system, which may be diagnosed and serviced using normal brake system procedures, however, there is a need to determine whether the problem is related to the ABS components or not.
2. The electrical system which may be diagnosed using the charts and diagnostic tools.

Before diagnosing an apparent ABS problem, make absolutely certain that the normal braking system is in correct working order. Many common brake problems (dragging lining, seepage, etc.) will affect the ABS system. A visual check of specific system components may reveal problems creating an apparent ABS malfunction. Performing this inspection may reveal a simple failure, thus eliminating extended diagnostic time.
3. Inspect the brake fluid level in the reservoir.
4. Inspect brake lines, hoses, master cylinder assembly, and brake calipers for leakage.
5. Visually check brake lines and hoses for excessive wear, heat damage, punctures, contact with other parts, missing clips or holders, blockage or crimping.
6. Check the calipers for rust or corrosion. Check for proper sliding action if applicable.
7. Check the caliper pistons for freedom of motion during application and release.
8. Inspect the wheel speed sensors for proper mounting and connections.
9. Inspect the toothed wheels for broken teeth or poor mounting.
10. Inspect the wheels and tires on the vehicle. They must be of the same size and type to generate accurate speed signals. Check also for approximately equal tire pressures.
11. Confirm the fault occurrence with the operator. Certain driver induced faults may cause dash warning lamps to light. Excessive wheel spin on low-traction surfaces or high speed acceleration may also set fault codes and trigger a warning lamp. These induced faults are not system failures but examples of vehicle performance outside the parameters of the controller.

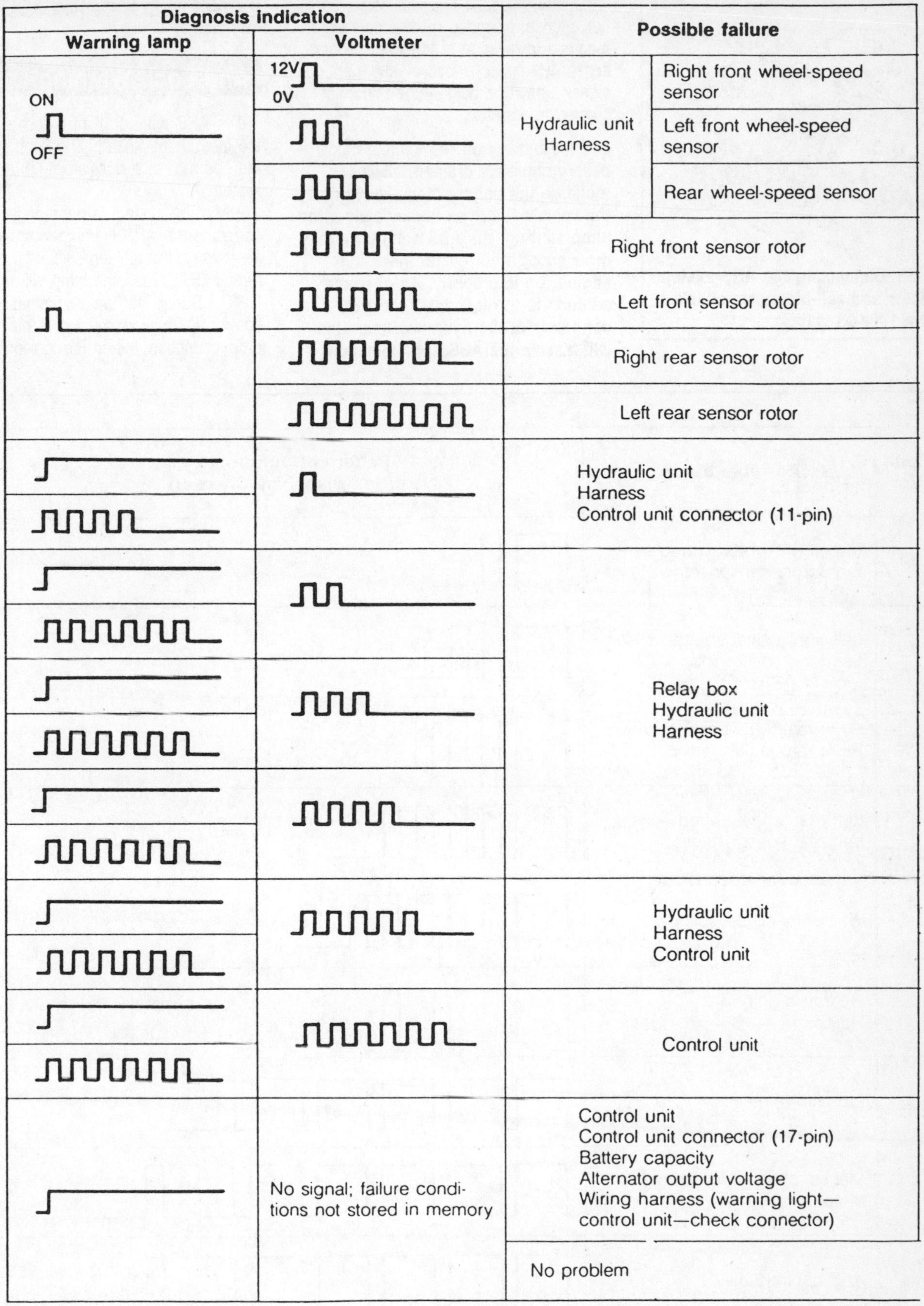

Diagnosis indication		Possible failure
Warning lamp	**Voltmeter**	
ON _⊓_ OFF	12V ⊓ 0V	Hydraulic unit / Harness — Right front wheel-speed sensor
	⊓⊓	Hydraulic unit / Harness — Left front wheel-speed sensor
	⊓⊓⊓	Hydraulic unit / Harness — Rear wheel-speed sensor
_⊓_	⊓⊓⊓⊓	Right front sensor rotor
	⊓⊓⊓⊓⊓	Left front sensor rotor
	⊓⊓⊓⊓⊓⊓	Right rear sensor rotor
	⊓⊓⊓⊓⊓⊓⊓	Left rear sensor rotor
⌐ / ⊓⊓⊓⊓	⊓	Hydraulic unit / Harness / Control unit connector (11-pin)
⌐ / ⊓⊓⊓⊓⊓⊓	⊓⊓	
⌐ / ⊓⊓⊓⊓⊓⊓⊓	⊓⊓⊓	Relay box / Hydraulic unit / Harness
⌐ / ⊓⊓⊓⊓⊓⊓⊓⊓	⊓⊓⊓⊓	
⌐ / ⊓⊓⊓⊓⊓⊓⊓⊓⊓	⊓⊓⊓⊓⊓	Hydraulic unit / Harness / Control unit
⌐ / ⊓⊓⊓⊓⊓⊓⊓	⊓⊓⊓⊓⊓⊓	Control unit
⌐	No signal; failure conditions not stored in memory	Control unit / Control unit connector (17-pin) / Battery capacity / Alternator output voltage / Wiring harness (warning light—control unit—check connector)
		No problem

Fig. 34 ABS trouble codes — 1990-91 models

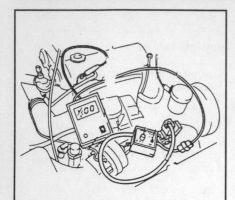

Fig. 35 Connecting the ABS system selector and self-diagnosis checker to the 1992-93 vehicles

12. The most common cause of intermittent faults is not a failed sensor but a loose, corroded or dirty connector. Incorrect installation of the wheel speed sensor will cause a loss of wheel speed signal. Check harness and component connectors carefully.

➡ If the battery on the vehicle has been completely drained, always recharge the battery before driving. If the vehicle is driven immediately after jump starting, the ABS self-check may draw enough current to make the engine run improperly. An alternate solution is to disconnect the ABS connector at the hydraulic unit. This will disable the ABS and illuminate the dash warning lamp. Reconnect the ABS when the battery is sufficiently charged.

Anti-Lock Warning Lamp

The ABS warning light is located in the instrument cluster. The lamp warns the operator of a possible fault in the system.

When the system is operating correctly, the ABS warning lamp will flash when the ignition switch is initially turned **ON**, then the lamp will turn **OFF**. During the lamp illumination the control unit checks the valve relays for proper function. When the ignition is

Code No.	Possible cause	Pattern of output signal (Self-Diagnosis Checker)
11	Right front wheel speed sensor Right front sensor rotor	
12	Left front wheel speed sensor Left front sensor rotor	
13	Right rear wheel speed sensor Right rear sensor rotor	
14	Left rear wheel speed sensor Left rear sensor rotor	
15	Wheel speed sensor	
22	Hydraulic unit Harness	
51	Fail-safe relay	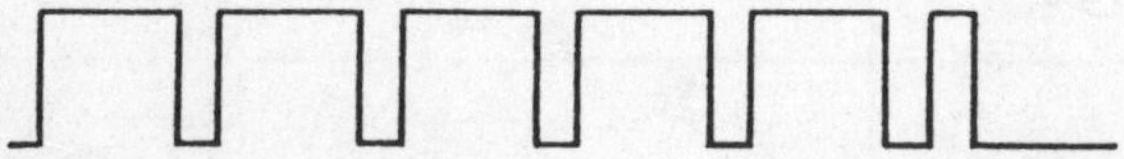
53	Motor Motor relay	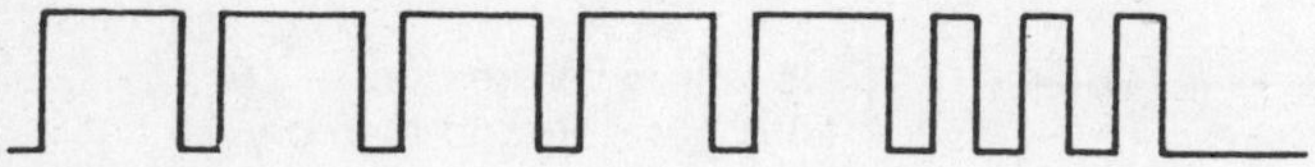
61	ABS control unit	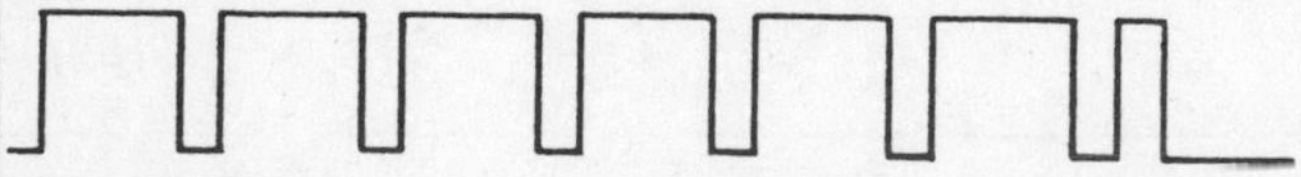

Fig. 36 ABS diagnostic trouble codes 1992-93 vehicles

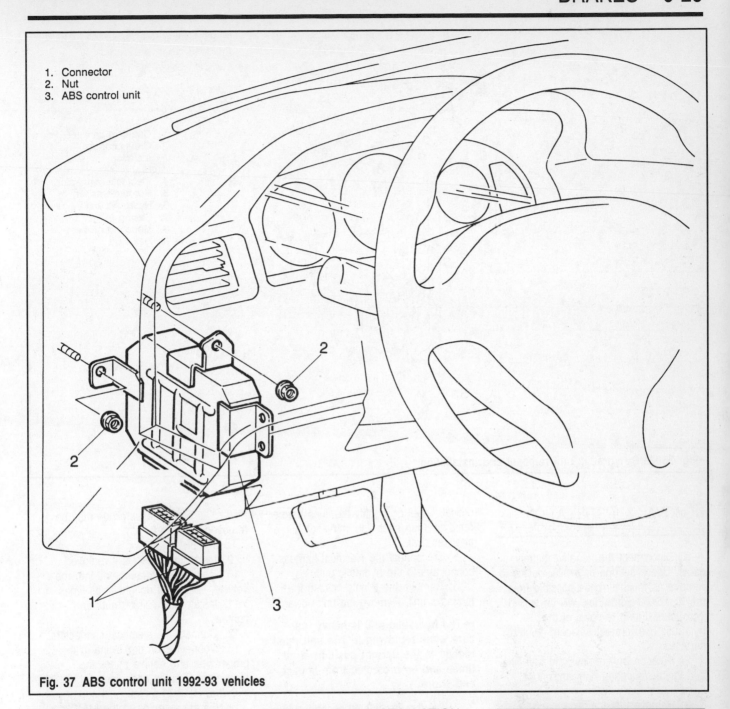

1. Connector
2. Nut
3. ABS control unit

Fig. 37 ABS control unit 1992-93 vehicles

turned to **START**, power to the ABS controller is interrupted and the warning lamp stays **ON**. Once the ignition returns to the **ON** position, power is restored and the system re-checks itself. The warning lamp goes out and should stay off during operation of the vehicle.

Control Unit

▶ **See Figure 37**

The control unit is located under the dash at the left side above the fuse panel.

REMOVAL AND INSTALLATION

1. Disconnect the negative battery cable.
2. Disconnect the electrical connectors from the ABS control unit.
3. Remove the ABS control unit mounting bolts and remove the ABS control unit.
4. Installation is the reverse of removal procedure.

Hydraulic Unit

▶ **See Figure 38**

The hydraulic unit is located in the engine compartment. It contains the solenoid valves and the pump/motor assembly which provides pressurized fluid for the anti-lock system when necessary. Hydraulic units are not interchangeable on any vehicles. Neither unit is serviceable; if any fault occurs within the hydraulic unit, the entire unit must be replaced.

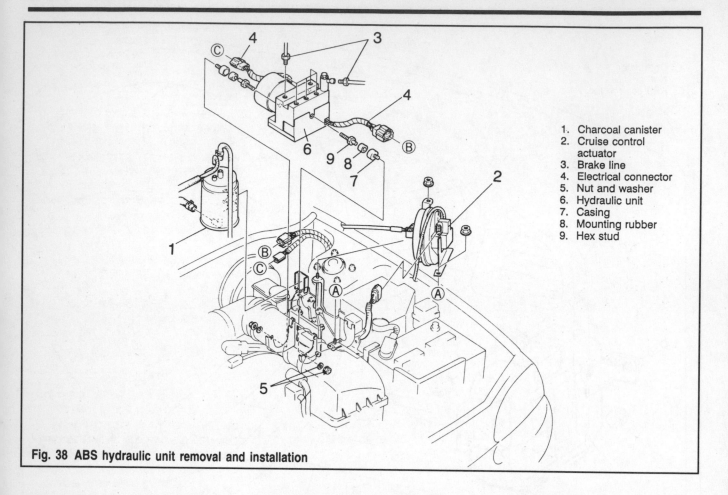

1. Charcoal canister
2. Cruise control actuator
3. Brake line
4. Electrical connector
5. Nut and washer
6. Hydraulic unit
7. Casing
8. Mounting rubber
9. Hex stud

Fig. 38 ABS hydraulic unit removal and installation

REMOVAL & INSTALLATION

1. Disconnect the negative battery cable. Use a syringe or similar device to remove as much fluid as possible from the reservoir. Some fluid will be spilled from lines during removal of the hydraulic unit; protect adjacent painted surfaces.

2. If necessary, remove the fuel filter and igniter mounting nuts and move them out of the way.

3. Remove the charcaoal canister from the vehicle and if the vehicle is equipped with cruise control, remove the cruise control actuator.

4. Disconnect the brake lines from the hydraulic unit. Correct reassembly is critical. Label or identify the lines before removal. Plug each line immediately after removal.

5. Disconnect the electrical harness connectors to the hydraulic unit.

6. Remove the 2 nuts holding the hydraulic unit. Remove the unit upwards.

➡The hydraulic unit is heavy; use care when removing it. The unit must remain in the upright position at all times and be protected from impact and shock.

7. Set the unit upright supported by blocks on the workbench. The hydraulic unit must not be tilted or turned upside down. No component of the hydraulic unit should be loosened or disassembled.

8. The bracket assemblies may be removed if desired.

To install:

9. Install the brackets if removed.

10. Install the hydraulic unit into the vehicle, keeping it upright at all times.

11. Install the retaining nuts and tighten.

12. Connect the electrical connectors.

13. Connect each brake line to the proper port and double check the placement. Tighten each line to 113-190 inch lbs. (12.9-21.5 Nm).

14. Fill the reservoir to the MAX line with brake fluid.

15. Bleed the master cylinder, then bleed the brake lines.

16. If removed, install the cruise control actuator and the charcoal canister.

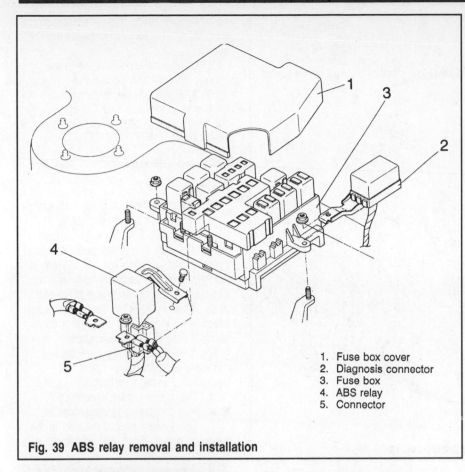

1. Fuse box cover
2. Diagnosis connector
3. Fuse box
4. ABS relay
5. Connector

Fig. 39 ABS relay removal and installation

ABS Relay

REMOVAL &INSTALLATION

▶ **See Figure 39**

1. Remove the underhood fuse box cover.

2. Remove the diagnosis connector attaching bolt and move the connector to the side.

3. Remove the under hood fuse panel mounting nuts and move the fuse panel to the side.

4. Remove the ABS relay mounting bolt and disconnect the relay electrical connector. Remove the relay.

5. Installation is the reverse of the removal procedure.

Wheel Speed Sensors

▶ **See Figures 40 and 41**

Each wheel is equipped with a magnetic sensor mounted a fixed distance from a toothed ring which rotates with the wheel. The sensors are replaceable but not interchangeable; each must be fitted to its correct location. The toothed rings are

replaceable although disassembly of the hub or axle shaft is required.

REMOVAL & INSTALLATION

1. Elevate and safely support the vehicle.

2. Remove the wheel and tire assembly.

3. Remove the inner fender or splash shield.

4. Beginning at the sensor end, carefully disconnect or release each clip and retainer along the sensor wire. Take careful note of the exact position of each clip; they must be reinstalled in the identical position.

5. Disconnect the sensor connector at the end of the harness.

6. Remove the two bolts holding the speed sensor bracket to the knuckle and remove the assembly from the vehicle.

➡**The speed sensor has a pole piece projecting from it. This exposed tip must be protected from impact or scratches. Do not allow the pole piece to contact the toothed wheel during removal or installation.**

To install:

7. Assemble the sensor onto the bracket. Note that the brackets are different for the left and right front wheels, as well as both side rear wheels.

8. Route the cable correctly and loosely install the clips and retainers. All clips must be in their original position and the sensor cable must not be twisted. Improper installation may cause cable damage and system failure.

9. Tighten the screws and bolts for the cable retaining clips.

10. Install the inner fender or splash shield.

11. Install the wheel and tire assembly. Lower the vehicle to the ground.

12. Inspect the brake system for proper operation.

FILLING THE SYSTEM

The brake fluid reservoir is part of the normal brake system and is filled or checked in the usual manner. Always clean the reservoir cap and surrounding area thoroughly before removing the cap. Fill the reservoir only to the FULL mark; do not overfill. Use only fresh DOT 3 brake fluid from unopened containers. Do not use any fluid containing a petroleum base. Do not use any fluid which has been exposed to water or moisture. Failure to use the correct fluid will affect system function and component life.

BLEEDING THE SYSTEM

Master Cylinder

If the master cylinder has been emptied of fluid or replaced, it must be bled separately from the rest of the system. Since the cylinder has no check valve, air can become trapped within it. To bleed the brake master cylinder after it has been drained, proceed as follows:

1. Disconnect the 2 brake lines from the master cylinder. Plug the lines immediately. The brake fluid reservoir should be in place and connected to the master cylinder. Check the fluid level before beginning.

2. An assistant should slowly depress and hold the brake pedal.

3. With the pedal held down, use 2 fingers to plug each outlet port on the master cylinder and release the brake pedal.

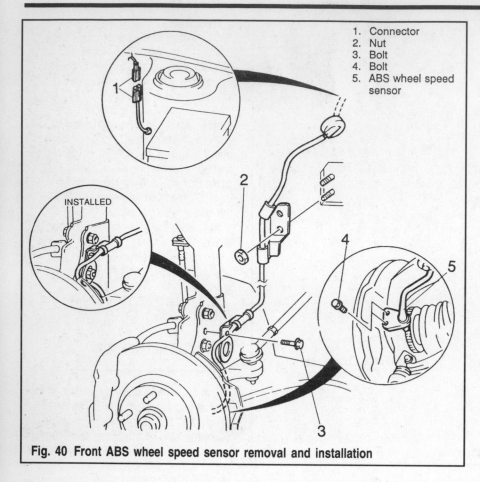

1. Connector
2. Nut
3. Bolt
4. Bolt
5. ABS wheel speed sensor

INSTALLED

Fig. 40 Front ABS wheel speed sensor removal and installation

4. Repeat Steps 2 and 3 three or four times. The air will be bled from the cylinder.

5. Connect the brake lines to the master cylinder and tighten the fittings.

6. Start the engine, allowing the system to pressurize and self-check. Shut the ignition **OFF** and bleed the brake lines.

Lines and Calipers
▶ **See Figure 42**

The brake system must be bled any time a line, hose or component is loosened or removed. Any air trapped within the lines can affect pedal feel and system function. Bleeding the system is performed in the usual manner with an assistant in the car to pump the brake pedal. Make certain the fluid level in the reservoir is maintained at or near correct levels during bleeding operations.

The individual lines may be bled manually at each wheel using the traditional 2 person method.

1. The ignition must remain **OFF** throughout the bleeding procedure.

2. The system should be bled in the following order: Right rear, left front, left rear and right front.

3. Connect a transparent hose to the caliper bleed screw. Submerge the other

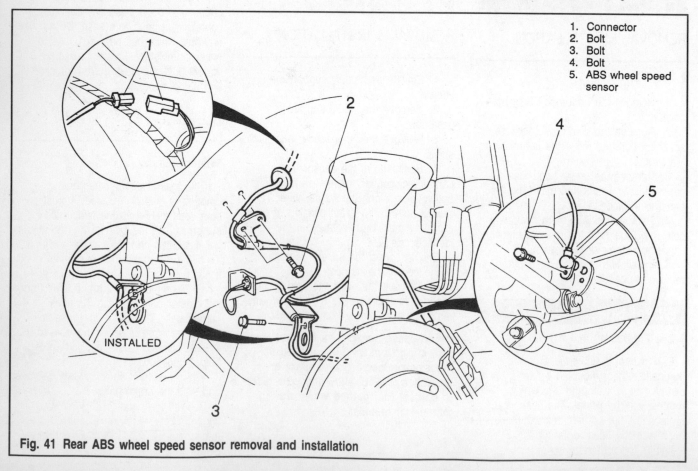

1. Connector
2. Bolt
3. Bolt
4. Bolt
5. ABS wheel speed sensor

INSTALLED

Fig. 41 Rear ABS wheel speed sensor removal and installation

end of the hose in clean brake fluid in a clear glass container.

4. Slowly pump the brake pedal several times. Use full strokes of the pedal and allow 5 seconds between strokes. After 2 or 3 strokes, hold pressure on the pedal keeping it at the bottom of its travel.

5. With pressure held on the pedal, open the bleed screw ½-¾turn. Leave the bleed screw open until fluid stops flowing from the hose. Tighten the bleed screw and release the pedal.

6. Repeat Steps 3 and 4 until air-free fluid flows from the hose. Tighten the caliper bleed screw to 7.5 ft. lbs. (10 Nm).

7. Repeat the sequence at each remaining wheel.

➥**Check the fluid level in the reservoir frequently and maintain it near the full level.**

8. When bleeding is complete, bring fluid level in the reservoir to the correct level. Install the reservoir cap.

Fig. 42 Bleeding brake system at the front caliper

BRAKE SPECIFICATIONS

All measurements in inches unless noted.

Year	Model	Master Cylinder Bore	Brake Disc Original Thickness	Brake Disc Minimum Thickness	Maximum Runout	Brake Drum Diameter Original Inside Diameter	Brake Drum Diameter Max. Wear Limit	Brake Drum Diameter Maximum Machine Diameter	Minimum Lining Thickness Front	Minimum Lining Thickness Rear
1989	323	0.875	①	②	0.004	7.870	7.910	NA	0.079	0.039
	626	0.875	③	④	0.004	9.000	9.060	NA	0.080	0.040
	MX6	0.875	③	④	0.004	9.000	9.060	NA	0.080	0.040
1990	323	0.875	⑤	⑥	0.004	9.000	9.040	NA	0.080	0.040
	Protege	0.875	⑤	⑥	0.004	9.000	9.040	NA	0.080	0.040
	Miata	0.875	⑦	⑧	0.004	—	—	—	0.040	0.040
	626	0.875	③	④	0.004	9.000	9.060	NA	0.080	0.040
	MX6	0.875	③	④	0.004	9.000	9.060	NA	0.080	0.040
1991	323	0.875	⑤	⑥	0.004	9.000	9.040	NA	0.080	0.040
	Protege	0.875	⑤	⑥	0.004	9.000	9.040	NA	0.080	0.040
	Miata	0.875	⑦	⑧	0.004	—	—	—	0.040	0.040
	626	0.875	③	④	0.004	9.000	9.060	NA	0.080	0.040
	MX6	0.875	③	④	0.004	9.000	9.060	NA	0.080	0.040
1992	323	0.875	⑤	⑥	0.004	7.874	7.913	NA	0.080	0.040
	Protege	0.875	⑤	⑥	0.004	7.874	7.913	NA	0.080	0.040
	Miata	0.875	⑦	⑧	0.004	—	—	—	0.040	0.040
	MX3	⑨	⑤	⑩	0.004	7.874	7.913	NA	0.080	0.040
	626	0.875	③	④	0.004	9.000	9.060	NA	0.080	0.040
	MX6	0.875	③	④	0.004	9.000	9.060	NA	0.080	0.040
1993	323	0.875	⑤	⑥	0.004	7.874	7.913	NA	0.080	0.040
	Protege	0.875	⑤	⑥	0.004	7.874	7.913	NA	0.080	0.040
	Miata	0.875	⑦	⑧	0.004	—	—	—	0.040	0.040
	MX3	⑨	⑤	⑩	0.004	7.874	7.913	NA	0.080	0.040
	626	0.937	③	④	0.004	9.000	9.060	NA	0.080	0.040
	MX6	0.937	③	④	0.004	9.000	9.060	NA	0.080	0.040

NA—Not available
① Front: 0.710
  Rear: 0.390
② Front: 0.630
  Rear: 0.310
③ Front: 0.940
  Rear: 0.390
④ Front: 0.870
  Rear: 0.310
⑤ Front: 0.870
  Rear: 0.350
⑥ Front: 0.790
  Rear: 0.280
⑦ Front: 0.710
  Rear: 0.350
⑧ Front: 0.630
  Rear: 0.280
⑨ 1.6L engine: 0.875
  1.8L engine: 0.937
⑩ Front: 0.790
  Rear: 0.310

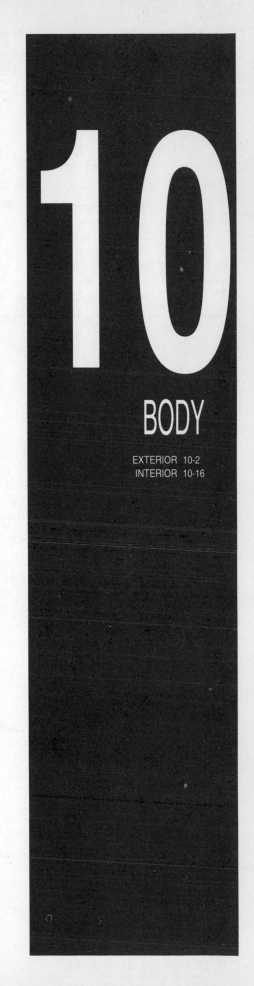

10
BODY

EXTERIOR

Doors

REMOVAL & INSTALLATION

▶ **See Figure 1**

1. Disconnect the negative battery cable.

2. At the door crease, pull back the rubber covering the electrical connector and disconnect the electrical connector.

3. Remove the checker pin from the door checker assembly.

4. Mark the relationship of the door to the hinge with a crayon or marker for installation purposes.

5. Have an assistant support the door and remove the upper and lower hinge mounting bolts.

6. Remove the door from the vehicle.

To install:

7. Have an assistant support the door in place and install the mounting bolts.

8. Align the hinge and the door with the previously made marks. Tighten the hinge bolts to 13-22 ft. lbs. (18-29 Nm).

9. Install the checker pin to the door checker.

10. Connect the door electrical connector to the chassis connector. Install the rubber boot.

11. Connect the negative battery cable.

1. Electrical harness connector
2. Checker pin
3. Hinge
4. Door
5. Door lock striker
6. Checker

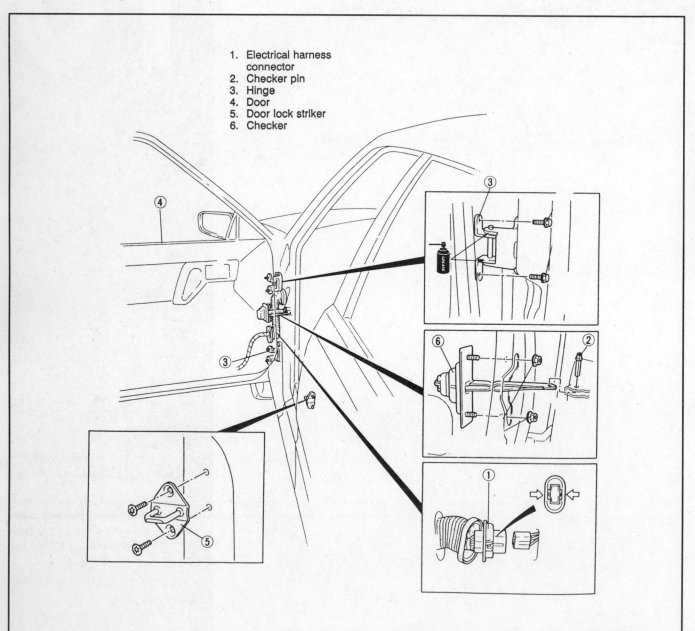

Fig. 1 Door removal procedure

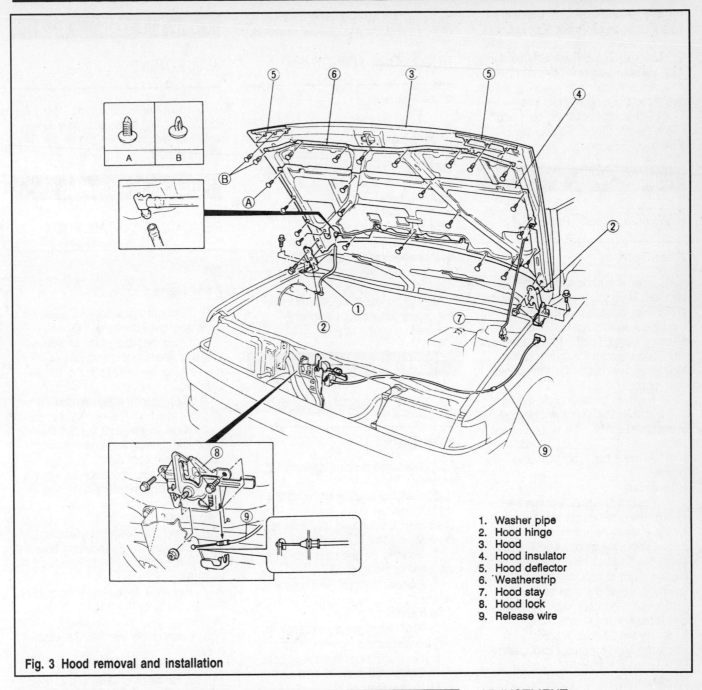

Fig. 3 Hood removal and installation

1. Washer pipe
2. Hood hinge
3. Hood
4. Hood insulator
5. Hood deflector
6. Weatherstrip
7. Hood stay
8. Hood lock
9. Release wire

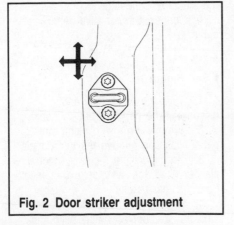

Fig. 2 Door striker adjustment

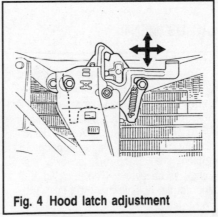

Fig. 4 Hood latch adjustment

ADJUSTMENT

Door Latch Striker and Door Alignment

The door latch striker can be adjusted laterally and vertically as well as fore and aft. The striker should not be adjusted to correct door sag.

ALL MODELS

▶ See Figure 2

1. Loosen the striker attaching screws and move the striker as required.

2. Tighten the attaching screws and check the door for fit. Repeat the procedure if necessary.

The door hinges provide sufficient adjustment latitude to correct most door misalignment conditions. Do not cover up a poor door alignment with the door latch striker adjustment.

3. Loosen the hinge attaching bolts and move the hinge as required.

4. Tighten the attaching bolts and check the door for fit. Repeat the procedure if necessary.

Hood

REMOVAL & INSTALLATION

▶ **See Figure 3**

1. Open the hood and support it securely. Mark the hinge location on the hood. If so equipped, disconnect the windshield washer hose from its retaining clamp, hood insulator fasteners and hood insulator (using the proper tool), front seal rubber insulators and seal rubber.

2. Have an assistant hold the hood in the up position. Remove the hood support and remove the hinge to hood bolts.

3. Remove the hood from the vehicle.

To install:

4. Position the hood against the hinges, using the marks made previously on the hood to help with alignment.

5. Have an assistant hold the hood. Install the hinge to hood bolts, the hood support and the hood support bolts. If so equipped, install the front seal rubber, seal rubber insulators, hood insulator and fasteners and washer hose.

6. Tighten all bolts securely and check the hood for proper alignment.

ALIGNMENT

The hood is provided with up-and-down and side-to-side adjustments.**To make the side-to-side adjustments:**

1. Loosen the hood attaching bolts and move the hood to the proper position, then tighten the attaching bolts.

2. Repeat the procedure if necessary.

To make the up-and-down adjustment (at the rear of the hood):

3. Loosen the hood stop bolts.

4. Using a screwdriver, turn the hood stop screws clockwise to lower the hood and counterclockwise to raise the hood. Hood is at the proper height when it is flush with the fenders.

5. Tighten the hood stop bolts.

6. Repeat the procedure if necessary.

HOOD LOCK ADJUSTMENT

▶ **See Figure 4**

1. Make sure that the hood is properly aligned.

2. Remove the hood latch attaching bolts. Move them as necessary to align with the latch dowel. Tighten the attaching bolts.

3. Remove the lock nut on the hood latch dowel, and turn the dowel clockwise to pull the hood tighter and counterclockwise to loosen it. The proper height is when the top of the hood is flush with the fenders.

4. Tighten the dowel lock nut after the proper adjustment has been obtained.

Trunk Lid

REMOVAL & INSTALLATION

▶ **See Figure 5**

1. Open and support the trunk lid securely.

2. Mark the position of the trunk lid hinge in relation to the trunk lid. Disconnect the trunk lid stay from its mounting bracket, if so equipped.

3. Remove the two bolts attaching the hinge to the trunk lid.

4. Remove the trunk lid from the vehicle.

To install:

5. Align the marks on the trunk lid with the hinges.

6. Install the hinge-to-trunk lid bolts.

7. Tighten the trunk lid bolts and adjust if necessary.

ADJUSTMENT

To make the side-to-side adjustment, loosen the trunk lid attaching bolts and move the trunk lid as necessary. Tighten the trunk lid attaching bolts.

To make the up-and-down adjustment, loosen the hinge-to-hinge support attaching bolts and raise or lower the hinge as necessary. The trunk lid is at the correct height when it is flush with the trunk deck.

Trunk Lid Lock

ADJUSTMENT

To adjust the trunk lid lock, loosen the striker attaching bolts, and move the striker as required, then tighten the attaching bolts.

Hatchback Assembly

REMOVAL & INSTALLATION

323

▶ **See Figure 6**

1. Disconnect the negative battery cable and open the hatch fully.

2. Disconnect the electrical harness that is located on the right side of the hatch. Feed the harness out of the channel.

3. Disconnect the rear window washer hose from the rear hatch.

4. Have an assistant support the rear hatch and remove the strut/damper supports from both sides.

5. From under the hatch lip, remove the hatch hinge mounting bolts and lift the hatch away from the vehicle.

To install:

6. Lower the hatch into place and install the hatch hinge mounting bolts. Tighten the bolts to 78-113 inch lbs. (9-13 Nm).

7. Install the strut/damper assemblies. Tighten the bolts to 69-104 inch lbs. (8-12 Nm).

8. Connect the rear window washer hose.

9. Feed the electrical harness through the hatch channel and connect the electrical connector.

10. Connect the negative battery cable.

MX-3

▶ **See Figure 7**

1. Open the hatch fully and disconnect the negative battery cable.

2. Remove the inside hatch trim panel clips and remove the trim panels.

3. Disconnect the the rear window washer hose and the electrical connector from the rear hatch.

4. Support the hatch. Remove the strut/stay damper assembly bolts and remove the assemblies from the hatch.

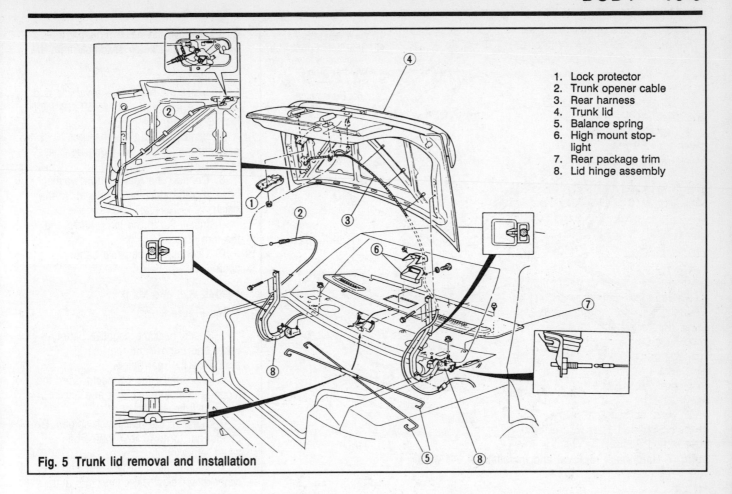

1. Lock protector
2. Trunk opener cable
3. Rear harness
4. Trunk lid
5. Balance spring
6. High mount stop-light
7. Rear package trim
8. Lid hinge assembly

Fig. 5 Trunk lid removal and installation

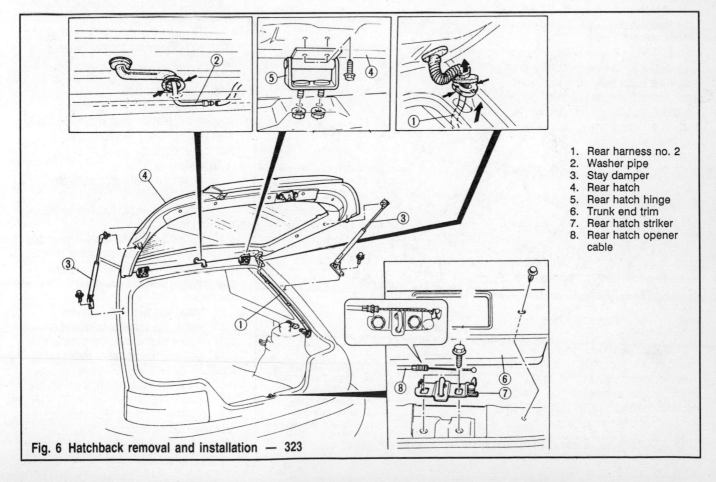

1. Rear harness no. 2
2. Washer pipe
3. Stay damper
4. Rear hatch
5. Rear hatch hinge
6. Trunk end trim
7. Rear hatch striker
8. Rear hatch opener cable

Fig. 6 Hatchback removal and installation — 323

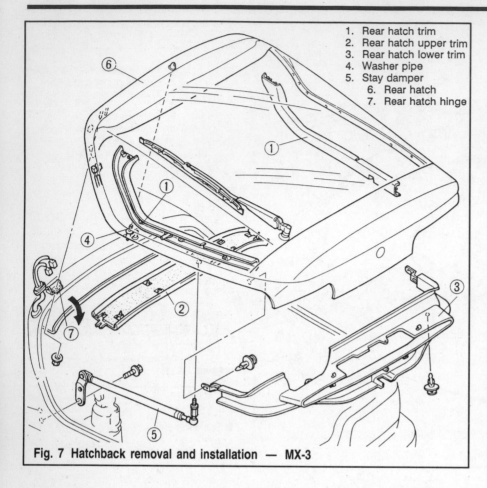

1. Rear hatch trim
2. Rear hatch upper trim
3. Rear hatch lower trim
4. Washer pipe
5. Stay damper
6. Rear hatch
7. Rear hatch hinge

Fig. 7 Hatchback removal and installation — MX-3

1. Rear hatch
2. Upper trim
3. Side trim
4. Lower trim
5. Rear finisher
6. Rear hatch lock

7. Lock controller
8. Rear hatch outer handle
9. Stay damper
10. Key cylinder
11. Rear hatch screen

Fig. 8 Hatchback removal and installation — 1990-92 626/MX-6

5. Remove the hatch mounting nuts and remove the hatch assembly from the vehicle.
   To install:
6. Install the hatch to the vehicle and tighten the mounting nuts to 69-104 inch lbs. (8-12 Nm).
7. Install the strut/stay damper assemblies. Tighten the mounting bolts to 13-16 ft. lbs. (18-22 Nm).
8. Connect the rear window washer hose and the electrical connector to the hatch.
9. Install the inside trim panels and the trim clips.
10. Connect the negative battery cable.

1990-92 626 and MX-6
▶ **See Figure 8**

1. Disconnect the negative battery cable and remove the trim that surrounds the rear hatch.
2. Disconnect the connector from the luggage compartment light and unscrew the light from its socket.
3. Remove the rear hatch screen. Be careful not to rip or tear the screen when removing it.
4. Locate the rear defroster and wiper motor electrical connectors and disconnect them. Pull the wiring through the rear hatch.
5. Remove the stay damper mounting bolts and disconnect the rear washer hose.
6. Remove the wiring harness and route it off to the side.
7. Have an assistant grasp and support the rear hatch and remove the rear hatch-to-hinge mounting bolts. Remove the hatch.
   To install:
8. Install the rear hatch assembly and install the hatch to hinge bolts.
9. Route the wiring harness to the side of the hatch.
10. Connect the rear washer hose and install the stay damper mounting bolts.
11. Connect the rear defroster and rear windshield wiper electrical connector.
12. Install the rear hatch screen.
13. Install the luggage compartment light and install the rear trim panels.
14. Connect the negative battery cable.

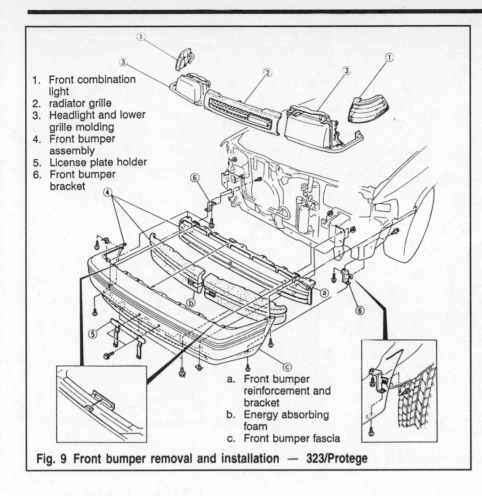

1. Front combination light
2. radiator grille
3. Headlight and lower grille molding
4. Front bumper assembly
5. License plate holder
6. Front bumper bracket

a. Front bumper reinforcement and bracket
b. Energy absorbing foam
c. Front bumper fascia

Fig. 9 Front bumper removal and installation — 323/Protege

ALIGNMENT

1. To align the side to side position of the door, loosen the hinge attaching bolts on both the hatch and the body.

2. To adjust the door for the up and down position, loosen the hinge attaching bolts on the hatch side, the lock attaching bolts, and the striker attaching bolts.

3. Adjust the rear for closing, by moving the lock and striker.

4. Make all necessary adjustments by moving the rear hatch in the appropriate directions for the desired adjustments and tighten the attaching bolts. Open and close the hatch several times to ensure proper operation.

Front Bumper

REMOVAL & INSTALLATION

323/Protege
▶ **See Figure 9**

1. Disconnect the negative battery cable.

2. Remove the front corner lights by first removing the attaching screws.

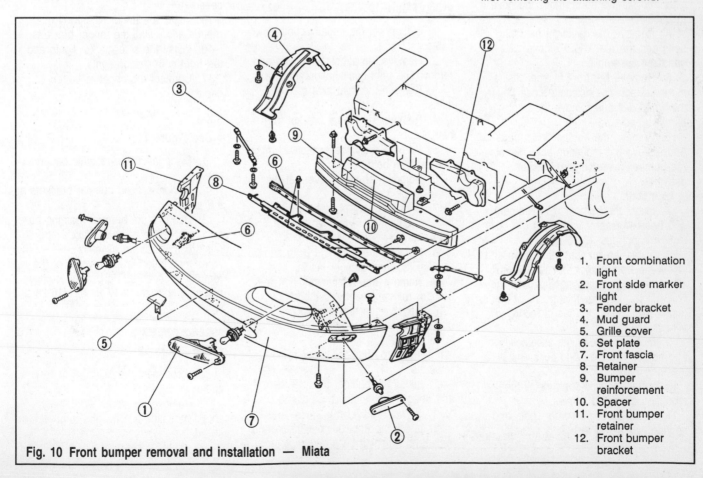

1. Front combination light
2. Front side marker light
3. Fender bracket
4. Mud guard
5. Grille cover
6. Set plate
7. Front fascia
8. Retainer
9. Bumper reinforcement
10. Spacer
11. Front bumper retainer
12. Front bumper bracket

Fig. 10 Front bumper removal and installation — Miata

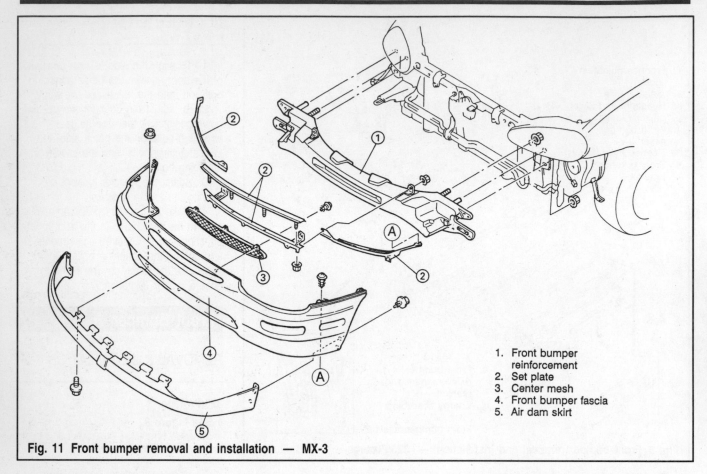

1. Front bumper reinforcement
2. Set plate
3. Center mesh
4. Front bumper fascia
5. Air dam skirt

Fig. 11 Front bumper removal and installation — MX-3

3. Remove the front grille mounting clips and screws and remove the grille assembly.

4. Remove the headlight mounting bolts and the rear clip. Remove the headlight assemblies.

5. Remove the front bumper fascia mounting screws, including those under the wheelwell and remove the front bumper fascia.

6. Remove the bumper foam pads and remove the mounting bolts. Remove the bumper reinforcement bracket assembly.

To install:

7. Install the bumper reinforcement and bracket assembly. Tighten the bolts to 61-87 inch lbs. (7-10 Nm).

8. Install the bumper foam pads and install the front bumper fascia. Carefully align the fascia mounting clips with the holes in the bumper reinforcement unit. Install and tighten the fascia mounting screws.

9. Install the headlight assemblies and tighten the mounting bolts. Install the rear retaining clip.

10. Install the grille and install the mounting clips and screws.

11. Install the front corner lights and connect the negative battery cable.

Miata

▶ **See Figure 10**

1. Disconnect the negative battery cable.

2. Remove the attaching screws and remove the front combination light.

3. Remove the front side marker lights.

4. Remove the fender bracket from both sides.

5. Remove the under wheelwell mud guards from both sides.

6. Remove the grille covers at the grille opening.

7. Unbolt the set plate from the bumper retainer and remove the set plate.

8. Remove the attaching bolts and remove the front bumper fascia.

9. Remove the bumper retainer, the bumper reinforcement and the spacer.

10. Remove the remaining bumper brackets and retainers.

To install:

11. Install the bumper brackets and retainers.

12. Install the bumper reinforcement and spacer and tighten the bolts to 12-17 ft. lbs. (16-23 Nm).

13. Install the front bumper fascia and install the retaining bolts and clips.

14. Install the set plate and the grille covers.

15. Install the under wheelwell mud guards and install the fender brackets.

16. Install the side marker lights and the front combination lights.

17. Connect the negative battery cable.

MX-3

▶ **See Figure 11**

1. Disconnect the negative battery cable.

2. Disconnect the bumper brackets at the side.

3. Remove the bumper reataing bolts and remove the complete fascia and reinforcement as an assembly.

4. Installation is the reverse of the removal procedure. Tighten the bumper retaining bolts to 12-17 ft. lbs. (16-23 Nm).

1990-92 626/MX-6

▶ **See Figure 12**

1. Disconnect the negative battery cable.

2. Remove the under side splash shleld mounting screws and remove the shield.

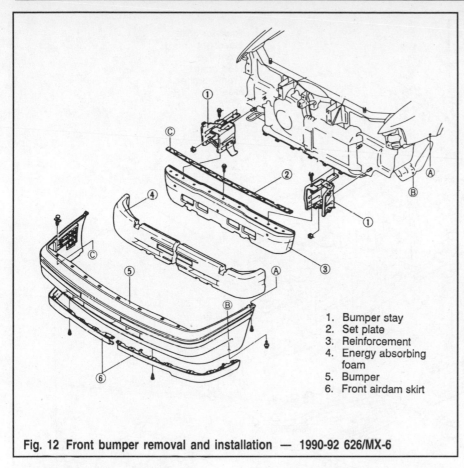

1. Bumper stay
2. Set plate
3. Reinforcement
4. Energy absorbing foam
5. Bumper
6. Front airdam skirt

Fig. 12 Front bumper removal and installation — 1990-92 626/MX-6

3. From under the wheelwell remove the front fascia mounting screws.

4. Disconnect the side turn signal electrical connectors.

5. Remove the front bumper stay mounting bolts, located behind the headlight assemblies. Loosen the rear side bolts.

6. Remove the complete bumper assembly from the vehicle.

7. Installation is the reverse of the removal procedure. Tighten the stay bolts to 23-34 ft. lbs. (31-46 Nm).

1993 626
▶ See Figure 13

1. Disconnect the negative battery cable.

2. Open the hood and remove the grille. In order to remove the grille, the clips must first be released and the mounting screws must be removed.

3. Remove the headlight mounting screws and remove the headlight assemblies.

4. Remove the front mud flaps and remove the inner fender mud guard.

5. Remove the mounting nuts and remove the complete front bumper assembly.

6. Installation is the reverse of the removal procedure. Tighten the mounting nuts to 12-16 ft. lbs. (16-22 Nm).

1993 MX-6
▶ See Figure 14

1. Disconnect the negative battery cable.

2. Remove the splash guard from under the bumper.

3. Remove both corner lamp assemblies. Remove the headlight assemblies.

4. Remove the bumper mounting nuts and remove the bumper assembly.

5. Disconnect the bumper mounted turn signal electrical connectors.

6. Installation is the reverse of the removal procedure. Tighten the mounting nuts to 12-16 ft. lbs. (16-22 Nm).

Rear Bumper

REMOVAL & INSTALLATION

323/Protege
▶ See Figure 15

1. Remove the inside trunk/hatch back trim panel.

2. On the Protege, remove the bumper bracket cover.

3. Remove the side reflector lights from the rear bumper.

4. On the 323, remove the rear liscence plate light assembly.

5. Remove the rear bumper mounting nuts and remove the rear bumper assembly.

6. Installation is the reverse of the removal procedure. Tighten the mounting nuts to 12-17 ft. lbs. (16-23 Nm).

Miata
▶ See Figure 16

1. Remove the bumper fascia retaining clips and remove the bumper fascia.

2. Remove the bumper reinforcement assembly bolts and remove the bumper reinforcement assembly.

3. Installation is the reverse of the removal procedure. Tighten the mounting bolts to 12-17 ft. lbs. (16-23 Nm).

MX-3
▶ See Figure 17

1. Disconnect the negative battery cable.

2. Remove the rear taillight assemblies.

3. Remove the rear inside hatch trim panel.

4. Remove the rear bumper mounting nuts, bolts and clips.

5. Remove the rear bumper assembly.

6. Installation is the reverse of the removal procedure. Tighten the bumper mounting nuts to 12-17 ft. lbs. (16-23 Nm).

1990-92 626/MX-6
▶ See Figure 18

1. Remove the rear mud flap assemblies.

2. Remove the inside trunk/hatch trim panel and remove the bumper mounting nuts from inside the trunk.

3. Remove the bumper from the vehicle.

4. Installation is the reverse of the removal procedure. Tighten the mounting nuts to 23-34 ft. lbs. (31-46 Nm).

1993 626/MX-6
▶ See Figures 19 and 20

1. Disconnect the negative battery cable.

2. Remove the rear light assemblies. On the MX-6, remove the license plate light assembly.

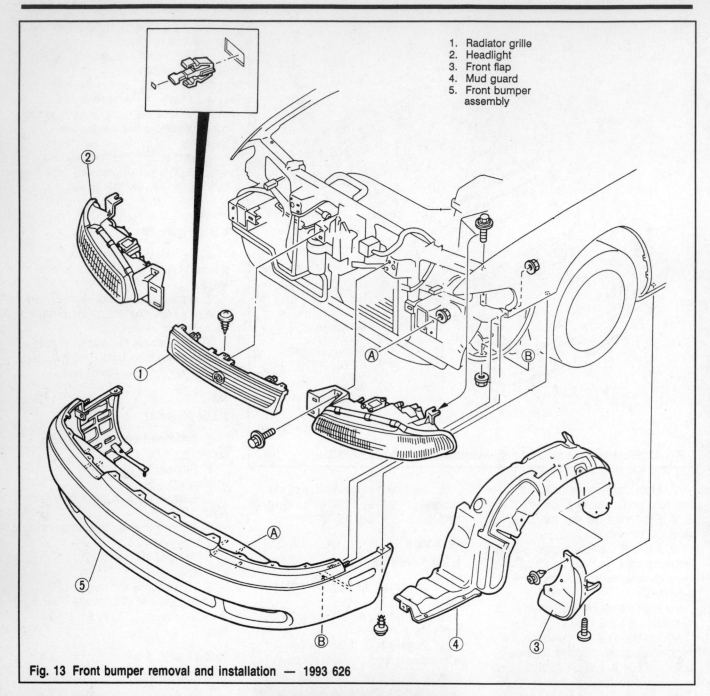

1. Radiator grille
2. Headlight
3. Front flap
4. Mud guard
5. Front bumper assembly

Fig. 13 Front bumper removal and installation — 1993 626

3. From inside the trunk, remove the rear bumper mounting nuts and remove the bumper assembly.

4. Installation is the reverse of the removal procedure. Tighten the 626 outer mounting nuts and the MX-6 inner mounting nuts to 12-16 ft. lbs. (16-22 Nm). Tighten the 626 inner mounting nuts and the MX-6 outer mounting nuts to 61-86 inch lbs. (7-10 Nm).

Grille

REMOVAL & INSTALLATION

323/Protege

1. Remove the single screw from the center of the radiator.

2. Open the tabs of the three radiator fasteners using a small flat blade screwdriver and remove the radiator grille.

3. To install, position the grllle and align the fastener holes with the holes in the body. Once they are aligned, press

the fasteners into place and install the center installation screw.

1990-92 626 and MX-6

1. Using the tip of a small flat bladed screwdriver, open the tabs of the fasteners and remove the radiator grille. The number of fasteners will vary depending on year.

2. To install, position the grille and align the fastener holes with the holes in the body. Once they are aligned, press the fasteners into place.

1993 626

1. Using the tip of a small flat bladed screwdriver, open the tabs of the grille

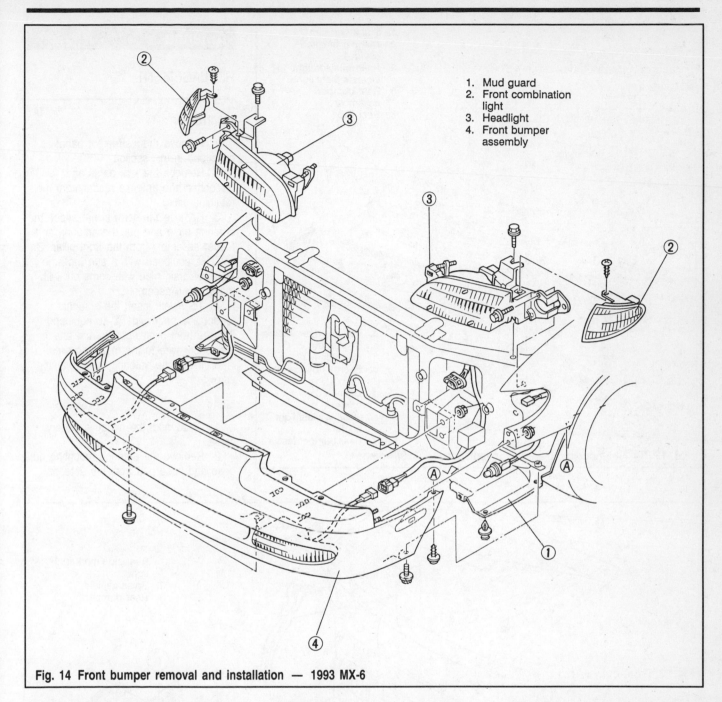

1. Mud guard
2. Front combination light
3. Headlight
4. Front bumper assembly

Fig. 14 Front bumper removal and installation — 1993 MX-6

fasteners. Remove the mounting screws and remove the grille.

2. To install, position the grille and align the fastener holes with the holes in the body. Press the fasteners into place and install the grille screws.

Outside Mirrors

REMOVAL & INSTALLATION

Power Mirror

1. Disconnect the negative battery cable.

2. Remove the trim panel from inside the mirror.

3. Remove the mirror mounting screws and pull the mirror away from the door. Disconnect the electrical connector and remove the mirror.

4. Installation is the reverse of the removal procedure.

Manual Mirror

ALL EXCEPT MIATA

1. Remove the cap from the mirror adjustment knob and remove the knob.

2. Remove the trim panel from inside the mirror.

3. Remove the mirror mounting screws and remove the mirror.

4. Installation is the reverse of the removal procedure.

MIATA

1. From outside the vehicle, carefully insert a flat edged screwdriver under the mirror base covering and pop it off.

2. Remove the mirror mounting screws and remove the mirror.

3. Installation is the reverse of the removal procedure.

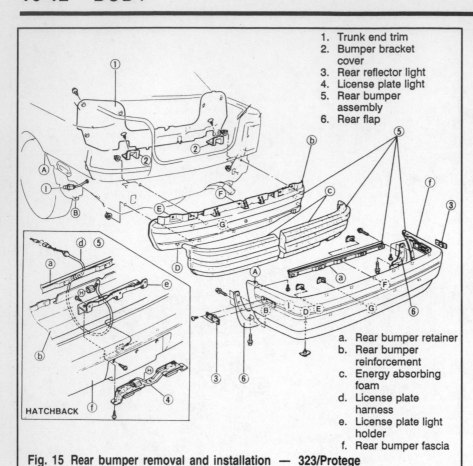

1. Trunk end trim
2. Bumper bracket cover
3. Rear reflector light
4. License plate light
5. Rear bumper assembly
6. Rear flap

a. Rear bumper retainer
b. Rear bumper reinforcement
c. Energy absorbing foam
d. License plate harness
e. License plate light holder
f. Rear bumper fascia

HATCHBACK

Fig. 15 Rear bumper removal and installation — 323/Protege

Antenna

REPLACEMENT

323/Protege

1. Remove the instrument panel as described in this section.

2. Remove the kick panel and disconnect the antenna feeder from the retaining clips.

3. Remove the screws that attach the antenna base and pull the antenna and feeder assembly from the front pillar. On vehicles equipped with a sun roof, the sun roof drain pipe with come out with the antenna assembly.

4. To install, insert the antenna feeder and drain pipe (if so equipped) into the front pillar opening and attach the feeder wire to the mounting clips.

5. Install the antenna base retaining screws.

Miata

1. Disconnect the negative battery cable.

2. Remove the antenna mounting nut, base and base pad from the antenna.

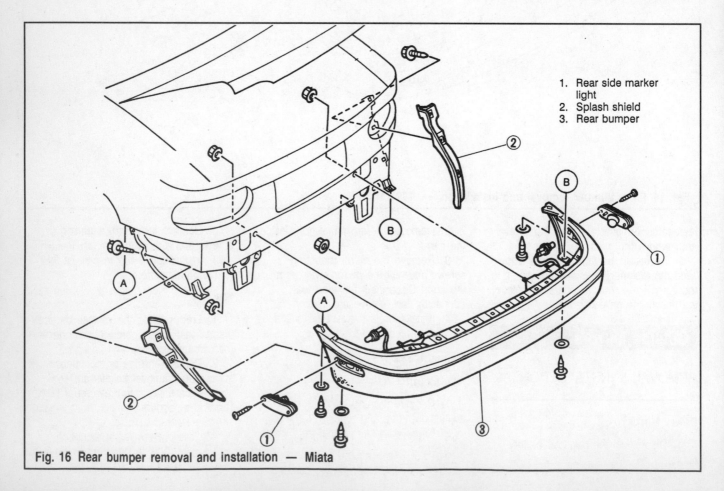

1. Rear side marker light
2. Splash shield
3. Rear bumper

Fig. 16 Rear bumper removal and installation — Miata

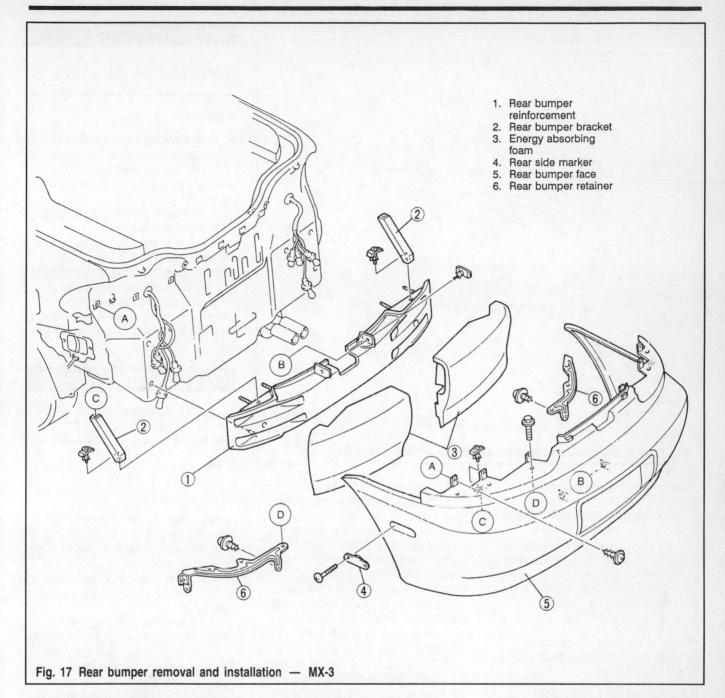

1. Rear bumper reinforcement
2. Rear bumper bracket
3. Energy absorbing foam
4. Rear side marker
5. Rear bumper face
6. Rear bumper retainer

Fig. 17 Rear bumper removal and installation — MX-3

3. Disconnect the antenna electrical connector and antenna coaxial cable.

4. Remove the antenna mounting bolt and remove the antenna and motor assembly.

5. Installation is the reverse of the removal procedure. Tighten the antenna mounting bolt and connect the cable and connector.

MX-3

1. Disconnect the negative battery cable.

2. Disconnect the antenna wire from the back of the radio.

3. Remove the antenna mounting screws and remove the antenna from the vehicle.

4. Installation is the reverse of the removal procedure.

626 and MX-6

1. Remove the front side trim.

2. Remove the undercover and loosen the nut and remove the hood release knob.

3. Disconnect the negative battery cable. Locate the central processing unit which is part of the joint box. The joint box is attached to the driver's side wheel well in the engine compartment across from the brake power booster.

Disconnect the connectors from the CPU. Release the locking clip using moderate finger pressure pull the unit from the joint box.

4. Disconnect the harness connectors from the joint box. Remove the joint box mounting bracket nut. Release the lock at the back of the joint box and remove the joint box.

5. Below the steering column and air duct, you will find the antenna feeder connector. Disconnect the feeder wire from the plug. Disconnect the connector from the antenna motor.

6. Remove the motor mounting bracket bolt and screws, and remove the antenna motor with the antenna mast.

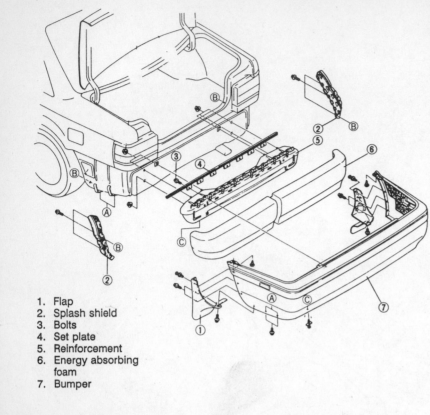

1. Flap
2. Splash shield
3. Bolts
4. Set plate
5. Reinforcement
6. Energy absorbing foam
7. Bumper

Fig. 18 Rear bumper removal and installation — 1990-92 626/MX-6

Slide the joint sleeve upward to disengage the motor from the mast.

7. Connect a 12 volt battery and a ground wire to the **R** and **W** terminals of the motor service connector to operate the motor. Connect the negative cable to the **W** terminal and the positive cable to the **R** terminal. Carefully pull the cable from the motor housing with the motor running.

➡**Even if the mast is broken or missing, make sure that all the cable is fed from the motor.**

8. Remove the antenna base mounting screws and withdraw the antenna from the front pillar.

9. A temporary protective cover is attached with tape to each new mast kit. The cover is there to protect the plastic rack cable and to make the installation easier. Before beginning the installation, extend the mast fully.

10. Take the plastic protective cover and install it over the base of the mast to protect the plastic cable. Use the tape provided in the kit to hold the tube in place.

11. Tape the antenna plug to the tip of the protector tube so that it will not be damaged or catch on body during installation.

12. Insert the antenna mast into the roof opening and carefully and slowly feed it down at the same angle as the windshield pillar. When the mast is fully inserted into the windshield pillar, remove the plastic tube and pull the antenna lead inside the passenger compartment. Carefully feed the plastic rack cable into the motor housing. The serrated side of the cable must face toward the motor as shown in the illustration.

13. Using the 12 volt battery, connect the positive lead to the **W** terminal and the negative lead to the **R** terminal on the antenna motor service connector. Operate the motor until all of the new cable is reeled into the motor housing.

14. Push the mast base into the motor housing joint. When the mast is locked properly, a faint click will be heard. Jiggle the mast base back and forth a few times to verify that the base is locked properly.

15. Check the operation of the antenna mast. The cable slack can be self adjusted by operating the motor a few times until the mast is fully extended. Complete the installation of the remaining components by reversing the removal procedure.

Fenders

REMOVAL & INSTALLATION

Front

1. Remove the front corner turn signal assemblies.

2. Remove the headlight lens assembly by first removing the clip and the mounting bolts.

3. Remove the lower grille molding from below the headlight.

4. Remove the front mud guard and the inner fender plastic liner.

5. Remove the fender mounting bolts and remove the fender assembly.

6. Installation is the reverse of the removal procedure. Tighten the fender mounting bolts to 61-87 inch lbs. (7-10 Nm).

Convertible Top

REMOVAL & INSTALLATION

Miata

▶ **See Figure 21**

1. Release the convertible top latches, unzip the rear windows and lower the top fully.

2. Remove the beltline cover and the beltline protector.

3. Remove the door sill scuff plate and the seam welt that runs along the body seam.

4. Remove the rear quarter trim panels and the rear package trim panel.

5. Remove the set plate from around the base of the convertible top.

6. Remove the convertible top mounting nuts from around the base and the side link mounting nuts. Remove the top from the vehicle.

To install:

7. Install the convertible top to the vehicle. Make sure that the rain rail is inserted into the beltline molding lip.

8. Make sure to align the link bracket over the studs so that there is no clearance between the studs and the bracket. Tighten the link bracket bolts to 14-19 ft. lbs. (19-25 Nm).

9. Install the set plate and tighten the top mounting nuts to 69-95 inch lbs. (8-11 Nm).

10. Install the rear package trim and inside quarter trim panels.

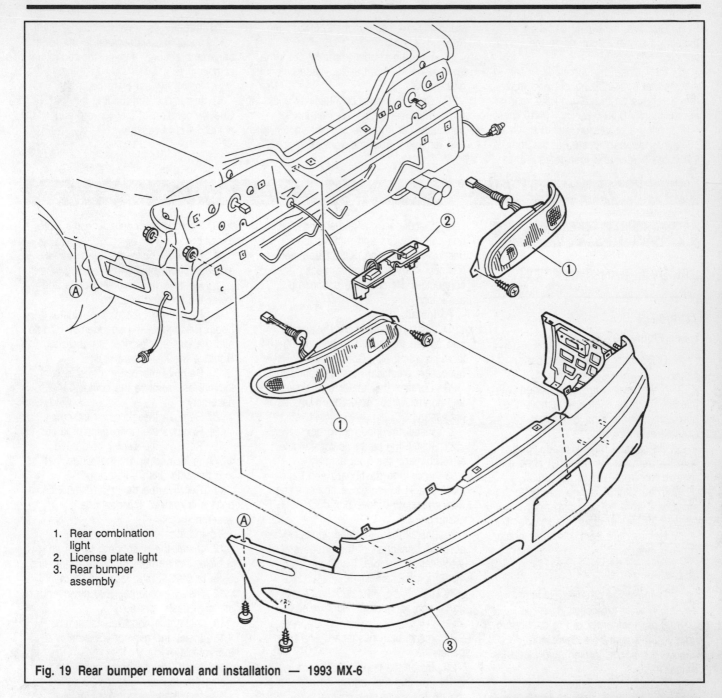

1. Rear combination light
2. License plate light
3. Rear bumper assembly

Fig. 19 Rear bumper removal and installation — 1993 MX-6

11. Install the seam welting and install the door sill scuff plates.

12. Install the beltline protector and the beltline cover.

Detachable Hard Top

REMOVAL & INSTALLATION

Miata

▶ **See Figure 22**

1. Remove the striker assemblies from the front and rear of the roof.

2. Remove the top latch assembly.

3. Remove the side latch assembly.

4. Remove the hard top mounting bolts and remove the top assembly.

5. Installation is the reverse of the removal procedure. Tighten the top and the side latch mounting bolts to 37-55 inch lbs. (4-6 Nm). Tighten the striker mounting bolts to 87-130 inch lbs. (10-15 Nm).

Power Sunroof

REMOVAL & INSTALLATION

▶ **See Figures 23, 24, 25, 26 and 27**

1. Slide the sunshade all the way to the rear position.

2. Fully close the glass sliding panel.

3. Remove the left, the right and the lower trim covers from around the sunroof perimeter.

4. Remove the 8 installation nuts from around the sliding sunroof panel and the lower panel.

5. Remove the sliding panel by pushing it upward from inside the vehicle.

6. Fully close the sunshade. Insert the manual operation handle and move the sunshade so that it is to the rear approximately 0.19-0.39 inch (5-10 mm).

7. Using a regular screwdriver, lift the sunshade stopper, located at the rear of the cable holder and then release the stopper. Move the sunshade toward the front.

8. Turn the handle and fully open the lower panel. Leave the sunshade fully closed.

9. Open the sunshade halfway and remove the set plate cap. Pull the sunshade out from the set plate notch and remove it from the vehicle.

To install:

10. Install the slide panel to the lower panel and securely tighten the mounting screws.

11. Install the set plate cap.

12. Install the surrounding trim panels. Check operation of the sunroof and adjust as is necessary.

INTERIOR

Dashboard Assembly

REMOVAL & INSTALLATION

323/Protege

▶ **See Figure 28**

1. Disconnect the negative battery cable.

2. If the vehicle is not equipped with passive restraint seatbelts, remove the rear ashtray and remove the rear console assembly.

3. On manual transaxle equipped vehicles, remove the gearshift knob and remove the front console assembly.

4. If the vehicle is equipped with the small type front console assembly, remove the center control box assembly.

5. Remove the front assembly center console inner walls.

6. Remove the glovebox under cover plate.

7. Remove the steering column assembly, refer to section 8.

8. From the center of the dashboard, remove the upper hole cover and remove the upper garnish strip along the windshield.

9. Remove the dashboard side panels.

10. Remove the hood release knob from its mounting point on the dashboard.

11. Remove the under steering column lower panel.

12. Remove the instrument cluster hood assembly.

13. Remove the instrument cluster assembly.

14. Remove the glove box door.

15. Remove the right side lower panel, located next to the glove box opening.

16. Remove the front ashtray and the center lower console assembly.

17. Remove the inner glove box cover from inside the glove box opening.

18. Disconnect the heater and blower unit control wires and remove the dashboard mounting bolts. Disconnect the necessary electrical harness connectors. Remove the dashboard assembly.

To install:

19. Install the dashboard assembly and tighten the mounting bolts to 69-104 inch lbs. (8-12 Nm).Connect the necessary electrical harness connectors.

20. Connect the heater and blower unit control wires. Adjust the wires as is necessary.

21. Install the inner glove box cover.

22. Install the center lower console assembly and the front ashtray.

23. install the dashboard end panel, located next to the glove box opening.

24. Install the glove box door assembly.

25. Install the instrument cluster. Make sure to connect all of the gauge and electrical connectors. Install the instrument cluster cover.

26. Install the left side lower trim panel and connect the hood release lever.

27. Install both dashboard end trim panels.

28. Install the upper dashboard garnish, along the windshield and install the center upper hole cover.

29. Install the steering column assembly.

30. Install the undercover panel below the glovebox.

31. Install the center console side walls.

32. Install the front and rear center console units. Install the gearshift knob.

33. Install the rear ashtray and connect the negative battery cable.

Miata

▶ **See Figure 29**

1. Disconnect the negative battery cable.

2. Remove the ashtray and remove the gearshift knob.

3. Remove the center console assembly.

4. Remove the center lower panel assembly from below the steering wheel.

5. Remove the mounting bolts and lower the steering column.

6. Remove the instrument cluster hood. Disconnect the speedometer cable and the cluster electrical connectors. Remove the instrument cluster.

7. Remove the center console vent louvers and remove the center panel assembly.

8. Remove the glovebox assembly.

9. Remove the hood release knob.

10. Remove the center hole cover which is located up by the windshield and the side dash hole covers.

11. Remove the dashboard mounting bolts and remove the dashboard assembly.

To install:

12. Install the dashboard to the vehicle. Tighten the dashboard mounting bolts to 69-104 inch lbs. (8-12 Nm).

13. Install the center hole cover and the side dash hole covers.

14. Install the hood release knob.

15. Install the glovebox assembly to the vehicle.

16. Install the panel assembly and install the console vent louvres.

17. Install the instrument cluster. Connect the speedometer cable and the electrical connectors. Install instrument cluster hood.

18. Raise the steering shaft into position and tighten the bolts to 78-122 inch lbs. (9-14 Nm).

19. Install the center lower panel to below the steering wheel.

20. Install the center console assembly.

21. Install the gearshift knob and the ashtray.

22. Connect the negative battery cable.

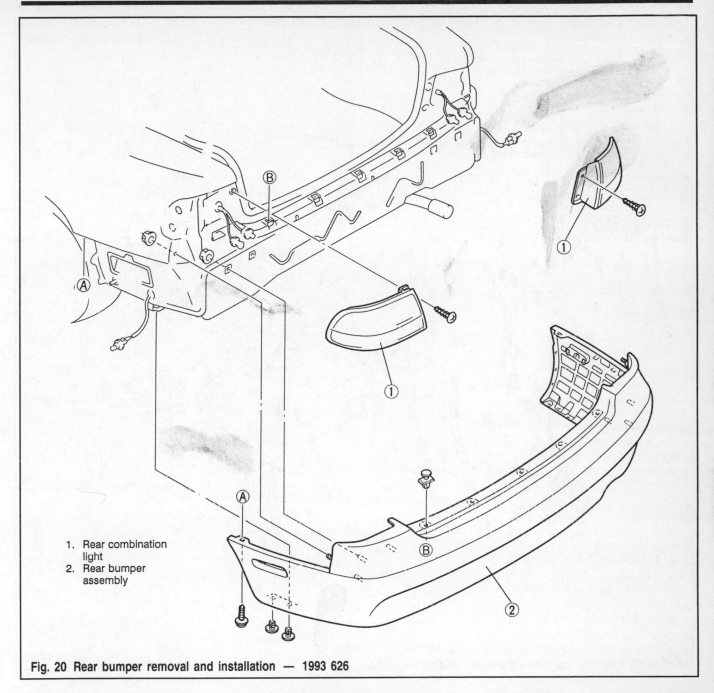

1. Rear combination light
2. Rear bumper assembly

Fig. 20 Rear bumper removal and installation — 1993 626

MX-3

▶ **See Figure 30**

1. Disconnect the negative battery cable.

2. Remove the rear ashtray and the rear portion of the center console.

3. Remove the front ashtray and the front portion of the center console.

4. Remove the front console side covers.

5. Remove the trim strip from below the glovebox.

6. Remove the steering wheel center cover and the steering wheel. Use a steering wheel puller to remove the steering wheel.

7. Remove the upper and lower steering column covers.

8. Remove the instrument cluster cover and disconnect the speedometer cable and electrical connectors from the instrument cluster.

9. Remove the instrument cluster.

10. Remove the center trim panel from around the heater controls.

11. Remove the center vent assembly from above the heater controls.

12. Remove the lower center panel assembly.

13. Remove the garnish panel along the inside of the windshield.

14. Remove the glove box assembly and remove the trim panel located next to the glove box.

15. Remove the inner glove box cover.

16. Disconnect the heater control cables from the heater unit and the blower unit and remove the heater control unit.

17. Remove the dashboard mounting bolts and remove the dashboard assembly.

To install:

18. Install the dashboard to the vehicle. Tighten the dashboard mounting bolts to 69-104 inch lbs. (8-12 Nm).

19. Connect the heater control cables and install the heater control unit. Inspect the operation of the heater control unit.

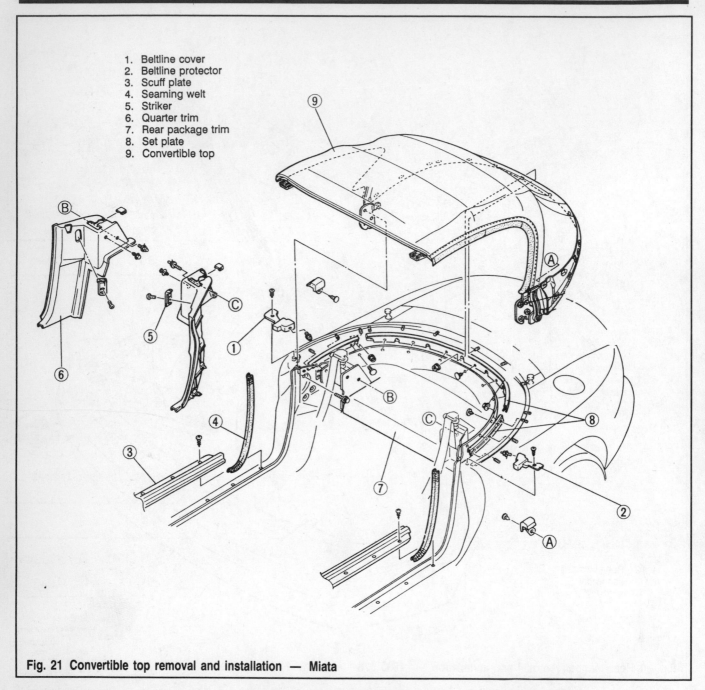

1. Beltline cover
2. Beltline protector
3. Scuff plate
4. Seaming welt
5. Striker
6. Quarter trim
7. Rear package trim
8. Set plate
9. Convertible top

Fig. 21 Convertible top removal and installation — Miata

20. Install the inner glove box panel and the trim panel located to the right of the glove box opening.

21. Install the glovebox assembly.

22. Install the left side lower trim panel, located below the steering column.

23. Install the side panels to both ends of the dashboard.

24. Install the upper garnish strip along the windshield.

25. Install the lower center panel assembly and install the vent panel above it.

26. Install the center panel to the position around the heater controls.

27. Connect the speedometer cable and electrical connectors to the

instrument cluster. Install the instrument cluster and install the cover.

28. Install the upper and lower steering column covers.

29. Install the under cover strip to below the glovebox.

30. Install the side center console panels and install the front portion of the center console.

31. Install the rear console portion and install the ashtrays.

32. Connect the negative battery cable and check to make sure all accessories are properly working.

1990-92 626/MX-6

▶ See Figure 31

1. Disconnect the negative battery cable.

2. If the vehicle is equipped with an automatic transaxle, remove the screws and shift lever knob. If the vehicle is equipped with a manual transaxle, twist off the shifter knob.

3. Remove the rear center console mounting screws and remove the rear center console.

4. Remove the front center console mounting screws.

5. Remove the steering wheel center ornament and remove the mounting nut. From the back of the steering wheel,

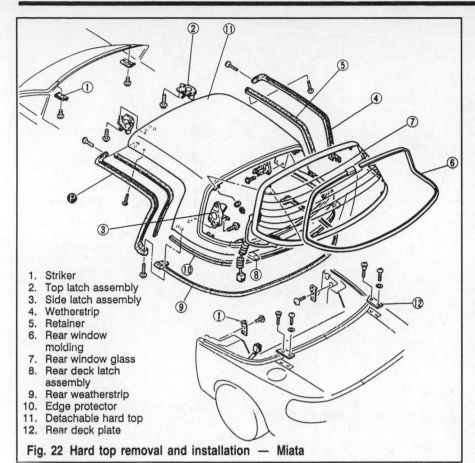

1. Striker
2. Top latch assembly
3. Side latch assembly
4. Wetherstrip
5. Retainer
6. Rear window molding
7. Rear window glass
8. Rear deck latch assembly
9. Rear weatherstrip
10. Edge protector
11. Detachable hard top
12. Rear deck plate

Fig. 22 Hard top removal and installation — Miata

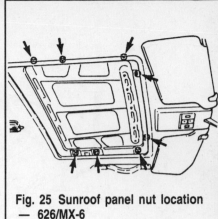

Fig. 25 Sunroof panel nut location — 626/MX-6

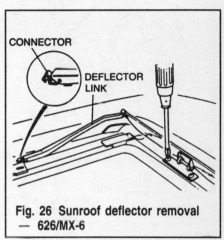

Fig. 26 Sunroof deflector removal — 626/MX-6

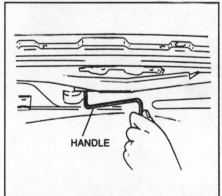

HANDLE

Fig. 23 Turning the sunroof override handle to move the sunshade to the rear for sunroof removal — 626/MX-6

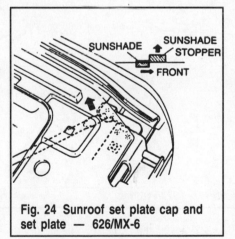

SUNSHADE   SUNSHADE STOPPER
FRONT

Fig. 24 Sunroof set plate cap and set plate — 626/MX-6

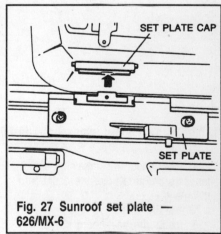

SET PLATE CAP

SET PLATE

Fig. 27 Sunroof set plate — 626/MX-6

remove the center cap mounting screws and remove the center cap.

6. Using a steering wheel puller, remove the steering wheel puller.

7. Remove the upper and lower steering column covers.

8. Remove the under column panel mounting screws and remove the panel. Remove the hood release.

9. Remove the instrument cluster screws and pull the cluster away from the dashboard. Disconnect the electrical connectors and the speedometer cable

and remove the instrument cluster assembly.

10. Remove the lower dash panel mounting screws and pull the panel away so that the switch electrical connectors can be disconnected. Disconnect the switches and remove the panel.

11. Remove the glove box assembly and disconnect the glove box light connector.

12. Remove the center trim panel, around the radio and the heater controls.

13. Remove the heater control assembly screws and slide the assembly

out to disconnect the electrical and/or control cables.

14. Remove the center dashboard cap from near the windshield and remove the dashboard mounting bolt.

15. Remove the side dashboard and the center mounting bolts from below the center console.

16. From under the dashboard, remove the steering shaft mounting bolts.

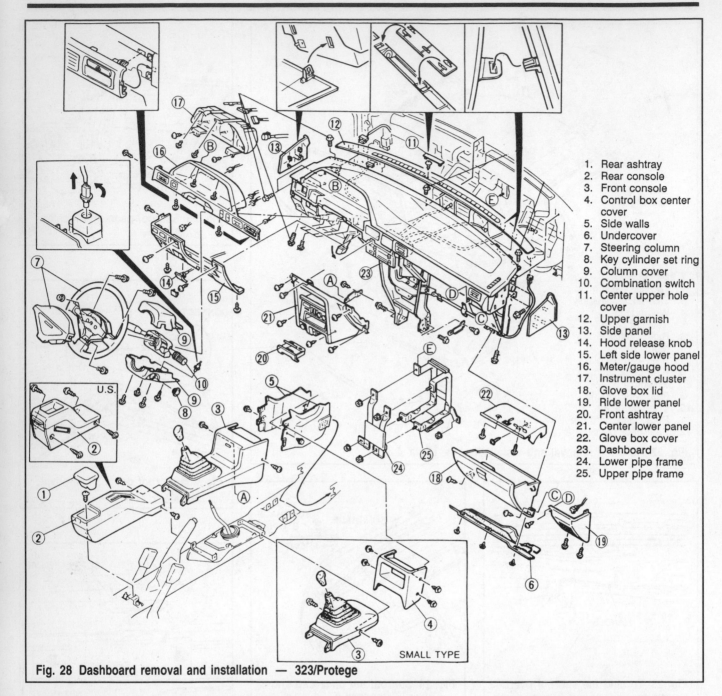

Fig. 28 Dashboard removal and installation — 323/Protege

1. Rear ashtray
2. Rear console
3. Front console
4. Control box center cover
5. Side walls
6. Undercover
7. Steering column
8. Key cylinder set ring
9. Column cover
10. Combination switch
11. Center upper hole cover
12. Upper garnish
13. Side panel
14. Hood release knob
15. Left side lower panel
16. Meter/gauge hood
17. Instrument cluster
18. Glove box lid
19. Ride lower panel
20. Front ashtray
21. Center lower panel
22. Glove box cover
23. Dashboard
24. Lower pipe frame
25. Upper pipe frame

17. Disconnect the remaining electrical connectors and remove the dashboard assembly.

To install:

18. Install the dashboard to the vehicle. Connect the electrical connectors. Install the top center bolt and tighten to 3-5 ft. lbs. (4-6 Nm).

19. Install the end dashboard and center console mounting bolts and tighten to 7-10 ft. lbs. (9-14 Nm).

20. Install the steering column mounting bolts and tighten to 7-10 ft. lbs. (9-14 Nm).

21. Connect the heater control cables/connector and adjust as necessary.

22. Install the center trim panel to around the radio and heater control panel.

23. Install the glove box assembly and connect the glove box light connector.

24. Connect the switch panel electrical connectors and install the lower dash panel.

25. Connect the speedometer cable and the instrument cluster connectors. Install the instrument cluster assembly and the instrument cluster hood.

26. Connect the hood release knob to the under dash cover and install the cover.

27. Install the steering column upper and lower covers.

28. Install the steering wheel and tighten the center bolt to 29-36 ft. lbs. (39-49 Nm).

29. Install the steering wheel caps.

30. Install the center console unit and install the shift lever knob. Connect the negative battery cable and check all accesories for proper operation.

1993 626/MX-6

▶ **See Figures 32 and 33**

1. Disconnect the negative battery cable and properly disengage the airbag.

2. Remove the steering wheel pad/air bag module. Refer to section 6.

3. Remove the steering wheel, using a steering wheel puller.

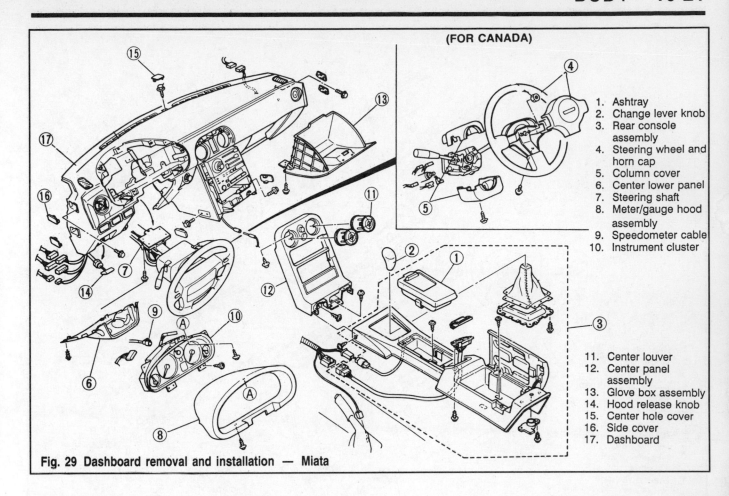

(FOR CANADA)

1. Ashtray
2. Change lever knob
3. Rear console assembly
4. Steering wheel and horn cap
5. Column cover
6. Center lower panel
7. Steering shaft
8. Meter/gauge hood assembly
9. Speedometer cable
10. Instrument cluster

11. Center louver
12. Center panel assembly
13. Glove box assembly
14. Hood release knob
15. Center hole cover
16. Side cover
17. Dashboard

Fig. 29 Dashboard removal and installation — Miata

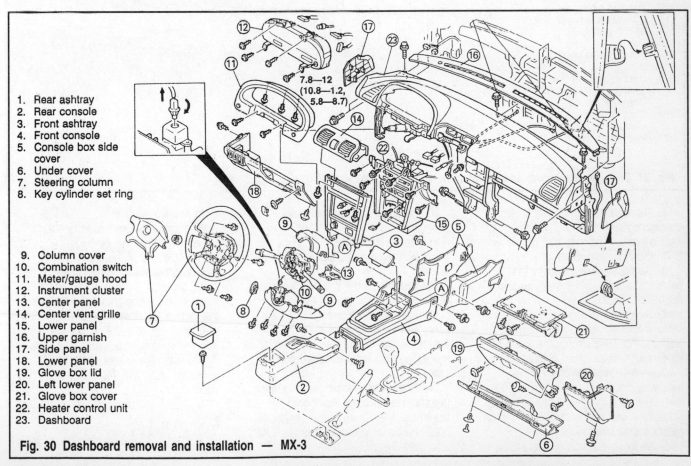

1. Rear ashtray
2. Rear console
3. Front ashtray
4. Front console
5. Console box side cover
6. Under cover
7. Steering column
8. Key cylinder set ring

9. Column cover
10. Combination switch
11. Meter/gauge hood
12. Instrument cluster
13. Center panel
14. Center vent grille
15. Lower panel
16. Upper garnish
17. Side panel
18. Lower panel
19. Glove box lid
20. Left lower panel
21. Glove box cover
22. Heater control unit
23. Dashboard

7.8—12
(10.8—1.2,
5.8—8.7)

Fig. 30 Dashboard removal and installation — MX-3

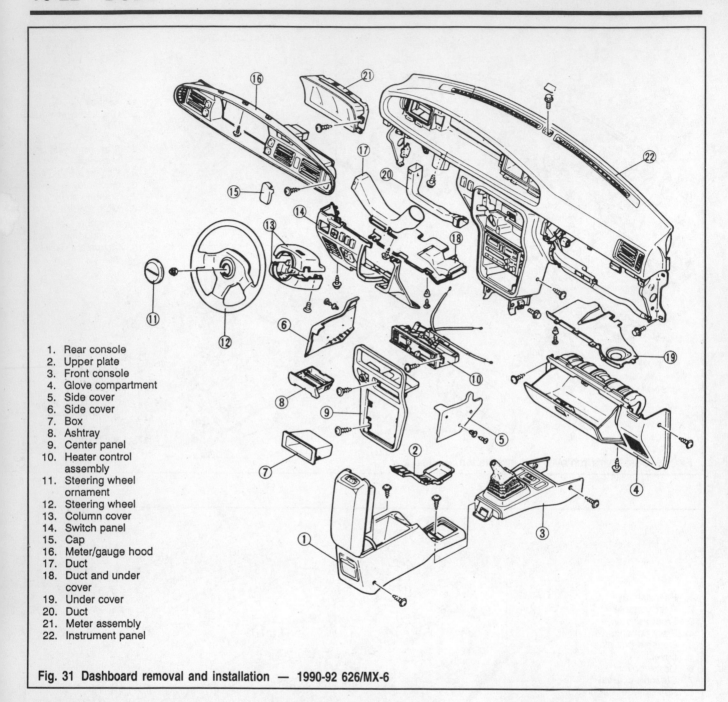

1. Rear console
2. Upper plate
3. Front console
4. Glove compartment
5. Side cover
6. Side cover
7. Box
8. Ashtray
9. Center panel
10. Heater control assembly
11. Steering wheel ornament
12. Steering wheel
13. Column cover
14. Switch panel
15. Cap
16. Meter/gauge hood
17. Duct
18. Duct and under cover
19. Under cover
20. Duct
21. Meter assembly
22. Instrument panel

Fig. 31 Dashboard removal and installation — 1990-92 626/MX-6

4. Remove the upper and lower steering column covers.

5. Remove the side trim panels from both ends of the dashboard.

6. Remove the emergency brake handle and remove the left side lower dash trim panel.

7. Remove the dash switch panel screws, located above the steering column. Pull the switch panel out and disconnect the electrical connectors. Remove the dash switch panel assembly.

8. Remove the gearshift knob as is necessary and remove the front portion of the center console.

9. Remove the rear portion of the center console unit.

10. Remove the center console sidewalls.

11. Remove the under glovebox trim panel and remove the glovebox assembly.

12. Disconnect the connections and remove the heater control assembly.

13. Remove the instrument cluster hood and the instrument cluster assembly. Make sure to disconnect all of the connectors and the speedometer cable.

14. Remove the dashboard mounting bolts and remove the dashboard assembly. Make sure to disconnect all necessary electrical connectors.

To install:

15. Install the dashboard to the vehicle. Connect the electrical connectors. Install the dashboard mounting bolts and tighten to 6-8 ft. lbs. (8-11 Nm).

16. Install the instrument cluster and the instrument cluster hood. Make sure to connect all of the electrical connectors and the speedometer cable.

17. Install the heater control unit assembly. Connect the electrical connectors.

18. Install the glove compartment and the undercovering.

19. Install the center console assembly.

20. Install the gearshift knob assembly.

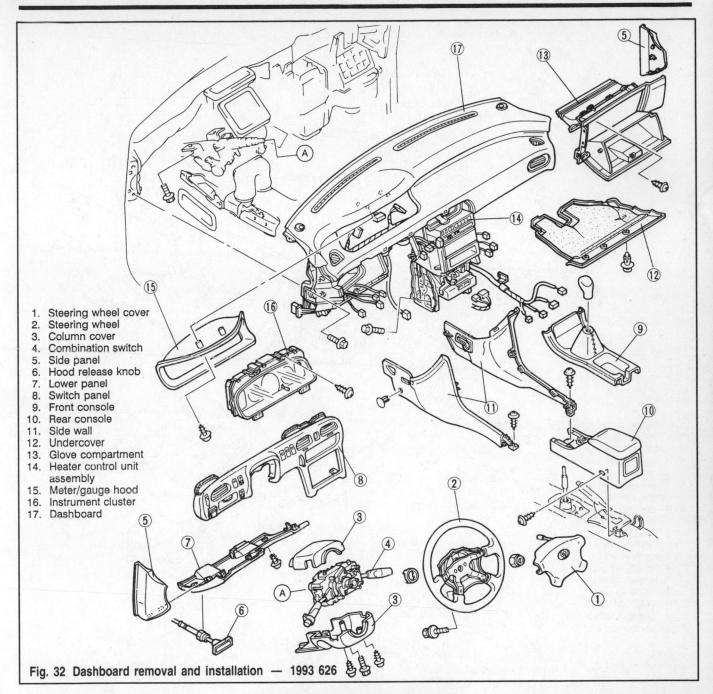

1. Steering wheel cover
2. Steering wheel
3. Column cover
4. Combination switch
5. Side panel
6. Hood release knob
7. Lower panel
8. Switch panel
9. Front console
10. Rear console
11. Side wall
12. Undercover
13. Glove compartment
14. Heater control unit
    assembly
15. Meter/gauge hood
16. Instrument cluster
17. Dashboard

Fig. 32 Dashboard removal and installation — 1993 626

21. Install the dash switch panel assembly.

22. Install the emergency brake handle and the left side lower dash trim panel.

23. Install the end dashboard trim panels.

24. Install the upper and lower steering column covers and the steering wheel. Tighten the steering wheel nut to 29-36 ft. lbs. (39-49 Nm).

25. Install the steering wheel pad/air bag module, refer to section 6.

26. Connect the negative battery cable and check all accesories for proper operation.

Door Panels

REMOVAL & INSTALLATION

▶ See Figure 34

1. Remove the window regulator handle, on non-power window equipped vehicles.

2. Remove the arm rest as required.

3. Remove the door lock knob if necessary.

4. Remove the inner door handle cover.

5. Using a flat screwdriver with the blade wrapped in tape, gently separate the door trim panel clips from the door.

6. Remove the door trim panel.

To install:

7. Place the door trim panel into position on the door.

8. Apply pressure to the trim panel in the areas where the trim panel clips attach to the door.

9. Install the inner door handle cover, door lock knob and the arm rest.

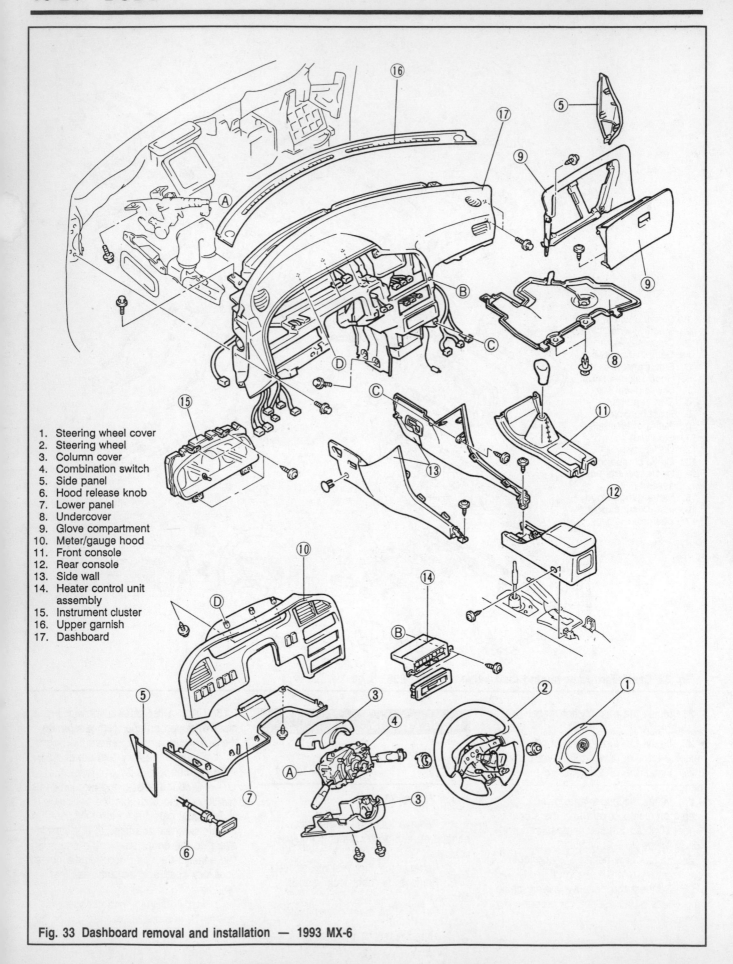

1. Steering wheel cover
2. Steering wheel
3. Column cover
4. Combination switch
5. Side panel
6. Hood release knob
7. Lower panel
8. Undercover
9. Glove compartment
10. Meter/gauge hood
11. Front console
12. Rear console
13. Side wall
14. Heater control unit assembly
15. Instrument cluster
16. Upper garnish
17. Dashboard

Fig. 33 Dashboard removal and installation — 1993 MX-6

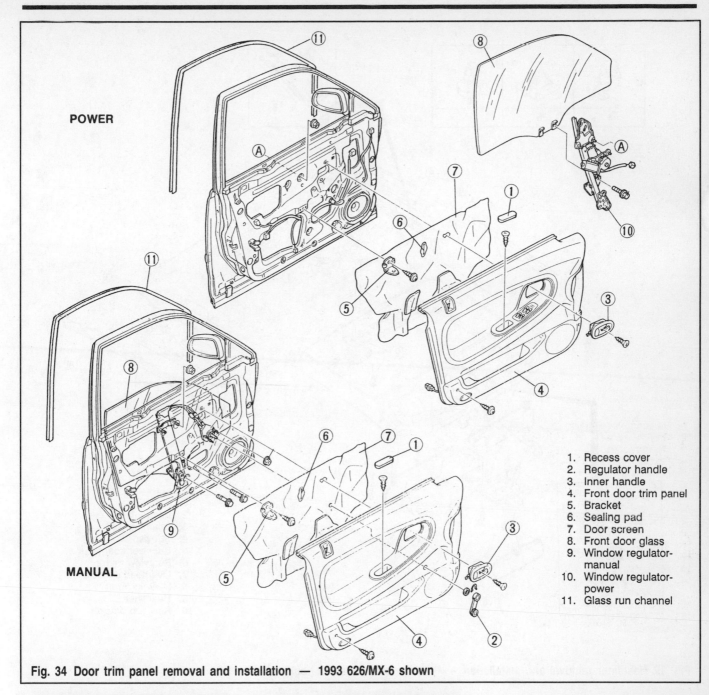

POWER

MANUAL

1. Recess cover
2. Regulator handle
3. Inner handle
4. Front door trim panel
5. Bracket
6. Sealing pad
7. Door screen
8. Front door glass
9. Window regulator-manual
10. Window regulator-power
11. Glass run channel

Fig. 34 Door trim panel removal and installation — 1993 626/MX-6 shown

Interior Trim Panels

REMOVAL & INSTALLATION

1. Pull up or out on the trim panel to remove the trim panel.

2. To install, simply align the push clips with the mounting holes and press into place until the clip engages.

Headliner

REMOVAL & INSTALLATION

323/Protege

▶ **See Figures 35 and 36**

1. Remove the rear assist handles.

2. Remove the interior lamp lens and remove the lamp assembly.

3. If the vehicle is equipped with a sunroof, remove the seaming welt from around the sunroof.

4. Remove the front sunvisors and the front sunvisor side clips.

5. Remove the rearview mirror and if the vehicle is equipped with a sunroof, remove the overhead console.

6. On the Protege, remove the pillar seaming welt. Carefully peel back the edges of the headliner and remove the headliner assembly from the vehicle.

To install:

7. Install the headliner to the vehicle, apply double sided tape to the edges of the headliner.

8. Make sure to seat all headliner fasteners.

9. Install the overhead console (if equipped) and install the rearview mirror.

10. Install the sunvisors and sunvisor clips.

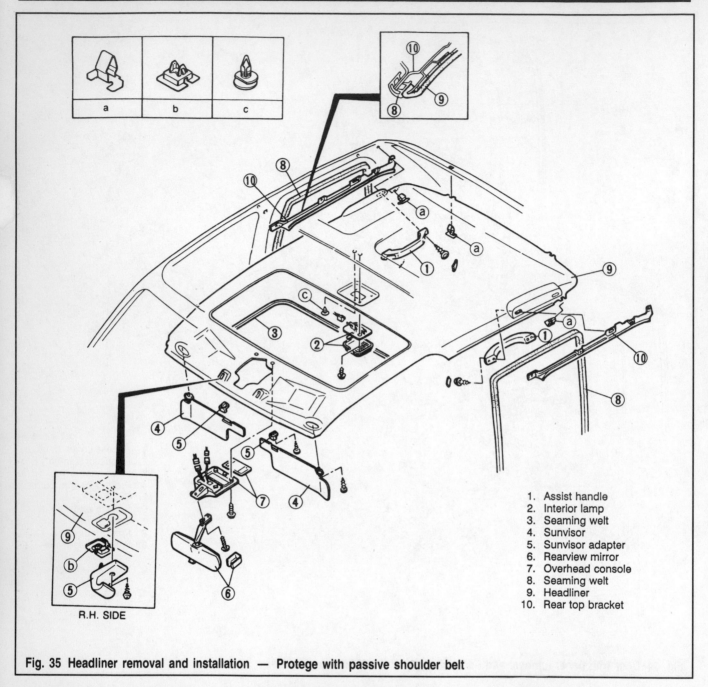

Fig. 35 Headliner removal and installation — Protege with passive shoulder belt

1. Assist handle
2. Interior lamp
3. Seaming welt
4. Sunvisor
5. Sunvisor adapter
6. Rearview mirror
7. Overhead console
8. Seaming welt
9. Headliner
10. Rear top bracket

R.H. SIDE

11. Install the sunroof and pillar seaming welt.

12. Install the interior lamp assembly and install the rear assist handles.

MX-3

▶ **See Figures 37 and 38**

1. Disconnect the negative battery cable.

2. Remove the rearview mirror.

3. Remove the sunvisors and side clips.

4. Remove the overhead console/light assembly and the assist handle.

5. Remove the seaming welt from along the door edges.

6. Remove the A-pillar trim from along the windshield.

7. Remove the rear quarter trim panel from next to the rear seat.

8. Remove the B-pillar trim panel from along the rear window.

9. Remove the headliner fastener from below the sunvisor side clips.

10. If the vehicle is equipped with a sunroof, remove the sunroof seaming welt from around the sunroof and unfold the clips at the sunroof edge.

11. Carefully pull down on the headliner to disengage the mounting clips and remove the headliner.

To install:

12. Install the headliner to the vehicle and align the clips with the holes and engage the mounting clips.

13. If the vehicle is equipped with a sunroof, fold the headliner hooks onto the sunroof frame flange. Install the sunroof seaming welt.

14. Install the front headliner fastening clips.

15. Install the B-pillar trim panel, the rear quarter trim panel and the A-pillar trim panel.

16. Install the seaming welt along the door edges.

17. Install the overhead console/light assembly and the assist handle.

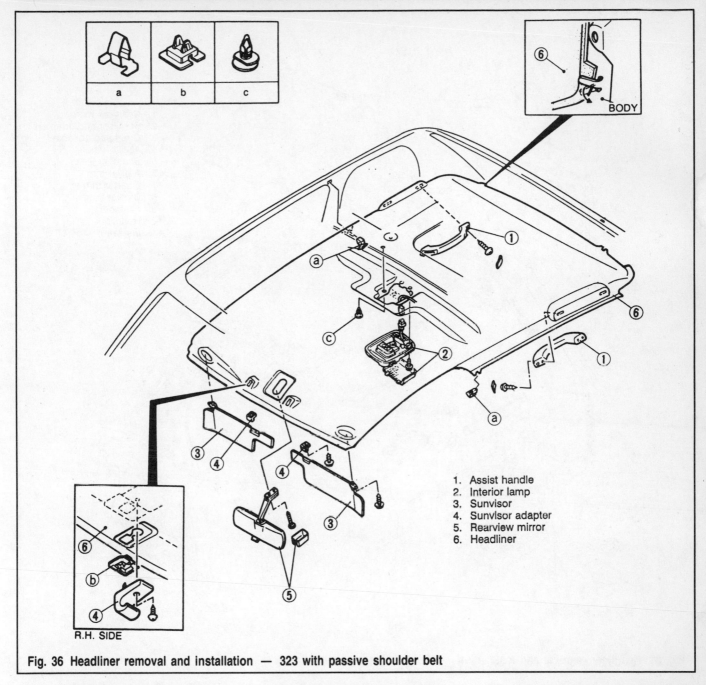

Fig. 36 Headliner removal and installation — 323 with passive shoulder belt

1. Assist handle
2. Interior lamp
3. Sunvisor
4. Sunvisor adapter
5. Rearview mirror
6. Headliner

18. Install the sunvisors with the side clips and install the rearview mirror.
19. Connect the negative battery cable.

1990-92 626/MX-6
▶ See Figures 39 and 40

1. Remove the rearview mirror and center overhead console.
2. Remove the sunvisors and side clips.
3. Remove the overhead assist handles.
4. Remove the interior light assembly and the front header trim strip along the top of the windshield.

5. Remove the front pillar trim and the rear pillar trim panel.
6. Remove the rear header trim strip from along the top of the rear windshield.
7. Remove the sunroof fasteners from along the sides of the headliner and remove the headliner.

To install:

8. Install the headliner to the vehicle and install the clips.
9. Install the rear header trim strip.
10. Install the front and rear pillar trim panels.
11. Install the front trim strip to along the windshield and install the interior light.

12. Install the overhead assist handles and the sunvisors.
13. Install the rearview mirror and the center overhead console.

1993 626/MX-6
▶ See Figure 41

1. Disconnect the negative battery cable.
2. On the 626, remove the center overhead console unit.
3. Remove the sunvisors and side clips.
4. Remove the assist handle(s).
5. On the 626, remove the interior lamp assembly.

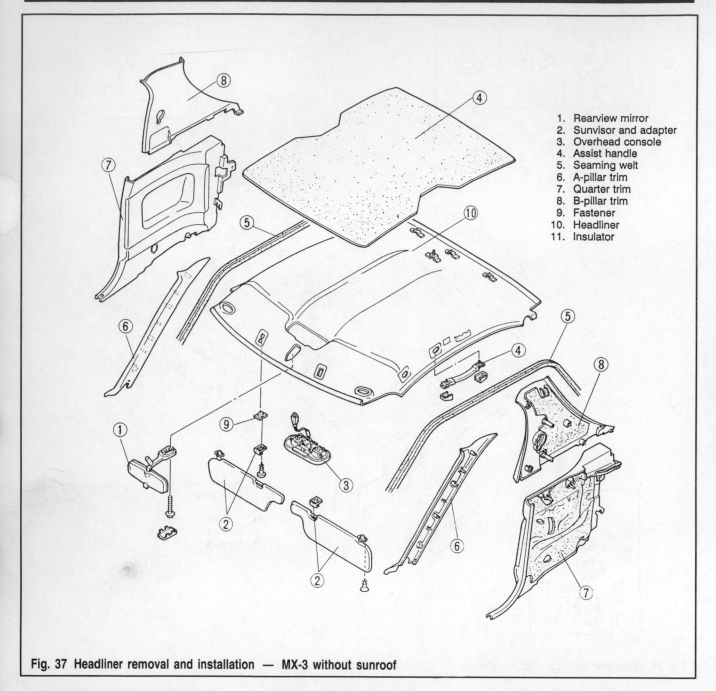

1. Rearview mirror
2. Sunvisor and adapter
3. Overhead console
4. Assist handle
5. Seaming welt
6. A-pillar trim
7. Quarter trim
8. B-pillar trim
9. Fastener
10. Headliner
11. Insulator

Fig. 37 Headliner removal and installation — MX-3 without sunroof

6. Remove the seaming welt from around the sunroof, if so equipped.

7. Remove the headliner mounting clips and screws and remove the headliner assembly.

To install:

8. Install the headliner and install the clips and screws. Make sure that all of the clips are fully seated.

9. If equipped with a sunroof, install the seaming welt to the sunroof perimeter.

10. Install the interior light assembly to the 626.

11. Install the assist handle(s).

12. Install the sunvisors and the side clips. On the 626, install the center overhead console unit.

13. Connect the negative battery cable.

Door Locks

REMOVAL & INSTALLATION

1. Disconnect the negative battery cable.

2. Remove the inner door panel and remove the inner door screening.

3. If the locks are power, disconnect the power lock controller from the lock assembly.

4. Remove the door lock mounting screws and disconnect the linkage.

Remove the lock assembly from the door.

5. Installation is the reverse of the removal procedure. Tighten the door lock mounting screw(s) to 37-55 inch lbs. (4.2-6.2 Nm).

Door Glass and Regulator

REMOVAL & INSTALLATION

▶ See Figures 42, 43 and 44

1. Lower the window glass and remove the inner handle cover, door lock

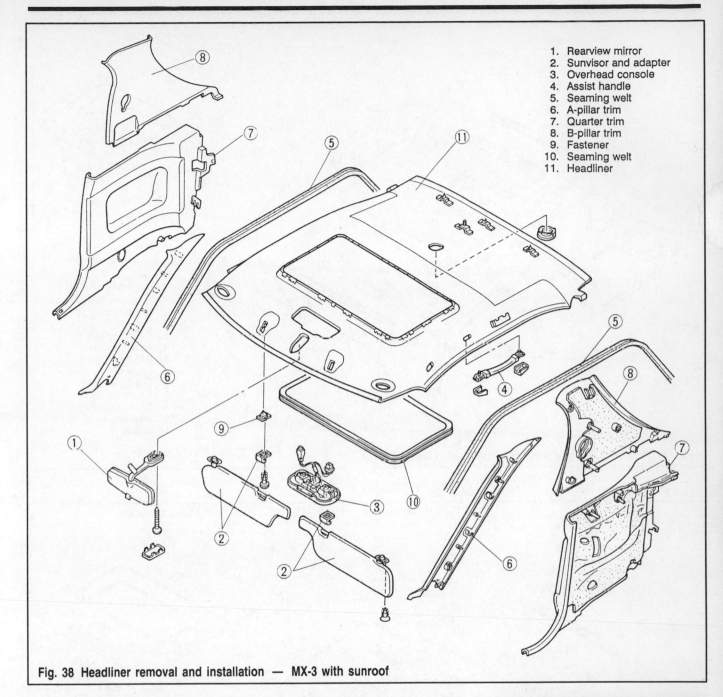

1. Rearview mirror
2. Sunvisor and adapter
3. Overhead console
4. Assist handle
5. Seaming welt
6. A-pillar trim
7. Quarter trim
8. B-pillar trim
9. Fastener
10. Seaming welt
11. Headliner

Fig. 38 Headliner removal and installation — MX-3 with sunroof

knob (if necessary), the window regulator handle and the door trim panel.

➡On vehicles with power windows, disconnect the wiring couplings.

2. Carefully peel off the door screen so that it can be reused.

3. Replace the window regulator handle and position the door glass so that the door glass installation bolts can be removed from the service hole.

4. Remove the door glass installation bolts.

5. Remove the door glass. Remove the regulator installation bolts, and then remove the regulator through the service access hole. Remove the window motor

mounting bolts and separate the motor from the regulator.

6. Installation is the reverse of the removal procedure. If the the vehicle is equipped with power windows, connect the leads of the motor to a battery and run the regulator to the down position before installing the motor. Cycle the window several times to make sure that everything is in good working order.

Electric Window Motor

REMOVAL & INSTALLATION

1. Disconnect the negative battery cable.

2. Remove the door panel and the inner door sheilding from the door.

3. Disconnect the power window motor electrical connector from inside the door.

4. Prop the window in the up position and remove the window motor mounting bolts from the door. Remove the window motor from the door.

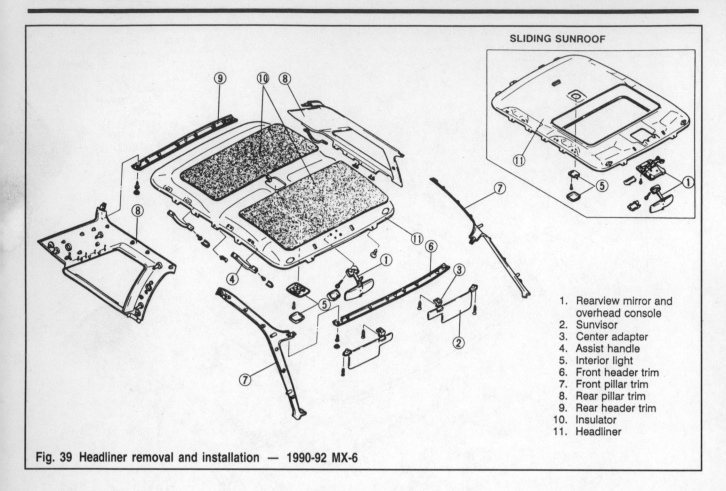

SLIDING SUNROOF

1. Rearview mirror and overhead console
2. Sunvisor
3. Center adapter
4. Assist handle
5. Interior light
6. Front header trim
7. Front pillar trim
8. Rear pillar trim
9. Rear header trim
10. Insulator
11. Headliner

Fig. 39 Headliner removal and installation — 1990-92 MX-6

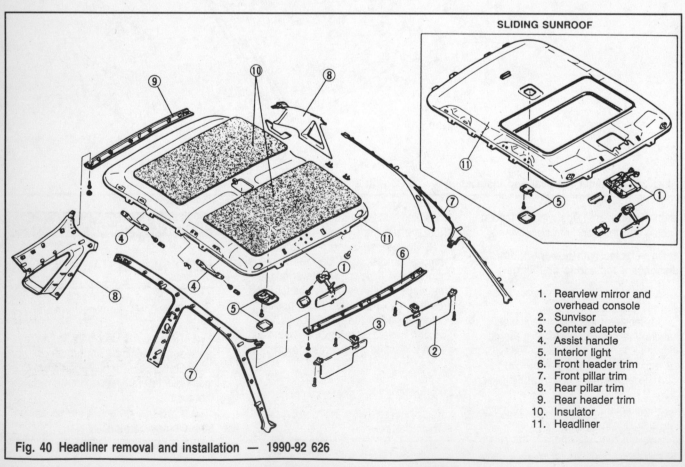

SLIDING SUNROOF

1. Rearview mirror and overhead console
2. Sunvisor
3. Center adapter
4. Assist handle
5. Interior light
6. Front header trim
7. Front pillar trim
8. Rear pillar trim
9. Rear header trim
10. Insulator
11. Headliner

Fig. 40 Headliner removal and installation — 1990-92 626

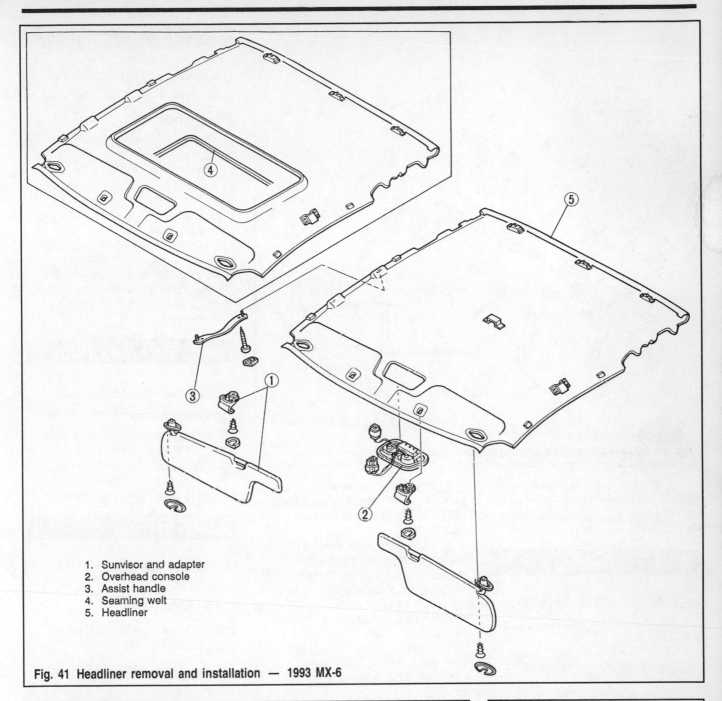

1. Sunvisor and adapter
2. Overhead console
3. Assist handle
4. Seaming welt
5. Headliner

Fig. 41 Headliner removal and installation — 1993 MX-6

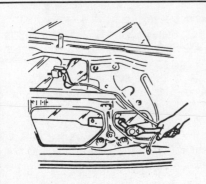

Fig. 42 Removing the door glass from the window regulator

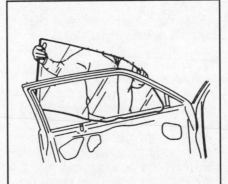

Fig. 43 Removing the door glass from the door

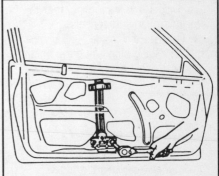

Fig. 44 Removal and installation of the window regulator

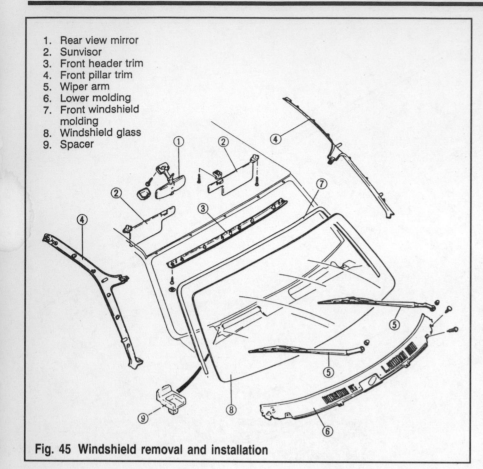

1. Rear view mirror
2. Sunvisor
3. Front header trim
4. Front pillar trim
5. Wiper arm
6. Lower molding
7. Front windshield molding
8. Windshield glass
9. Spacer

Fig. 45 Windshield removal and installation

5. Installation is the reverse of the removal procedure. Tighten the motor mounting bolts to 61-87 inch lbs. (6.9-9.8 Nm).

Windshield Glass

REMOVAL & INSTALLATION

▶ **See Figure 45**

1. Disconnect the negative battery cable.
2. From inside the vehicle, remove the sunvisors and visor clips, rearview mirror and overhead console.
3. Remove the inside A-pillar trim and the molding strip along the bottom of the windshield and the dashboard.
4. From outside of the vehicle, remove the windshield wiper arms and the cowl panel along the front of the windshield.
5. From under the cowl panel, remove the glass stopper strip.
6. Carefully remove the top windshield trim strip.
7. Apply protective tape along all exposed body areas and along the inside of the headliner.

8. From inside the vehicle, use an awl and carefully punch a hole through the windshield sealant at the edge of the body.
9. Insert a length of piano wire through the hole and working with an assistant, carefully guide the wire around the perimeter of the windshield glass.
10. With an assistant helping lift the windshield out and away from the vehicle.
   To install:
11. Clean the old sealant material from around the inside windshield perimeter.
12. Apply the bonding material to the perimeter of the windshield glass and apply the primer agent to around the edge of the body. Allow the primer to dry for approximately 30 minutes.
13. Apply a continuous bead of sealant around the windshield and immediately install the upper windshield molding.
14. Install the glass stopper strip to it's position below the windshield. Install the cowl panel and the wiper arms.
15. Install the A-pillar trim panels and the sunvisors.
16. Install the rearview mirror and the overhead console assembly. Connect the negative battery cable.

Rear Quarter Glass

REMOVAL & INSTALLATION

Pop-Out Type

1. From inside the vehicle, remove the seat belt anchor from in front of the side window.
2. Remove the interior pillar trim panel from in front of the window.
3. Remove the quarter window latch from the window.
4. Remove the window hinge bolts and remove the window assembly.
5. Installation is the reverse of the removal procedure. Tighten the window hinge mounting bolts to 69-95 inch lbs. (7.8-11 Nm).

Inside Rear View Mirror

REMOVAL & INSTALLATION

Removal of the rearview mirror is simply a matter of removing the mounting screws and removing the mirror assembly. Installation is the reverse of the removal procedure.

Seats

REMOVAL & INSTALLATION

▶ **See Figures 46 and 47**

323/Protege and 1993 626/MX-6

FRONT

1. If the vehicle is equipped with passive shoulder belt type seat belts, disconnect the buckle switch electrical connector from under the seat.
2. Remove the seat slide rear covers.
3. Slide the seat forward and remove the rear mounting bolts.
4. Slide the seat to the rear and remove the front mounting bolts.
5. Remove the seat(s) from the vehicle.
6. Installation is the reverse of the removal procedure. Tighten the mounting bolts to 28-38 ft. lbs. (38-51 Nm).

REAR

1. From under the front of the rear seat bottom cushion, release the seat cushion locks by pushing the latch in.

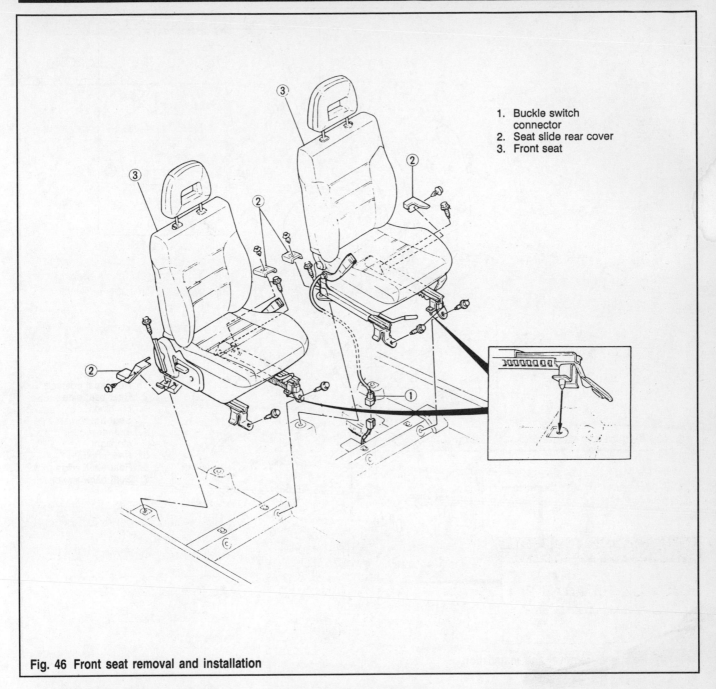

1. Buckle switch connector
2. Seat slide rear cover
3. Front seat

Fig. 46 Front seat removal and installation

2. If the vehicle has the folding rear seat, remove the side cushion peices first by removing the bolts and lifting up.

3. Remove the bolts and/or nuts from the base of the back cushion(s) and lift the back cushion up and off of the fastening hooks.

4. Installation is the reverse of the removal procedure. Tighten the seat back bolts to 12-17 ft. lbs. (16-23 Nm).

Miata

1. Slide the seat forward and remove the rear mounting bolts.

2. Slide the seat to the rear and remove the front mounting bolts.

3. Remove the seat(s) from the vehicle.

4. Installation is the reverse of removal procedure. Tighten the mounting bolts to 28-38 ft. lbs. (38-51 Nm).

MX-3 and 1990-92 626/MX-6

FRONT

1. Slide the seat forward and remove the rear mounting bolts.

2. Slide the seat to the rear and remove the front mounting bolts.

3. Remove the seat(s) from the vehicle.

4. Installation is the reverse of the removal procedure. Tighten the mounting bolts to 28-38 ft. lbs. (38-51 Nm).

REAR

1. From under the front of the rear seat bottom cushion, release the seat cushion locks by sliding them to the center.

2. Lift the cushion up and out of the vehicle.

3. Remove the bolts from the back cushion and lift the back cushion up and off of the fastening hooks.

4. Installation is the reverse of the removal procedure. Tighten the seat back bolts to 12-17 ft. lbs. (16-23 Nm).

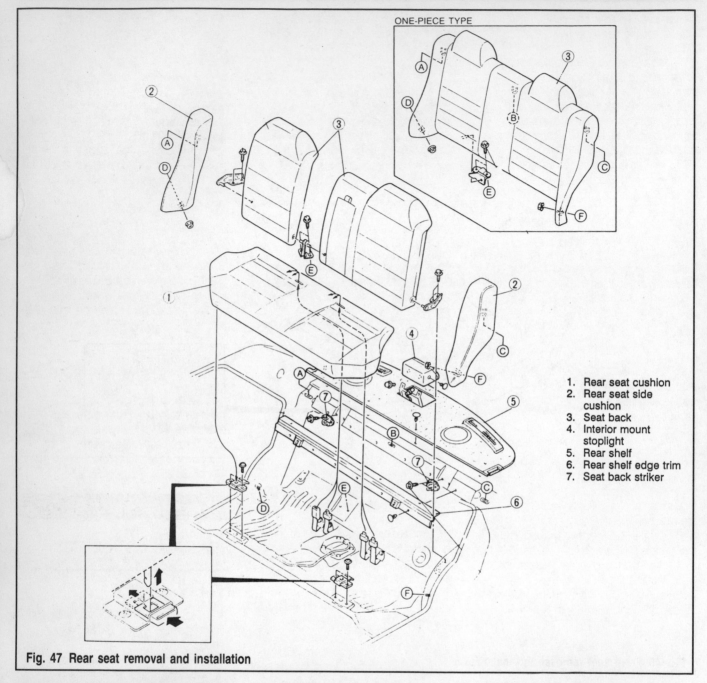

ONE-PIECE TYPE

1. Rear seat cushion
2. Rear seat side cushion
3. Seat back
4. Interior mount stoplight
5. Rear shelf
6. Rear shelf edge trim
7. Seat back striker

Fig. 47 Rear seat removal and installation

Seat Belt Systems

REMOVAL & INSTALLATION

▶ See Figure 48

323/Protege

FRONT — NON-MOTORIZED SEAT BELT SYSTEM

1. From inside the door, remove the lower scuff plate.

2. On the Protege, remove the lower B-pillar trim panel and on the 323, remove the rear quarter trim panel.

3. Remove the front seat belt retaining bolts and remove the seat belt assembly.

4. Installation is the reverse of the removal procedure. Tighten the mounting bolts to 28-58 ft. lbs. (38-78 Nm).

FRONT — MOTORIZED PASSIVE SEAT BELT SYSTEM

1. Disconnect the negative battery cable.

2. From inside the door, remove the lower scuff plate.

3. On the Protege, remove the lower B-pillar trim panel and on the 323, remove the rear quarter trim panel.

4. Remove the A-pillar trim panel from around the inside of the door.

5. Disconnect the electrical connectors at the shoulder belt system and remove the mounting bolts. Remove the passive shoulder belt system.

6. Remove the lap belt mounting bolts and remove the lap belt assembly.

7. Unbolt the lap belt buckle and remove the lap belt buckle assembly.

8. Remove the rear center console mounting screws and lift the console out of the way.

9. Disconnect the electrical connector at the center passive shoulder belt unit assembly and remove the unit mounting bolts. Remove the passive shoulder belt unit.

10. Remove the front seat as described earlier in this section. Remove

the passive shoulder belt control unit from under the seat.

To install:

11. Install the passive shoulder belt control unit to under the seat. Install the front seat.

12. Install the passive shoulder belt retractor unit. Connect the electrical connector and tighten the mounting bolts to 28-58 ft. lbs. (38-78 Nm).

13. Install the rear center console unit.

14. Install the lap belt buckle and tighten the mounting bolts to 28-58 ft. lbs. (38-78 Nm).

15. Install the lap belt assembly and tighten the mounting bolts to 28-58 ft. lbs. (38-78 Nm).

16. Install the passive shoulder belt assembly and tighten the mounting bolts. Tighten the 3 top bolts and the lower bolt to 69-104 inch lbs. (8-12 Nm). Tighten the 2 side bolts, closest to the seat belt buckle to 13-19 ft. lbs. (18-25 Nm).

17. Install the A-pillar trim, the B-pillar trim and the lower scuff plate.

18. Connect the negative battery cable.

REAR

1. Remove the rear seat cushion assembly.

2. On the Protege, remove the high mount center brake light assembly and the rear shelf assembly.

3. On the 323, remove the rear trunk trim panels.

4. Remove the seat belt assemblies.

5. Installation is the reverse of the removal procedure. Tighten the mounting bolts to 28-58 ft. lbs. (38-78 Nm).

Miata

1. Remove the rear quarter interior trim panel.

2. Remove the seat belt anchor cover and remove the seat belt assembly mounting bolts.

3. Remove the seat belt assembly.

4. Installation is the reverse of the removal procedure. Tighten the mounting bolts to 28-58 ft. lbs. (38-78 Nm).

MX-3

FRONT

1. From inside the door, remove the lower scuff plate.

2. Remove the rear quarter trim panel.

3. Remove the upper anchor bolt and the lower slide bar bolt. Remove the seat belt assembly.

4. Installation is the reverse of the removal procedure. Tighten the mounting bolts to 28-58 ft. lbs. (38-78 Nm).

REAR

1. Remove the rear seat cushion assembly.

2. Remove the rear speaker covers.

3. Remove the seat belt assemblies.

4. Installation is the reverse of the removal procedure. Tighten the mounting bolts to 28-58 ft. lbs. (38-78 Nm).

1990-92 626/MX-6

FRONT — NON-MOTORIZED SEAT BELT SYSTEM

1. Remove the seat belt bolt caps and remove the front seat belt retaining bolts. Remove the seat belt assembly.

2. Installation is the reverse of the removal procedure. Tighten the mounting bolts to 28-39 ft. lbs. (39-55 Nm).

FRONT — MOTORIZED PASSIVE SEAT BELT SYSTEM

1. Disconnect the negative battery cable.

2. From inside the door, remove the front pillar trim panel. Remove the rear pillar trim panel the side trim.

3. Disconnect the electrical connectors at the shoulder belt system and remove the mounting bolts. Remove the passive shoulder belt system.

4. Remove the lap belt mounting bolts and remove the lap belt assembly.

5. Unbolt the lap belt buckle and remove the lap belt buckle assembly.

6. Remove the rear center console mounting screws and lift the console out of the way.

7. Disconnect the electrical connector at the center passive shoulder belt unit assembly and remove the unit mounting bolts. Remove the passive shoulder belt unit.**To install:**

8. Install the passive shoulder belt retractor unit. Connect the electrical connector and tighten the mounting bolts to 28-58 ft. lbs. (38-78 Nm).

9. Install the rear center console unit.

10. Install the lap belt buckle and tighten the mounting bolts to 28-58 ft. lbs. (38-78 Nm).

11. Install the lap belt assembly and tighten the mounting bolts to 28-58 ft. lbs. (38-78 Nm).

12. Install the passive shoulder belt assembly and tighten the mounting bolts. Tighten the bolts to 69-104 inch lbs. (8-12 Nm).

13. Install the pillar trim panels.

14. Connect the negative battery cable.

REAR

1. Remove the rear seat cushion assembly.

2. Remove the upper seat belt mounting bolts and remove the seat belt assemblies.

3. Installation is the reverse of the removal procedure. Tighten the mounting bolts to 28-39 ft. lbs. (39-55 Nm).

1993 626

FRONT

1. Remove the B-pillar trim cover and remove the seat belt mounting bolts.

2. Remove the seat belt assembly.

3. Installation is the reverse of the removal procedure. Tighten the mounting bolts to 29-57 ft. lbs. (39-78 Nm).

REAR

1. Remove the rear seat cushion assembly.

2. Remove the upper seat belt mounting bolts and remove the seat belt assemblies.

3. Installation is the reverse of the removal procedure. Tighten the mounting bolts to 28-39 ft. lbs. (39-55 Nm).

Power Seat Motor

REMOVAL & INSTALLATION

Driver's Seat

1. Remove the driver's seat from the vehicle and set it on a clean, flat surface.

2. To remove and install the sliding and reclining motor, perform the following:

   a. Unscrew the cable from the motor using pliers.

   b. Remove the retaining screws and remove the motor from its mounting.

   c. Position the motor onto the mounting and install the attaching screws.

   d. Connect the cable to the motor and tighten it properly.

3. To remove and install the reclining motor, perform the following:

   a. Pull the head rest and the two headrest mounting poles from the seat.

   b. Remove the bolts from the front part of the reclining knuckles.

c. Loosen but do not remove the rear reclining knuckle bolts.

d. Remove the seat back cushion from the seat back frame.

e. Unbolt and remove the reclining knuckle (3 bolts).

f. Remove the three attaching screws and remove the motor from the reclining knuckle.

g. Unscrew and remove the bracket from the motor. Transfer the existing bracket to the new motor.

h. Complete the installation in reverse of the removal procedure.

4. Installation is the reverse of removal. Make sure that all the motors are functioning properly.

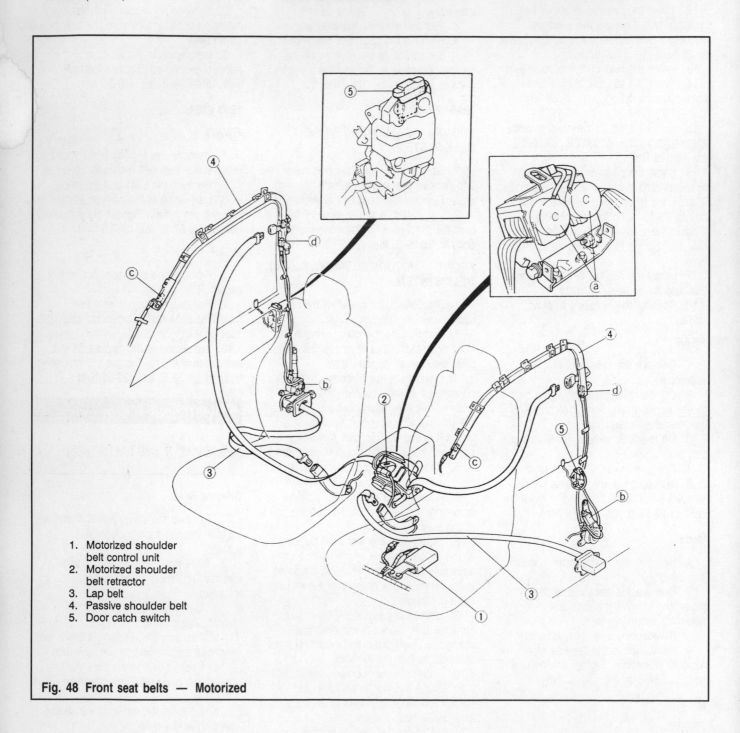

1. Motorized shoulder belt control unit
2. Motorized shoulder belt retractor
3. Lap belt
4. Passive shoulder belt
5. Door catch switch

Fig. 48 Front seat belts — Motorized

TORQUE SPECIFICATIONS

Component	U.S.	Metric
Hood to hood hinge bolts		
All	14–19 ft. lbs.	19–25 Nm
Hood lock to vehicle bolts		
All	69–95 inch lbs.	8–11 Nm
Fender mounting bolts		
All	61–87 inch lbs.	7–10 Nm
Door mounting bolts		
All	13–22 ft. lbs.	18–29 Nm
Door lock striker torx screws		
All	13–20 ft. lbs.	18–26 Nm
Door checker nuts		
All	78–113 inch lbs.	9–13 Nm
Window regulator bolts		
All	61–87 inch lbs.	7–10 Nm
Rear hatch to hinge mounting bolts		
All	78–113 inch lbs.	9–13 Nm
Rear hatch strut bolts		
All	69–104 inch lbs.	8–12 Nm
Trunk hinge mounting bolts/nuts		
All	69–95 inch lbs.	8–11 Nm
Front bumper mounting bolts/nuts		
All	61–87 inch lbs.	7–10 Nm
Rear bumper mounting bolts/nuts		
All	12–17 ft. lbs.	16–23 Nm
Dashboard mounting bolts		
All	69–104 inch lbs.	8–12 Nm
Seatbelt mounting bolts		
All	28–58 ft. lbs.	38–78 Nm
Front seat mounting bolts		
All	28–38 ft. lbs.	38–51 Nm

Hood, Trunk Lid, Hatch Lid, Glass and Doors

Problem	Possible Cause	Correction
HOOD/TRUNK/HATCH LID		
Improper closure.	• Striker and latch not properly aligned.	• Adjust the alignment.
Difficulty locking and unlocking.	• Striker and latch not properly aligned.	• Adjust the alignment.
Uneven clearance with body panels.	• Incorrectly installed hood or trunk lid.	• Adjust the alignment.
WINDOW/WINDSHIELD GLASS		
Water leak through windshield	• Defective seal. • Defective body flange.	• Fill sealant • Correct.
Water leak through door window glass.	• Incorrect window glass installation. • Gap at upper window frame.	• Adjust position. • Adjust position.
Water leak through quarter window.	• Defective seal. • Defective body flange.	• Replace seal. • Correct.
Water leak through rear window.	• Defective seal. • Defective body flange.	• Replace seal. • Correct.
FRONT/REAR DOORS		
Door window malfunction.	• Incorrect window glass installation. • Damaged or faulty regulator.	• Adjust position. • Correct or replace.
Water leak through door edge.	• Cracked or faulty weatherstrip.	• Replace.
Water leak from door center.	• Drain hole clogged. • Inadequate waterproof skeet contact or damage.	• Remove foreign objects. • Correct or replace.
Door hard to open.	• Incorrect latch or striker adjustment.	• Adjust.
Door does not open or close completely.	• Incorrect door installation. • Defective door check strap. • Door check strap and hinge require grease.	• Adjust position. • Correct or replace. • Apply grease.
Uneven gap between door and body.	• Incorrect door installation.	• Adjust position.
Wind noise around door.	• Improperly installed weatherstrip. • Improper clearance between door glass and door weatherstrip. • Deformed door.	• Repair or replace. • Adjust. • Repair or replace.

GLOSSARY

AIR/FUEL RATIO: The ratio of air to gasoline by weight in the fuel mixture drawn into the engine.

AIR INJECTION: One method of reducing harmful exhaust emissions by injecting air into each of the exhaust ports of an engine. The fresh air entering the hot exhaust manifold causes any remaining fuel to be burned before it can exit the tailpipe.

ALTERNATOR: A device used for converting mechanical energy into electrical energy.

AMMETER: An instrument, calibrated in amperes, used to measure the flow of an electrical current in a circuit. Ammeters are always connected in series with the circuit being tested.

AMPERE: The rate of flow of electrical current present when one volt of electrical pressure is applied against one ohm of electrical resistance.

ANALOG COMPUTER: Any microprocessor that uses similar (analogous) electrical signals to make its calculations.

ARMATURE: A laminated, soft iron core wrapped by a wire that converts electrical energy to mechanical energy as in a motor or relay. When rotated in a magnetic field, it changes mechanical energy into electrical energy as in a generator.

ATMOSPHERIC PRESSURE: The pressure on the Earth's surface caused by the weight of the air in the atmosphere. At sea level, this pressure is 14.7 psi at 32{248}F (101 kPa at 0{248}C).

ATOMIZATION: The breaking down of a liquid into a fine mist that can be suspended in air.

AXIAL PLAY: Movement parallel to a shaft or bearing bore.

BACKFIRE: The sudden combustion of gases in the intake or exhaust system that results in a loud explosion.

BACKLASH: The clearance or play between two parts, such as meshed gears.

BACKPRESSURE: Restrictions in the exhaust system that slow the exit of exhaust gases from the combustion chamber.

BAKELITE: A heat resistant, plastic insulator material commonly used in printed circuit boards and transistorized components.

BALL BEARING: A bearing made up of hardened inner and outer races between which hardened steel balls roll.

BALLAST RESISTOR: A resistor in the primary ignition circuit that lowers voltage after the engine is started to reduce wear on ignition components.

BEARING: A friction reducing, supportive device usually located between a stationary part and a moving part.

BIMETAL TEMPERATURE SENSOR: Any sensor or switch made of two dissimilar types of metal that bend when heated or cooled due to the different expansion rates of the alloys. These types of sensors usually function as an on/off switch.

BLOWBY: Combustion gases, composed of water vapor and unburned fuel, that leak past the piston rings into the crankcase during normal engine operation. These gases are removed by the PCV system to prevent the buildup of harmful acids in the crankcase.

BRAKE PAD: A brake shoe and lining assembly used with disc brakes.

BRAKE SHOE: The backing for the brake lining. The term is, however, usually applied to the assembly of the brake backing and lining.

BUSHING: A liner, usually removable, for a bearing; an anti-friction liner used in place of a bearing.

BYPASS: System used to bypass ballast resistor during engine cranking to increase voltage supplied to the coil.

CALIPER: A hydraulically activated device in a disc brake system, which is mounted straddling the brake rotor (disc). The caliper contains at least one piston and two brake pads. Hydraulic pressure on the piston(s) forces the pads against the rotor.

CAMSHAFT: A shaft in the engine on which are the lobes (cams) which operate the valves. The camshaft is driven by the crankshaft, via a belt, chain or gears, at one half the crankshaft speed.

CAPACITOR: A device which stores an electrical charge.

CARBON MONOXIDE (CO): A colorless, odorless gas given off as a normal byproduct of combustion. It is poisonous and extremely dangerous in confined areas, building up slowly to toxic levels without warning if adequate ventilation is not available.

CARBURETOR: A device, usually mounted on the intake manifold of an engine, which mixes the air and fuel in the proper proportion to allow even combustion.

CATALYTIC CONVERTER: A device installed in the exhaust system, like a muffler, that converts harmful byproducts of combustion into carbon dioxide and water vapor by means of a heat-producing chemical reaction.

CENTRIFUGAL ADVANCE: A mechanical method of advancing the spark timing by using flyweights in the distributor that react to centrifugal force generated by the distributor shaft rotation.

CHECK VALVE: Any one-way valve installed to permit the flow of air, fuel or vacuum in one direction only.

CHOKE: A device, usually a moveable valve, placed in the intake path of a carburetor to restrict the flow of air.

CIRCUIT: Any unbroken path through which an electrical current can flow. Also used to describe fuel flow in some instances.

CIRCUIT BREAKER: A switch which protects an electrical circuit from overload by opening the circuit when the current flow exceeds a predetermined level. Some circuit breakers must be reset manually, while most reset automatically

COIL (IGNITION): A transformer in the ignition circuit which steps up the voltage provided to the spark plugs.

COMBINATION MANIFOLD: An assembly which includes both the intake and exhaust manifolds in one casting.

COMBINATION VALVE: A device used in some fuel systems that routes fuel vapors to a charcoal storage canister instead of venting them into the atmosphere. The valve relieves fuel tank pressure and allows fresh air into the tank as the fuel level drops to prevent a vapor lock situation.

COMPRESSION RATIO: The comparison of the total volume of the cylinder and combustion chamber with the piston at BDC and the piston at TDC.

CONDENSER: 1. An electrical device which acts to store an electrical charge, preventing voltage surges.
2. A radiator-like device in the air conditioning system in which refrigerant gas condenses into a liquid, giving off heat.

CONDUCTOR: Any material through which an electrical current can be transmitted easily.

CONTINUITY: Continuous or complete circuit. Can be checked with an ohmmeter.

COUNTERSHAFT: An intermediate shaft which is rotated by a mainshaft and transmits, in turn, that rotation to a working part.

CRANKCASE: The lower part of an engine in which the crankshaft and related parts operate.

CRANKSHAFT: The main driving shaft of an engine which receives reciprocating motion from the pistons and converts it to rotary motion.

CYLINDER: In an engine, the round hole in the engine block in which the piston(s) ride.

CYLINDER BLOCK: The main structural member of an engine in which is found the cylinders, crankshaft and other principal parts.

CYLINDER HEAD: The detachable portion of the engine, fastened, usually, to the top of the cylinder block, containing all or most of the combustion chambers. On overhead valve engines, it contains the valves and their operating parts. On overhead cam engines, it contains the camshaft as well.

DEAD CENTER: The extreme top or bottom of the piston stroke.

DETONATION: An unwanted explosion of the air/fuel mixture in the combustion chamber caused by excess heat and compression, advanced timing, or an overly lean mixture. Also referred to as "ping".

DIAPHRAGM: A thin, flexible wall separating two cavities, such as in a vacuum advance unit.

DIESELING: A condition in which hot spots in the combustion chamber cause the engine to run on after the key is turned off.

DIFFERENTIAL: A geared assembly which allows the transmission of motion between drive axles, giving one axle the ability to turn faster than the other.

DIODE: An electrical device that will allow current to flow in one direction only.

DISC BRAKE: A hydraulic braking assembly consisting of a brake disc, or rotor, mounted on an axle, and a caliper assembly containing, usually two brake pads which are activated by hydraulic pressure. The pads are forced against the sides of the disc, creating friction which slows the vehicle.

DISTRIBUTOR: A mechanically driven device on an engine which is responsible for electrically firing the spark plug at a predetermined point of the piston stroke.

DOWEL PIN: A pin, inserted in mating holes in two different parts allowing those parts to maintain a fixed relationship.

DRUM BRAKE: A braking system which consists of two brake shoes and one or two wheel cylinders, mounted on a fixed backing plate, and a brake drum, mounted on an axle, which revolves around the assembly. Hydraulic action applied to the wheel cylinders forces the shoes outward against the drum, creating friction, slowing the vehicle.

DWELL: The rate, measured in degrees of shaft rotation, at which an electrical circuit cycles on and off.

ELECTRONIC CONTROL UNIT (ECU): Ignition module, module, amplifier or igniter. See Module for definition.

ELECTRONIC IGNITION: A system in which the timing and firing of the spark plugs is controlled by an electronic control unit, usually called a module. These systems have no points or condenser.

ENDPLAY: The measured amount of axial movement in a shaft.

ENGINE: A device that converts heat into mechanical energy.

EXHAUST MANIFOLD: A set of cast passages or pipes which conduct exhaust gases from the engine.

FEELER GAUGE: A blade, usually metal, of precisely predetermined thickness, used to measure the clearance between two parts. These blades usually are available in sets of assorted thicknesses.

FIRING ORDER: The order in which combustion occurs in the cylinders of an engine. Also the order in which spark is distributed to the plugs by the distributor.

FLATHEAD: An engine configuration in which the camshaft and all the valves are located in the cylinder block.

FLOODING: The presence of too much fuel in the intake manifold and combustion chamber which prevents the air/fuel mixture from firing, thereby causing a no-start situation.

FLYWHEEL: A disc shaped part bolted to the rear end of the crankshaft. Around the outer perimeter is affixed the ring gear. The starter drive engages the ring gear, turning the flywheel, which rotates the crankshaft, imparting the initial starting motion to the engine.

FOOT POUND (ft.lb. or sometimes, ft. lbs.): The amount of energy or work needed to raise an item weighing one pound, a distance of one foot.

FUSE: A protective device in a circuit which prevents circuit overload by breaking the circuit when a specific amperage is present. The device is constructed around a strip or wire of a lower amperage rating than the circuit it is designed to protect. When an amperage higher than that stamped on the fuse is present in the circuit, the strip or wire melts, opening the circuit.

GEAR RATIO: The ratio between the number of teeth on meshing gears.

GENERATOR: A device which converts mechanical energy into electrical energy.

HEAT RANGE: The measure of a spark plug's ability to dissipate heat from its firing end. The higher the heat range, the hotter the plug fires.

HUB: The center part of a wheel or gear.

HYDROCARBON (HC): Any chemical compound made up of hydrogen and carbon. A major pollutant formed by the engine as a byproduct of combustion.

HYDROMETER: An instrument used to measure the specific gravity of a solution.

INCH POUND (in.lb. or sometimes, in. lbs.): One twelfth of a foot pound.

INDUCTION: A means of transferring electrical energy in the form of a magnetic field. Principle used in the ignition coil to increase voltage.

INJECTION PUMP: A device, usually mechanically operated, which meters and delivers fuel under pressure to the fuel injector.

INJECTOR: A device which receives metered fuel under relatively low pressure and is activated to inject the fuel into the engine under relatively high pressure at a predetermined time.

INPUT SHAFT: The shaft to which torque is applied, usually carrying the driving gear or gears.

INTAKE MANIFOLD: A casting of passages or pipes used to conduct air or a fuel/air mixture to the cylinders.

JOURNAL: The bearing surface within which a shaft operates.

KEY: A small block usually fitted in a notch between a shaft and a hub to prevent slippage of the two parts.

MANIFOLD: A casting of passages or set of pipes which connect the cylinders to an inlet or outlet source.

MANIFOLD VACUUM: Low pressure in an engine intake manifold formed just below the throttle plates. Manifold vacuum is highest at idle and drops under acceleration.

MASTER CYLINDER: The primary fluid pressurizing device in a hydraulic system. In automotive use, it is found in brake and hydraulic clutch systems and is pedal activated, either directly or, in a power brake system, through the power booster.

MODULE: Electronic control unit, amplifier or igniter of solid state or integrated design which controls the current flow in the ignition primary circuit based on input from the pick-up coil. When the module opens the primary circuit, the high secondary voltage is induced in the coil.

NEEDLE BEARING: A bearing which consists of a number (usually a large number) of long, thin rollers.

OHM:(Ω) The unit used to measure the resistance of conductor to electrical flow. One ohm is the amount of resistance that limits current flow to one ampere in a circuit with one volt of pressure.

OHMMETER: An instrument used for measuring the resistance, in ohms, in an electrical circuit.

OUTPUT SHAFT: The shaft which transmits torque from a device, such as a transmission.

OVERDRIVE: A gear assembly which produces more shaft revolutions than that transmitted to it.

OVERHEAD CAMSHAFT (OHC): An engine configuration in which the camshaft is mounted on top of the cylinder head and operates the valve either directly or by means of rocker arms.

OVERHEAD VALVE (OHV): An engine configuration in which all of the valves are located in the cylinder head and the camshaft is located in the cylinder block. The camshaft operates the valves via lifters and pushrods.

OXIDES OF NITROGEN (NOx): Chemical compounds of nitrogen produced as a byproduct of combustion. They combine with hydrocarbons to produce smog.

OXYGEN SENSOR: Used with the feedback system to sense the presence of oxygen in the exhaust gas and signal the computer which can reference the voltage signal to an air/fuel ratio.

PINION: The smaller of two meshing gears.

PISTON RING: An open ended ring which fits into a groove on the outer diameter of the piston. Its chief function is to form a seal between the piston and cylinder wall. Most automotive pistons have three rings: two for compression sealing; one for oil sealing.

PRELOAD: A predetermined load placed on a bearing during assembly or by adjustment.

PRIMARY CIRCUIT: Is the low voltage side of the ignition system which consists of the ignition switch, ballast resistor or resistance wire, bypass, coil, electronic control unit and pick-up coil as well as the connecting wires and harnesses.

PRESS FIT: The mating of two parts under pressure, due to the inner diameter of one being smaller than the outer diameter of the other, or vice versa; an interference fit.

RACE: The surface on the inner or outer ring of a bearing on which the balls, needles or rollers move.

REGULATOR: A device which maintains the amperage and/or voltage levels of a circuit at predetermined values.

RELAY: A switch which automatically opens and/or closes a circuit.

RESISTANCE: The opposition to the flow of current through a circuit or electrical device, and is measured in ohms. Resistance is equal to the voltage divided by the amperage.

RESISTOR: A device, usually made of wire, which offers a preset amount of resistance in an electrical circuit.

RING GEAR: The name given to a ring-shaped gear attached to a differential case, or affixed to a flywheel or as part a planetary gear set.

ROLLER BEARING: A bearing made up of hardened inner and outer races between which hardened steel rollers move.

ROTOR: 1. The disc-shaped part of a disc brake assembly, upon which the brake pads bear; also called, brake disc. 2. The device mounted atop the distributor shaft, which passes current to the distributor cap tower contacts.

SECONDARY CIRCUIT: The high voltage side of the ignition system, usually above 20,000 volts. The secondary includes the ignition coil, coil wire, distributor cap and rotor, spark plug wires and spark plugs.

SENDING UNIT: A mechanical, electrical, hydraulic or electromagnetic device which transmits information to a gauge.

SENSOR: Any device designed to measure engine operating conditions or ambient pressures and temperatures. Usually electronic in nature and designed to send a voltage signal to an on-board computer, some sensors may operate as a simple on/off switch or they may provide a variable voltage signal (like a potentiometer) as conditions or measured parameters change.

SHIM: Spacers of precise, predetermined thickness used between parts to establish a proper working relationship.

SLAVE CYLINDER: In automotive use, a device in the hydraulic clutch system which is activated by hydraulic force, disengaging the clutch.

SOLENOID: A coil used to produce a magnetic field, the effect of which is produce work.

SPARK PLUG: A device screwed into the combustion chamber of a spark ignition engine. The basic construction is a conductive core inside of a ceramic insulator, mounted in an outer conductive base. An electrical charge from the spark plug wire travels along the conductive core and jumps a preset air gap to a grounding point or points at the end of the conductive base. The resultant spark ignites the fuel/air mixture in the combustion chamber.

SPLINES: Ridges machined or cast onto the outer diameter of a shaft or inner diameter of a bore to enable parts to mate without rotation.

TACHOMETER: A device used to measure the rotary speed of an engine, shaft, gear, etc., usually in rotations per minute.

THERMOSTAT: A valve, located in the cooling system of an engine, which is closed when cold and opens gradually in response to engine heating, controlling the temperature of the coolant and rate of coolant flow.

TOP DEAD CENTER (TDC): The point at which the piston reaches the top of its travel on the compression stroke.

TORQUE: The twisting force applied to an object.

TORQUE CONVERTER: A turbine used to transmit power from a driving member to a driven member via hydraulic action, providing changes in drive ratio and torque. In automotive use, it links the driveplate at the rear of the engine to the automatic transmission.

TRANSDUCER: A device used to change a force into an electrical signal.

TRANSISTOR: A semi-conductor component which can be actuated by a small voltage to perform an electrical switching function.

TUNE-UP: A regular maintenance function, usually associated with the replacement and adjustment of parts and components in the electrical and fuel systems of a vehicle for the purpose of attaining optimum performance.

TURBOCHARGER: An exhaust driven pump which compresses intake air and forces it into the combustion chambers at higher than atmospheric pressures. The increased air pressure allows more fuel to be burned and results in increased horsepower being produced.

VACUUM ADVANCE: A device which advances the ignition timing in response to increased engine vacuum.

VACUUM GAUGE: An instrument used to measure the presence of vacuum in a chamber.

VALVE: A device which control the pressure, direction of flow or rate of flow of a liquid or gas.

VALVE CLEARANCE: The measured gap between the end of the valve stem and the rocker arm, cam lobe or follower that activates the valve.

VISCOSITY: The rating of a liquid's internal resistance to flow.

VOLTMETER: An instrument used for measuring electrical force in units called volts. Voltmeters are always connected parallel with the circuit being tested.

WHEEL CYLINDER: Found in the automotive drum brake assembly, it is a device, actuated by hydraulic pressure, which, through internal pistons, pushes the brake shoes outward against the drums.

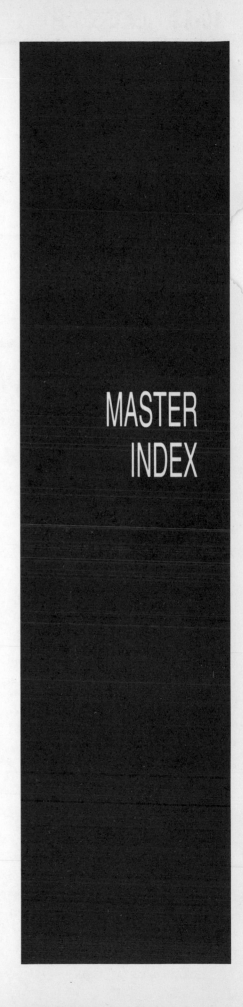

MASTER INDEX